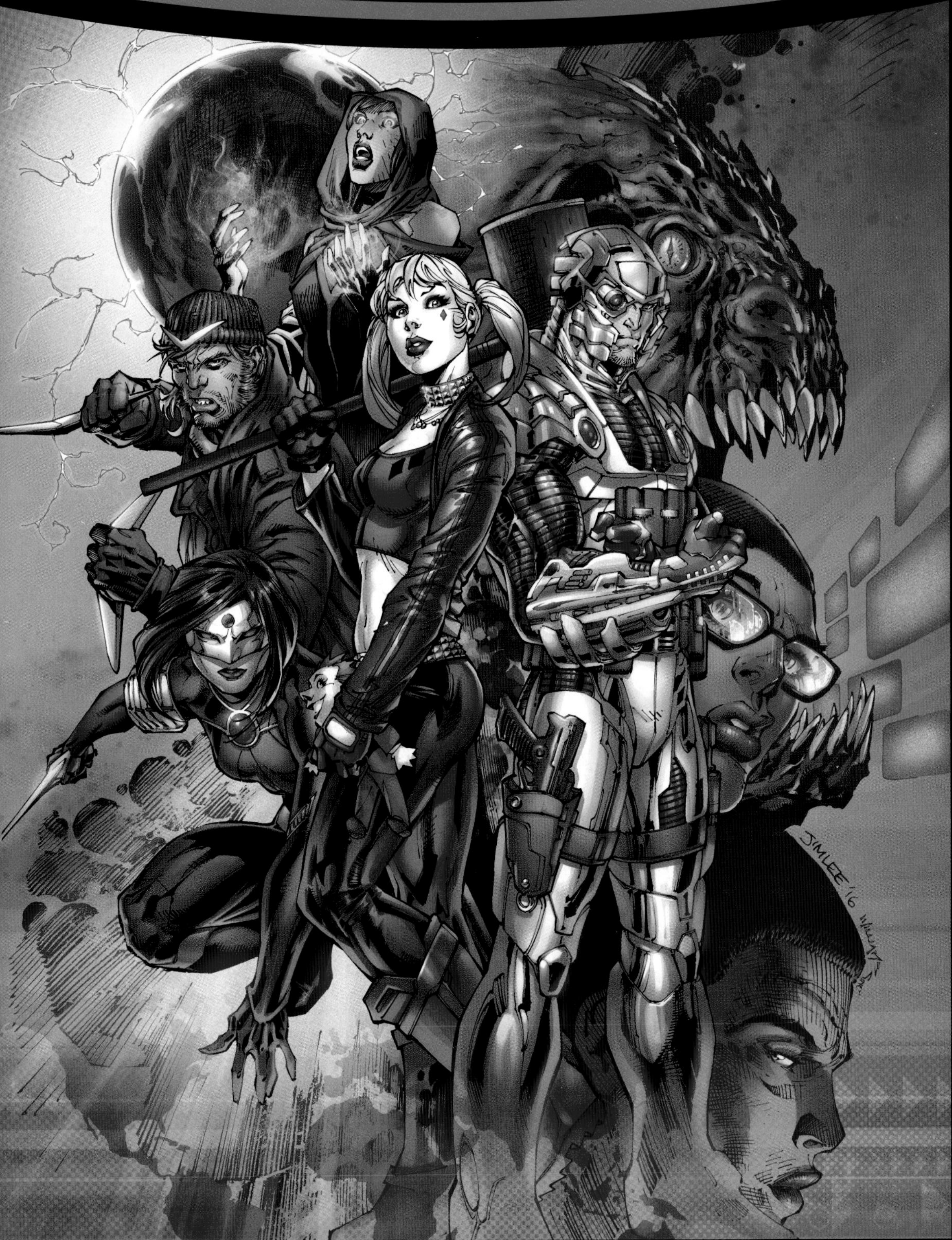

SUICIDE SQUAD

REBIRTH DELUXE EDITION

BOOK 1

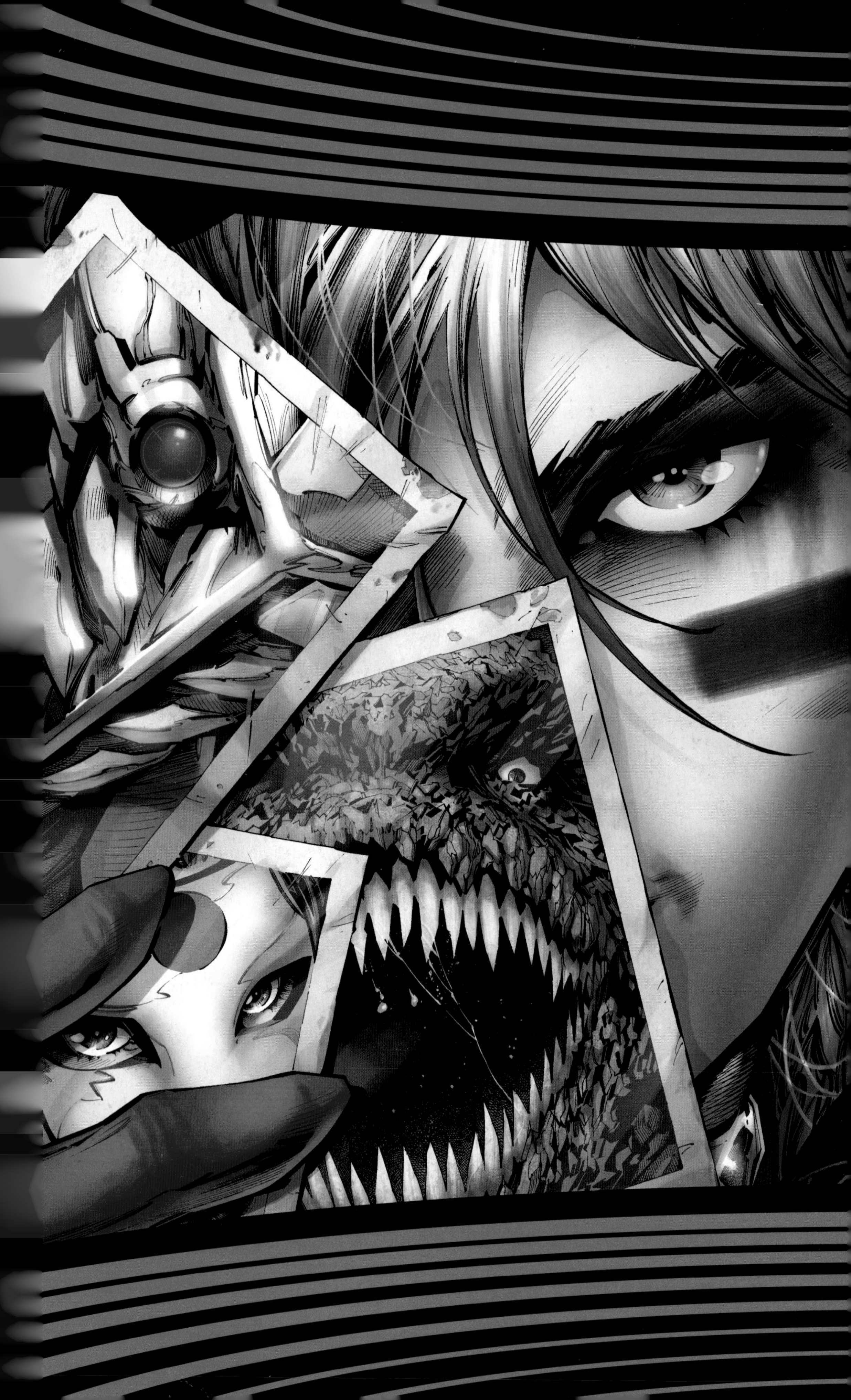

SUICIDE SQUAD
REBIRTH DELUXE EDITION
BOOK 1

ROB WILLIAMS
writer

JIM LEE * PHILIP TAN * SEAN "CHEEKS" GALLOWAY * JASON FABOK * IVAN REIS * GARY FRANK
STEPHEN BYRNE * CARLOS D'ANDA * CHRISTIAN WARD * GIUSEPPE CAMUNCOLI
FRANCESCO MATTINA * SCOTT WILLIAMS * SANDRA HOPE * RICHARD FRIEND * JONATHAN GLAPION
SCOTT HANNA * SANDU FLOREA * MATT BANNING * OCLAIR ALBERT * TREVOR SCOTT
artists

ALEX SINCLAIR * BRAD ANDERSON * MARCELO MAIOLO * ELMER SANTOS * HI-FI * STEPHEN BYRNE
GABE ELTAEB * JEREMIAH SKIPPER * CHRISTIAN WARD * SEAN "CHEEKS" GALLOWAY
colorists

ROB LEIGH * TRAVIS LANHAM * NATE PIEKOS * PAT BROSSEAU * JOSH REED * DAVE SHARPE
letterers

JIM LEE, SCOTT WILLIAMS and ALEX SINCLAIR
collection cover artists

JIM LEE, SCOTT WILLIAMS and ALEX SINCLAIR
PHILIP TAN, JONATHAN GLAPION and ALEX SINCLAIR
original series covers

HARLEY QUINN created by PAUL DINI and BRUCE TIMM

SUPERMAN created by JERRY SIEGEL and JOE SHUSTER
BY SPECIAL ARRANGEMENT WITH THE JERRY SIEGEL FAMILY

ANDY KHOURI BRIAN CUNNINGHAM Editors - Original Series * HARVEY RICHARDS Associate Editor - Original Series * DIEGO LOPEZ Assistant Editor - Original Series
JEB WOODARD Group Editor - Collected Editions * SCOTT NYBAKKEN Editor - Collected Edition
STEVE COOK Design Director - Books * DAMIAN RYLAND Publication Design

BOB HARRAS Senior VP - Editor-in-Chief, DC Comics
PAT McCALLUM Executive Editor, DC Comics

DIANE NELSON President * DAN DiDIO Publisher * JIM LEE Publisher * GEOFF JOHNS President & Chief Creative Officer
AMIT DESAI Executive VP - Business & Marketing Strategy, Direct to Consumer & Global Franchise Management * SAM ADES Senior VP & General Manager, Digital Services
BOBBIE CHASE VP & Executive Editor, Young Reader & Talent Development * MARK CHIARELLO Senior VP - Art, Design & Collected Editions
JOHN CUNNINGHAM Senior VP - Sales & Trade Marketing * ANNE DePIES Senior VP - Business Strategy, Finance & Administration
DON FALLETTI VP - Manufacturing Operations * LAWRENCE GANEM VP - Editorial Administration & Talent Relations
ALISON GILL Senior VP - Manufacturing & Operations * HANK KANALZ Senior VP - Editorial Strategy & Administration * JAY KOGAN VP - Legal Affairs
JACK MAHAN VP - Business Affairs * NICK J. NAPOLITANO VP - Manufacturing Administration * EDDIE SCANNELL VP - Consumer Marketing
COURTNEY SIMMONS Senior VP - Publicity & Communications * JIM (SKI) SOKOLOWSKI VP - Comic Book Specialty Sales & Trade Marketing
NANCY SPEARS VP - Mass, Book, Digital Sales & Trade Marketing * MICHELE R. WELLS VP – Content Strategy

SUICIDE SQUAD: THE REBIRTH DELUXE EDITION BOOK 1

DC Comics, 2900 West Alameda Ave., Burbank, CA 91505. Printed by Transcontinental Interglobe, Beauceville, QC, Canada. 9/15/17.
First Printing. ISBN: 978-1-4012-7421-4

Library of Congress Cataloging-in-Publication Data is available.

PEFC Certified
Printed on paper from
sustainably managed
forests and controlled
sources
PEFC/01-31-106   www.pefc.org

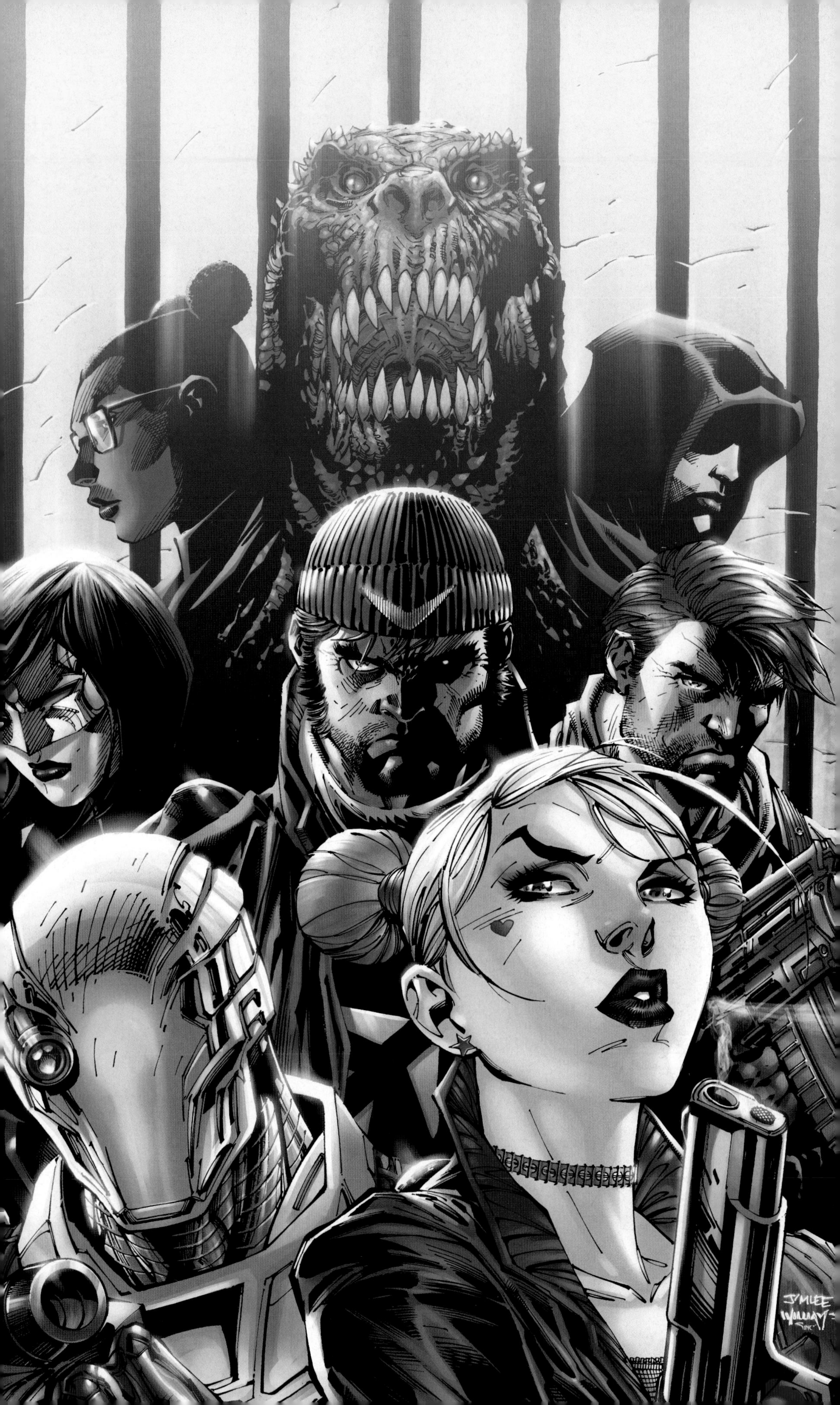

PROLOGUE
EVIL ANONYMOUS

ROB WILLIAMS
writer

JIM LEE
penciller (pages 8-17, 28-37)

SCOTT WILLIAMS * **SANDRA HOPE** * **RICHARD FRIEND**
inkers (pages 8-17, 28-37)

ALEX SINCLAIR
colorist (pages 8-17, 28-37)

SEAN "CHEEKS" GALLOWAY
artist (pages 18-27)

TRAVIS LANHAM
letterer

JIM LEE, SCOTT WILLIAMS and ALEX SINCLAIR
cover art

HARVEY RICHARDS
associate editor

ANDY KHOURI
editor

BRIAN CUNNINGHAM
group editor

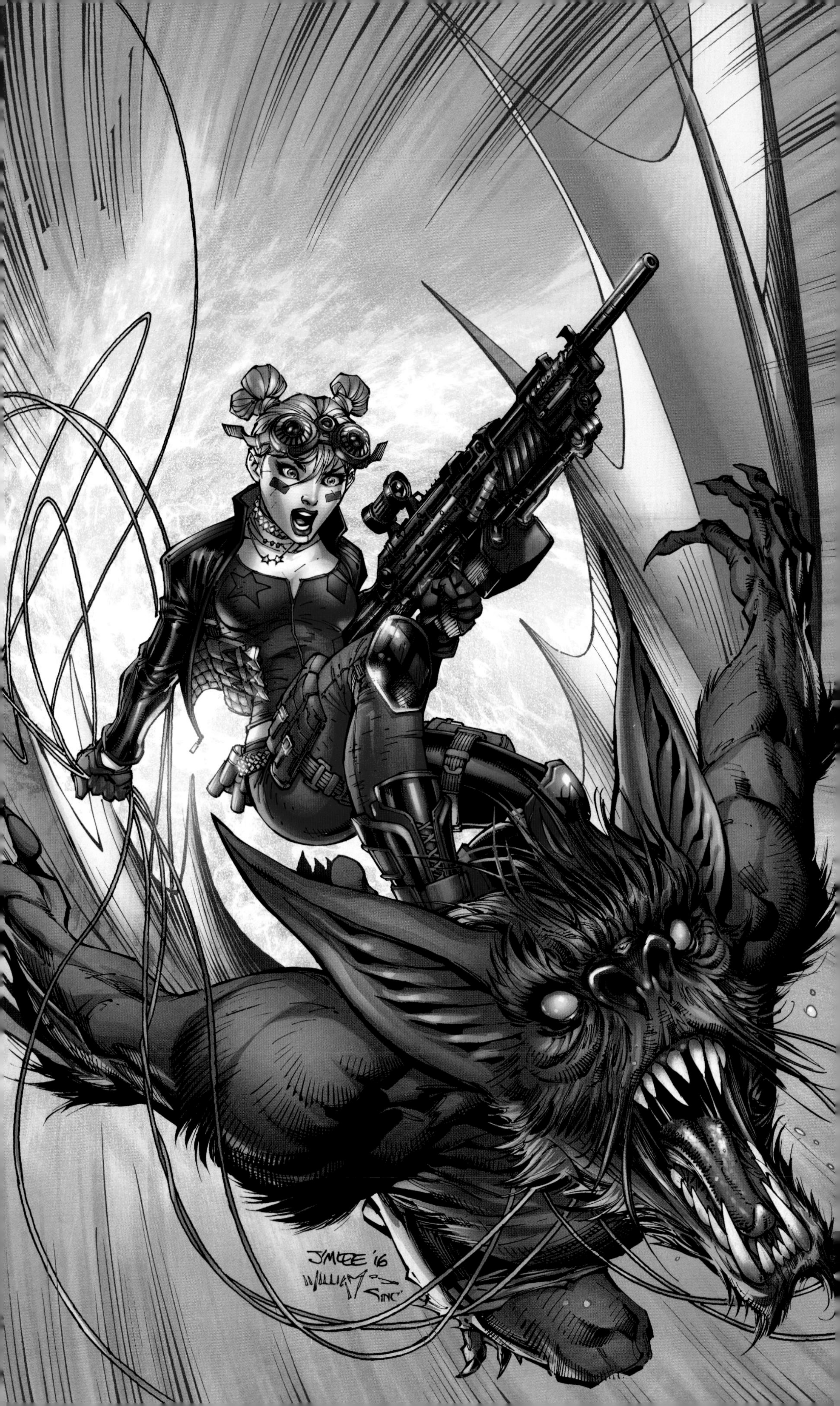

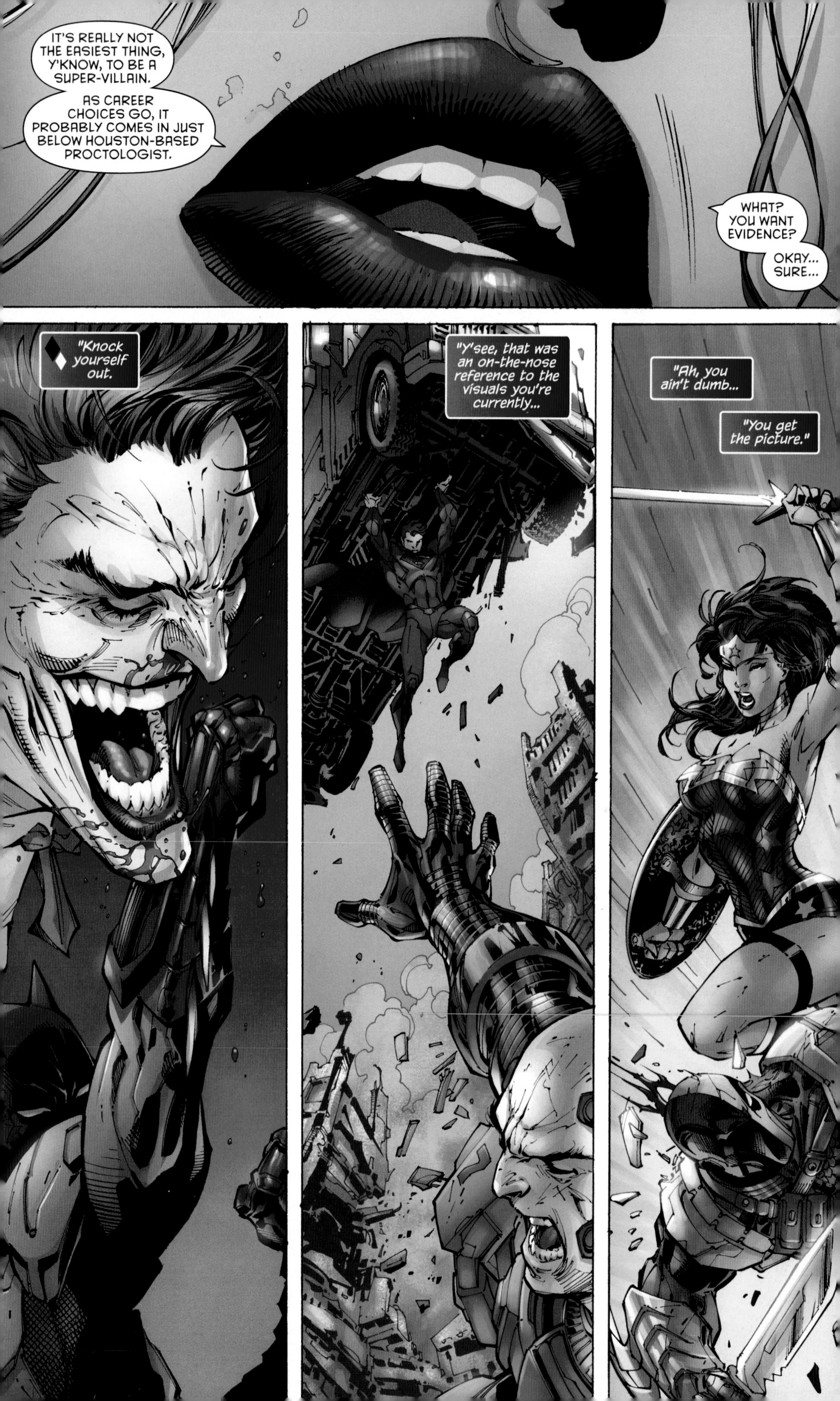

IT'S REALLY NOT THE EASIEST THING, Y'KNOW, TO BE A SUPER-VILLAIN.
AS CAREER CHOICES GO, IT PROBABLY COMES IN JUST BELOW HOUSTON-BASED PROCTOLOGIST.
WHAT? YOU WANT EVIDENCE?
OKAY... SURE...
"Knock yourself out.
"Y'see, that was an on-the-nose reference to the visuals you're currently...
"Ah, you ain't dumb...
"You get the picture."

"All them beatings...

"...it'd be enough to make me cry...

"...if I wasn't an *extraordinarily* bored psychopath."

WHO'S THE JOKE *REALLY* ON, HUH, HARLEY? ANSWER ME... **WHO?!**

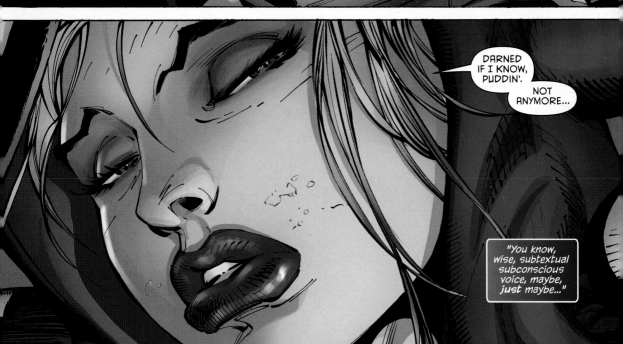

DARNED IF I KNOW, PUDDIN'. NOT ANYMORE...

"You know, wise, subtextual subconscious voice, maybe, *just maybe...*"

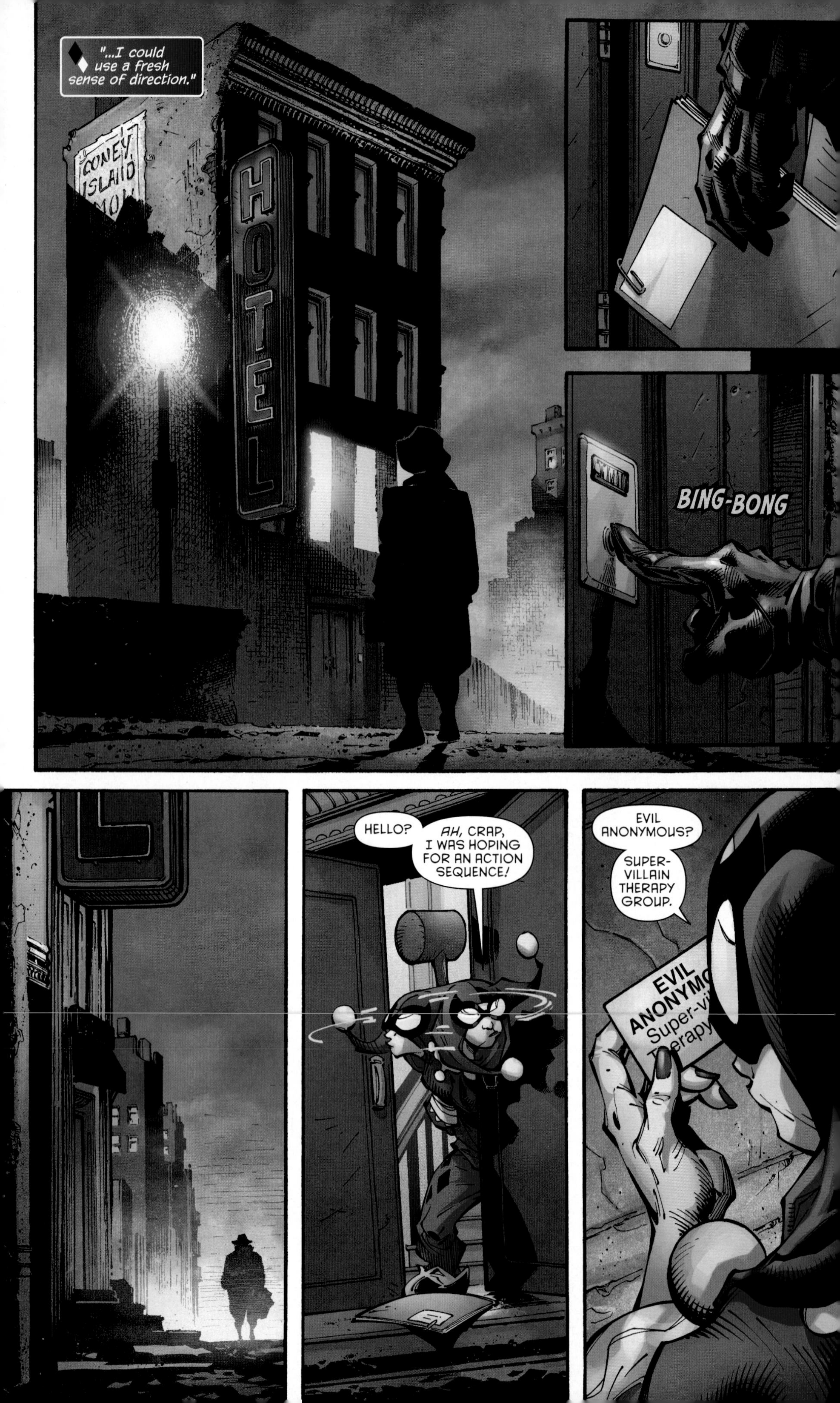
"...I could use a fresh sense of direction."
CONEY ISLAND
HOTEL
BING-BONG
HELLO?
AH, CRAP, I WAS HOPING FOR AN ACTION SEQUENCE!
EVIL ANONYMOUS?
SUPER-VILLAIN THERAPY GROUP.

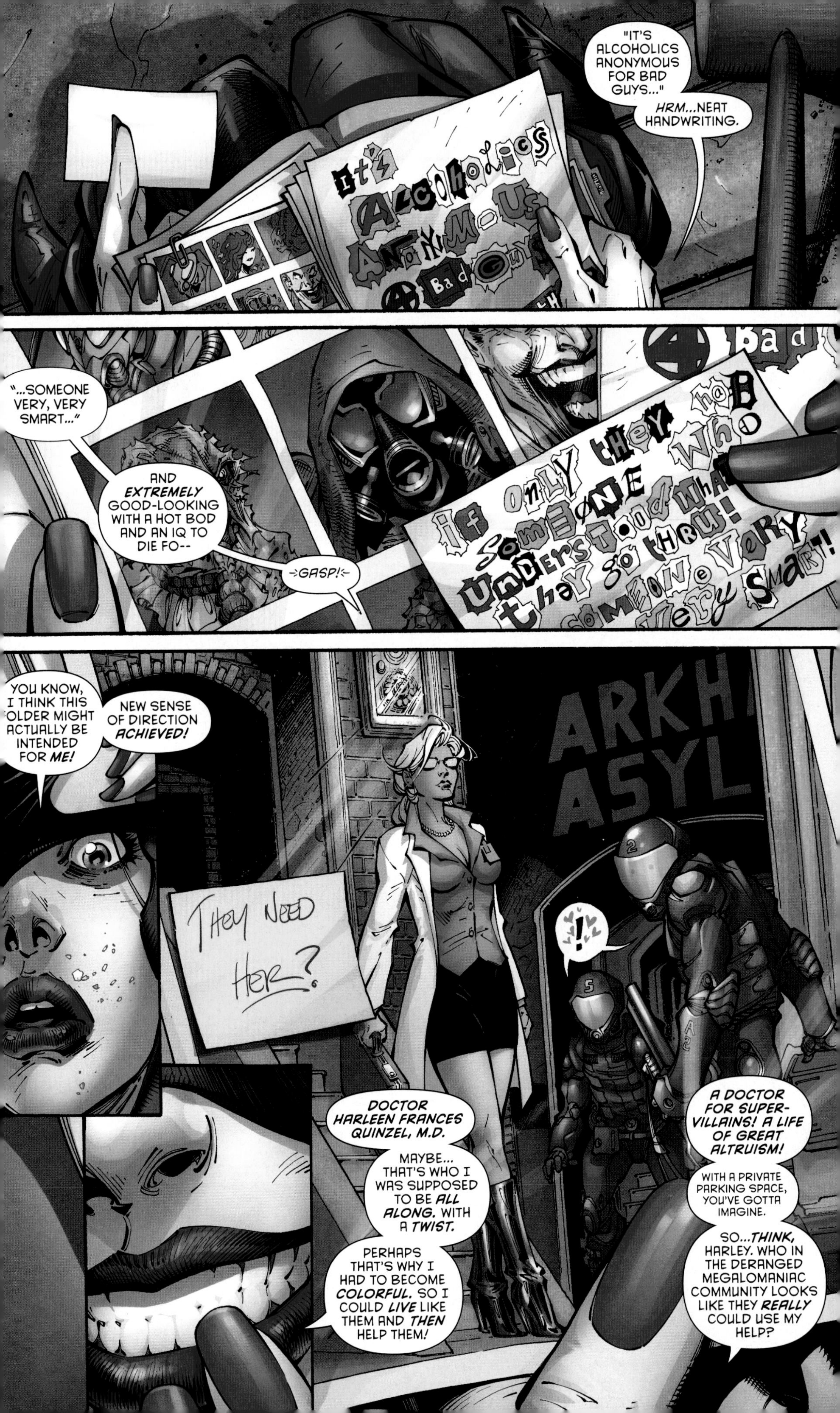
"IT'S ALCOHOLICS ANONYMOUS FOR BAD GUYS..."
HRM...NEAT HANDWRITING.
It's Alcoholics Anonymous 4 Bad Guys
"...SOMEONE VERY, VERY SMART..."
AND EXTREMELY GOOD-LOOKING WITH A HOT BOD AND AN IQ TO DIE FO--
-GASP!-
Bad
If only they had someone who understood what they go thru! Someone very very smart!
YOU KNOW, I THINK THIS FOLDER MIGHT ACTUALLY BE INTENDED FOR ME!
NEW SENSE OF DIRECTION ACHIEVED!
THEY NEED HER?
ARKH
ASYL
!
DOCTOR HARLEEN FRANCES QUINZEL, M.D.
MAYBE... THAT'S WHO I WAS SUPPOSED TO BE ALL ALONG. WITH A TWIST.
PERHAPS THAT'S WHY I HAD TO BECOME COLORFUL. SO I COULD LIVE LIKE THEM AND THEN HELP THEM!
A DOCTOR FOR SUPER-VILLAINS! A LIFE OF GREAT ALTRUISM!
WITH A PRIVATE PARKING SPACE, YOU'VE GOTTA IMAGINE.
SO...THINK, HARLEY. WHO IN THE DERANGED MEGALOMANIAC COMMUNITY LOOKS LIKE THEY REALLY COULD USE MY HELP?

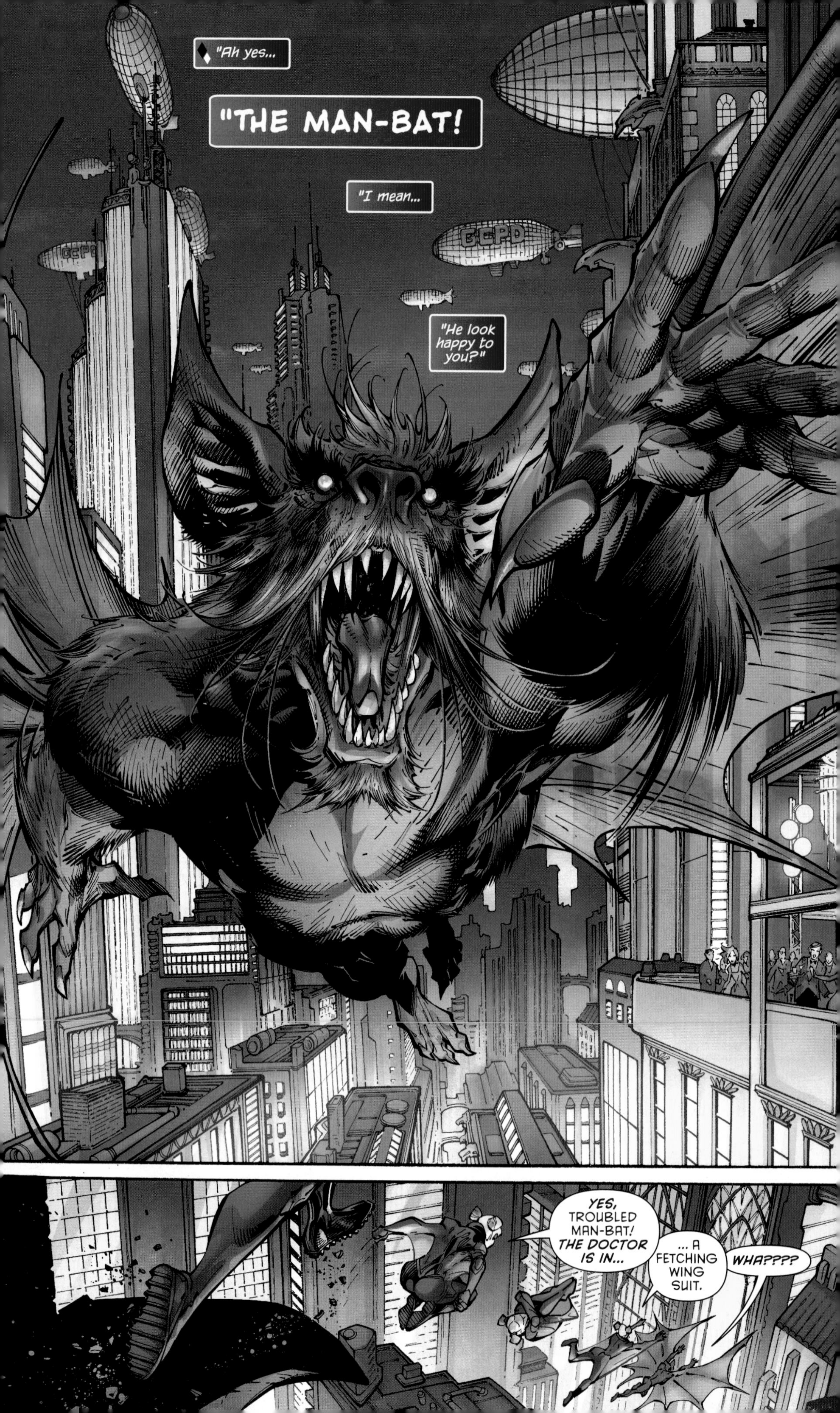
"Ah yes...
"THE MAN-BAT!
"I mean...
"He look happy to you?"
GCPD
GCPD
YES, TROUBLED MAN-BAT! THE DOCTOR IS IN...
... A FETCHING WING SUIT.
WHA????

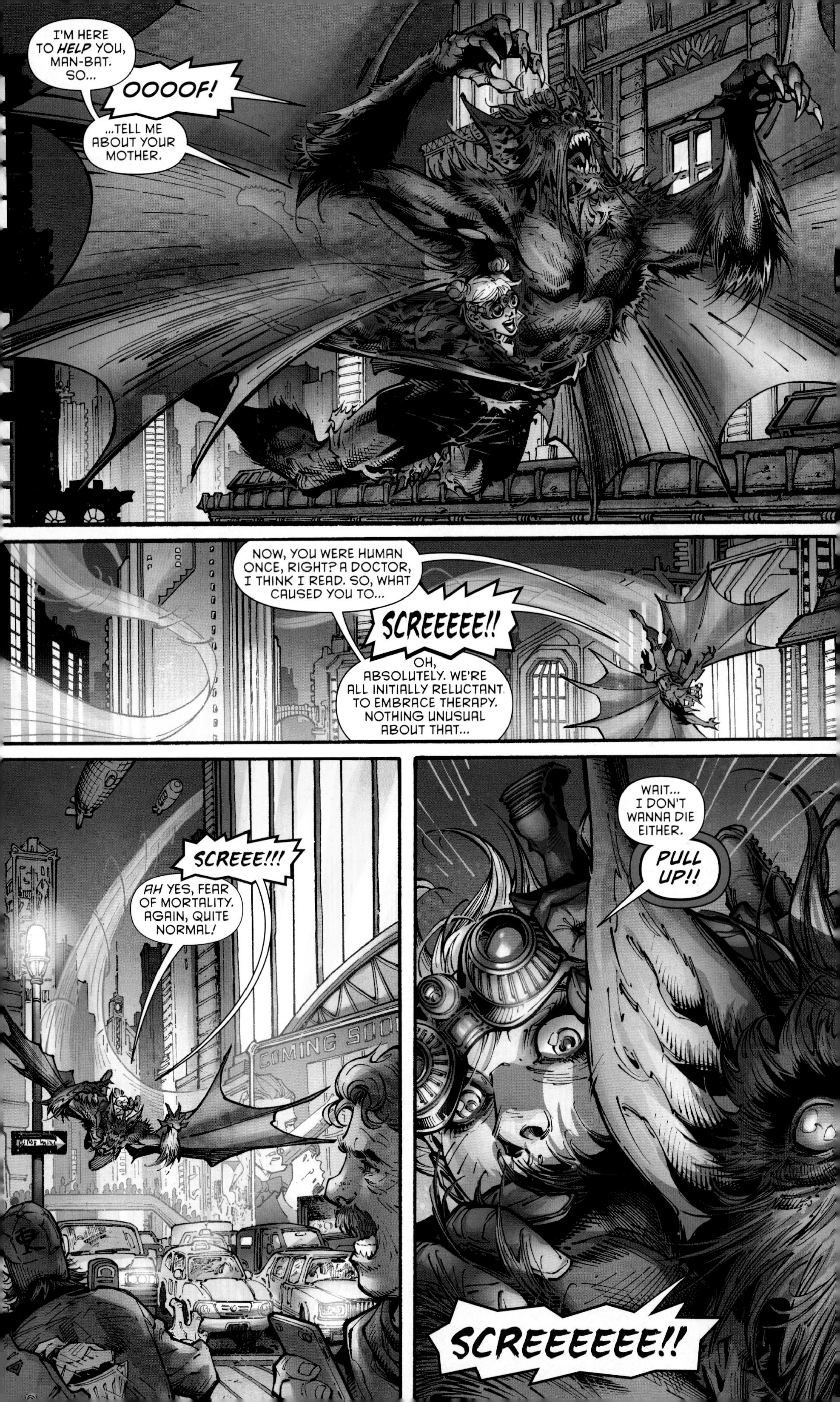

I'M HERE TO *HELP* YOU, MAN-BAT. SO...
OOOOF!
...TELL ME ABOUT YOUR MOTHER.
NOW, YOU WERE HUMAN ONCE, RIGHT? A DOCTOR, I THINK I READ. SO, WHAT CAUSED YOU TO...
SCREEEEE!!
OH, ABSOLUTELY. WE'RE ALL INITIALLY RELUCTANT TO EMBRACE THERAPY. NOTHING UNUSUAL ABOUT THAT...
SCREEE!!!
AH YES, FEAR OF MORTALITY. AGAIN, QUITE NORMAL!
COMING SOO
WAIT... I DON'T WANNA DIE EITHER.
PULL UP!!
SCREEEEEEE!!

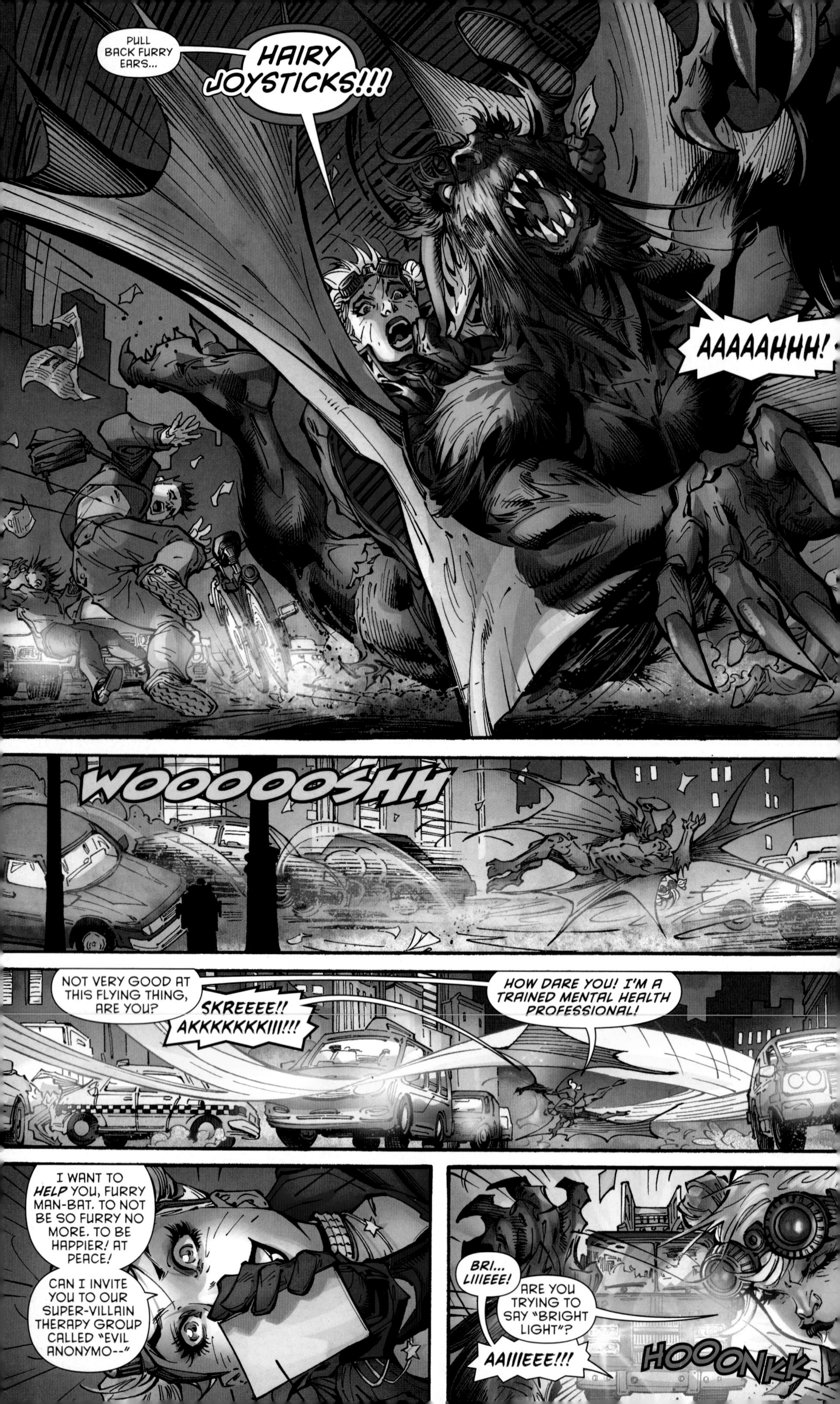
PULL BACK FURRY EARS...
HAIRY JOYSTICKS!!!
AAAAAHHH!
WOOOOOSHH
NOT VERY GOOD AT THIS FLYING THING, ARE YOU?
SKREEEE!! AKKKKKKIII!!!
HOW DARE YOU! I'M A TRAINED MENTAL HEALTH PROFESSIONAL!
I WANT TO HELP YOU, FURRY MAN-BAT. TO NOT BE SO FURRY NO MORE. TO BE HAPPIER! AT PEACE!
CAN I INVITE YOU TO OUR SUPER-VILLAIN THERAPY GROUP CALLED "EVIL ANONYMO--"
BRI... LIIIEEE!
ARE YOU TRYING TO SAY "BRIGHT LIGHT"?
AAIIIEEE!!!
HOOONKK

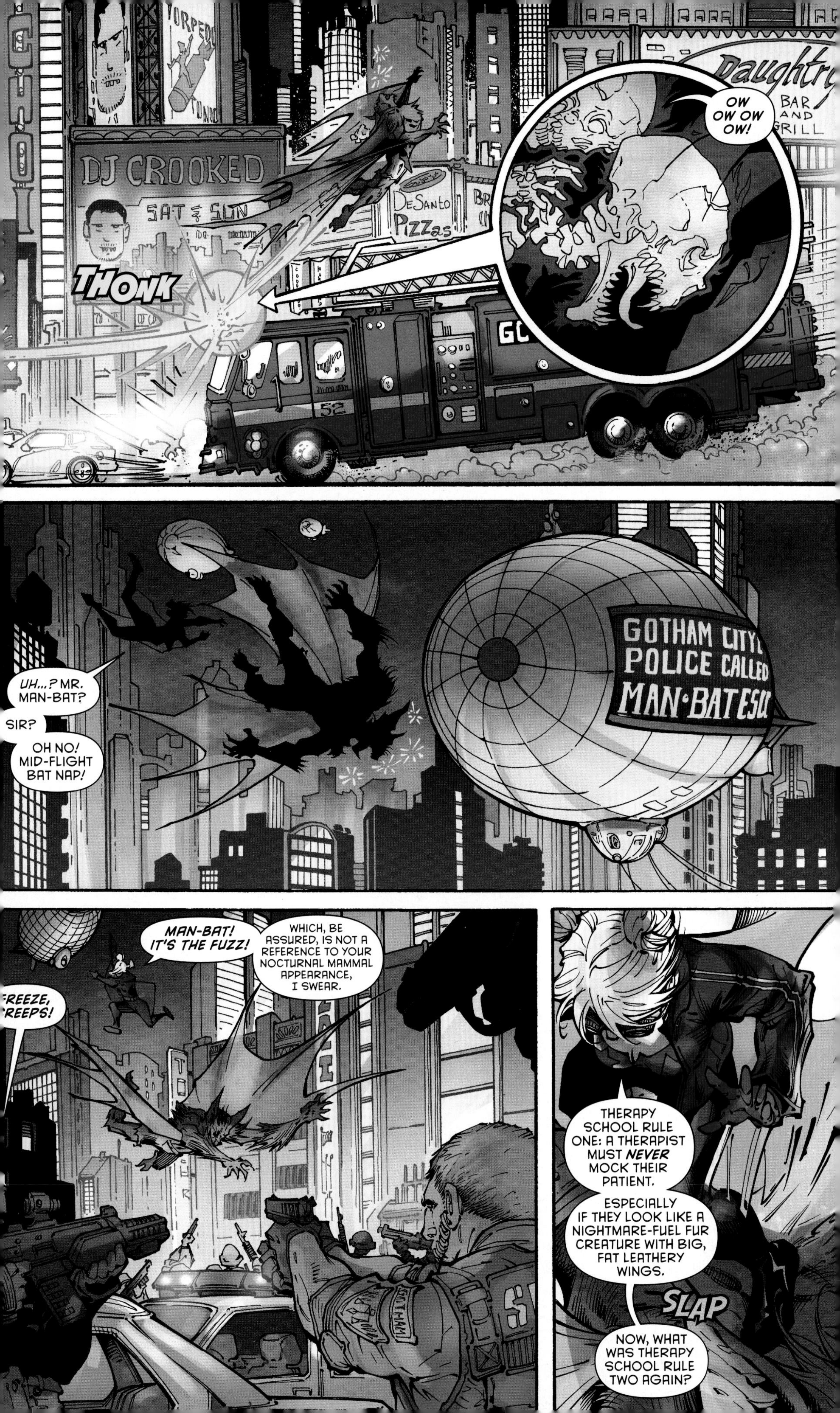

DJ CROOKED
SAT & SUN
DeSanto Pizzas
Daughtry BAR AND GRILL
THONK
OW OW OW OW!
GOTHAM CITY POLICE CALLED MAN-BAT ESC
UH...? MR. MAN-BAT?
SIR?
OH NO! MID-FLIGHT BAT NAP!
MAN-BAT! IT'S THE FUZZ!
WHICH, BE ASSURED, IS NOT A REFERENCE TO YOUR NOCTURNAL MAMMAL APPEARANCE, I SWEAR.
FREEZE, CREEPS!
THERAPY SCHOOL RULE ONE: A THERAPIST MUST NEVER MOCK THEIR PATIENT.
ESPECIALLY IF THEY LOOK LIKE A NIGHTMARE-FUEL FUR CREATURE WITH BIG, FAT LEATHERY WINGS.
SLAP
NOW, WHAT WAS THERAPY SCHOOL RULE TWO AGAIN?

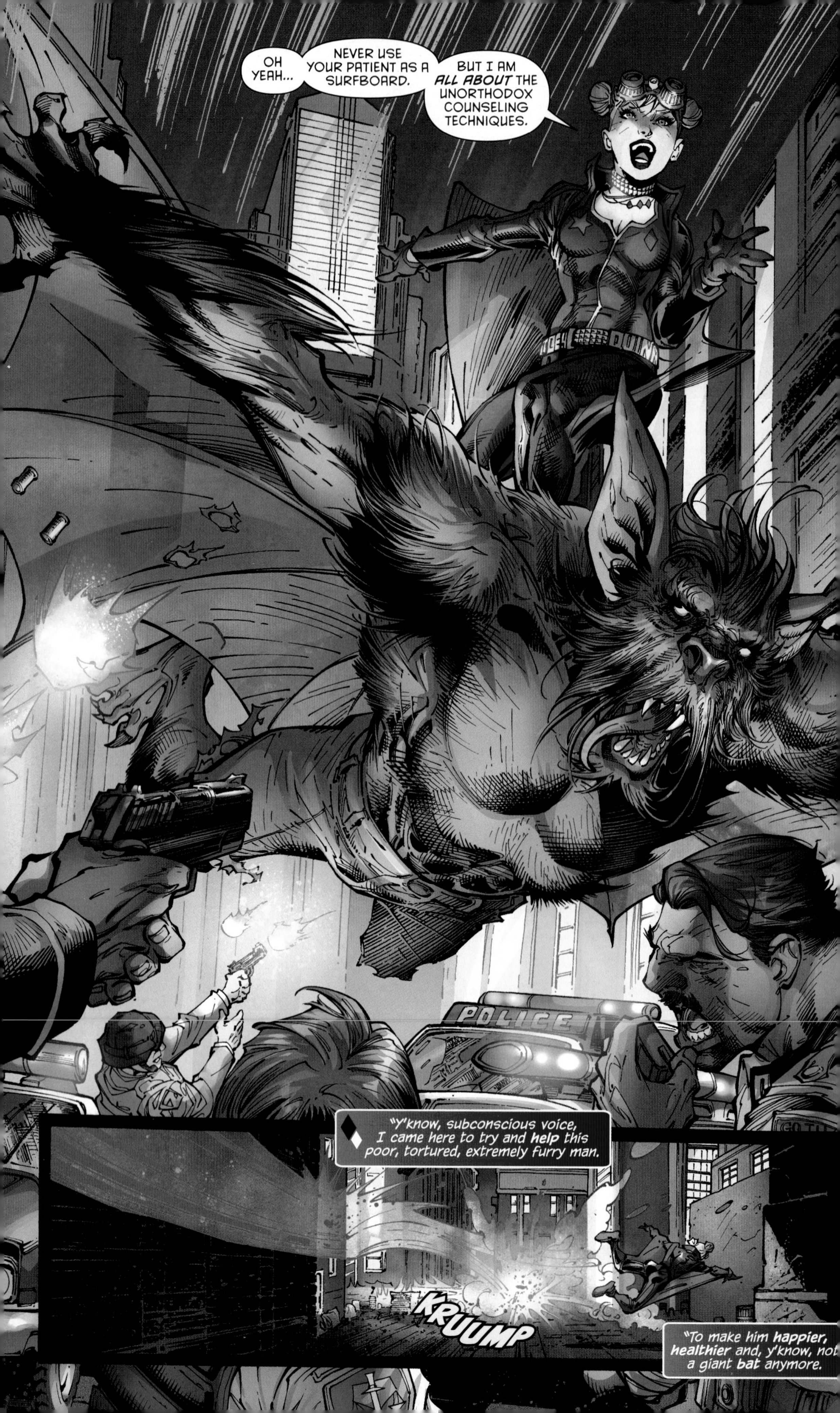
OH YEAH...
NEVER USE YOUR PATIENT AS A SURFBOARD.
BUT I AM ALL ABOUT THE UNORTHODOX COUNSELING TECHNIQUES.
POLICE
"Y'know, subconscious voice, I came here to try and help this poor, tortured, extremely furry man.
KRUUMP
"To make him happier, healthier and, y'know, not a giant bat anymore.

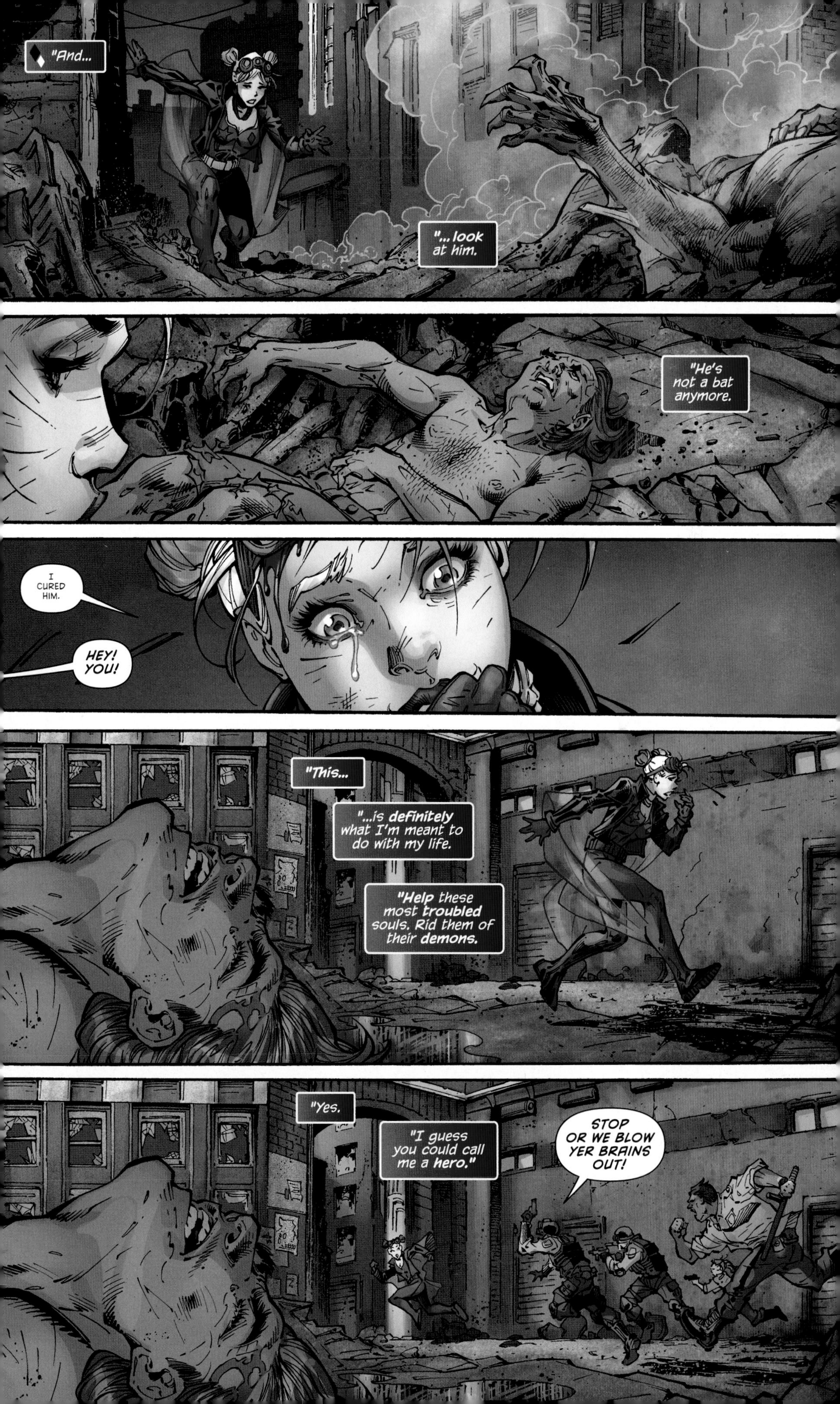
"And...
"...look at him.
"He's not a bat anymore.
I CURED HIM.
HEY! YOU!
"This...
"...is definitely what I'm meant to do with my life.
"Help these most troubled souls. Rid them of their demons.
"Yes.
"I guess you could call me a hero."
STOP OR WE BLOW YER BRAINS OUT!

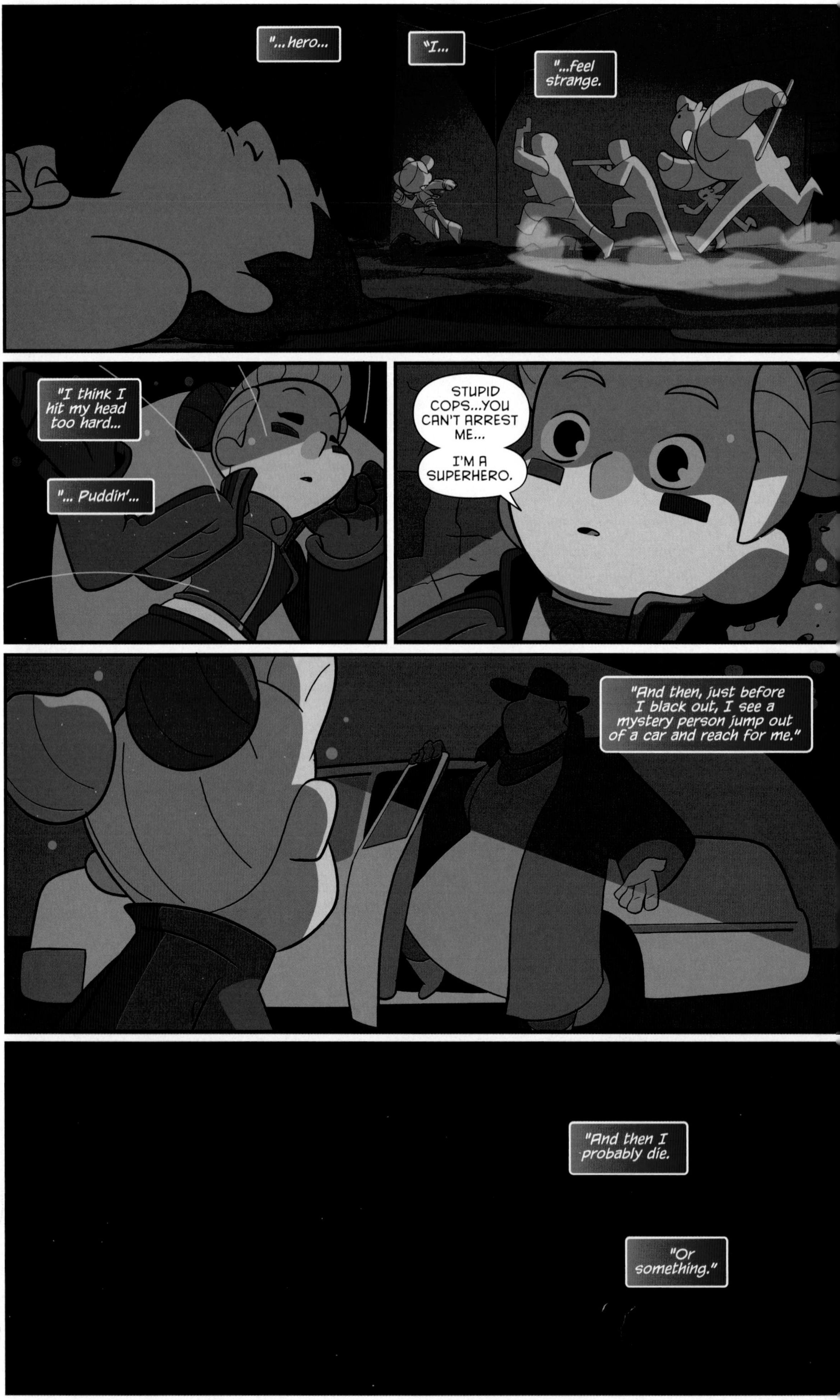
"...hero...
"I...
"...feel strange.
"I think I hit my head too hard...
"... Puddin'...
STUPID COPS...YOU CAN'T ARREST ME...
I'M A SUPERHERO.
"And then, just before I black out, I see a mystery person jump out of a car and reach for me."
"And then I probably die.
"Or something."

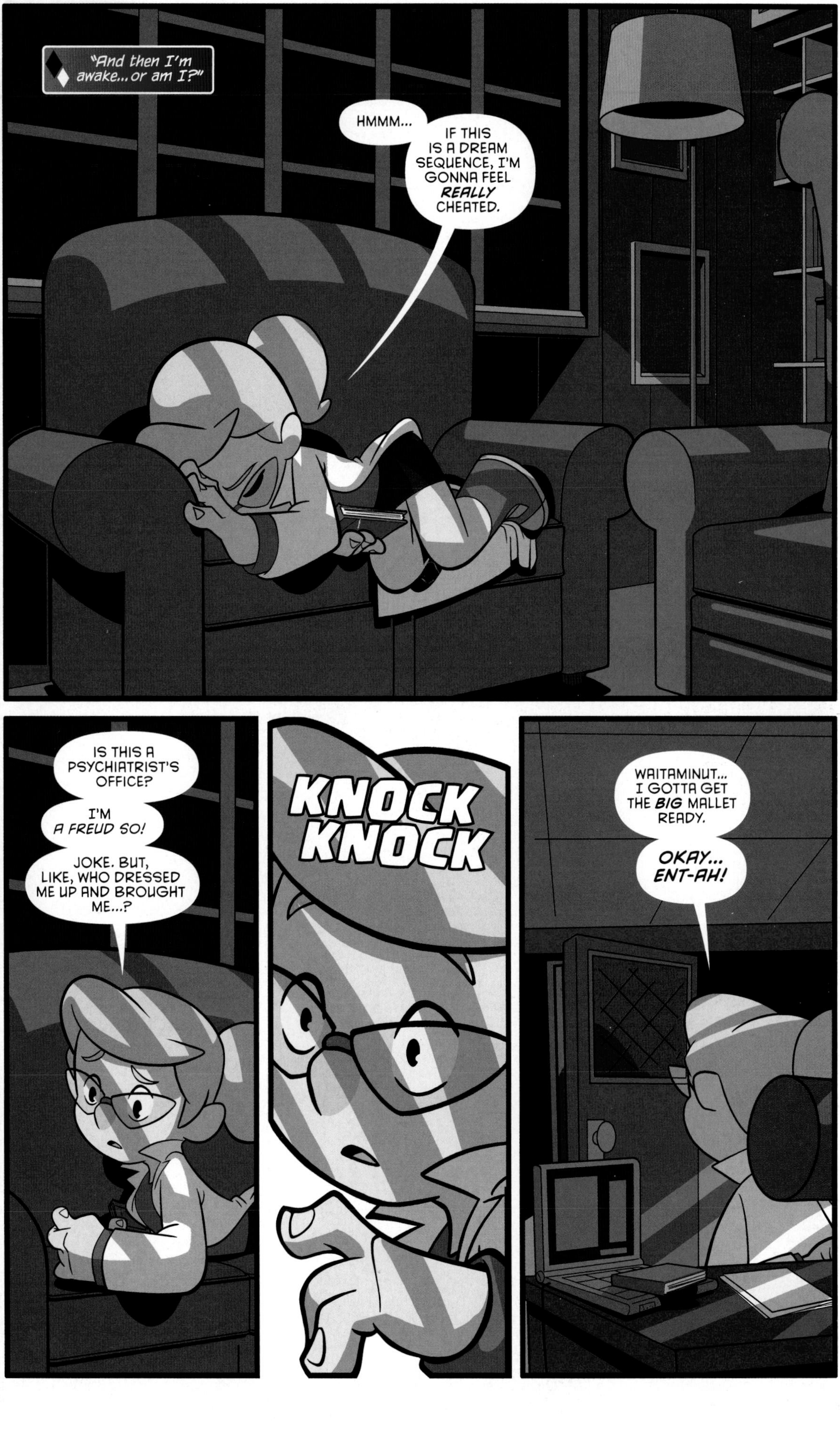
"And then I'm awake...or am I?"
HMMM...
IF THIS IS A DREAM SEQUENCE, I'M GONNA FEEL *REALLY* CHEATED.
IS THIS A PSYCHIATRIST'S OFFICE?
I'M *A FREUD SO!*
JOKE. BUT, LIKE, WHO DRESSED ME UP AND BROUGHT ME...?
KNOCK KNOCK
WAITAMINUT... I GOTTA GET THE *BIG* MALLET READY.
OKAY... ENT-AH!

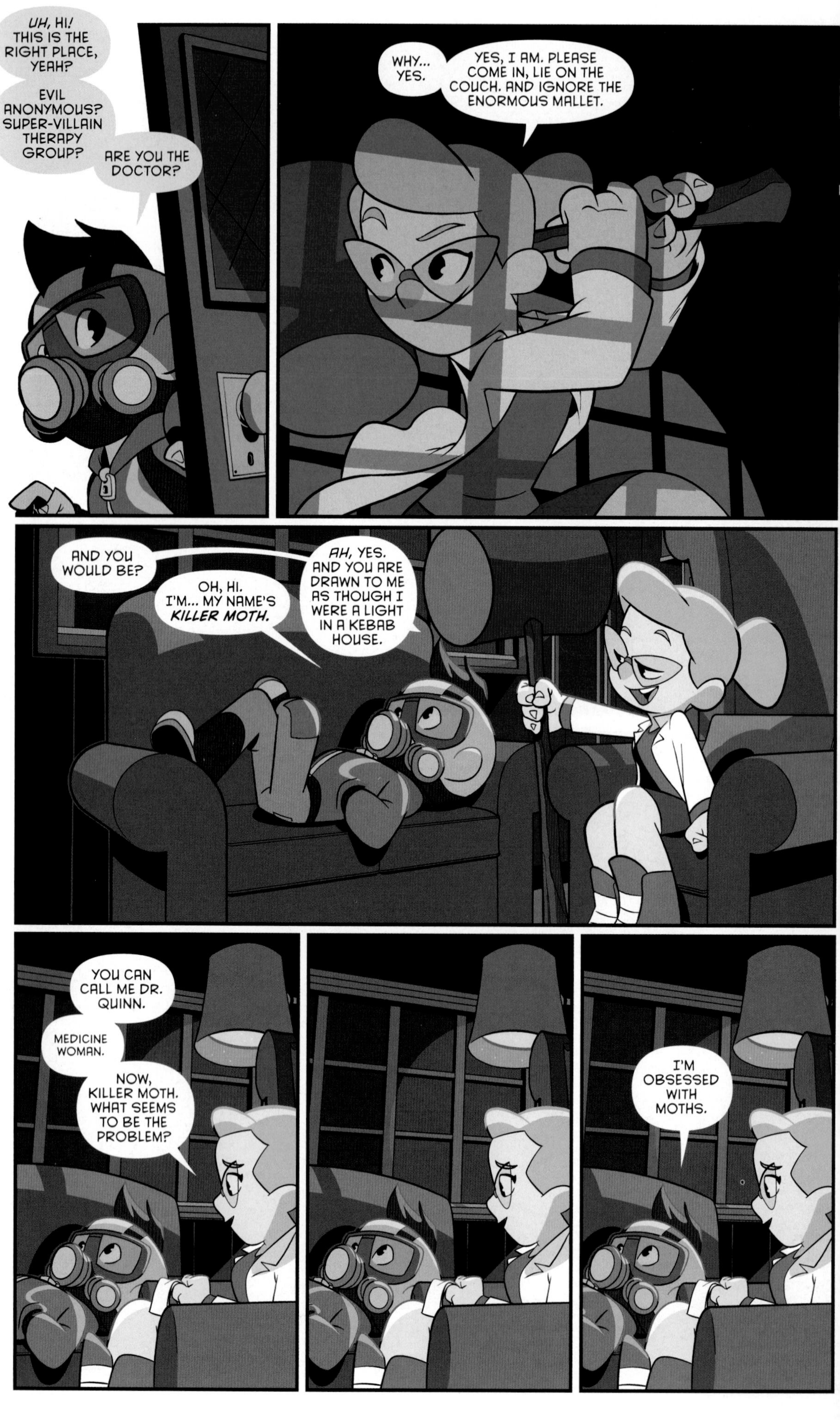
UH, HI!
THIS IS THE RIGHT PLACE, YEAH?
EVIL ANONYMOUS? SUPER-VILLAIN THERAPY GROUP?
ARE YOU THE DOCTOR?
WHY... YES.
YES, I AM. PLEASE COME IN, LIE ON THE COUCH. AND IGNORE THE ENORMOUS MALLET.
AND YOU WOULD BE?
OH, HI. I'M... MY NAME'S KILLER MOTH.
AH, YES. AND YOU ARE DRAWN TO ME AS THOUGH I WERE A LIGHT IN A KEBAB HOUSE.
YOU CAN CALL ME DR. QUINN.
MEDICINE WOMAN.
NOW, KILLER MOTH. WHAT SEEMS TO BE THE PROBLEM?
I'M OBSESSED WITH MOTHS.

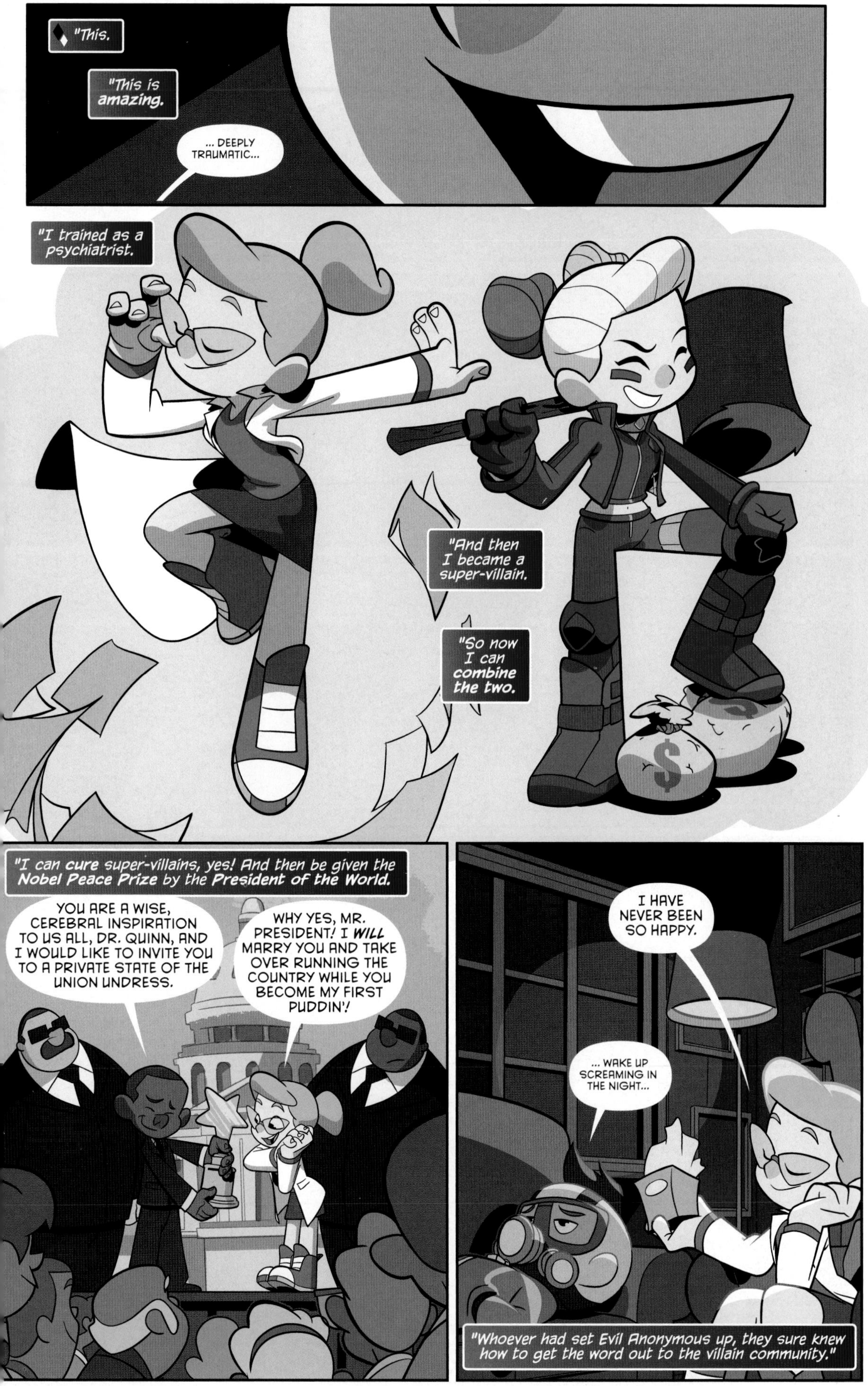

"This.
"This is amazing.
... DEEPLY TRAUMATIC...
"I trained as a psychiatrist.
"And then I became a super-villain.
"So now I can combine the two.
"I can cure super-villains, yes! And then be given the Nobel Peace Prize by the President of the World.
YOU ARE A WISE, CEREBRAL INSPIRATION TO US ALL, DR. QUINN, AND I WOULD LIKE TO INVITE YOU TO A PRIVATE STATE OF THE UNION UNDRESS.
WHY YES, MR. PRESIDENT! I WILL MARRY YOU AND TAKE OVER RUNNING THE COUNTRY WHILE YOU BECOME MY FIRST PUDDIN'!
I HAVE NEVER BEEN SO HAPPY.
... WAKE UP SCREAMING IN THE NIGHT...
"Whoever had set Evil Anonymous up, they sure knew how to get the word out to the villain community."

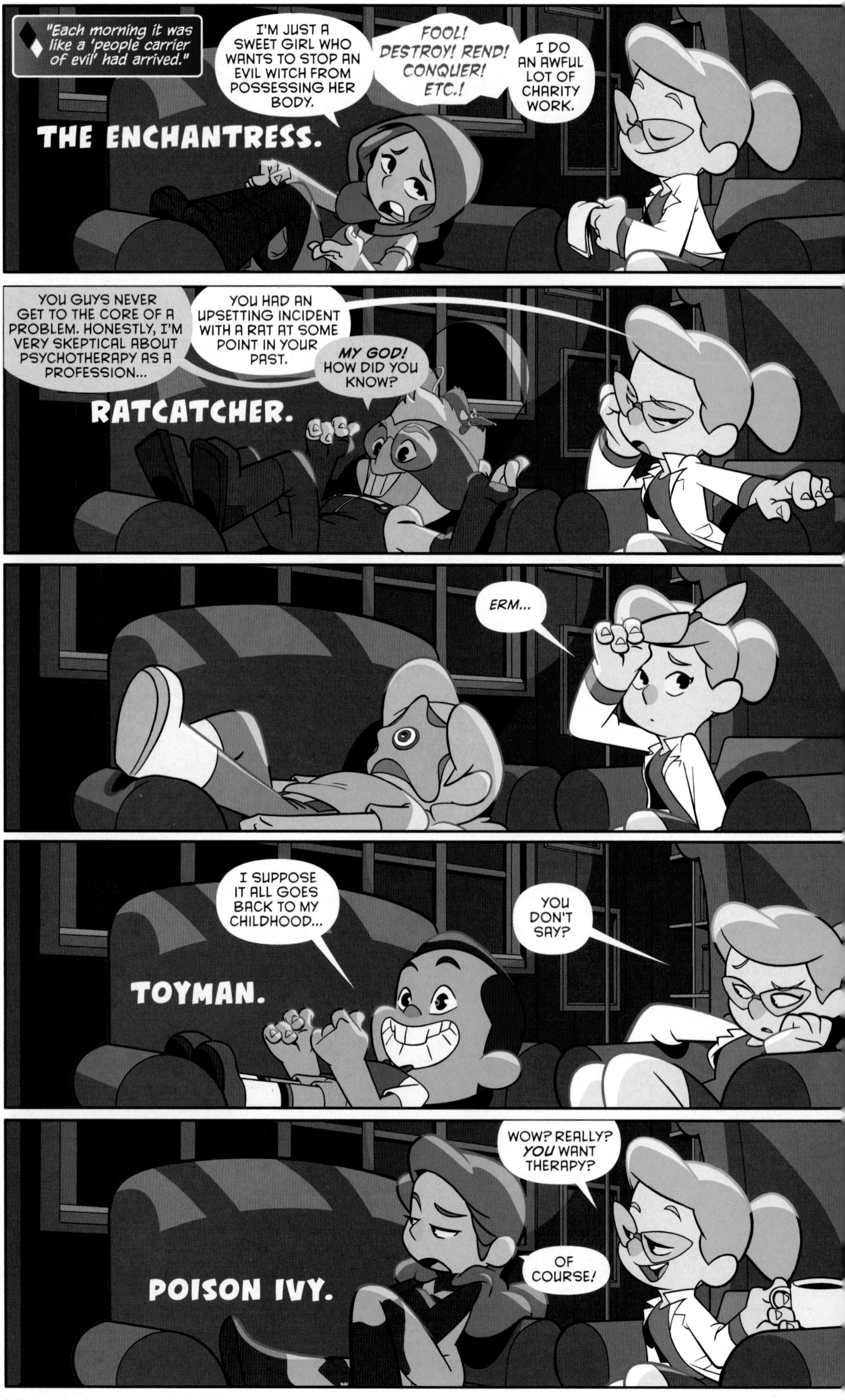

"Each morning it was like a 'people carrier of evil' had arrived."
I'M JUST A SWEET GIRL WHO WANTS TO STOP AN EVIL WITCH FROM POSSESSING HER BODY.
FOOL! DESTROY! REND! CONQUER! ETC.!
I DO AN AWFUL LOT OF CHARITY WORK.
THE ENCHANTRESS.
YOU GUYS NEVER GET TO THE CORE OF A PROBLEM. HONESTLY, I'M VERY SKEPTICAL ABOUT PSYCHOTHERAPY AS A PROFESSION...
YOU HAD AN UPSETTING INCIDENT WITH A RAT AT SOME POINT IN YOUR PAST.
MY GOD! HOW DID YOU KNOW?
RATCATCHER.
ERM...
I SUPPOSE IT ALL GOES BACK TO MY CHILDHOOD...
YOU DON'T SAY?
TOYMAN.
WOW? REALLY? YOU WANT THERAPY?
OF COURSE!
POISON IVY.

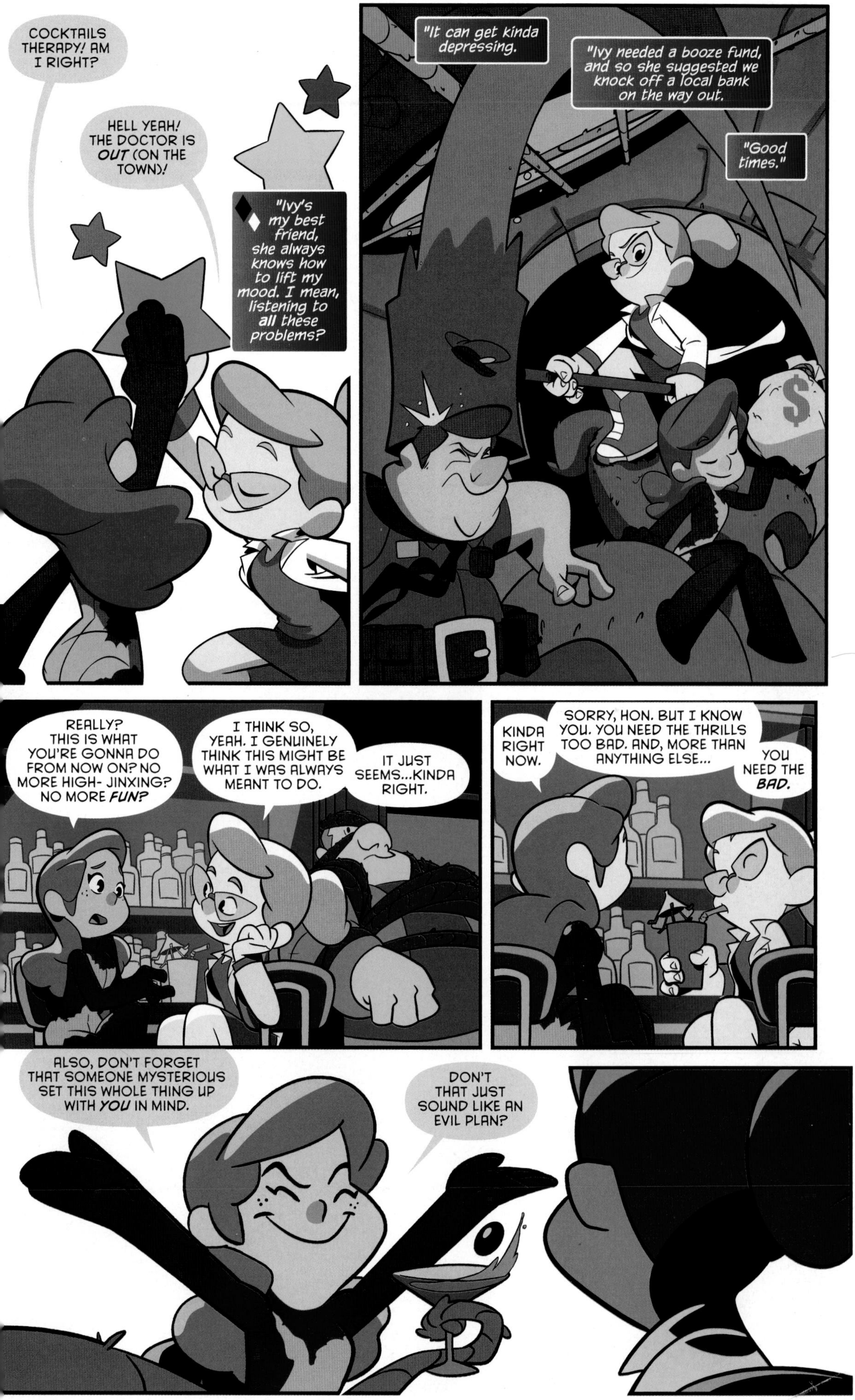
COCKTAILS THERAPY! AM I RIGHT?
HELL YEAH! THE DOCTOR IS *OUT* (ON THE TOWN)!
"Ivy's my best friend, she always knows how to lift my mood. I mean, listening to *all* these problems?
"It can get kinda depressing.
"Ivy needed a booze fund, and so she suggested we knock off a local bank on the way out.
"Good times."
REALLY? THIS IS WHAT YOU'RE GONNA DO FROM NOW ON? NO MORE HIGH- JINXING? NO MORE *FUN*?
I THINK SO, YEAH. I GENUINELY THINK THIS MIGHT BE WHAT I WAS ALWAYS MEANT TO DO.
IT JUST SEEMS...KINDA RIGHT.
KINDA RIGHT NOW.
SORRY, HON. BUT I KNOW YOU. YOU NEED THE THRILLS TOO BAD. AND, MORE THAN ANYTHING ELSE...
YOU NEED THE *BAD*.
ALSO, DON'T FORGET THAT SOMEONE MYSTERIOUS SET THIS WHOLE THING UP WITH *YOU* IN MIND.
DON'T THAT JUST SOUND LIKE AN EVIL PLAN?

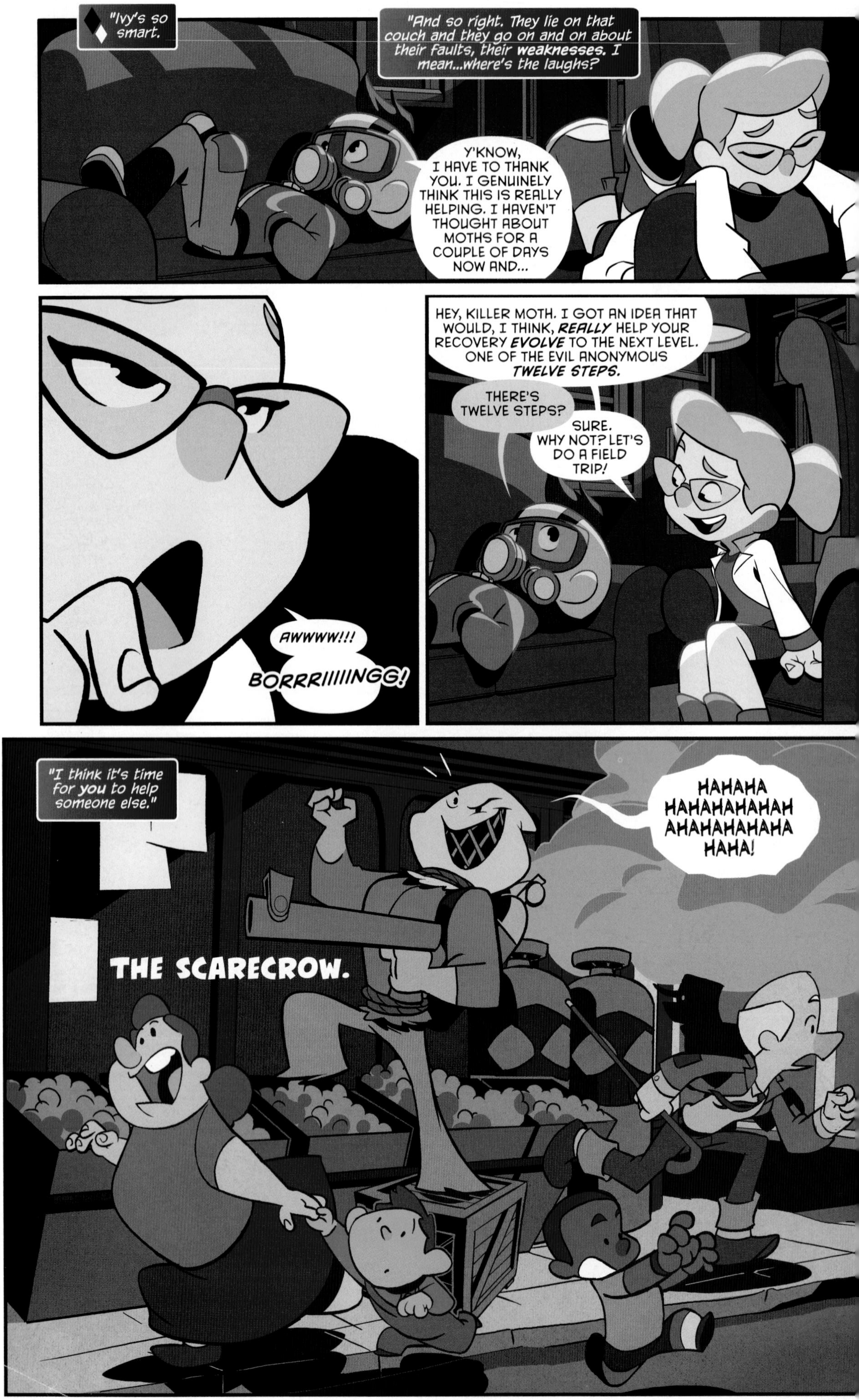
"Ivy's so smart.
"And so right. They lie on that couch and they go on and on about their faults, their **weaknesses.** I mean...where's the laughs?
Y'KNOW, I HAVE TO THANK YOU. I GENUINELY THINK THIS IS REALLY HELPING. I HAVEN'T THOUGHT ABOUT MOTHS FOR A COUPLE OF DAYS NOW AND...
AWWWW!!!
BORRRIIIIINGG!
HEY, KILLER MOTH. I GOT AN IDEA THAT WOULD, I THINK, ***REALLY*** HELP YOUR RECOVERY ***EVOLVE*** TO THE NEXT LEVEL. ONE OF THE EVIL ANONYMOUS ***TWELVE STEPS.***
THERE'S TWELVE STEPS?
SURE. WHY NOT? LET'S DO A FIELD TRIP!
"I think it's time for **you** to help someone else."
HAHAHA HAHAHAHAHAH AHAHAHAHAHA HAHA!
THE SCARECROW.

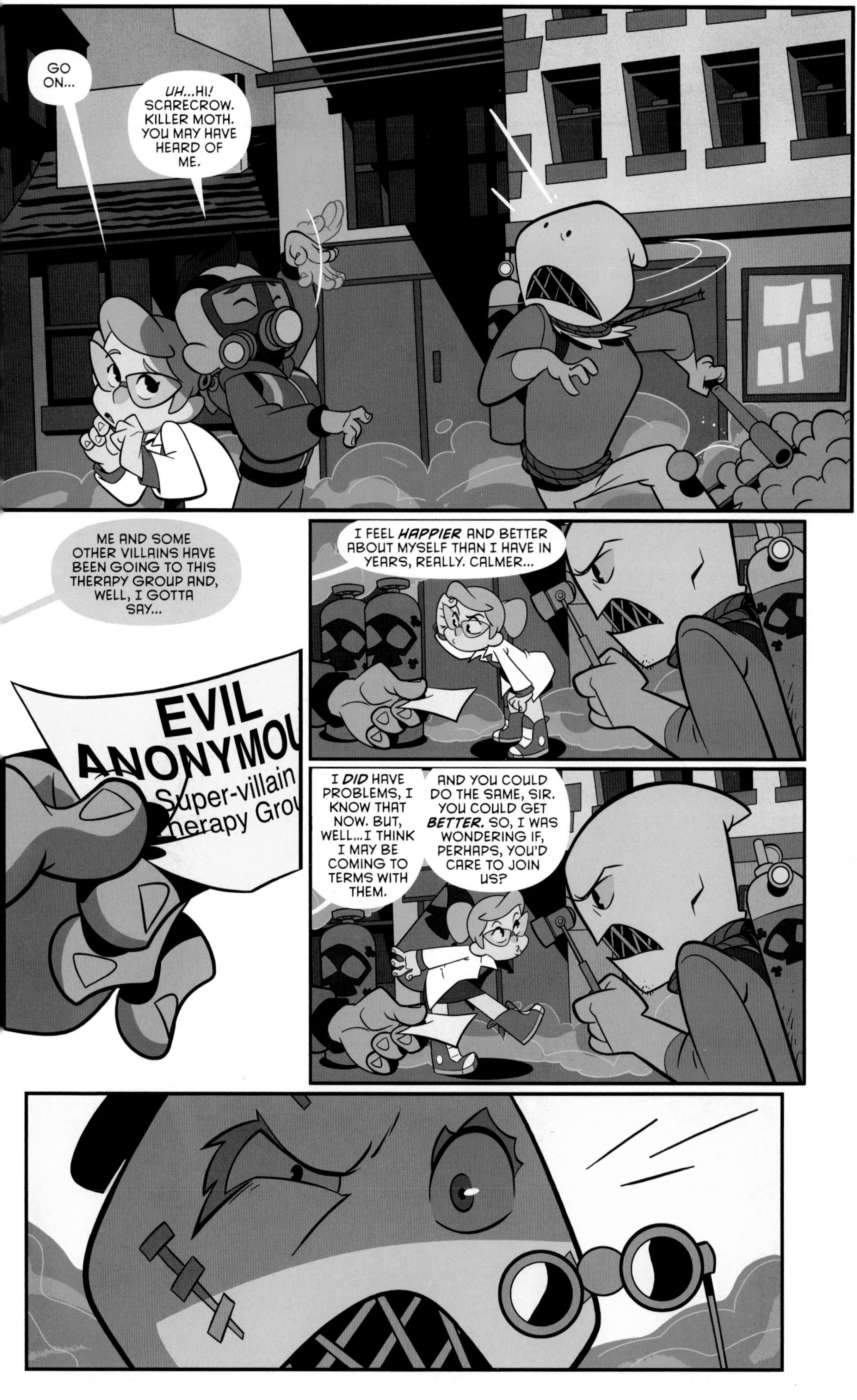
GO ON...
UH...HI! SCARECROW. KILLER MOTH. YOU MAY HAVE HEARD OF ME.
ME AND SOME OTHER VILLAINS HAVE BEEN GOING TO THIS THERAPY GROUP AND, WELL, I GOTTA SAY...
I FEEL HAPPIER AND BETTER ABOUT MYSELF THAN I HAVE IN YEARS, REALLY. CALMER...
EVIL ANONYMOU
Super-villain
herapy Grou
I DID HAVE PROBLEMS, I KNOW THAT NOW. BUT, WELL...I THINK I MAY BE COMING TO TERMS WITH THEM.
AND YOU COULD DO THE SAME, SIR. YOU COULD GET BETTER. SO, I WAS WONDERING IF, PERHAPS, YOU'D CARE TO JOIN US?

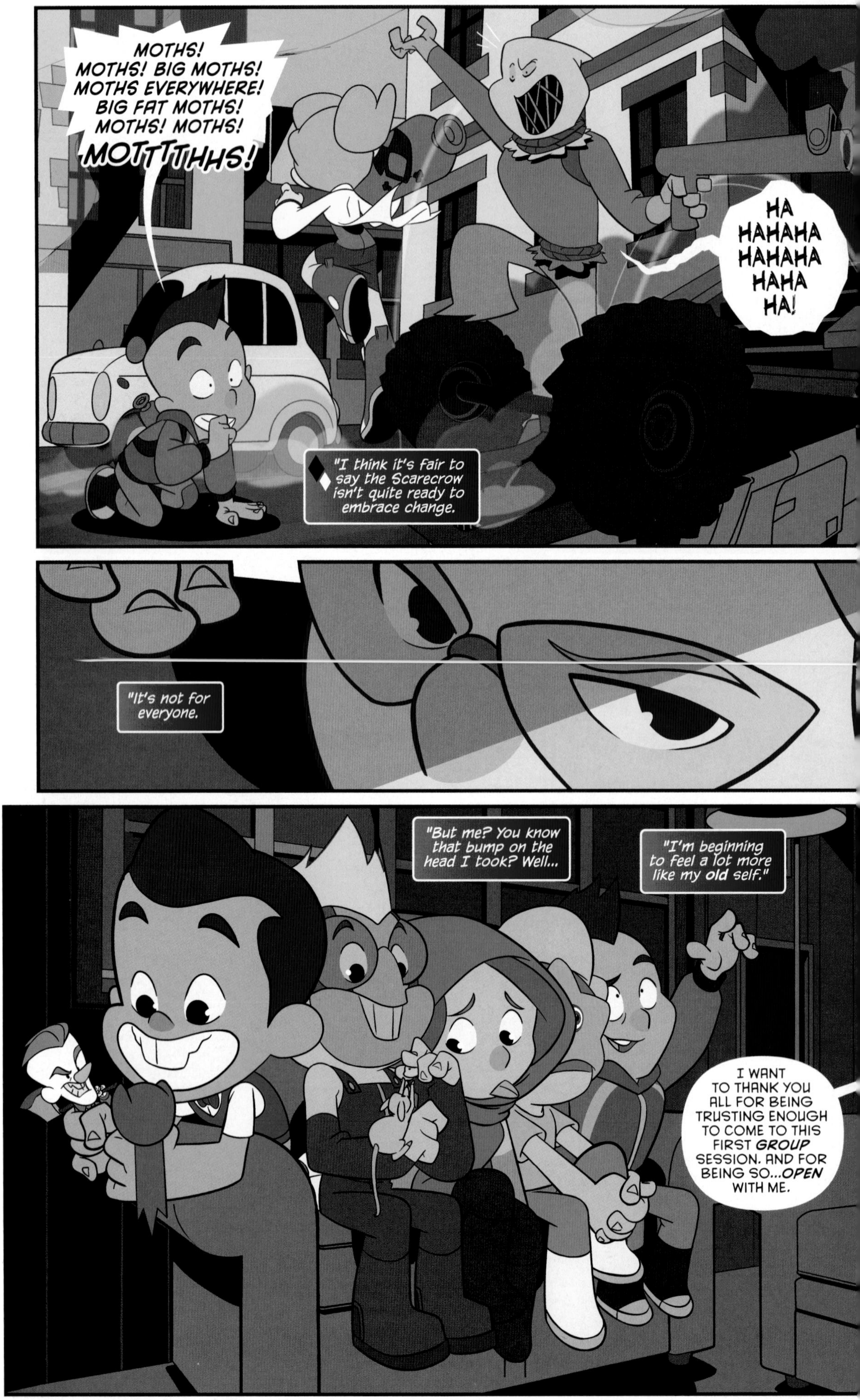
MOTHS! MOTHS! BIG MOTHS! MOTHS EVERYWHERE! BIG FAT MOTHS! MOTHS! MOTHS! MOTTTTHHS!
HA HAHAHA HAHAHA HAHA HA!
"I think it's fair to say the Scarecrow isn't quite ready to embrace change.
"It's not for everyone.
"But me? You know that bump on the head I took? Well...
"I'm beginning to feel a lot more like my old self."
I WANT TO THANK YOU ALL FOR BEING TRUSTING ENOUGH TO COME TO THIS FIRST GROUP SESSION. AND FOR BEING SO...OPEN WITH ME.

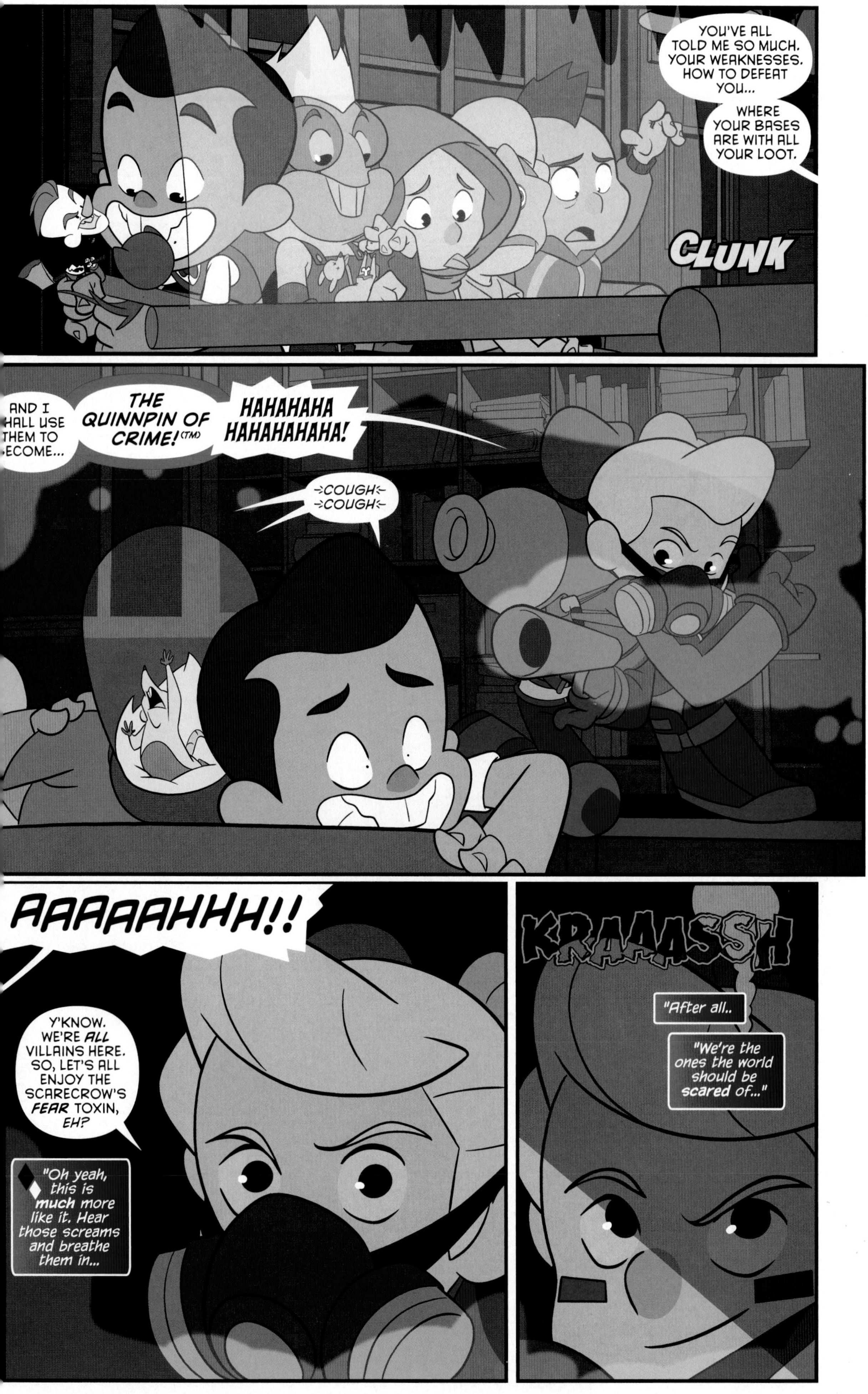

YOU'VE ALL TOLD ME SO MUCH. YOUR WEAKNESSES. HOW TO DEFEAT YOU...
WHERE YOUR BASES ARE WITH ALL YOUR LOOT.
CLUNK
AND I HALL USE THEM TO ECOME...
THE QUINNPIN OF CRIME!(TM)
HAHAHAHA HAHAHAHAHA!
COUGH COUGH
AAAAAHHH!!
Y'KNOW. WE'RE ALL VILLAINS HERE. SO, LET'S ALL ENJOY THE SCARECROW'S FEAR TOXIN, EH?
"Oh yeah, this is much more like it. Hear those screams and breathe them in...
KRAAASSH
"After all..
"We're the ones the world should be scared of..."

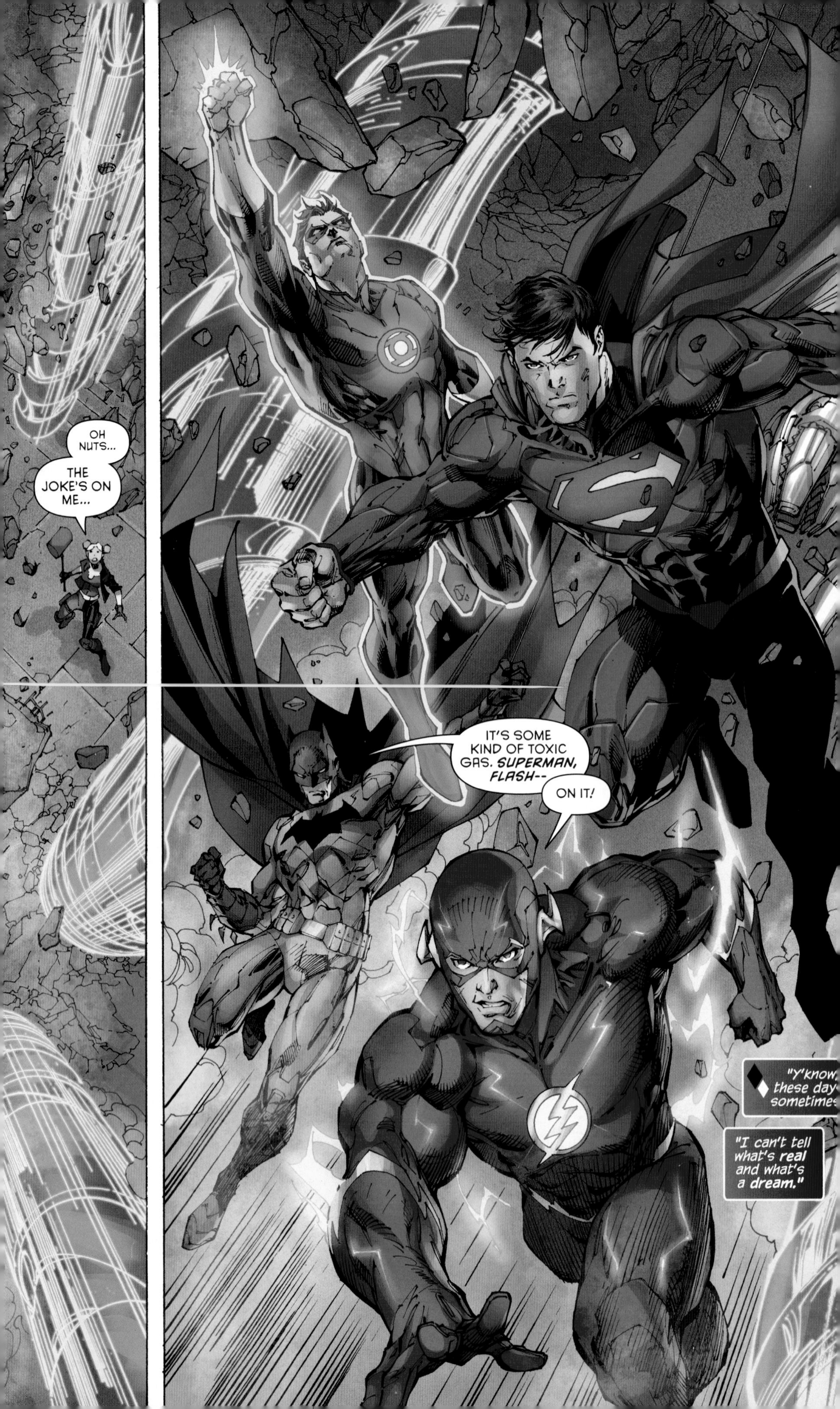
OH NUTS...
THE JOKE'S ON ME...
IT'S SOME KIND OF TOXIC GAS. *SUPERMAN, FLASH--*
ON IT!
"Y'know, these day sometimes
"I can't tell what's **real** and what's a **dream.**"

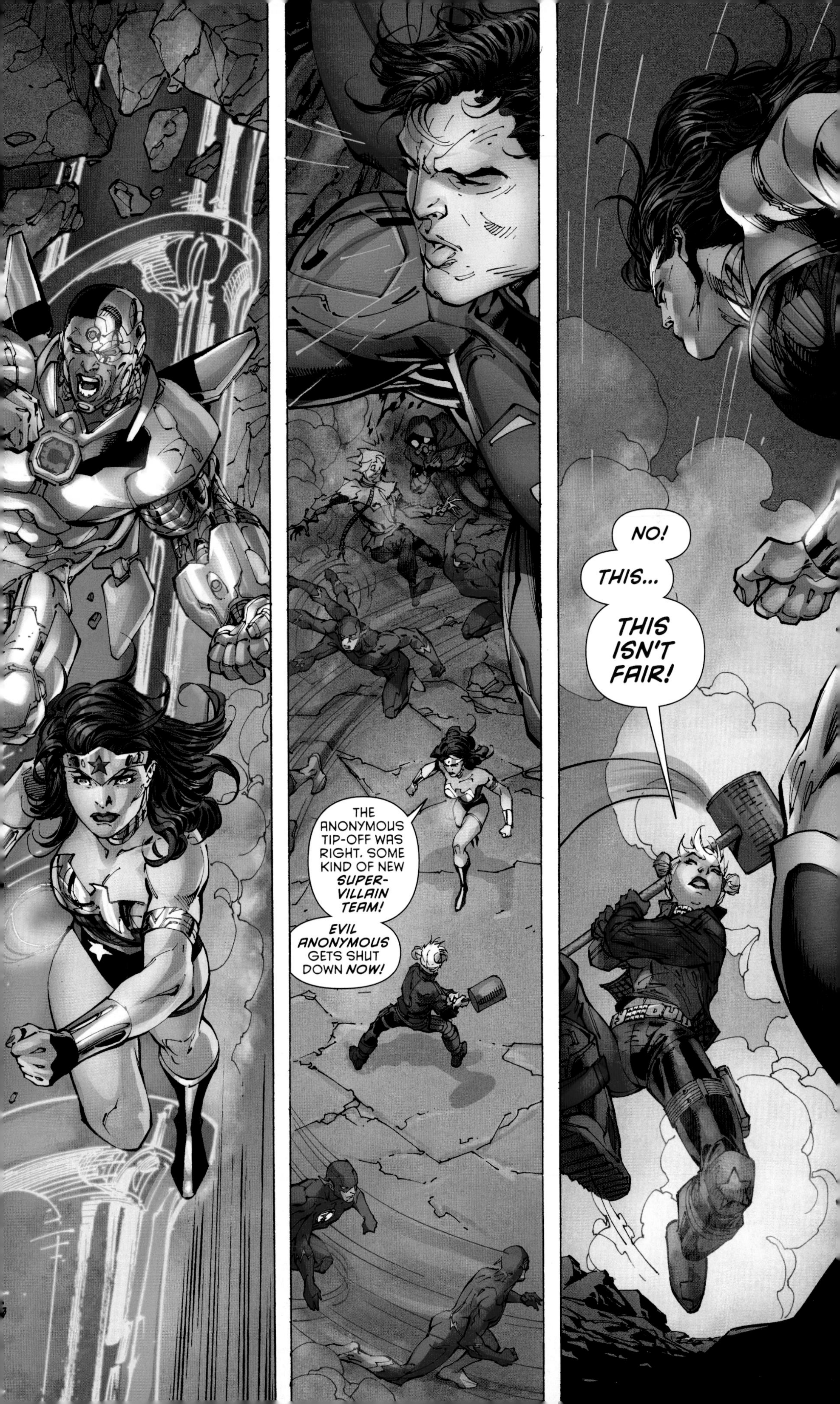
THE ANONYMOUS TIP-OFF WAS RIGHT. SOME KIND OF NEW SUPER-VILLAIN TEAM!
EVIL ANONYMOUS GETS SHUT DOWN NOW!
NO!
THIS...
THIS ISN'T FAIR!

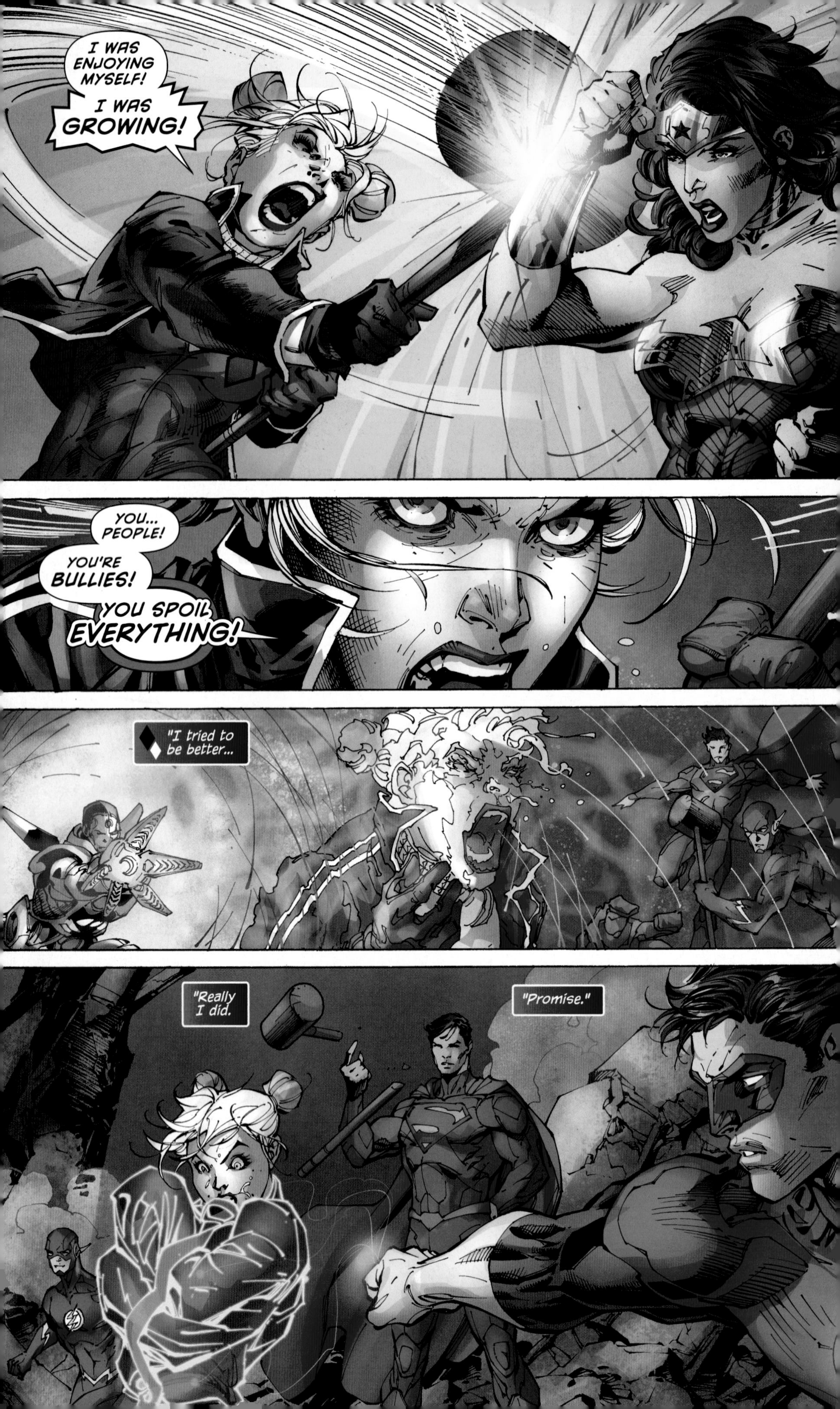
I WAS ENJOYING MYSELF!
I WAS GROWING!
YOU... PEOPLE!
YOU'RE BULLIES!
YOU SPOIL EVERYTHING!
"I tried to be better...
"Really I did.
"Promise."

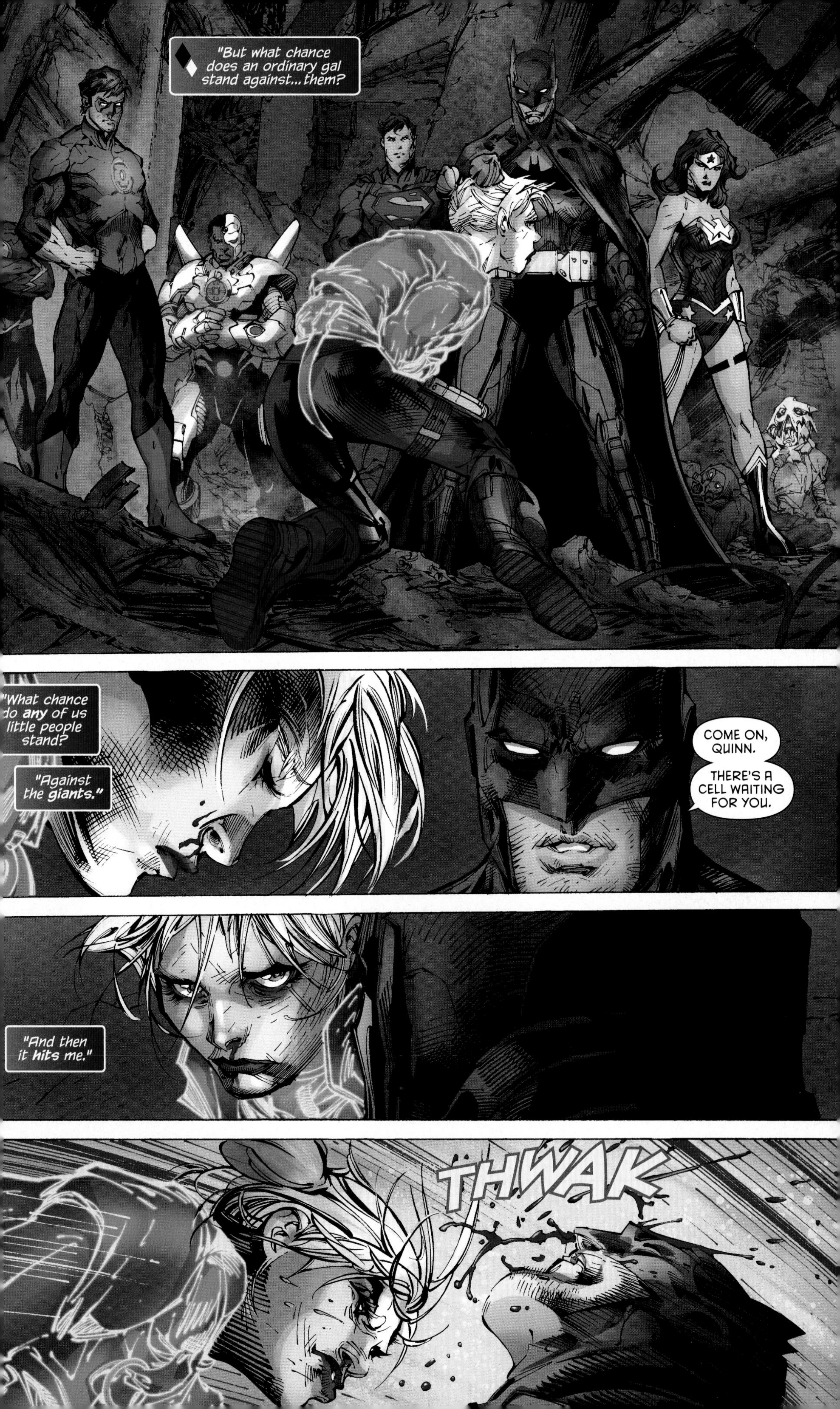
"But what chance does an ordinary gal stand against...them?
"What chance do any of us little people stand?
"Against the giants."
COME ON, QUINN.
THERE'S A CELL WAITING FOR YOU.
"And then it hits me."
THWAK

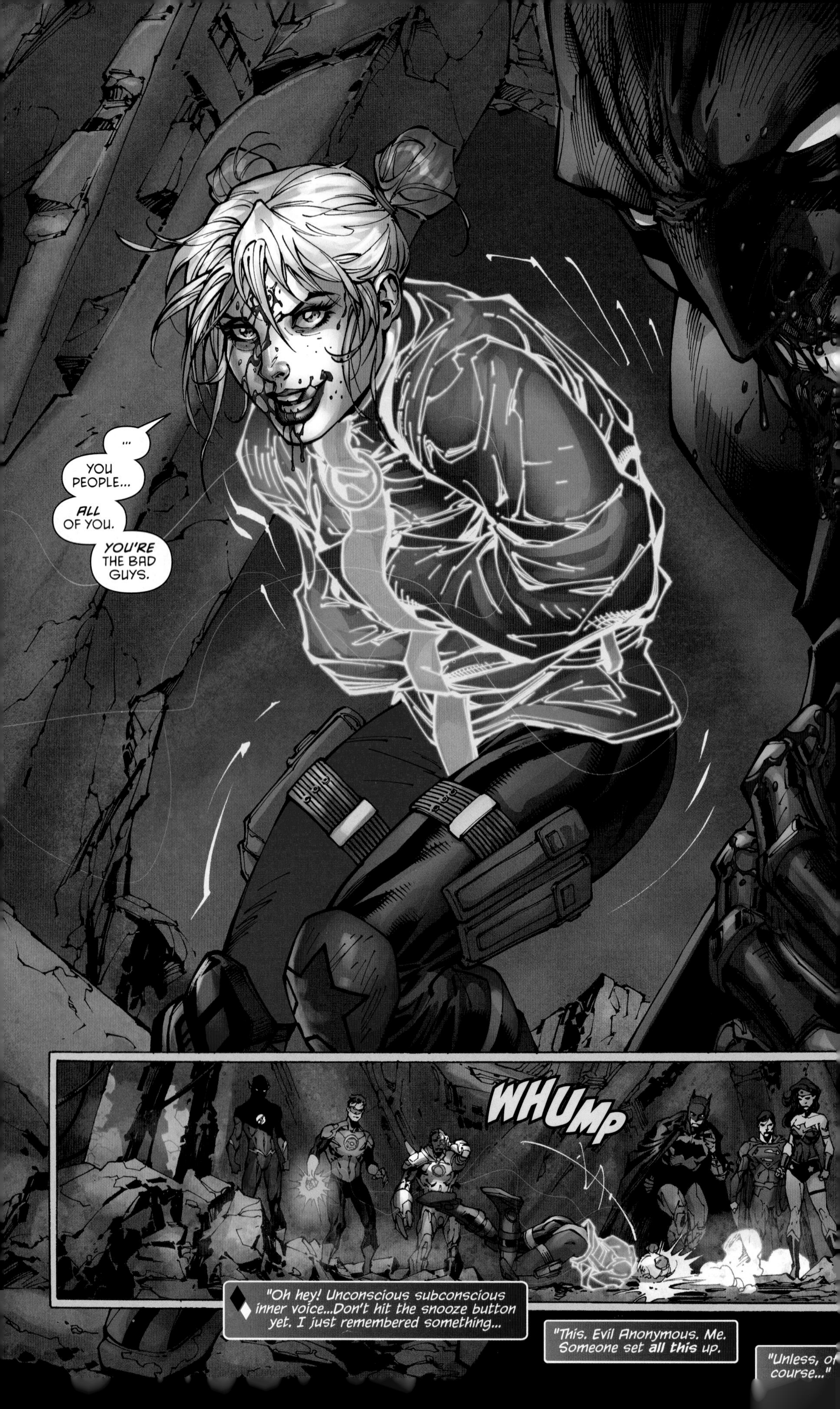

...
YOU PEOPLE...
ALL OF YOU.
YOU'RE THE BAD GUYS.
WHUMP
"Oh hey! Unconscious subconscious inner voice...Don't hit the snooze button yet. I just remembered something...
"This. Evil Anonymous. Me. Someone set all this up.
"Unless, of course..."

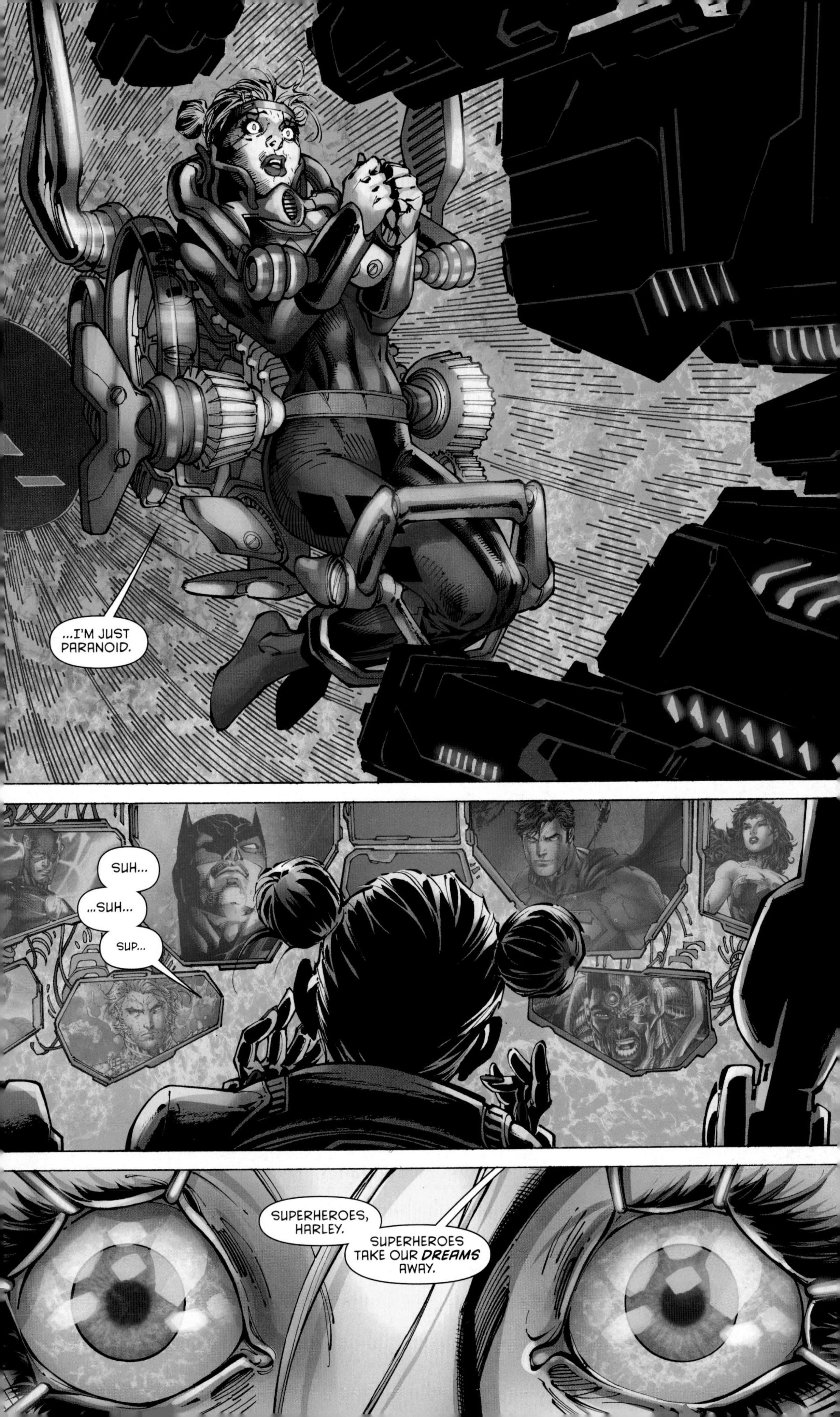
...I'M JUST PARANOID.
SUH...
...SUH...
SUP...
SUPERHEROES, HARLEY.
SUPERHEROES TAKE OUR DREAMS AWAY.

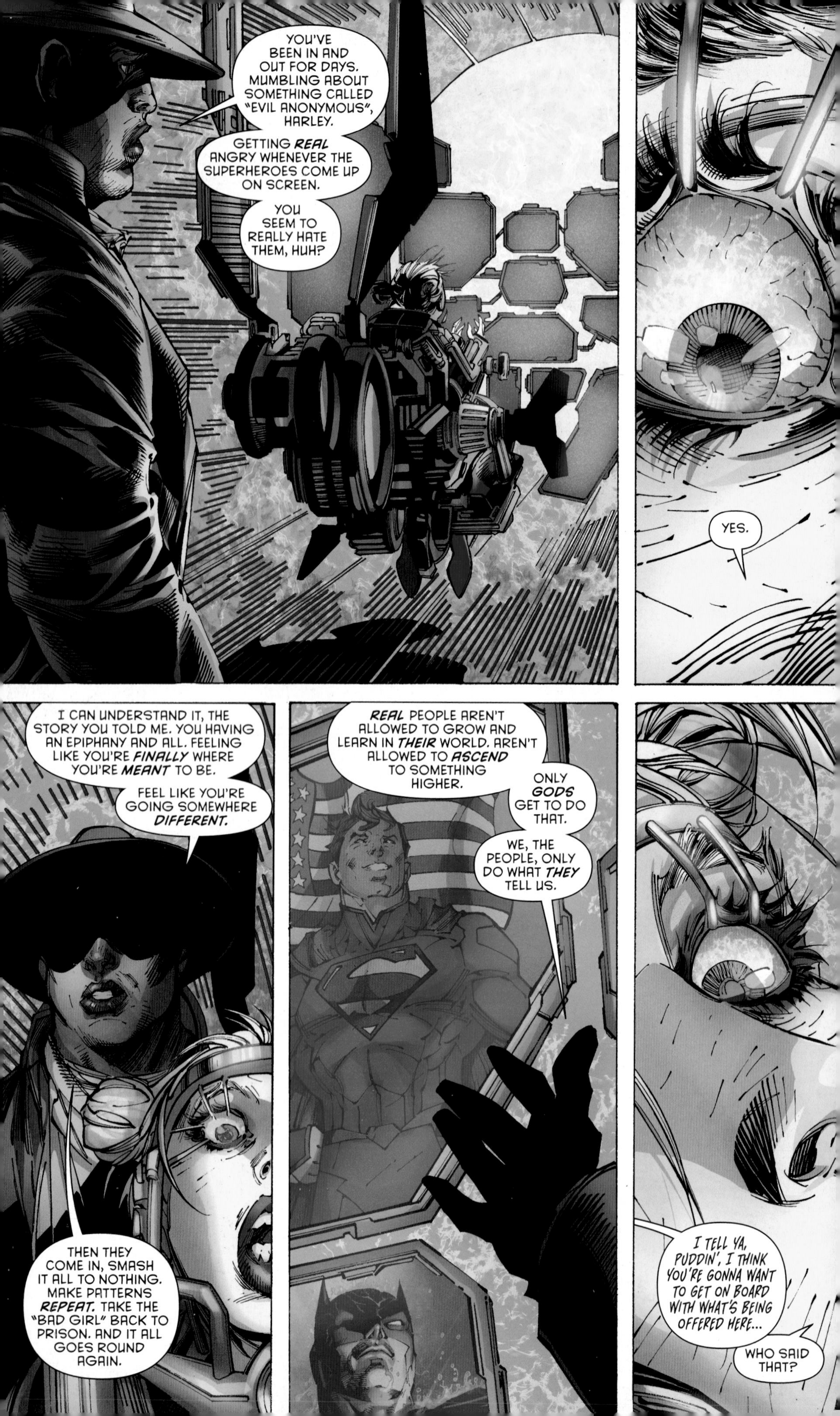
YOU'VE BEEN IN AND OUT FOR DAYS. MUMBLING ABOUT SOMETHING CALLED "EVIL ANONYMOUS", HARLEY.
GETTING REAL ANGRY WHENEVER THE SUPERHEROES COME UP ON SCREEN.
YOU SEEM TO REALLY HATE THEM, HUH?
YES.
I CAN UNDERSTAND IT, THE STORY YOU TOLD ME. YOU HAVING AN EPIPHANY AND ALL. FEELING LIKE YOU'RE FINALLY WHERE YOU'RE MEANT TO BE.
FEEL LIKE YOU'RE GOING SOMEWHERE DIFFERENT.
THEN THEY COME IN, SMASH IT ALL TO NOTHING. MAKE PATTERNS REPEAT. TAKE THE "BAD GIRL" BACK TO PRISON. AND IT ALL GOES ROUND AGAIN.
REAL PEOPLE AREN'T ALLOWED TO GROW AND LEARN IN THEIR WORLD. AREN'T ALLOWED TO ASCEND TO SOMETHING HIGHER.
ONLY GODS GET TO DO THAT.
WE, THE PEOPLE, ONLY DO WHAT THEY TELL US.
I TELL YA, PUDDIN', I THINK YOU'RE GONNA WANT TO GET ON BOARD WITH WHAT'S BEING OFFERED HERE...
WHO SAID THAT?

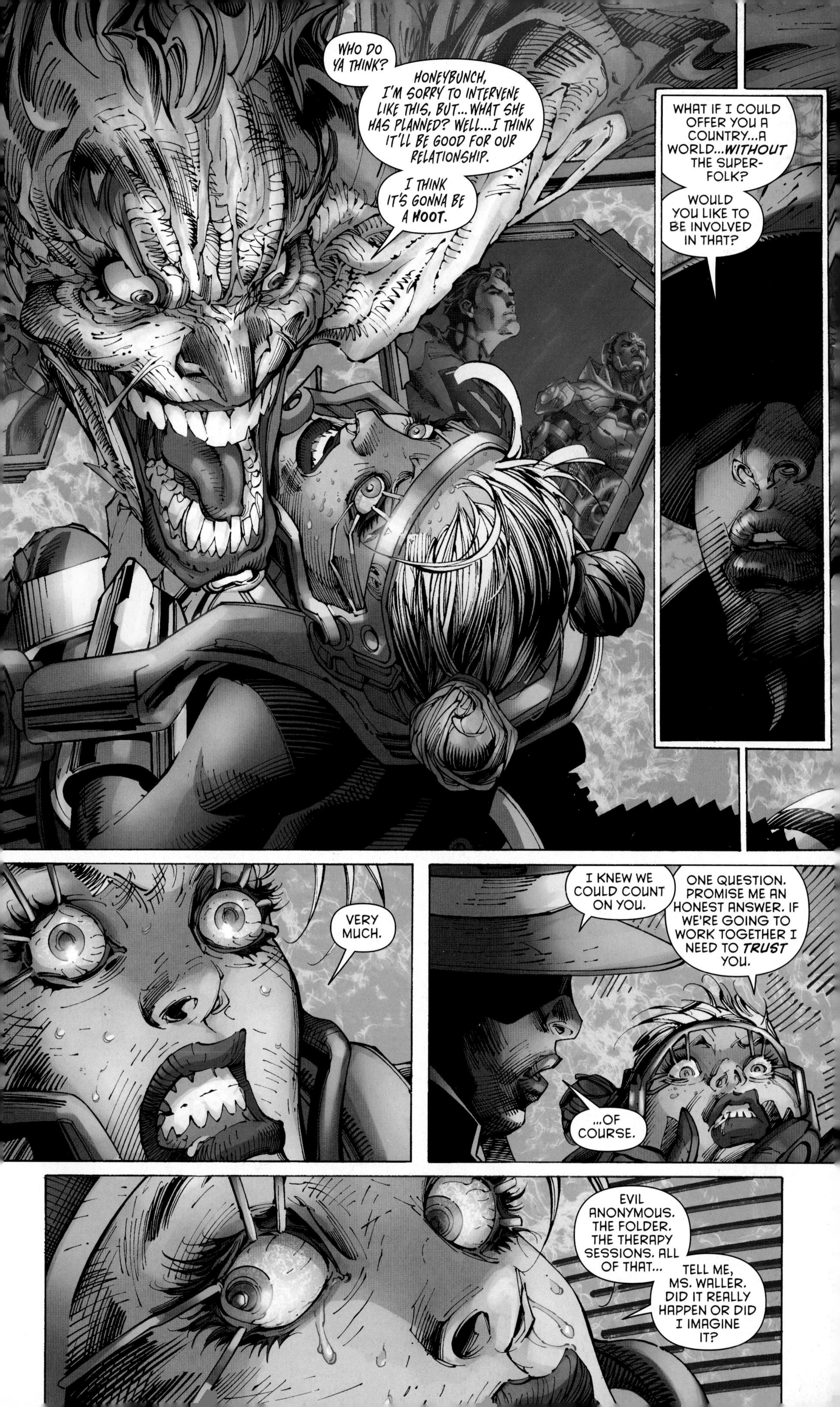
WHO DO YA THINK?
HONEYBUNCH, I'M SORRY TO INTERVENE LIKE THIS, BUT...WHAT SHE HAS PLANNED? WELL...I THINK IT'LL BE GOOD FOR OUR RELATIONSHIP.
I THINK IT'S GONNA BE A HOOT.
WHAT IF I COULD OFFER YOU A COUNTRY...A WORLD...WITHOUT THE SUPER-FOLK?
WOULD YOU LIKE TO BE INVOLVED IN THAT?
VERY MUCH.
I KNEW WE COULD COUNT ON YOU.
ONE QUESTION. PROMISE ME AN HONEST ANSWER. IF WE'RE GOING TO WORK TOGETHER I NEED TO TRUST YOU.
...OF COURSE.
EVIL ANONYMOUS. THE FOLDER. THE THERAPY SESSIONS. ALL OF THAT...
TELL ME, MS. WALLER. DID IT REALLY HAPPEN OR DID I IMAGINE IT?

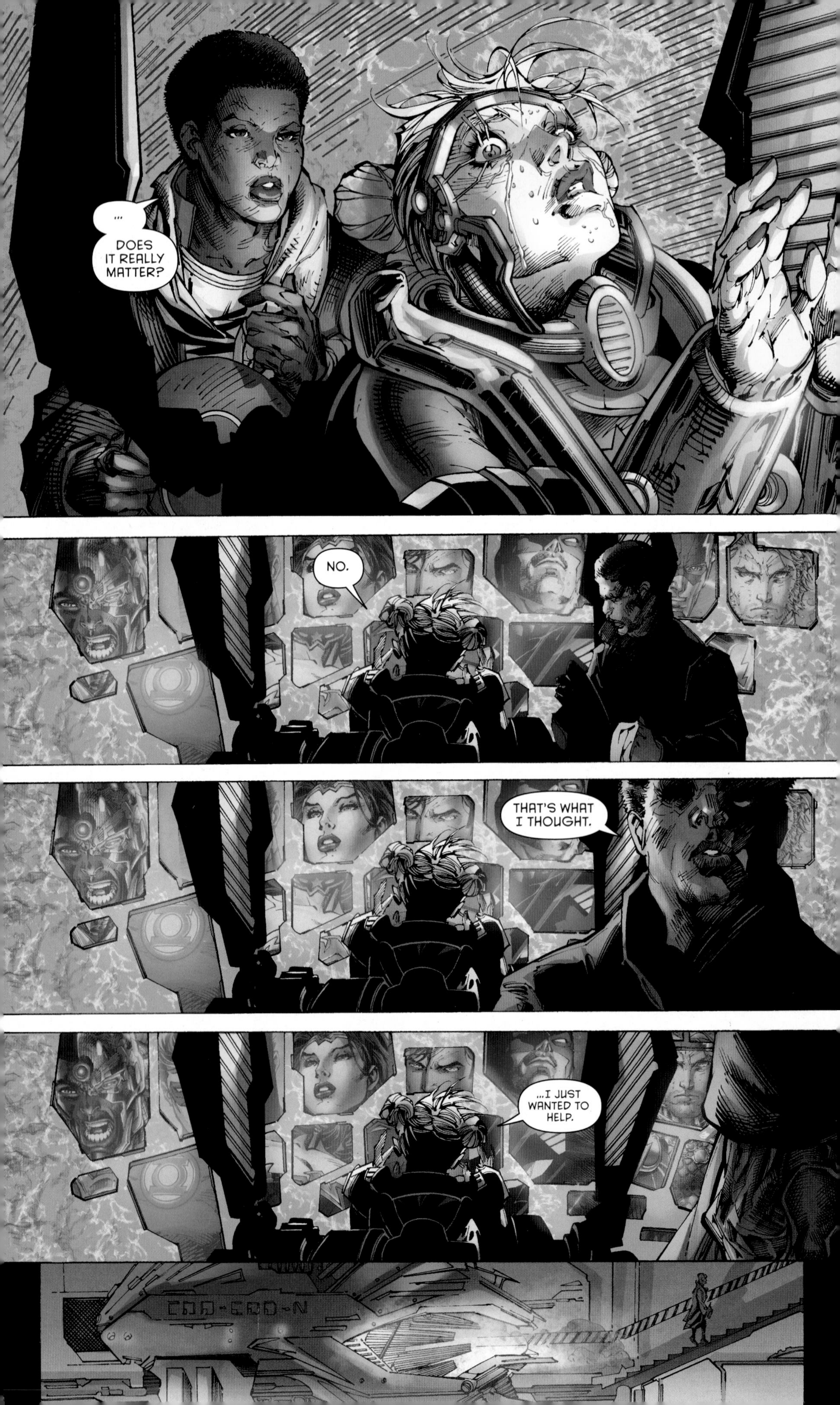
...
DOES IT REALLY MATTER?
NO.
THAT'S WHAT I THOUGHT.
...I JUST WANTED TO HELP.
COD-COD-N

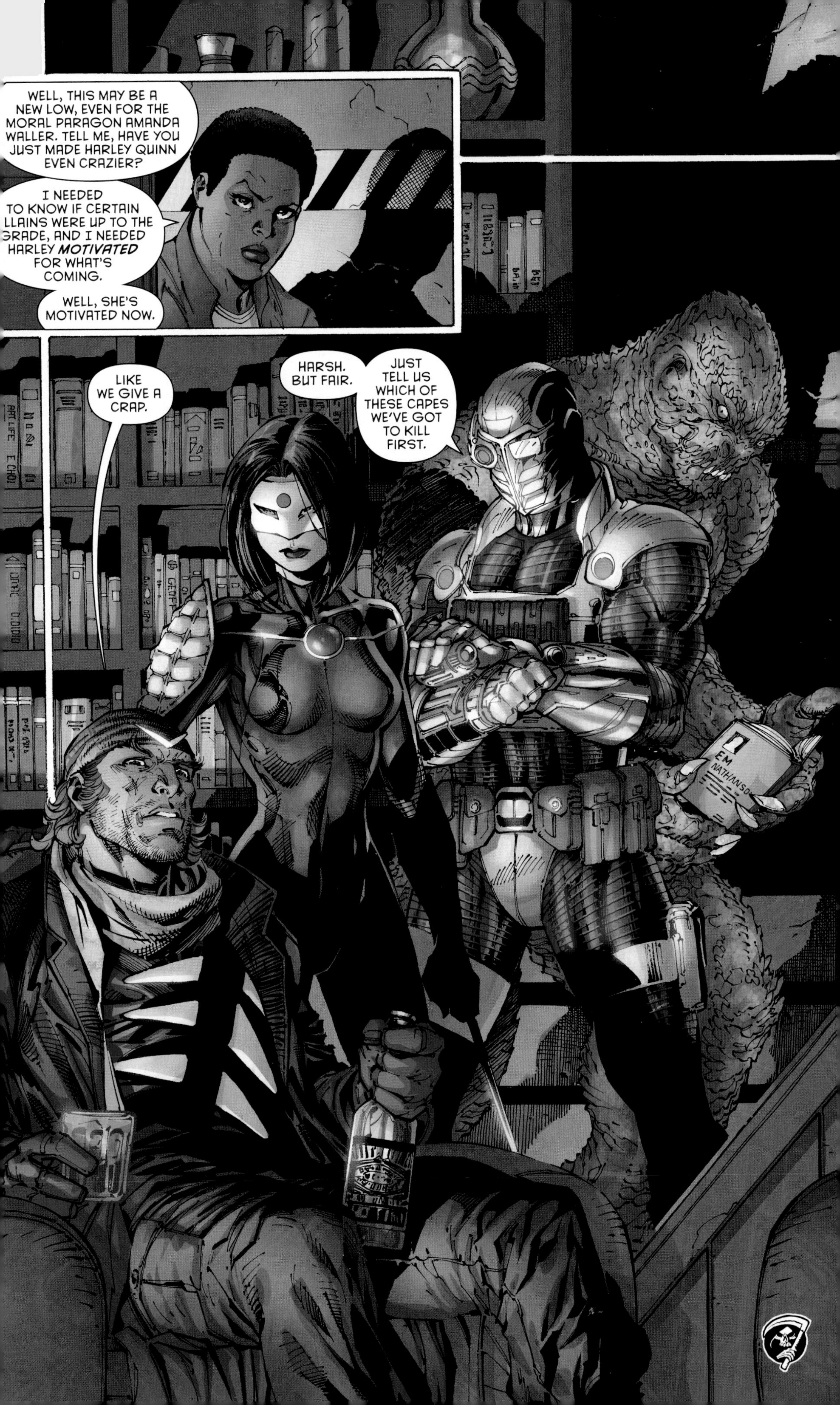

WELL, THIS MAY BE A NEW LOW, EVEN FOR THE MORAL PARAGON AMANDA WALLER. TELL ME, HAVE YOU JUST MADE HARLEY QUINN EVEN CRAZIER?
I NEEDED TO KNOW IF CERTAIN LLAINS WERE UP TO THE GRADE, AND I NEEDED HARLEY *MOTIVATED* FOR WHAT'S COMING.
WELL, SHE'S MOTIVATED NOW.
LIKE WE GIVE A CRAP.
HARSH. BUT FAIR.
JUST TELL US WHICH OF THESE CAPES WE'VE GOT TO KILL FIRST.

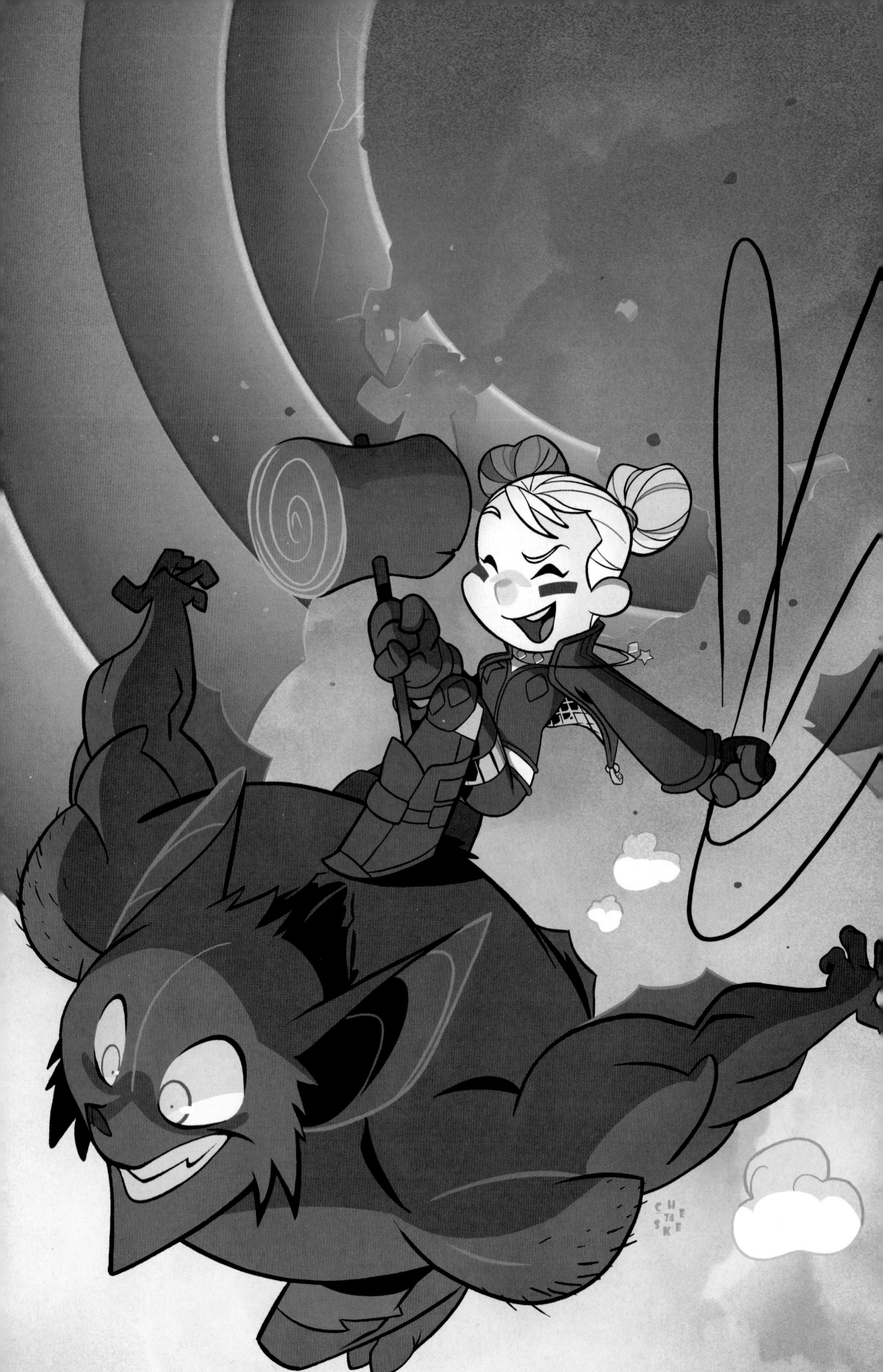
CHEESKE 74

Variant cover art for HARLEY QUINN AND THE SUICIDE SQUAD APRIL FOOLS' SPECIAL #1
by SEAN "CHEEKS" GALLOWAY

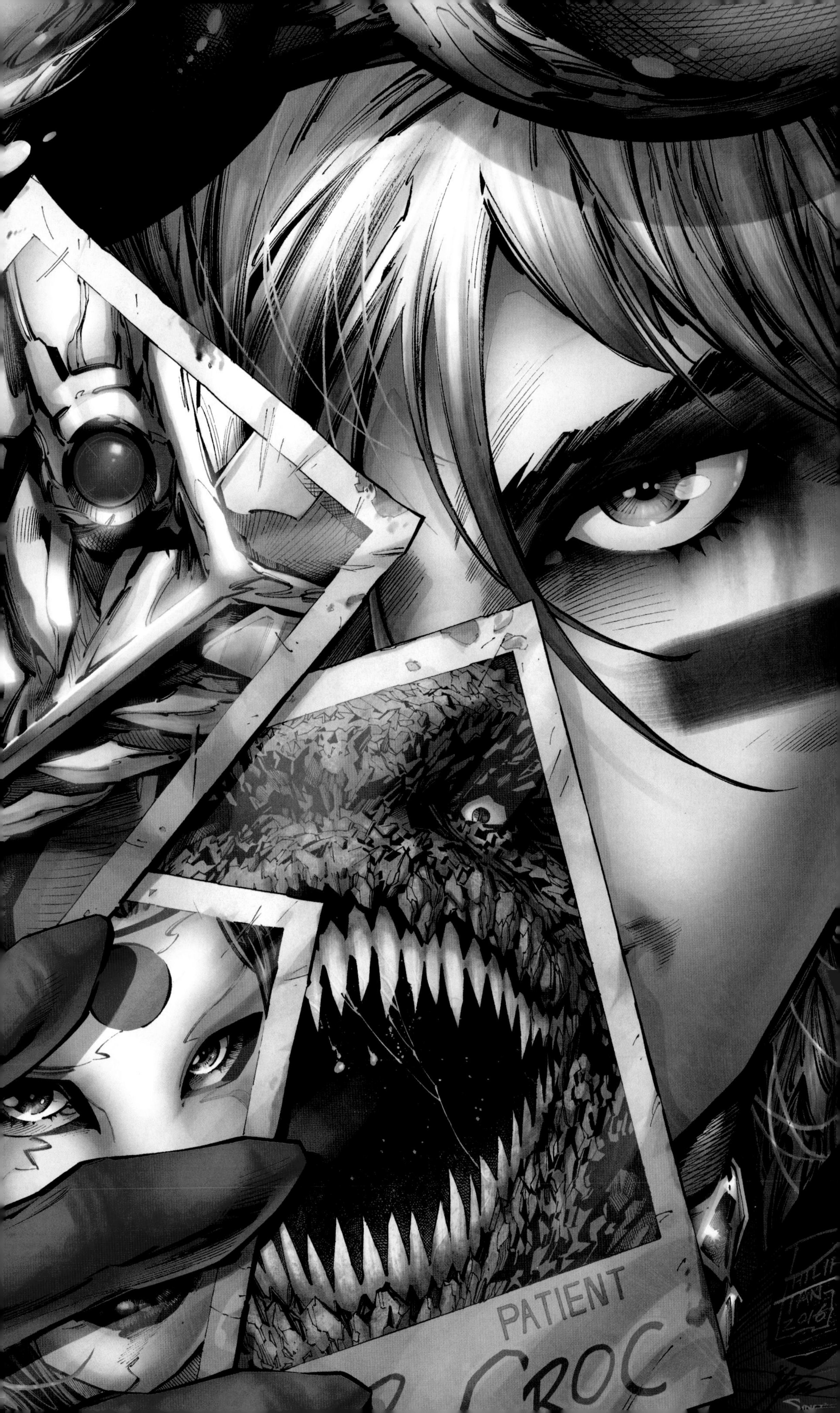
PATIENT
CROC

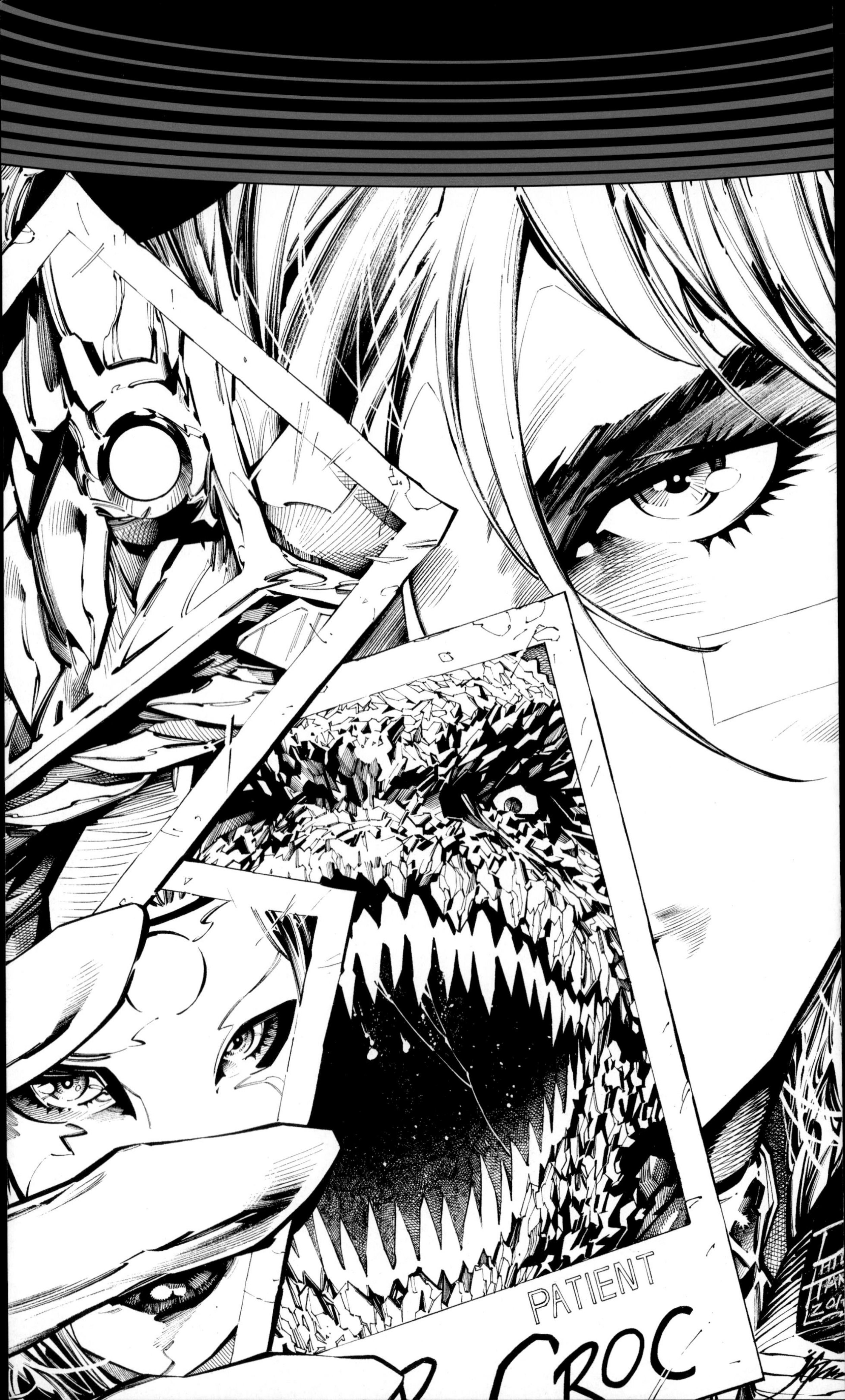
PATIENT
CROC

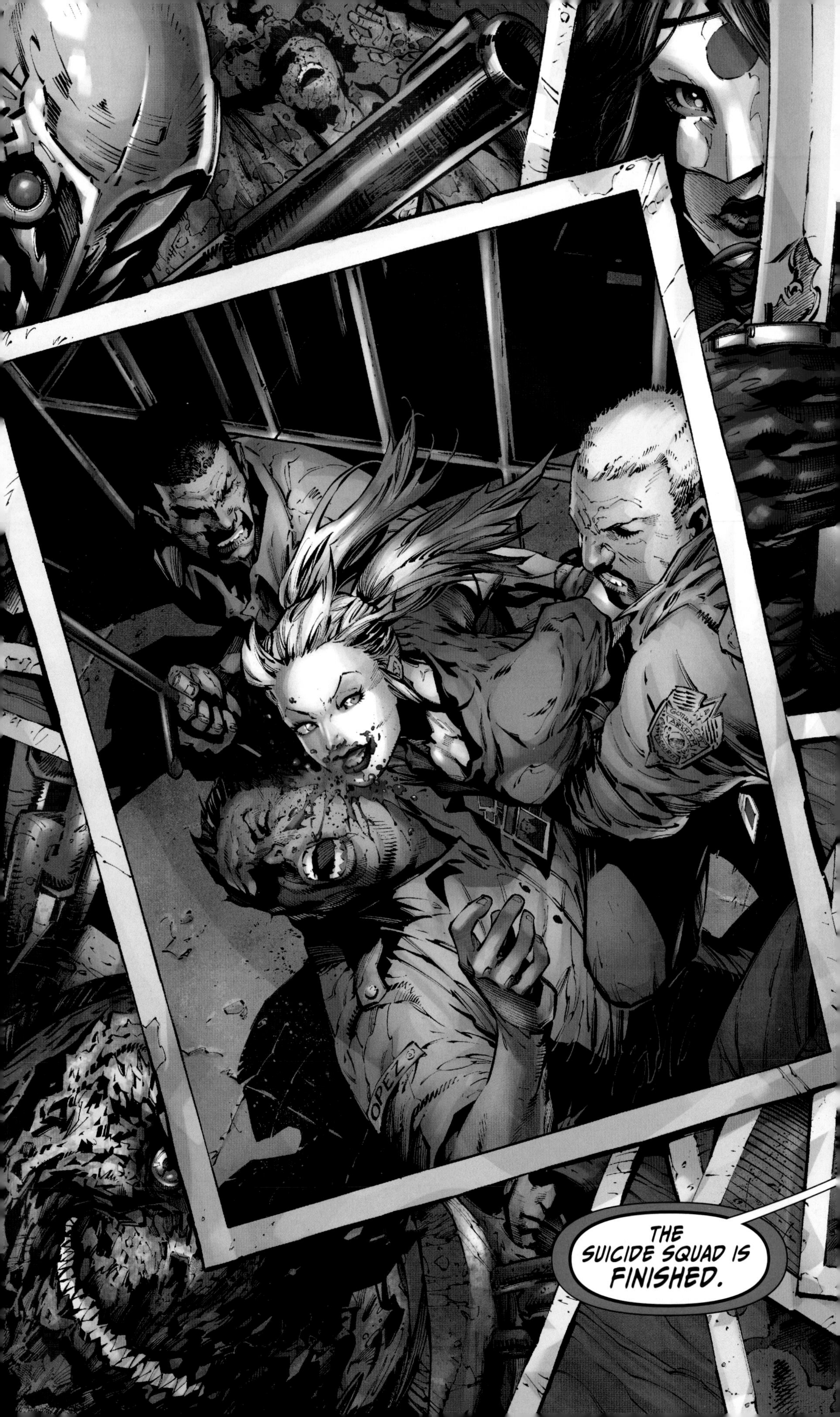
THE SUICIDE SQUAD IS FINISHED.

FINISHED, *DIRECTOR WALLER.* PERIOD.

FRANKLY, I WOULD HAVE MADE THIS DECISION A LOT SOONER, BUT IT WASN'T UNTIL I WAS ALREADY IN MY SECOND TERM THAT I WAS EVEN MADE AWARE OF YOUR... PROGRAM.

WHICH IS EXACTLY THE WAY YOU *LIKED* IT, I'M SURE.

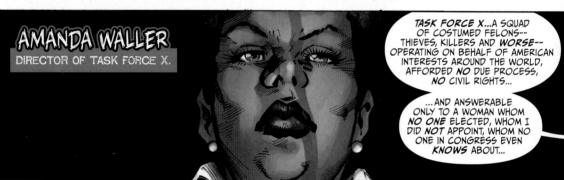

AMANDA WALLER
DIRECTOR OF TASK FORCE X.

TASK FORCE X...A SQUAD OF COSTUMED FELONS-- THIEVES, KILLERS AND *WORSE*-- OPERATING ON BEHALF OF AMERICAN INTERESTS AROUND THE WORLD, AFFORDED *NO* DUE PROCESS, *NO* CIVIL RIGHTS...

...AND ANSWERABLE ONLY TO A WOMAN WHOM *NO ONE* ELECTED, WHOM I DID *NOT* APPOINT, WHOM NO ONE IN CONGRESS EVEN *KNOWS* ABOUT...

...I DON'T KNOW HOW THIS WHOLE THING GOT STARTED, DIRECTOR WALLER, BUT THE SUICIDE SQUAD IS NOT ONLY A *BETRAYAL* OF OUR IDEALS...IT'S MANIFESTLY A *BOMB* WAITING TO BLOW UP IN OUR *FACES.*

I SWORE AN OATH TO DEFEND THIS *COUNTRY.* WE DO *NOT* DO THIS.

NOT *HERE.*

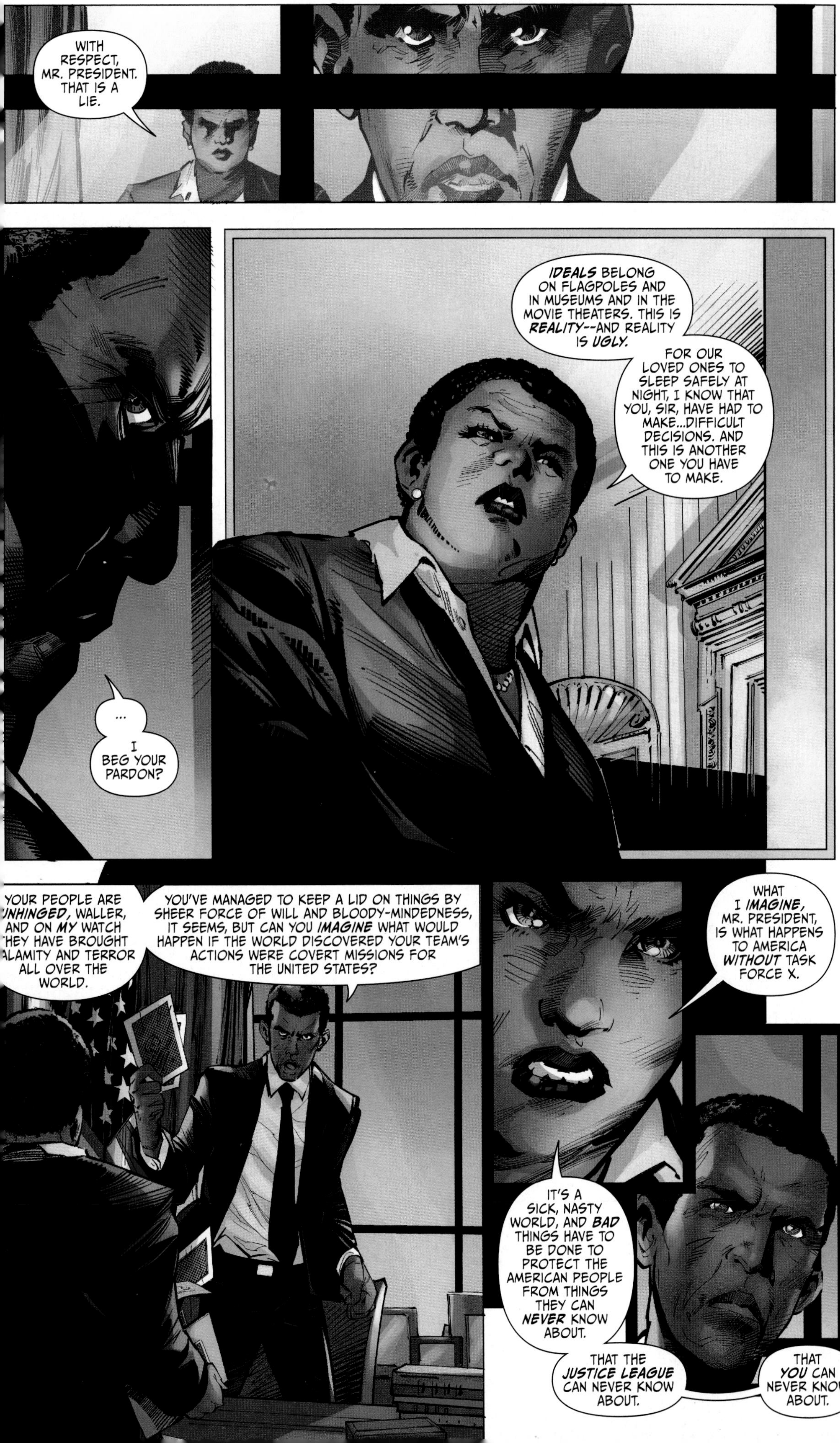
WITH RESPECT, MR. PRESIDENT. THAT IS A LIE.
IDEALS BELONG ON FLAGPOLES AND IN MUSEUMS AND IN THE MOVIE THEATERS. THIS IS REALITY--AND REALITY IS UGLY.
FOR OUR LOVED ONES TO SLEEP SAFELY AT NIGHT, I KNOW THAT YOU, SIR, HAVE HAD TO MAKE...DIFFICULT DECISIONS. AND THIS IS ANOTHER ONE YOU HAVE TO MAKE.
...
I BEG YOUR PARDON?
YOUR PEOPLE ARE UNHINGED, WALLER, AND ON MY WATCH THEY HAVE BROUGHT CALAMITY AND TERROR ALL OVER THE WORLD.
YOU'VE MANAGED TO KEEP A LID ON THINGS BY SHEER FORCE OF WILL AND BLOODY-MINDEDNESS, IT SEEMS, BUT CAN YOU IMAGINE WHAT WOULD HAPPEN IF THE WORLD DISCOVERED YOUR TEAM'S ACTIONS WERE COVERT MISSIONS FOR THE UNITED STATES?
WHAT I IMAGINE, MR. PRESIDENT, IS WHAT HAPPENS TO AMERICA WITHOUT TASK FORCE X.
IT'S A SICK, NASTY WORLD, AND BAD THINGS HAVE TO BE DONE TO PROTECT THE AMERICAN PEOPLE FROM THINGS THEY CAN NEVER KNOW ABOUT.
THAT THE JUSTICE LEAGUE CAN NEVER KNOW ABOUT.
THAT YOU CAN NEVER KNOW ABOUT.

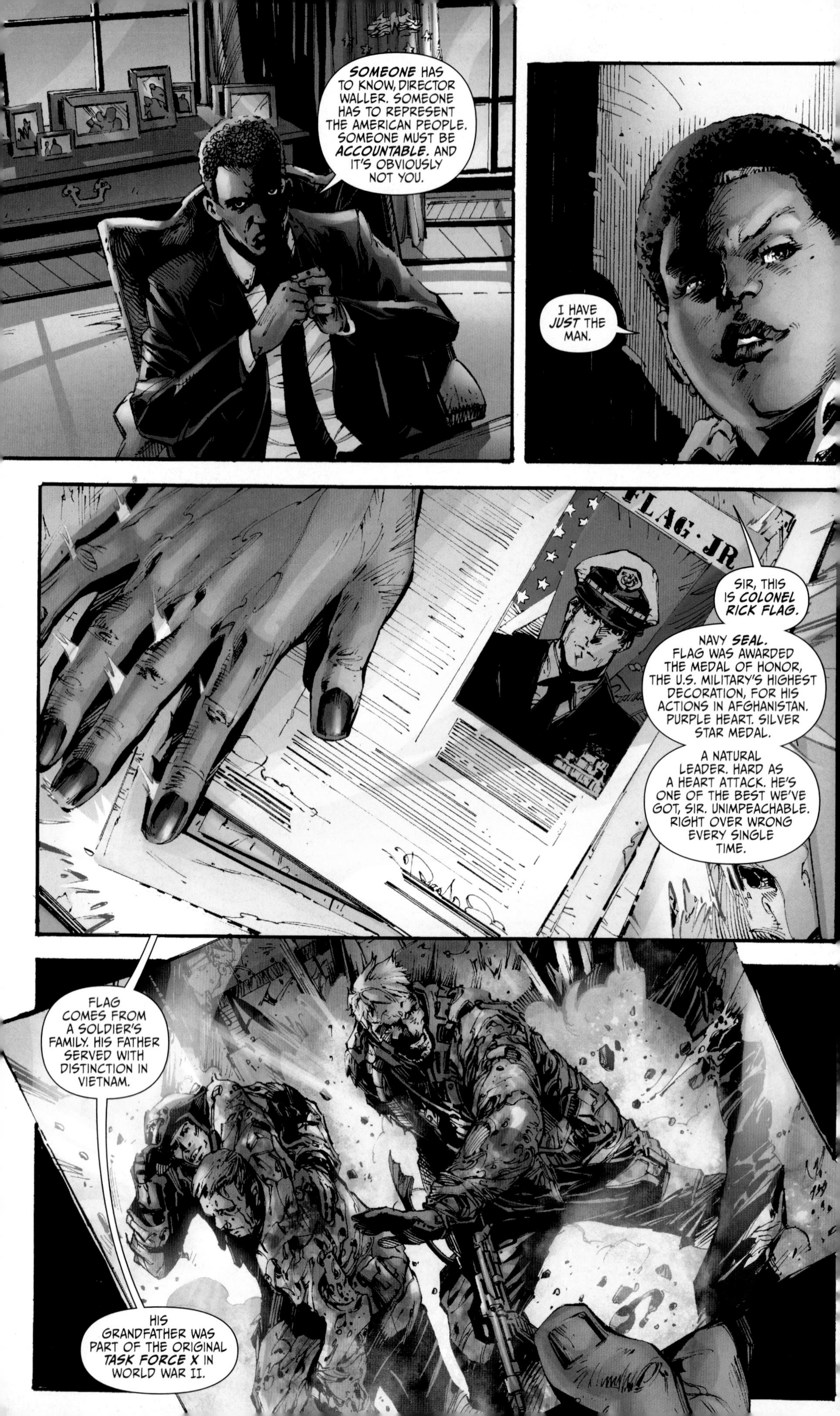
SOMEONE HAS TO KNOW, DIRECTOR WALLER. SOMEONE HAS TO REPRESENT THE AMERICAN PEOPLE. SOMEONE MUST BE ACCOUNTABLE. AND IT'S OBVIOUSLY NOT YOU.
I HAVE JUST THE MAN.
FLAG · JR
SIR, THIS IS COLONEL RICK FLAG.
NAVY SEAL. FLAG WAS AWARDED THE MEDAL OF HONOR, THE U.S. MILITARY'S HIGHEST DECORATION, FOR HIS ACTIONS IN AFGHANISTAN. PURPLE HEART. SILVER STAR MEDAL.
A NATURAL LEADER. HARD AS A HEART ATTACK. HE'S ONE OF THE BEST WE'VE GOT, SIR. UNIMPEACHABLE. RIGHT OVER WRONG EVERY SINGLE TIME.
FLAG COMES FROM A SOLDIER'S FAMILY. HIS FATHER SERVED WITH DISTINCTION IN VIETNAM.
HIS GRANDFATHER WAS PART OF THE ORIGINAL TASK FORCE X IN WORLD WAR II.

I'M AWARE OF THE HEROIC ACTIONS OF COLONEL FLAG. BUT I HAVEN'T HEARD ANYTHING FOR YEARS NOW. WHERE IS HE?

FLAG IS ON...*SPECIAL ASSIGNMENT.* BUT I CAN MAKE ARRANGEMENTS FOR HIM TO BE DETAILED TO ME *EXCLUSIVELY.* FOR THE *NEW* MISSION.

YOU JUST HAVE TO GIVE THE AUTHORIZATION, SIR.

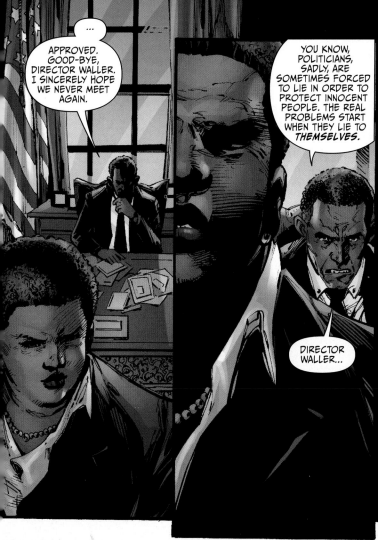

...

APPROVED. GOOD-BYE, DIRECTOR WALLER. I SINCERELY HOPE WE NEVER MEET AGAIN.

YOU KNOW, POLITICIANS, SADLY, ARE SOMETIMES FORCED TO LIE IN ORDER TO PROTECT INNOCENT PEOPLE. THE REAL PROBLEMS START WHEN THEY LIE TO *THEMSELVES.*

DIRECTOR WALLER...

...THIS COLONEL FLAG...

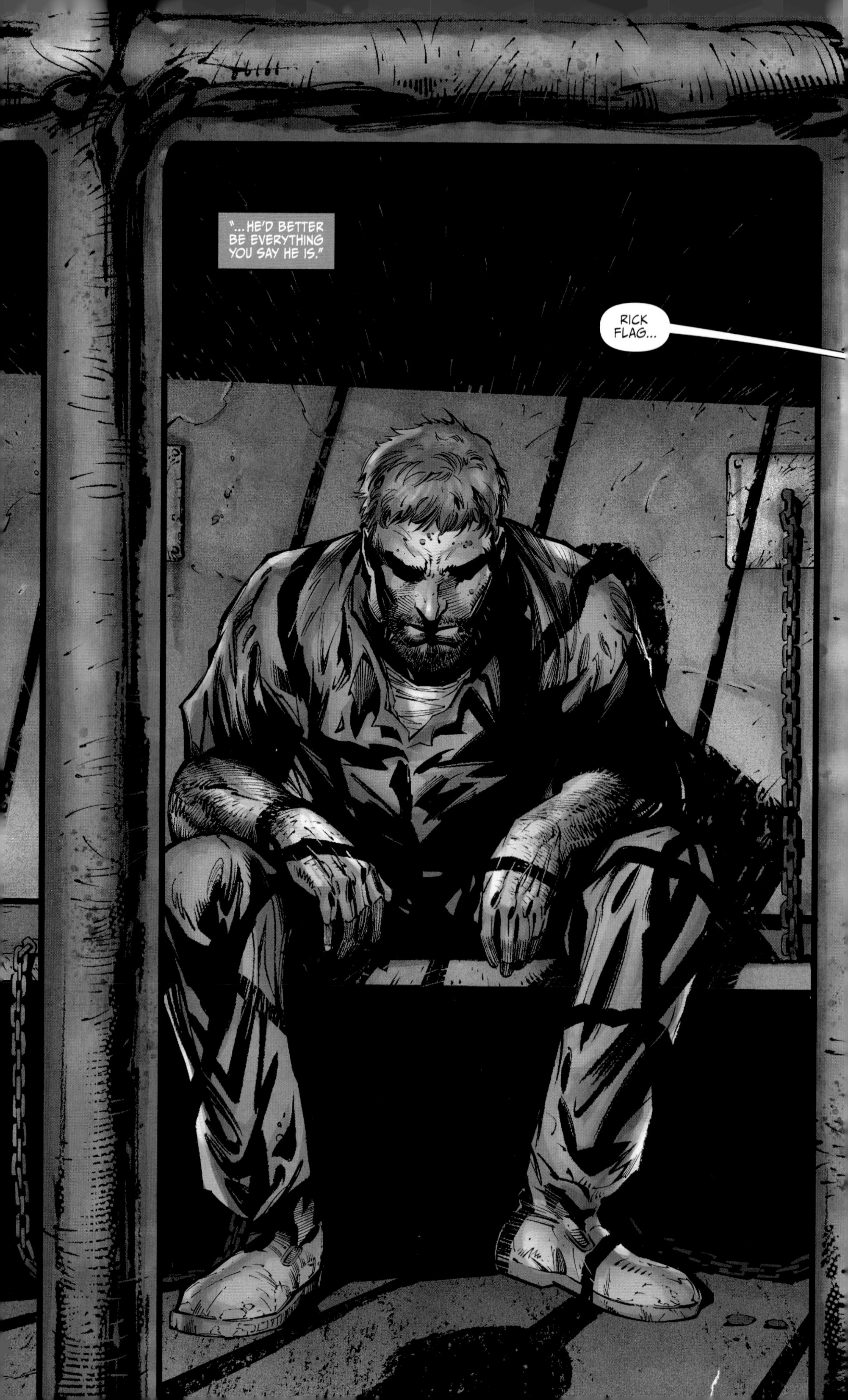
"...HE'D BETTER BE EVERYTHING YOU SAY HE IS."
RICK FLAG...

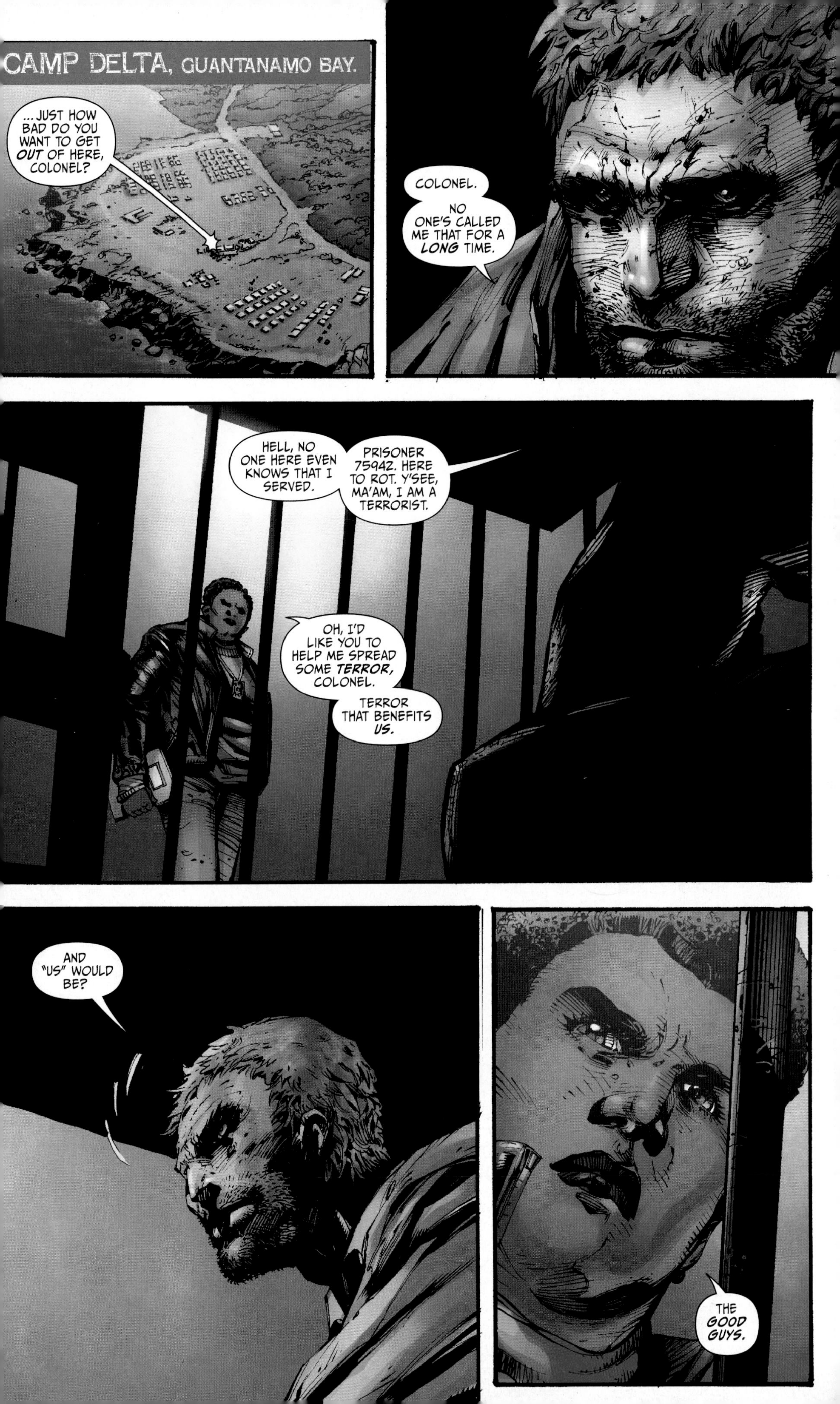
CAMP DELTA, GUANTANAMO BAY.
...JUST HOW BAD DO YOU WANT TO GET OUT OF HERE, COLONEL?
COLONEL.
NO ONE'S CALLED ME THAT FOR A LONG TIME.
HELL, NO ONE HERE EVEN KNOWS THAT I SERVED.
PRISONER 75942. HERE TO ROT. Y'SEE, MA'AM, I AM A TERRORIST.
OH, I'D LIKE YOU TO HELP ME SPREAD SOME TERROR, COLONEL.
TERROR THAT BENEFITS US.
AND "US" WOULD BE?
THE GOOD GUYS.

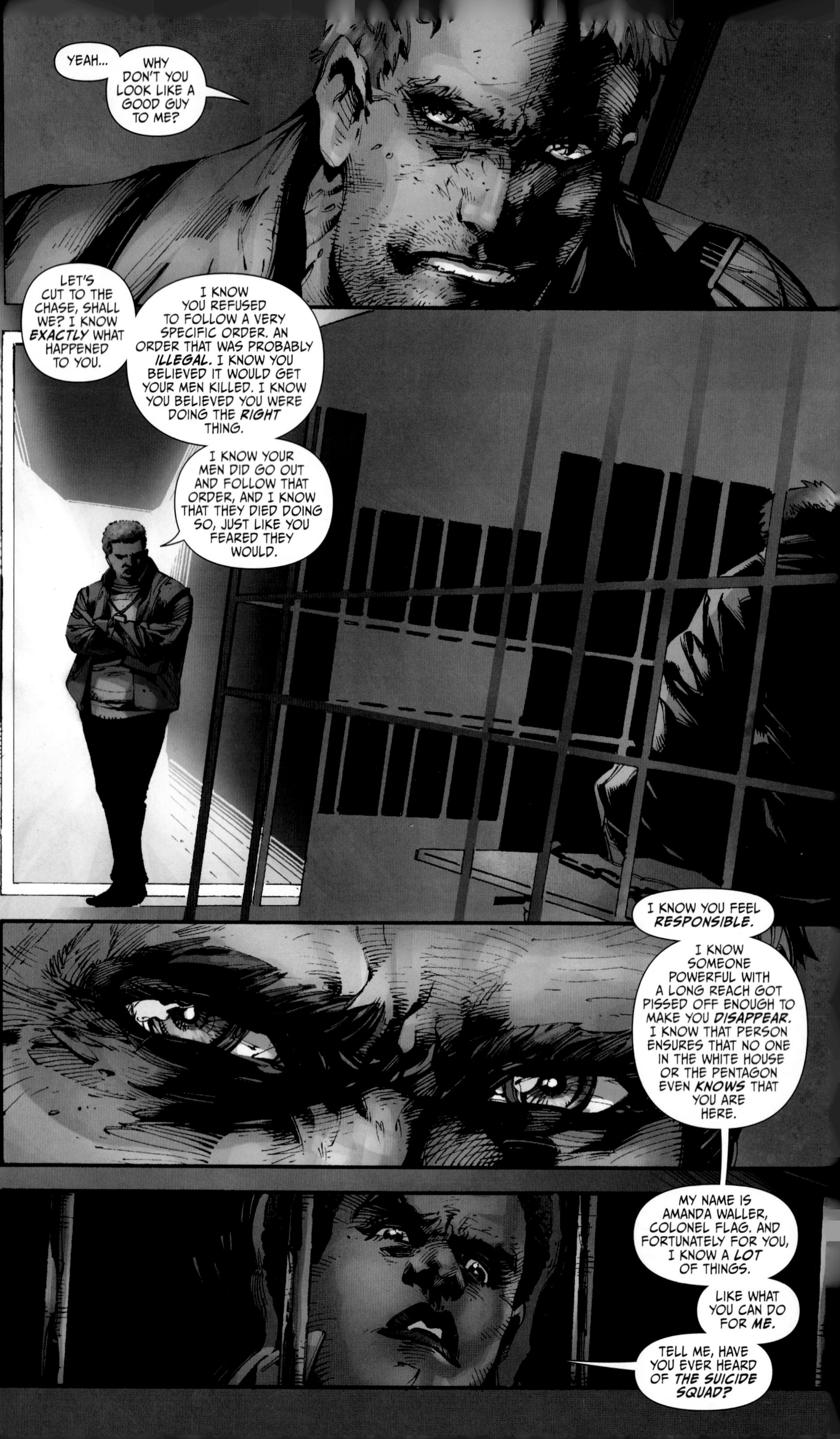

YEAH...
WHY DON'T YOU LOOK LIKE A GOOD GUY TO ME?
LET'S CUT TO THE CHASE, SHALL WE? I KNOW *EXACTLY* WHAT HAPPENED TO YOU.
I KNOW YOU REFUSED TO FOLLOW A VERY SPECIFIC ORDER. AN ORDER THAT WAS PROBABLY *ILLEGAL.* I KNOW YOU BELIEVED IT WOULD GET YOUR MEN KILLED. I KNOW YOU BELIEVED YOU WERE DOING THE *RIGHT* THING.
I KNOW YOUR MEN DID GO OUT AND FOLLOW THAT ORDER, AND I KNOW THAT THEY DIED DOING SO, JUST LIKE YOU FEARED THEY WOULD.
I KNOW YOU FEEL *RESPONSIBLE.*
I KNOW SOMEONE POWERFUL WITH A LONG REACH GOT PISSED OFF ENOUGH TO MAKE YOU *DISAPPEAR.* I KNOW THAT PERSON ENSURES THAT NO ONE IN THE WHITE HOUSE OR THE PENTAGON EVEN *KNOWS* THAT YOU ARE HERE.
MY NAME IS AMANDA WALLER, COLONEL FLAG. AND FORTUNATELY FOR YOU, I KNOW A *LOT* OF THINGS.
LIKE WHAT YOU CAN DO FOR *ME.*
TELL ME, HAVE YOU EVER HEARD OF *THE SUICIDE SQUAD?*

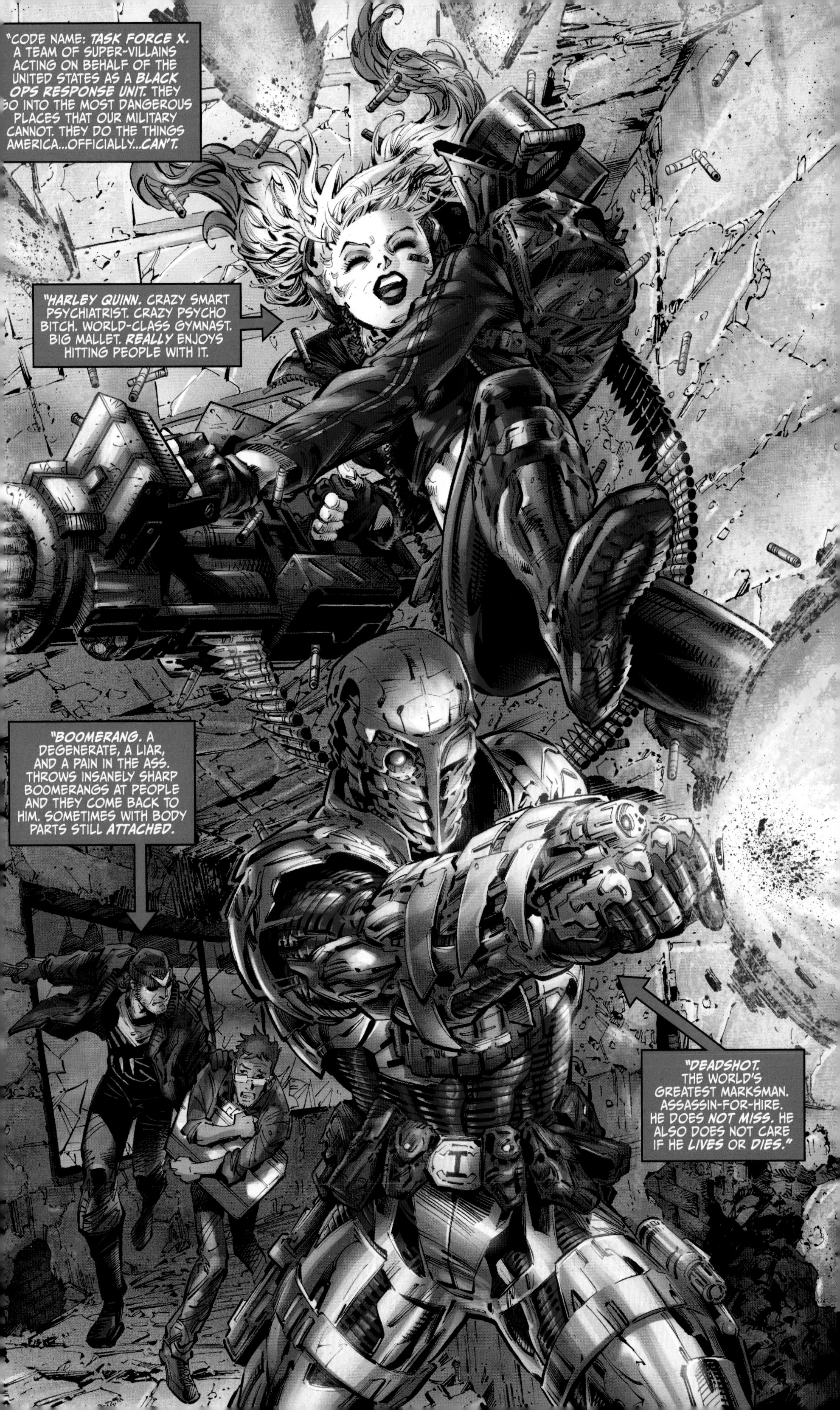
"CODE NAME: *TASK FORCE X.* A TEAM OF SUPER-VILLAINS ACTING ON BEHALF OF THE UNITED STATES AS A *BLACK OPS RESPONSE UNIT.* THEY GO INTO THE MOST DANGEROUS PLACES THAT OUR MILITARY CANNOT. THEY DO THE THINGS AMERICA...OFFICIALLY...*CAN'T.*
"*HARLEY QUINN.* CRAZY SMART PSYCHIATRIST. CRAZY PSYCHO BITCH. WORLD-CLASS GYMNAST. BIG MALLET. *REALLY* ENJOYS HITTING PEOPLE WITH IT.
"*BOOMERANG.* A DEGENERATE, A LIAR, AND A PAIN IN THE ASS. THROWS INSANELY SHARP BOOMERANGS AT PEOPLE AND THEY COME BACK TO HIM. SOMETIMES WITH BODY PARTS STILL *ATTACHED.*
"*DEADSHOT.* THE WORLD'S GREATEST MARKSMAN. ASSASSIN-FOR-HIRE. HE DOES *NOT MISS.* HE ALSO DOES NOT CARE IF HE *LIVES* OR *DIES.*"

THERE ARE OTHERS WHO WILL ALSO BE AT YOUR DISPOSAL...

THE SQUAD ALL HAVE EXPLOSIVES SURGICALLY IMPLANTED IN THEIR HEADS THAT YOU WILL HAVE CONTROL OF IN THE FIELD SHOULD THEY...STEP OUT OF LINE.

YOU'RE *CRAZY*, WALLER. I WILL NOT *LOWER* MYSELF TO BE ONE OF YOUR *BAD GUYS.*

OH, THEY *ARE* THE BAD GUYS. THAT'S WHY I NEED A *GOOD GUY* TO *LEAD* THEM.

BECAUSE RIGHT NOW, EVEN AS WE SPEAK, THERE'S A *BOMB* THAT THREATENS US.

AND, IN THIS WORLD, THERE IS *ALWAYS* A BOMB.

SO, COLONEL, HERE'S THE DEAL. YOU'RE *DAMNED* IF YOU *STAY* IN THAT CELL AND DAMNED IF YOU *DON'T.*

BUT BY ACCEPTING MY OFFER, AT LEAST YOU'LL BE SAVING SOME LIVES.

CASE IN POINT...

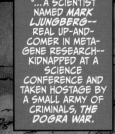

"...A SCIENTIST NAMED *MARK LJUNGBERG*-- REAL UP-AND-COMER IN META-GENE RESEARCH-- KIDNAPPED AT A SCIENCE CONFERENCE AND TAKEN HOSTAGE BY A SMALL ARMY OF CRIMINALS, *THE DOGRA WAR.*

MISSION OBJECTIVE

"THEY TRANSPORTED LJUNGBERG TO A PREVIOUSLY DESERTED *GHOST CITY* IN INNER MONGOLIA. THAT'S *CHINA* SO...AMERICA CAN'T JUST GO OPENLY STRIDING IN.

"EVEN THOUGH, LESS THAN 24 HOURS AGO OUR SATELLITES PICKED UP WHAT THEY BELIEVE TO BE A LOCALIZED *META-GENE BLAST* THERE."

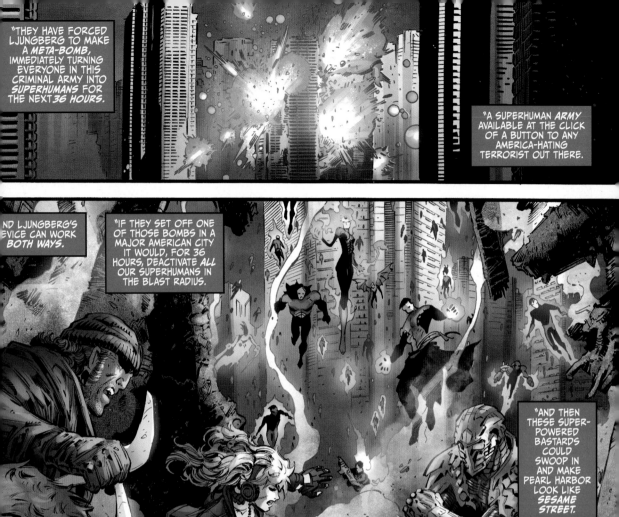

"THEY HAVE FORCED LJUNGBERG TO MAKE A *META-BOMB,* IMMEDIATELY TURNING EVERYONE IN THIS CRIMINAL ARMY INTO *SUPERHUMANS* FOR THE NEXT *36* HOURS.

"A SUPERHUMAN *ARMY* AVAILABLE AT THE CLICK OF A BUTTON TO ANY AMERICA-HATING TERRORIST OUT THERE.

ND LJUNGBERG'S EVICE CAN WORK *BOTH* WAYS.

"IF THEY SET OFF ONE OF THOSE BOMBS IN A MAJOR AMERICAN CITY IT WOULD, FOR 36 HOURS, DEACTIVATE *ALL* OUR SUPERHUMANS IN THE BLAST RADIUS.

"AND THEN THESE SUPER-POWERED BASTARDS COULD SWOOP IN AND MAKE *PEARL HARBOR* LOOK LIKE *SESAME STREET.*

BOOOM

WE *HAVE* TO GET UNGBERG AND HIS META- OMB OUT. NOW."

I NEVER WANTED THIS. I... I JUST WANTED TO HELP HUMANITY!

YEAH. THAT'S ADMIRABLE. :BURP:

KRAKAKA KAKAKAKA

HEY, THAT'S SO WEIRD. I JUST WANTED TO HELP HUMAN BEINGS, TOO!

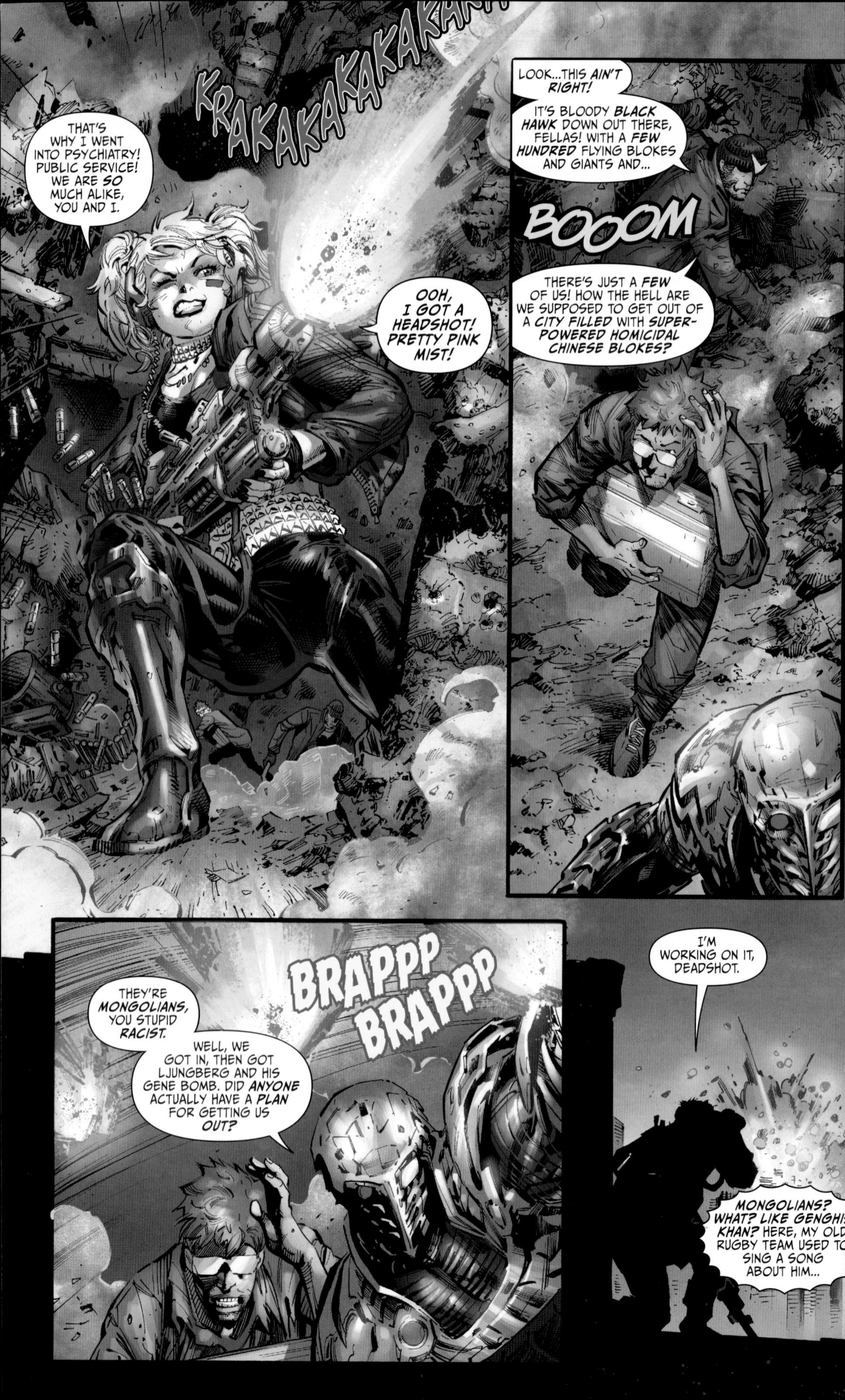
KRAKAKAKAKAKAKAKAKA
THAT'S WHY I WENT INTO PSYCHIATRY! PUBLIC SERVICE! WE ARE SO MUCH ALIKE, YOU AND I.
OOH, I GOT A HEADSHOT! PRETTY PINK MIST!
LOOK...THIS AIN'T RIGHT!
IT'S BLOODY BLACK HAWK DOWN OUT THERE, FELLAS! WITH A FEW HUNDRED FLYING BLOKES AND GIANTS AND...
BOOOM
THERE'S JUST A FEW OF US! HOW THE HELL ARE WE SUPPOSED TO GET OUT OF A CITY FILLED WITH SUPER-POWERED HOMICIDAL CHINESE BLOKES?
BRAPPP BRAPPP
THEY'RE MONGOLIANS, YOU STUPID RACIST.
WELL, WE GOT IN, THEN GOT LJUNGBERG AND HIS GENE BOMB. DID ANYONE ACTUALLY HAVE A PLAN FOR GETTING US OUT?
I'M WORKING ON IT, DEADSHOT.
MONGOLIANS? WHAT? LIKE GENGHIS KHAN? HERE, MY OLD RUGBY TEAM USED TO SING A SONG ABOUT HIM...

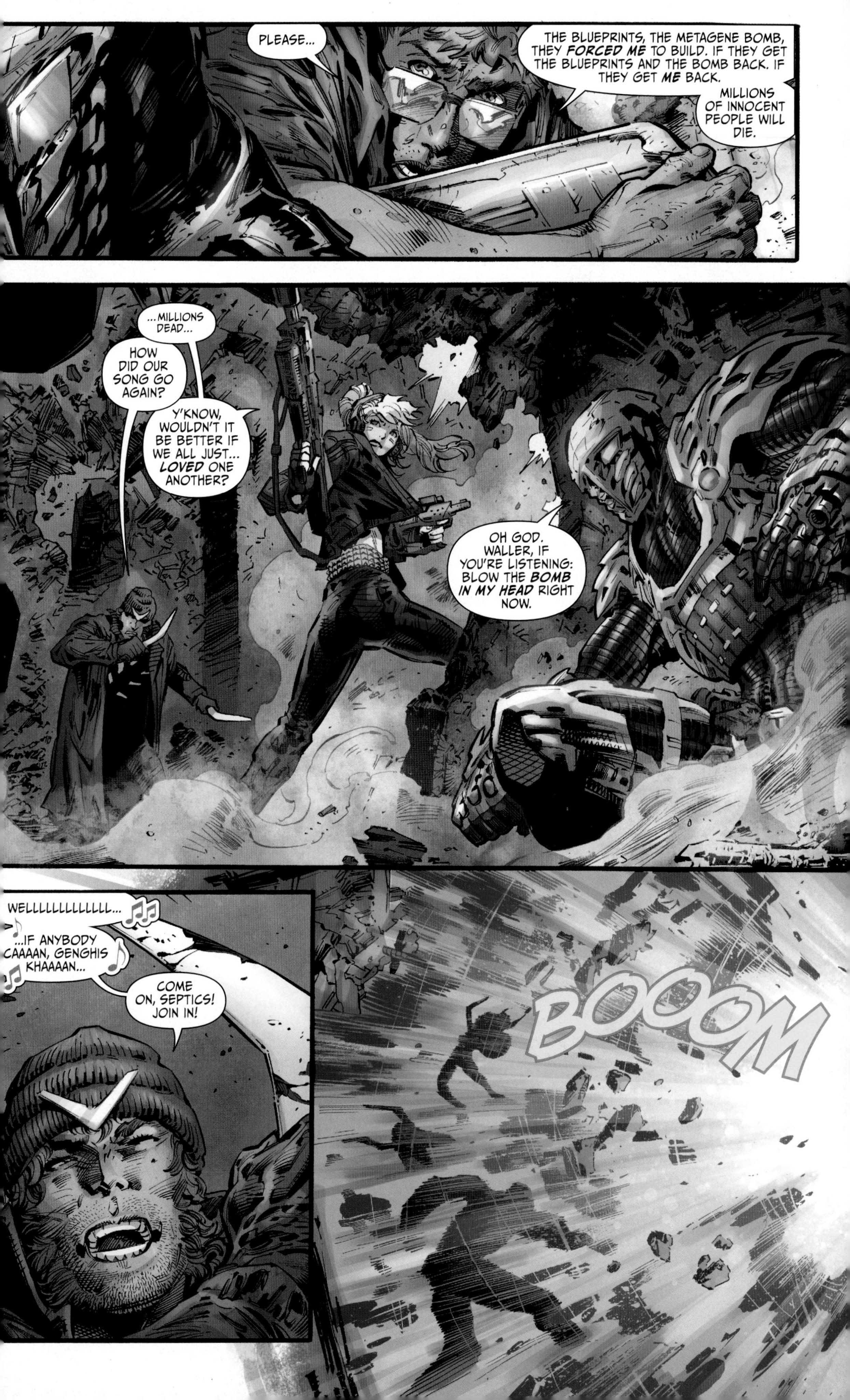

PLEASE...
THE BLUEPRINTS, THE METAGENE BOMB, THEY FORCED ME TO BUILD. IF THEY GET THE BLUEPRINTS AND THE BOMB BACK. IF THEY GET ME BACK.
MILLIONS OF INNOCENT PEOPLE WILL DIE.
...MILLIONS DEAD...
HOW DID OUR SONG GO AGAIN?
Y'KNOW, WOULDN'T IT BE BETTER IF WE ALL JUST... LOVED ONE ANOTHER?
OH GOD. WALLER, IF YOU'RE LISTENING: BLOW THE BOMB IN MY HEAD RIGHT NOW.
WELLLLLLLLLLLLLL...
...IF ANYBODY CAAAAN, GENGHIS KHAAAAN...
COME ON, SEPTICS! JOIN IN!
BOOOM

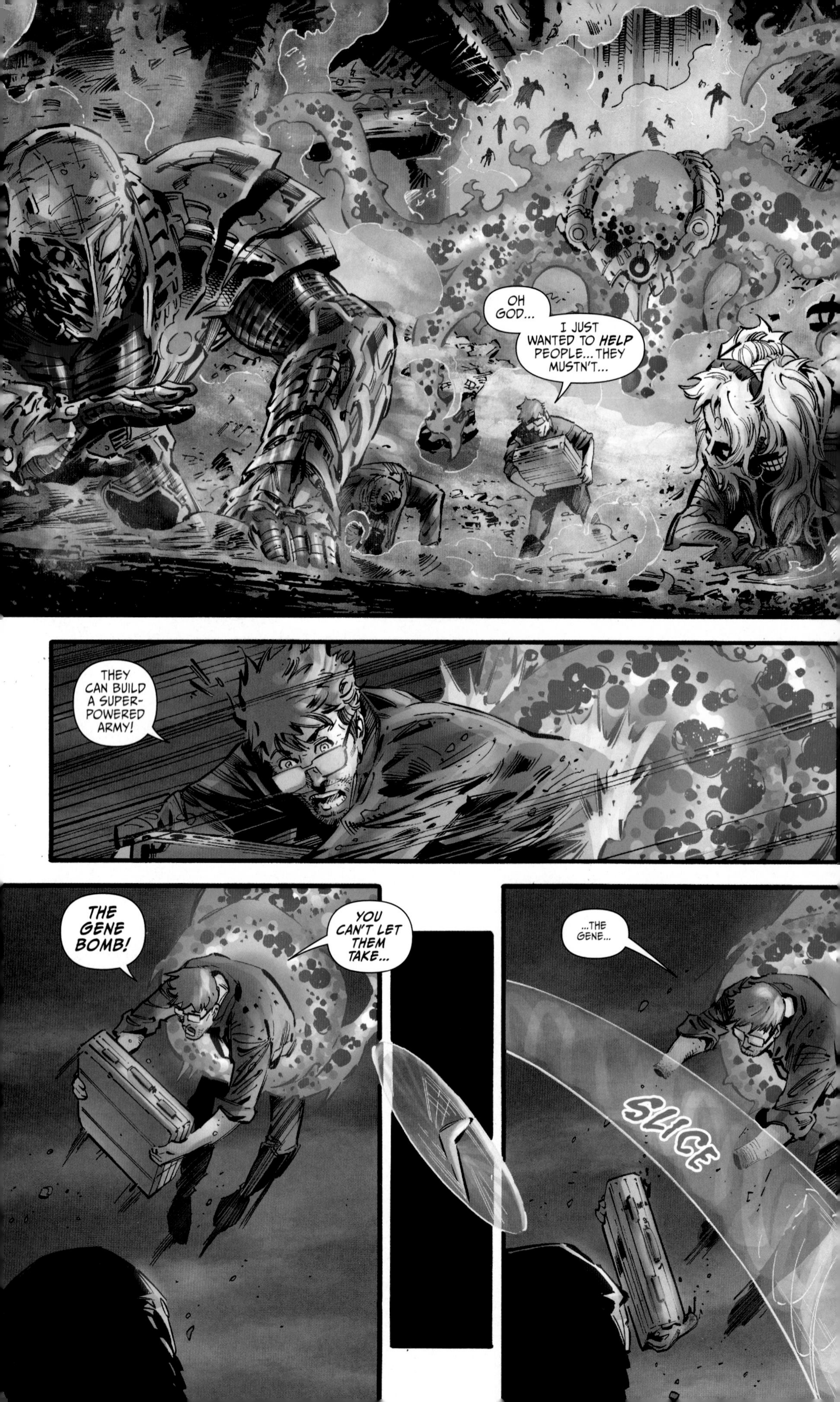
OH GOD...
I JUST WANTED TO HELP PEOPLE...THEY MUSTN'T...
THEY CAN BUILD A SUPER-POWERED ARMY!
THE GENE BOMB!
YOU CAN'T LET THEM TAKE...
...THE GENE...
SLICE

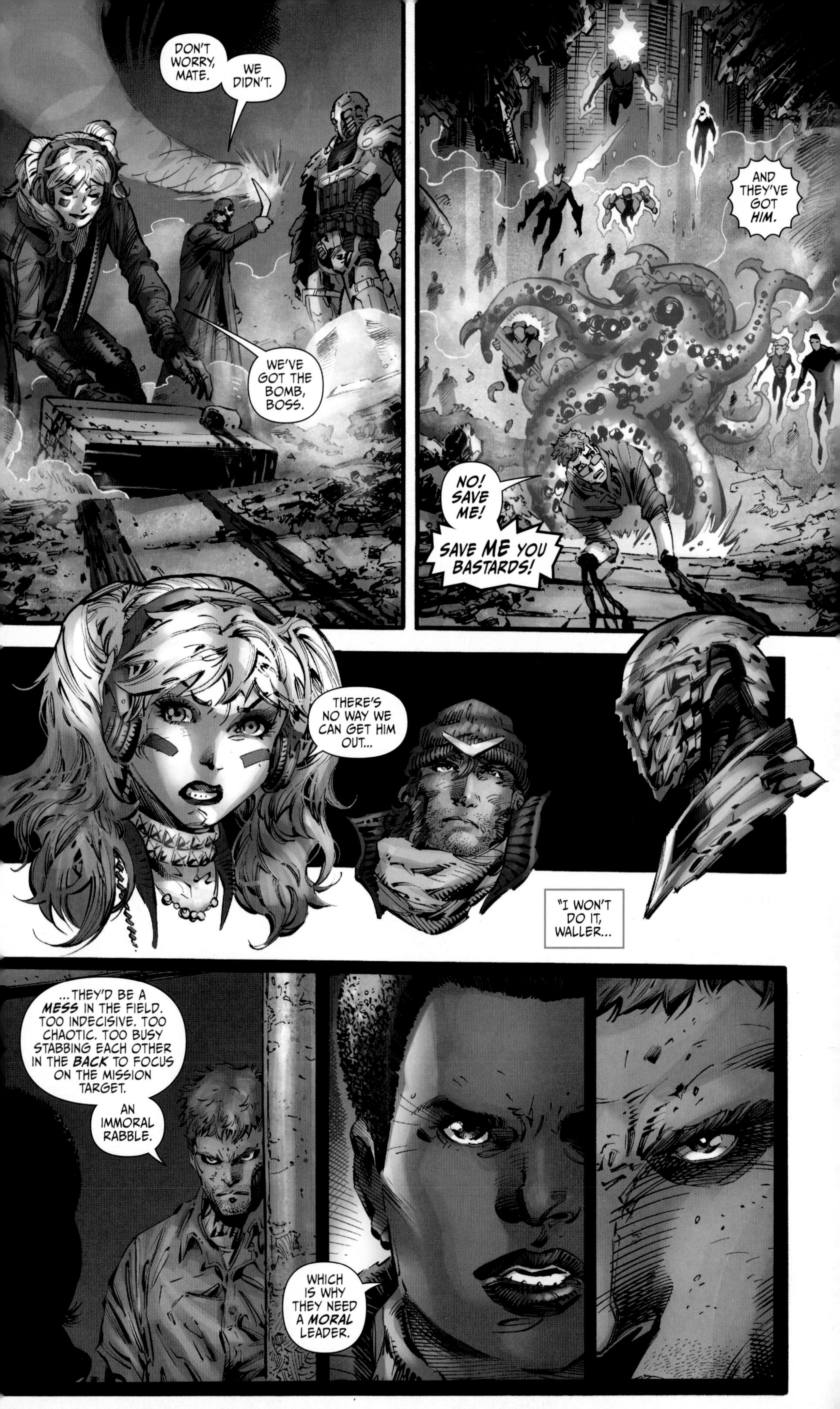
DON'T WORRY, MATE.
WE DIDN'T.
WE'VE GOT THE BOMB, BOSS.
AND THEY'VE GOT HIM.
NO! SAVE ME!
SAVE ME YOU BASTARDS!
THERE'S NO WAY WE CAN GET HIM OUT...
"I WON'T DO IT, WALLER...
...THEY'D BE A MESS IN THE FIELD. TOO INDECISIVE. TOO CHAOTIC. TOO BUSY STABBING EACH OTHER IN THE BACK TO FOCUS ON THE MISSION TARGET.
AN IMMORAL RABBLE.
WHICH IS WHY THEY NEED A MORAL LEADER.

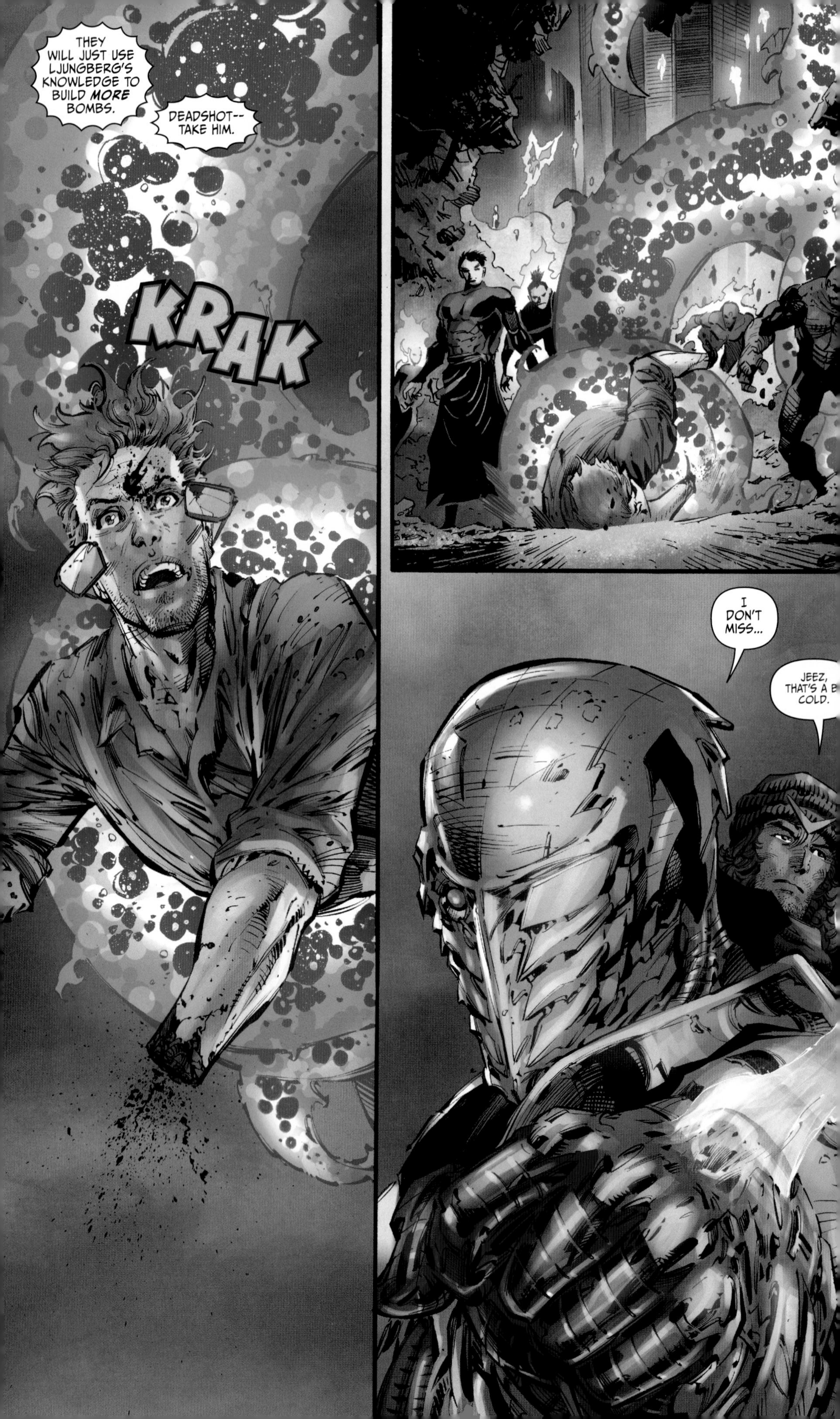
THEY WILL JUST USE LJUNGBERG'S KNOWLEDGE TO BUILD *MORE* BOMBS.
DEADSHOT-- TAKE HIM.
KRAK
I DON'T MISS...
JEEZ, THAT'S A B
COLD.

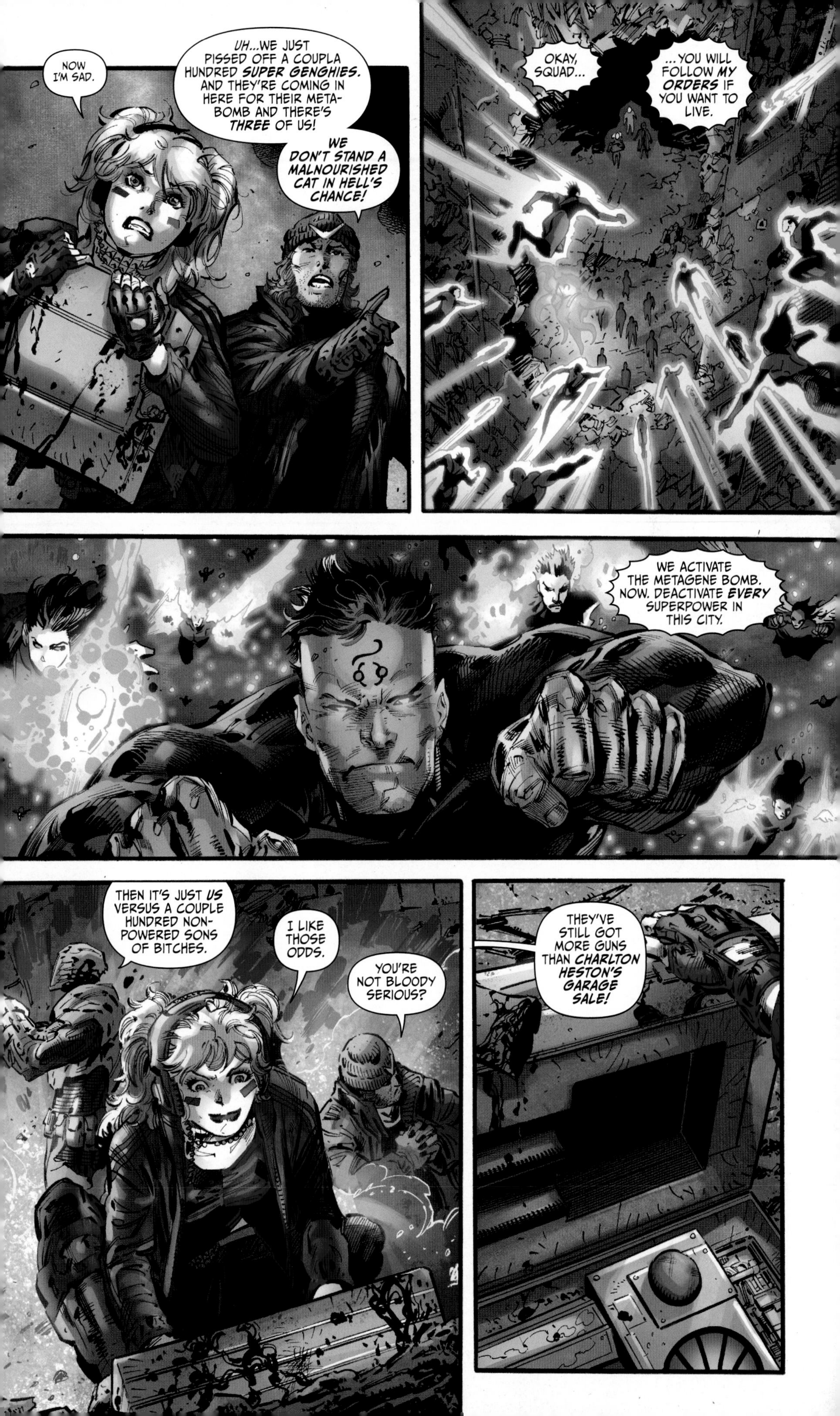
NOW I'M SAD.
UH...WE JUST PISSED OFF A COUPLA HUNDRED SUPER GENGHIES. AND THEY'RE COMING IN HERE FOR THEIR META-BOMB AND THERE'S THREE OF US!
WE DON'T STAND A MALNOURISHED CAT IN HELL'S CHANCE!
OKAY, SQUAD...
...YOU WILL FOLLOW MY ORDERS IF YOU WANT TO LIVE.
WE ACTIVATE THE METAGENE BOMB. NOW. DEACTIVATE EVERY SUPERPOWER IN THIS CITY.
THEN IT'S JUST US VERSUS A COUPLE HUNDRED NON-POWERED SONS OF BITCHES.
I LIKE THOSE ODDS.
YOU'RE NOT BLOODY SERIOUS?
THEY'VE STILL GOT MORE GUNS THAN CHARLTON HESTON'S GARAGE SALE!

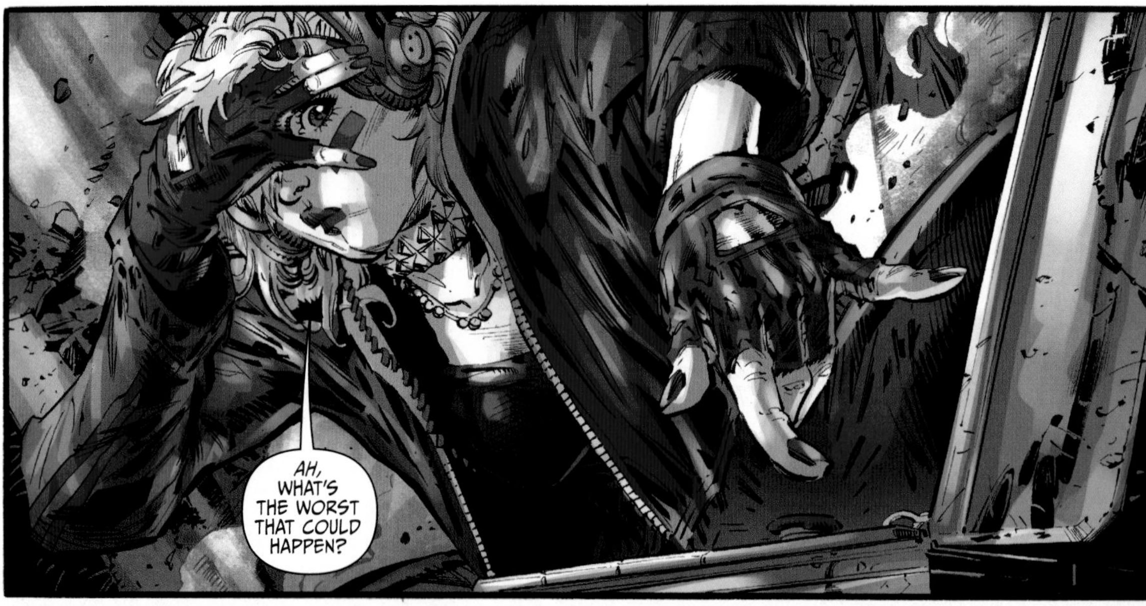
AH, WHAT'S THE WORST THAT COULD HAPPEN?

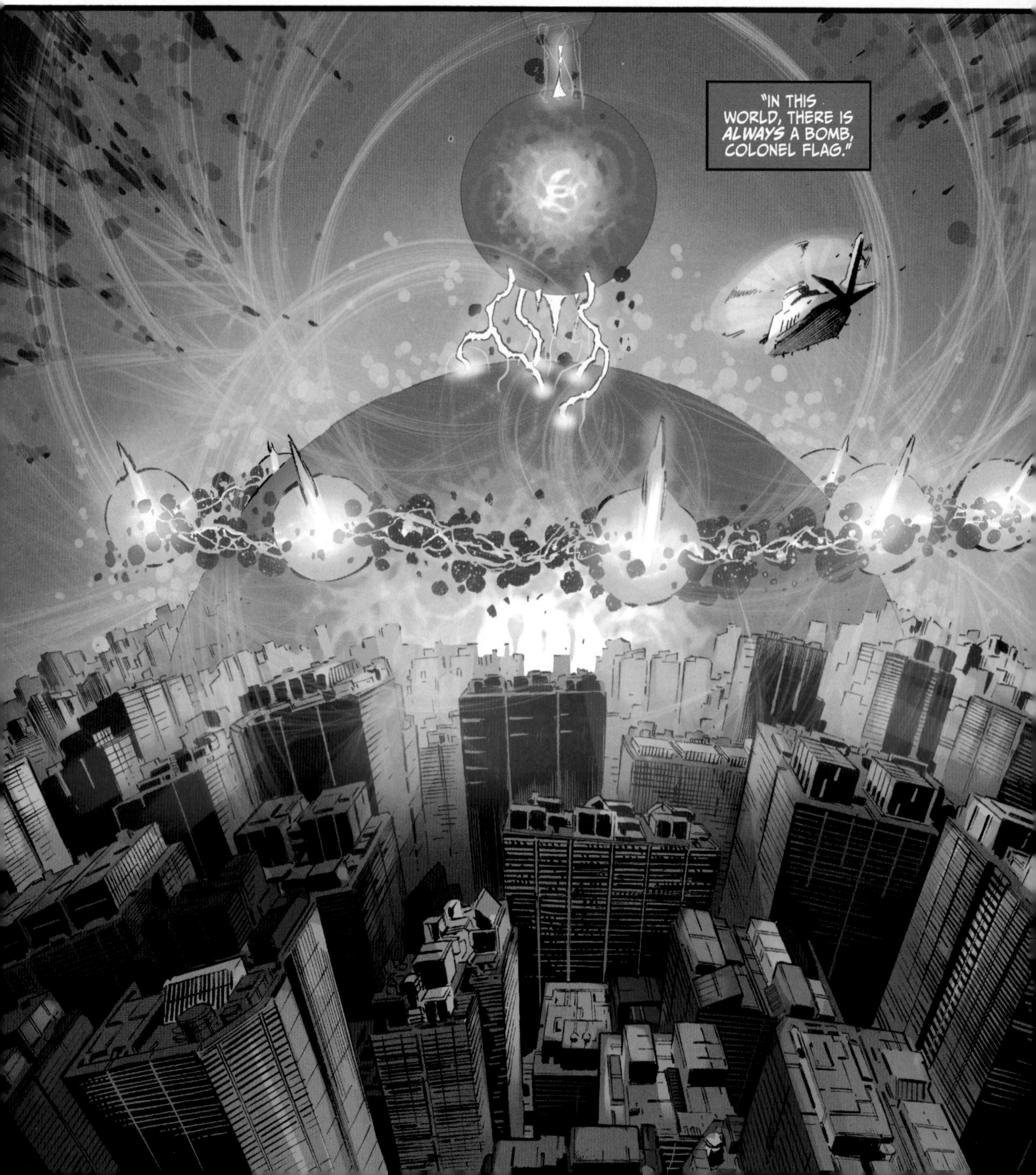
"IN THIS WORLD, THERE IS *ALWAYS* A BOMB, COLONEL FLAG."

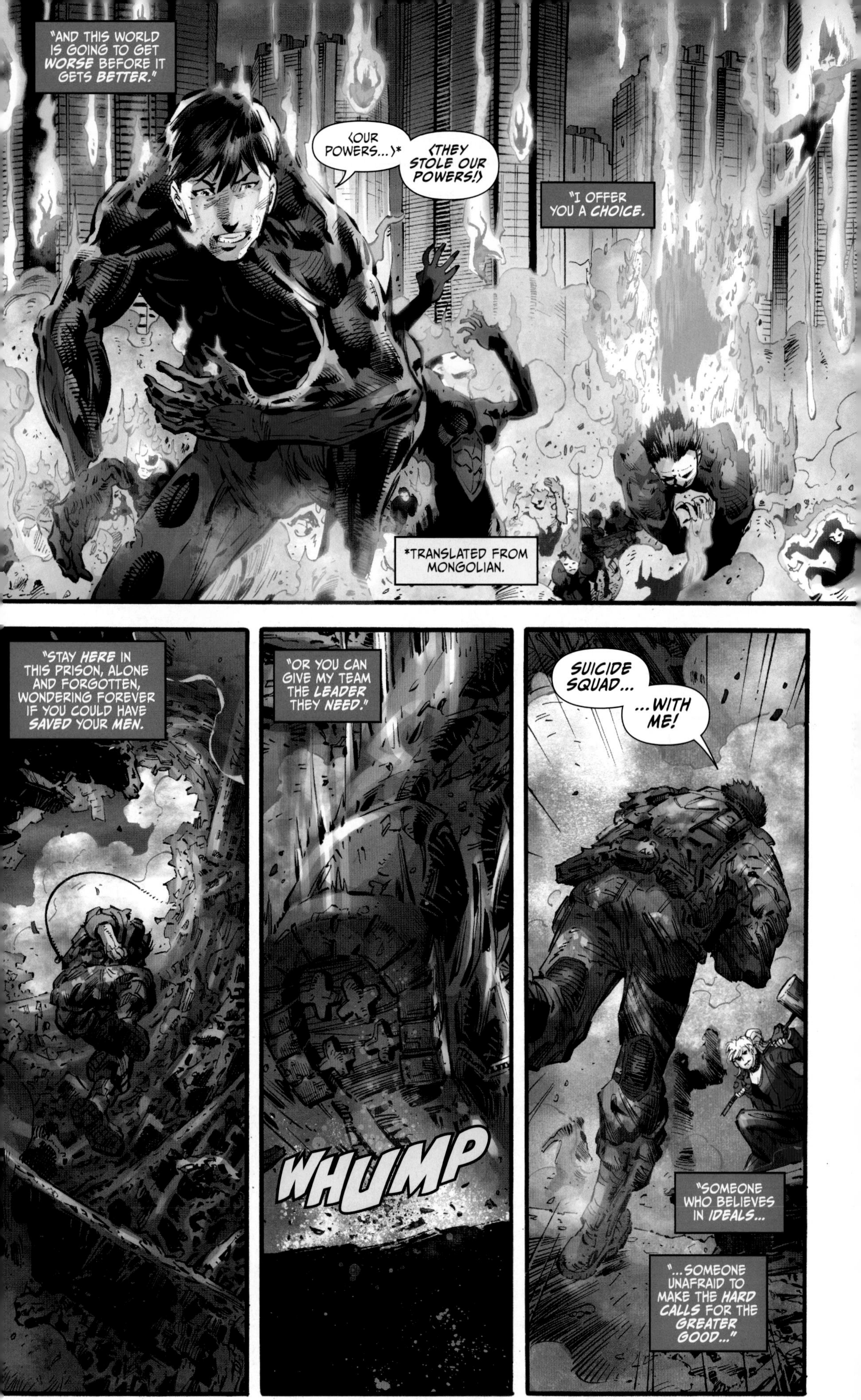
"AND THIS WORLD IS GOING TO GET WORSE BEFORE IT GETS BETTER."
‹OUR POWERS...›*
‹THEY STOLE OUR POWERS!›
"I OFFER YOU A CHOICE.
*TRANSLATED FROM MONGOLIAN.
"STAY HERE IN THIS PRISON, ALONE AND FORGOTTEN, WONDERING FOREVER IF YOU COULD HAVE SAVED YOUR MEN.
"OR YOU CAN GIVE MY TEAM THE LEADER THEY NEED."
WHUMP
SUICIDE SQUAD...
...WITH ME!
"SOMEONE WHO BELIEVES IN IDEALS...
"...SOMEONE UNAFRAID TO MAKE THE HARD CALLS FOR THE GREATER GOOD..."

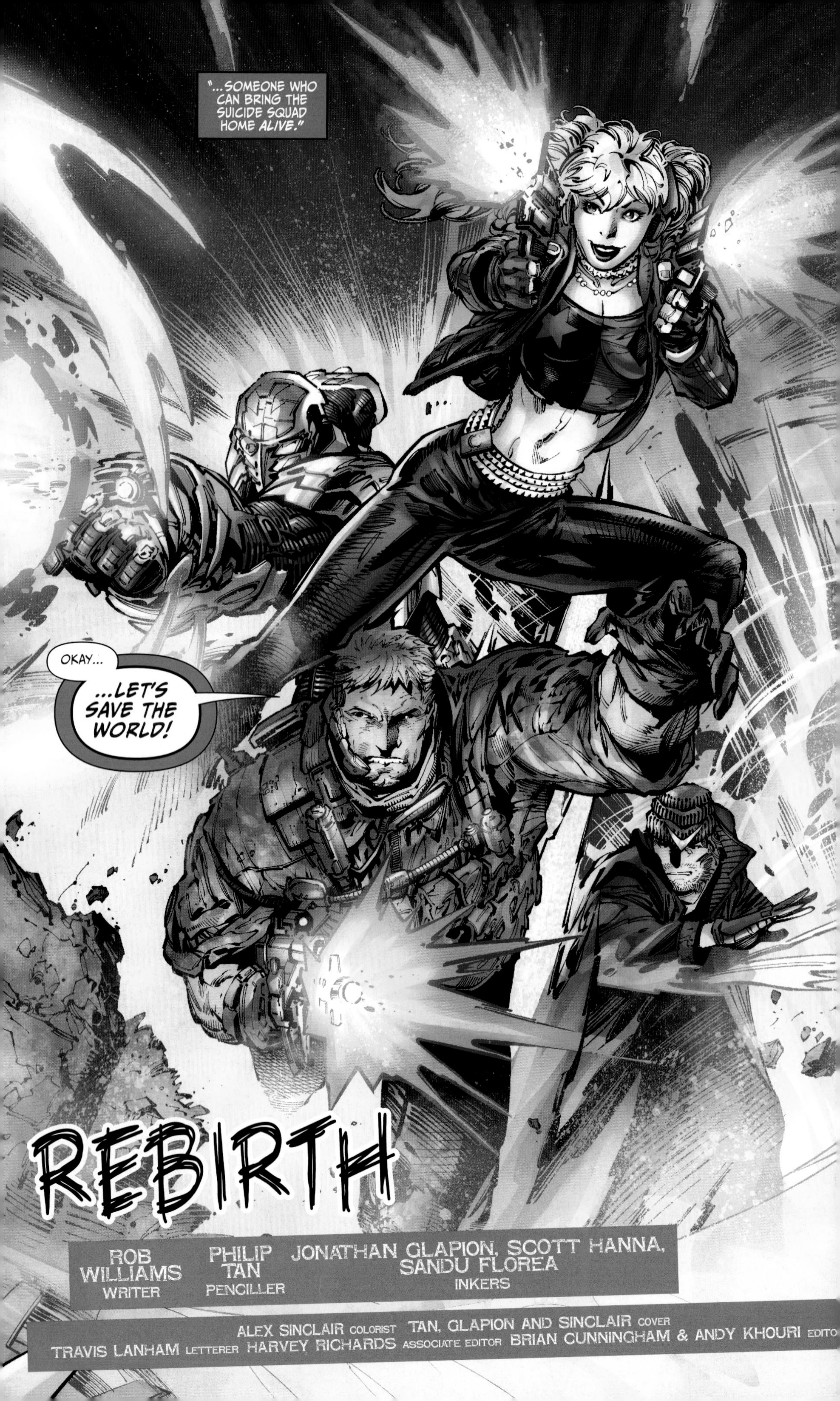
"...SOMEONE WHO CAN BRING THE SUICIDE SQUAD HOME ALIVE."
OKAY...
...LET'S SAVE THE WORLD!
REBIRTH
ROB WILLIAMS WRITER
PHILIP TAN PENCILLER
JONATHAN GLAPION, SCOTT HANNA, SANDU FLOREA INKERS
ALEX SINCLAIR COLORIST TAN, GLAPION AND SINCLAIR COVER
TRAVIS LANHAM LETTERER HARVEY RICHARDS ASSOCIATE EDITOR BRIAN CUNNINGHAM & ANDY KHOURI EDITO

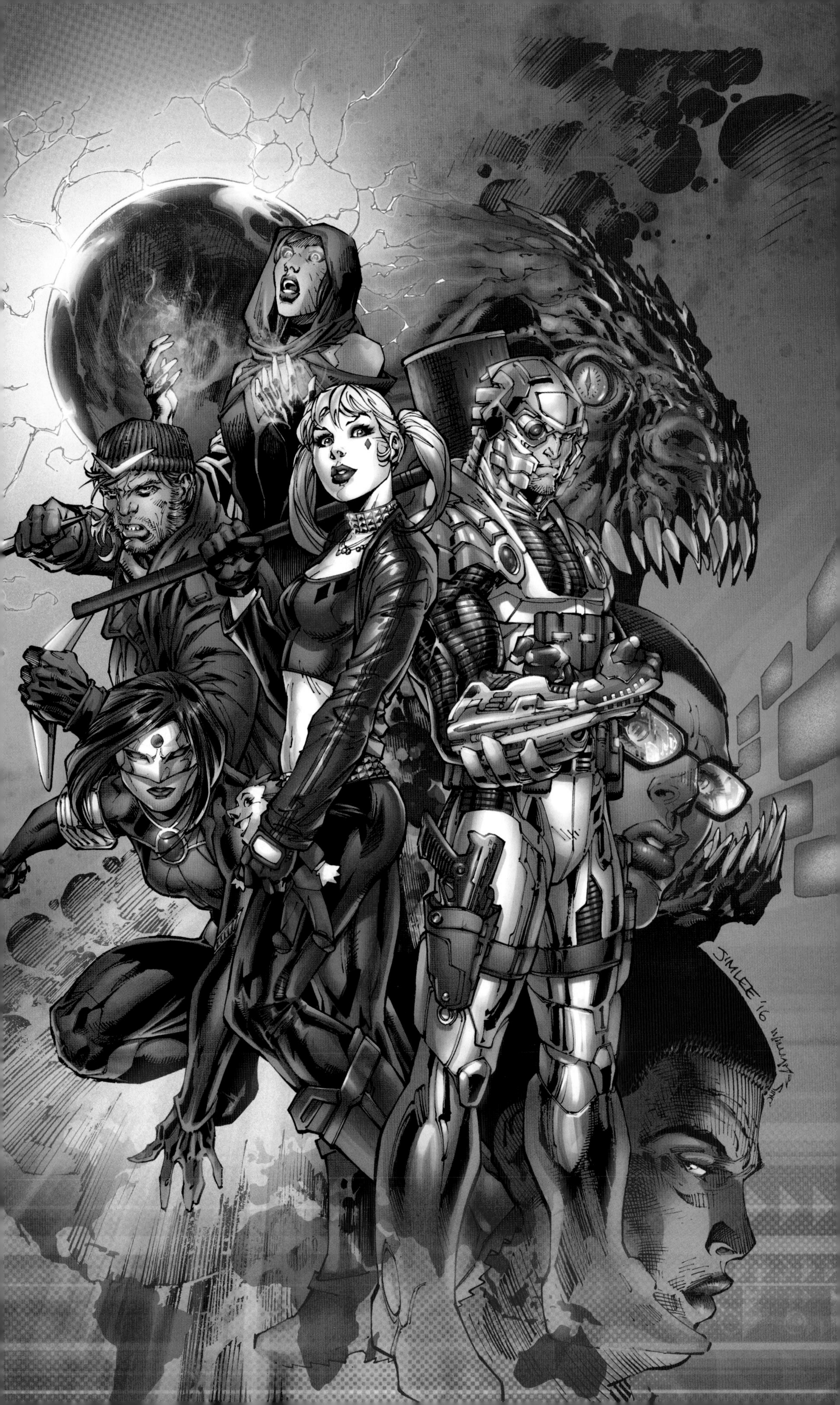

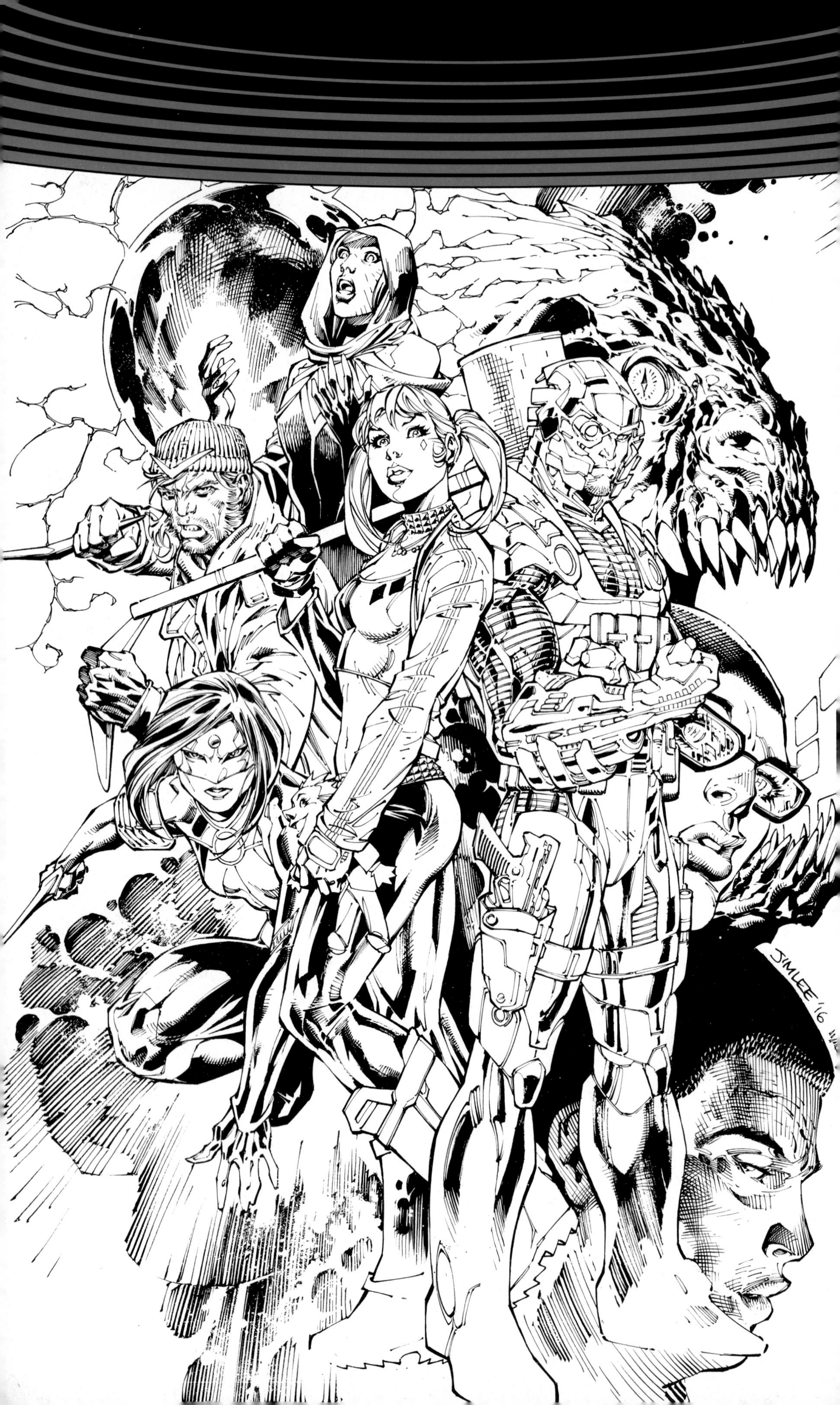
JIM LEE '16

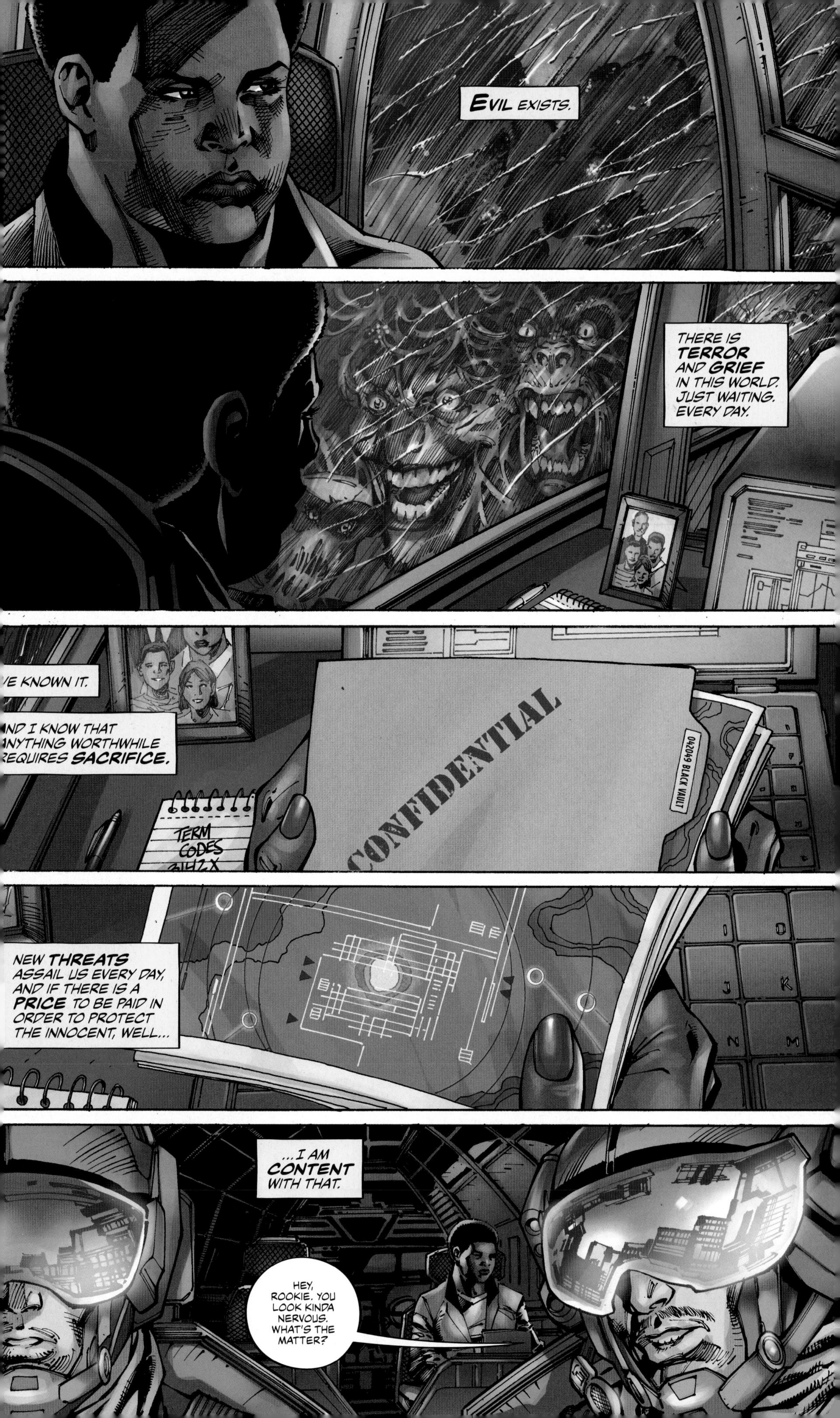
EVIL EXISTS.
THERE IS TERROR AND GRIEF IN THIS WORLD. JUST WAITING. EVERY DAY.
VE KNOWN IT.
ND I KNOW THAT NYTHING WORTHWHILE REQUIRES SACRIFICE.
TERM CODES 3142X
CONFIDENTIAL
042049 BLACK VAULT
NEW THREATS ASSAIL US EVERY DAY, AND IF THERE IS A PRICE TO BE PAID IN ORDER TO PROTECT THE INNOCENT, WELL...
...I AM CONTENT WITH THAT.
HEY, ROOKIE. YOU LOOK KINDA NERVOUS. WHAT'S THE MATTER?

YOU'VE NEVER DELIVERED THE DEVIL TO HELL BEFORE?
THE BLACK VAULT
PART ONE: I WANNA BE SEDATED
ROB WILLIAMS WRITER JIM LEE PENCILLER SCOTT WILLIAMS INKER ALEX SINCLAIR COLORIST NATE PIEKOS OF BLAMBOT® LETTE
LEE, WILLIAMS AND SINCLAIR COVER HARVEY RICHARDS ASSOCIATE EDITOR
BRIAN CUNNINGHAM AND ANDY KHOURI EDITORS

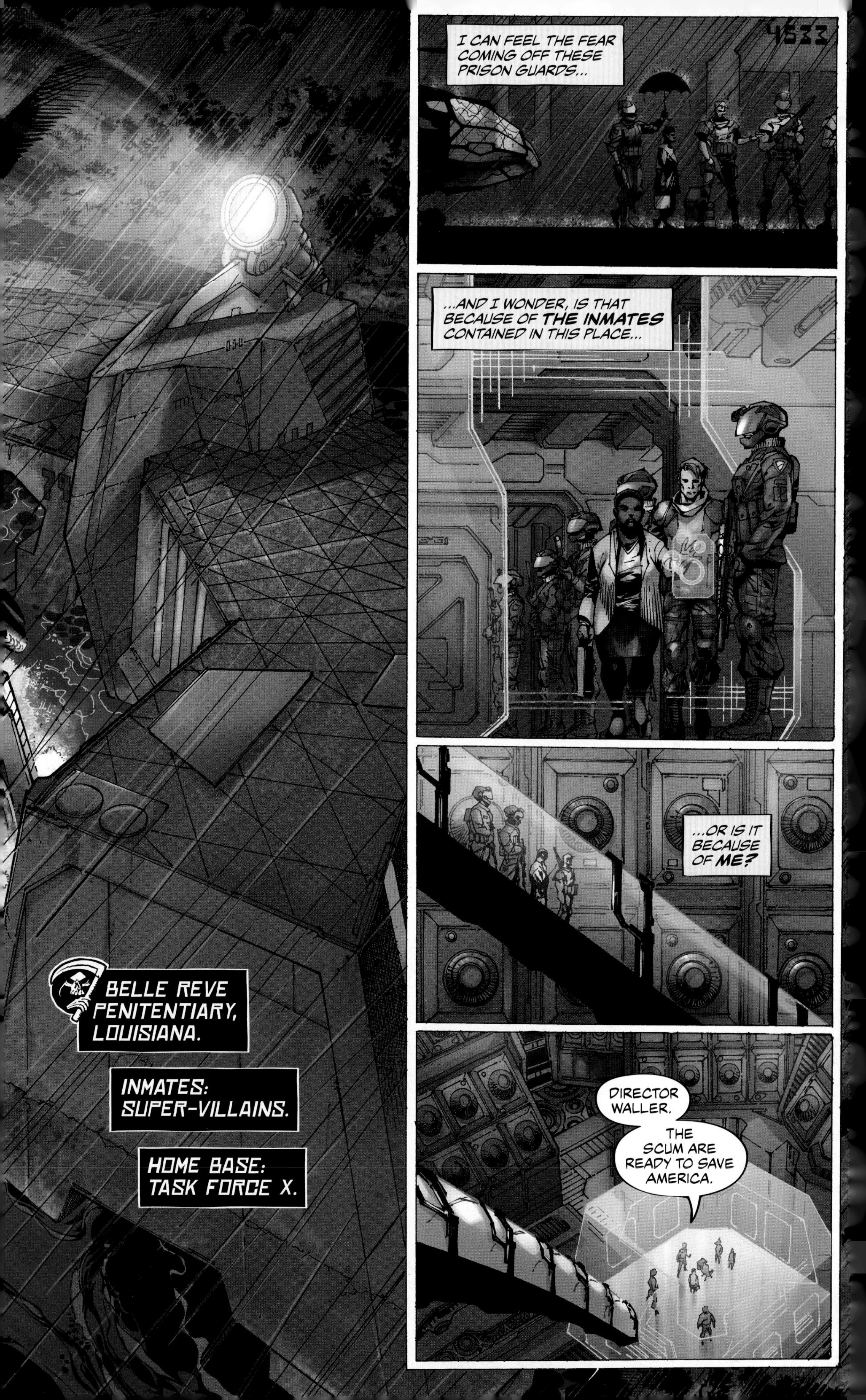

BELLE REVE PENITENTIARY, LOUISIANA.
INMATES: SUPER-VILLAINS.
HOME BASE: TASK FORCE X.
I CAN FEEL THE FEAR COMING OFF THESE PRISON GUARDS...
4533
...AND I WONDER, IS THAT BECAUSE OF THE INMATES CONTAINED IN THIS PLACE...
...OR IS IT BECAUSE OF ME?
DIRECTOR WALLER.
THE SCUM ARE READY TO SAVE AMERICA.

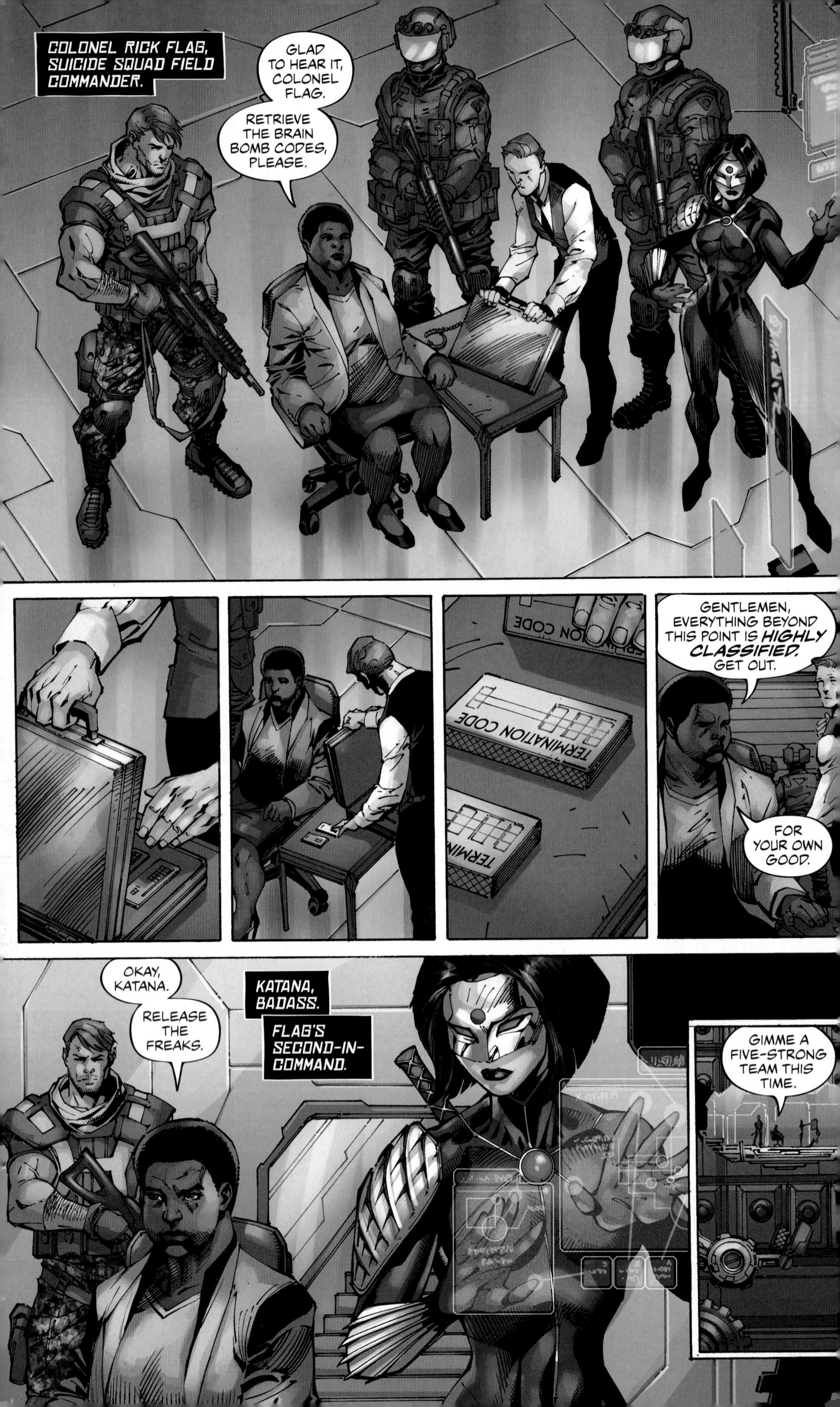
COLONEL RICK FLAG, SUICIDE SQUAD FIELD COMMANDER.
GLAD TO HEAR IT, COLONEL FLAG.
RETRIEVE THE BRAIN BOMB CODES, PLEASE.
TERMINATION CODE
TERMINATION CODE
GENTLEMEN, EVERYTHING BEYOND THIS POINT IS HIGHLY CLASSIFIED. GET OUT.
FOR YOUR OWN GOOD.
OKAY, KATANA.
RELEASE THE FREAKS.
KATANA, BADASS.
FLAG'S SECOND-IN-COMMAND.
GIMME A FIVE-STRONG TEAM THIS TIME.

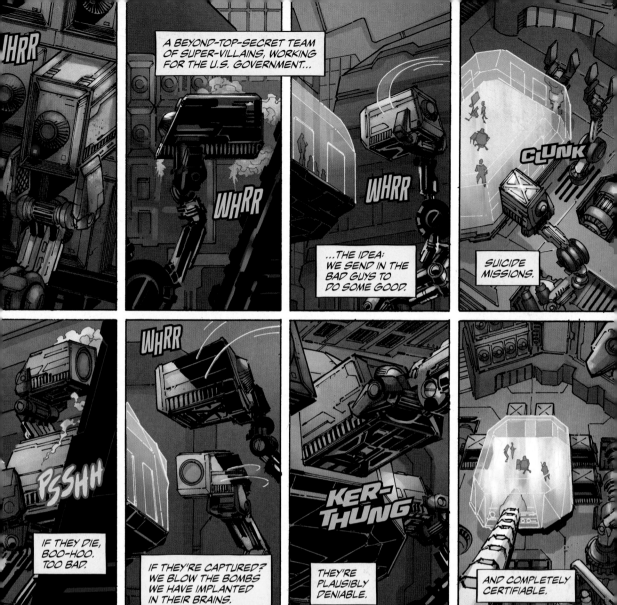

WHRR

A BEYOND-TOP-SECRET TEAM OF SUPER-VILLAINS, WORKING FOR THE U.S. GOVERNMENT...

WHRR

...THE IDEA: WE SEND IN THE BAD GUYS TO DO SOME GOOD.

WHRR

CLUNK

SUICIDE MISSIONS.

WHRR

PSSHH

IF THEY DIE, BOO-HOO. TOO BAD.

IF THEY'RE CAPTURED? WE BLOW THE BOMBS WE HAVE IMPLANTED IN THEIR BRAINS.

KER-THUNG

THEY'RE PLAUSIBLY DENIABLE.

AND COMPLETELY CERTIFIABLE.

WHY DID I SIGN UP FOR THIS, AGAIN?

FOR FREEDOM, FLAG.

REMEMBER?

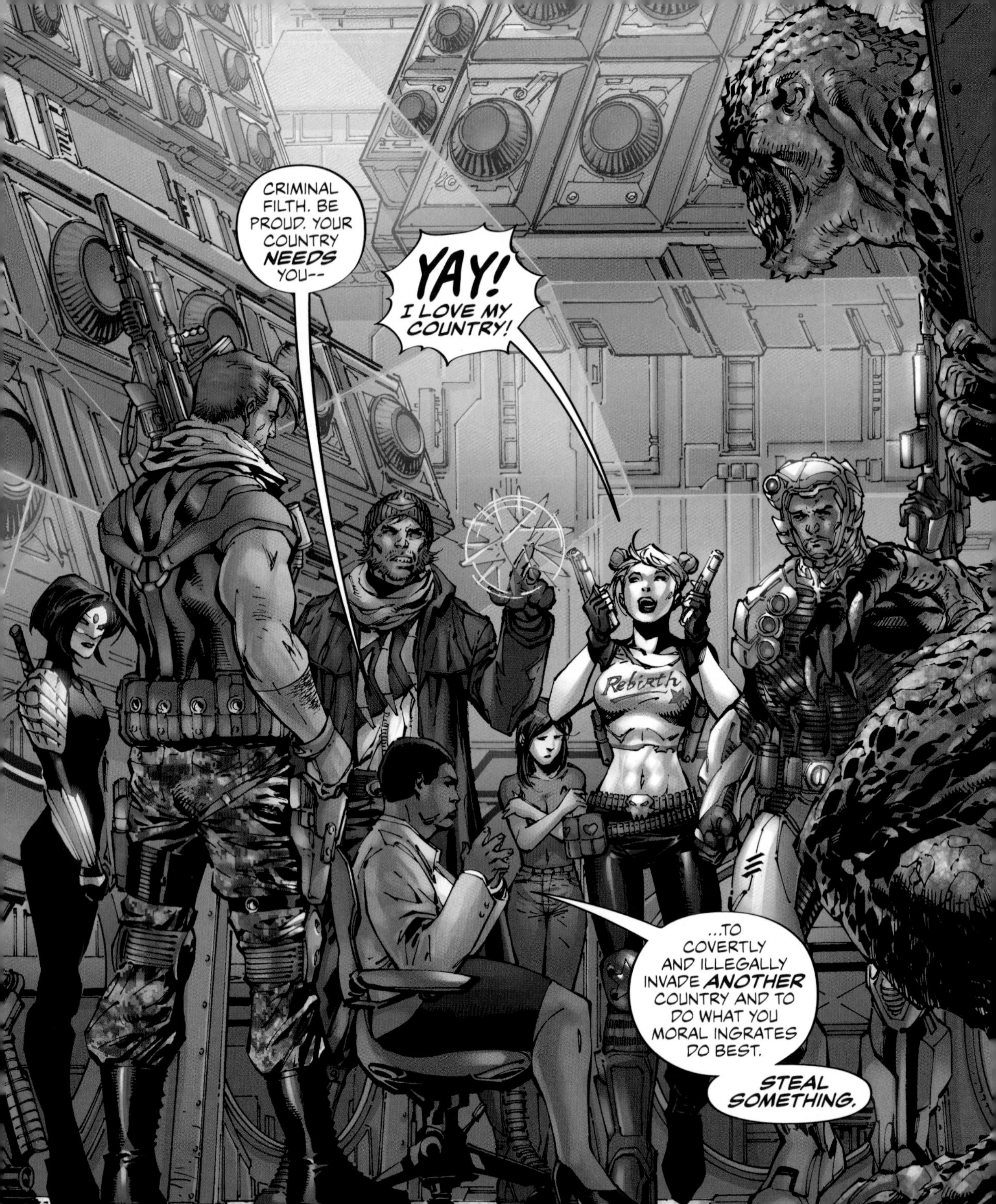
CRIMINAL FILTH. BE PROUD. YOUR COUNTRY NEEDS YOU--
YAY! I LOVE MY COUNTRY!
...TO COVERTLY AND ILLEGALLY INVADE ANOTHER COUNTRY AND TO DO WHAT YOU MORAL INGRATES DO BEST.
STEAL SOMETHING.
Rebirth
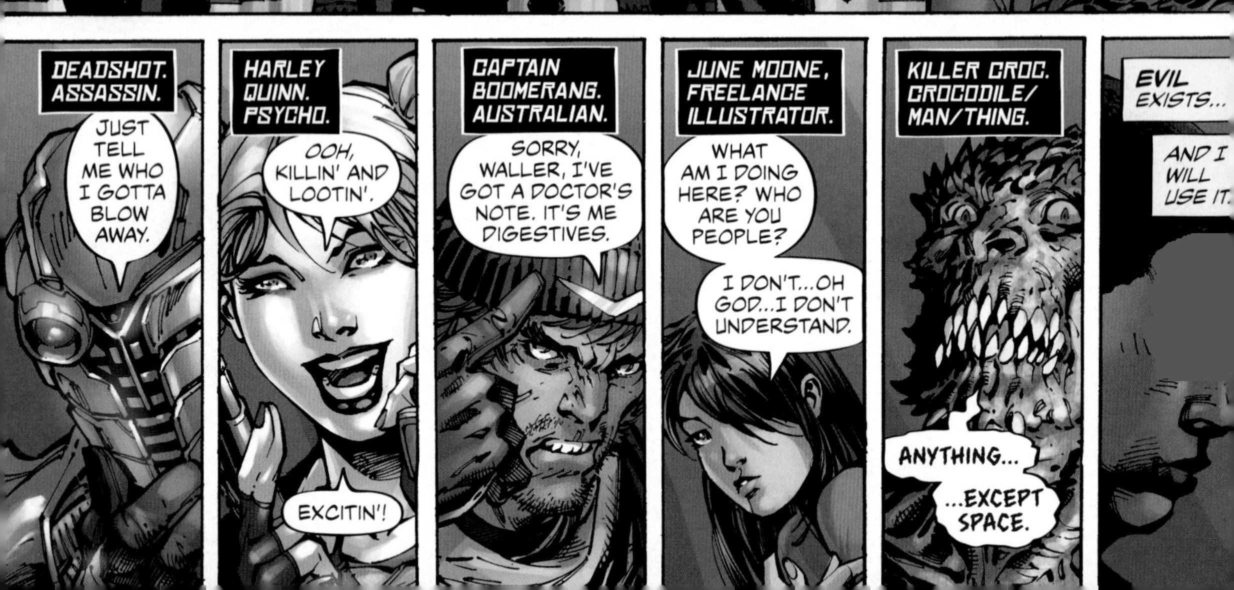
DEADSHOT. ASSASSIN.
JUST TELL ME WHO I GOTTA BLOW AWAY.
HARLEY QUINN. PSYCHO.
OOH, KILLIN' AND LOOTIN'.
EXCITIN'!
CAPTAIN BOOMERANG. AUSTRALIAN.
SORRY, WALLER, I'VE GOT A DOCTOR'S NOTE. IT'S ME DIGESTIVES.
JUNE MOONE, FREELANCE ILLUSTRATOR.
WHAT AM I DOING HERE? WHO ARE YOU PEOPLE?
I DON'T...OH GOD...I DON'T UNDERSTAND.
KILLER CROC. CROCODILE/ MAN/THING.
ANYTHING...
...EXCEPT SPACE.
EVIL EXISTS...
AND I WILL USE IT.

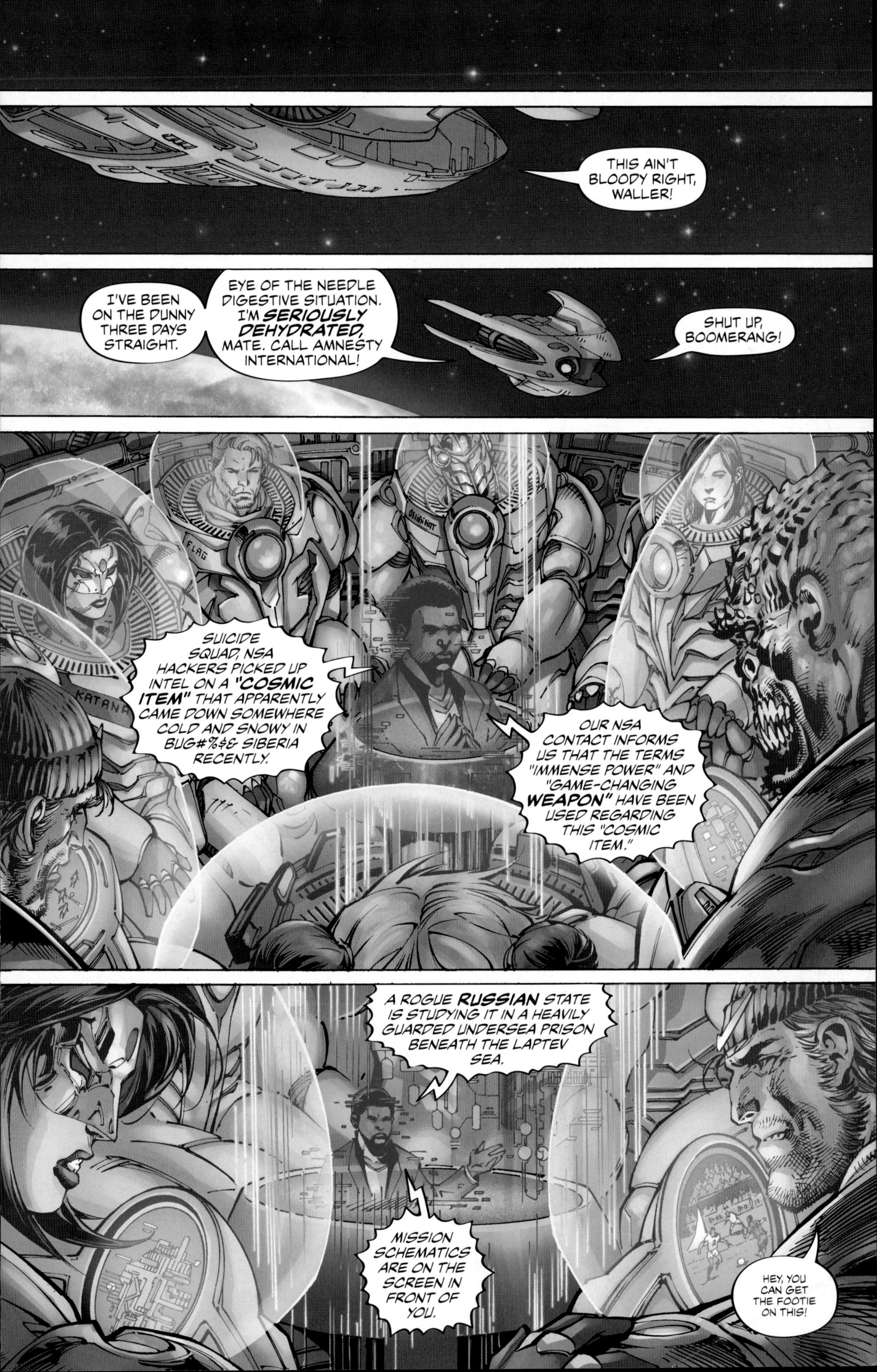

THIS AIN'T BLOODY RIGHT, WALLER!
I'VE BEEN ON THE DUNNY THREE DAYS STRAIGHT.
EYE OF THE NEEDLE DIGESTIVE SITUATION. I'M SERIOUSLY DEHYDRATED, MATE. CALL AMNESTY INTERNATIONAL!
SHUT UP, BOOMERANG!
FLAG
KATANA
SUICIDE SQUAD, NSA HACKERS PICKED UP INTEL ON A "COSMIC ITEM" THAT APPARENTLY CAME DOWN SOMEWHERE COLD AND SNOWY IN BUG#%$& SIBERIA RECENTLY.
OUR NSA CONTACT INFORMS US THAT THE TERMS "IMMENSE POWER" AND "GAME-CHANGING WEAPON" HAVE BEEN USED REGARDING THIS "COSMIC ITEM."
A ROGUE RUSSIAN STATE IS STUDYING IT IN A HEAVILY GUARDED UNDERSEA PRISON BENEATH THE LAPTEV SEA.
MISSION SCHEMATICS ARE ON THE SCREEN IN FRONT OF YOU.
HEY, YOU CAN GET THE FOOTIE ON THIS!

ANY ASSAULT VIA AIR OR SEA WOULD BE PICKED UP BY THEIR SENTRIES WAY BEFORE WE GOT WITHIN MILES. AND, BESIDES, THAT WOULD BE AN "ACT OF WAR," WHICH THE U.S. WOULD NEVER SANCTION.

ZZZZZ

BUT WE HAVE A WAY TO GET US ON-SITE FAST BEFORE THEY EVEN KNOW WE'RE THERE.

OH GOD. I SHOULDN'T BE HERE. I...THERE'S TOO MUCH DARKNESS, SHE'S INSIDE ME. I CAN FEEL IT. SHE'S INSIDE ME AND SHE WANTS TO EMERGE! TO TRANSCEND!

I FEEL A BIT... UNWELL.

I'LL SAY THIS IN TWO-SYLLABLE WORDS, FOR BOOMERANG...

OI!

OOOH, THERE'S A POKÉCUTEY UP HERE!

GET IN, STEAL OR DESTROY THIS COSMIC ITEM. ENSURE THIS RUSSIAN ROGUE STATE DOESN'T HAVE IT.

AND REMEMBER THAT IF YOU GET ANY IDEAS ABOUT RUNNING FOR IT...

...I WILL NOT HESITATE TO BLOW YOUR MINDS.

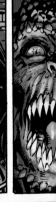

IN THE MOST LITERAL SENSE.

GOOD LUCK.

CLUNK

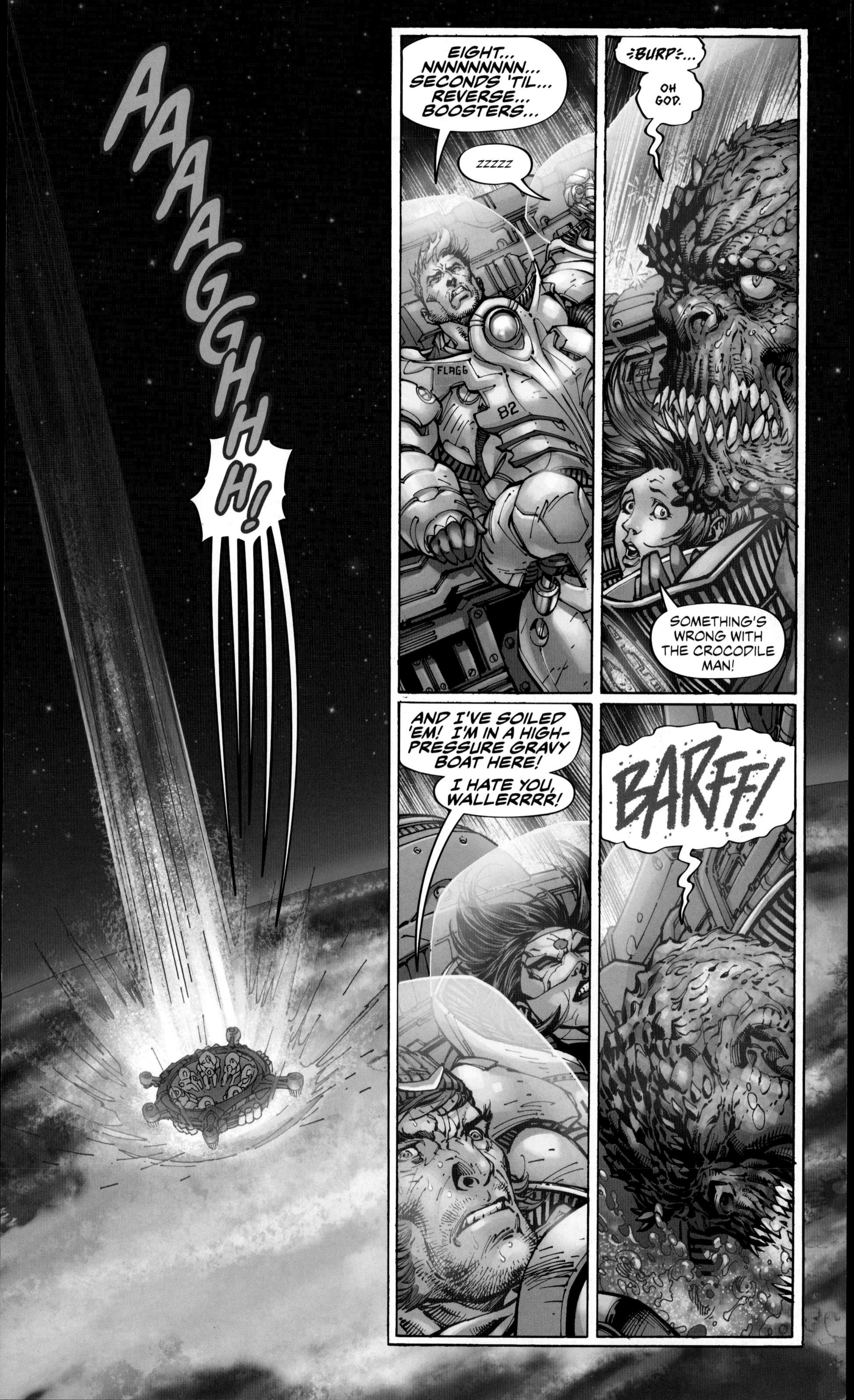
AAAAGGHHH!
EIGHT... NNNNNNNNN... SECONDS 'TIL... REVERSE... BOOSTERS...
ZZZZZ
FLAGG
82
BURP...
OH GOD.
SOMETHING'S WRONG WITH THE CROCODILE MAN!
AND I'VE SOILED 'EM! I'M IN A HIGH-PRESSURE GRAVY BOAT HERE!
I HATE YOU, WALLERRRR!
BARFF!

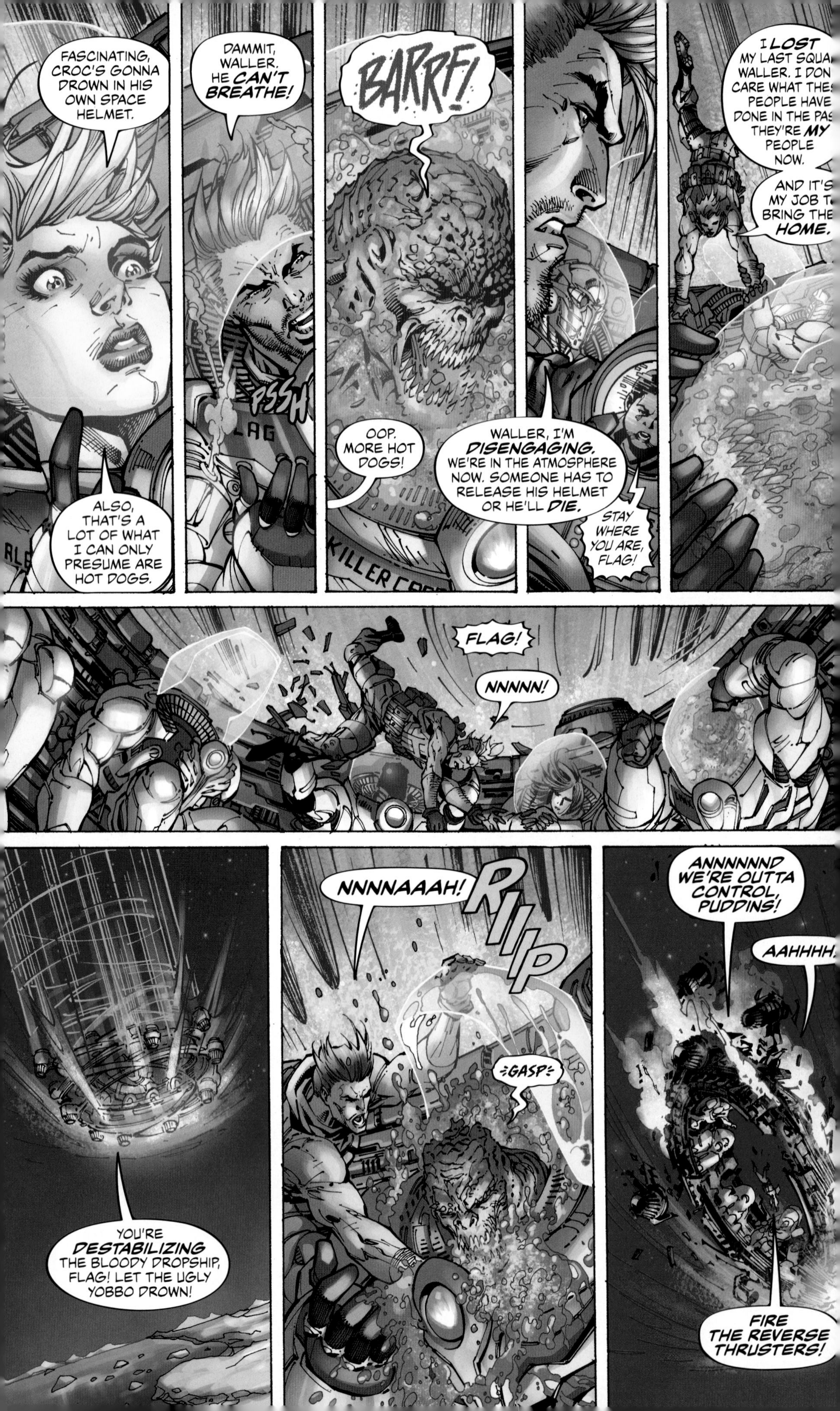
FASCINATING, CROC'S GONNA DROWN IN HIS OWN SPACE HELMET.
ALSO, THAT'S A LOT OF WHAT I CAN ONLY PRESUME ARE HOT DOGS.
DAMMIT, WALLER. HE *CAN'T BREATHE!*
PSSH
FLAG
BARRF!
OOP. MORE HOT DOGS!
WALLER, I'M *DISENGAGING.* WE'RE IN THE ATMOSPHERE NOW. SOMEONE HAS TO RELEASE HIS HELMET OR HE'LL *DIE.*
STAY WHERE YOU ARE, FLAG!
I *LOST* MY LAST SQUA WALLER. I DON CARE WHAT THES PEOPLE HAVE DONE IN THE PAS THEY'RE *MY* PEOPLE NOW.
AND IT'S MY JOB T BRING THE *HOME.*
FLAG!
NNNNN!
YOU'RE *DESTABILIZING* THE BLOODY DROPSHIP, FLAG! LET THE UGLY YOBBO DROWN!
NNNNAAAH!
RIIIP
GASP
ANNNNNND WE'RE OUTTA CONTROL, PUDDINS!
AAHHHH
FIRE THE REVERSE THRUSTERS!

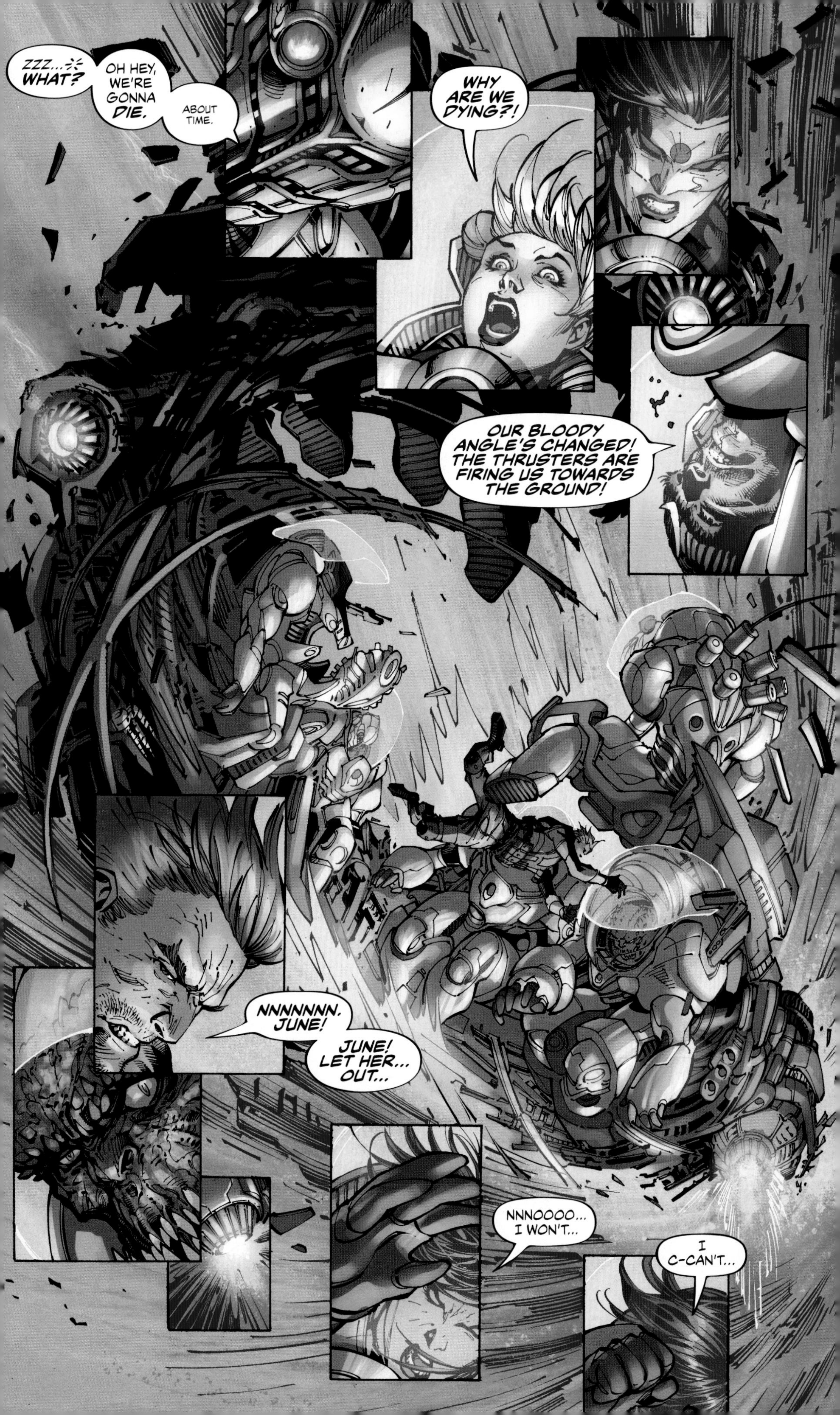
ZZZ... WHAT?
OH HEY, WE'RE GONNA DIE.
ABOUT TIME.
WHY ARE WE DYING?!
OUR BLOODY ANGLE'S CHANGED! THE THRUSTERS ARE FIRING US TOWARDS THE GROUND!
NNNNNNN. JUNE!
JUNE! LET HER... OUT...
NNNOOOO... I WON'T...
I C-CAN'T...

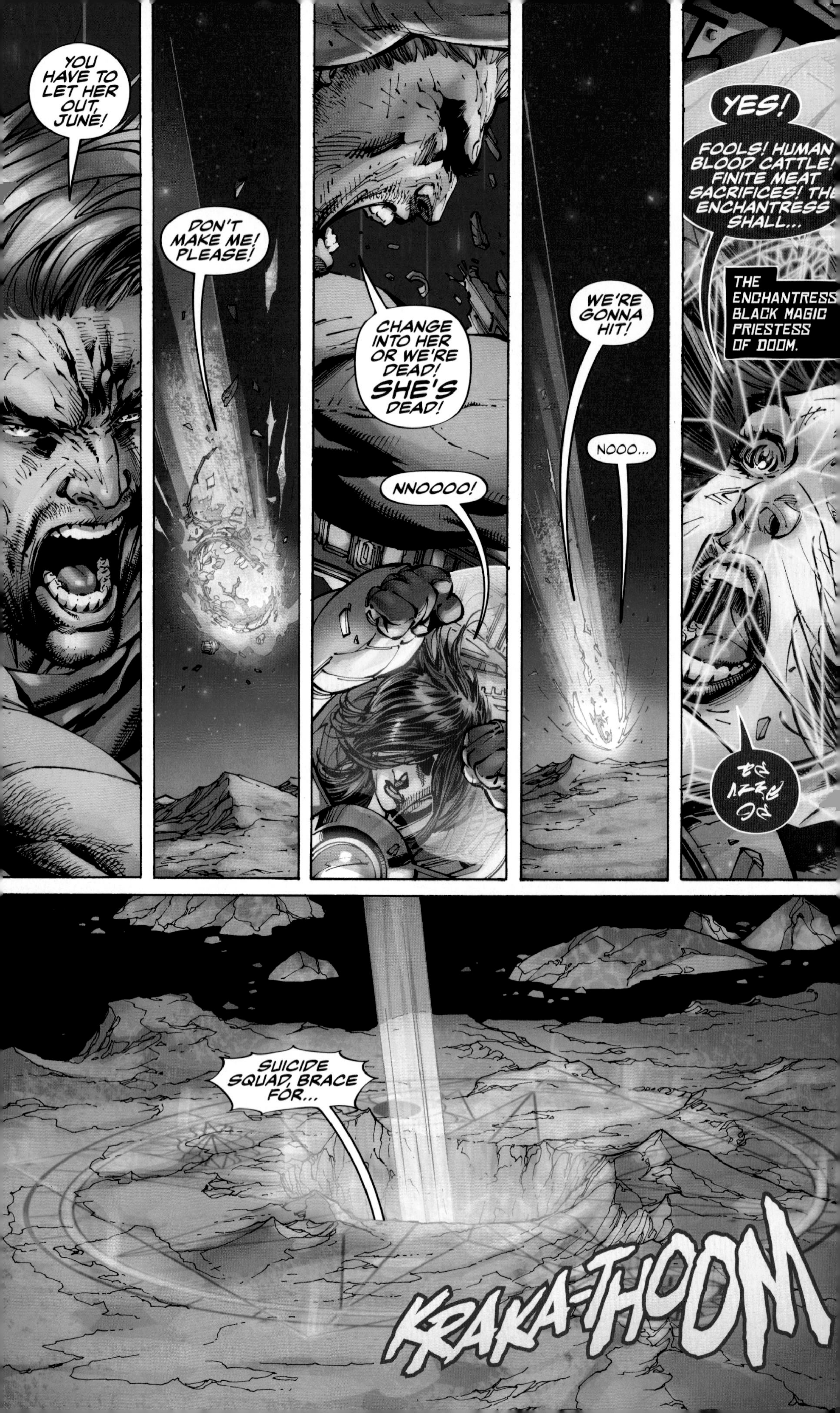
YOU HAVE TO LET HER OUT, JUNE!
DON'T MAKE ME! PLEASE!
CHANGE INTO HER OR WE'RE DEAD! SHE'S DEAD!
NNOOOO!
WE'RE GONNA HIT!
NOOO...
YES!
FOOLS! HUMAN BLOOD CATTLE! FINITE MEAT SACRIFICES! THE ENCHANTRESS SHALL...
THE ENCHANTRESS BLACK MAGIC PRIESTESS OF DOOM.
SUICIDE SQUAD, BRACE FOR...
KRAKA-THOOM

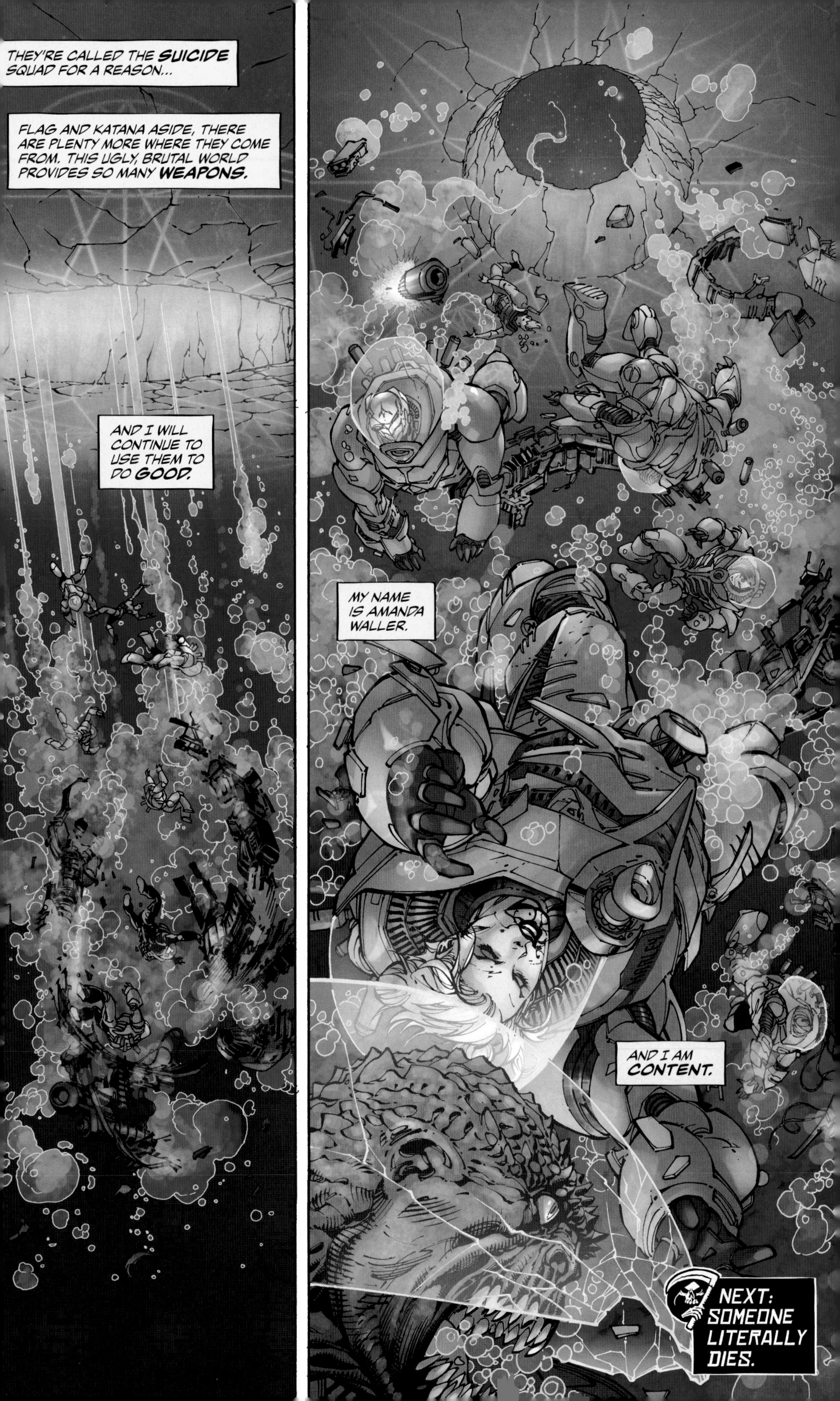
THEY'RE CALLED THE SUICIDE SQUAD FOR A REASON...
FLAG AND KATANA ASIDE, THERE ARE PLENTY MORE WHERE THEY COME FROM. THIS UGLY, BRUTAL WORLD PROVIDES SO MANY WEAPONS.
AND I WILL CONTINUE TO USE THEM TO DO GOOD.
MY NAME IS AMANDA WALLER.
AND I AM CONTENT.
NEXT: SOMEONE LITERALLY DIES.

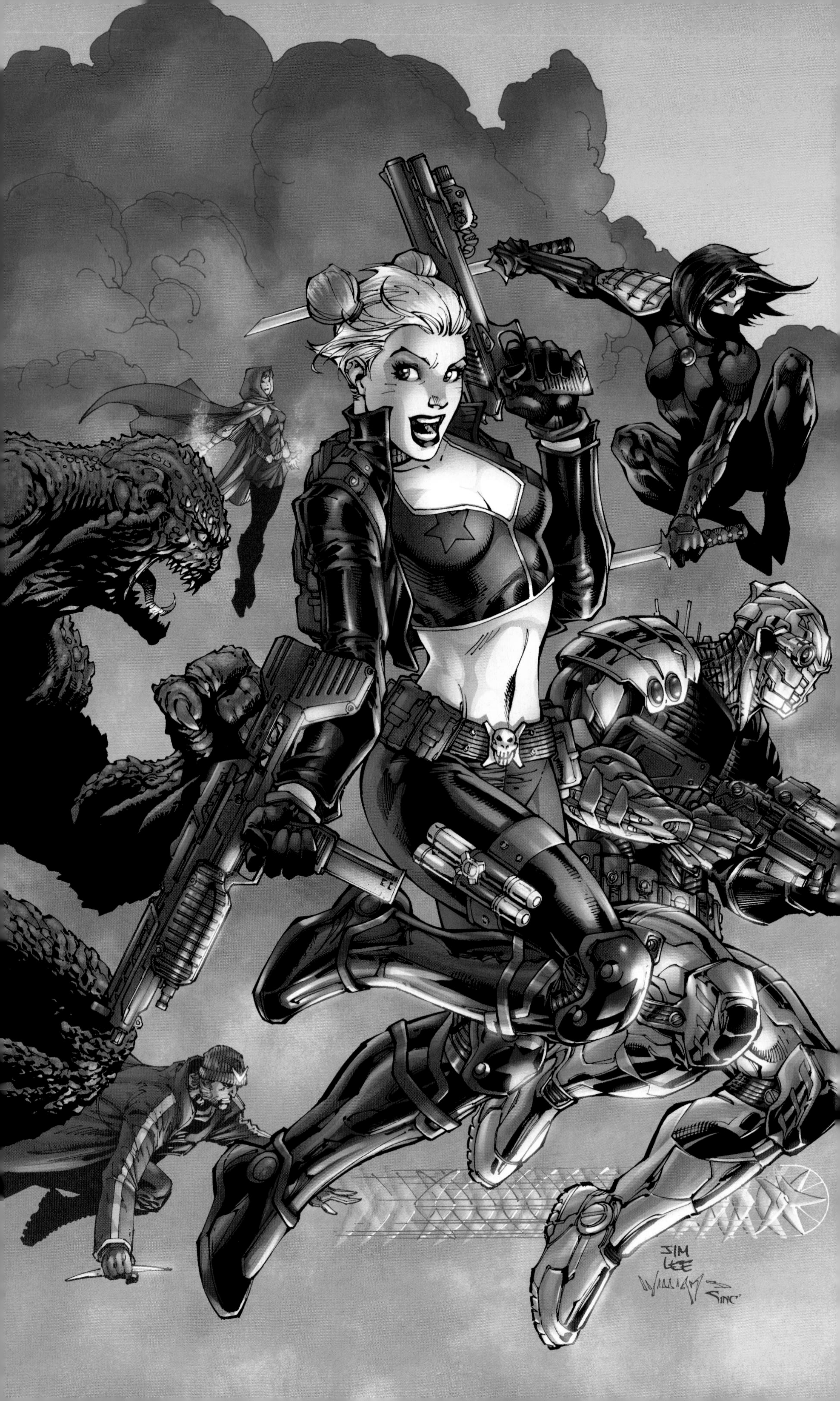
JIM LEE

THE BLACK...

...VAULT.

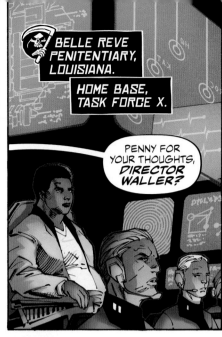

BELLE REVE PENITENTIARY, LOUISIANA.

HOME BASE, TASK FORCE X.

PENNY FOR YOUR THOUGHTS, *DIRECTOR WALLER?*

I'M WONDERING WHY *THE NSA* FELT THE NEED TO SEND SOMEONE LIKE *YOU* TO *MY* PRISON TO DELIVER MISSION INTEL. BELLE REVE IS A *VERY* DANGEROUS PLACE.

"THE WEAK GET *RIPPED TO SHREDS* HERE."

YOU DON'T JUDGE A BOOK BY ITS COVER, MS. WALLER. YOU KNOW THAT BETTER THAN MOST.

YOU CAN CALL ME *HARCOURT.* AND I CAN LOOK AFTER MYSELF.

I *REQUESTED* TO COME HERE BECAUSE I'M A FAN. I WANTED TO SEE IF THE TALES ABOUT YOU WERE TRUE.

"AND TO SEE THE *SUICIDE SQUAD* IN ACTION FIRSTHAND."

RETINAL CAMER LAG. RICK

BUT IT SEEMS I'M WATCHING THE SUICIDE SQUAD *DIE* FIRSTHAND.

"YOUR TEAM CRASHED INTO ARCTIC WATERS, SEVERAL OF THEIR PRESSURE SUITS ARE COMPROMISED, ONE OF THE DROP SHIPS' *ROCKETS* IS CIRCLING WILDLY...

"...WITH THREE OF YOUR PEOPLE TRYING TO *RIDE IT* TOWARD THEIR TARGET?!"

THEY ARE SCUMBAGS, BUT THEY ARE *RESOURCEFUL* SCUMBAGS. HAVE FAITH, HARCOURT.

BUT THE OTHERS...

"WATER HAS FILLED THEIR SUITS. THEY'RE DROWNING...

...SINKING TO THE BOTTOM OF THE LAPTEV SEA LIKE *CONCRETE COFFINS.*

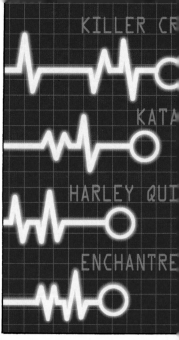

KILLER CR

KATA

HARLEY QUI

ENCHANTRE

KILLER CROC

KATANA

HARLEY QUINN

ENCHANTRESS

"YOUR GIRL KATANA WILL LAST 60 SECONDS-- *TOPS*--IN THAT ICE-COLD WATER WITHOUT HER SUIT.

"SELF-SACRIFICE...

"IT SEEMS EVEN VILLAINS ARE WORTH *DYING* FOR.

I THINK YOU JUST LOST OVER HALF YOUR TEAM, MS. WALLER.

THE OTHERS HAD BETTER GET THE JOB DONE.

"OUR ENEMIES *CANNOT* POSSESS THE COSMIC ITEM."

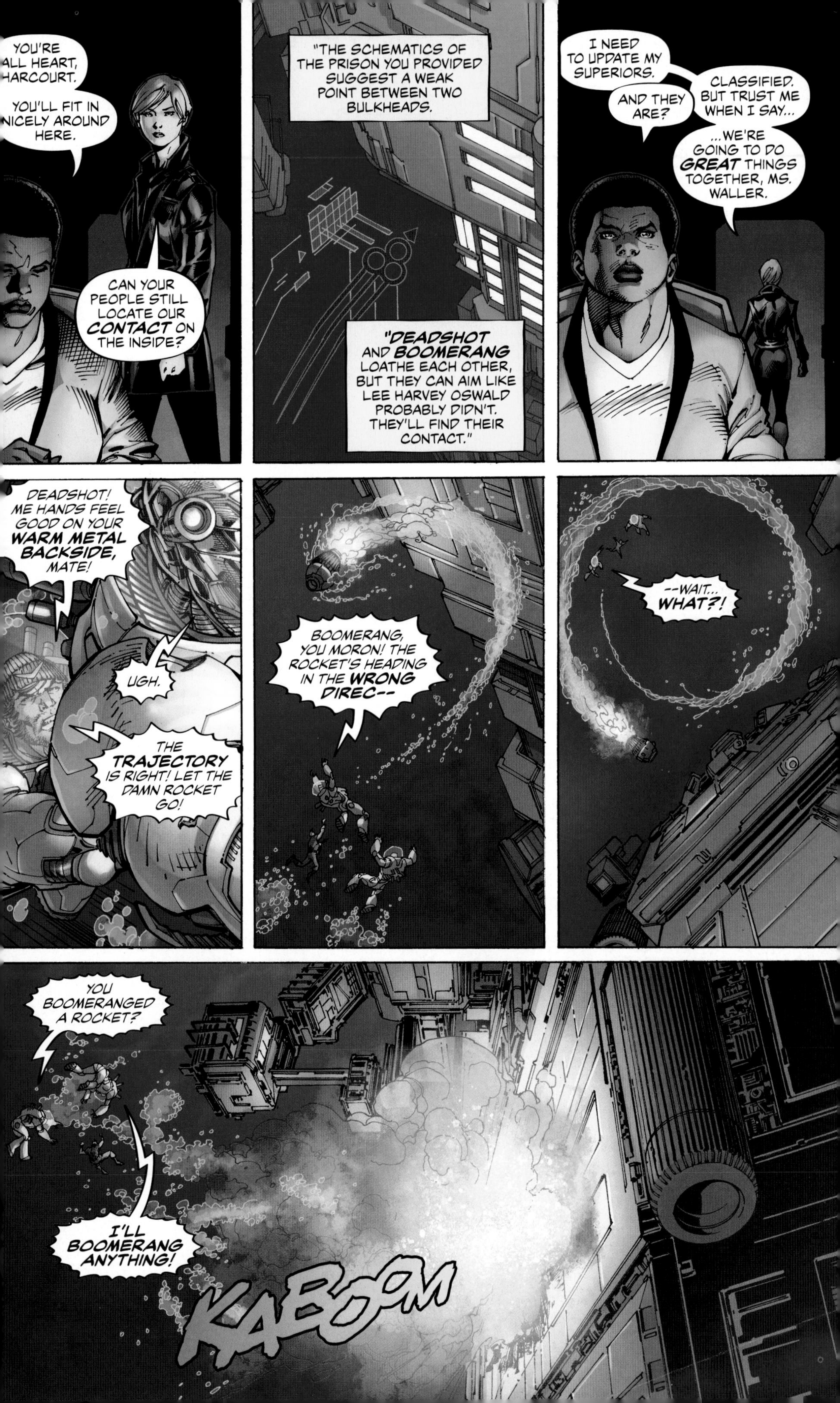
YOU'RE ALL HEART, HARCOURT.
YOU'LL FIT IN NICELY AROUND HERE.
CAN YOUR PEOPLE STILL LOCATE OUR CONTACT ON THE INSIDE?
"THE SCHEMATICS OF THE PRISON YOU PROVIDED SUGGEST A WEAK POINT BETWEEN TWO BULKHEADS.
"DEADSHOT AND BOOMERANG LOATHE EACH OTHER, BUT THEY CAN AIM LIKE LEE HARVEY OSWALD PROBABLY DIDN'T. THEY'LL FIND THEIR CONTACT."
I NEED TO UPDATE MY SUPERIORS.
AND THEY ARE?
CLASSIFIED. BUT TRUST ME WHEN I SAY...
...WE'RE GOING TO DO GREAT THINGS TOGETHER, MS. WALLER.
DEADSHOT! ME HANDS FEEL GOOD ON YOUR WARM METAL BACKSIDE, MATE!
UGH.
THE TRAJECTORY IS RIGHT! LET THE DAMN ROCKET GO!
BOOMERANG, YOU MORON! THE ROCKET'S HEADING IN THE WRONG DIREC--
--WAIT... WHAT?!
YOU BOOMERANGED A ROCKET?
I'LL BOOMERANG ANYTHING!
KABOOM

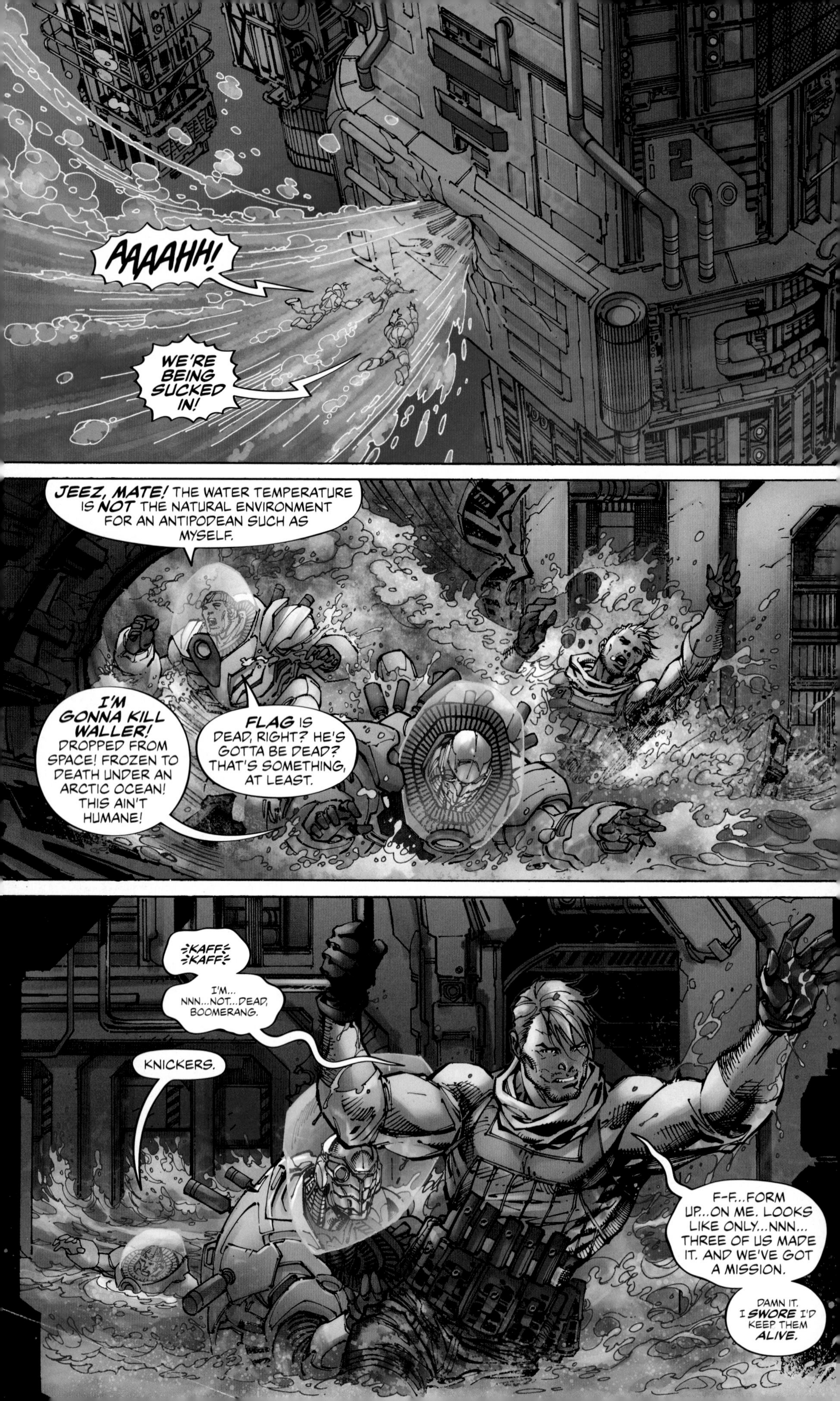
AAAAHH!
WE'RE BEING SUCKED IN!
JEEZ, MATE! THE WATER TEMPERATURE IS NOT THE NATURAL ENVIRONMENT FOR AN ANTIPODEAN SUCH AS MYSELF.
I'M GONNA KILL WALLER! DROPPED FROM SPACE! FROZEN TO DEATH UNDER AN ARCTIC OCEAN! THIS AIN'T HUMANE!
FLAG IS DEAD, RIGHT? HE'S GOTTA BE DEAD? THAT'S SOMETHING, AT LEAST.
KAFF KAFF
I'M... NNN...NOT...DEAD, BOOMERANG.
KNICKERS.
F-F...FORM UP...ON ME. LOOKS LIKE ONLY...NNN... THREE OF US MADE IT. AND WE'VE GOT A MISSION.
DAMN IT. I SWORE I'D KEEP THEM ALIVE.

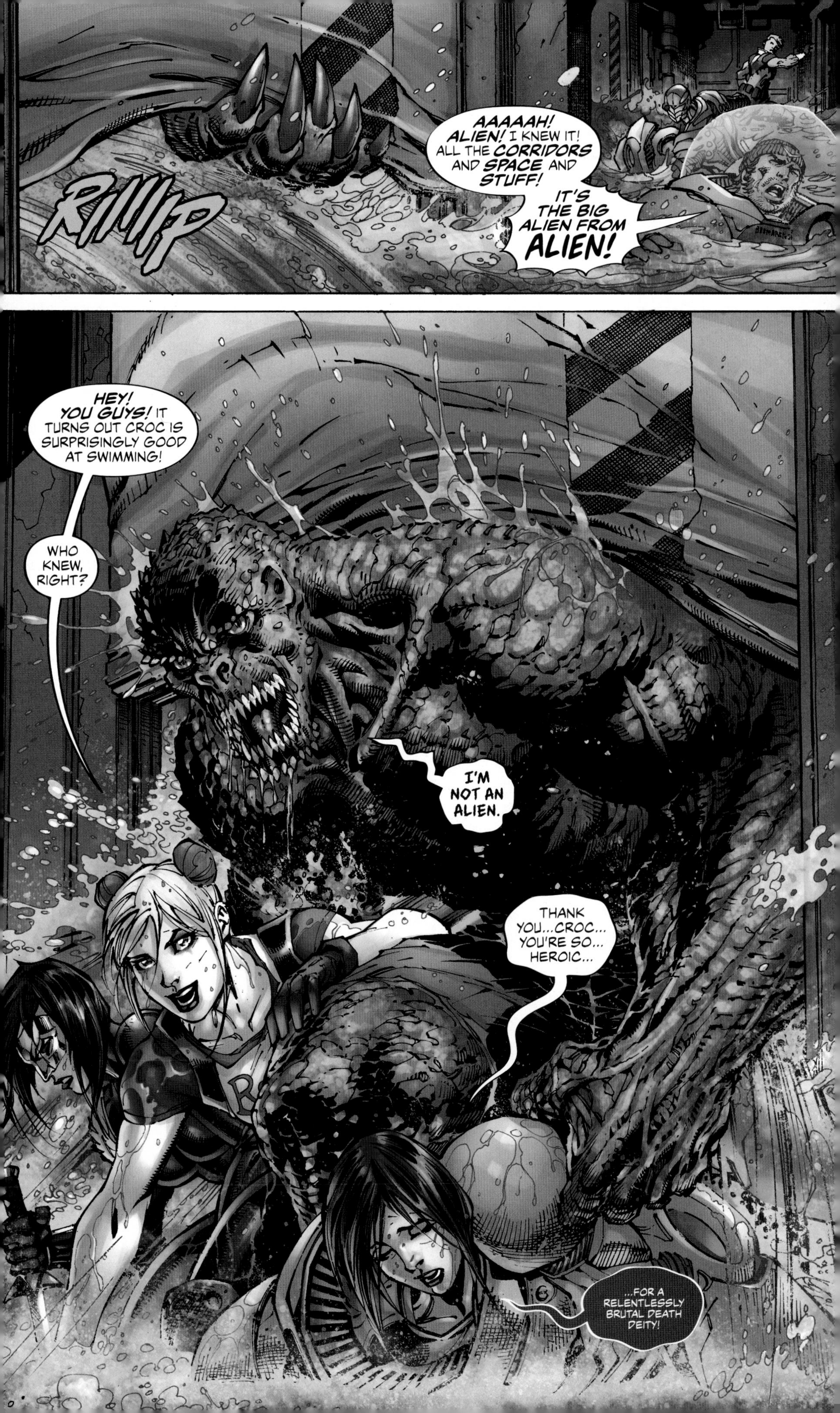
RIIIIP
AAAAAH! ALIEN! I KNEW IT! ALL THE CORRIDORS AND SPACE AND STUFF!
IT'S THE BIG ALIEN FROM ALIEN!
HEY! YOU GUYS! IT TURNS OUT CROC IS SURPRISINGLY GOOD AT SWIMMING!
WHO KNEW, RIGHT?
I'M NOT AN ALIEN.
THANK YOU...CROC... YOU'RE SO... HEROIC...
...FOR A RELENTLESSLY BRUTAL DEATH DEITY!

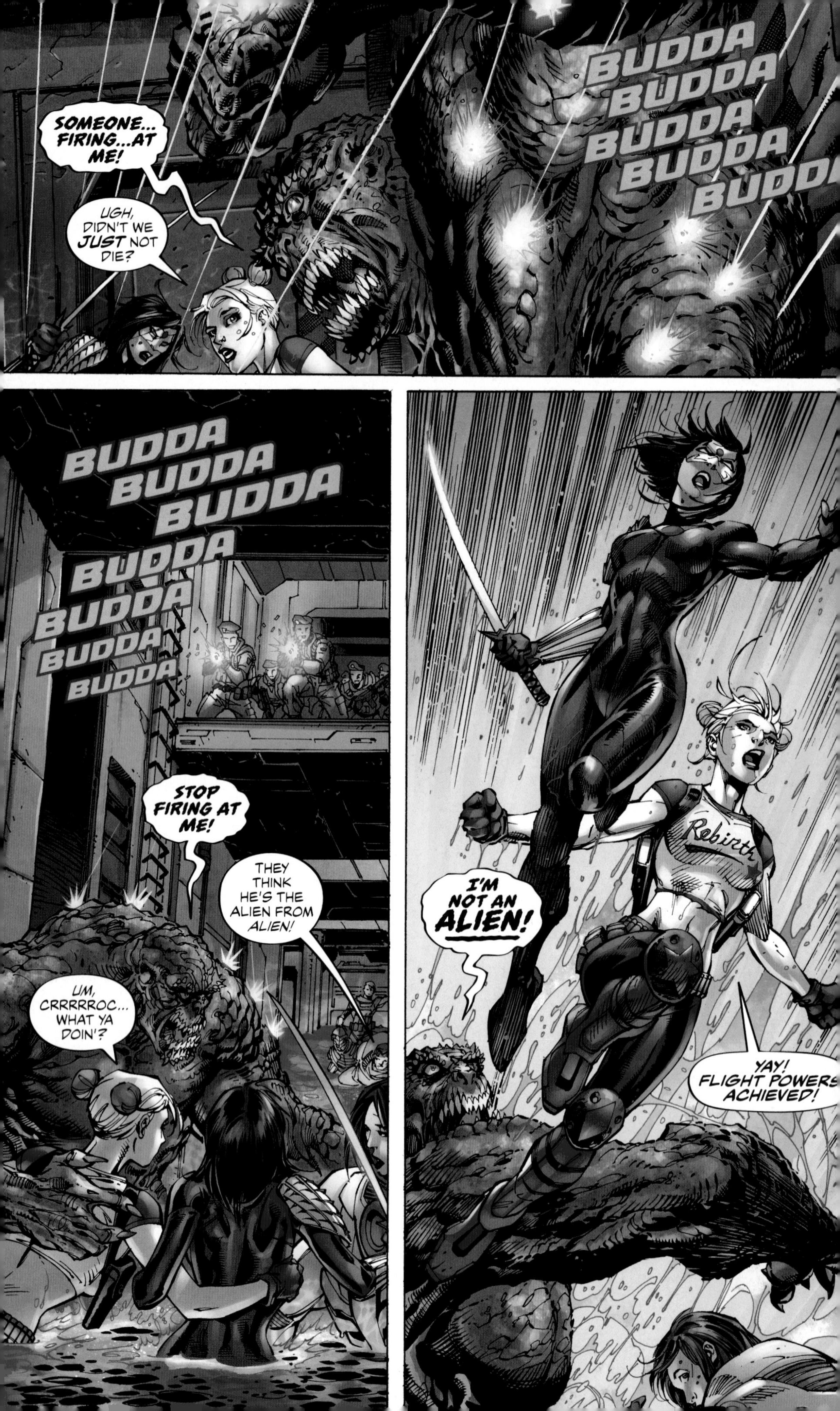
SOMEONE... FIRING...AT ME!
UGH, DIDN'T WE JUST NOT DIE?
BUDDA BUDDA BUDDA BUDDA BUDD
BUDDA BUDDA BUDDA BUDDA BUDDA BUDDA BUDDA
STOP FIRING AT ME!
THEY THINK HE'S THE ALIEN FROM ALIEN!
UM, CRRRRROC... WHAT YA DOIN'?
Rebirth
I'M NOT AN ALIEN!
YAY! FLIGHT POWERS ACHIEVED!

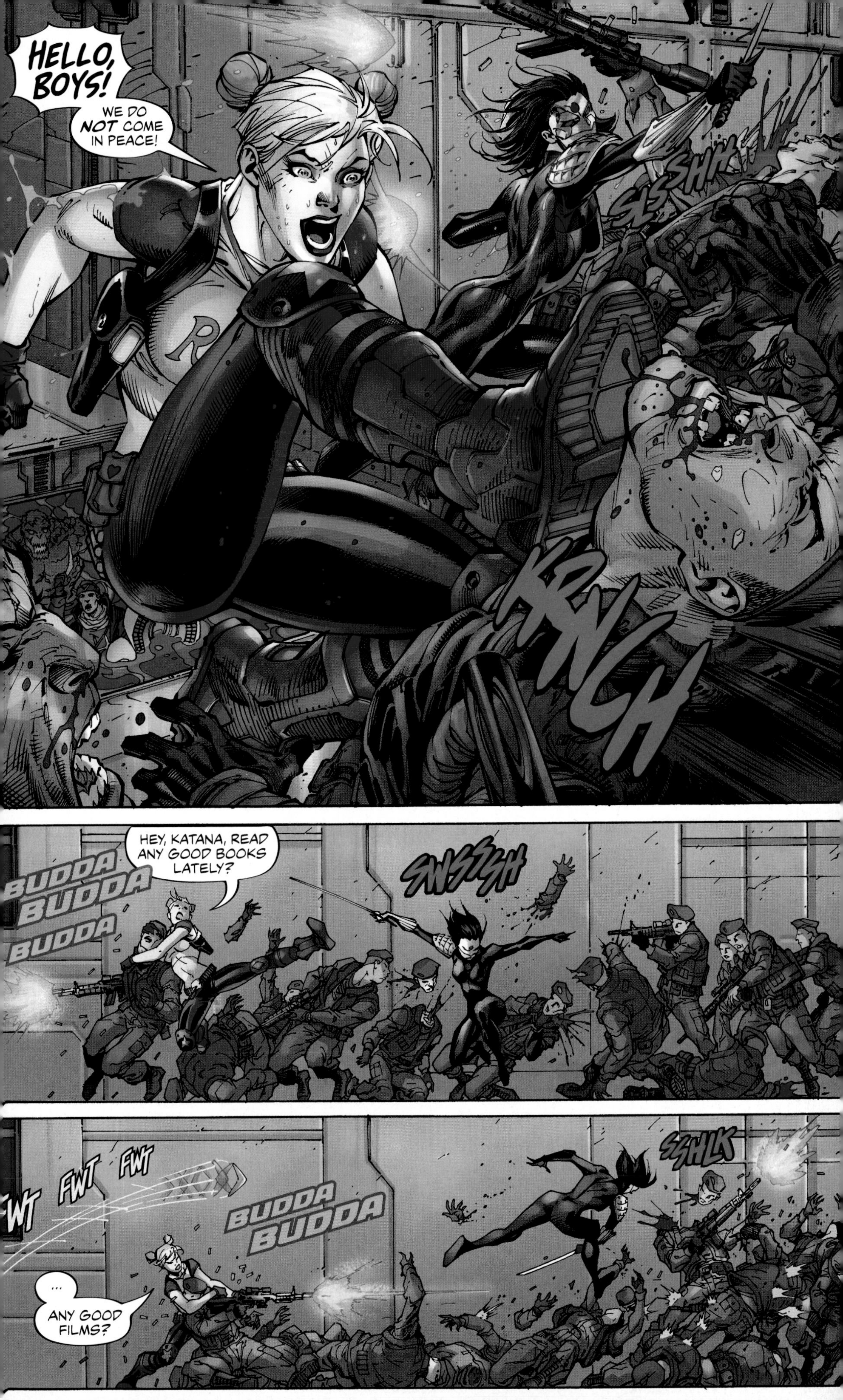
HELLO, BOYS!
WE DO *NOT* COME IN PEACE!
SLSSHH
KRNCH
BUDDA BUDDA BUDDA
HEY, KATANA, READ ANY GOOD BOOKS LATELY?
SWSSH
FWT FWT
BUDDA BUDDA
SSHLK
... ANY GOOD FILMS?

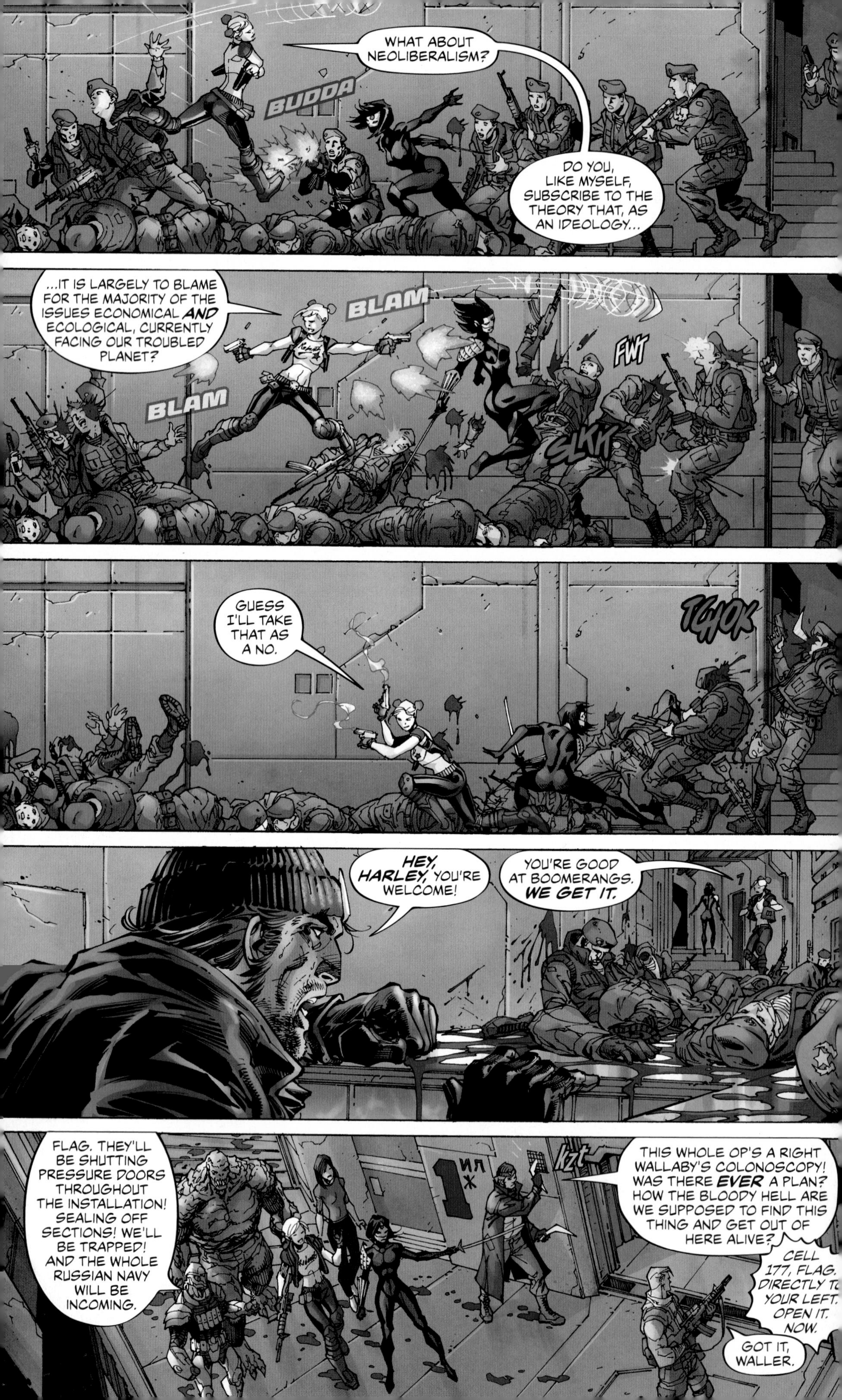

WHAT ABOUT NEOLIBERALISM?
BUDDA
DO YOU, LIKE MYSELF, SUBSCRIBE TO THE THEORY THAT, AS AN IDEOLOGY...
...IT IS LARGELY TO BLAME FOR THE MAJORITY OF THE ISSUES ECONOMICAL AND ECOLOGICAL, CURRENTLY FACING OUR TROUBLED PLANET?
BLAM
BLAM
FWT
SLKK
GUESS I'LL TAKE THAT AS A NO.
TCHOK
HEY, HARLEY, YOU'RE WELCOME!
YOU'RE GOOD AT BOOMERANGS. WE GET IT.
FLAG. THEY'LL BE SHUTTING PRESSURE DOORS THROUGHOUT THE INSTALLATION! SEALING OFF SECTIONS! WE'LL BE TRAPPED! AND THE WHOLE RUSSIAN NAVY WILL BE INCOMING.
kzt
THIS WHOLE OP'S A RIGHT WALLABY'S COLONOSCOPY! WAS THERE EVER A PLAN? HOW THE BLOODY HELL ARE WE SUPPOSED TO FIND THIS THING AND GET OUT OF HERE ALIVE?
CELL 177, FLAG. DIRECTLY T YOUR LEFT. OPEN IT. NOW.
GOT IT, WALLER.

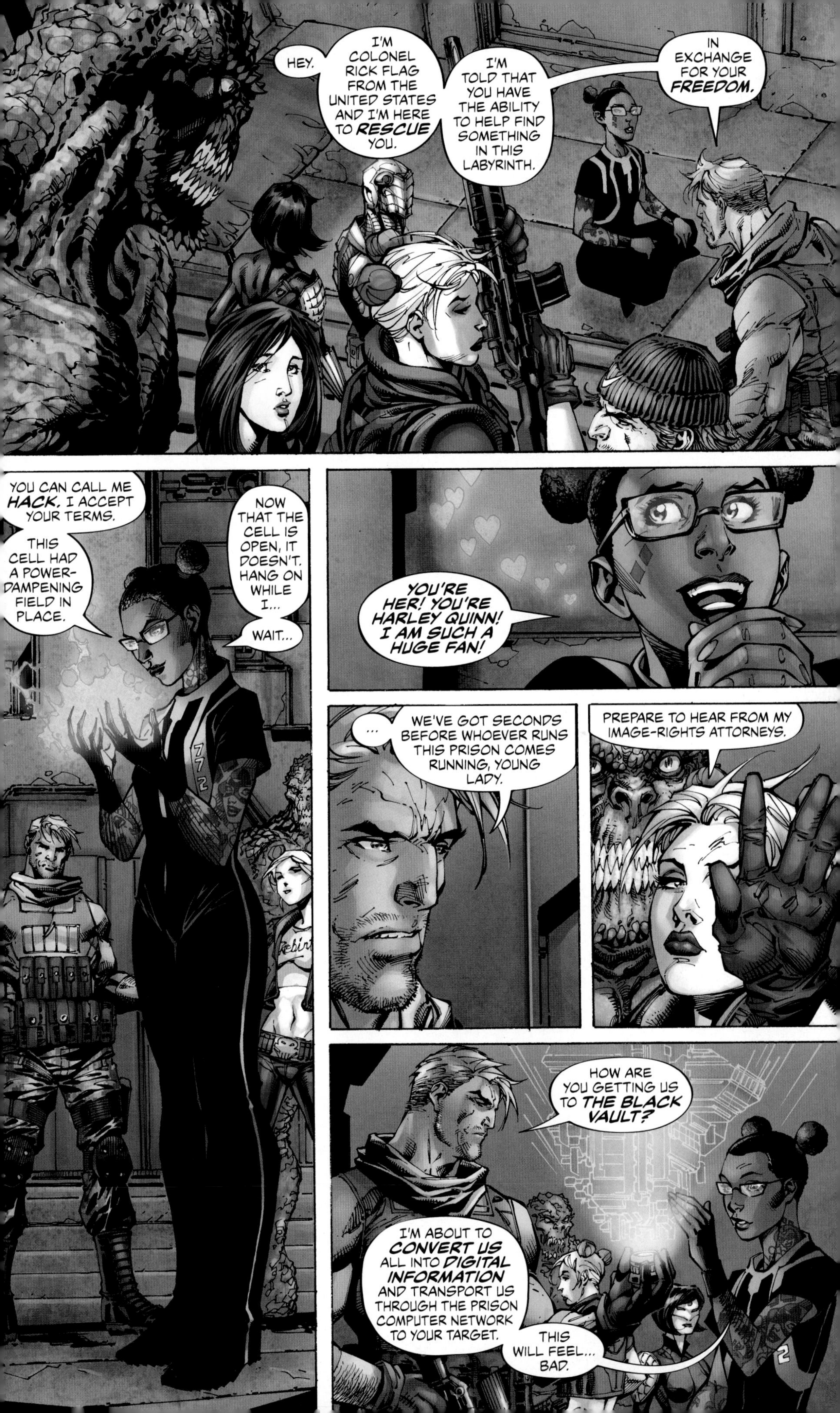
HEY.
I'M COLONEL RICK FLAG FROM THE UNITED STATES AND I'M HERE TO RESCUE YOU.
I'M TOLD THAT YOU HAVE THE ABILITY TO HELP FIND SOMETHING IN THIS LABYRINTH.
IN EXCHANGE FOR YOUR FREEDOM.
YOU CAN CALL ME HACK. I ACCEPT YOUR TERMS.
THIS CELL HAD A POWER-DAMPENING FIELD IN PLACE.
NOW THAT THE CELL IS OPEN, IT DOESN'T. HANG ON WHILE I...
WAIT...
YOU'RE HER! YOU'RE HARLEY QUINN! I AM SUCH A HUGE FAN!
...
WE'VE GOT SECONDS BEFORE WHOEVER RUNS THIS PRISON COMES RUNNING, YOUNG LADY.
PREPARE TO HEAR FROM MY IMAGE-RIGHTS ATTORNEYS.
HOW ARE YOU GETTING US TO THE BLACK VAULT?
I'M ABOUT TO CONVERT US ALL INTO DIGITAL INFORMATION AND TRANSPORT US THROUGH THE PRISON COMPUTER NETWORK TO YOUR TARGET.
THIS WILL FEEL... BAD.

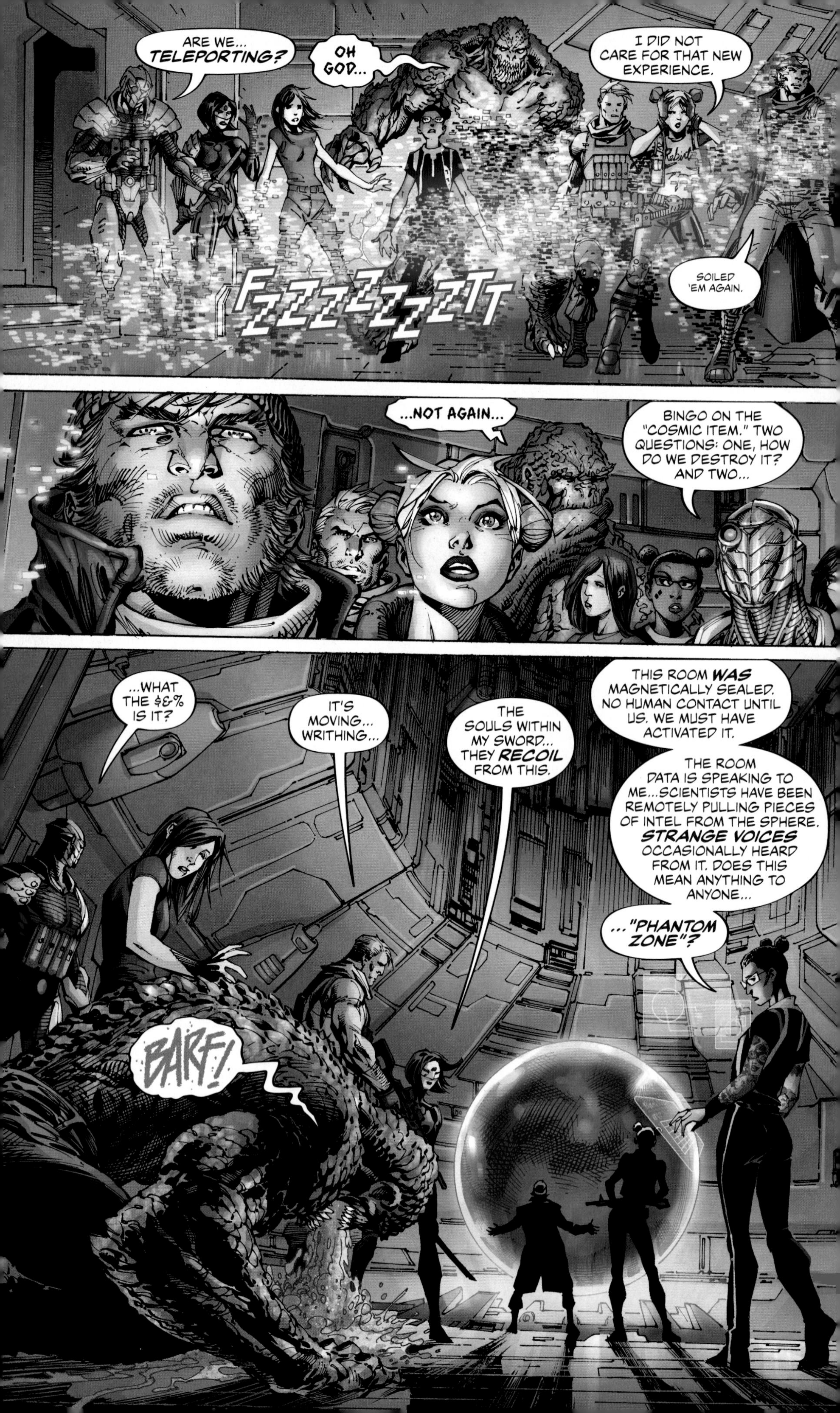
ARE WE... TELEPORTING?
OH GOD...
I DID NOT CARE FOR THAT NEW EXPERIENCE.
FZZZZZZZZTT
SOILED 'EM AGAIN.
...NOT AGAIN...
BINGO ON THE "COSMIC ITEM." TWO QUESTIONS: ONE, HOW DO WE DESTROY IT? AND TWO...
...WHAT THE $&% IS IT?
IT'S MOVING... WRITHING...
THE SOULS WITHIN MY SWORD... THEY RECOIL FROM THIS.
THIS ROOM WAS MAGNETICALLY SEALED. NO HUMAN CONTACT UNTIL US. WE MUST HAVE ACTIVATED IT.
THE ROOM DATA IS SPEAKING TO ME...SCIENTISTS HAVE BEEN REMOTELY PULLING PIECES OF INTEL FROM THE SPHERE. STRANGE VOICES OCCASIONALLY HEARD FROM IT. DOES THIS MEAN ANYTHING TO ANYONE...
..."PHANTOM ZONE"?
BARF!

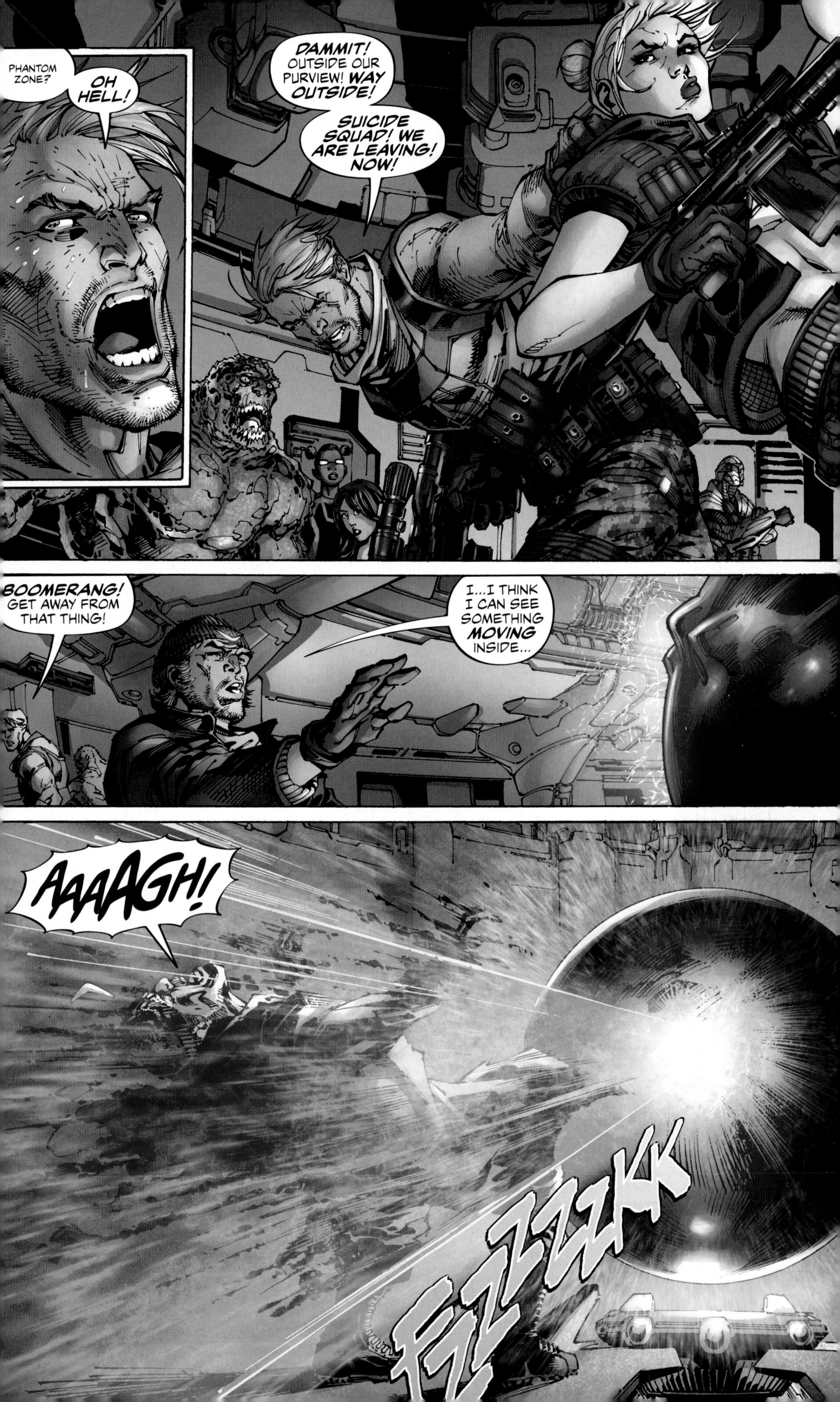
PHANTOM ZONE?
OH HELL!
DAMMIT! OUTSIDE OUR PURVIEW! WAY OUTSIDE!
SUICIDE SQUAD! WE ARE LEAVING! NOW!
BOOMERANG! GET AWAY FROM THAT THING!
I...I THINK I CAN SEE SOMETHING MOVING INSIDE...
AAAAGH!
FZZZZZKK

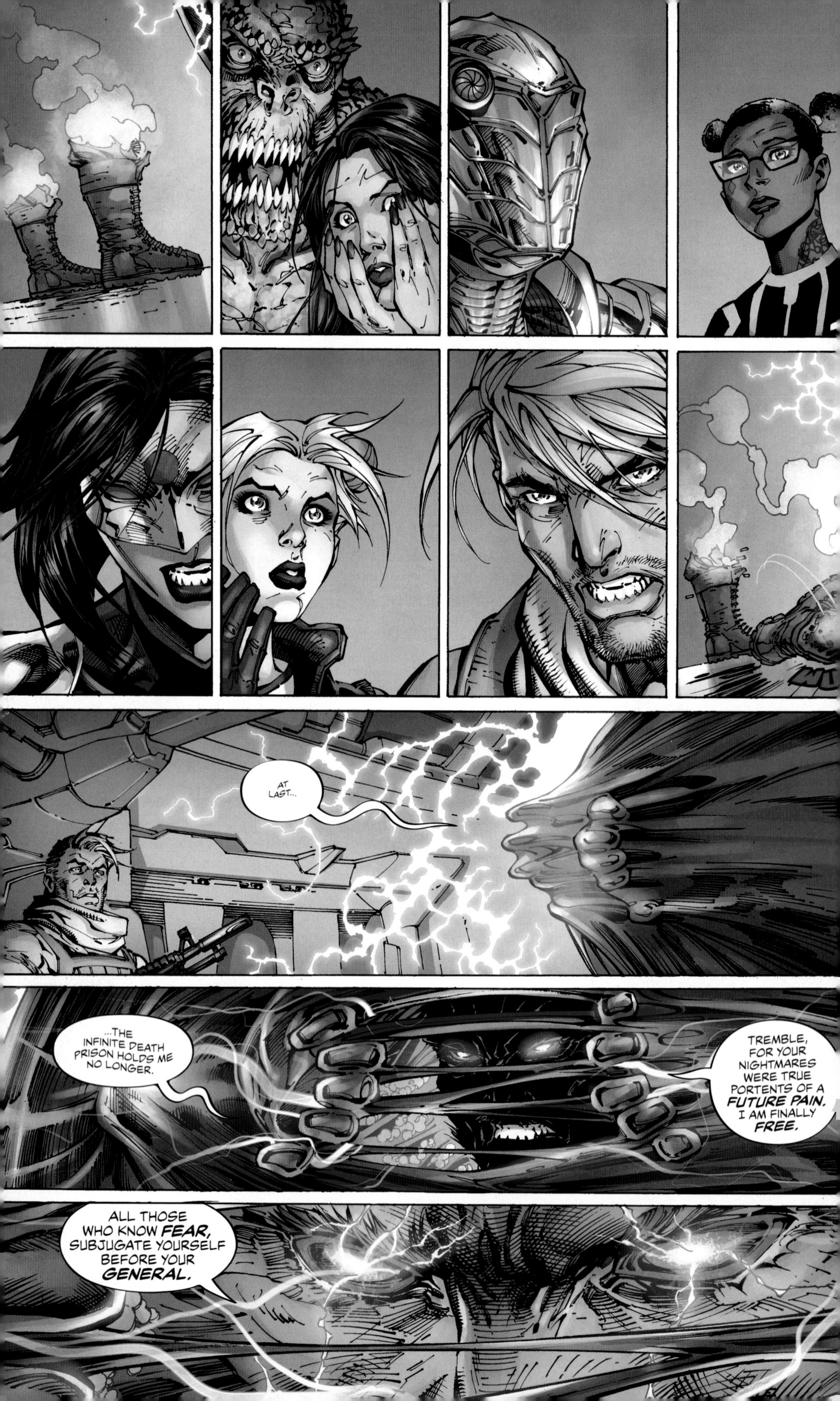
AT LAST...
...THE INFINITE DEATH PRISON HOLDS ME NO LONGER.
TREMBLE, FOR YOUR NIGHTMARES WERE TRUE PORTENTS OF A FUTURE PAIN. I AM FINALLY FREE.
ALL THOSE WHO KNOW FEAR, SUBJUGATE YOURSELF BEFORE YOUR GENERAL.

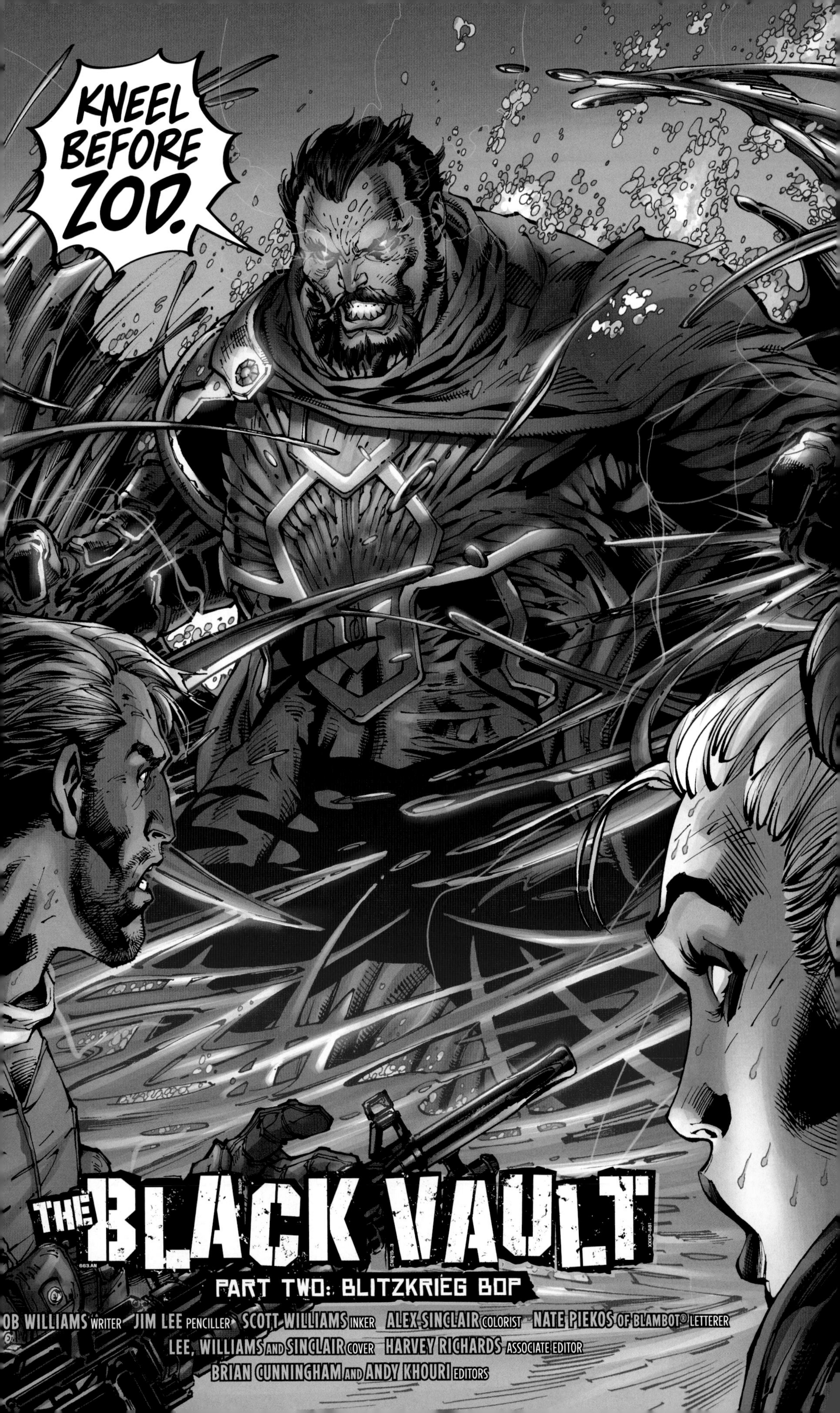
KNEEL BEFORE ZOD.
THE BLACK VAULT
PART TWO: BLITZKRIEG BOP
OB WILLIAMS WRITER JIM LEE PENCILLER SCOTT WILLIAMS INKER ALEX SINCLAIR COLORIST NATE PIEKOS OF BLAMBOT® LETTERER
LEE, WILLIAMS AND SINCLAIR COVER HARVEY RICHARDS ASSOCIATE EDITOR
BRIAN CUNNINGHAM AND ANDY KHOURI EDITORS

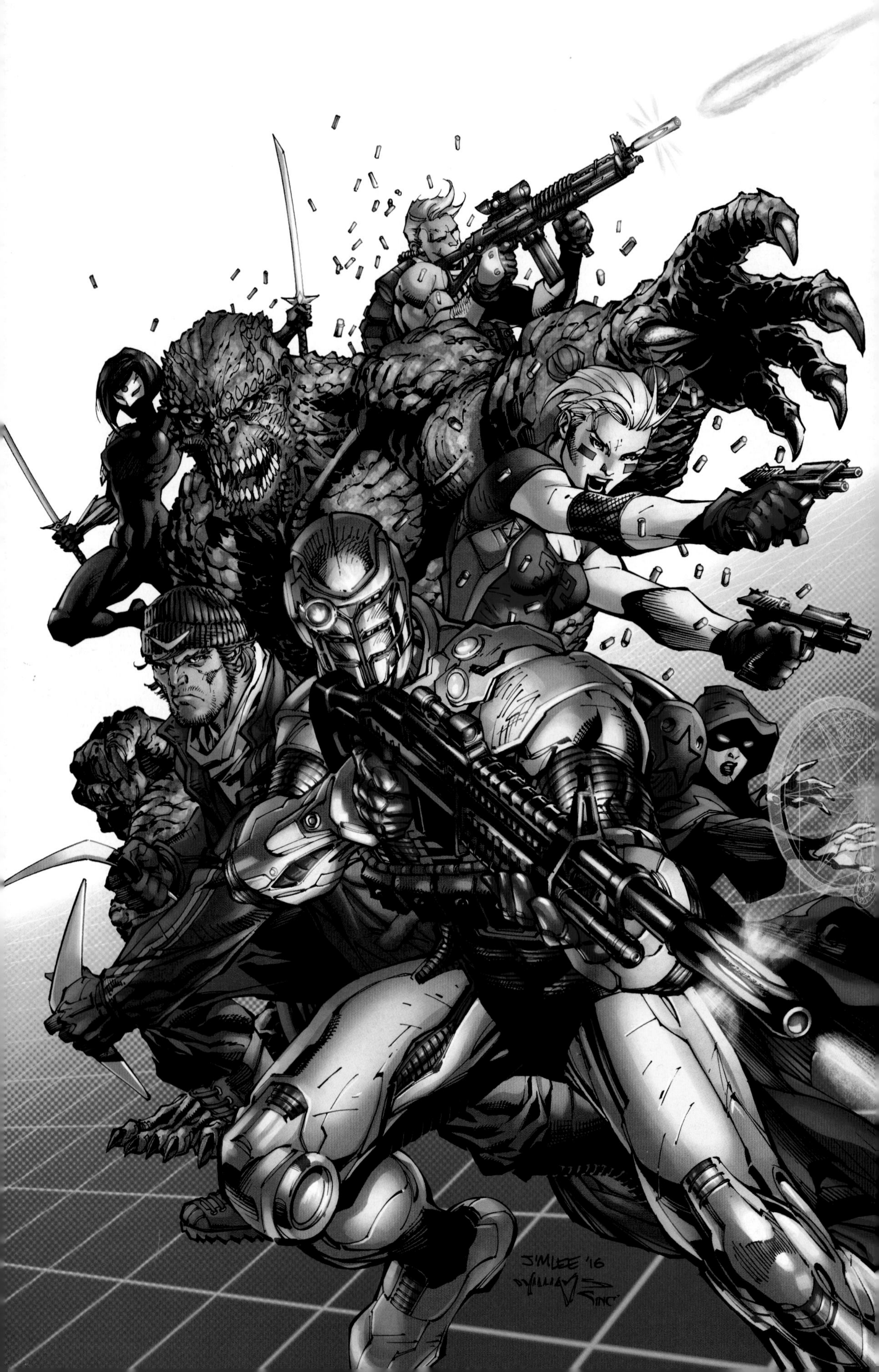

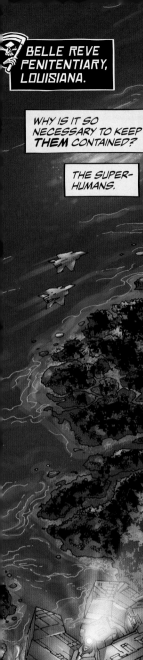

BELLE REVE PENITENTIARY, LOUISIANA.

WHY IS IT SO NECESSARY TO KEEP **THEM** CONTAINED?

THE SUPER-HUMANS.

I REMEMBER THE FIRST TIME MY DADDY TOOK ME DOWNTOWN, AND I DID WHAT ALL CHILDREN DO. I LOOKED UP AT THE SKYSCRAPERS LIKE THEY WERE CASTLES.

I ASKED, IN AWE, WHO BUILT THEM? AND DADDY SAID, "**WE** DID, **AMANDA.** ORDINARY **HUMAN BEINGS** JUST LIKE YOU AND ME."

LIKE WE WERE REACHING UP FOR THE SKY.

HERE'S DOWNTOWN TODAY, IN THE AFTERMATH OF THE RECENT BATTLE BETWEEN **DARKSEID** AND THE **ANTI-MONITOR.** *

THE TYPE OF DESTRUCTION THAT COULD FALL **UPON** US AT ANY MOMENT...

*JUSTICE LEAGUE: THE DARKSEID WAR --ANDY

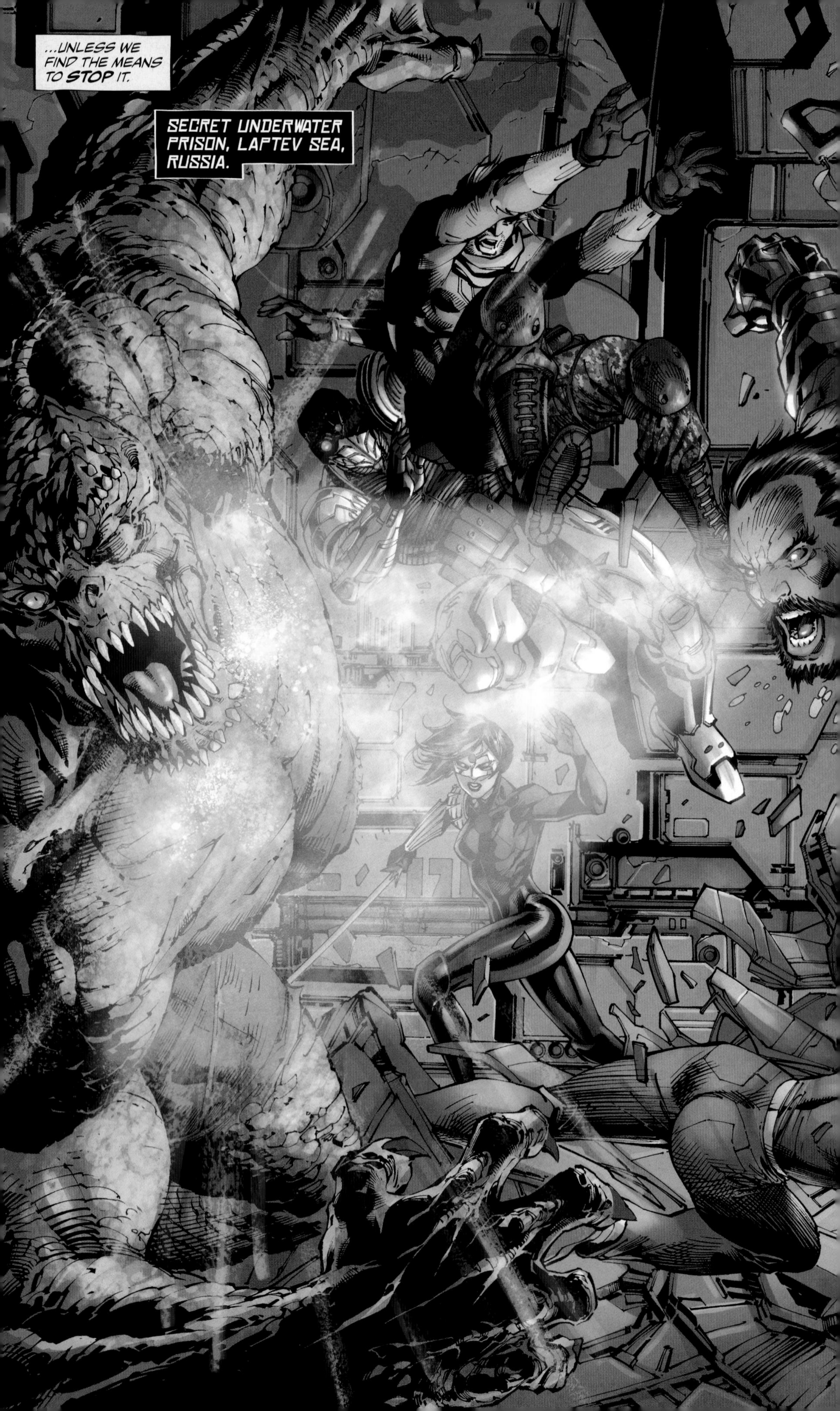
...UNLESS WE FIND THE MEANS TO STOP IT.
SECRET UNDERWATER PRISON, LAPTEV SEA, RUSSIA.

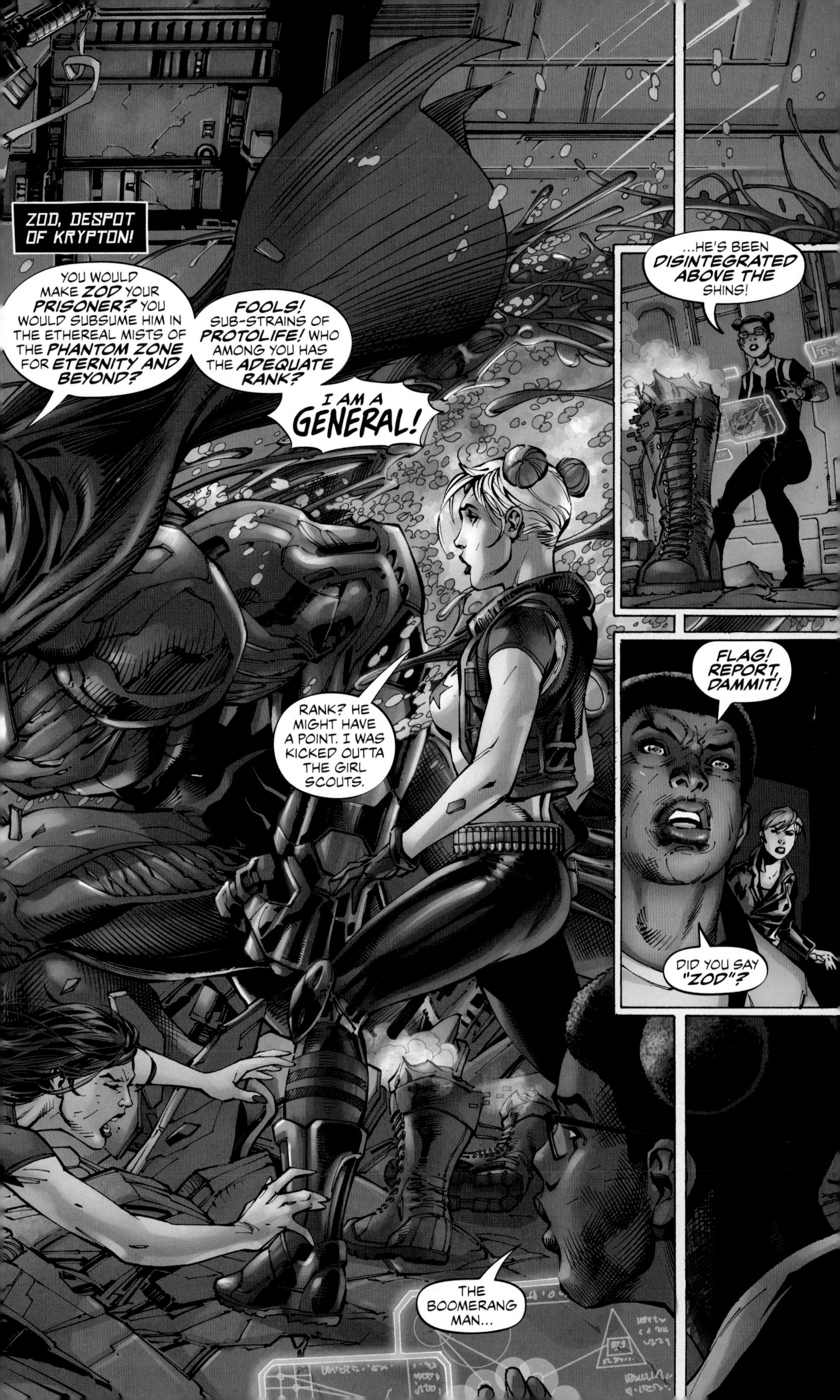
ZOD, DESPOT OF KRYPTON!
YOU WOULD MAKE ZOD YOUR PRISONER? YOU WOULD SUBSUME HIM IN THE ETHEREAL MISTS OF THE PHANTOM ZONE FOR ETERNITY AND BEYOND?
FOOLS! SUB-STRAINS OF PROTOLIFE! WHO AMONG YOU HAS THE ADEQUATE RANK?
I AM A GENERAL!
RANK? HE MIGHT HAVE A POINT. I WAS KICKED OUTTA THE GIRL SCOUTS.
...HE'S BEEN DISINTEGRATED ABOVE THE SHINS!
FLAG! REPORT, DAMMIT!
DID YOU SAY "ZOD"?
THE BOOMERANG MAN...

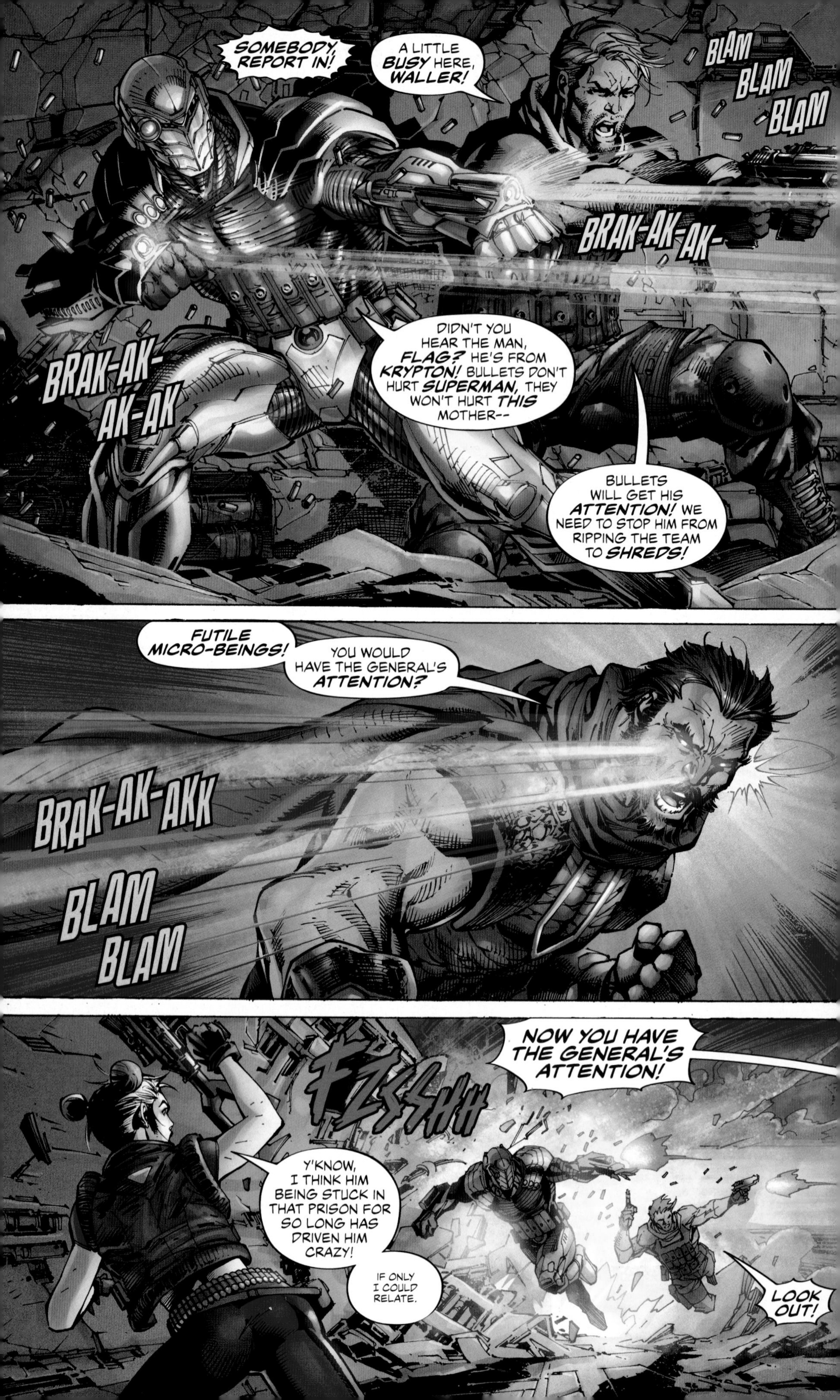
SOMEBODY, REPORT IN!
A LITTLE BUSY HERE, WALLER!
BLAM BLAM BLAM
BRAK-AK-AK-
BRAK-AK-AK-AK
DIDN'T YOU HEAR THE MAN, FLAG? HE'S FROM KRYPTON! BULLETS DON'T HURT SUPERMAN, THEY WON'T HURT THIS MOTHER--
BULLETS WILL GET HIS ATTENTION! WE NEED TO STOP HIM FROM RIPPING THE TEAM TO SHREDS!
FUTILE MICRO-BEINGS!
YOU WOULD HAVE THE GENERAL'S ATTENTION?
BRAK-AK-AKK
BLAM BLAM
NOW YOU HAVE THE GENERAL'S ATTENTION!
FZSSHH
Y'KNOW, I THINK HIM BEING STUCK IN THAT PRISON FOR SO LONG HAS DRIVEN HIM CRAZY!
IF ONLY I COULD RELATE.
LOOK OUT!

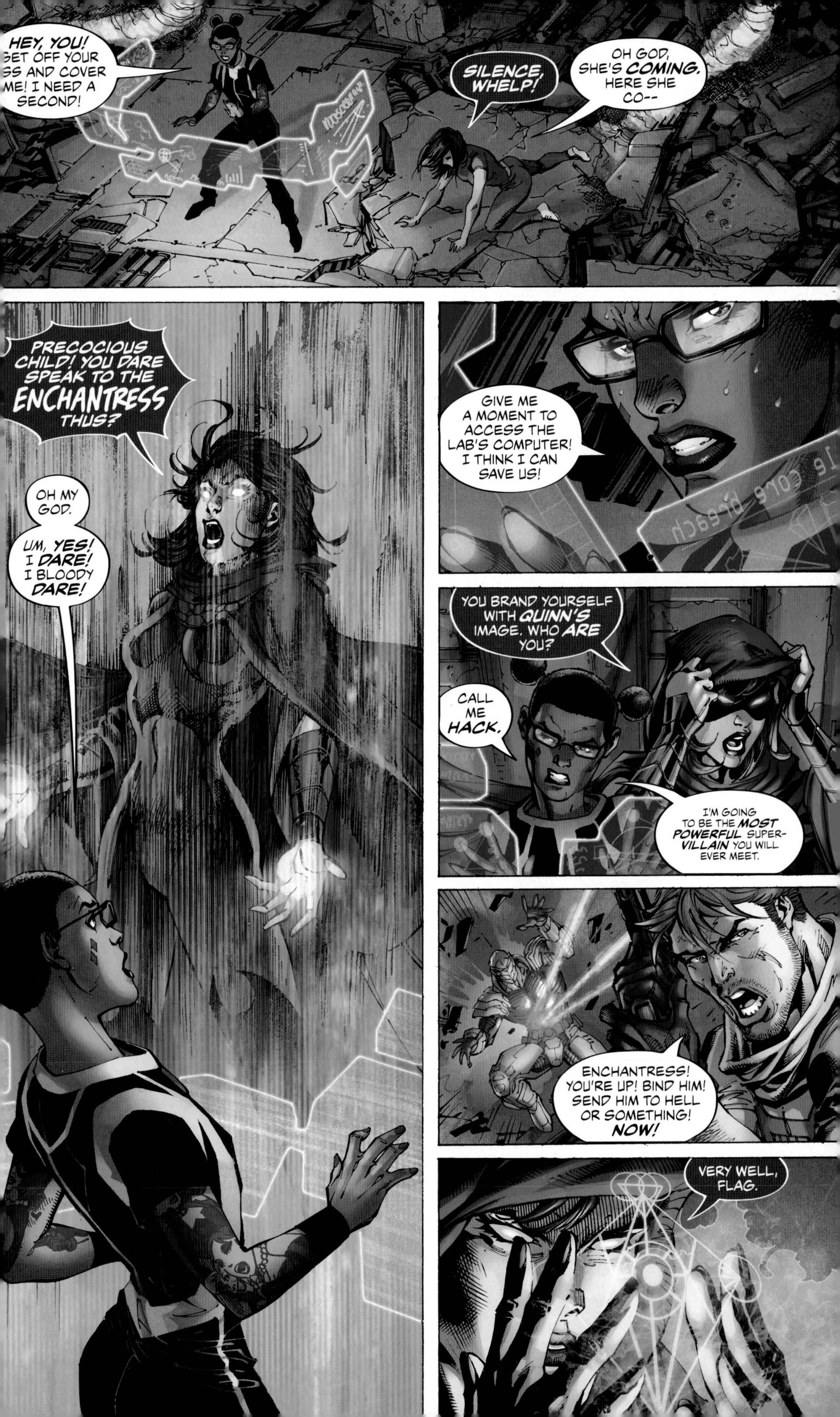

HEY, YOU! GET OFF YOUR SS AND COVER ME! I NEED A SECOND!
SILENCE, WHELP!
OH GOD, SHE'S COMING. HERE SHE CO--
PRECOCIOUS CHILD! YOU DARE SPEAK TO THE ENCHANTRESS THUS?
OH MY GOD.
UM, YES! I DARE! I BLOODY DARE!
GIVE ME A MOMENT TO ACCESS THE LAB'S COMPUTER! I THINK I CAN SAVE US!
YOU BRAND YOURSELF WITH QUINN'S IMAGE. WHO ARE YOU?
CALL ME HACK.
I'M GOING TO BE THE MOST POWERFUL SUPER-VILLAIN YOU WILL EVER MEET.
ENCHANTRESS! YOU'RE UP! BIND HIM! SEND HIM TO HELL OR SOMETHING! NOW!
VERY WELL, FLAG.

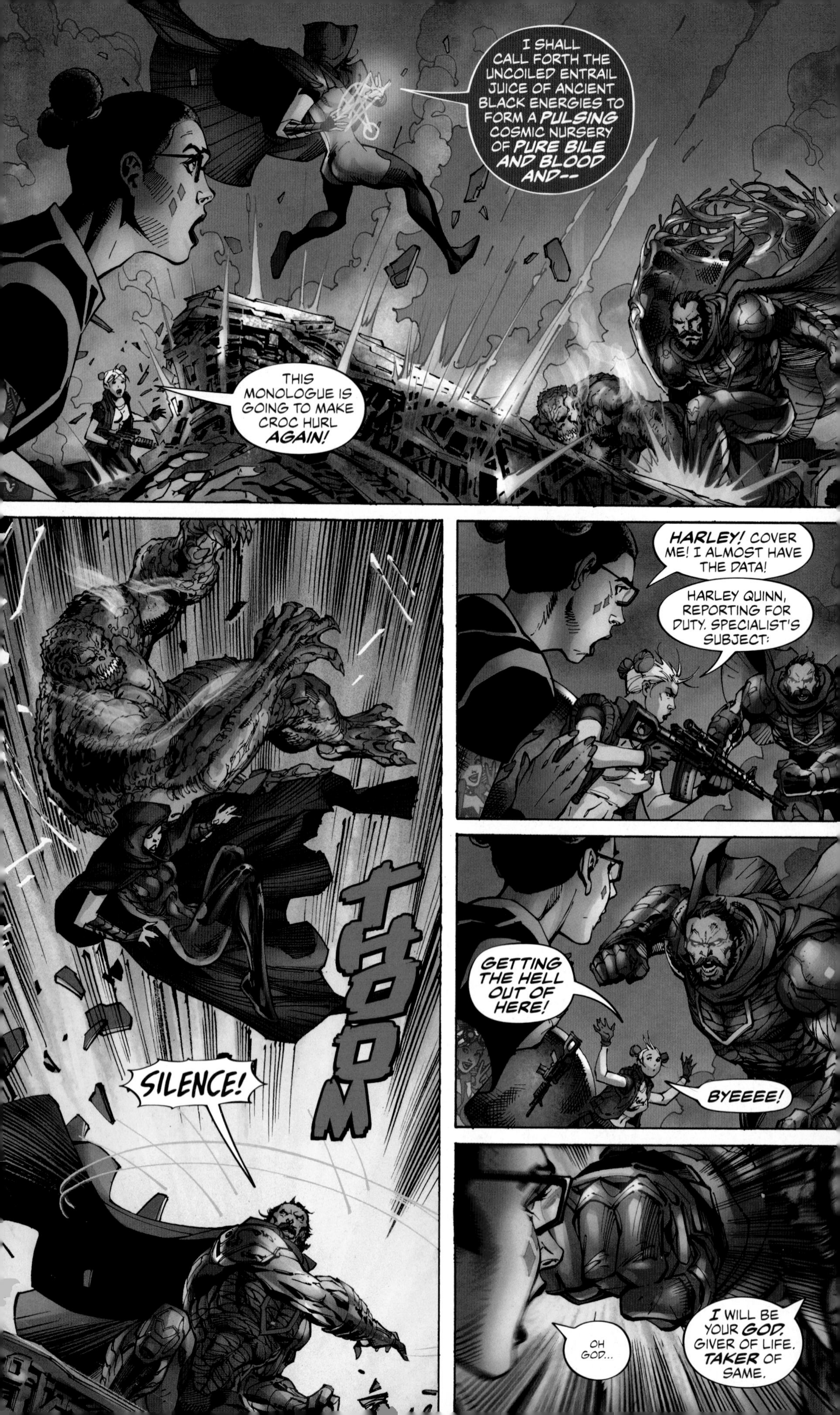
I SHALL CALL FORTH THE UNCOILED ENTRAIL JUICE OF ANCIENT BLACK ENERGIES TO FORM A PULSING COSMIC NURSERY OF PURE BILE AND BLOOD AND--
THIS MONOLOGUE IS GOING TO MAKE CROC HURL AGAIN!
THOOM
SILENCE!
HARLEY! COVER ME! I ALMOST HAVE THE DATA!
HARLEY QUINN, REPORTING FOR DUTY. SPECIALIST'S SUBJECT:
GETTING THE HELL OUT OF HERE!
BYEEEE!
OH GOD...
I WILL BE YOUR GOD. GIVER OF LIFE. TAKER OF SAME.

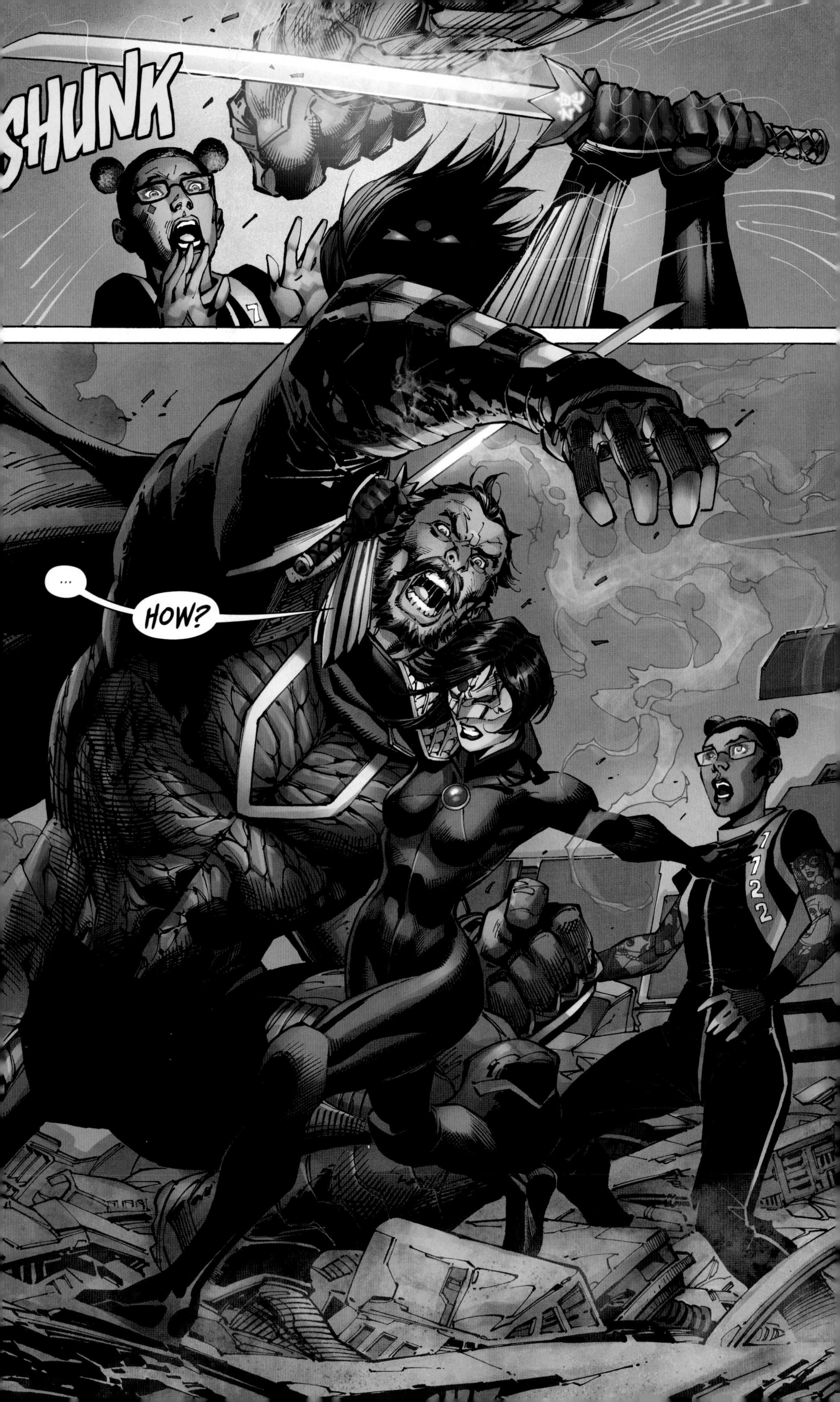
SHUNK
...
HOW?

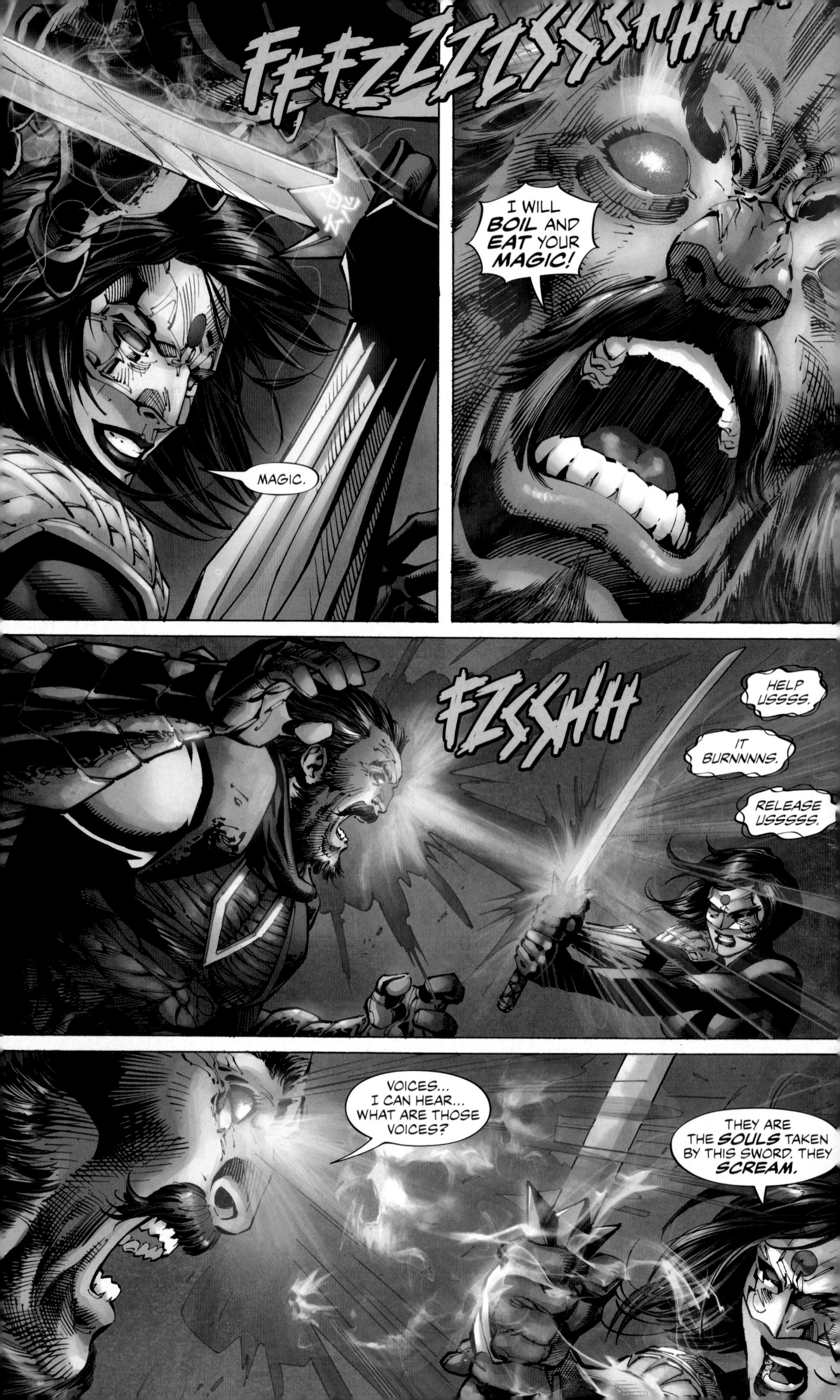
FFFZZZZSSSHHH
MAGIC.
I WILL BOIL AND EAT YOUR MAGIC!
FZSSHH
HELP USSSS.
IT BURNNNNS.
RELEASE USSSSS.
VOICES... I CAN HEAR... WHAT ARE THOSE VOICES?
THEY ARE THE SOULS TAKEN BY THIS SWORD. THEY SCREAM.

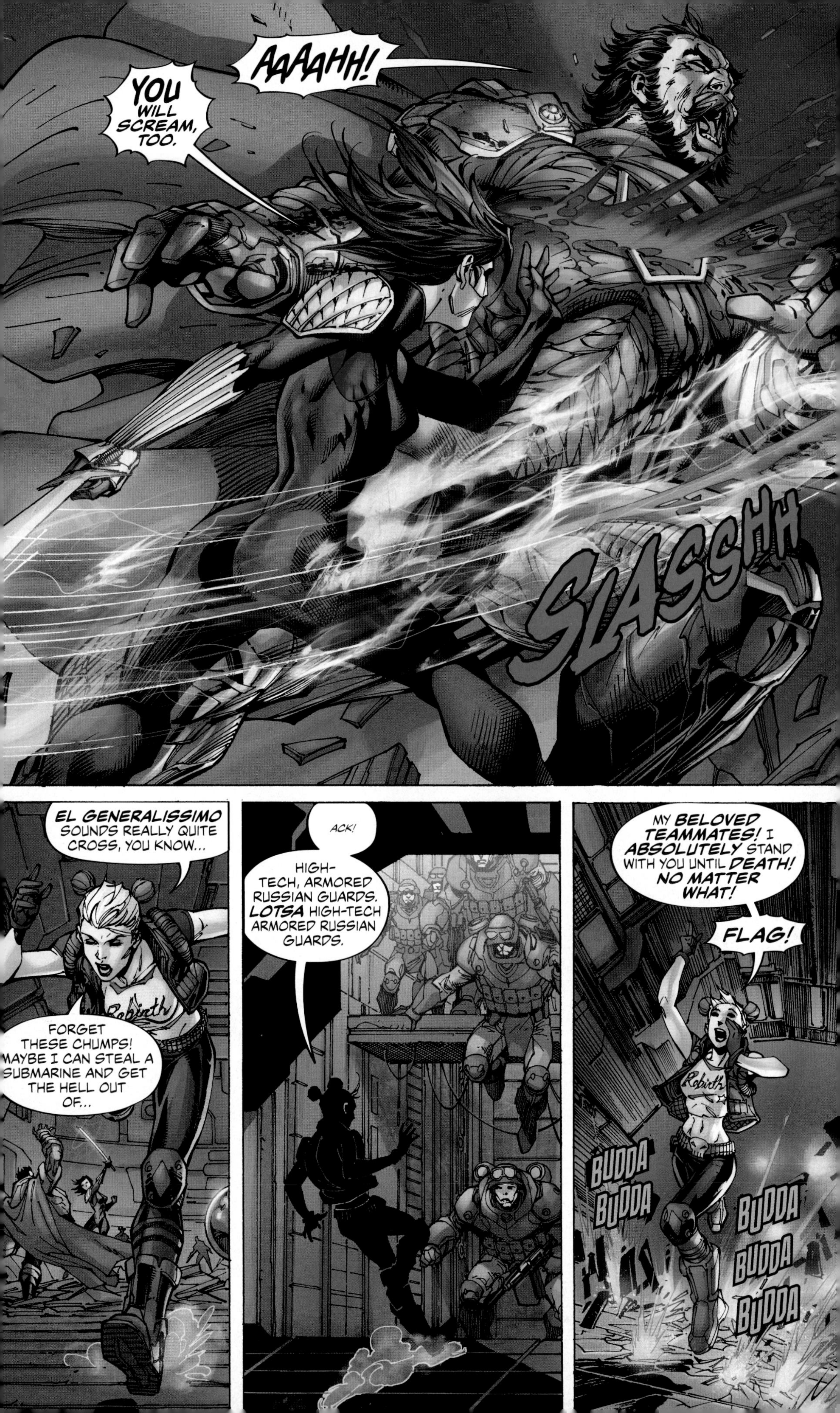
AAAAHH!
YOU WILL SCREAM, TOO.
SLASSHH
EL GENERALISSIMO SOUNDS REALLY QUITE CROSS, YOU KNOW...
FORGET THESE CHUMPS! MAYBE I CAN STEAL A SUBMARINE AND GET THE HELL OUT OF...
ACK!
HIGH-TECH, ARMORED RUSSIAN GUARDS. LOTSA HIGH-TECH ARMORED RUSSIAN GUARDS.
MY BELOVED TEAMMATES! I ABSOLUTELY STAND WITH YOU UNTIL DEATH! NO MATTER WHAT!
FLAG!
BUDDA BUDDA
BUDDA BUDDA BUDDA

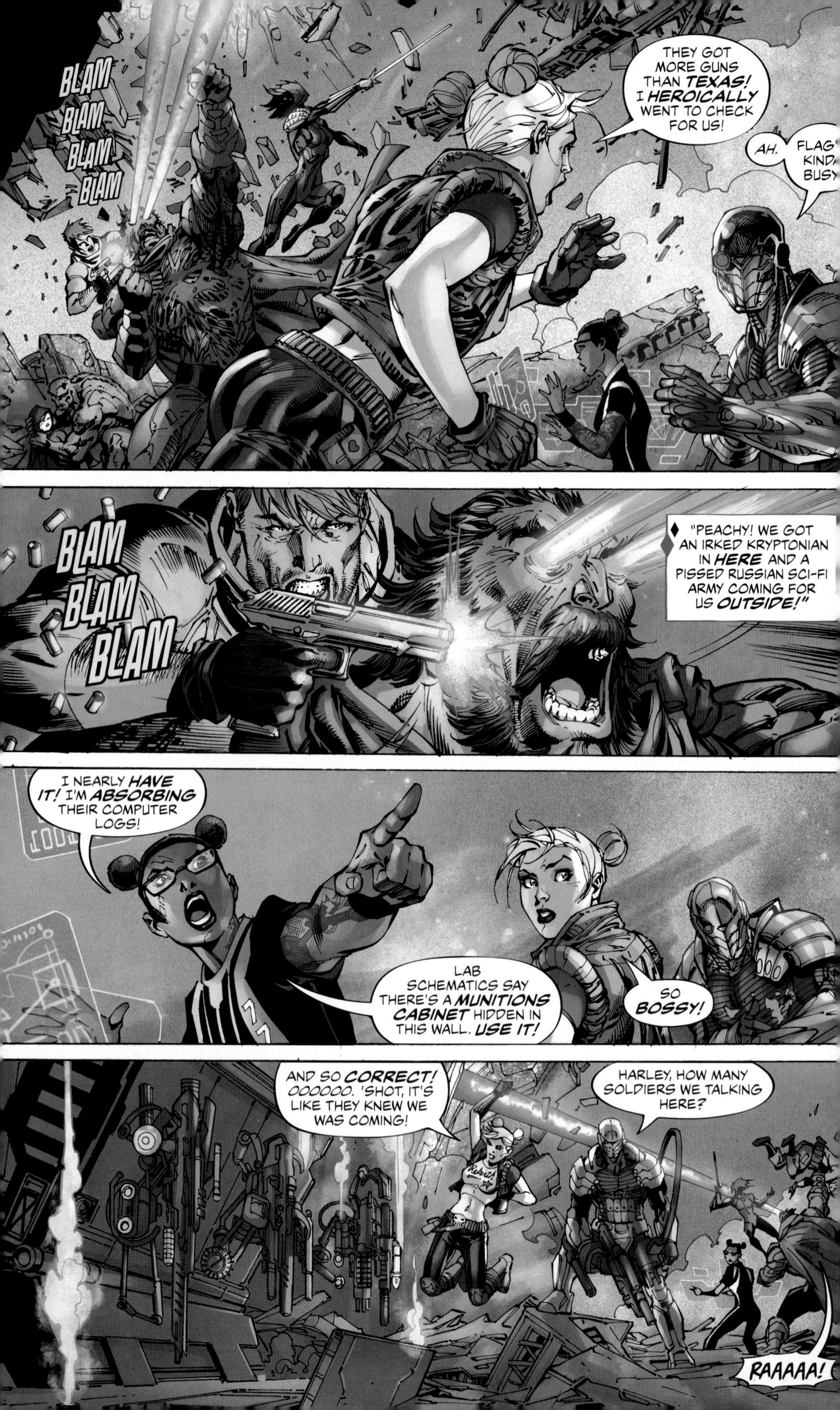
BLAM
BLAM
BLAM
BLAM
THEY GOT MORE GUNS THAN TEXAS! I HEROICALLY WENT TO CHECK FOR US!
AH.
FLAG KIND BUSY
BLAM
BLAM
BLAM
"PEACHY! WE GOT AN IRKED KRYPTONIAN IN HERE AND A PISSED RUSSIAN SCI-FI ARMY COMING FOR US OUTSIDE!"
I NEARLY HAVE IT! I'M ABSORBING THEIR COMPUTER LOGS!
LAB SCHEMATICS SAY THERE'S A MUNITIONS CABINET HIDDEN IN THIS WALL. USE IT!
SO BOSSY!
AND SO CORRECT! OOOOOOO. 'SHOT, IT'S LIKE THEY KNEW WE WAS COMING!
HARLEY, HOW MANY SOLDIERS WE TALKING HERE?
RAAAAA!

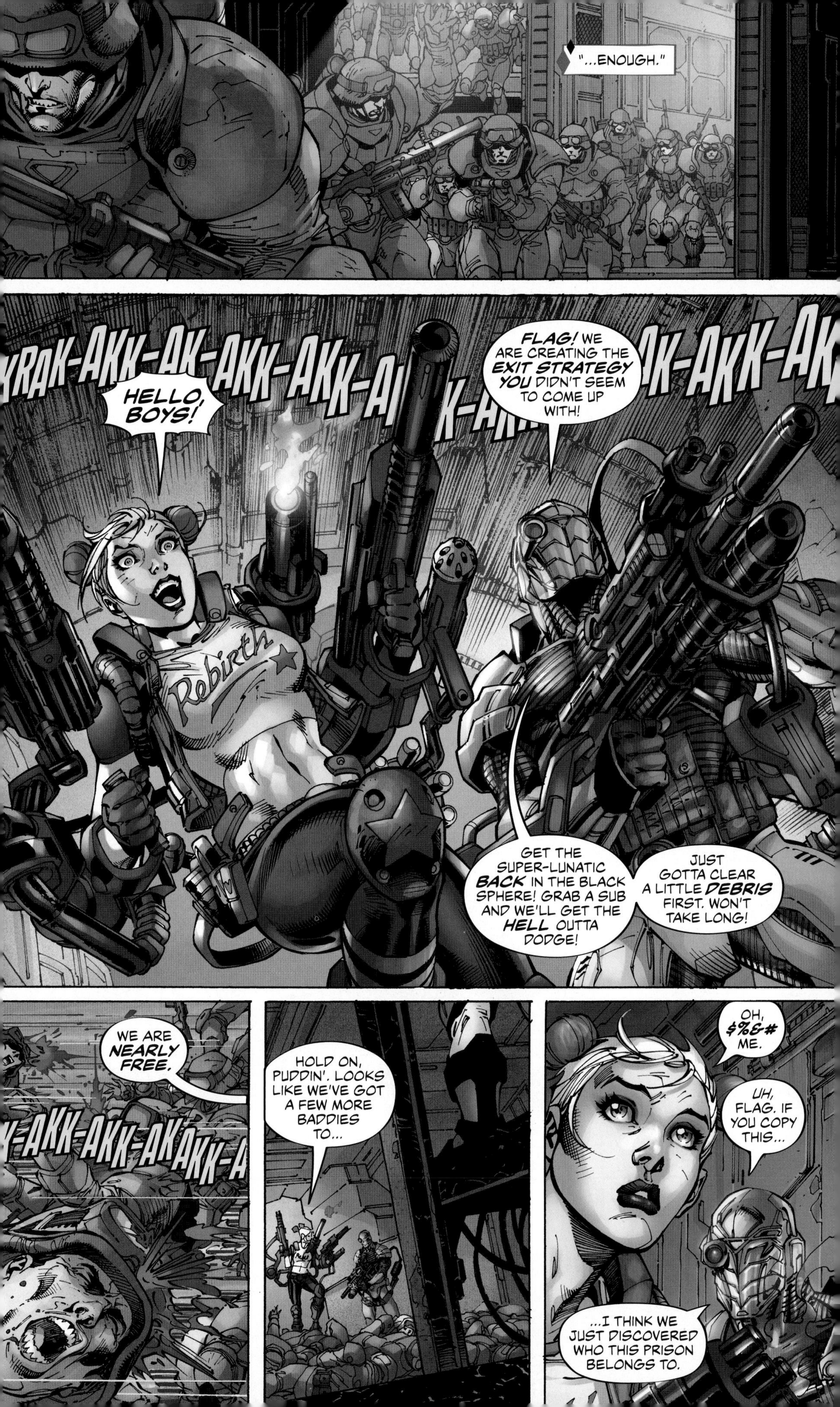
"...ENOUGH."
KRAK-AKK-AK-AKK-AKK-AKK-AKK-AKK-AK
HELLO, BOYS!
FLAG! WE ARE CREATING THE EXIT STRATEGY YOU DIDN'T SEEM TO COME UP WITH!
GET THE SUPER-LUNATIC BACK IN THE BLACK SPHERE! GRAB A SUB AND WE'LL GET THE HELL OUTTA DODGE!
JUST GOTTA CLEAR A LITTLE DEBRIS FIRST. WON'T TAKE LONG!
WE ARE NEARLY FREE.
AKK-AKK-AKAKK-A
HOLD ON, PUDDIN'. LOOKS LIKE WE'VE GOT A FEW MORE BADDIES TO...
OH, $%&# ME.
UH, FLAG. IF YOU COPY THIS...
...I THINK WE JUST DISCOVERED WHO THIS PRISON BELONGS TO.

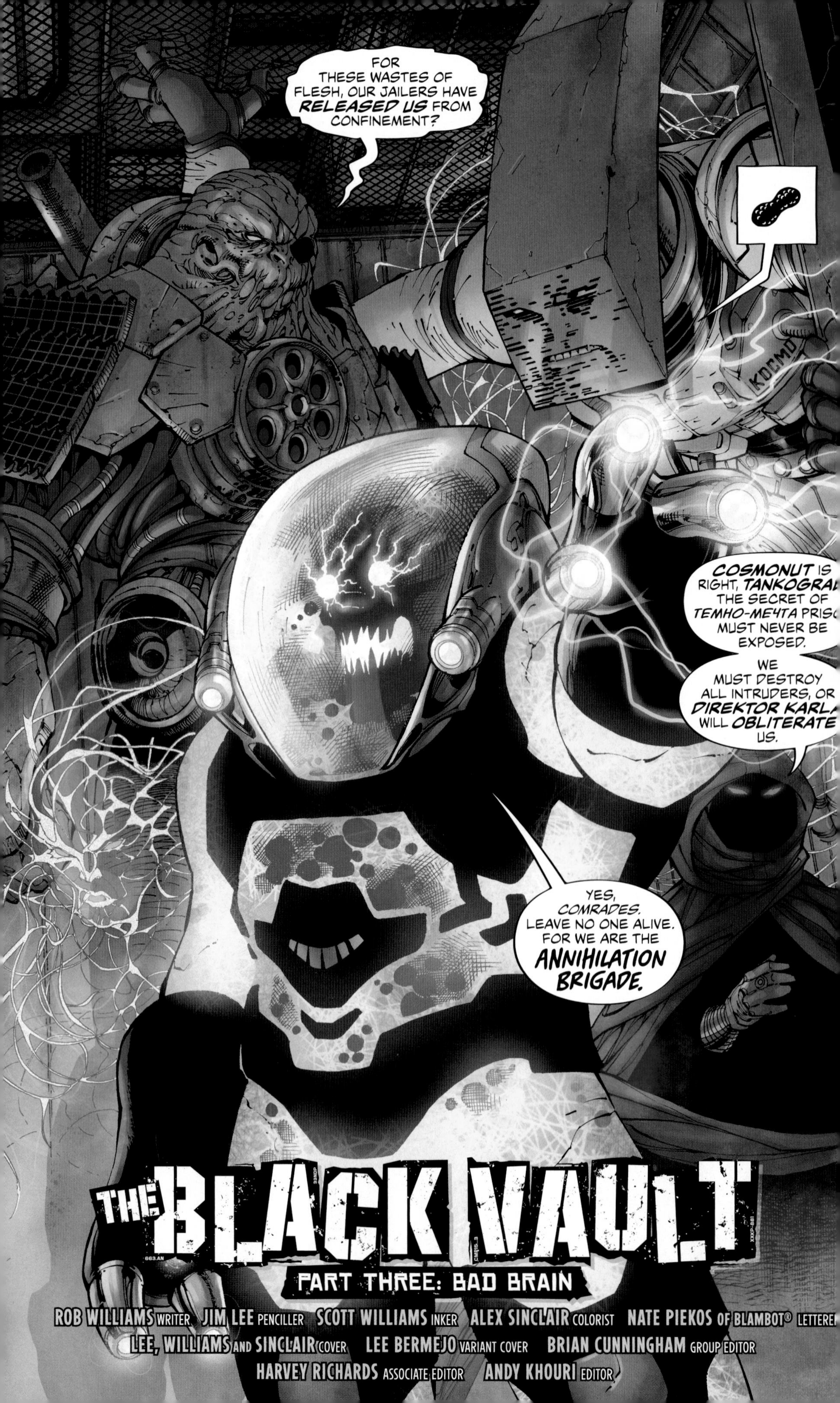

FOR THESE WASTES OF FLESH, OUR JAILERS HAVE RELEASED US FROM CONFINEMENT?
COSMONUT IS RIGHT, TANKOGRA THE SECRET OF TEMHO-ME4TA PRIS MUST NEVER BE EXPOSED.
WE MUST DESTROY ALL INTRUDERS, OR DIREKTOR KARL WILL OBLITERATE US.
YES, COMRADES. LEAVE NO ONE ALIVE. FOR WE ARE THE ANNIHILATION BRIGADE.
KOCMO
THE BLACK VAULT
PART THREE: BAD BRAIN
ROB WILLIAMS WRITER JIM LEE PENCILLER SCOTT WILLIAMS INKER ALEX SINCLAIR COLORIST NATE PIEKOS OF BLAMBOT® LETTERE
LEE, WILLIAMS AND SINCLAIR COVER LEE BERMEJO VARIANT COVER BRIAN CUNNINGHAM GROUP EDITOR
HARVEY RICHARDS ASSOCIATE EDITOR ANDY KHOURI EDITOR

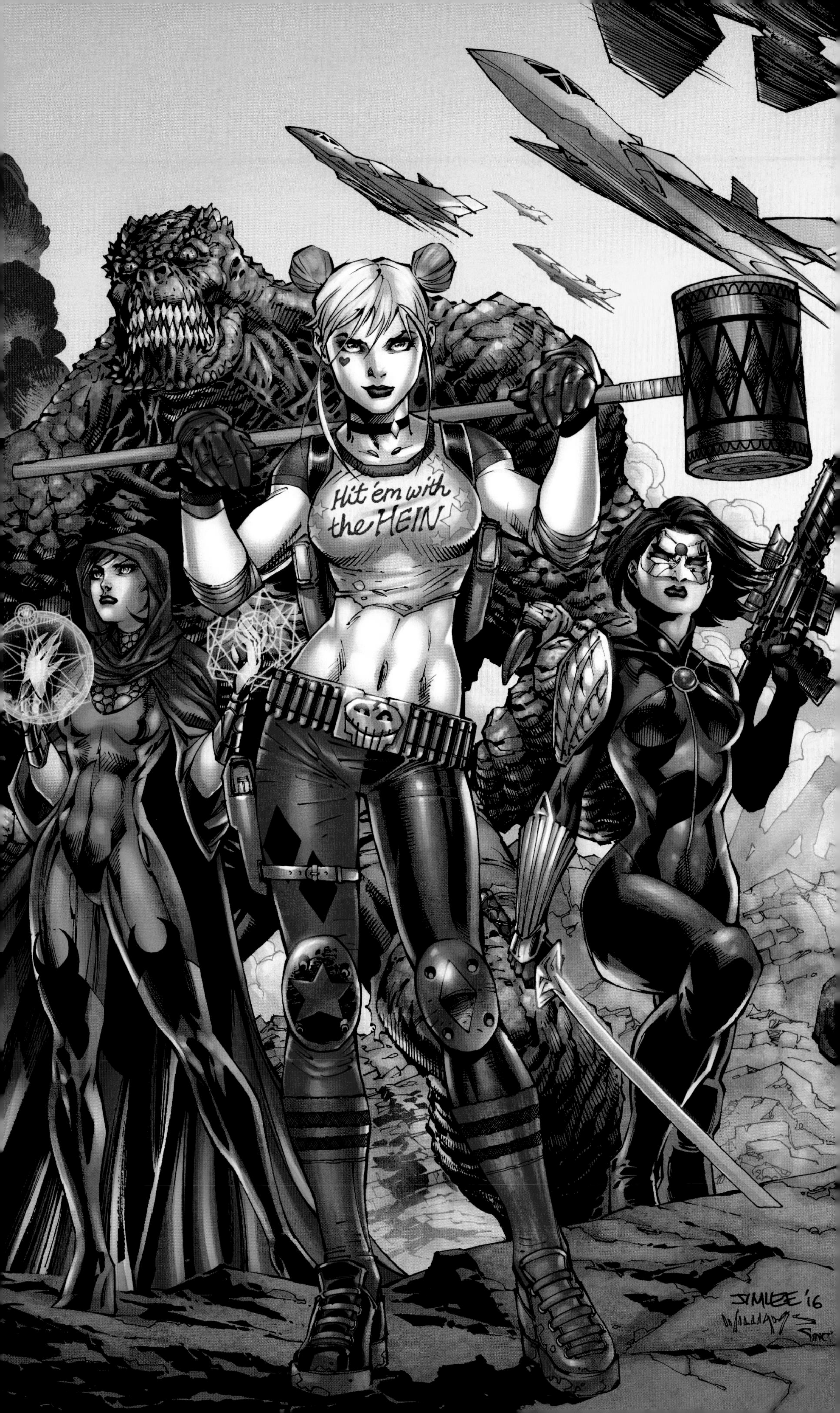
Hit 'em with the HEIN
JIM LEE '16

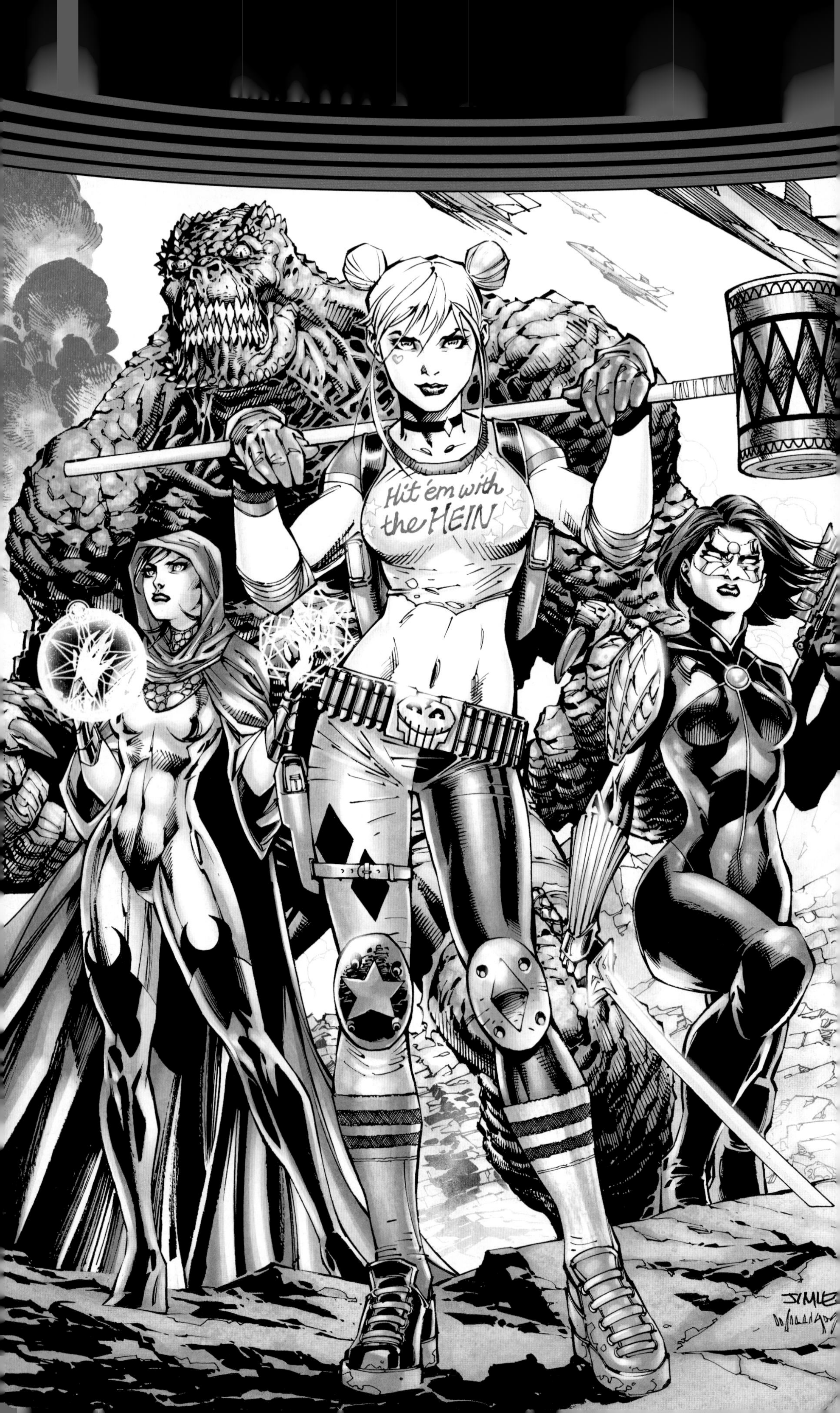
Hit 'em with
the HEIN

LAPTEV SEA, SIBERIA.

MY NAME IS AMANDA WALLER, AND THE DEFINITION OF A SUICIDE MISSION IS:

A LOCATION THAT DOES NOT SUSTAIN HUMAN LIFE.

UNIDENTIFIED UNDERSEA PRISON.

NO POSSIBLE ESCAPE.

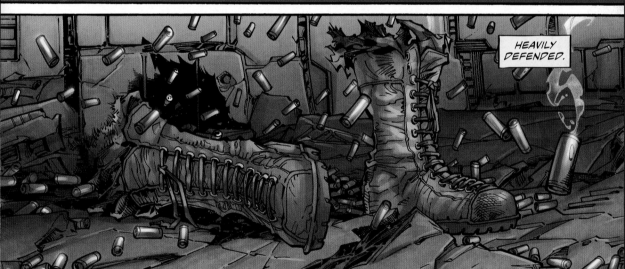

HEAVILY DEFENDED.

HIGHLY ERRATIC TARGET.

PROSTRATE YOURSELF BEFORE YOUR GENERAL, SUB-CREATURES!

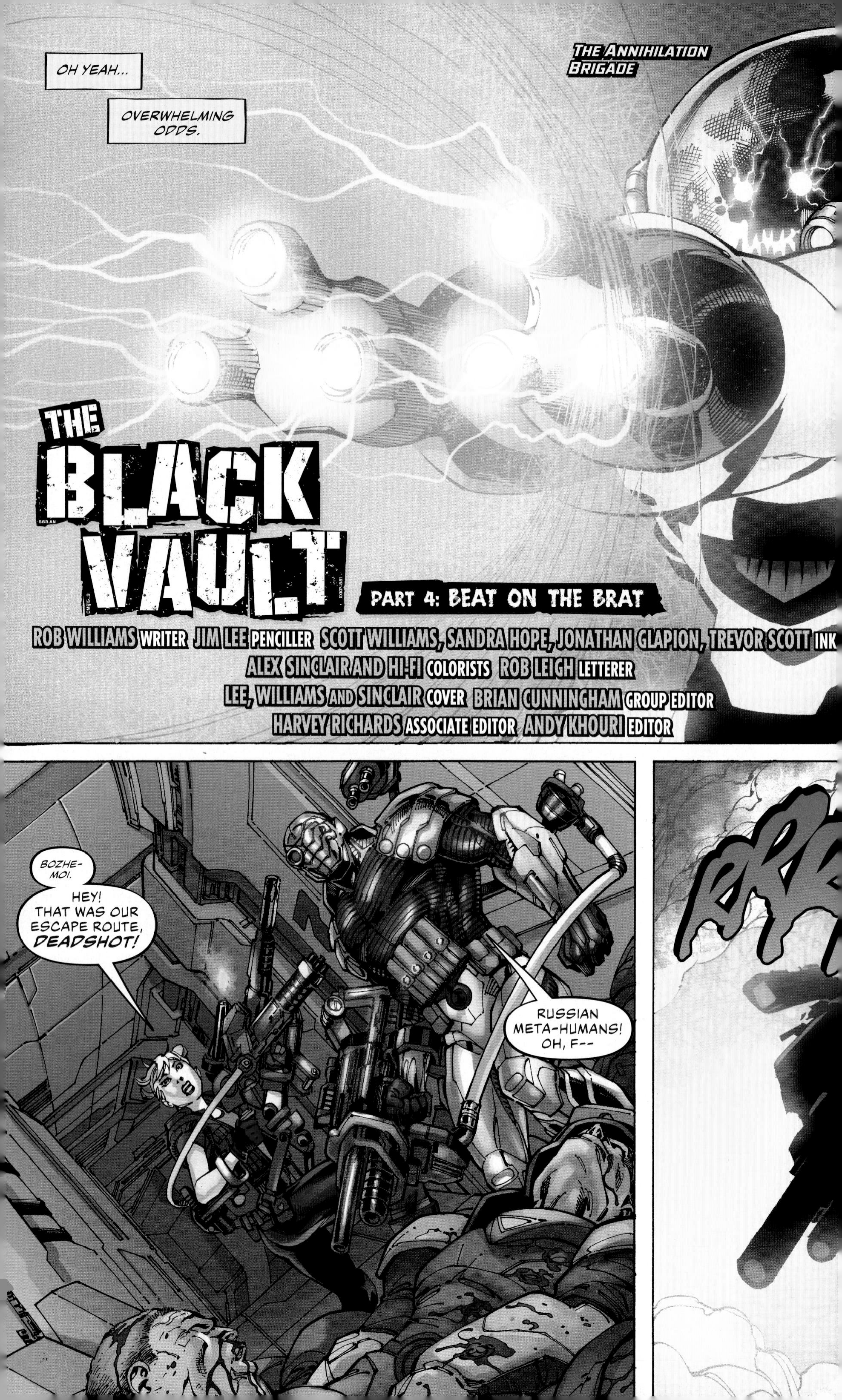

OH YEAH...
OVERWHELMING ODDS.
THE ANNIHILATION BRIGADE
THE BLACK VAULT
PART 4: BEAT ON THE BRAT
ROB WILLIAMS WRITER JIM LEE PENCILLER SCOTT WILLIAMS, SANDRA HOPE, JONATHAN GLAPION, TREVOR SCOTT INK
ALEX SINCLAIR AND HI-FI COLORISTS ROB LEIGH LETTERER
LEE, WILLIAMS AND SINCLAIR COVER BRIAN CUNNINGHAM GROUP EDITOR
HARVEY RICHARDS ASSOCIATE EDITOR ANDY KHOURI EDITOR
BOZHE-MOI.
HEY! THAT WAS OUR ESCAPE ROUTE, DEADSHOT!
RUSSIAN META-HUMANS! OH, F--

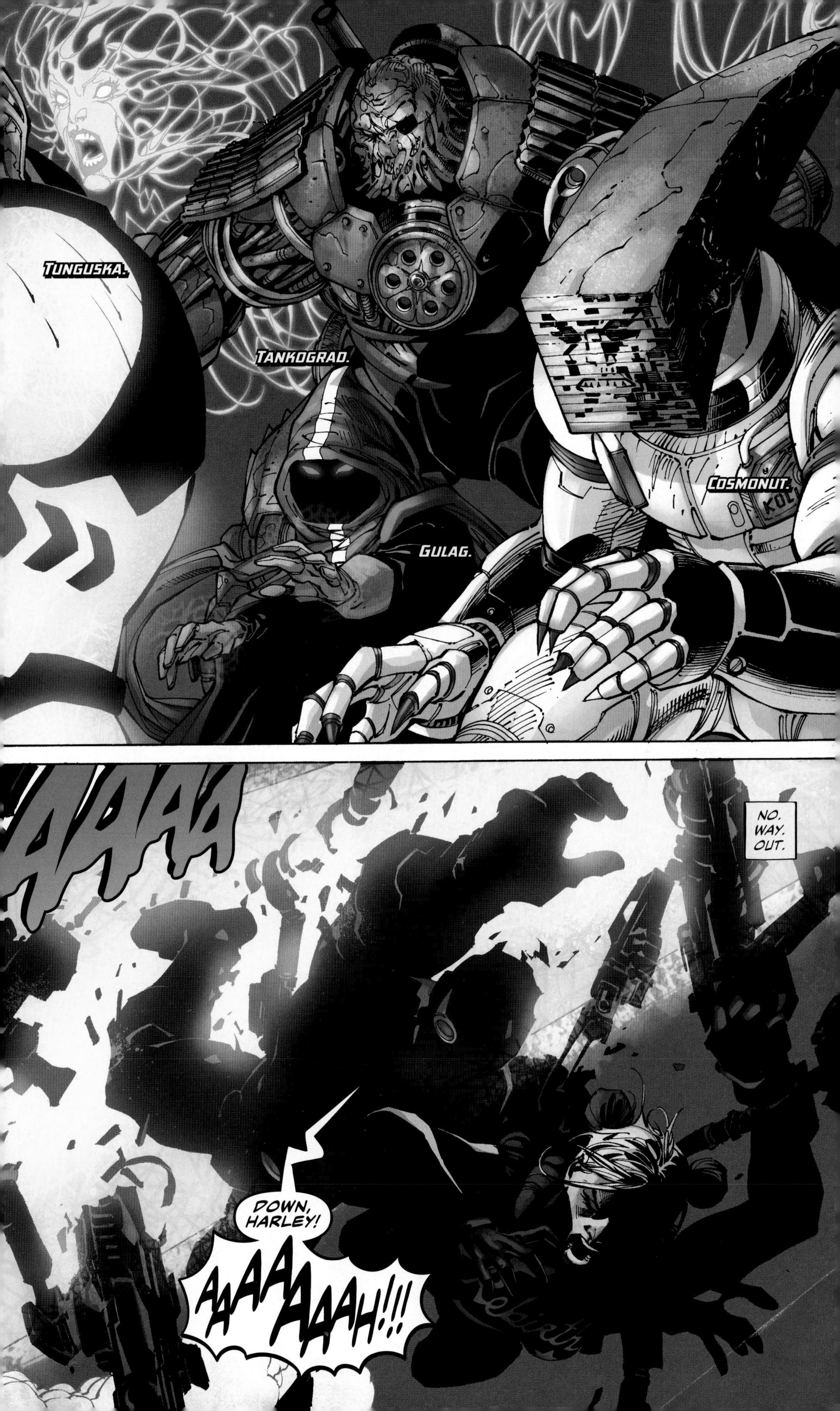
TUNGUSKA.
TANKOGRAD.
COSMONUT.
GULAG.
AAAA
NO. WAY. OUT.
DOWN, HARLEY!
AAAAAAAH!!!

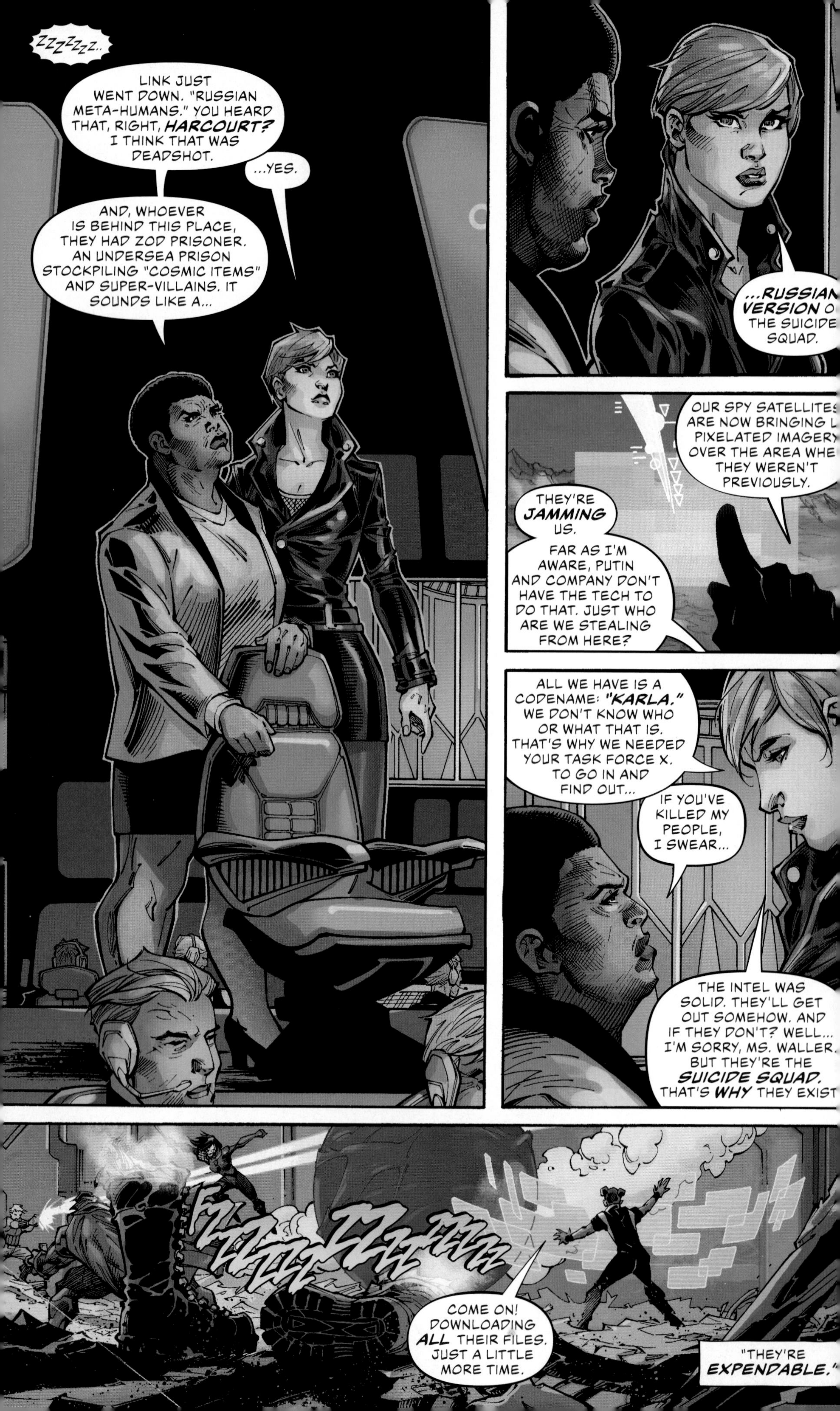
ZZZZZZZ..
LINK JUST WENT DOWN. "RUSSIAN META-HUMANS." YOU HEARD THAT, RIGHT, HARCOURT? I THINK THAT WAS DEADSHOT.
...YES.
AND, WHOEVER IS BEHIND THIS PLACE, THEY HAD ZOD PRISONER. AN UNDERSEA PRISON STOCKPILING "COSMIC ITEMS" AND SUPER-VILLAINS. IT SOUNDS LIKE A...
...RUSSIAN VERSION O THE SUICIDE SQUAD.
OUR SPY SATELLITES ARE NOW BRINGING PIXELATED IMAGERY OVER THE AREA WHE THEY WEREN'T PREVIOUSLY.
THEY'RE JAMMING US.
FAR AS I'M AWARE, PUTIN AND COMPANY DON'T HAVE THE TECH TO DO THAT. JUST WHO ARE WE STEALING FROM HERE?
ALL WE HAVE IS A CODENAME: "KARLA." WE DON'T KNOW WHO OR WHAT THAT IS. THAT'S WHY WE NEEDED YOUR TASK FORCE X. TO GO IN AND FIND OUT...
IF YOU'VE KILLED MY PEOPLE, I SWEAR...
THE INTEL WAS SOLID. THEY'LL GET OUT SOMEHOW. AND IF THEY DON'T? WELL... I'M SORRY, MS. WALLER. BUT THEY'RE THE SUICIDE SQUAD. THAT'S WHY THEY EXIST
COME ON! DOWNLOADING ALL THEIR FILES. JUST A LITTLE MORE TIME.
"THEY'RE EXPENDABLE."

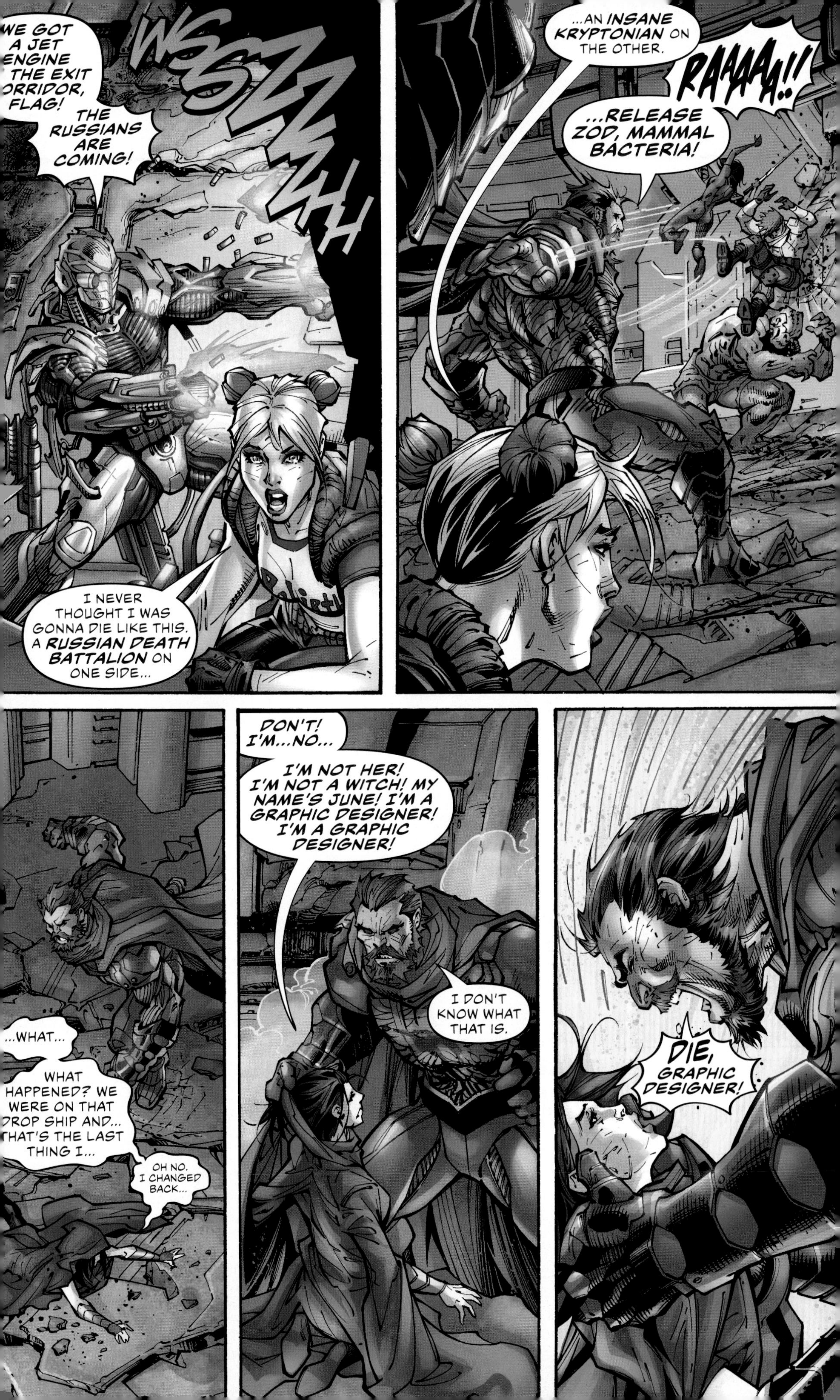
WE GOT A JET ENGINE THE EXIT ORRIDOR, FLAG!
THE RUSSIANS ARE COMING!
WSSZWWHH
I NEVER THOUGHT I WAS GONNA DIE LIKE THIS. A RUSSIAN DEATH BATTALION ON ONE SIDE...
...AN INSANE KRYPTONIAN ON THE OTHER.
RAAAAAA!!
...RELEASE ZOD, MAMMAL BACTERIA!
...WHAT...
WHAT HAPPENED? WE WERE ON THAT DROP SHIP AND... THAT'S THE LAST THING I...
OH NO. I CHANGED BACK...
DON'T! I'M...NO...
I'M NOT HER! I'M NOT A WITCH! MY NAME'S JUNE! I'M A GRAPHIC DESIGNER! I'M A GRAPHIC DESIGNER!
I DON'T KNOW WHAT THAT IS.
DIE, GRAPHIC DESIGNER!

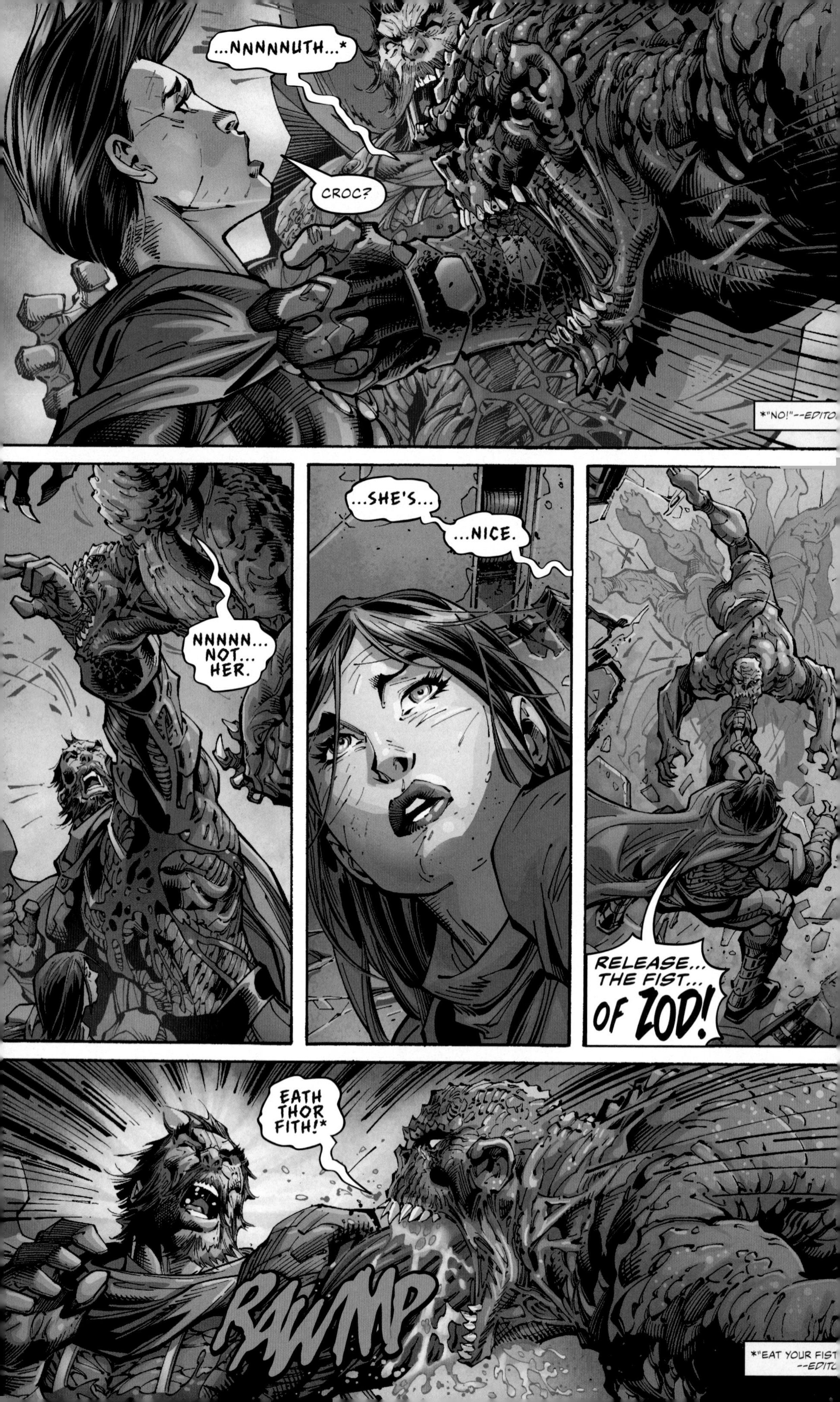
...NNNNNUTH...*
CROC?
*"NO!"--EDITO
NNNNN... NOT... HER.
...SHE'S...
...NICE.
RELEASE... THE FIST... OF ZOD!
EATH THOR FITH!*
RAWMP
*"EAT YOUR FIST --EDITO

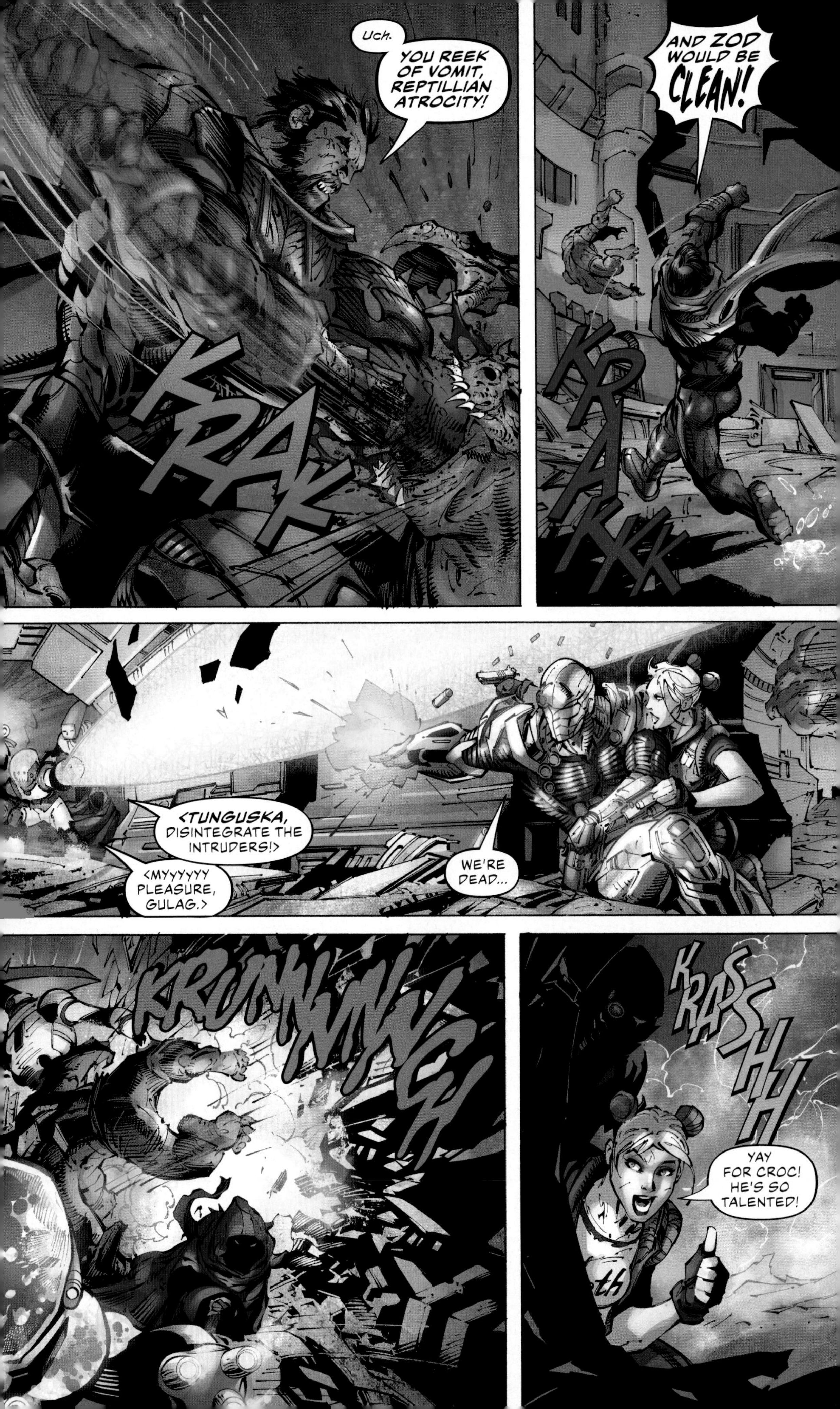
Uch.
YOU REEK OF VOMIT, REPTILLIAN ATROCITY!
KRAK
AND ZOD WOULD BE CLEAN!
KRAKKK
<TUNGUSKA, DISINTEGRATE THE INTRUDERS!>
<MYYYYYY PLEASURE, GULAG.>
WE'RE DEAD...
KRASHH
YAY FOR CROC! HE'S SO TALENTED!

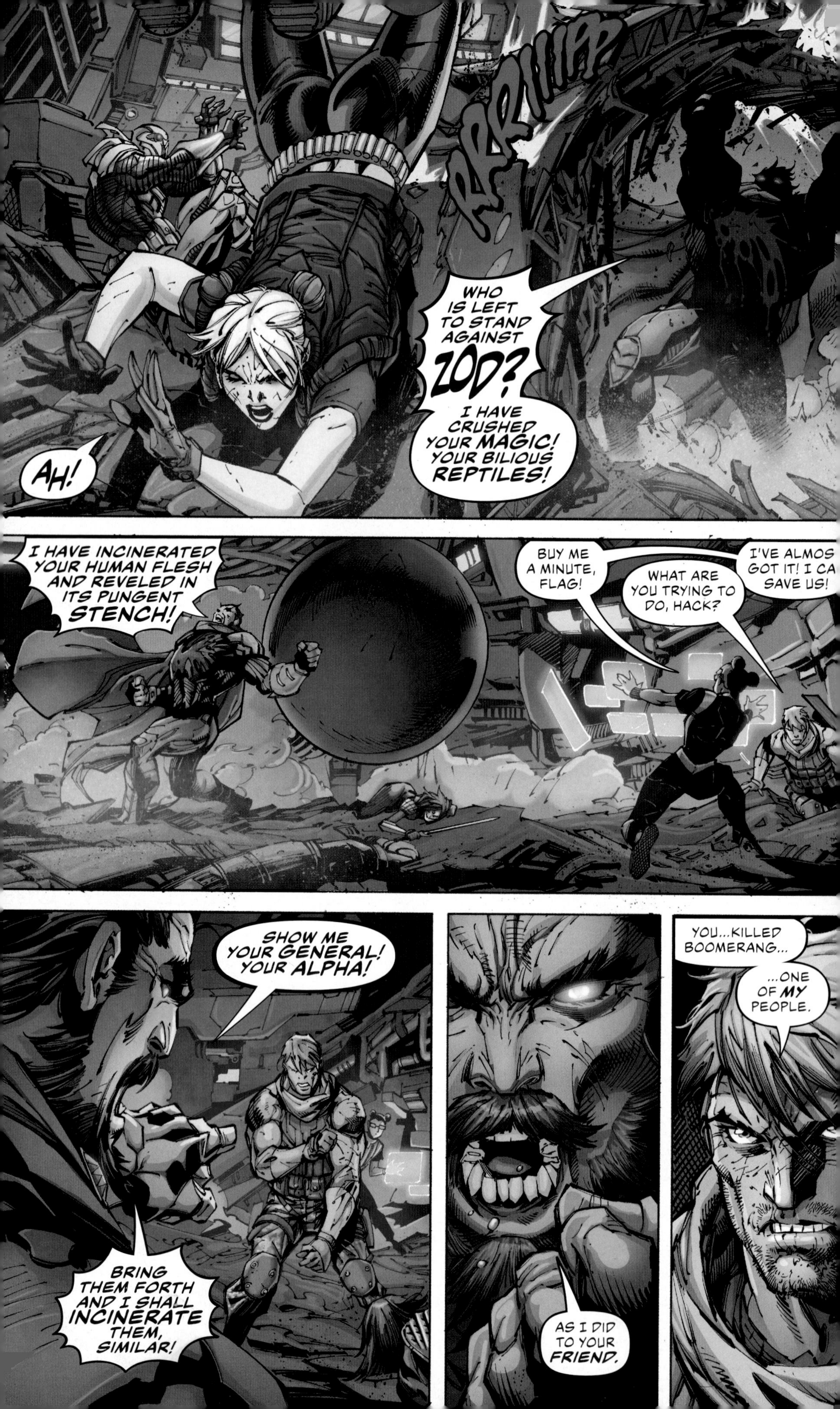

BRRRIIIIIP
AH!
WHO IS LEFT TO STAND AGAINST ZOD?
I HAVE CRUSHED YOUR MAGIC! YOUR BILIOUS REPTILES!
I HAVE INCINERATED YOUR HUMAN FLESH AND REVELED IN ITS PUNGENT STENCH!
BUY ME A MINUTE, FLAG!
WHAT ARE YOU TRYING TO DO, HACK?
I'VE ALMOS GOT IT! I CA SAVE US!
SHOW ME YOUR GENERAL! YOUR ALPHA!
BRING THEM FORTH AND I SHALL INCINERATE THEM, SIMILAR!
AS I DID TO YOUR FRIEND.
YOU...KILLED BOOMERANG...
...ONE OF MY PEOPLE.

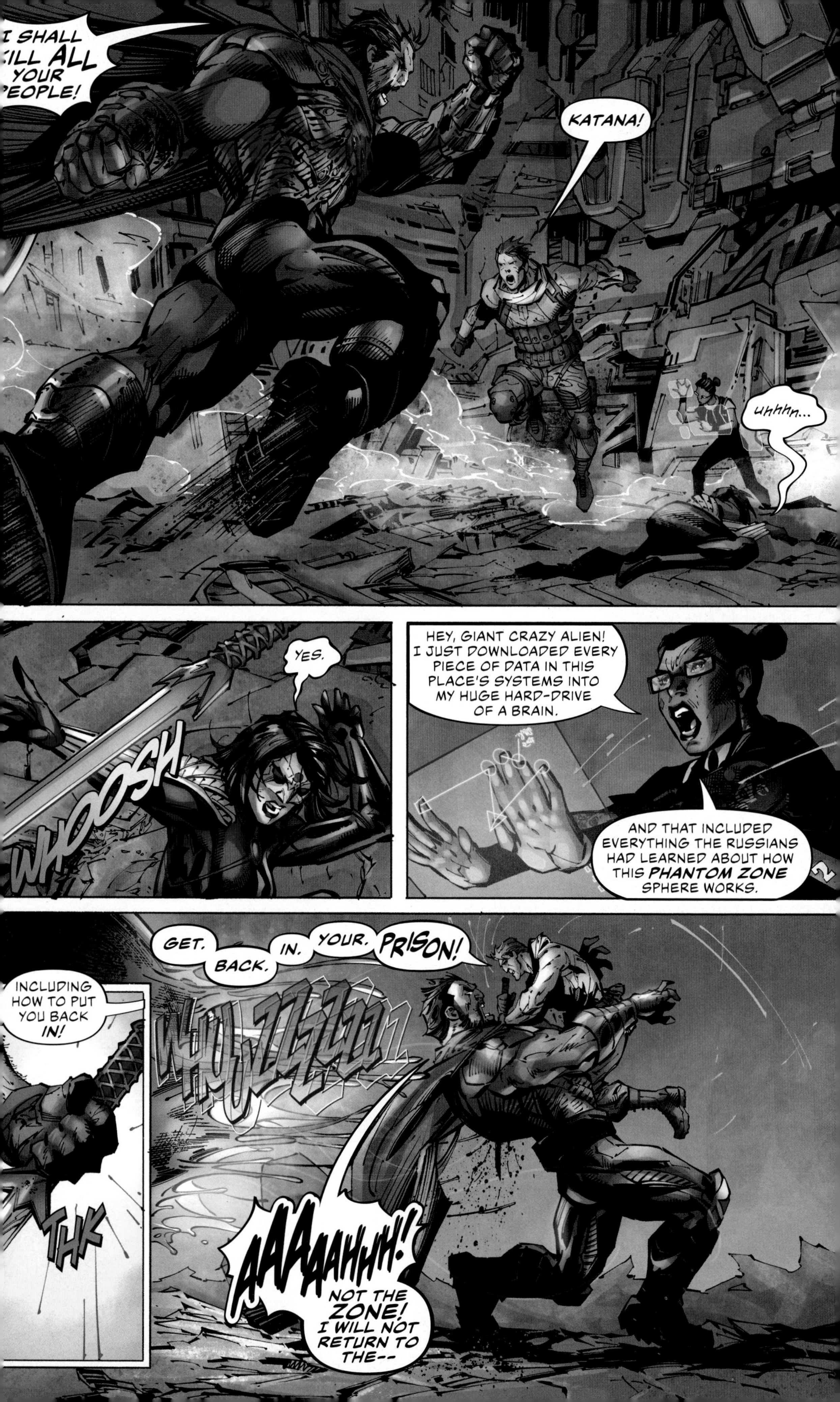
I SHALL KILL ALL YOUR PEOPLE!
KATANA!
uhhhn...
YES.
WHOOSH
HEY, GIANT CRAZY ALIEN! I JUST DOWNLOADED EVERY PIECE OF DATA IN THIS PLACE'S SYSTEMS INTO MY HUGE HARD-DRIVE OF A BRAIN.
AND THAT INCLUDED EVERYTHING THE RUSSIANS HAD LEARNED ABOUT HOW THIS PHANTOM ZONE SPHERE WORKS.
GET.
BACK.
IN.
YOUR.
PRISON!
INCLUDING HOW TO PUT YOU BACK IN!
THK
AAAAAHHH!
NOT THE ZONE! I WILL NOT RETURN TO THE--

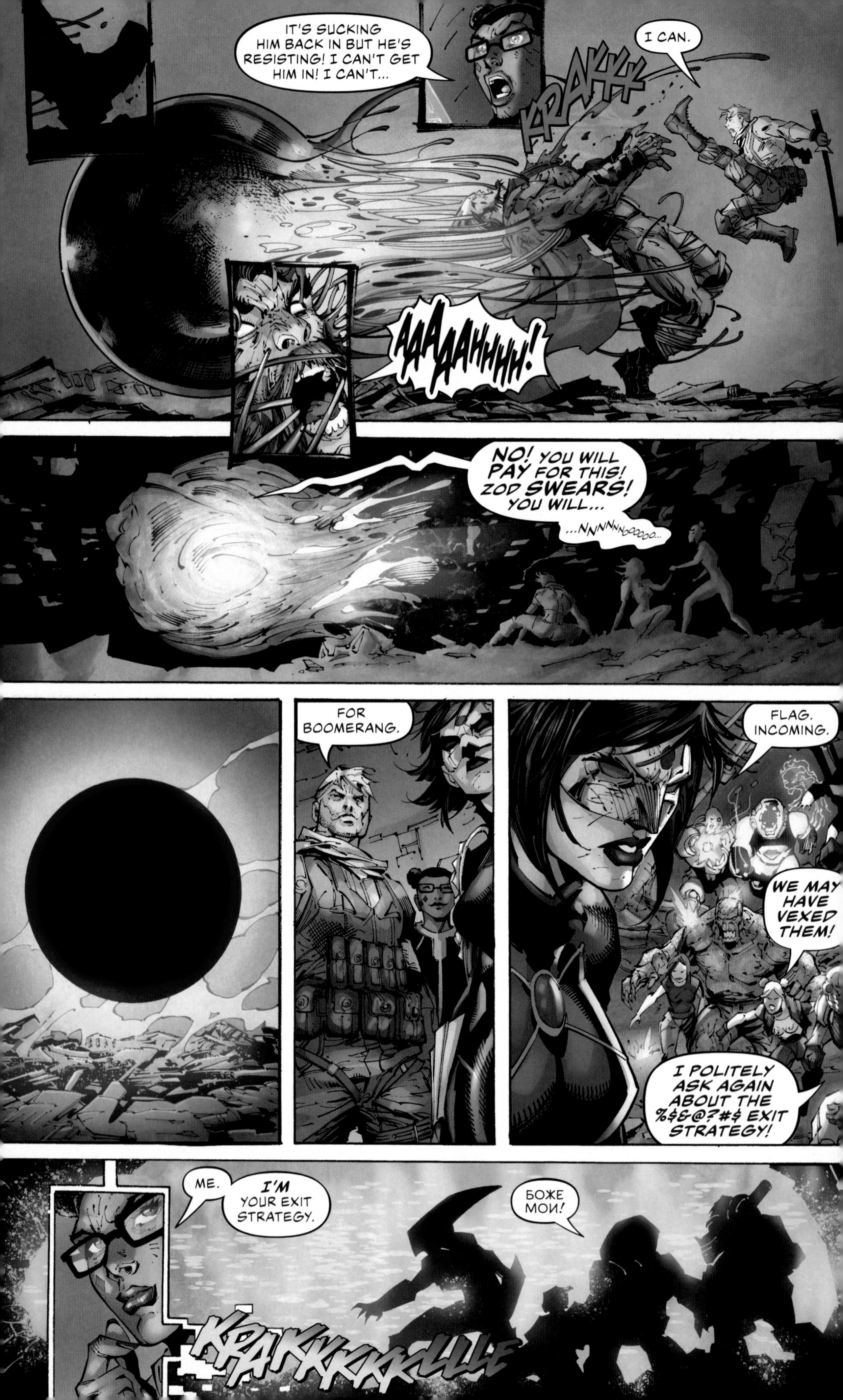
IT'S SUCKING HIM BACK IN BUT HE'S RESISTING! I CAN'T GET HIM IN! I CAN'T...
I CAN.
KRAKK
AAAAAHHHH!
NO! YOU WILL PAY FOR THIS! ZOD SWEARS! YOU WILL...
...NNNNNNOOOOOO...
FOR BOOMERANG.
FLAG. INCOMING.
WE MAY HAVE VEXED THEM!
I POLITELY ASK AGAIN ABOUT THE %$&@?#$ EXIT STRATEGY!
ME.
I'M YOUR EXIT STRATEGY.
БОЖЕ МОИ!
KRAKKKKKKRUUUE

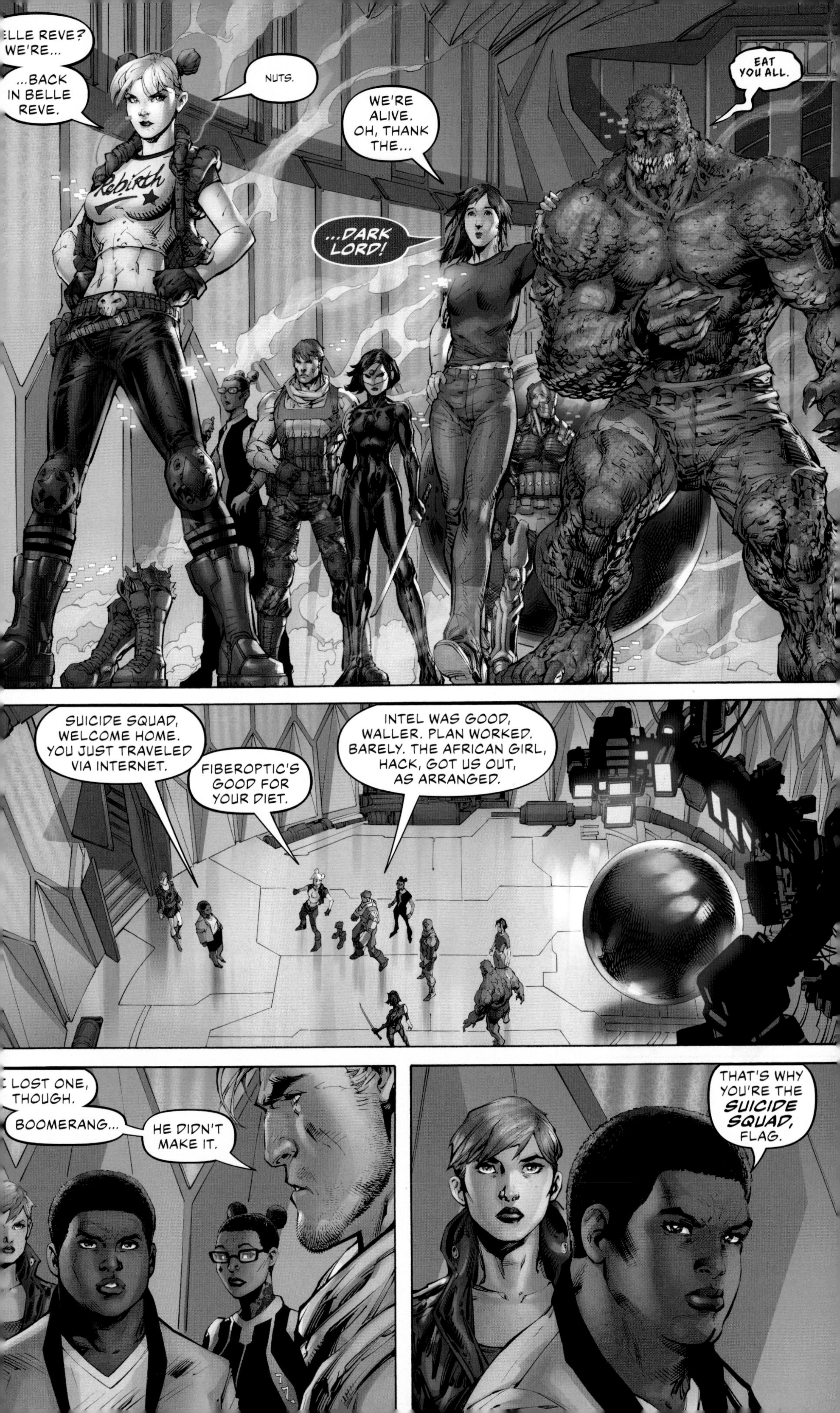
ELLE REVE? WE'RE...
...BACK IN BELLE REVE.
NUTS.
WE'RE ALIVE. OH, THANK THE...
...DARK LORD!
EAT YOU ALL.
SUICIDE SQUAD, WELCOME HOME. YOU JUST TRAVELED VIA INTERNET.
FIBEROPTIC'S GOOD FOR YOUR DIET.
INTEL WAS GOOD, WALLER. PLAN WORKED. BARELY. THE AFRICAN GIRL, HACK, GOT US OUT, AS ARRANGED.
LOST ONE, THOUGH.
BOOMERANG...
HE DIDN'T MAKE IT.
THAT'S WHY YOU'RE THE SUICIDE SQUAD, FLAG.

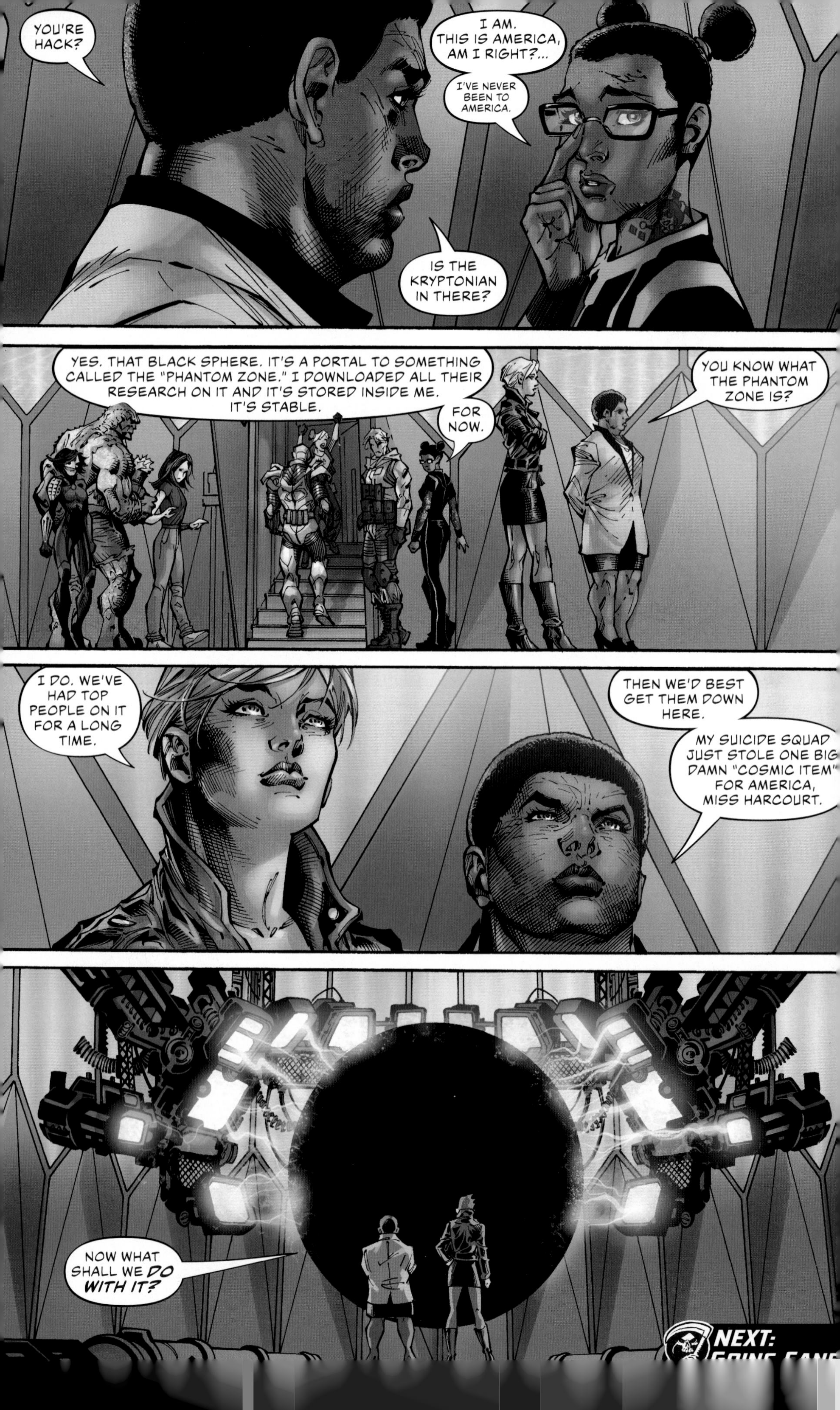
YOU'RE HACK?
I AM. THIS IS AMERICA, AM I RIGHT?...
I'VE NEVER BEEN TO AMERICA.
IS THE KRYPTONIAN IN THERE?
YES. THAT BLACK SPHERE. IT'S A PORTAL TO SOMETHING CALLED THE "PHANTOM ZONE." I DOWNLOADED ALL THEIR RESEARCH ON IT AND IT'S STORED INSIDE ME. IT'S STABLE.
FOR NOW.
YOU KNOW WHAT THE PHANTOM ZONE IS?
I DO. WE'VE HAD TOP PEOPLE ON IT FOR A LONG TIME.
THEN WE'D BEST GET THEM DOWN HERE.
MY SUICIDE SQUAD JUST STOLE ONE BIG DAMN "COSMIC ITEM" FOR AMERICA, MISS HARCOURT.
NOW WHAT SHALL WE *DO WITH IT?*
NEXT:

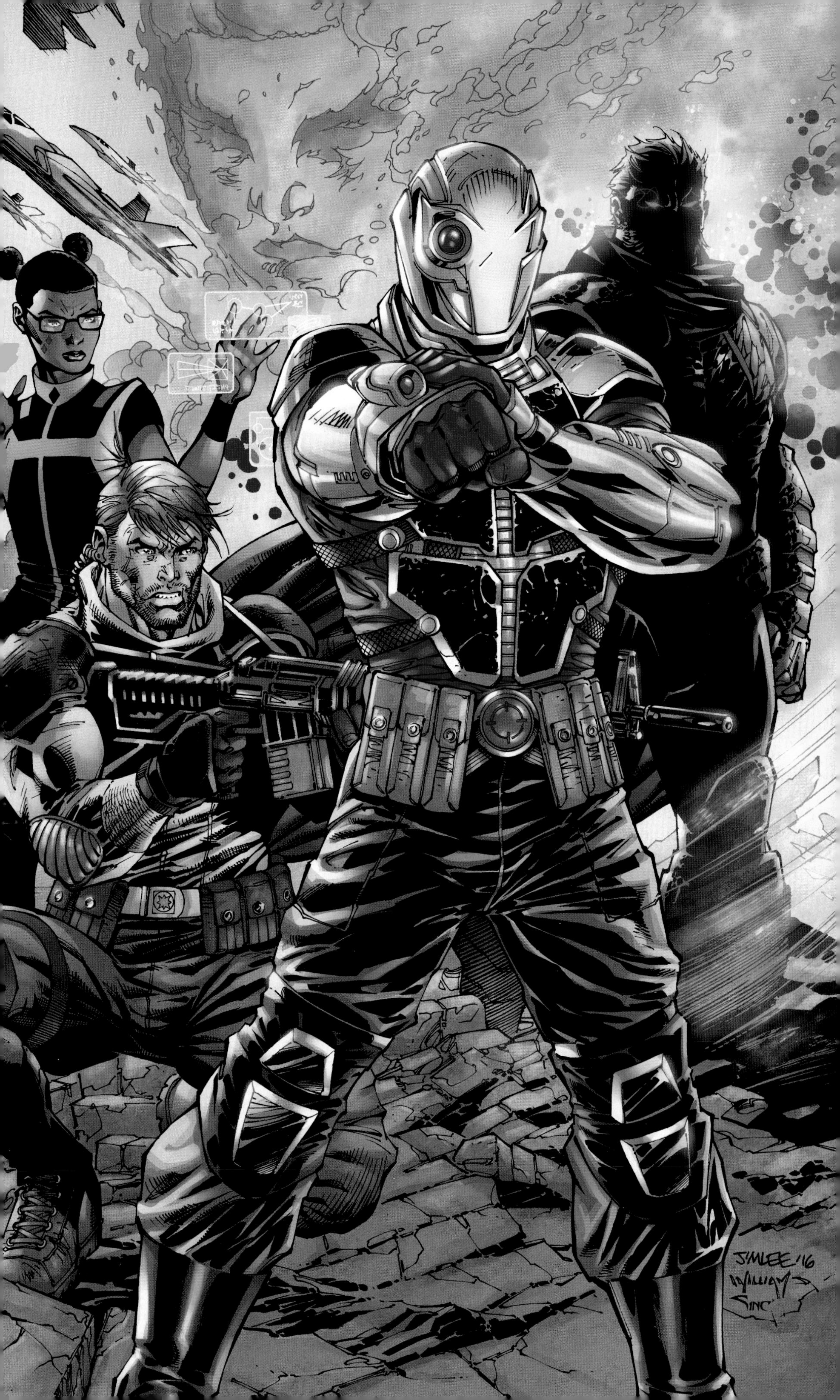
JIMLEE '16

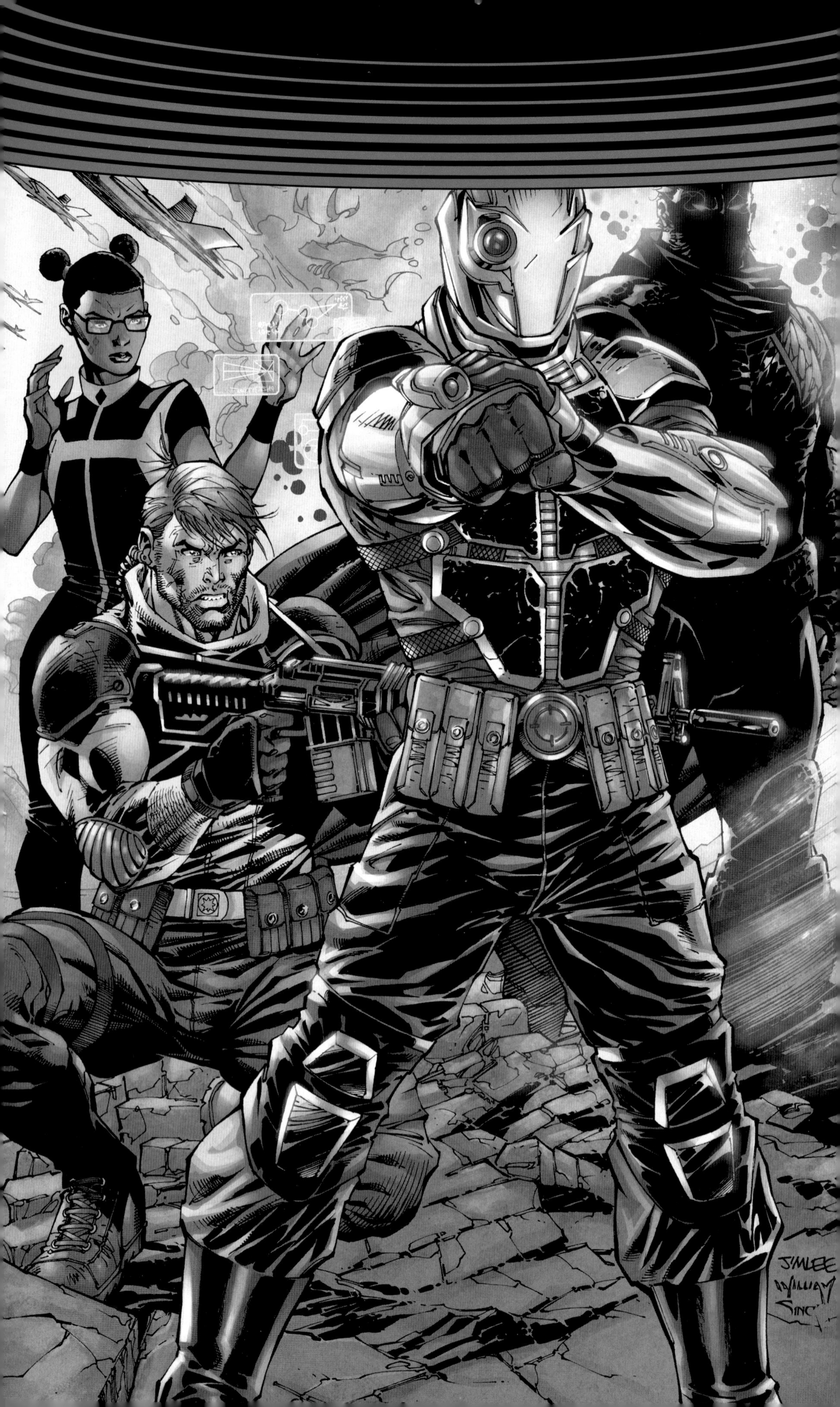

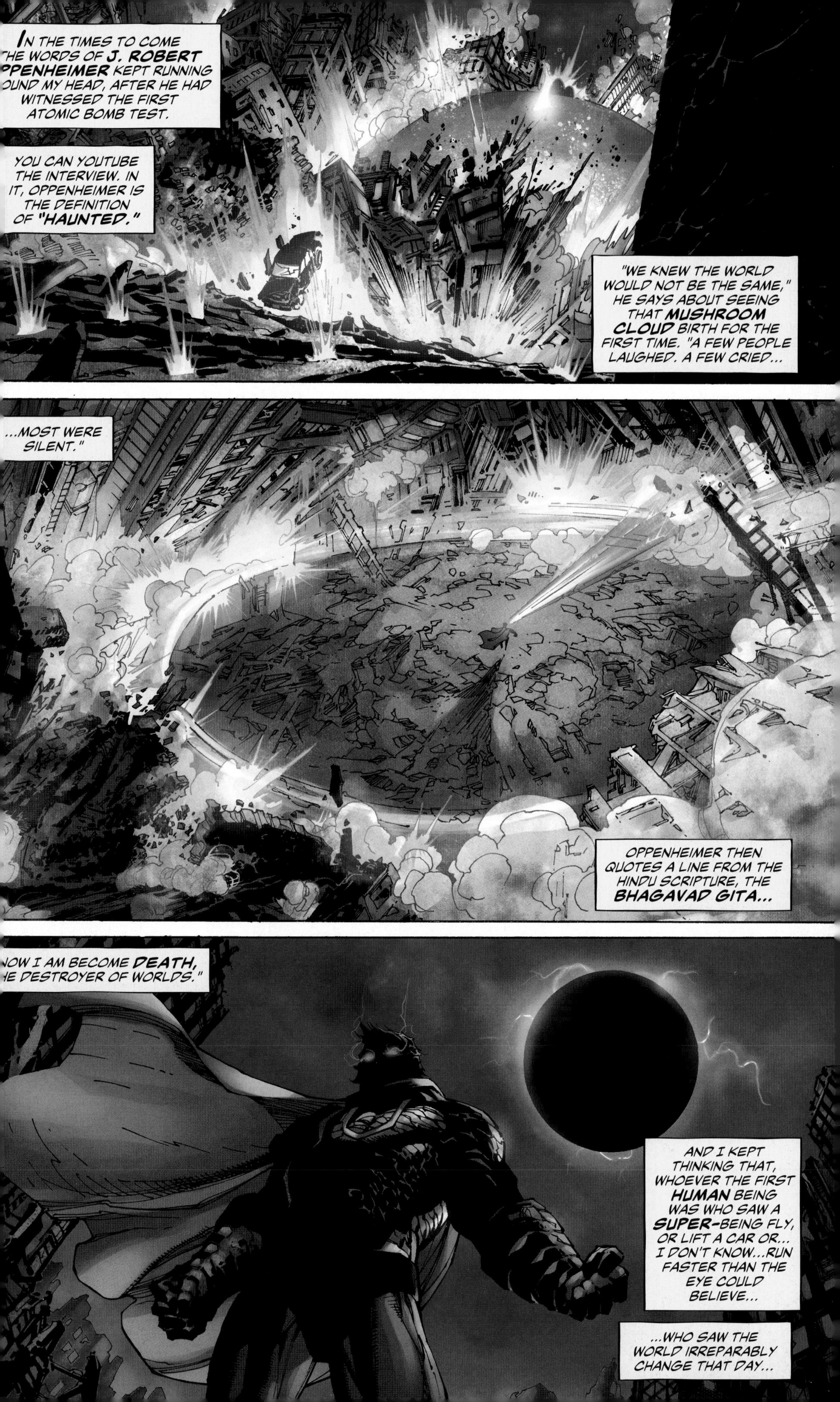

IN THE TIMES TO COME THE WORDS OF J. ROBERT OPPENHEIMER KEPT RUNNING 'ROUND MY HEAD, AFTER HE HAD WITNESSED THE FIRST ATOMIC BOMB TEST.
YOU CAN YOUTUBE THE INTERVIEW. IN IT, OPPENHEIMER IS THE DEFINITION OF "HAUNTED."
"WE KNEW THE WORLD WOULD NOT BE THE SAME," HE SAYS ABOUT SEEING THAT MUSHROOM CLOUD BIRTH FOR THE FIRST TIME. "A FEW PEOPLE LAUGHED. A FEW CRIED...
...MOST WERE SILENT."
OPPENHEIMER THEN QUOTES A LINE FROM THE HINDU SCRIPTURE, THE BHAGAVAD GITA...
"NOW I AM BECOME DEATH, THE DESTROYER OF WORLDS."
AND I KEPT THINKING THAT, WHOEVER THE FIRST HUMAN BEING WAS WHO SAW A SUPER-BEING FLY, OR LIFT A CAR OR... I DON'T KNOW...RUN FASTER THAN THE EYE COULD BELIEVE...
...WHO SAW THE WORLD IRREPARABLY CHANGE THAT DAY...

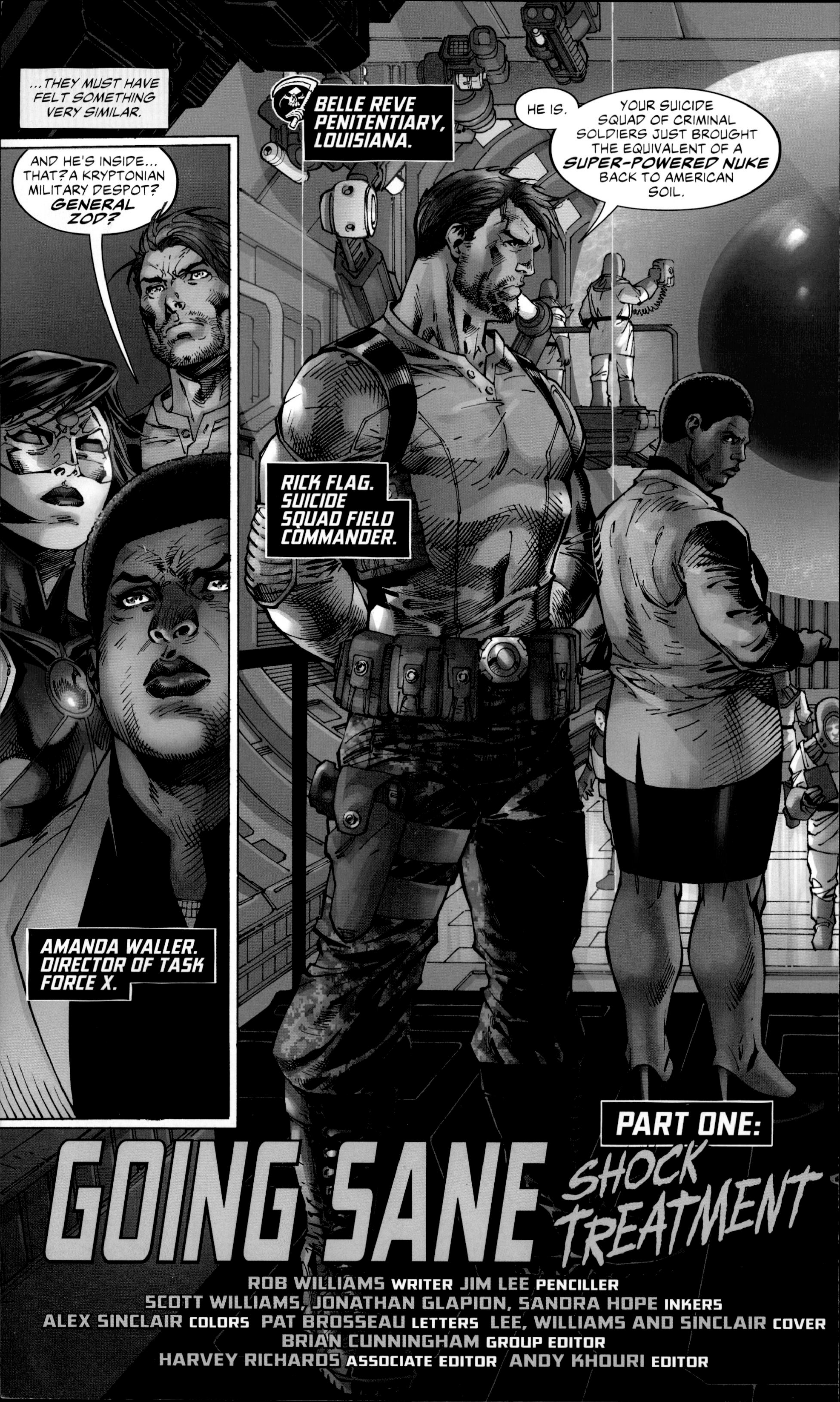

...THEY MUST HAVE FELT SOMETHING VERY SIMILAR.
AND HE'S INSIDE... THAT? A KRYPTONIAN MILITARY DESPOT? GENERAL ZOD?
AMANDA WALLER. DIRECTOR OF TASK FORCE X.
BELLE REVE PENITENTIARY, LOUISIANA.
RICK FLAG. SUICIDE SQUAD FIELD COMMANDER.
HE IS.
YOUR SUICIDE SQUAD OF CRIMINAL SOLDIERS JUST BROUGHT THE EQUIVALENT OF A SUPER-POWERED NUKE BACK TO AMERICAN SOIL.
PART ONE:
GOING SANE
SHOCK TREATMENT
ROB WILLIAMS WRITER JIM LEE PENCILLER
SCOTT WILLIAMS, JONATHAN GLAPION, SANDRA HOPE INKERS
ALEX SINCLAIR COLORS PAT BROSSEAU LETTERS LEE, WILLIAMS AND SINCLAIR COVER
BRIAN CUNNINGHAM GROUP EDITOR
HARVEY RICHARDS ASSOCIATE EDITOR ANDY KHOURI EDITOR

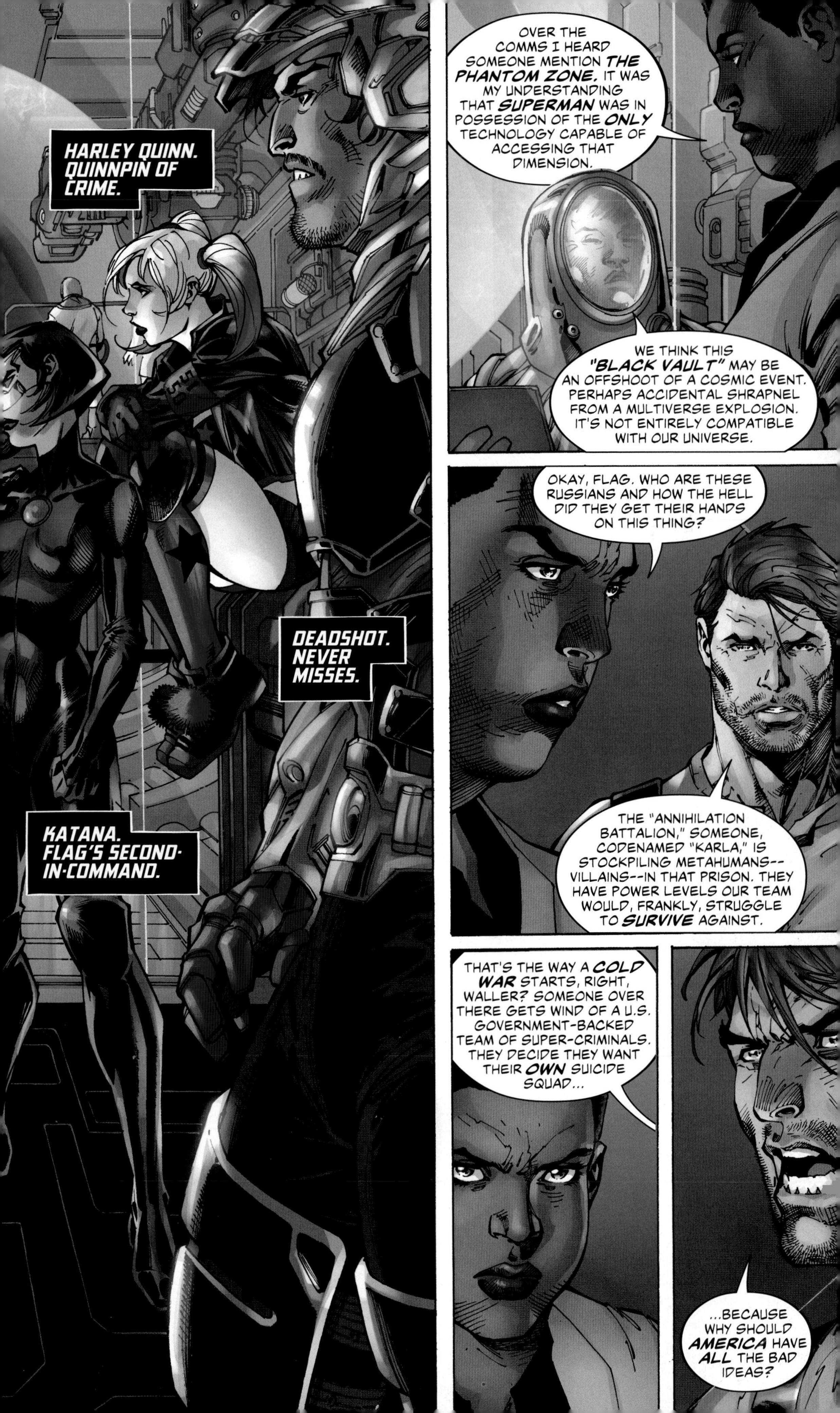
HARLEY QUINN. QUINNPIN OF CRIME.
DEADSHOT. NEVER MISSES.
KATANA. FLAG'S SECOND-IN-COMMAND.
OVER THE COMMS I HEARD SOMEONE MENTION THE PHANTOM ZONE. IT WAS MY UNDERSTANDING THAT SUPERMAN WAS IN POSSESSION OF THE ONLY TECHNOLOGY CAPABLE OF ACCESSING THAT DIMENSION.
WE THINK THIS "BLACK VAULT" MAY BE AN OFFSHOOT OF A COSMIC EVENT. PERHAPS ACCIDENTAL SHRAPNEL FROM A MULTIVERSE EXPLOSION. IT'S NOT ENTIRELY COMPATIBLE WITH OUR UNIVERSE.
OKAY, FLAG. WHO ARE THESE RUSSIANS AND HOW THE HELL DID THEY GET THEIR HANDS ON THIS THING?
THE "ANNIHILATION BATTALION," SOMEONE, CODENAMED "KARLA," IS STOCKPILING METAHUMANS--VILLAINS--IN THAT PRISON. THEY HAVE POWER LEVELS OUR TEAM WOULD, FRANKLY, STRUGGLE TO SURVIVE AGAINST.
THAT'S THE WAY A COLD WAR STARTS, RIGHT, WALLER? SOMEONE OVER THERE GETS WIND OF A U.S. GOVERNMENT-BACKED TEAM OF SUPER-CRIMINALS. THEY DECIDE THEY WANT THEIR OWN SUICIDE SQUAD...
...BECAUSE WHY SHOULD AMERICA HAVE ALL THE BAD IDEAS?

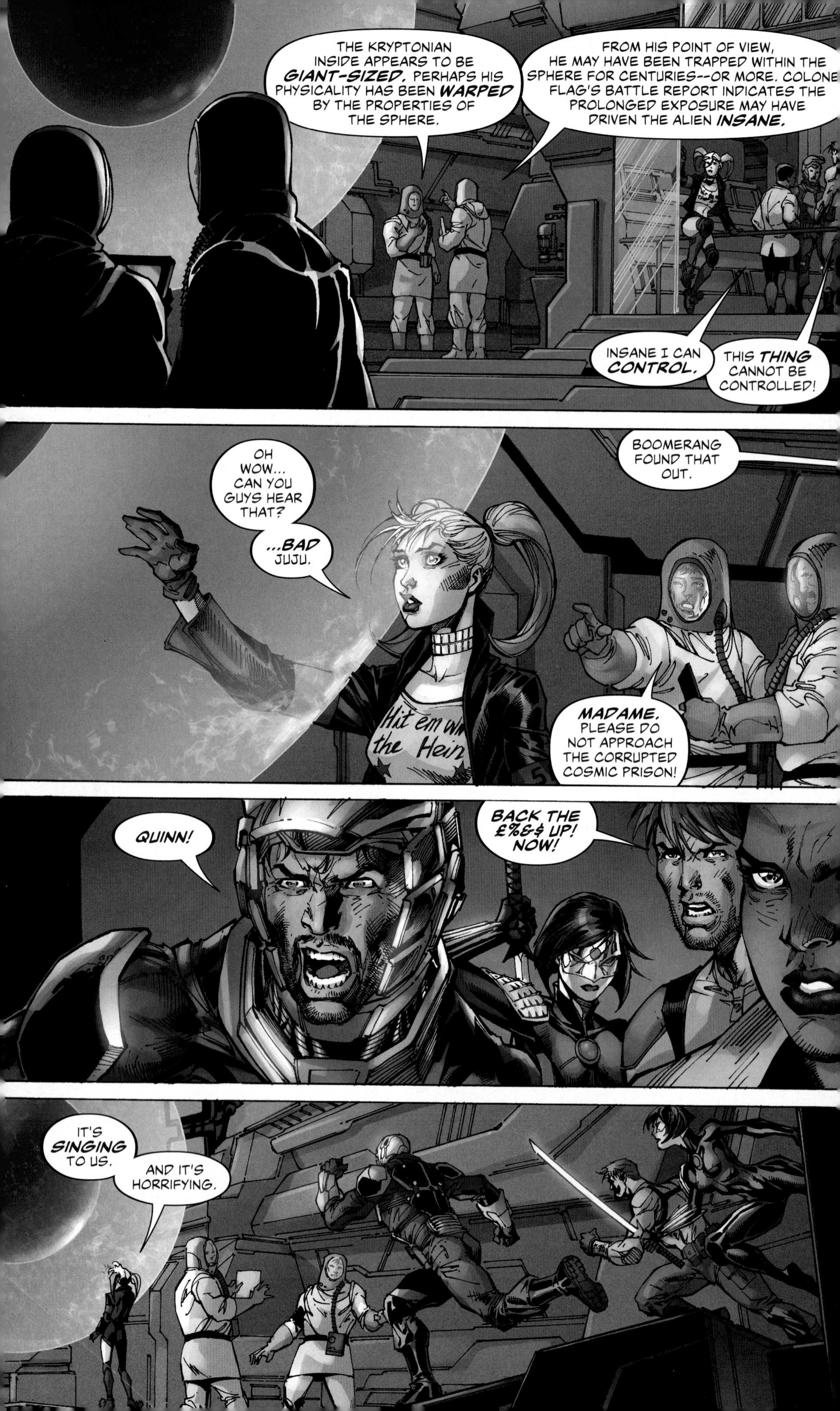
THE KRYPTONIAN INSIDE APPEARS TO BE GIANT-SIZED. PERHAPS HIS PHYSICALITY HAS BEEN WARPED BY THE PROPERTIES OF THE SPHERE.
FROM HIS POINT OF VIEW, HE MAY HAVE BEEN TRAPPED WITHIN THE SPHERE FOR CENTURIES--OR MORE. COLONEL FLAG'S BATTLE REPORT INDICATES THE PROLONGED EXPOSURE MAY HAVE DRIVEN THE ALIEN INSANE.
INSANE I CAN CONTROL.
THIS THING CANNOT BE CONTROLLED!
BOOMERANG FOUND THAT OUT.
OH WOW... CAN YOU GUYS HEAR THAT?
...BAD JUJU.
MADAME. PLEASE DO NOT APPROACH THE CORRUPTED COSMIC PRISON!
QUINN!
BACK THE £%&$ UP! NOW!
IT'S SINGING TO US.
AND IT'S HORRIFYING.

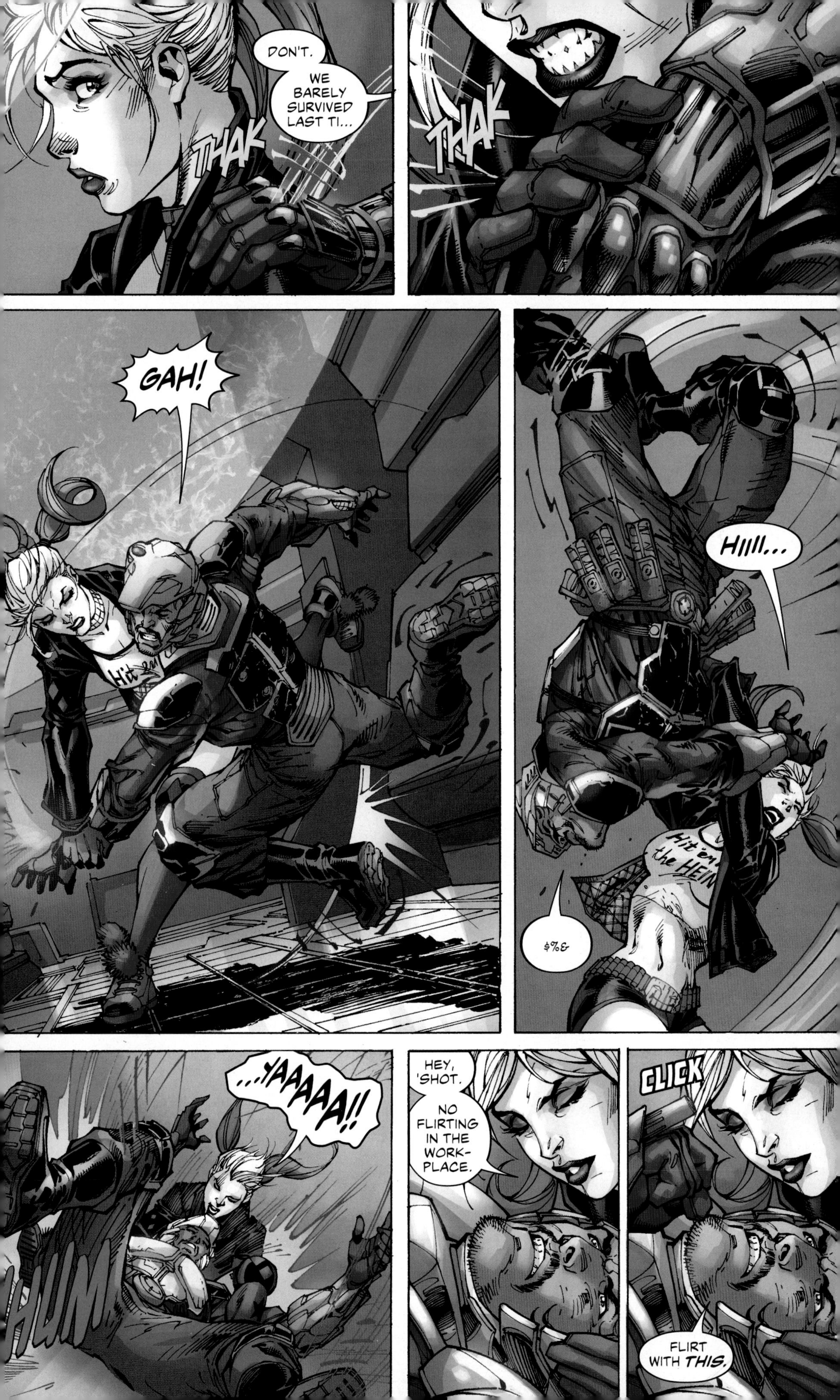

DON'T.
WE BARELY SURVIVED LAST TI...
THAK
THAK
GAH!
HIIII...
$%&
...YAAAAA!!
HUM
HEY, 'SHOT.
NO FLIRTING IN THE WORK-PLACE.
CLICK
FLIRT WITH THIS.

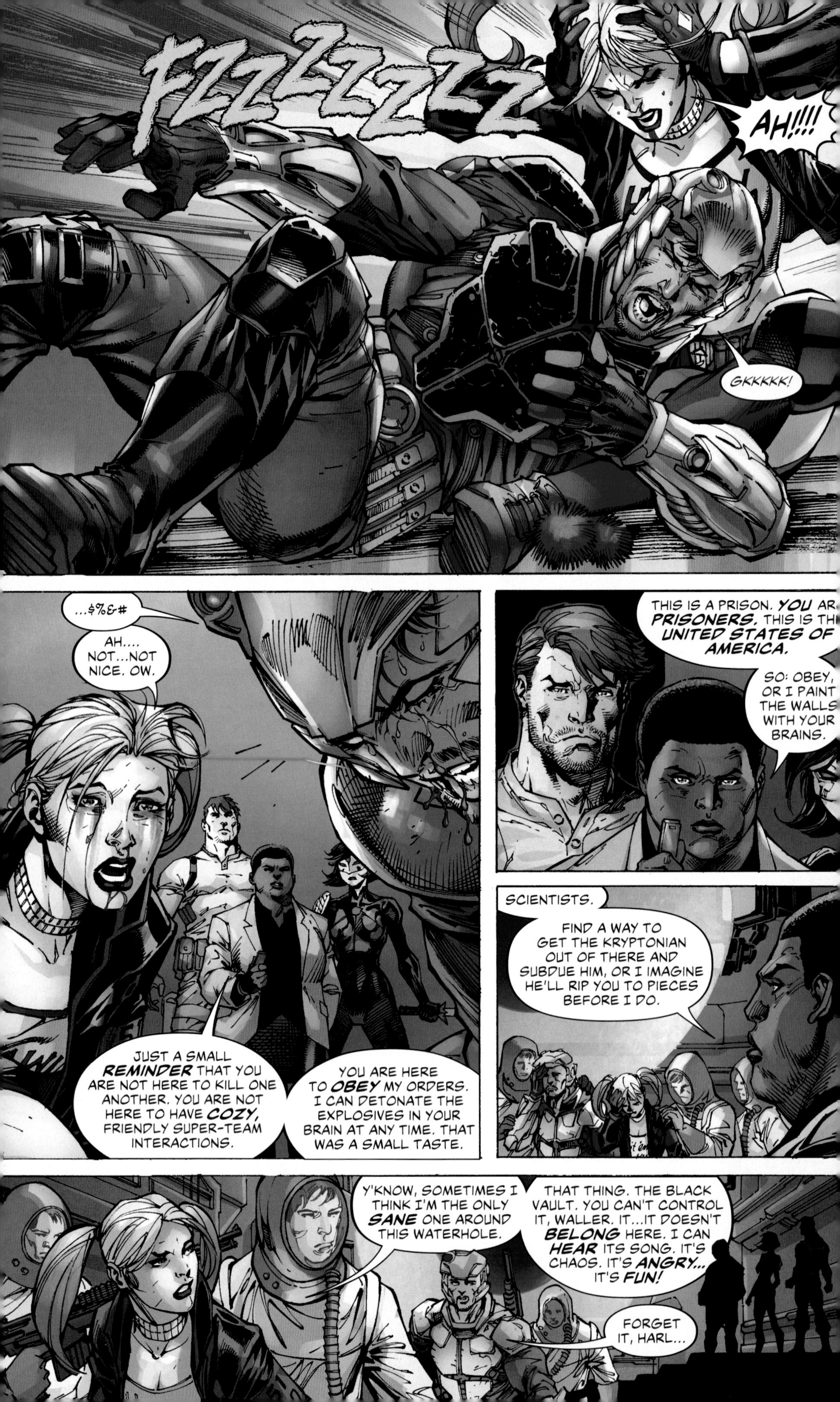

FZZZZZZZZ
AH!!!!
GKKKKK!
...$%&#
AH.... NOT...NOT NICE. OW.
JUST A SMALL REMINDER THAT YOU ARE NOT HERE TO KILL ONE ANOTHER. YOU ARE NOT HERE TO HAVE COZY, FRIENDLY SUPER-TEAM INTERACTIONS.
YOU ARE HERE TO OBEY MY ORDERS. I CAN DETONATE THE EXPLOSIVES IN YOUR BRAIN AT ANY TIME. THAT WAS A SMALL TASTE.
THIS IS A PRISON. YOU AR PRISONERS. THIS IS TH UNITED STATES OF AMERICA.
SO: OBEY, OR I PAINT THE WALLS WITH YOUR BRAINS.
SCIENTISTS.
FIND A WAY TO GET THE KRYPTONIAN OUT OF THERE AND SUBDUE HIM, OR I IMAGINE HE'LL RIP YOU TO PIECES BEFORE I DO.
Y'KNOW, SOMETIMES I THINK I'M THE ONLY SANE ONE AROUND THIS WATERHOLE.
THAT THING. THE BLACK VAULT. YOU CAN'T CONTROL IT, WALLER. IT...IT DOESN'T BELONG HERE. I CAN HEAR ITS SONG. IT'S CHAOS. IT'S ANGRY... IT'S FUN!
FORGET IT, HARL...

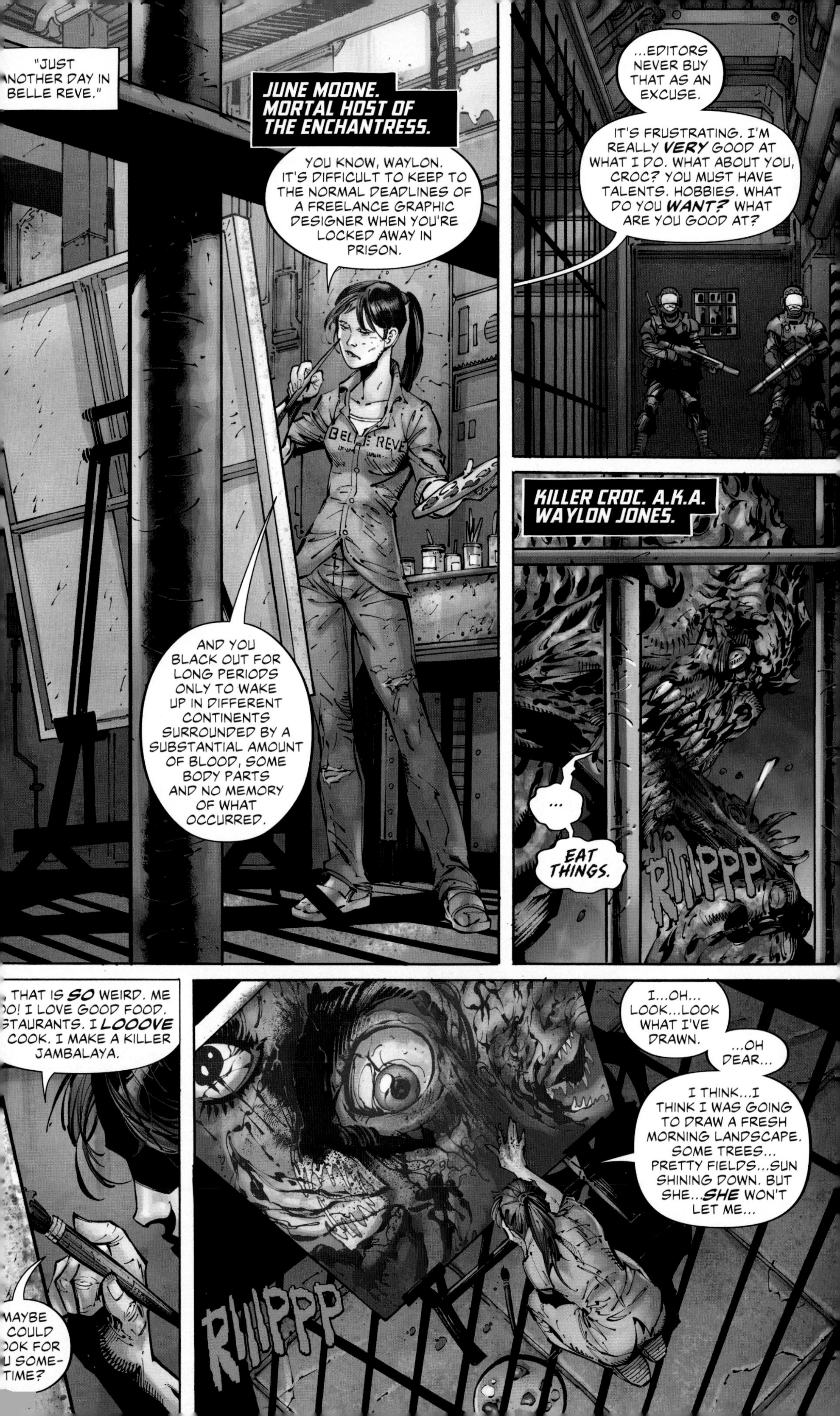
"JUST
ANOTHER DAY IN
BELLE REVE."
JUNE MOONE. MORTAL HOST OF THE ENCHANTRESS.
YOU KNOW, WAYLON. IT'S DIFFICULT TO KEEP TO THE NORMAL DEADLINES OF A FREELANCE GRAPHIC DESIGNER WHEN YOU'RE LOCKED AWAY IN PRISON.
AND YOU BLACK OUT FOR LONG PERIODS ONLY TO WAKE UP IN DIFFERENT CONTINENTS SURROUNDED BY A SUBSTANTIAL AMOUNT OF BLOOD, SOME BODY PARTS AND NO MEMORY OF WHAT OCCURRED.
...EDITORS NEVER BUY THAT AS AN EXCUSE.
IT'S FRUSTRATING. I'M REALLY VERY GOOD AT WHAT I DO. WHAT ABOUT YOU, CROC? YOU MUST HAVE TALENTS. HOBBIES. WHAT DO YOU WANT? WHAT ARE YOU GOOD AT?
KILLER CROC. A.K.A. WAYLON JONES.
...
EAT THINGS.
RIIPPP
THAT IS SO WEIRD. ME
I LOVE GOOD FOOD.
I LOOOVE
COOK. I MAKE A KILLER JAMBALAYA.
COULD
SOME-
TIME?
I...OH... LOOK...LOOK WHAT I'VE DRAWN.
...OH DEAR...
I THINK...I THINK I WAS GOING TO DRAW A FRESH MORNING LANDSCAPE. SOME TREES... PRETTY FIELDS...SUN SHINING DOWN. BUT SHE...SHE WON'T LET ME...
RIIPPP

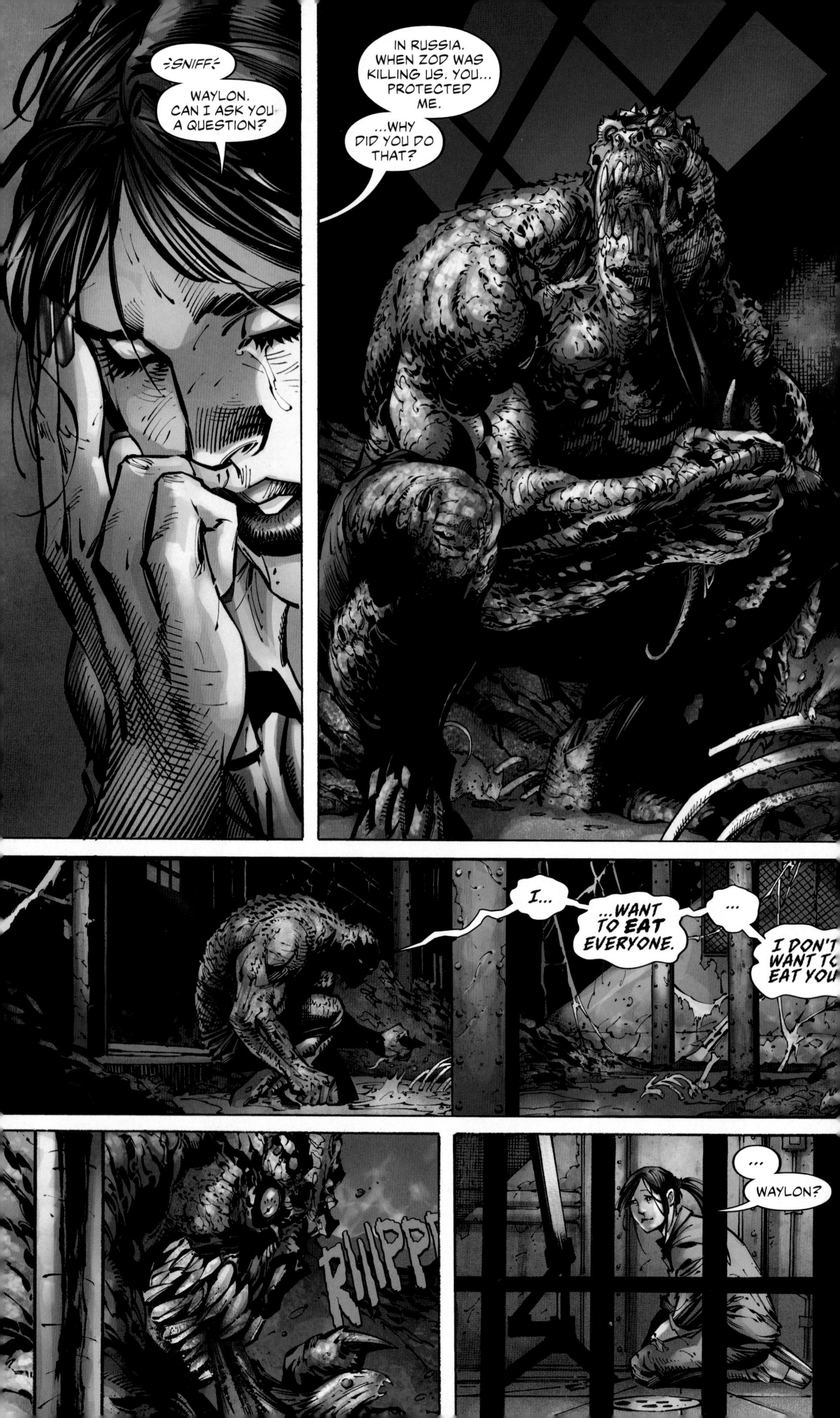

-SNIFF-
WAYLON. CAN I ASK YOU A QUESTION?
IN RUSSIA. WHEN ZOD WAS KILLING US. YOU... PROTECTED ME.
...WHY DID YOU DO THAT?
I...
...WANT TO EAT EVERYONE.
...
I DON'T WANT TO EAT YOU
RIIPP
...
WAYLON?

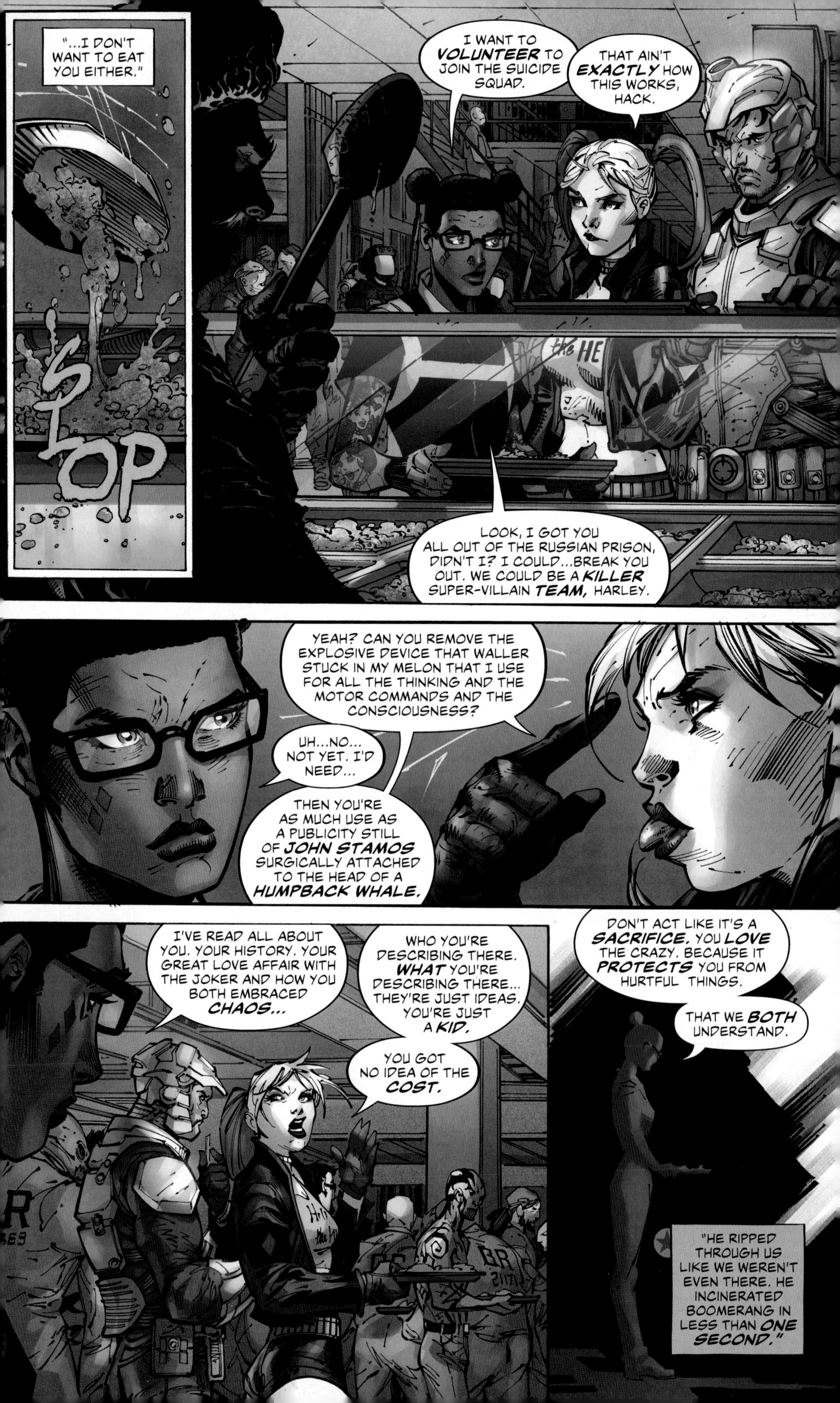
"...I DON'T WANT TO EAT YOU EITHER."
SLOP
I WANT TO VOLUNTEER TO JOIN THE SUICIDE SQUAD.
THAT AIN'T EXACTLY HOW THIS WORKS, HACK.
LOOK, I GOT YOU ALL OUT OF THE RUSSIAN PRISON, DIDN'T I? I COULD...BREAK YOU OUT. WE COULD BE A KILLER SUPER-VILLAIN TEAM, HARLEY.
YEAH? CAN YOU REMOVE THE EXPLOSIVE DEVICE THAT WALLER STUCK IN MY MELON THAT I USE FOR ALL THE THINKING AND THE MOTOR COMMANDS AND THE CONSCIOUSNESS?
UH...NO... NOT YET. I'D NEED...
THEN YOU'RE AS MUCH USE AS A PUBLICITY STILL OF JOHN STAMOS SURGICALLY ATTACHED TO THE HEAD OF A HUMPBACK WHALE.
I'VE READ ALL ABOUT YOU. YOUR HISTORY. YOUR GREAT LOVE AFFAIR WITH THE JOKER AND HOW YOU BOTH EMBRACED CHAOS...
WHO YOU'RE DESCRIBING THERE. WHAT YOU'RE DESCRIBING THERE... THEY'RE JUST IDEAS. YOU'RE JUST A KID.
YOU GOT NO IDEA OF THE COST.
DON'T ACT LIKE IT'S A SACRIFICE. YOU LOVE THE CRAZY. BECAUSE IT PROTECTS YOU FROM HURTFUL THINGS.
THAT WE BOTH UNDERSTAND.
"HE RIPPED THROUGH US LIKE WE WEREN'T EVEN THERE. HE INCINERATED BOOMERANG IN LESS THAN ONE SECOND."

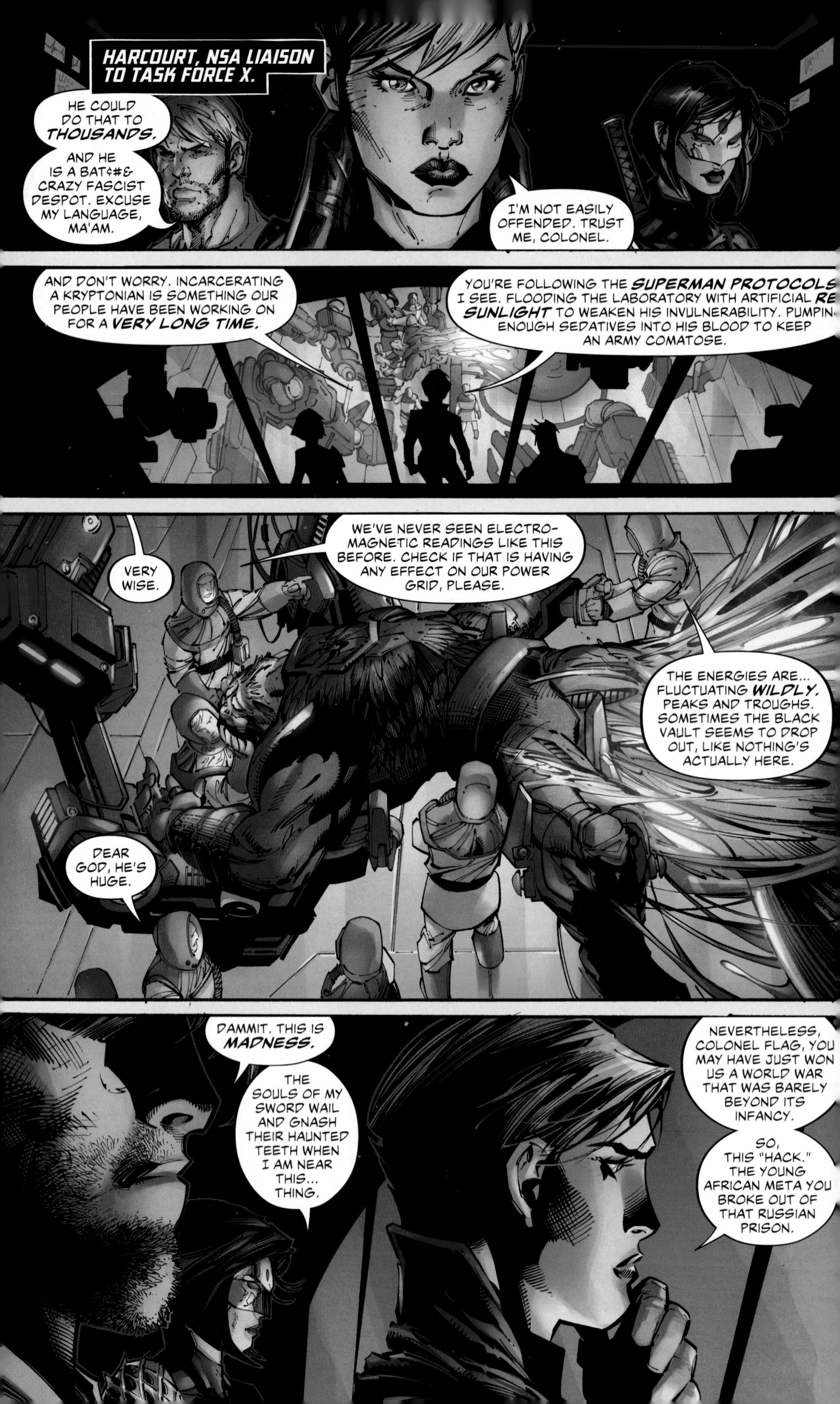
HARCOURT, NSA LIAISON TO TASK FORCE X.
HE COULD DO THAT TO THOUSANDS.
AND HE IS A BAT¢#& CRAZY FASCIST DESPOT. EXCUSE MY LANGUAGE, MA'AM.
I'M NOT EASILY OFFENDED. TRUST ME, COLONEL.
AND DON'T WORRY. INCARCERATING A KRYPTONIAN IS SOMETHING OUR PEOPLE HAVE BEEN WORKING ON FOR A VERY LONG TIME.
YOU'RE FOLLOWING THE SUPERMAN PROTOCOLS I SEE. FLOODING THE LABORATORY WITH ARTIFICIAL RE SUNLIGHT TO WEAKEN HIS INVULNERABILITY. PUMPIN ENOUGH SEDATIVES INTO HIS BLOOD TO KEEP AN ARMY COMATOSE.
VERY WISE.
WE'VE NEVER SEEN ELECTRO-MAGNETIC READINGS LIKE THIS BEFORE. CHECK IF THAT IS HAVING ANY EFFECT ON OUR POWER GRID, PLEASE.
THE ENERGIES ARE... FLUCTUATING WILDLY. PEAKS AND TROUGHS. SOMETIMES THE BLACK VAULT SEEMS TO DROP OUT, LIKE NOTHING'S ACTUALLY HERE.
DEAR GOD, HE'S HUGE.
DAMMIT. THIS IS MADNESS.
THE SOULS OF MY SWORD WAIL AND GNASH THEIR HAUNTED TEETH WHEN I AM NEAR THIS... THING.
NEVERTHELESS, COLONEL FLAG, YOU MAY HAVE JUST WON US A WORLD WAR THAT WAS BARELY BEYOND ITS INFANCY.
SO, THIS "HACK." THE YOUNG AFRICAN META YOU BROKE OUT OF THAT RUSSIAN PRISON.

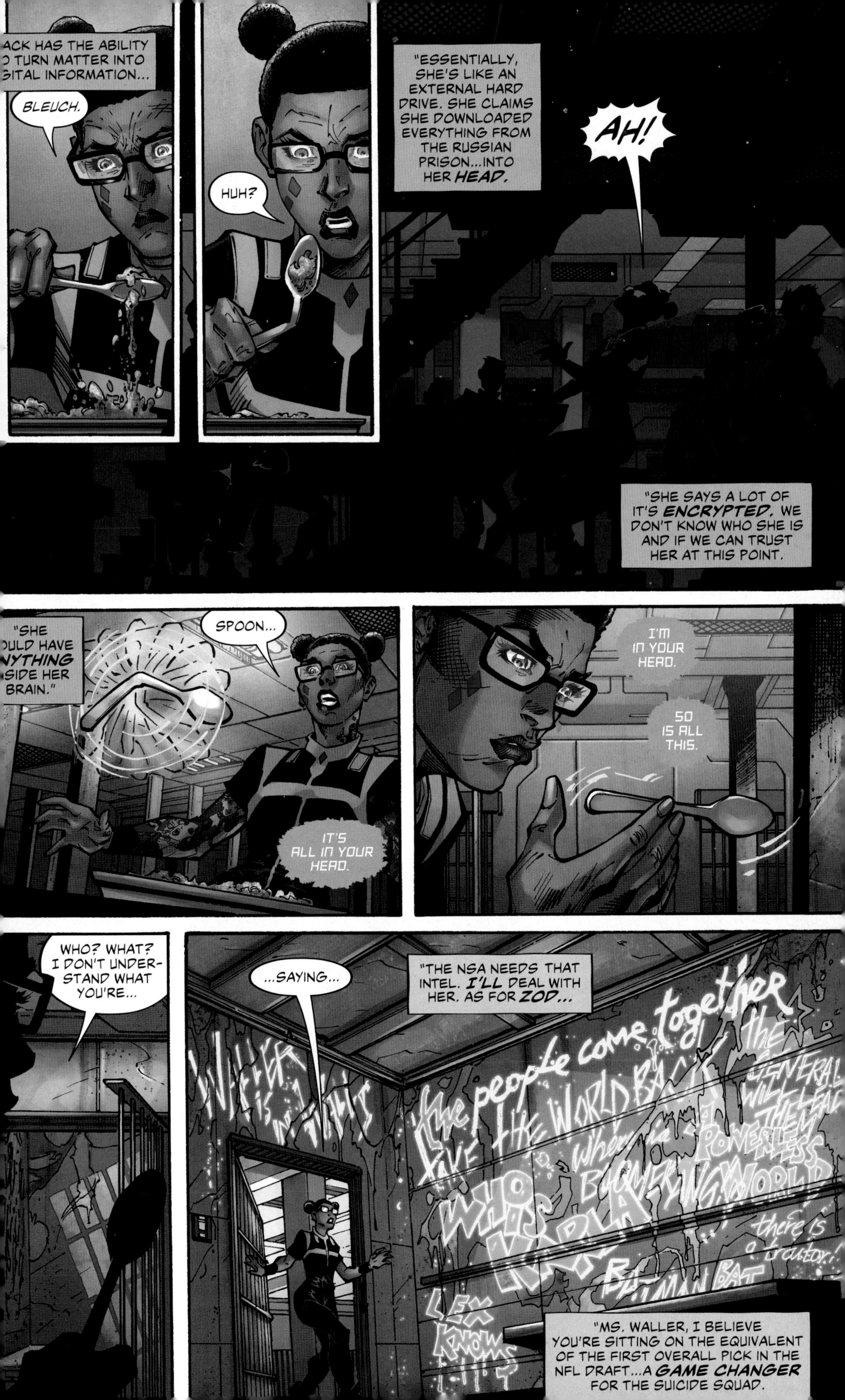
ACK HAS THE ABILITY O TURN MATTER INTO IGITAL INFORMATION...
BLEUCH.
HUH?
"ESSENTIALLY, SHE'S LIKE AN EXTERNAL HARD DRIVE. SHE CLAIMS SHE DOWNLOADED EVERYTHING FROM THE RUSSIAN PRISON...INTO HER HEAD.
AH!
"SHE SAYS A LOT OF IT'S ENCRYPTED. WE DON'T KNOW WHO SHE IS AND IF WE CAN TRUST HER AT THIS POINT.
"SHE OULD HAVE NYTHING SIDE HER BRAIN."
SPOON...
IT'S ALL IN YOUR HEAD.
I'M IN YOUR HEAD.
SO IS ALL THIS.
WHO? WHAT? I DON'T UNDER-STAND WHAT YOU'RE...
...SAYING...
"THE NSA NEEDS THAT INTEL. I'LL DEAL WITH HER. AS FOR ZOD...
the people come together
POWERLESS
there is a traitor!
LEX KNOWS
"MS. WALLER, I BELIEVE YOU'RE SITTING ON THE EQUIVALENT OF THE FIRST OVERALL PICK IN THE NFL DRAFT...A GAME CHANGER FOR THE SUICIDE SQUAD.

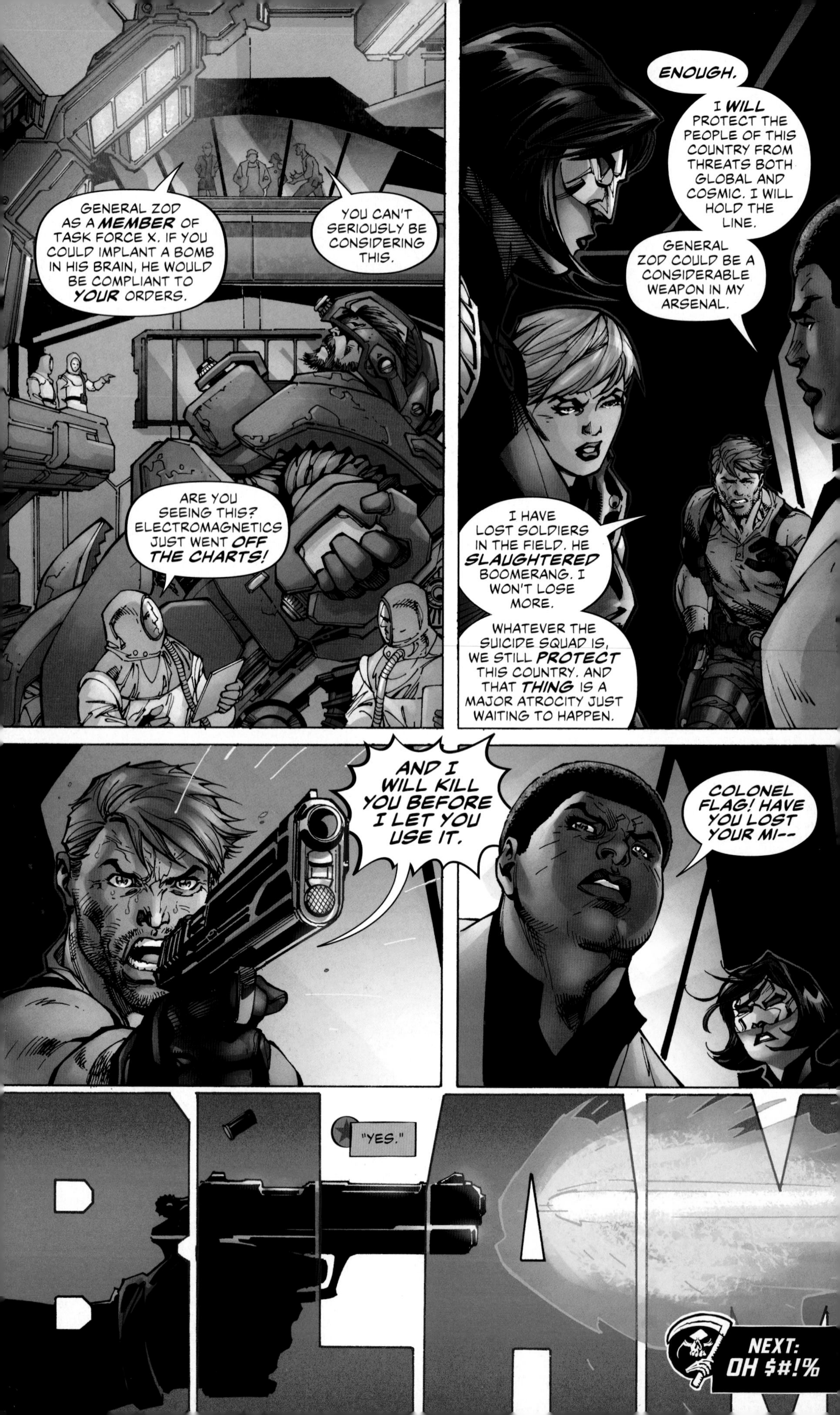
GENERAL ZOD AS A MEMBER OF TASK FORCE X. IF YOU COULD IMPLANT A BOMB IN HIS BRAIN, HE WOULD BE COMPLIANT TO YOUR ORDERS.
YOU CAN'T SERIOUSLY BE CONSIDERING THIS.
ARE YOU SEEING THIS? ELECTROMAGNETICS JUST WENT OFF THE CHARTS!
ENOUGH.
I WILL PROTECT THE PEOPLE OF THIS COUNTRY FROM THREATS BOTH GLOBAL AND COSMIC. I WILL HOLD THE LINE.
GENERAL ZOD COULD BE A CONSIDERABLE WEAPON IN MY ARSENAL.
I HAVE LOST SOLDIERS IN THE FIELD. HE SLAUGHTERED BOOMERANG. I WON'T LOSE MORE.
WHATEVER THE SUICIDE SQUAD IS, WE STILL PROTECT THIS COUNTRY. AND THAT THING IS A MAJOR ATROCITY JUST WAITING TO HAPPEN.
AND I WILL KILL YOU BEFORE I LET YOU USE IT.
COLONEL FLAG! HAVE YOU LOST YOUR MI--
"YES."
NEXT: OH $#!%

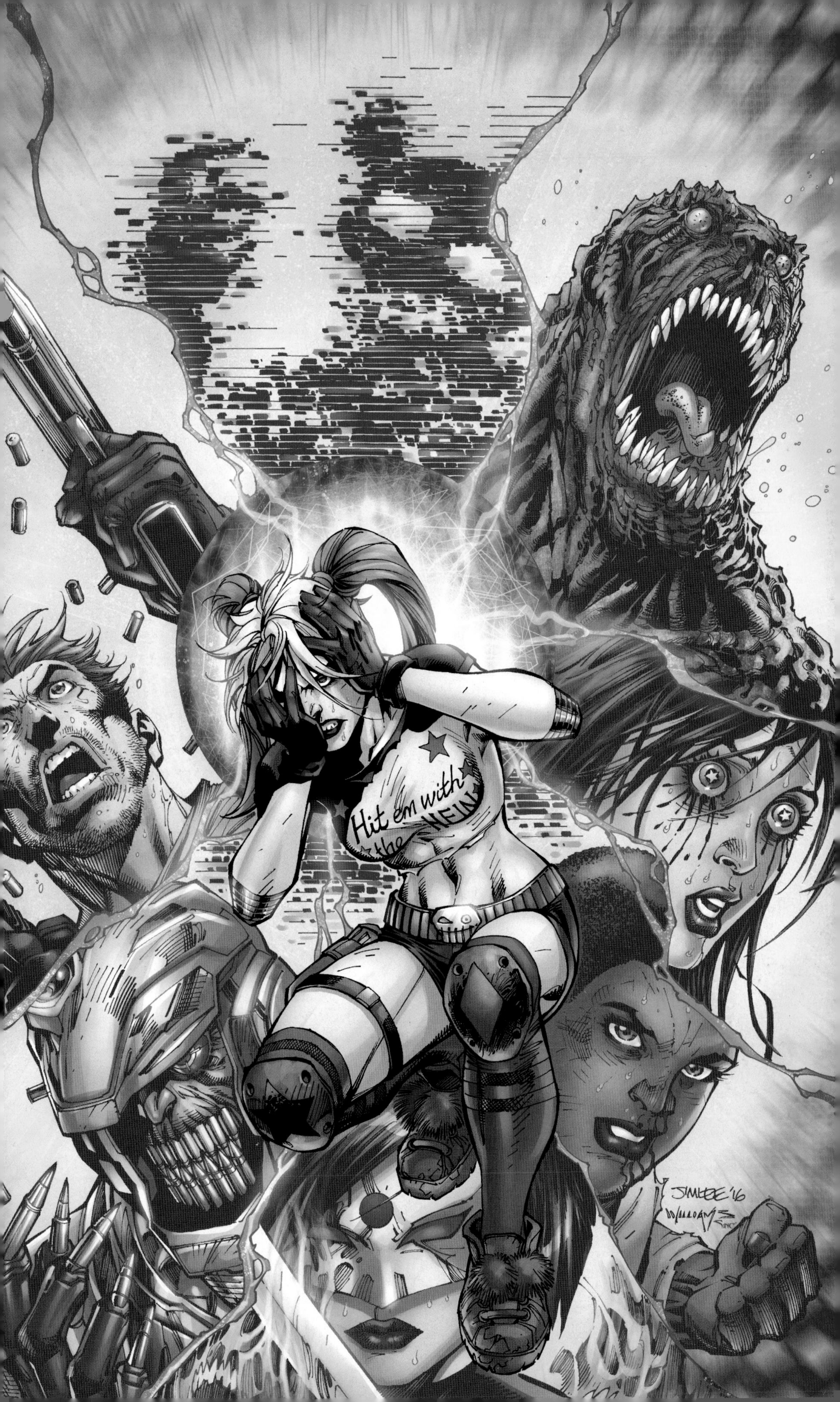
Hit em with
JIM LEE '16

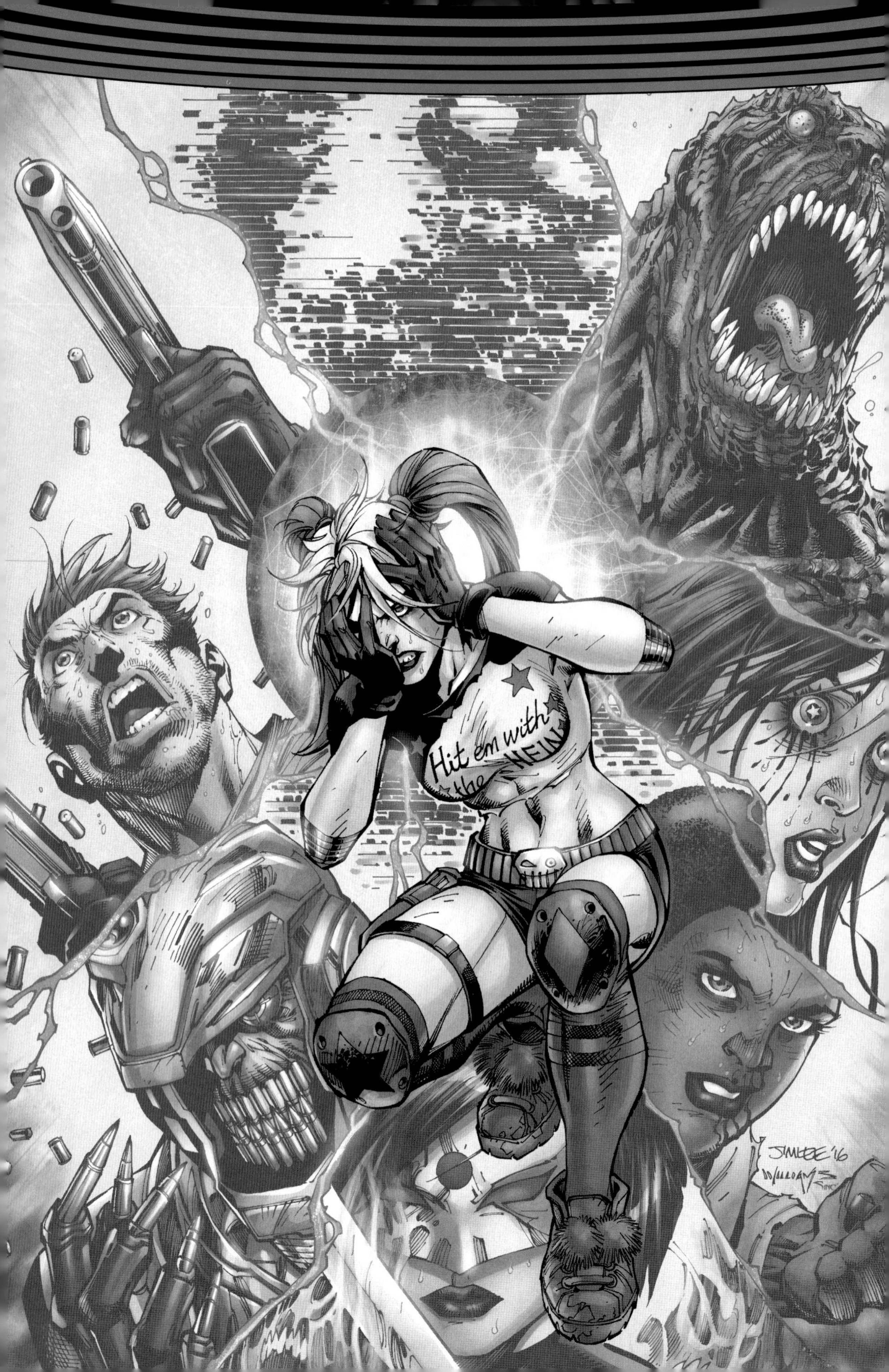

Hit em with the
JIMLEE '16

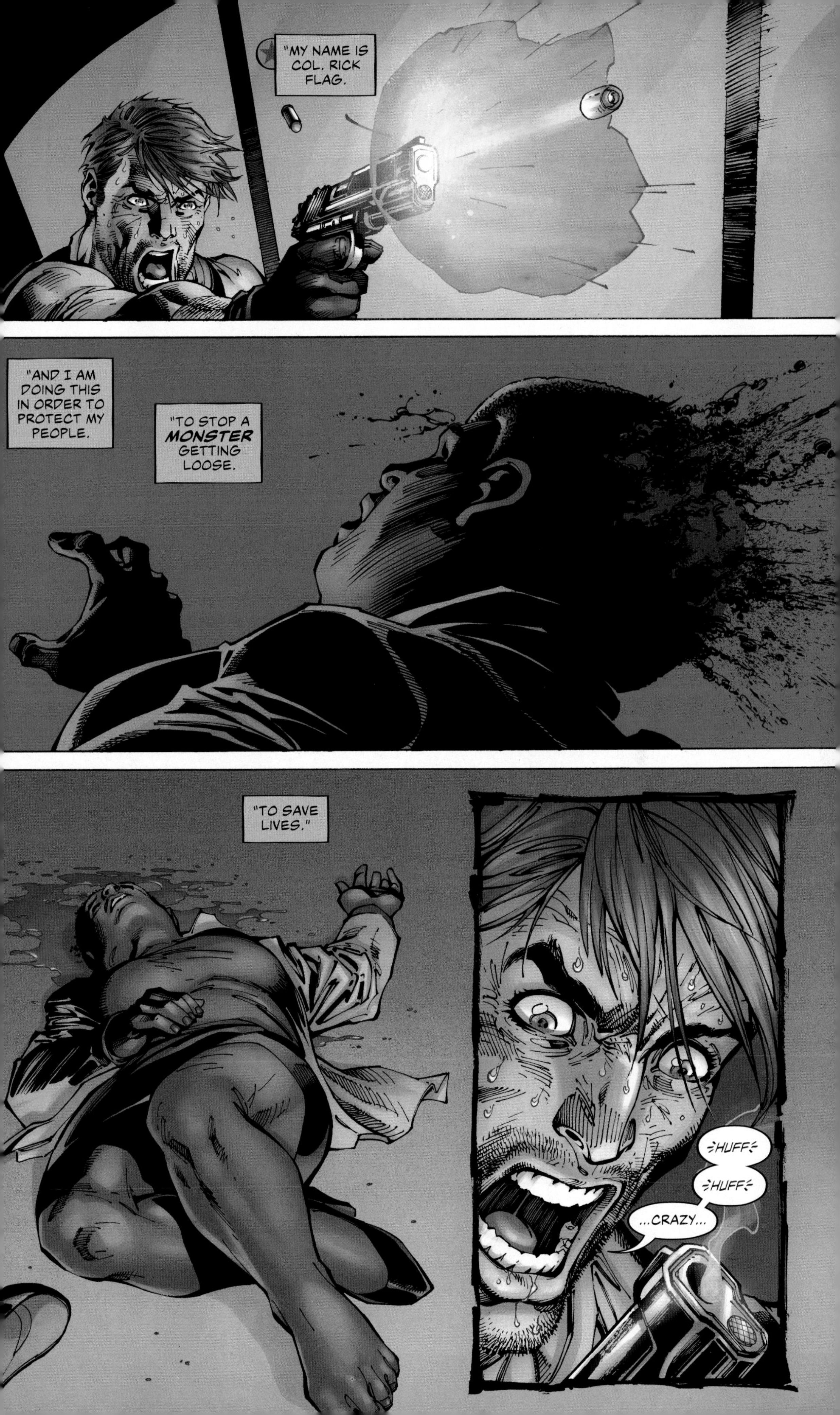
"MY NAME IS COL. RICK FLAG.
"AND I AM DOING THIS IN ORDER TO PROTECT MY PEOPLE.
"TO STOP A **MONSTER** GETTING LOOSE.
"TO SAVE LIVES."
HUFF
HUFF
...CRAZY...

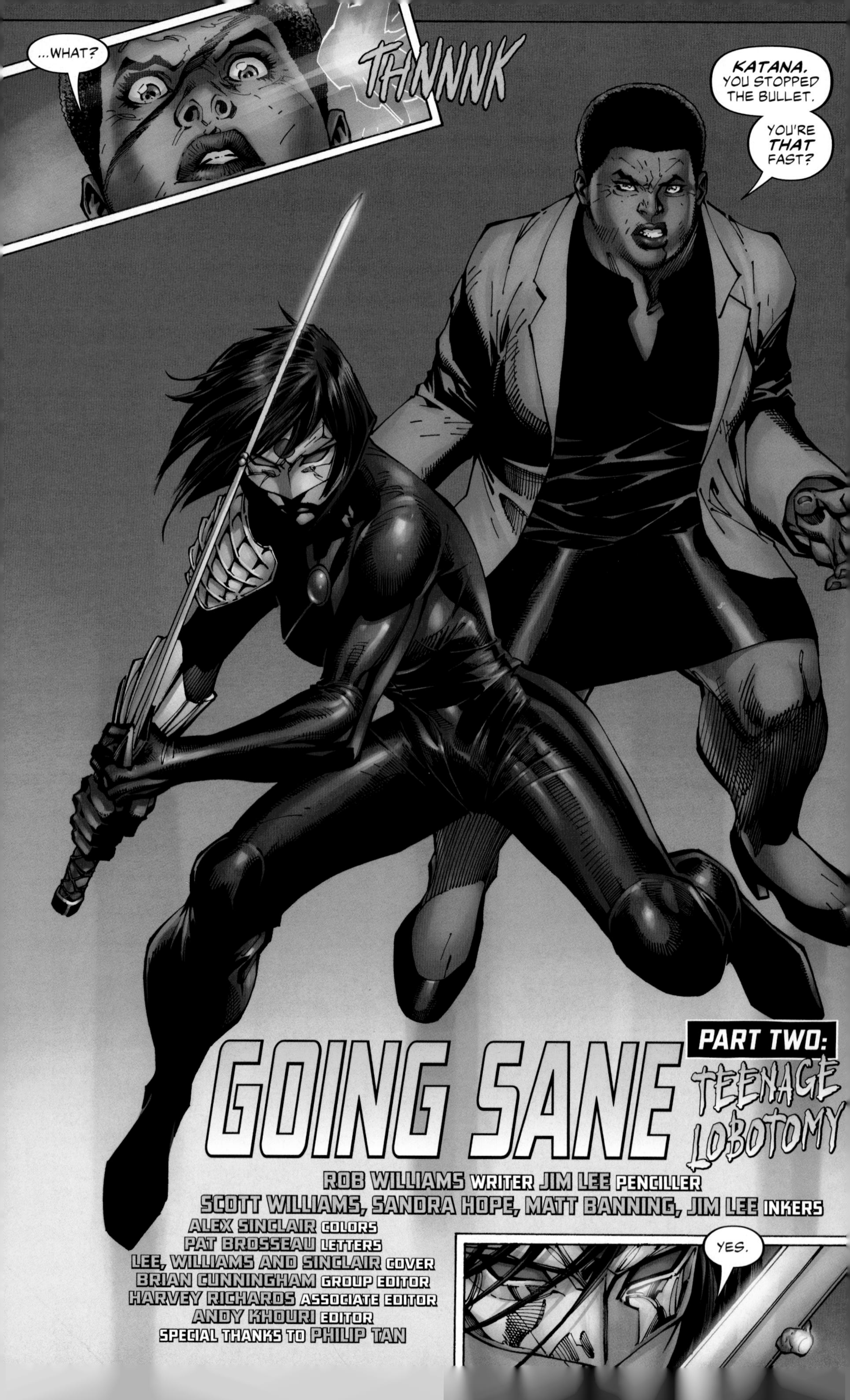

...WHAT?
THHNNNK
KATANA. YOU STOPPED THE BULLET.
YOU'RE THAT FAST?
GOING SANE
PART TWO: TEENAGE LOBOTOMY
ROB WILLIAMS WRITER JIM LEE PENCILLER
SCOTT WILLIAMS, SANDRA HOPE, MATT BANNING, JIM LEE INKERS
ALEX SINCLAIR COLORS
PAT BROSSEAU LETTERS
LEE, WILLIAMS AND SINCLAIR COVER
BRIAN CUNNINGHAM GROUP EDITOR
HARVEY RICHARDS ASSOCIATE EDITOR
ANDY KHOURI EDITOR
SPECIAL THANKS TO PHILIP TAN
YES.

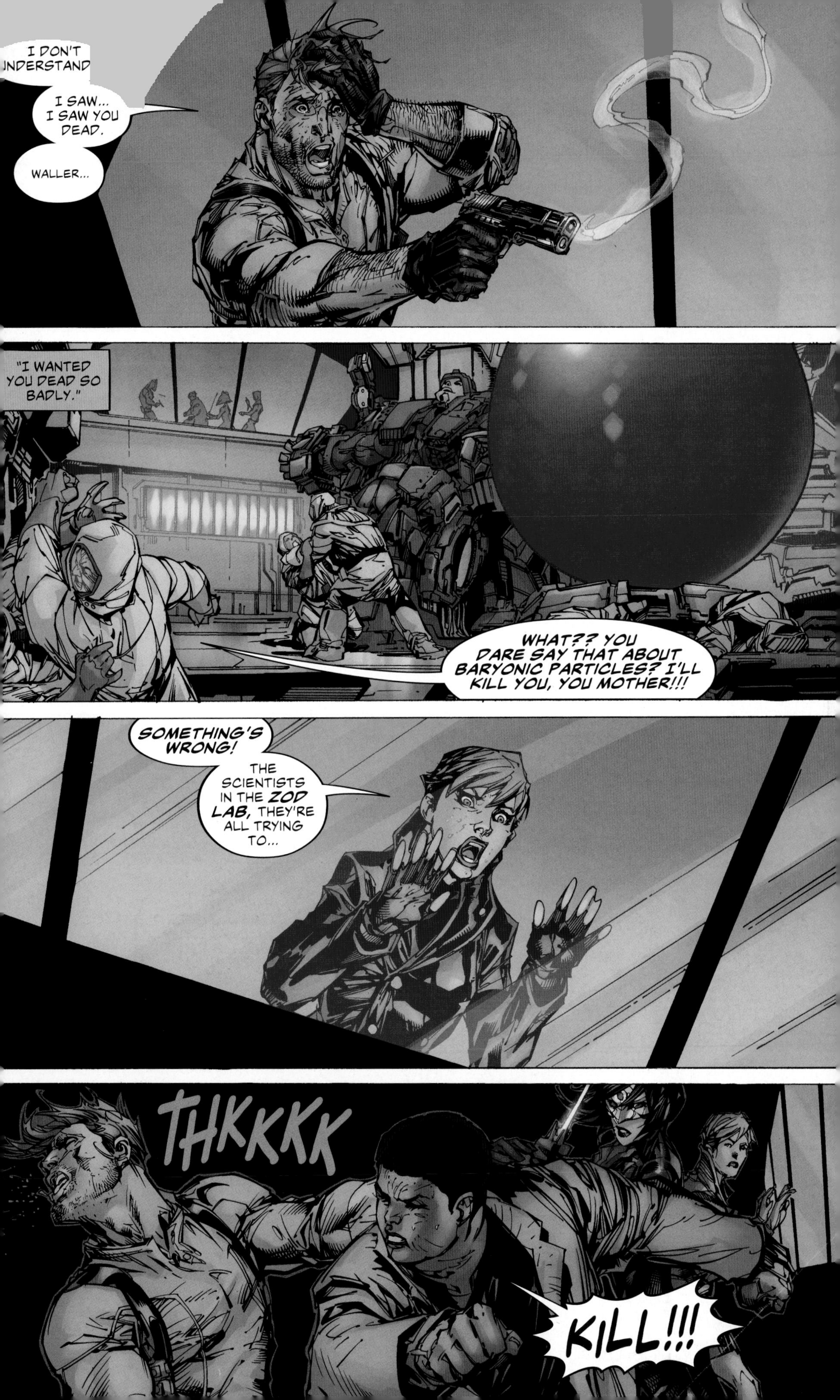

I DON'T
UNDERSTAND
I SAW... I SAW YOU DEAD.
WALLER...
"I WANTED YOU DEAD SO BADLY."
WHAT?? YOU DARE SAY THAT ABOUT BARYONIC PARTICLES? I'LL KILL YOU, YOU MOTHER!!!
SOMETHING'S WRONG!
THE SCIENTISTS IN THE ZOD LAB, THEY'RE ALL TRYING TO...
THKKKK
KILL!!!

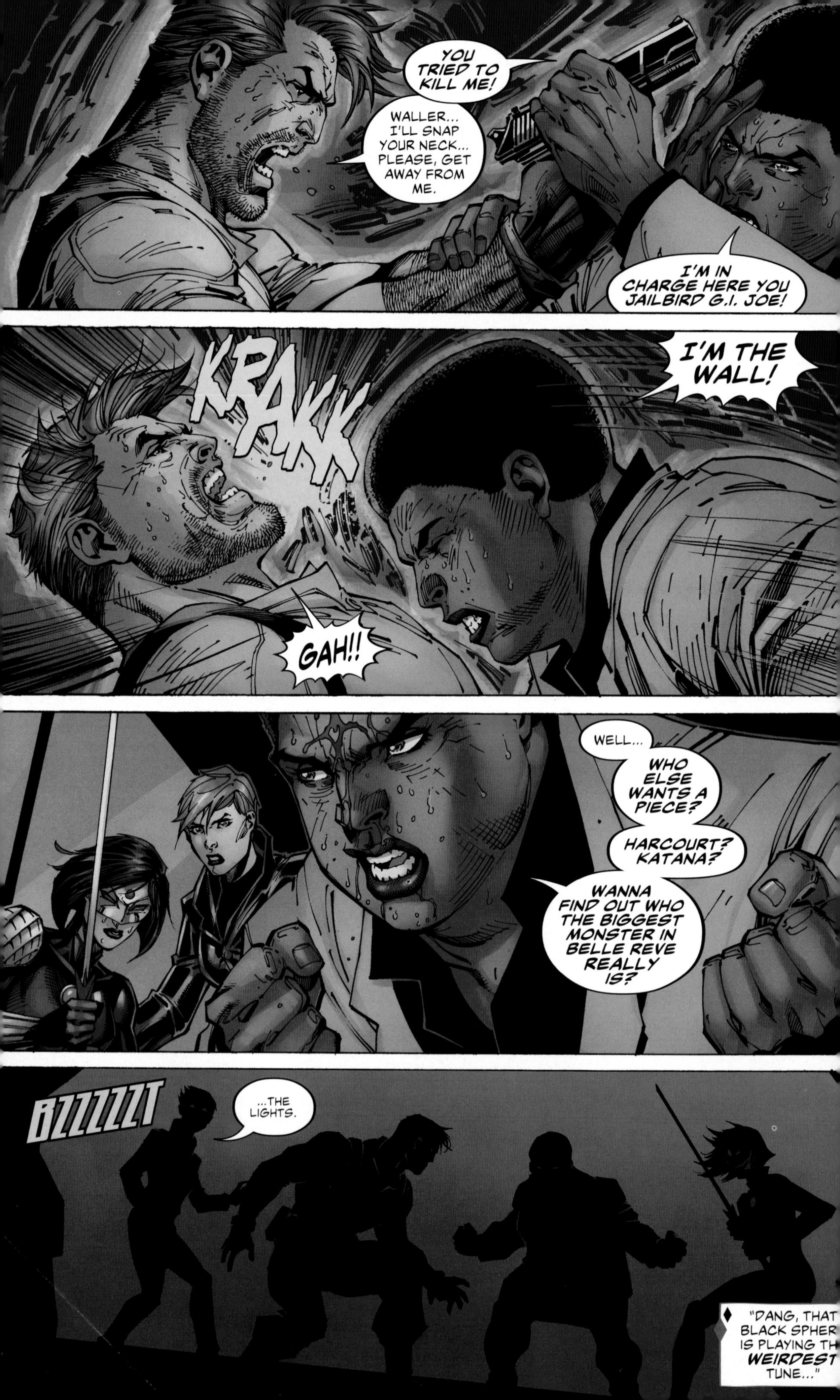
YOU TRIED TO KILL ME!
WALLER... I'LL SNAP YOUR NECK... PLEASE, GET AWAY FROM ME.
I'M IN CHARGE HERE YOU JAILBIRD G.I. JOE!
KRAKK
I'M THE WALL!
GAH!!
WELL...
WHO ELSE WANTS A PIECE?
HARCOURT? KATANA?
WANNA FIND OUT WHO THE BIGGEST MONSTER IN BELLE REVE REALLY IS?
BZZZZZZT
...THE LIGHTS.
"DANG, THAT BLACK SPHER IS PLAYING TH WEIRDEST TUNE..."

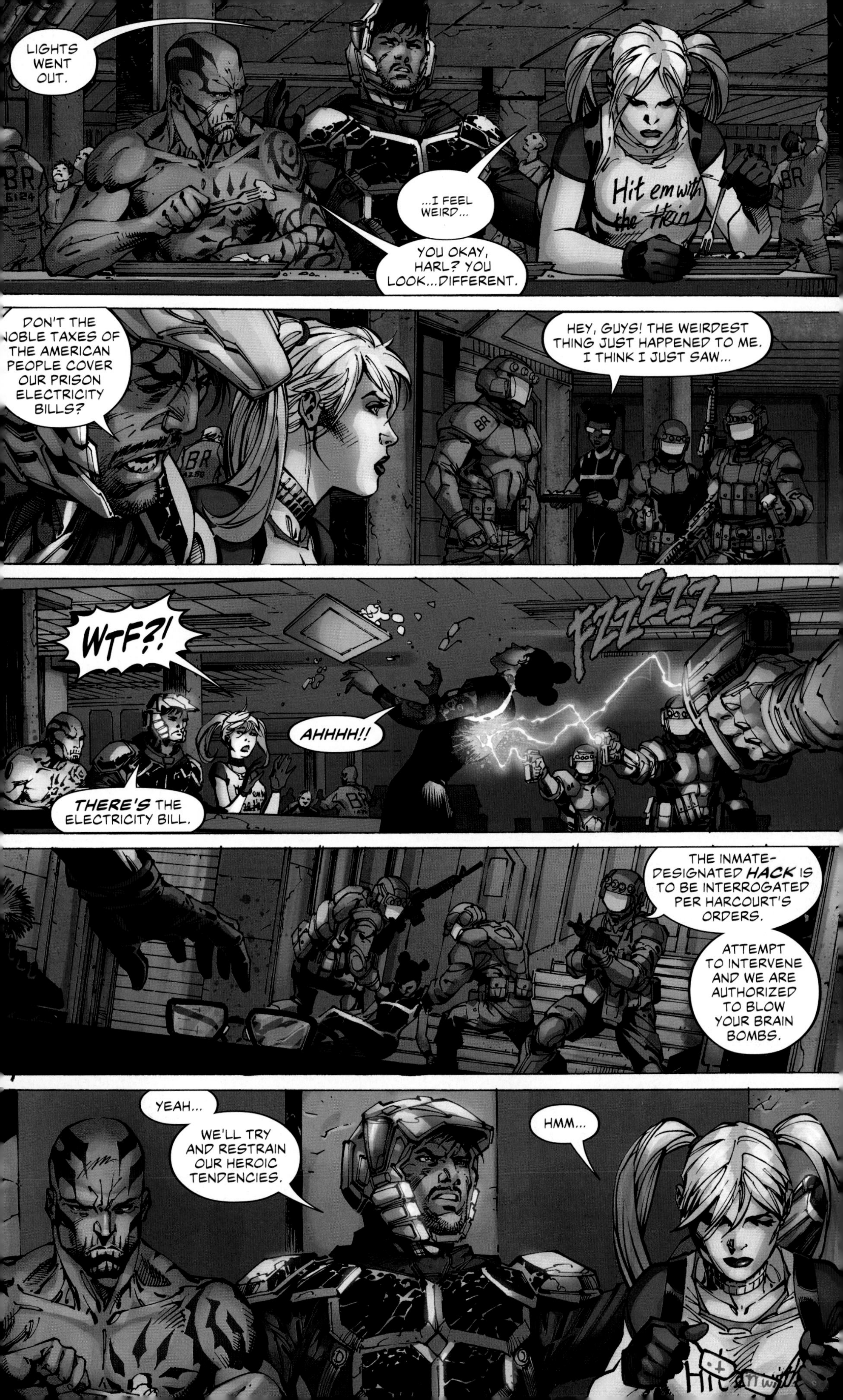
LIGHTS WENT OUT.
...I FEEL WEIRD...
YOU OKAY, HARL? YOU LOOK...DIFFERENT.
Hit em with the Hein
DON'T THE NOBLE TAXES OF THE AMERICAN PEOPLE COVER OUR PRISON ELECTRICITY BILLS?
HEY, GUYS! THE WEIRDEST THING JUST HAPPENED TO ME. I THINK I JUST SAW...
WTF?!
FZZZZZZ
AHHHH!!
THERE'S THE ELECTRICITY BILL.
THE INMATE-DESIGNATED HACK IS TO BE INTERROGATED PER HARCOURT'S ORDERS.
ATTEMPT TO INTERVENE AND WE ARE AUTHORIZED TO BLOW YOUR BRAIN BOMBS.
YEAH...
WE'LL TRY AND RESTRAIN OUR HEROIC TENDENCIES.
HMM...

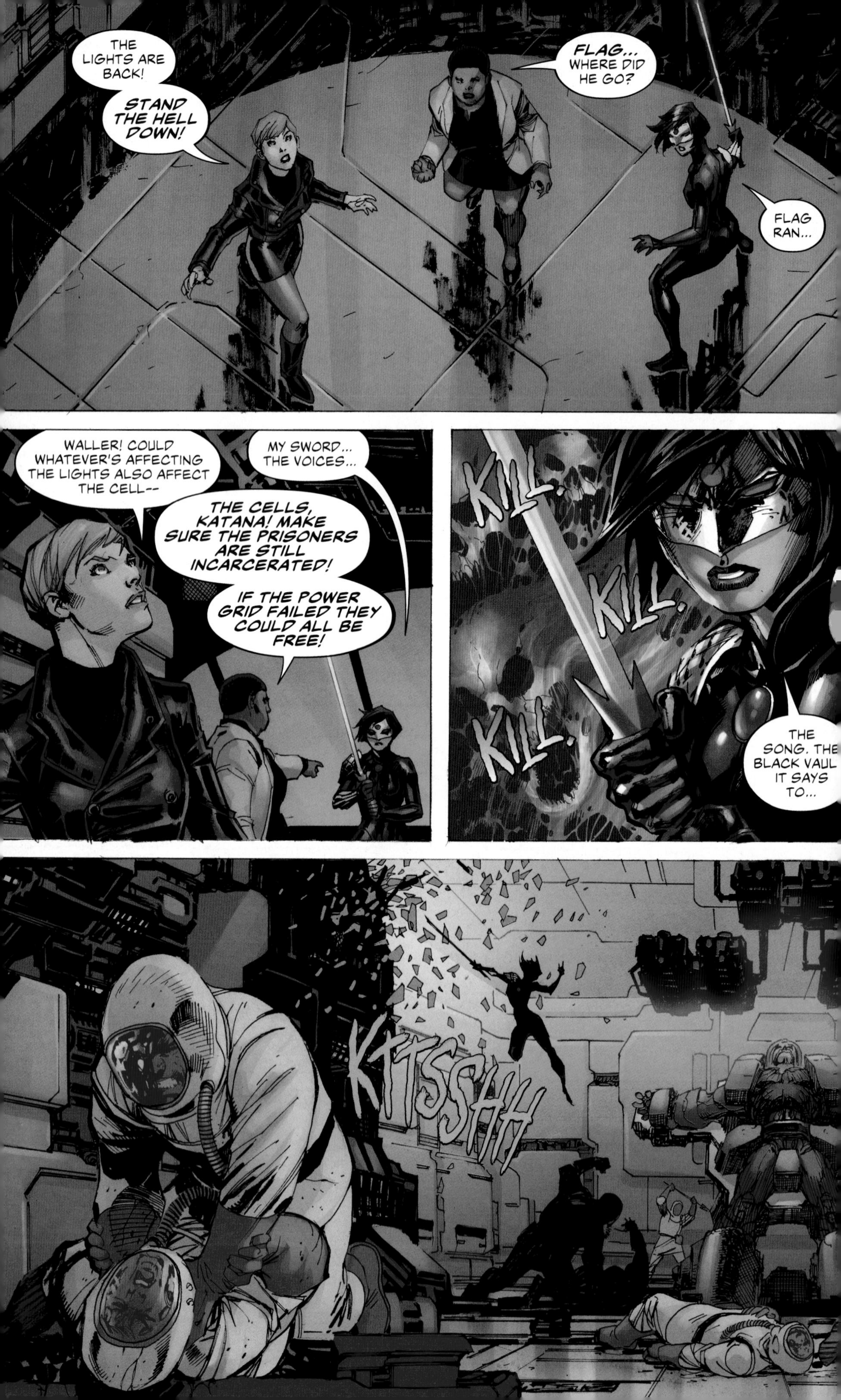
THE LIGHTS ARE BACK!
STAND THE HELL DOWN!
FLAG... WHERE DID HE GO?
FLAG RAN...
WALLER! COULD WHATEVER'S AFFECTING THE LIGHTS ALSO AFFECT THE CELL--
MY SWORD... THE VOICES...
THE CELLS, KATANA! MAKE SURE THE PRISONERS ARE STILL INCARCERATED!
IF THE POWER GRID FAILED THEY COULD ALL BE FREE!
KILL.
KILL.
KILL.
THE SONG. THE BLACK VAUL IT SAYS TO...
KTTSSHH

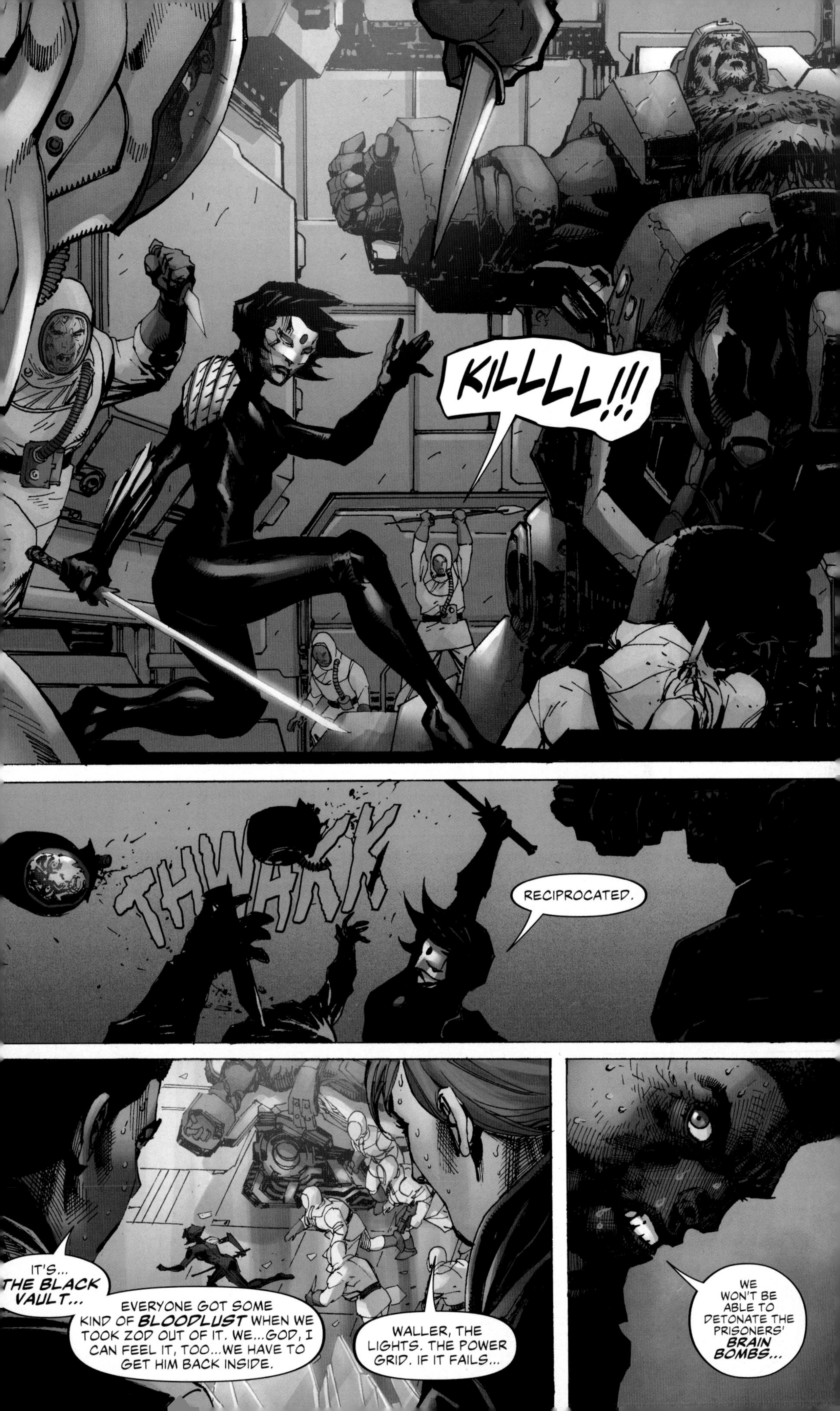

KILLLL!!!
THWAKK
RECIPROCATED.
IT'S... THE BLACK VAULT...
EVERYONE GOT SOME KIND OF BLOODLUST WHEN WE TOOK ZOD OUT OF IT. WE...GOD, I CAN FEEL IT, TOO...WE HAVE TO GET HIM BACK INSIDE.
WALLER, THE LIGHTS. THE POWER GRID. IF IT FAILS...
WE WON'T BE ABLE TO DETONATE THE PRISONERS' BRAIN BOMBS...

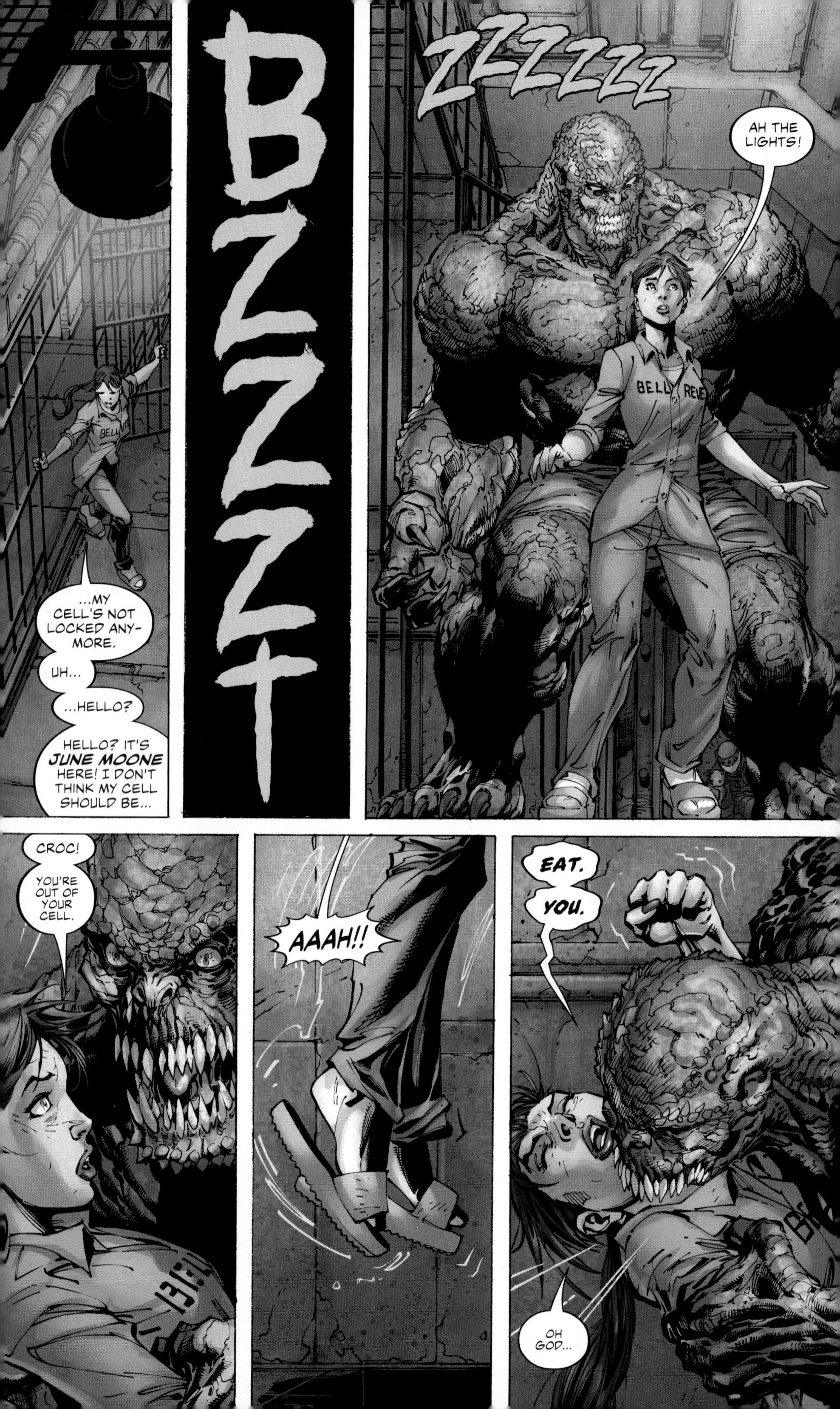

...MY CELL'S NOT LOCKED ANY-MORE.
UH...
...HELLO?
HELLO? IT'S ***JUNE MOONE*** HERE! I DON'T THINK MY CELL SHOULD BE...
BZZZZt
ZZZZZZZ
AH THE LIGHTS!
BELLE REVE
CROC!
YOU'RE OUT OF YOUR CELL.
AAAH!!
EAT.
YOU.
OH GOD...

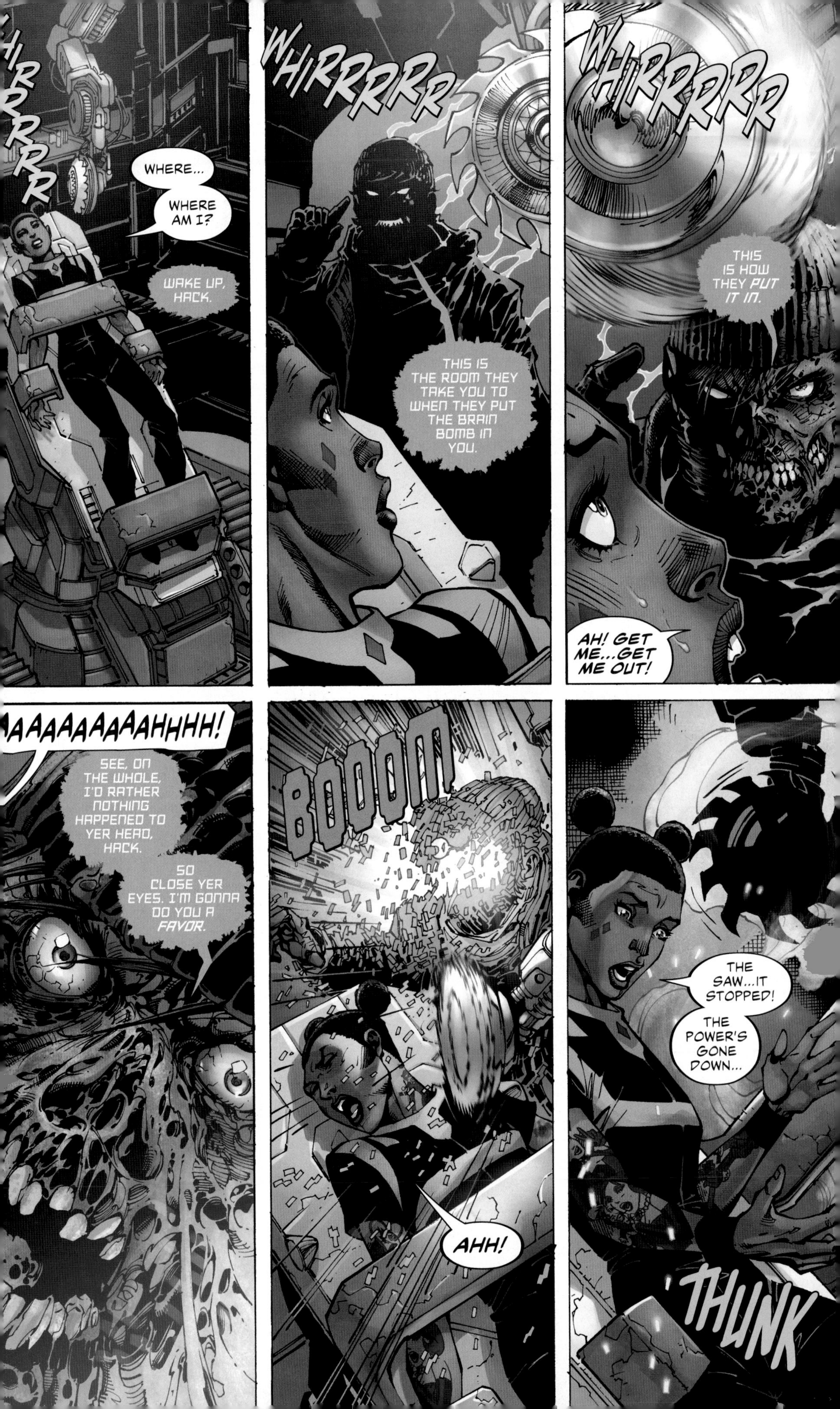
WHIRRRRR
WHERE...
WHERE AM I?
WAKE UP, HACK.
WHIRRRRRR
THIS IS THE ROOM THEY TAKE YOU TO WHEN THEY PUT THE BRAIN BOMB IN YOU.
WHIRRRRRR
THIS IS HOW THEY *PUT* *IT* *IN*.
AH! GET ME...GET ME OUT!
AAAAAAAAAAHHHH!
SEE, ON THE WHOLE, I'D RATHER NOTHING HAPPENED TO YER HEAD, HACK.
SO CLOSE YER EYES. I'M GONNA DO YOU A *FAVOR*.
BOOOM
AHH!
THE SAW...IT STOPPED!
THE POWER'S GONE DOWN...
THUNK

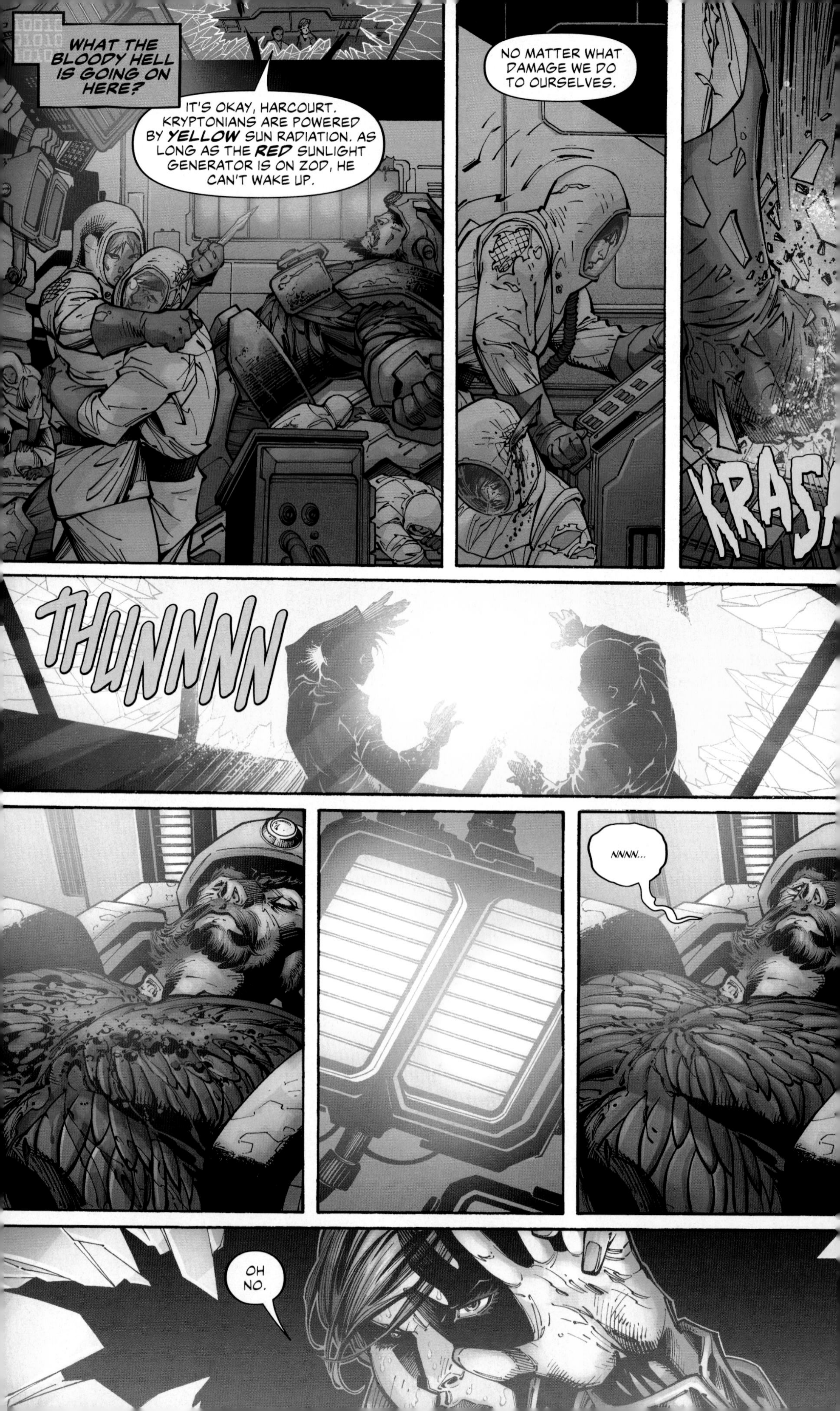
WHAT THE BLOODY HELL IS GOING ON HERE?
IT'S OKAY, HARCOURT. KRYPTONIANS ARE POWERED BY YELLOW SUN RADIATION. AS LONG AS THE RED SUNLIGHT GENERATOR IS ON ZOD, HE CAN'T WAKE UP.
NO MATTER WHAT DAMAGE WE DO TO OURSELVES.
KRAS
THUNNNNN
NNNN...
OH NO.

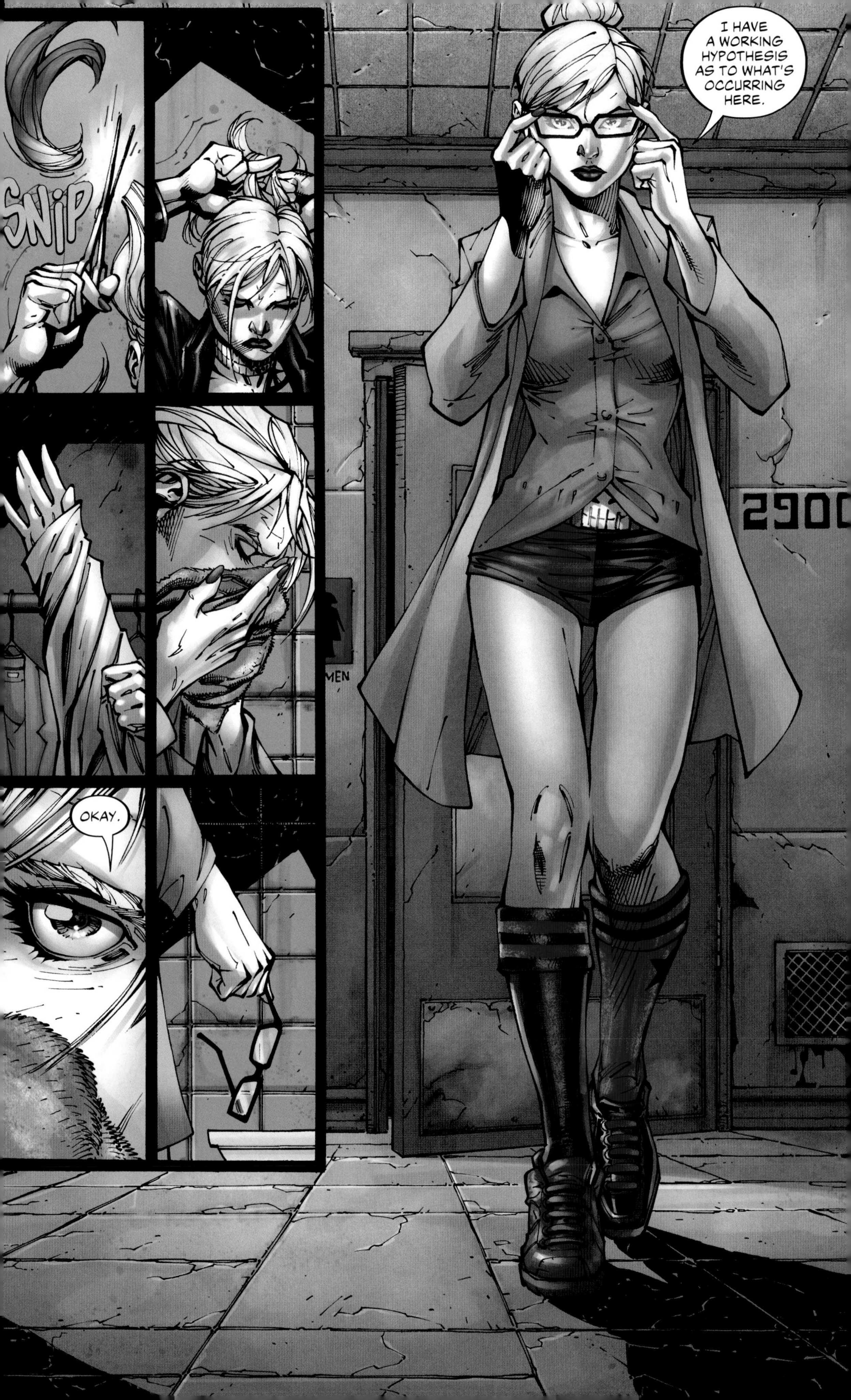
SNIP
OKAY.
I HAVE A WORKING HYPOTHESIS AS TO WHAT'S OCCURRING HERE.
2900
MEN

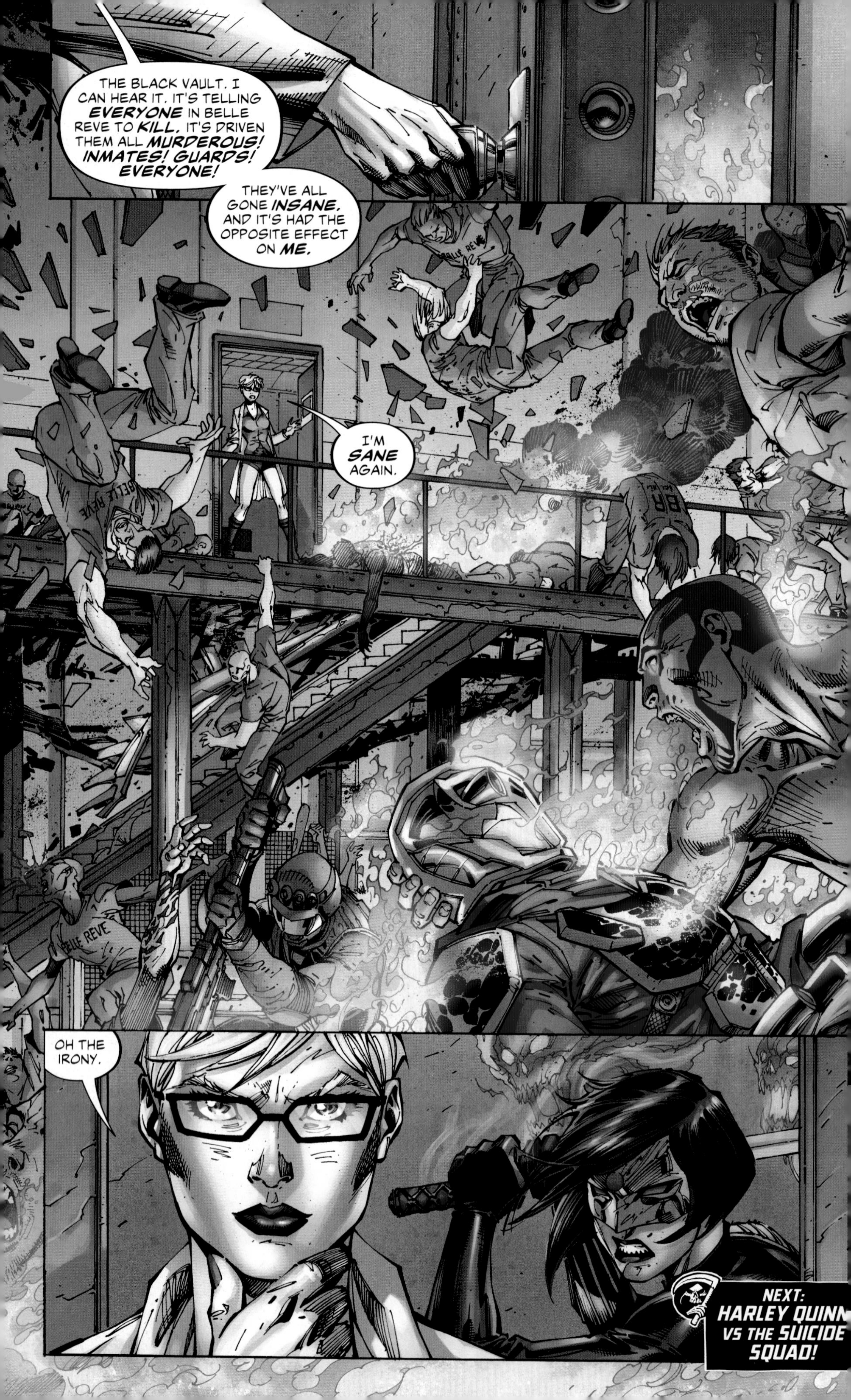

THE BLACK VAULT. I CAN HEAR IT. IT'S TELLING EVERYONE IN BELLE REVE TO KILL. IT'S DRIVEN THEM ALL MURDEROUS! INMATES! GUARDS! EVERYONE!
THEY'VE ALL GONE INSANE. AND IT'S HAD THE OPPOSITE EFFECT ON ME.
I'M SANE AGAIN.
BELLE REVE
BELLE REVE
OH THE IRONY.
NEXT: HARLEY QUINN VS THE SUICIDE SQUAD!

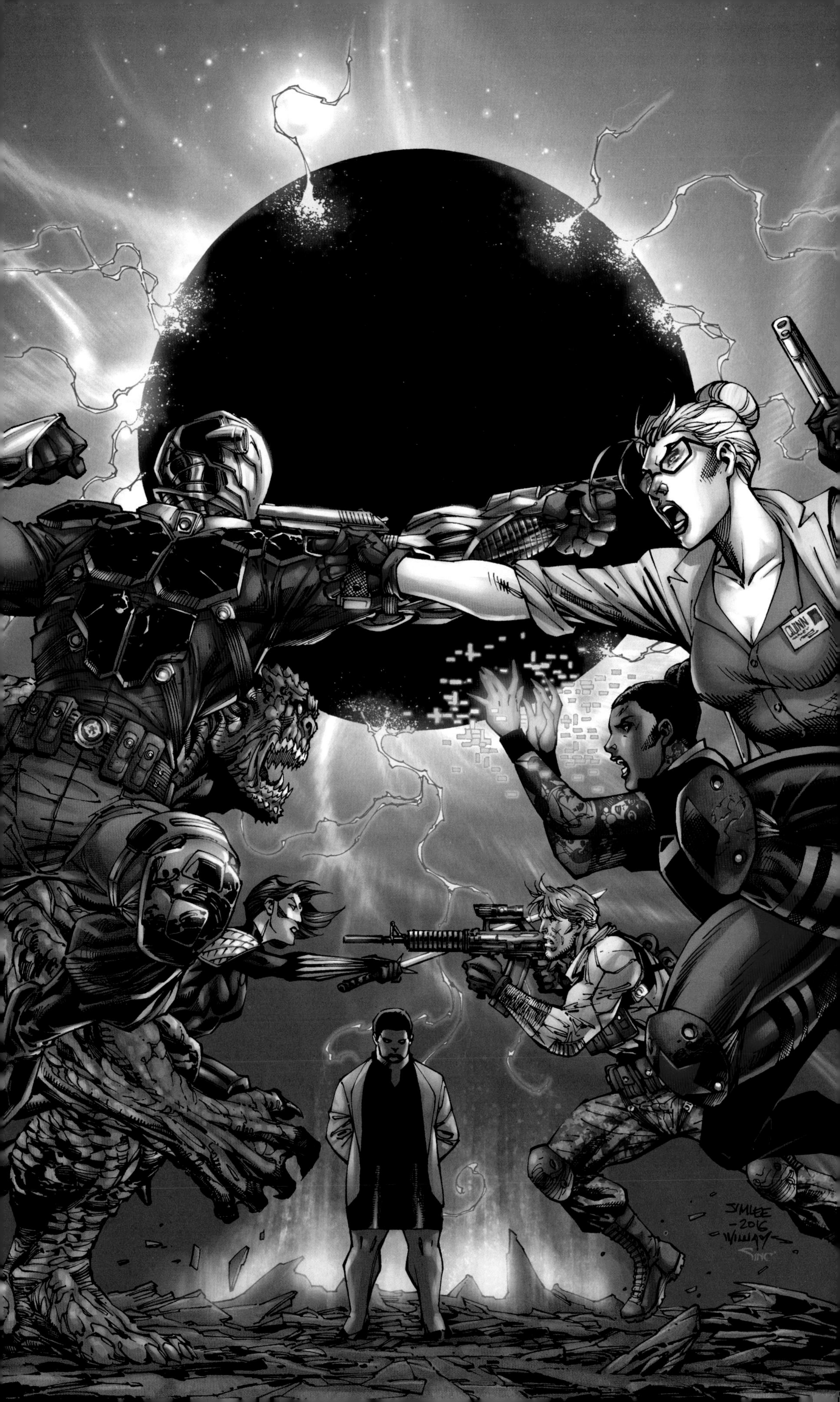
QUINN

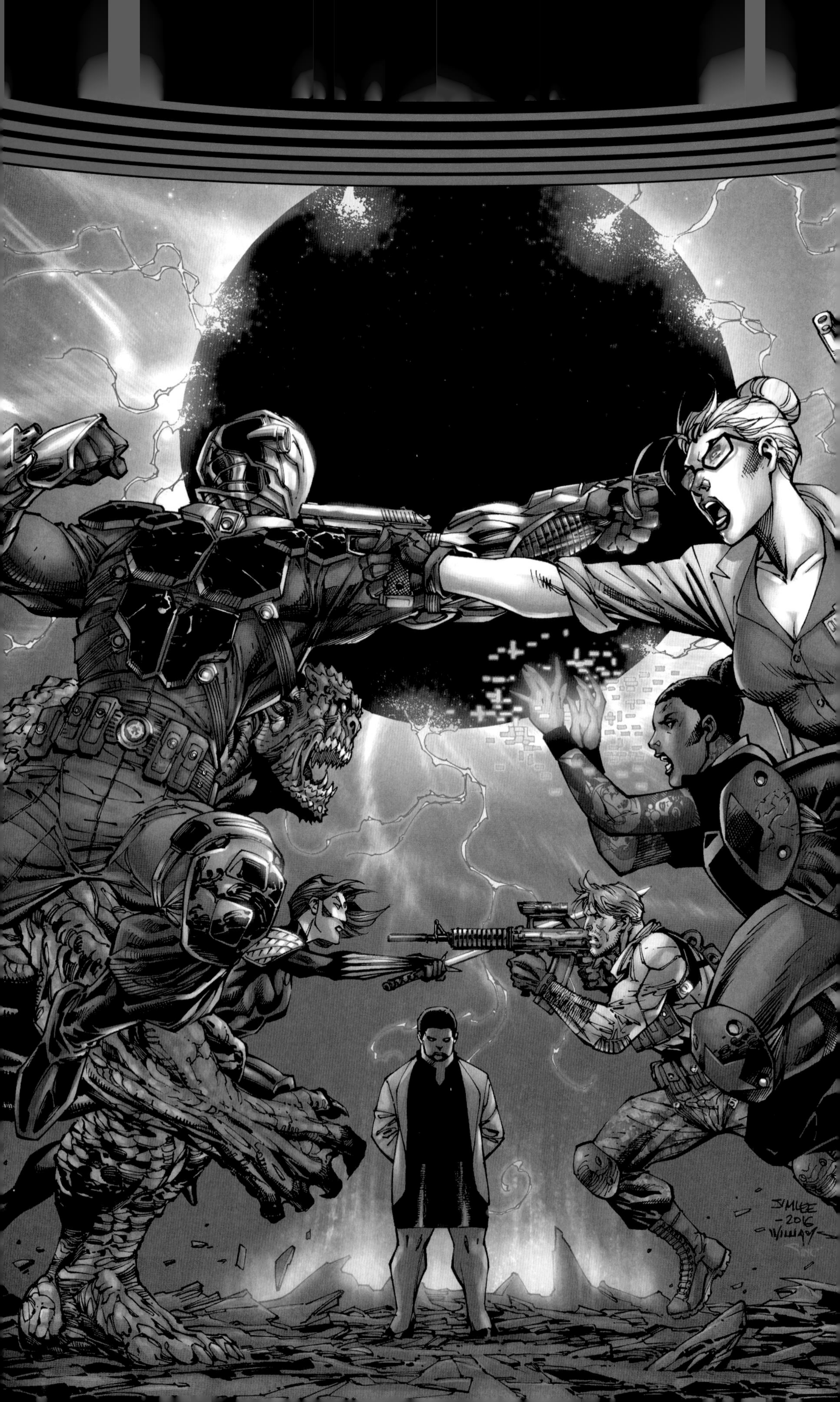

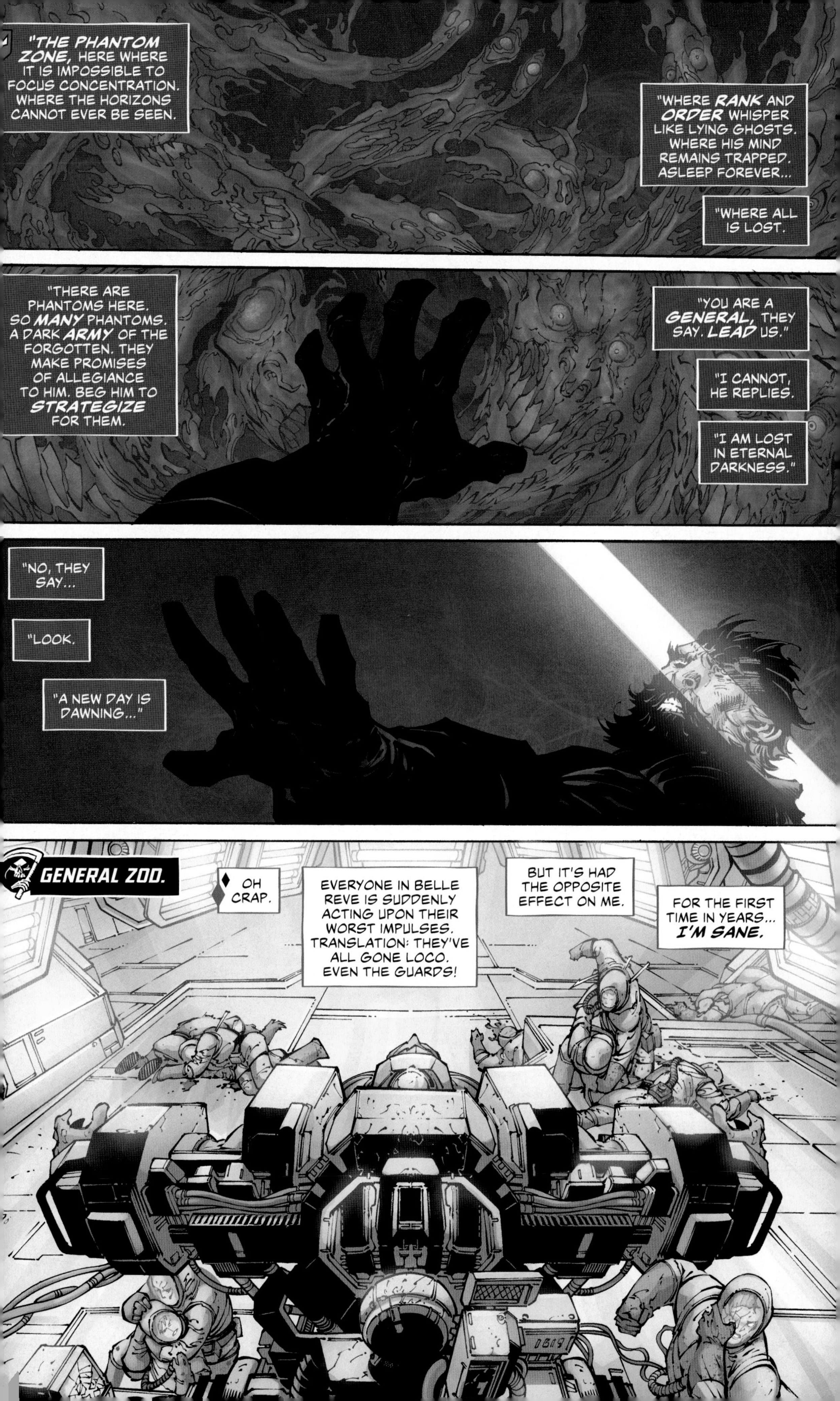
"THE PHANTOM ZONE, HERE WHERE IT IS IMPOSSIBLE TO FOCUS CONCENTRATION. WHERE THE HORIZONS CANNOT EVER BE SEEN.
"WHERE RANK AND ORDER WHISPER LIKE LYING GHOSTS. WHERE HIS MIND REMAINS TRAPPED. ASLEEP FOREVER...
"WHERE ALL IS LOST.
"THERE ARE PHANTOMS HERE. SO MANY PHANTOMS. A DARK ARMY OF THE FORGOTTEN. THEY MAKE PROMISES OF ALLEGIANCE TO HIM. BEG HIM TO STRATEGIZE FOR THEM.
"YOU ARE A GENERAL, THEY SAY. LEAD US."
"I CANNOT, HE REPLIES.
"I AM LOST IN ETERNAL DARKNESS."
"NO, THEY SAY...
"LOOK.
"A NEW DAY IS DAWNING..."
GENERAL ZOD.
OH CRAP.
EVERYONE IN BELLE REVE IS SUDDENLY ACTING UPON THEIR WORST IMPULSES. TRANSLATION: THEY'VE ALL GONE LOCO. EVEN THE GUARDS!
BUT IT'S HAD THE OPPOSITE EFFECT ON ME.
FOR THE FIRST TIME IN YEARS... I'M SANE.

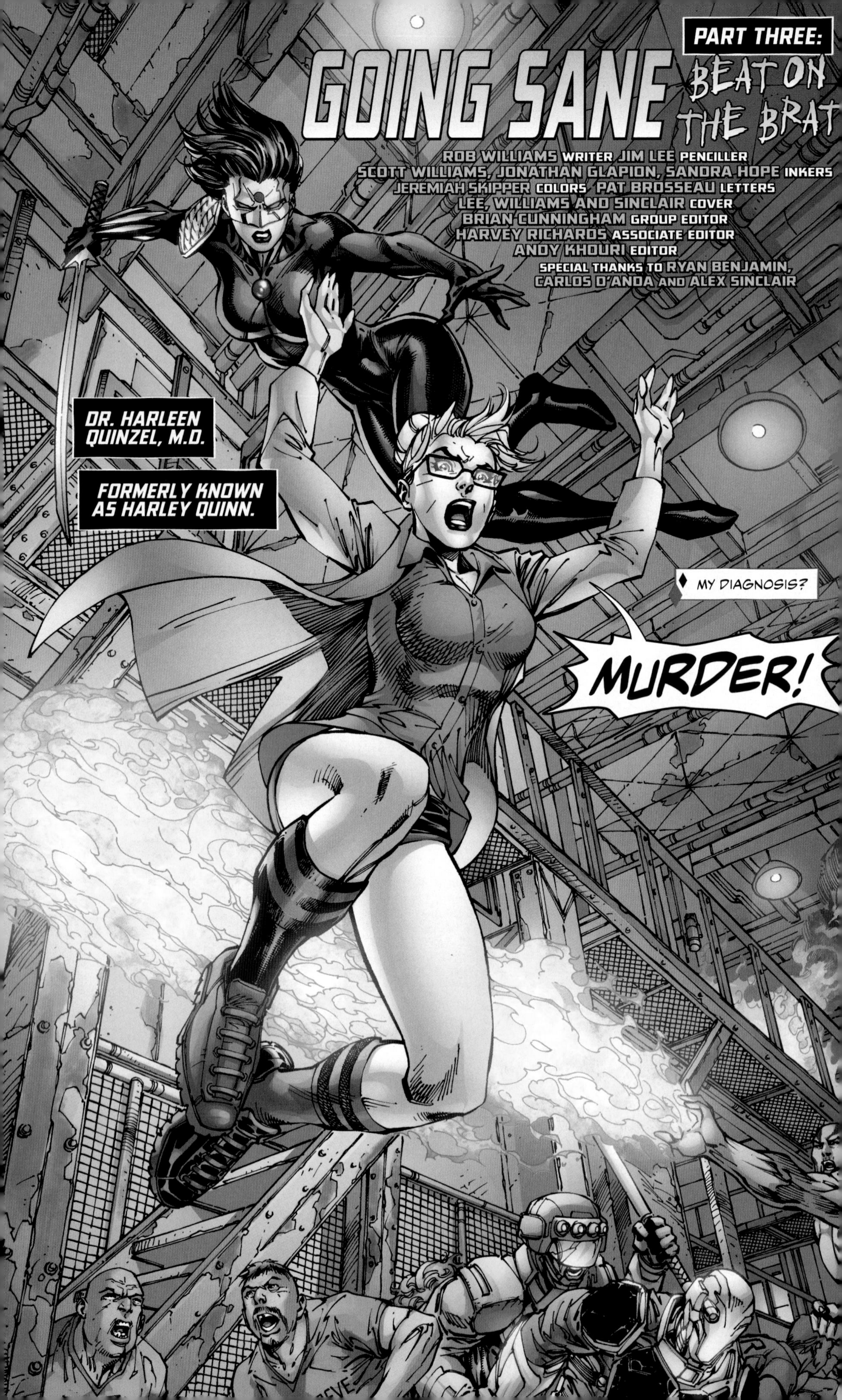

PART THREE:
GOING SANE
BEAT ON THE BRAT
ROB WILLIAMS WRITER JIM LEE PENCILLER
SCOTT WILLIAMS, JONATHAN GLAPION, SANDRA HOPE INKERS
JEREMIAH SKIPPER COLORS PAT BROSSEAU LETTERS
LEE, WILLIAMS AND SINCLAIR COVER
BRIAN CUNNINGHAM GROUP EDITOR
HARVEY RICHARDS ASSOCIATE EDITOR
ANDY KHOURI EDITOR
SPECIAL THANKS TO RYAN BENJAMIN, CARLOS D'ANDA AND ALEX SINCLAIR
DR. HARLEEN QUINZEL, M.D.
FORMERLY KNOWN AS HARLEY QUINN.
MY DIAGNOSIS?
MURDER!

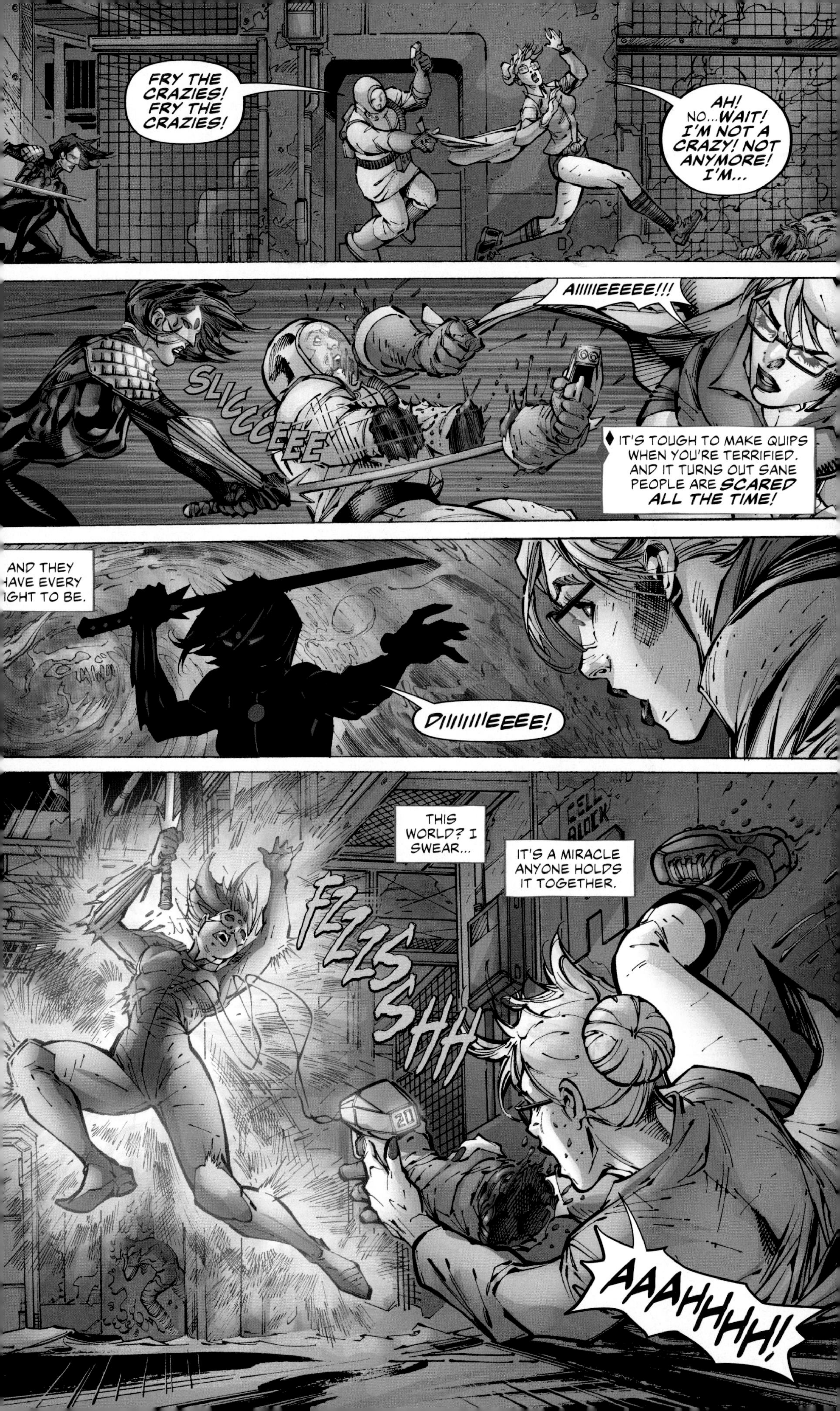
FRY THE CRAZIES! FRY THE CRAZIES!
AH! NO...WAIT! I'M NOT A CRAZY! NOT ANYMORE! I'M...
AIIIIEEEEE!!!
SLICCCEEE
IT'S TOUGH TO MAKE QUIPS WHEN YOU'RE TERRIFIED. AND IT TURNS OUT SANE PEOPLE ARE SCARED ALL THE TIME!
AND THEY HAVE EVERY RIGHT TO BE.
DIIIIIIEEEE!
CELL BLOCK
THIS WORLD? I SWEAR...
IT'S A MIRACLE ANYONE HOLDS IT TOGETHER.
FZZZSSHH
AAAHHHH!

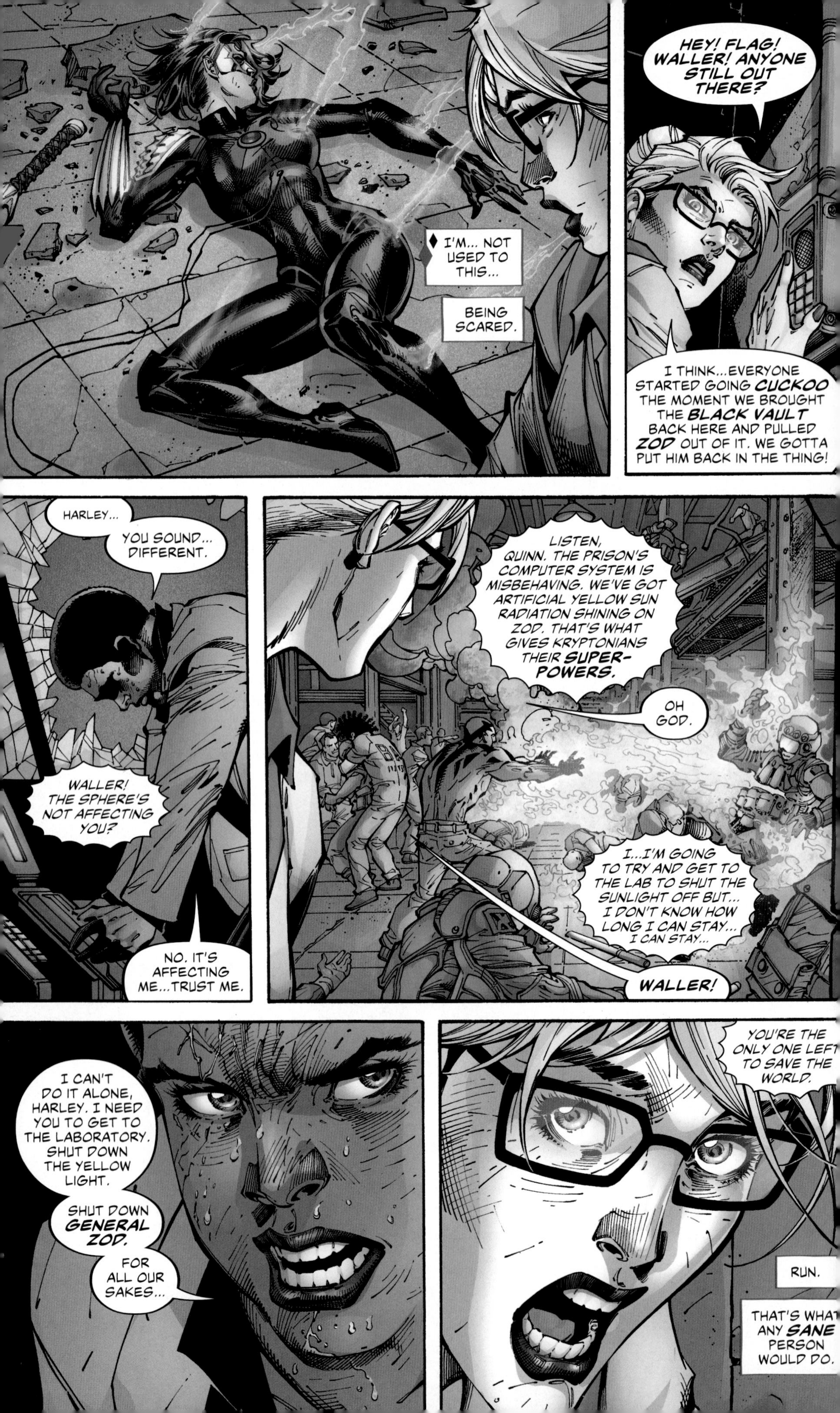
I'M... NOT USED TO THIS...
BEING SCARED.
HEY! FLAG! WALLER! ANYONE STILL OUT THERE?
I THINK...EVERYONE STARTED GOING CUCKOO THE MOMENT WE BROUGHT THE BLACK VAULT BACK HERE AND PULLED ZOD OUT OF IT. WE GOTTA PUT HIM BACK IN THE THING!
HARLEY...
YOU SOUND... DIFFERENT.
WALLER! THE SPHERE'S NOT AFFECTING YOU?
NO. IT'S AFFECTING ME...TRUST ME.
LISTEN, QUINN. THE PRISON'S COMPUTER SYSTEM IS MISBEHAVING. WE'VE GOT ARTIFICIAL YELLOW SUN RADIATION SHINING ON ZOD. THAT'S WHAT GIVES KRYPTONIANS THEIR SUPER-POWERS.
OH GOD.
I...I'M GOING TO TRY AND GET TO THE LAB TO SHUT THE SUNLIGHT OFF BUT... I DON'T KNOW HOW LONG I CAN STAY... I CAN STAY...
WALLER!
I CAN'T DO IT ALONE, HARLEY. I NEED YOU TO GET TO THE LABORATORY. SHUT DOWN THE YELLOW LIGHT.
SHUT DOWN GENERAL ZOD.
FOR ALL OUR SAKES...
YOU'RE THE ONLY ONE LEFT TO SAVE THE WORLD.
RUN.
THAT'S WHAT ANY SANE PERSON WOULD DO.

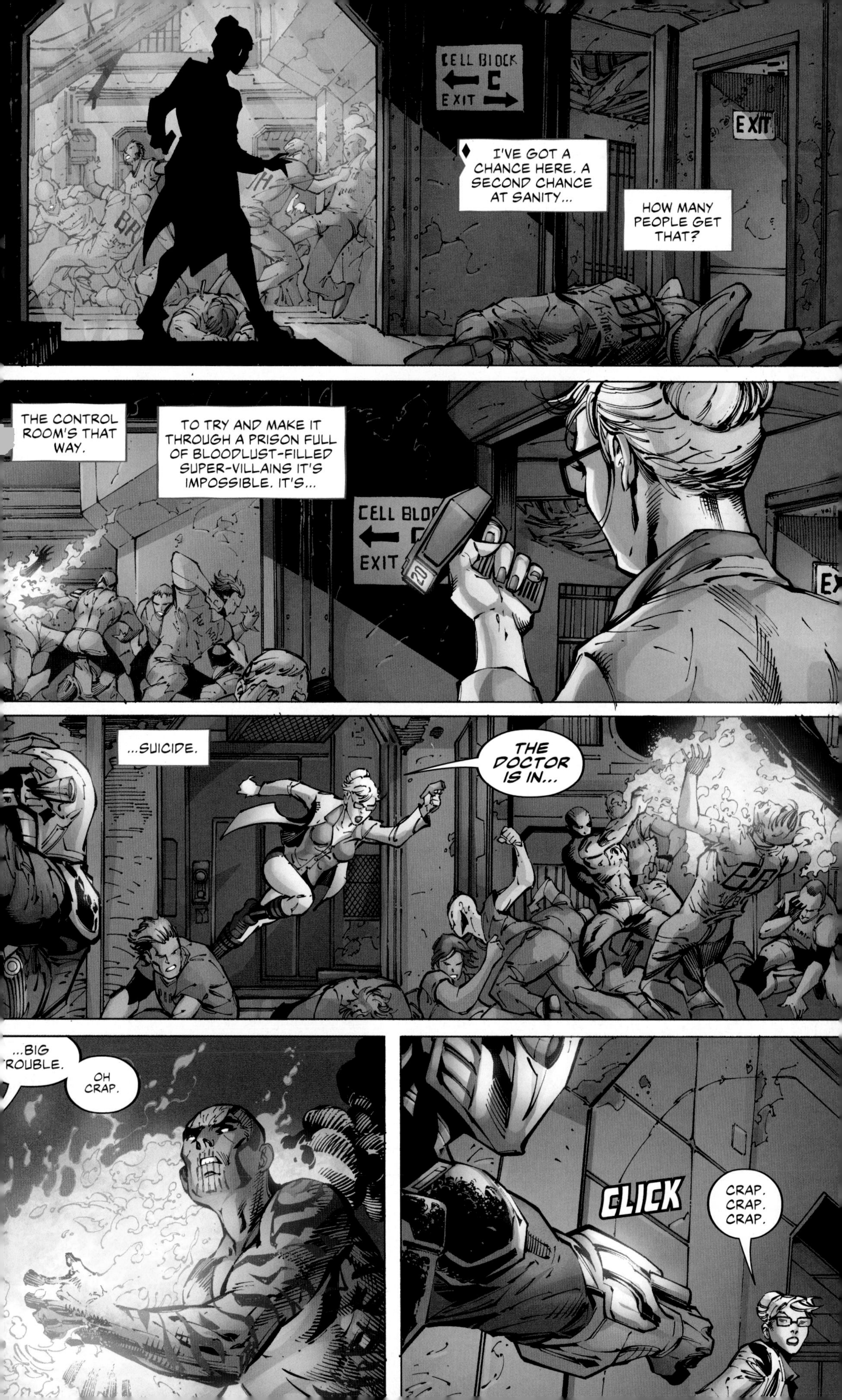
CELL BLOCK C
EXIT
EXIT
I'VE GOT A CHANCE HERE. A SECOND CHANCE AT SANITY...
HOW MANY PEOPLE GET THAT?
THE CONTROL ROOM'S THAT WAY.
TO TRY AND MAKE IT THROUGH A PRISON FULL OF BLOODLUST-FILLED SUPER-VILLAINS IT'S IMPOSSIBLE. IT'S...
CELL BLOC
EXIT
...SUICIDE.
THE DOCTOR IS IN...
...BIG ROUBLE.
OH CRAP.
CLICK
CRAP. CRAP. CRAP.

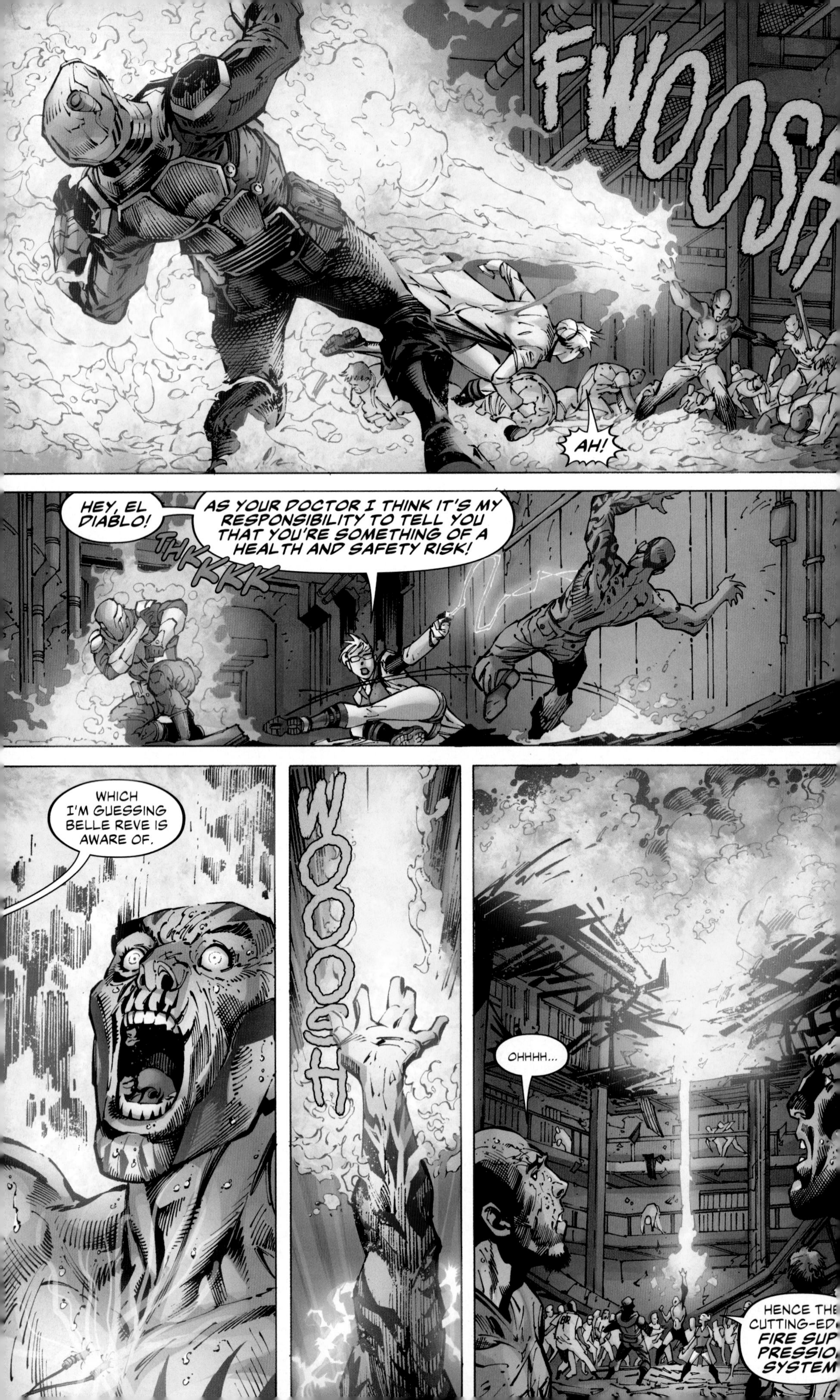

FWOOSH
AH!
HEY, EL DIABLO!
AS YOUR DOCTOR I THINK IT'S MY RESPONSIBILITY TO TELL YOU THAT YOU'RE SOMETHING OF A HEALTH AND SAFETY RISK!
THKKKK
WHICH I'M GUESSING BELLE REVE IS AWARE OF.
WOOOOSH
OHHHH...
HENCE THE CUTTING-ED FIRE SUP PRESSIO SYSTEM

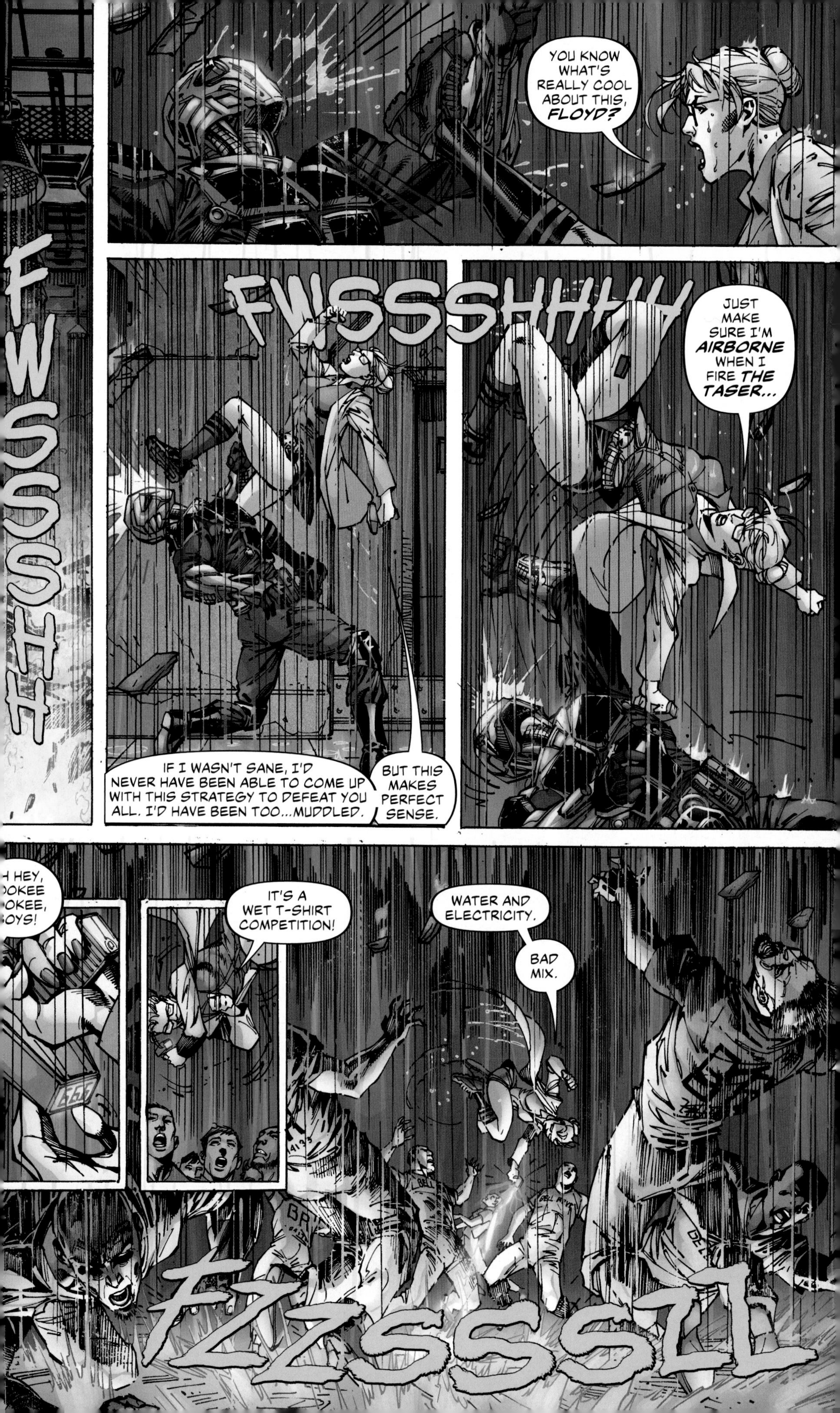
YOU KNOW WHAT'S REALLY COOL ABOUT THIS, FLOYD?
FWSSHH
FWSSSHHHH
IF I WASN'T SANE, I'D NEVER HAVE BEEN ABLE TO COME UP WITH THIS STRATEGY TO DEFEAT YOU ALL. I'D HAVE BEEN TOO...MUDDLED.
BUT THIS MAKES PERFECT SENSE.
JUST MAKE SURE I'M AIRBORNE WHEN I FIRE THE TASER...
IT'S A WET T-SHIRT COMPETITION!
WATER AND ELECTRICITY.
BAD MIX.
FZZSSSZZ

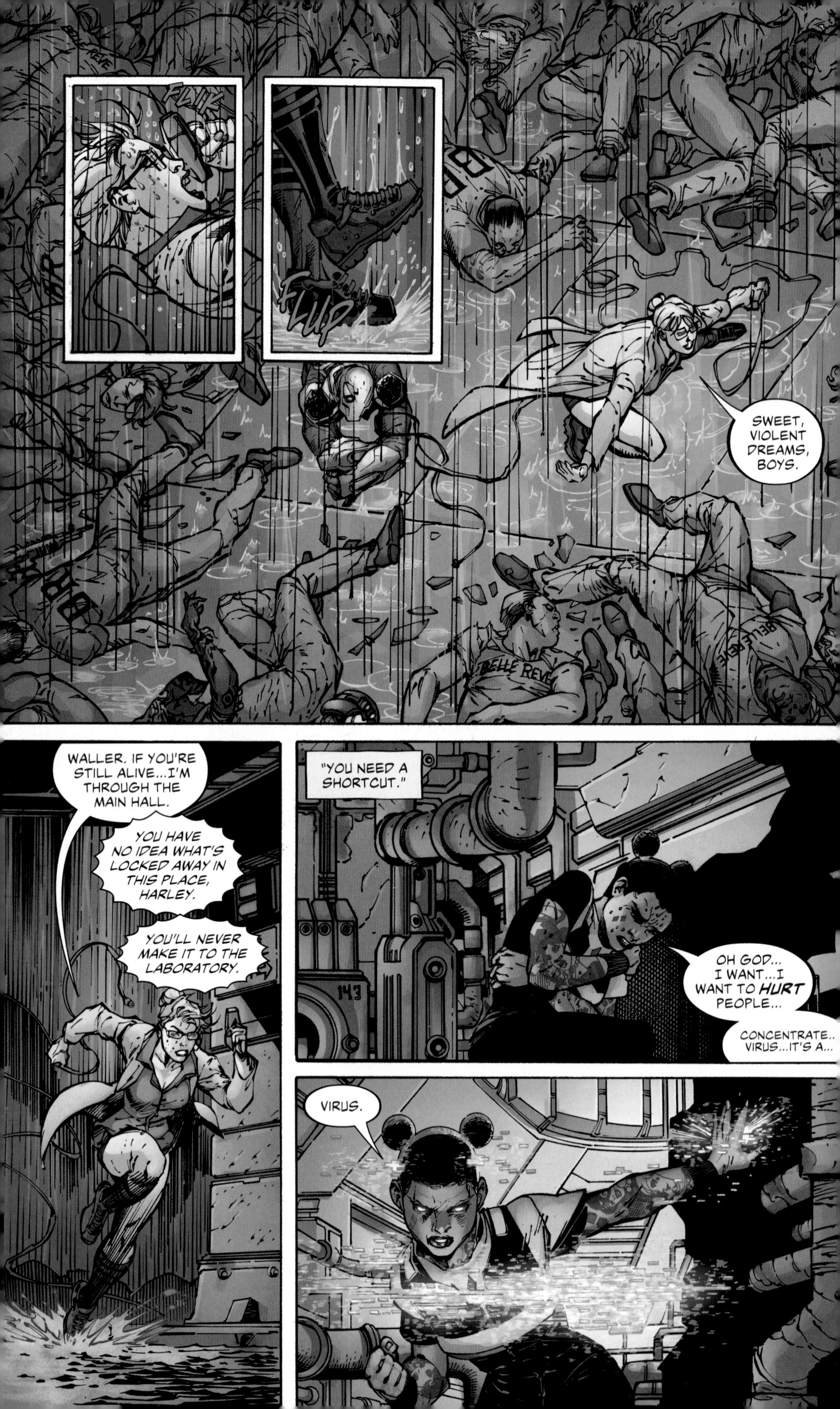
FLIK
FLUP
SWEET, VIOLENT DREAMS, BOYS.
BELLE REVE
WALLER. IF YOU'RE STILL ALIVE...I'M THROUGH THE MAIN HALL.
YOU HAVE NO IDEA WHAT'S LOCKED AWAY IN THIS PLACE, HARLEY.
YOU'LL NEVER MAKE IT TO THE LABORATORY.
"YOU NEED A SHORTCUT."
OH GOD... I WANT...I WANT TO HURT PEOPLE...
CONCENTRATE.. VIRUS...IT'S A...
143
VIRUS.

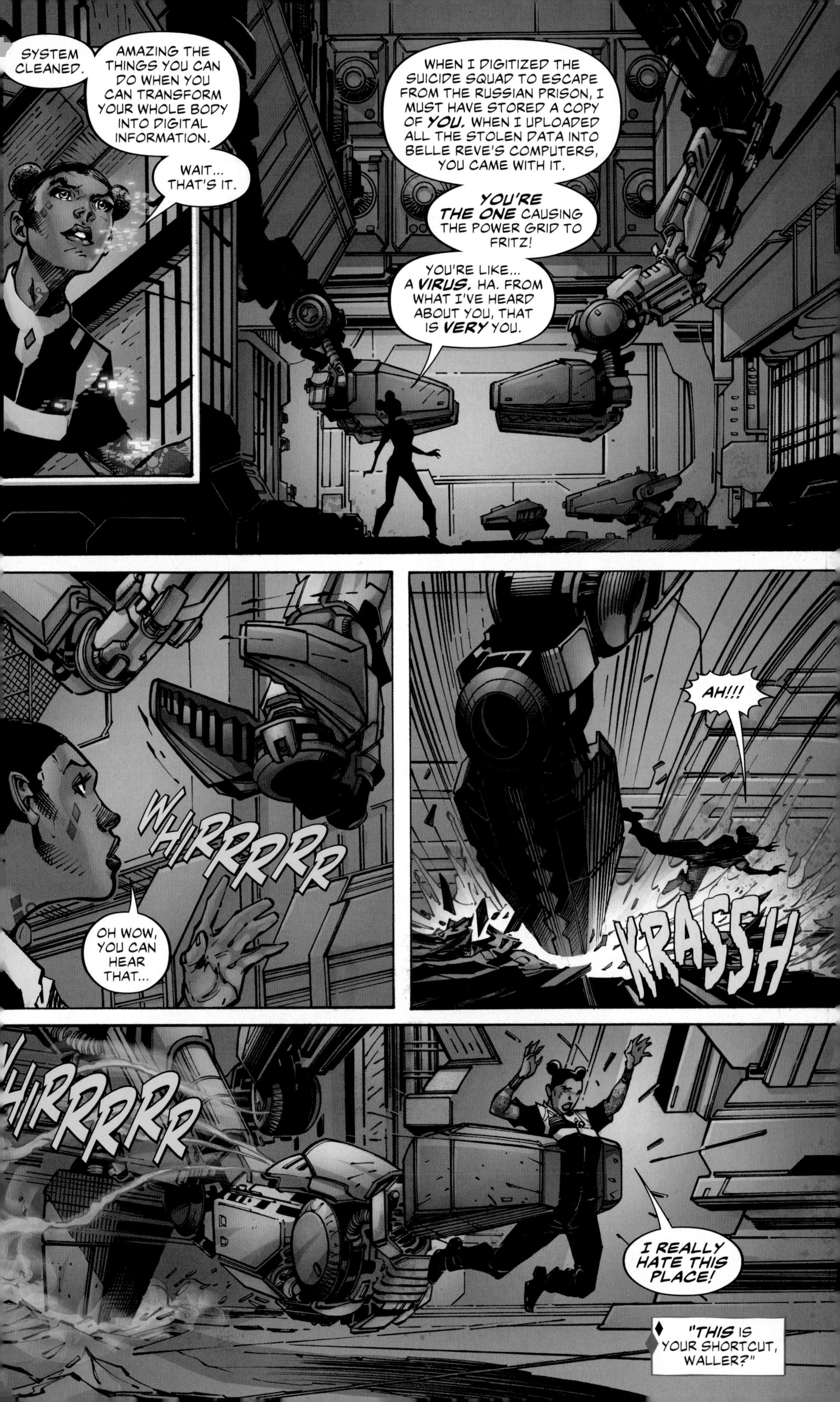
SYSTEM CLEANED.
AMAZING THE THINGS YOU CAN DO WHEN YOU CAN TRANSFORM YOUR WHOLE BODY INTO DIGITAL INFORMATION.
WAIT... THAT'S IT.
WHEN I DIGITIZED THE SUICIDE SQUAD TO ESCAPE FROM THE RUSSIAN PRISON, I MUST HAVE STORED A COPY OF YOU. WHEN I UPLOADED ALL THE STOLEN DATA INTO BELLE REVE'S COMPUTERS, YOU CAME WITH IT.
YOU'RE THE ONE CAUSING THE POWER GRID TO FRITZ!
YOU'RE LIKE... A VIRUS. HA. FROM WHAT I'VE HEARD ABOUT YOU, THAT IS VERY YOU.
WHIRRRRRR
OH WOW, YOU CAN HEAR THAT...
AH!!!
KRASSH
HIRRRRRR
I REALLY HATE THIS PLACE!
"THIS IS YOUR SHORTCUT, WALLER?"

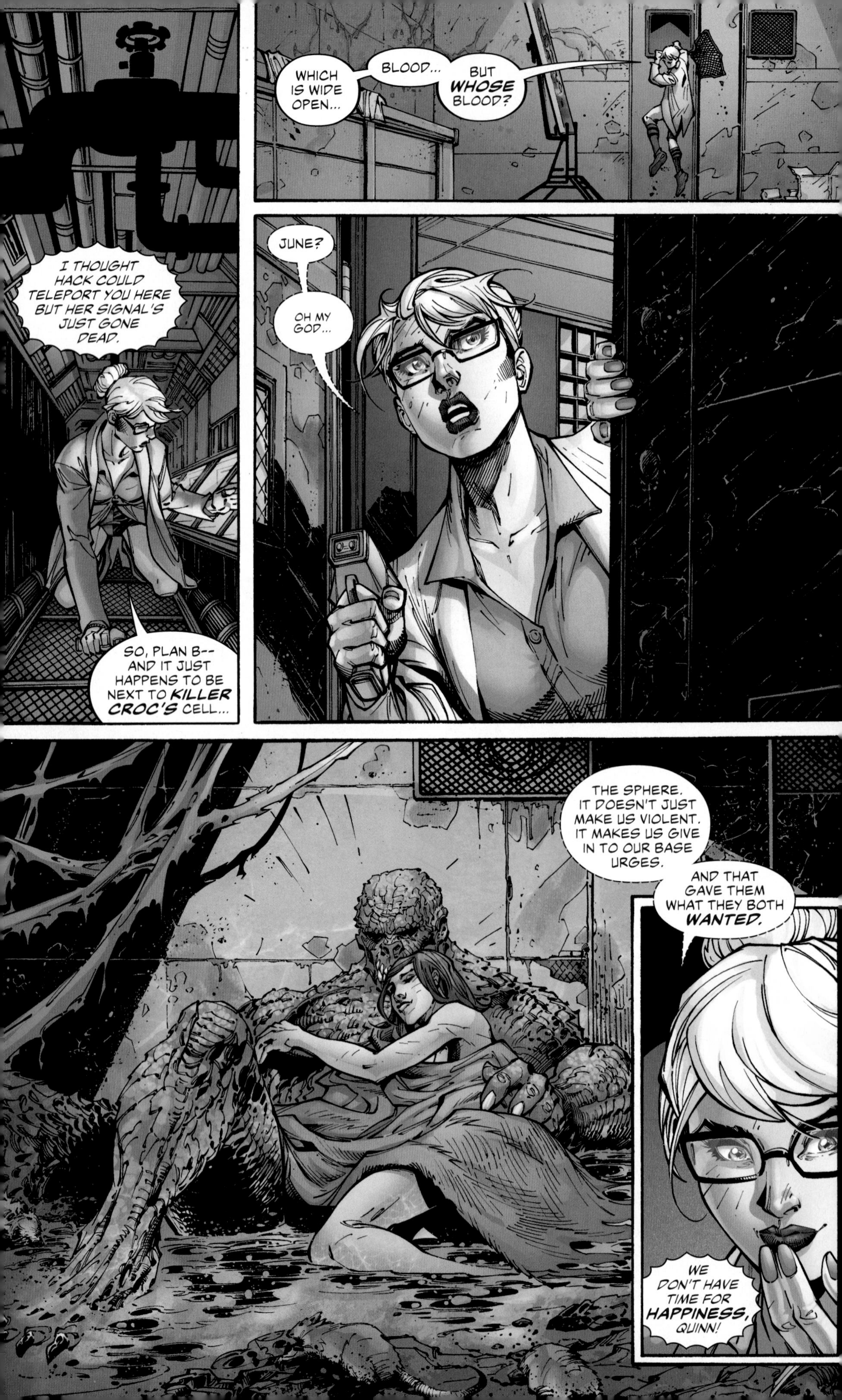

WHICH IS WIDE OPEN...
BLOOD... BUT WHOSE BLOOD?
I THOUGHT HACK COULD TELEPORT YOU HERE BUT HER SIGNAL'S JUST GONE DEAD.
SO, PLAN B--AND IT JUST HAPPENS TO BE NEXT TO KILLER CROC'S CELL...
JUNE?
OH MY GOD...
THE SPHERE. IT DOESN'T JUST MAKE US VIOLENT. IT MAKES US GIVE IN TO OUR BASE URGES.
AND THAT GAVE THEM WHAT THEY BOTH WANTED.
WE DON'T HAVE TIME FOR HAPPINESS, QUINN!

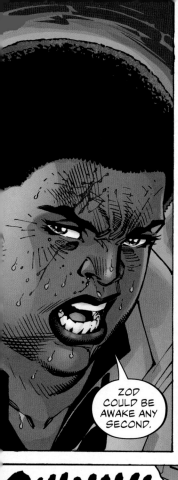

ZOD COULD BE AWAKE ANY SECOND.

THERE'S THE TRUTH...

JUNE...I'M REALLY SORRY... BUT WE DON'T HAVE MUCH TIME.

AND I'M GUESSING THIS IS THE QUICKEST WAY TO GET TO...

THE ENCHANTRESS...

AA!!EEEEE!

FZZSSHH

QUINN!!

SHE... LOVED ME...

AND YOU FRIED HER!!!!

AAKK...!

"OH...IT IS YOU..."

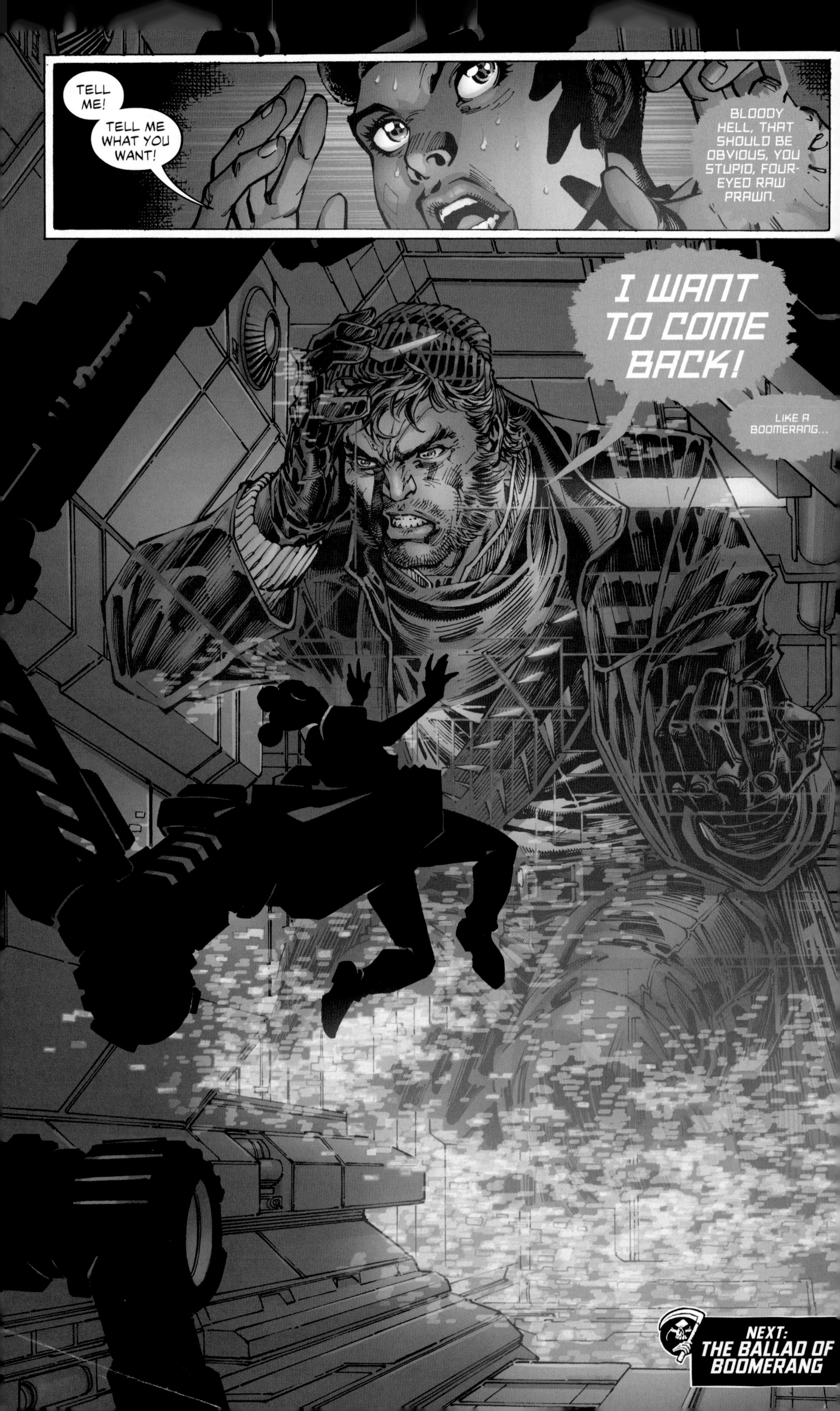
TELL ME!
TELL ME WHAT YOU WANT!
BLOODY HELL, THAT SHOULD BE OBVIOUS, YOU STUPID, FOUR-EYED RAW PRAWN.
I WANT TO COME BACK!
LIKE A BOOMERANG...
NEXT: THE BALLAD OF BOOMERANG

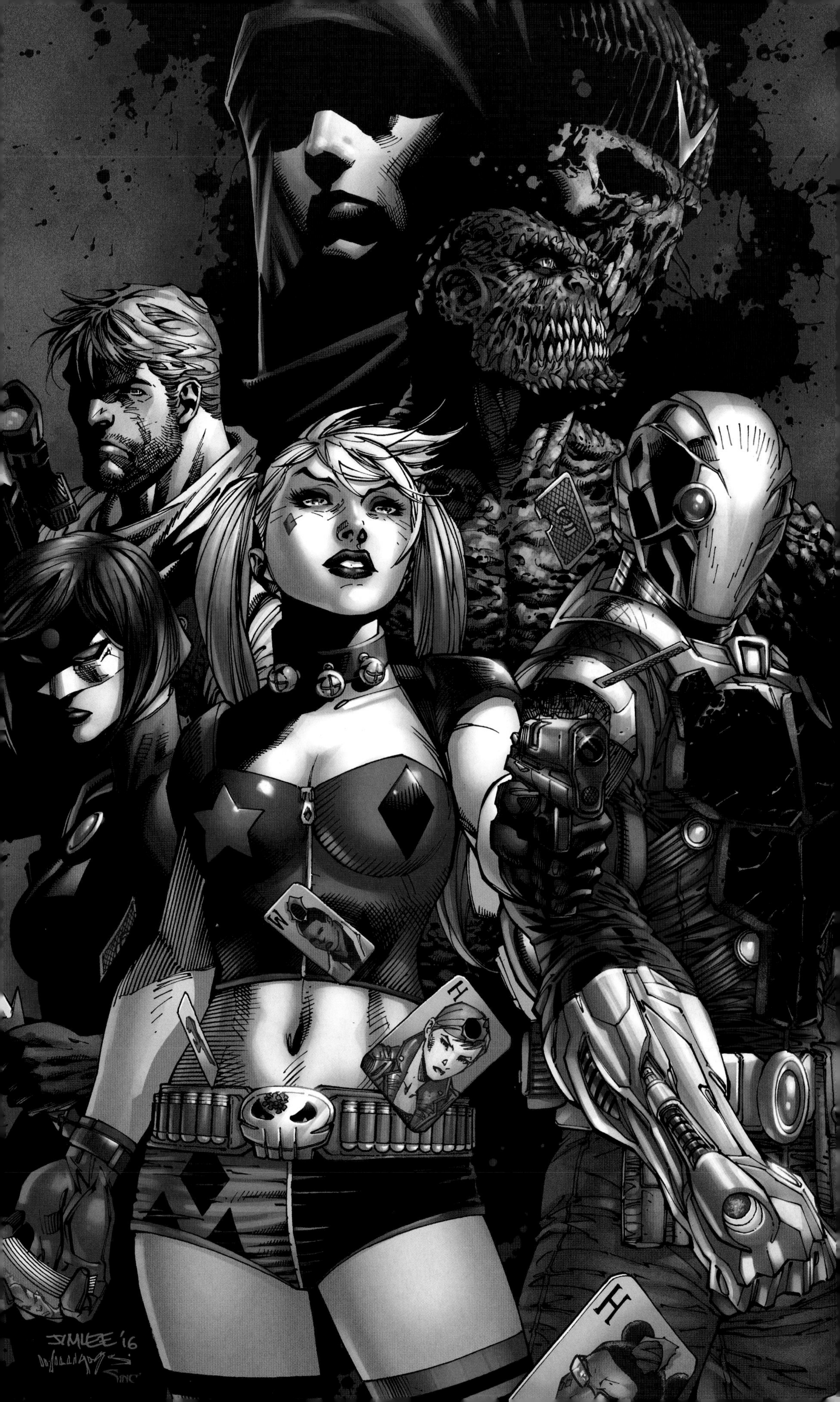

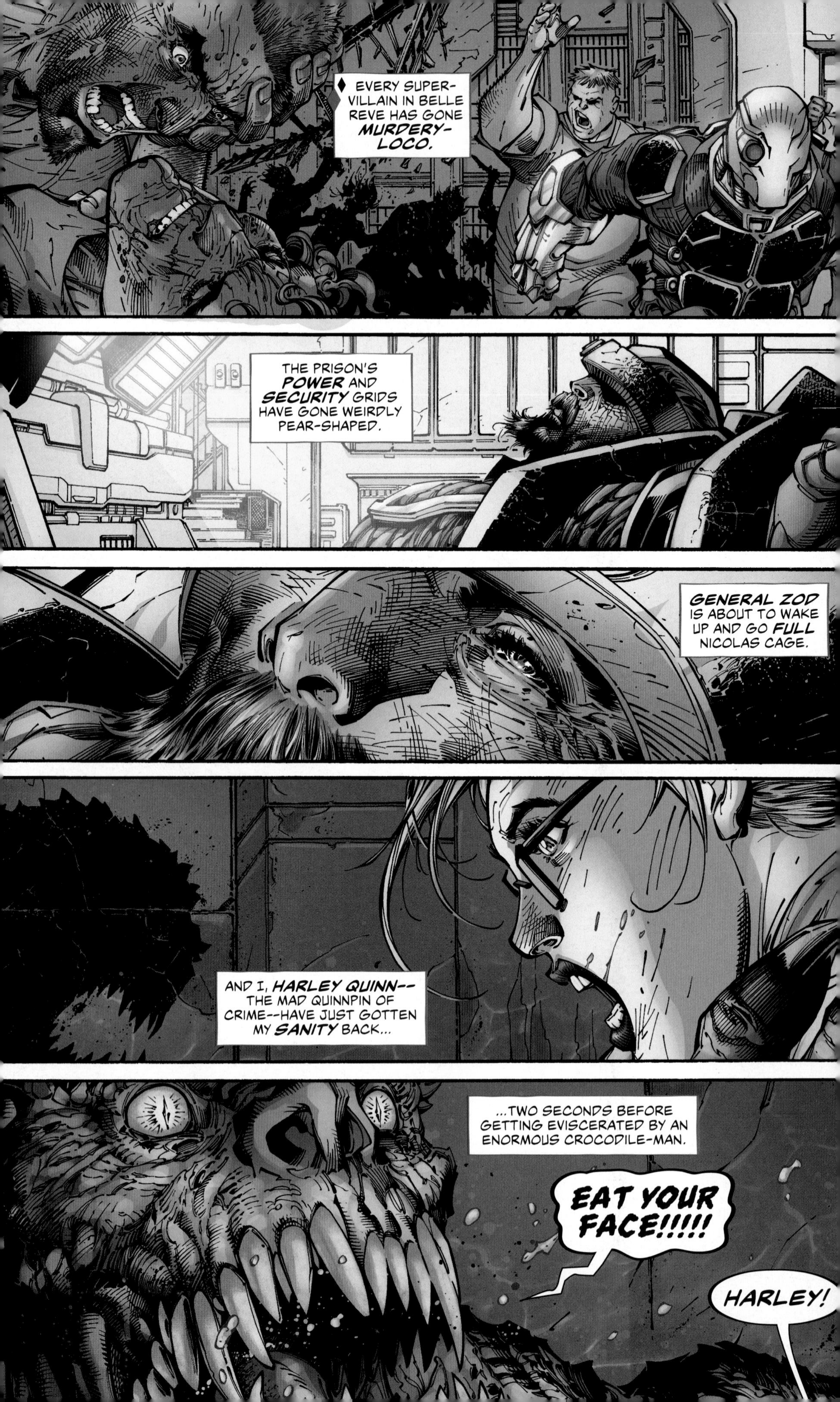
EVERY SUPER-VILLAIN IN BELLE REVE HAS GONE MURDERY-LOCO.
THE PRISON'S POWER AND SECURITY GRIDS HAVE GONE WEIRDLY PEAR-SHAPED.
GENERAL ZOD IS ABOUT TO WAKE UP AND GO FULL NICOLAS CAGE.
AND I, HARLEY QUINN--THE MAD QUINNPIN OF CRIME--HAVE JUST GOTTEN MY SANITY BACK...
...TWO SECONDS BEFORE GETTING EVISCERATED BY AN ENORMOUS CROCODILE-MAN.
EAT YOUR FACE!!!!!
HARLEY!

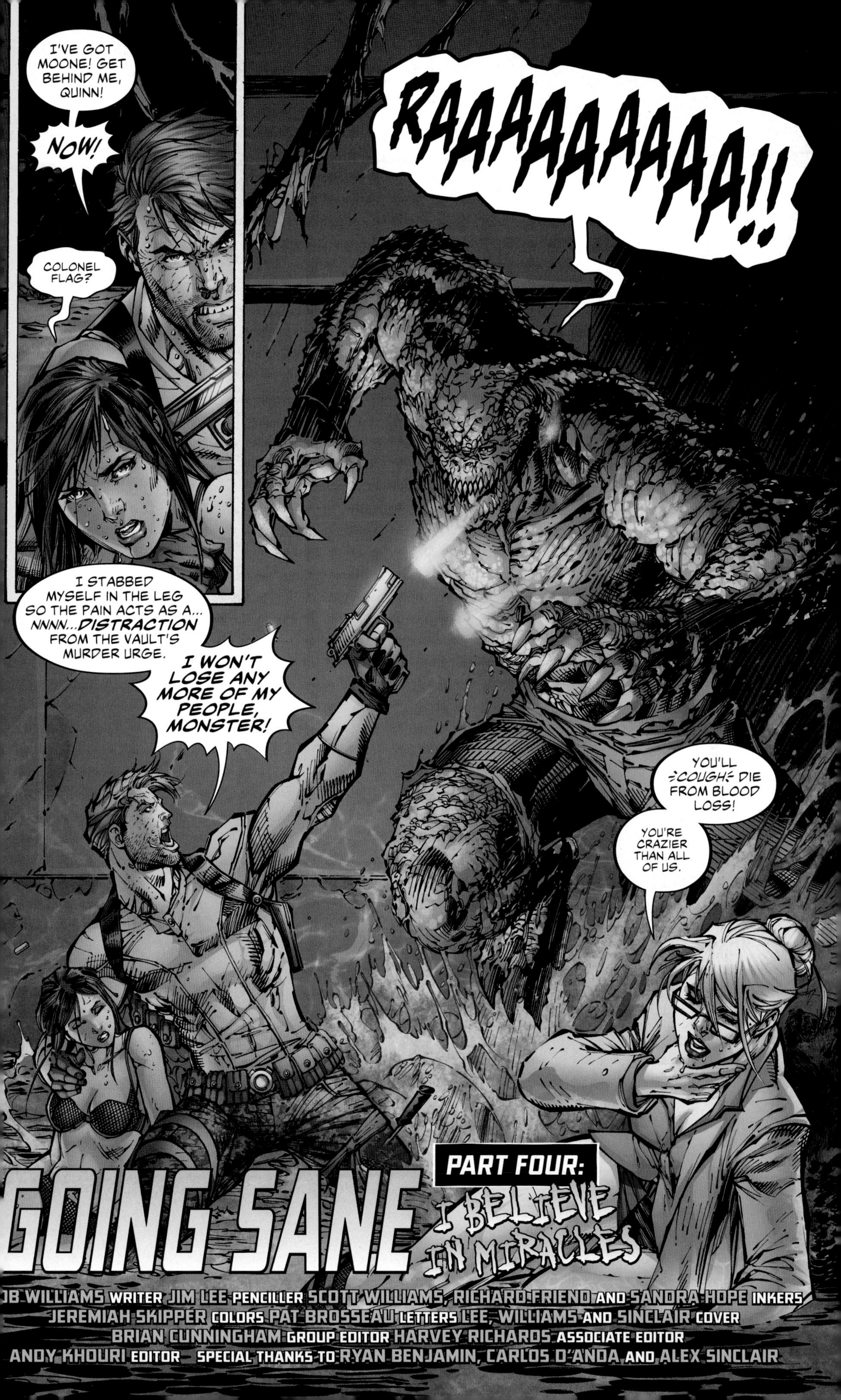
I'VE GOT MOONE! GET BEHIND ME, QUINN!
NOW!
COLONEL FLAG?
RAAAAAAAAAA!!
I STABBED MYSELF IN THE LEG SO THE PAIN ACTS AS A... NNNN...DISTRACTION FROM THE VAULT'S MURDER URGE.
I WON'T LOSE ANY MORE OF MY PEOPLE, MONSTER!
YOU'LL =COUGH= DIE FROM BLOOD LOSS!
YOU'RE CRAZIER THAN ALL OF US.
PART FOUR:
GOING SANE
I BELIEVE IN MIRACLES
OB WILLIAMS WRITER JIM LEE PENCILLER SCOTT WILLIAMS, RICHARD FRIEND AND SANDRA HOPE INKERS
JEREMIAH SKIPPER COLORS PAT BROSSEAU LETTERS LEE, WILLIAMS AND SINCLAIR COVER
BRIAN CUNNINGHAM GROUP EDITOR HARVEY RICHARDS ASSOCIATE EDITOR
ANDY KHOURI EDITOR SPECIAL THANKS TO RYAN BENJAMIN, CARLOS D'ANDA AND ALEX SINCLAIR

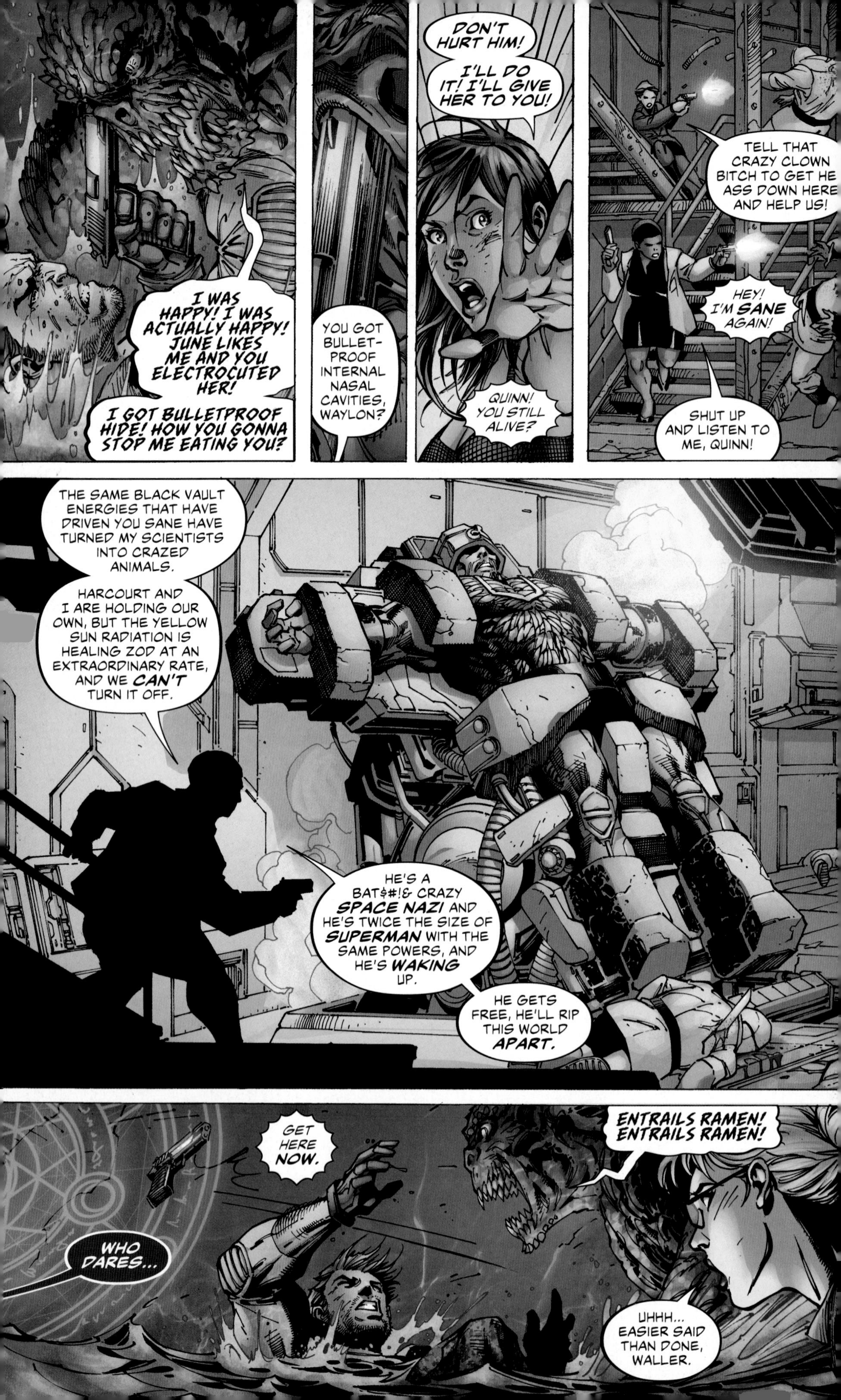
I WAS HAPPY! I WAS ACTUALLY HAPPY! JUNE LIKES ME AND YOU ELECTROCUTED HER!
I GOT BULLETPROOF HIDE! HOW YOU GONNA STOP ME EATING YOU?
YOU GOT BULLET-PROOF INTERNAL NASAL CAVITIES, WAYLON?
DON'T HURT HIM!
I'LL DO IT! I'LL GIVE HER TO YOU!
QUINN! YOU STILL ALIVE?
TELL THAT CRAZY CLOWN BITCH TO GET HER ASS DOWN HERE AND HELP US!
HEY! I'M SANE AGAIN!
SHUT UP AND LISTEN TO ME, QUINN!
THE SAME BLACK VAULT ENERGIES THAT HAVE DRIVEN YOU SANE HAVE TURNED MY SCIENTISTS INTO CRAZED ANIMALS.
HARCOURT AND I ARE HOLDING OUR OWN, BUT THE YELLOW SUN RADIATION IS HEALING ZOD AT AN EXTRAORDINARY RATE, AND WE CAN'T TURN IT OFF.
HE'S A BAT$#!& CRAZY SPACE NAZI AND HE'S TWICE THE SIZE OF SUPERMAN WITH THE SAME POWERS, AND HE'S WAKING UP.
HE GETS FREE, HE'LL RIP THIS WORLD APART.
GET HERE NOW.
ENTRAILS RAMEN! ENTRAILS RAMEN!
UHHH... EASIER SAID THAN DONE, WALLER.
WHO DARES...

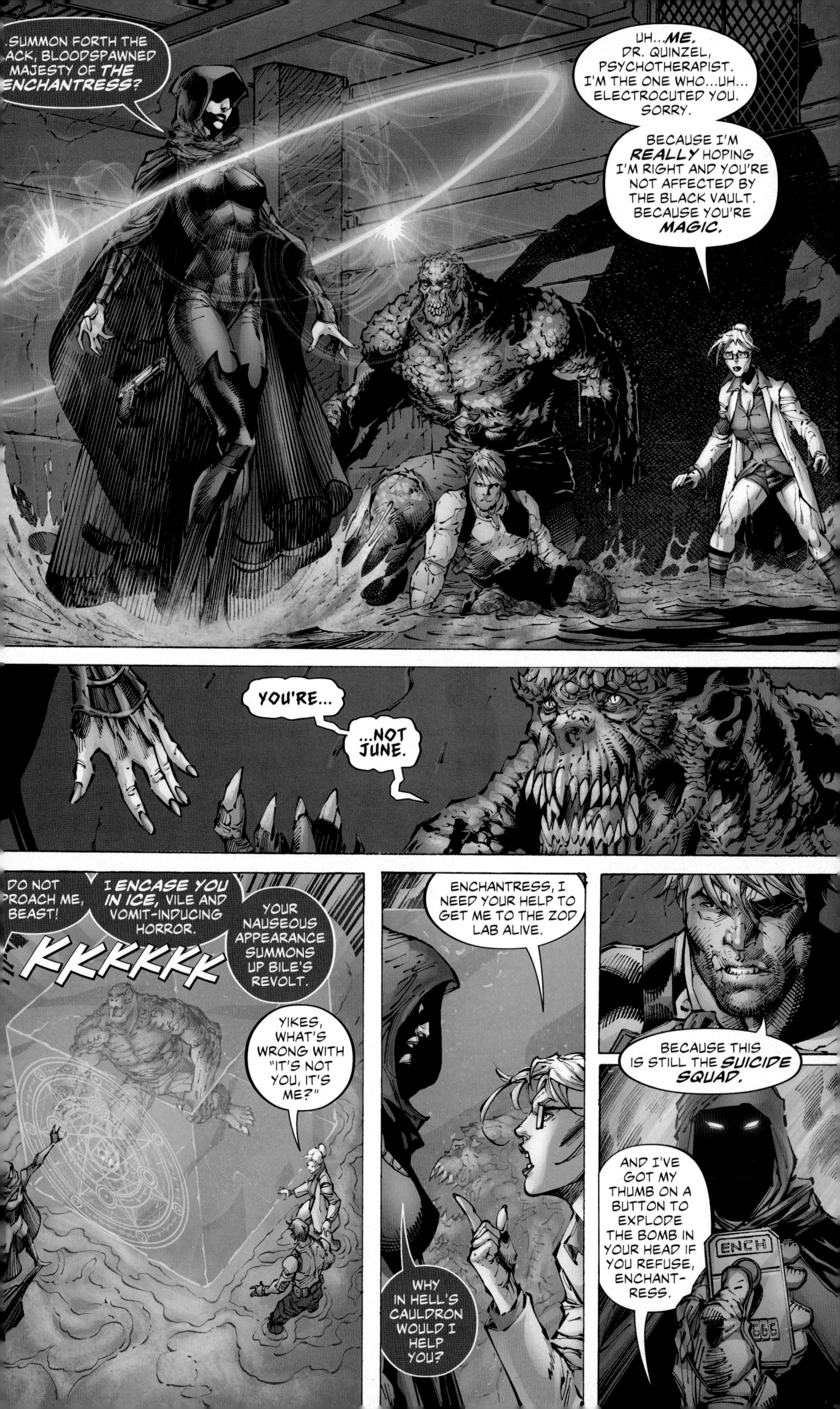
...SUMMON FORTH THE ...ACK, BLOODSPAWNED MAJESTY OF THE ENCHANTRESS?
UH...ME. DR. QUINZEL, PSYCHOTHERAPIST. I'M THE ONE WHO...UH... ELECTROCUTED YOU. SORRY.
BECAUSE I'M REALLY HOPING I'M RIGHT AND YOU'RE NOT AFFECTED BY THE BLACK VAULT. BECAUSE YOU'RE MAGIC.
YOU'RE...
...NOT JUNE.
DO NOT ...PROACH ME, BEAST!
I ENCASE YOU IN ICE, VILE AND VOMIT-INDUCING HORROR.
KKKKKK
YOUR NAUSEOUS APPEARANCE SUMMONS UP BILE'S REVOLT.
YIKES, WHAT'S WRONG WITH "IT'S NOT YOU, IT'S ME?"
ENCHANTRESS, I NEED YOUR HELP TO GET ME TO THE ZOD LAB ALIVE.
WHY IN HELL'S CAULDRON WOULD I HELP YOU?
BECAUSE THIS IS STILL THE SUICIDE SQUAD.
AND I'VE GOT MY THUMB ON A BUTTON TO EXPLODE THE BOMB IN YOUR HEAD IF YOU REFUSE, ENCHANT-RESS.
ENCH

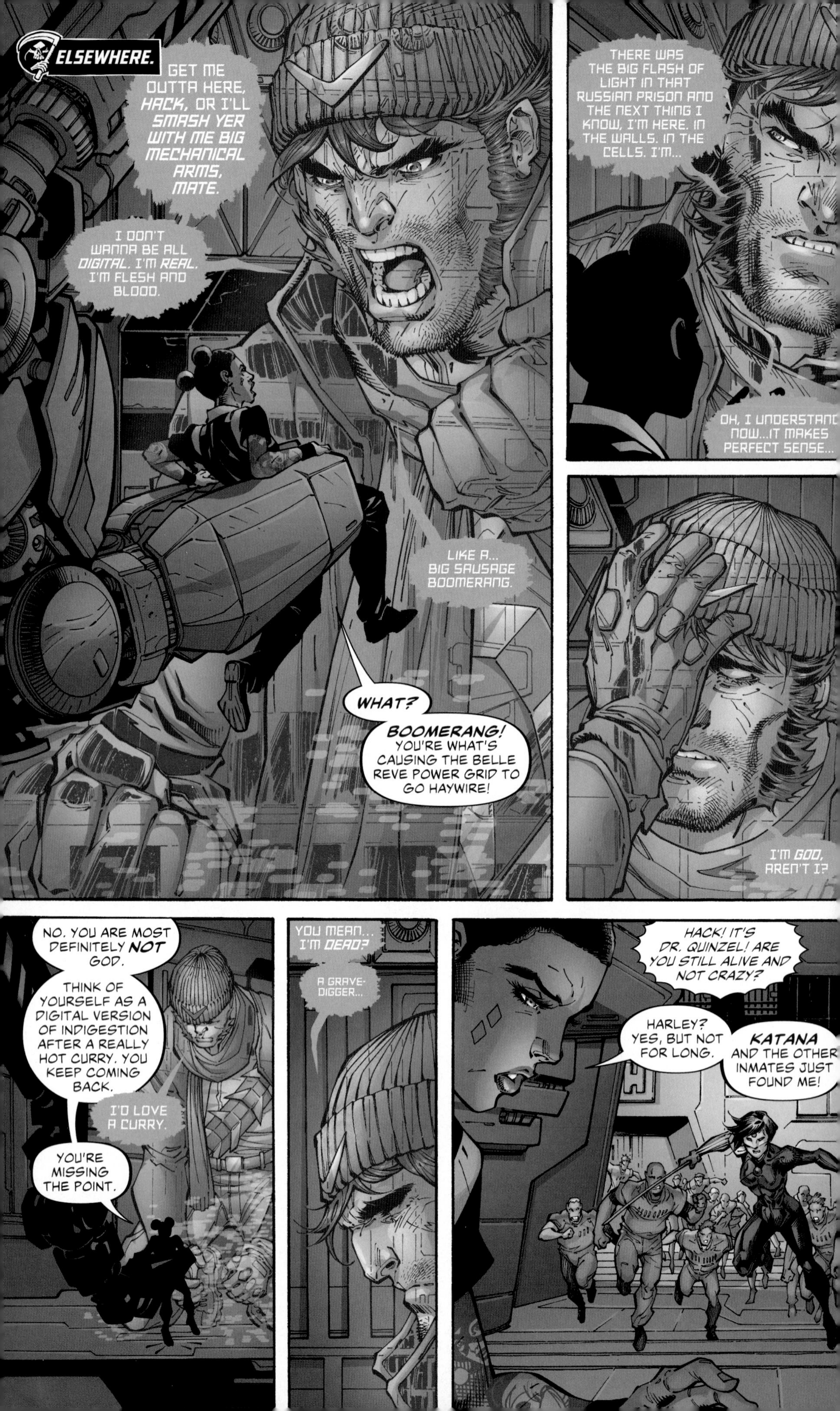

ELSEWHERE.
GET ME OUTTA HERE, HACK, OR I'LL SMASH YER WITH ME BIG MECHANICAL ARMS, MATE.
I DON'T WANNA BE ALL DIGITAL. I'M REAL. I'M FLESH AND BLOOD.
LIKE A... BIG SAUSAGE BOOMERANG.
WHAT?
BOOMERANG! YOU'RE WHAT'S CAUSING THE BELLE REVE POWER GRID TO GO HAYWIRE!
THERE WAS THE BIG FLASH OF LIGHT IN THAT RUSSIAN PRISON AND THE NEXT THING I KNOW, I'M HERE. IN THE WALLS. IN THE CELLS. I'M...
OH, I UNDERSTAND NOW...IT MAKES PERFECT SENSE...
I'M GOD, AREN'T I?
NO. YOU ARE MOST DEFINITELY NOT GOD.
THINK OF YOURSELF AS A DIGITAL VERSION OF INDIGESTION AFTER A REALLY HOT CURRY. YOU KEEP COMING BACK.
I'D LOVE A CURRY.
YOU'RE MISSING THE POINT.
YOU MEAN... I'M DEAD?
A GRAVE-DIGGER...
HACK! IT'S DR. QUINZEL! ARE YOU STILL ALIVE AND NOT CRAZY?
HARLEY? YES, BUT NOT FOR LONG.
KATANA AND THE OTHER INMATES JUST FOUND ME!

HACK. BRING ME BACK AND I'LL PROTECT YOU.

WALLER'S TRAPPED IN THE ZOD LAB TRYING TO GET BELLE REVE'S SYSTEMS BACK ONLINE.

COMPUTERS ARE *YOUR* THING. I NEED YOU TO MEET ME THERE!

I DON'T KNOW...I'M NOT POWERFUL ENOUGH...I'M NOT LIKE YOU...

YOU'RE A *SUPER-VILLAIN*, HACK. YOU'RE POWERFUL ENOUGH.

HARLEY QUINN SAYS SO.

QUINN...IT'S DEADSHOT...I'LL HOLD HIM HERE...GIVE YOU THE TIME YOU NEED IN THE LAB.

YOU'LL *BLEED OUT* BEFORE DEADSHOT KILLS YOU.

THEN WE'LL BOTH SACRIFICE SOMETHING PRECIOUS TODAY, HUH, QUINN?

RICK... IF WE MAKE IT OUT OF THIS...

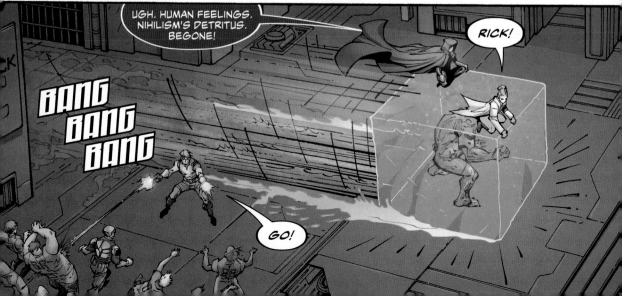

UGH. HUMAN FEELINGS. NIHILISM'S DETRITUS. BEGONE!

RICK!

BANG BANG BANG

GO!

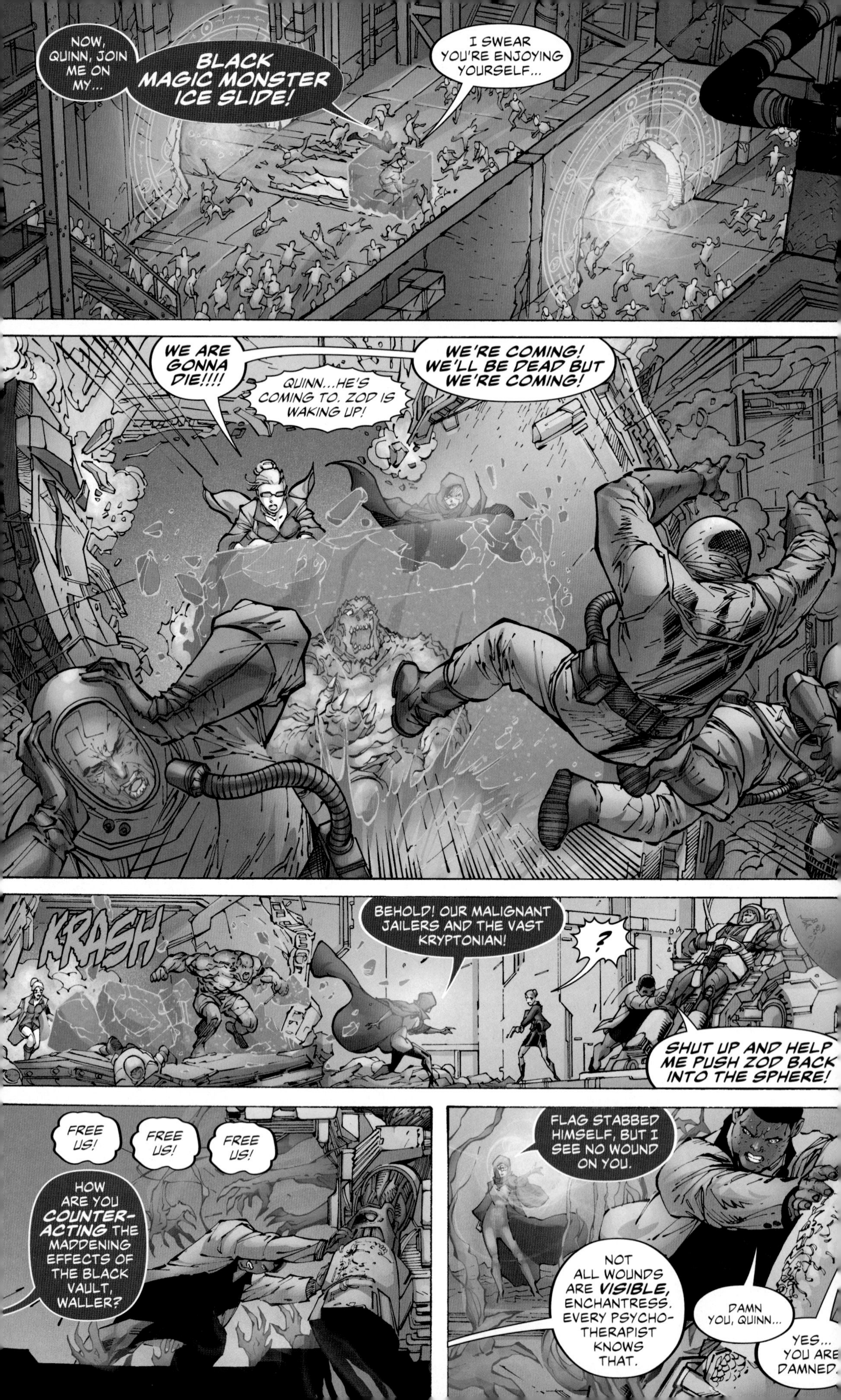
NOW, QUINN, JOIN ME ON MY...
BLACK MAGIC MONSTER ICE SLIDE!
I SWEAR YOU'RE ENJOYING YOURSELF...
WE ARE GONNA DIE!!!!
QUINN...HE'S COMING TO. ZOD IS WAKING UP!
WE'RE COMING! WE'LL BE DEAD BUT WE'RE COMING!
KRASH
BEHOLD! OUR MALIGNANT JAILERS AND THE VAST KRYPTONIAN!
?
SHUT UP AND HELP ME PUSH ZOD BACK INTO THE SPHERE!
FREE US!
FREE US!
FREE US!
HOW ARE YOU COUNTER-ACTING THE MADDENING EFFECTS OF THE BLACK VAULT, WALLER?
FLAG STABBED HIMSELF, BUT I SEE NO WOUND ON YOU.
NOT ALL WOUNDS ARE VISIBLE, ENCHANTRESS. EVERY PSYCHO-THERAPIST KNOWS THAT.
DAMN YOU, QUINN...
YES... YOU ARE DAMNED.

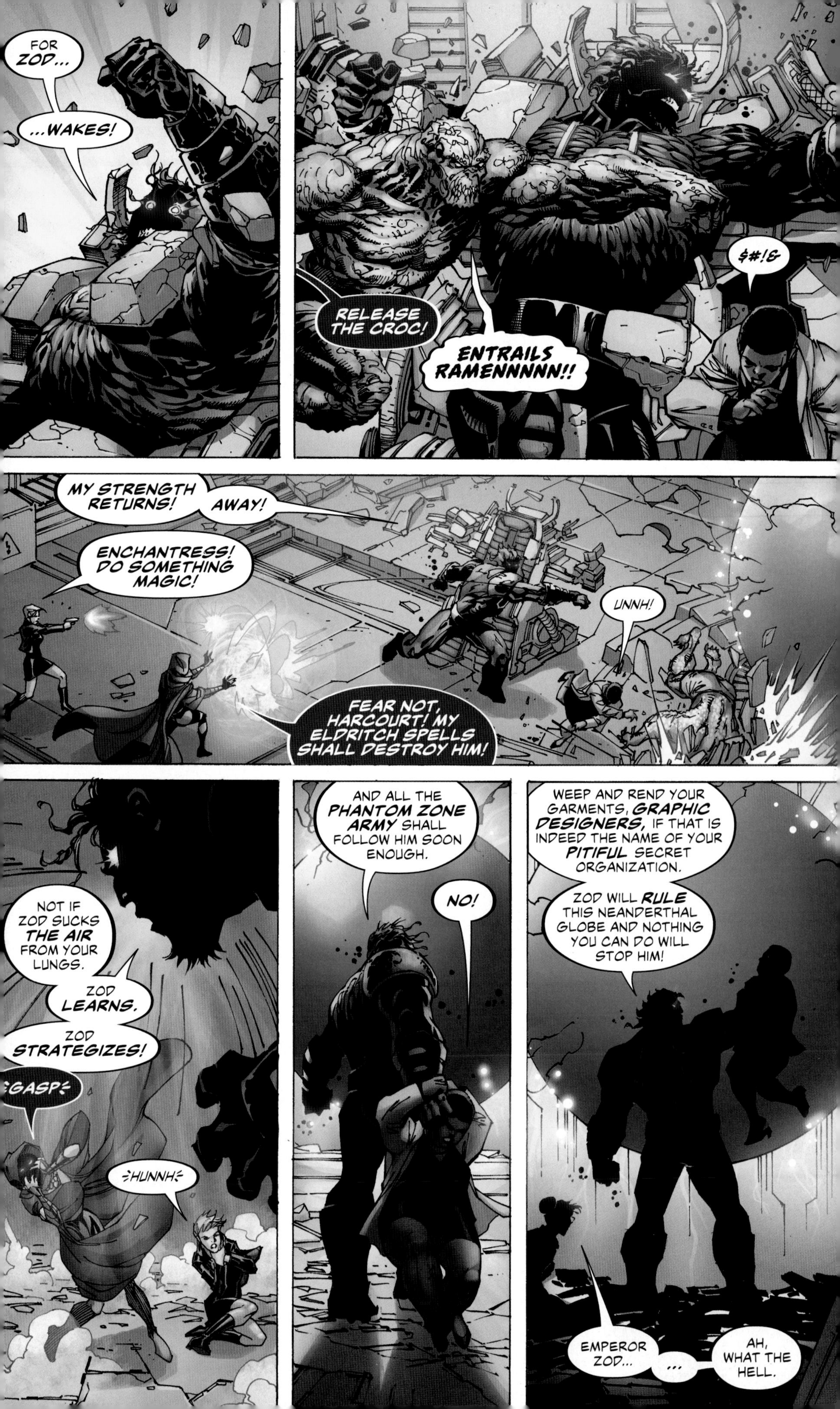

FOR ZOD...
...WAKES!
RELEASE THE CROC!
ENTRAILS RAMENNNNN!!
$#!&
MY STRENGTH RETURNS!
AWAY!
ENCHANTRESS! DO SOMETHING MAGIC!
UNNH!
FEAR NOT, HARCOURT! MY ELDRITCH SPELLS SHALL DESTROY HIM!
NOT IF ZOD SUCKS THE AIR FROM YOUR LUNGS.
ZOD LEARNS.
ZOD STRATEGIZES!
GASP
HUNNH
AND ALL THE PHANTOM ZONE ARMY SHALL FOLLOW HIM SOON ENOUGH.
NO!
WEEP AND REND YOUR GARMENTS, GRAPHIC DESIGNERS, IF THAT IS INDEED THE NAME OF YOUR PITIFUL SECRET ORGANIZATION.
ZOD WILL RULE THIS NEANDERTHAL GLOBE AND NOTHING YOU CAN DO WILL STOP HIM!
EMPEROR ZOD...
...
AH, WHAT THE HELL.

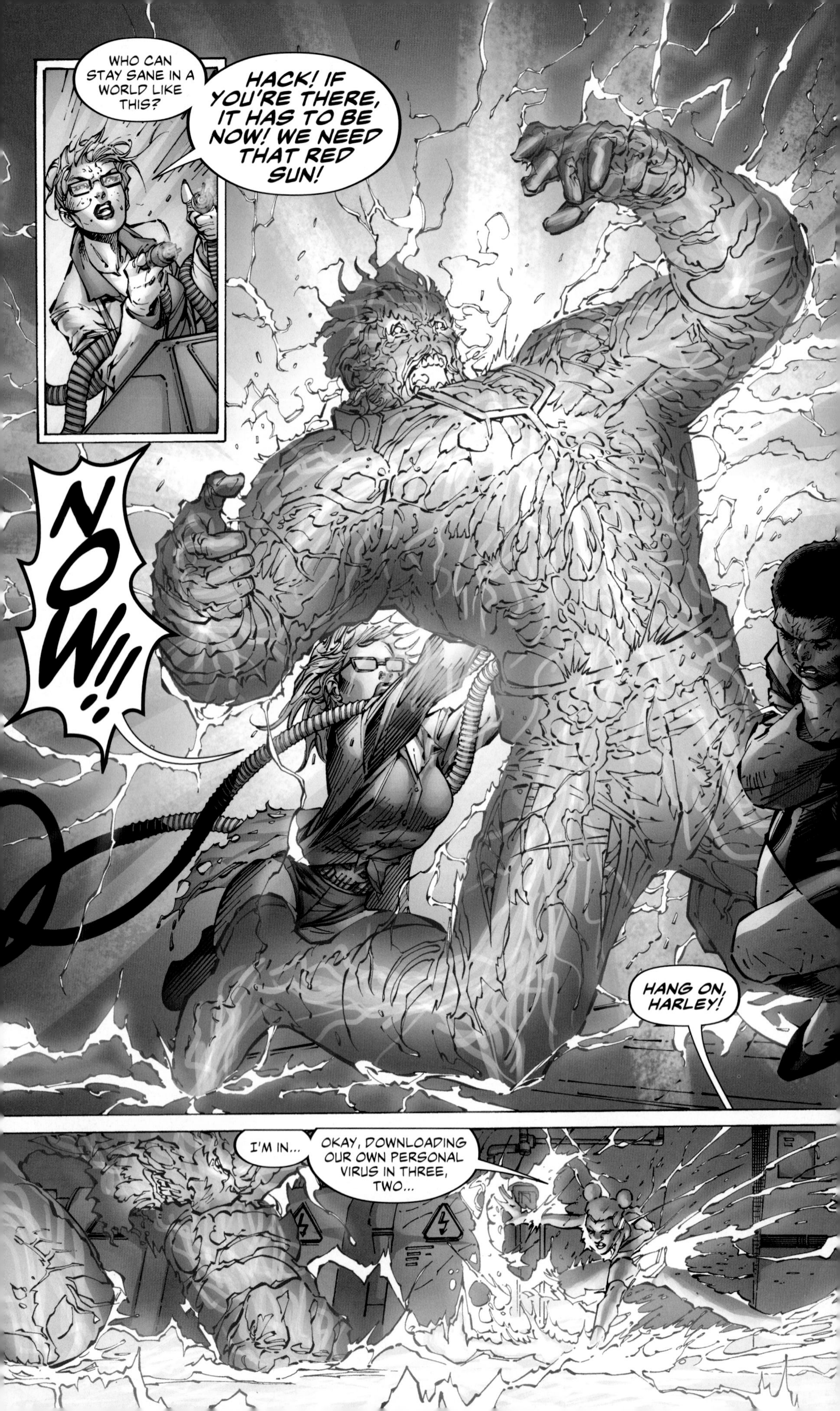

WHO CAN STAY SANE IN A WORLD LIKE THIS?
HACK! IF YOU'RE THERE, IT HAS TO BE NOW! WE NEED THAT RED SUN!
NOW!!!
HANG ON, HARLEY!
I'M IN...
OKAY, DOWNLOADING OUR OWN PERSONAL VIRUS IN THREE, TWO...

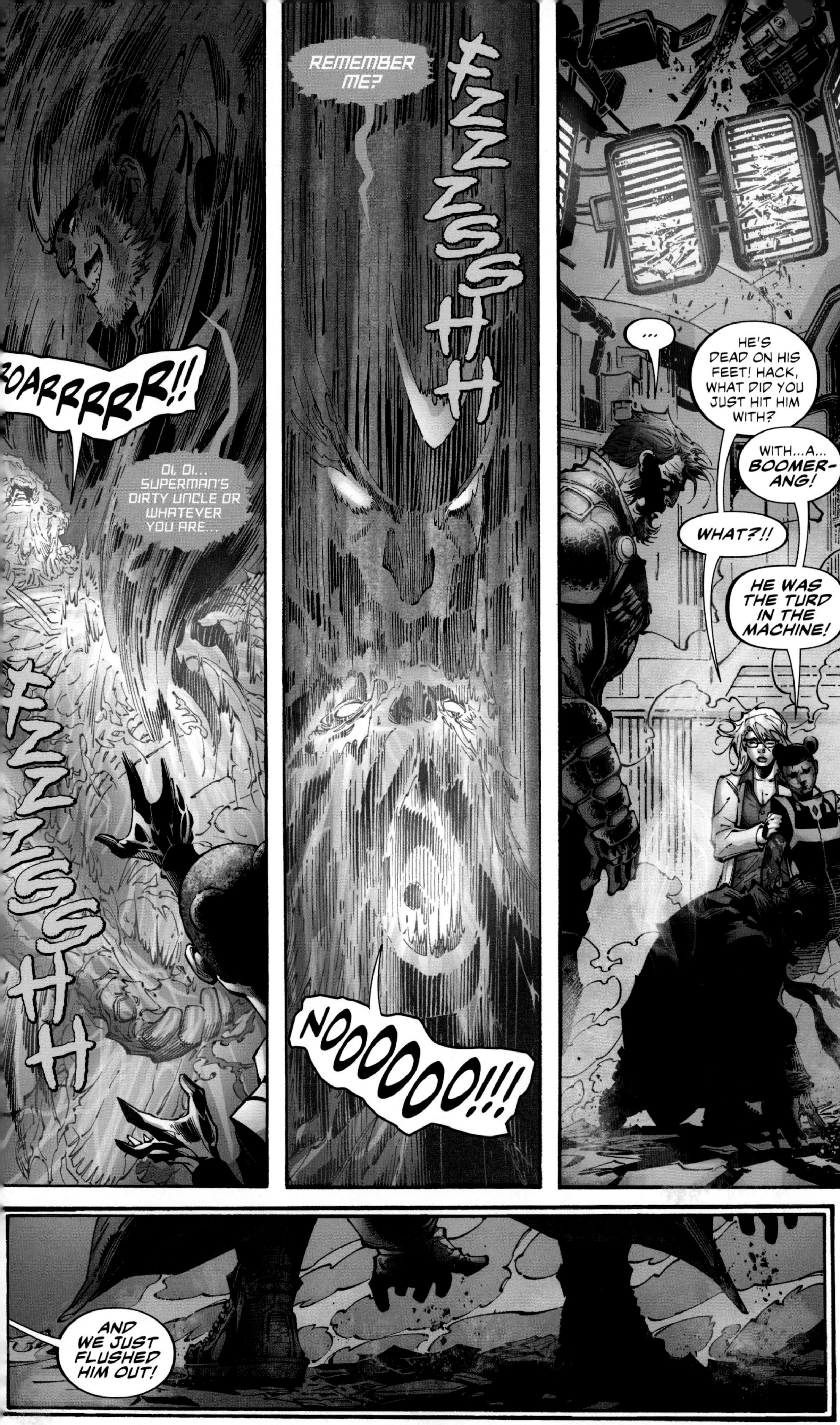
ROARRRRR!!
OI, OI... SUPERMAN'S DIRTY UNCLE OR WHATEVER YOU ARE...
FZZZSSHH
REMEMBER ME?
FZZZSSHH
NOOOOOO!!!
...
HE'S DEAD ON HIS FEET! HACK, WHAT DID YOU JUST HIT HIM WITH?
WITH...A... BOOMER-ANG!
WHAT?!!
HE WAS THE TURD IN THE MACHINE!
AND WE JUST FLUSHED HIM OUT!

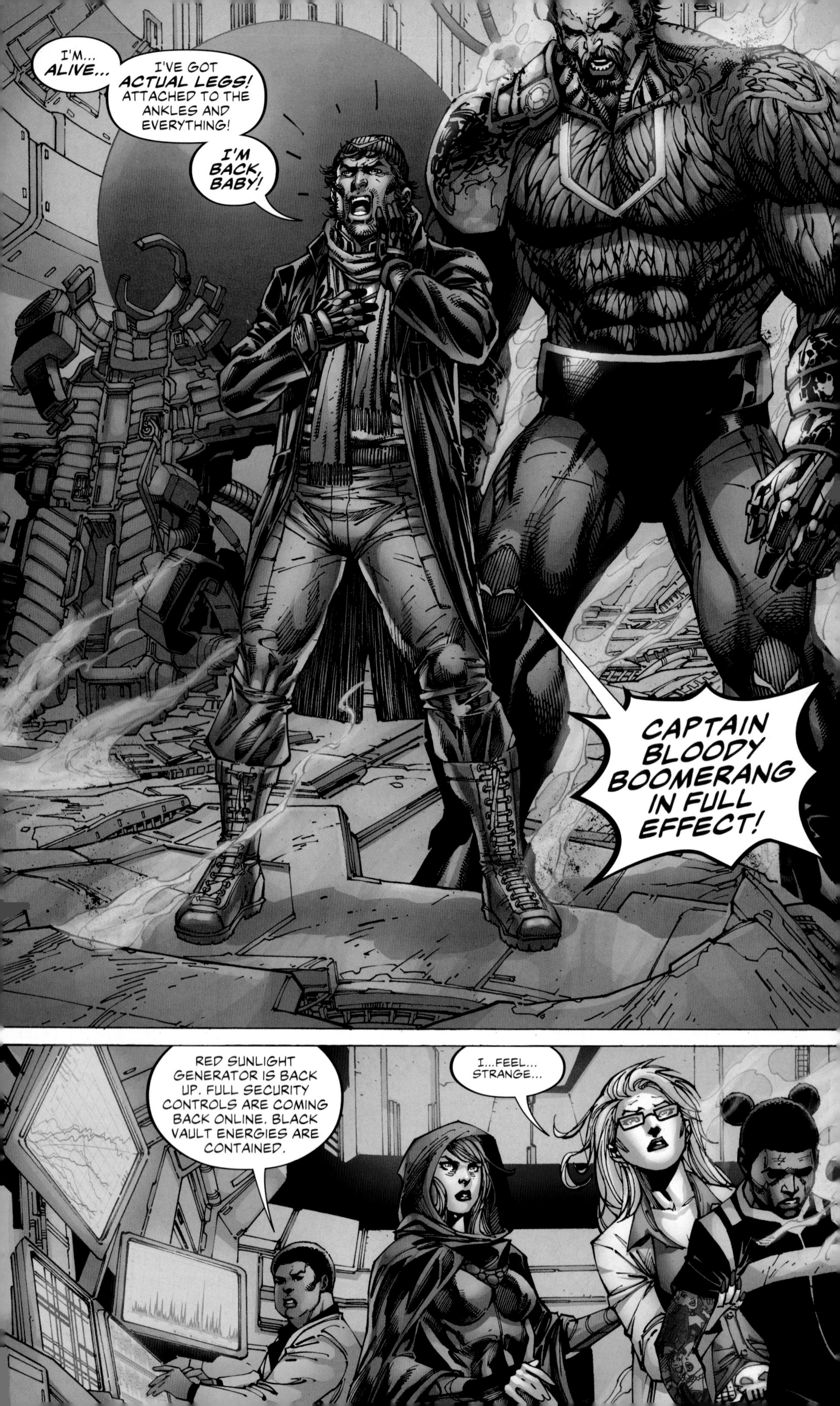
I'M... ALIVE...
I'VE GOT ACTUAL LEGS! ATTACHED TO THE ANKLES AND EVERYTHING!
I'M BACK, BABY!
CAPTAIN BLOODY BOOMERANG IN FULL EFFECT!
RED SUNLIGHT GENERATOR IS BACK UP. FULL SECURITY CONTROLS ARE COMING BACK ONLINE. BLACK VAULT ENERGIES ARE CONTAINED.
I...FEEL... STRANGE...

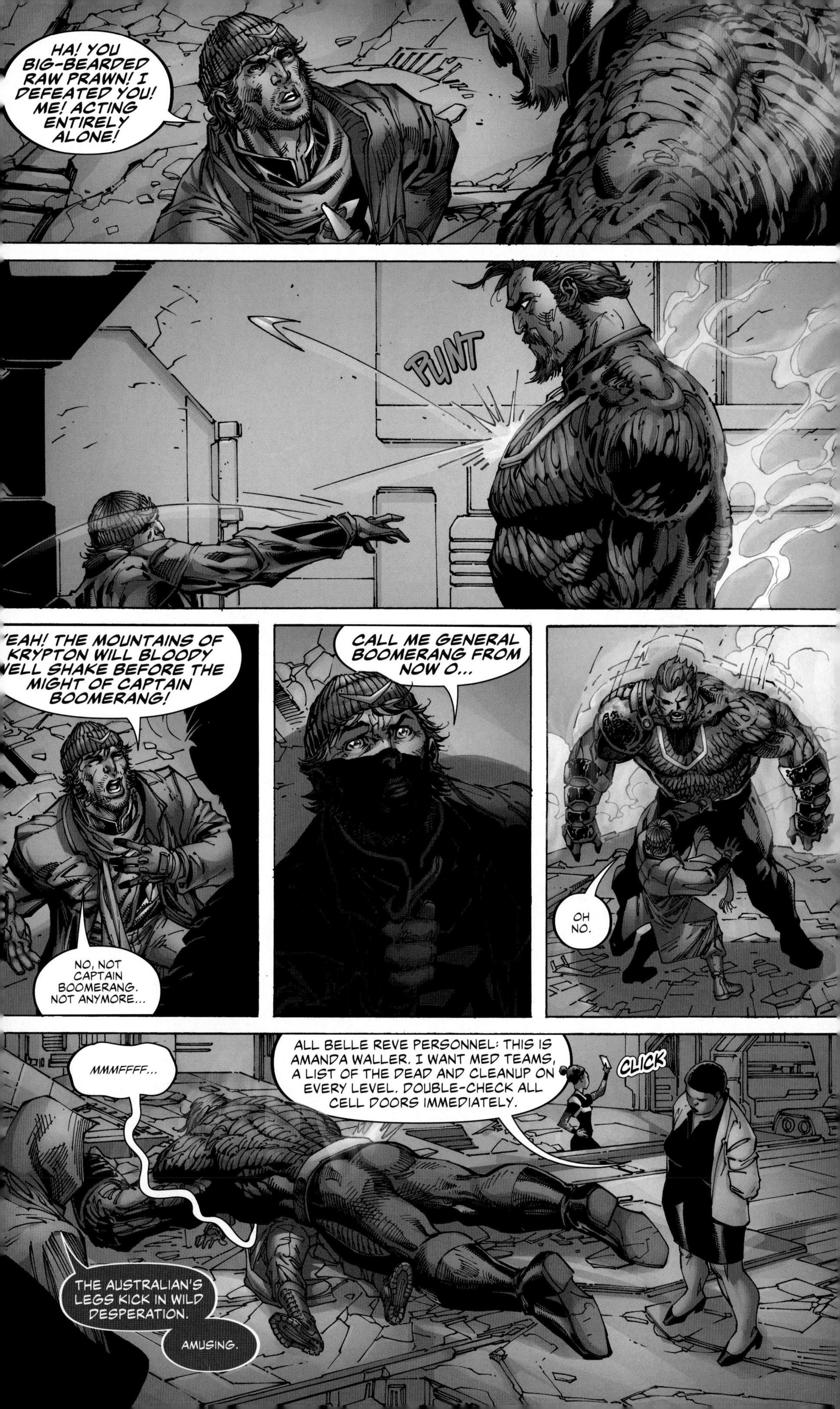
HA! YOU BIG-BEARDED RAW PRAWN! I DEFEATED YOU! ME! ACTING ENTIRELY ALONE!
PLINT
YEAH! THE MOUNTAINS OF KRYPTON WILL BLOODY WELL SHAKE BEFORE THE MIGHT OF CAPTAIN BOOMERANG!
NO, NOT CAPTAIN BOOMERANG. NOT ANYMORE...
CALL ME GENERAL BOOMERANG FROM NOW O...
OH NO.
MMMFFFF...
ALL BELLE REVE PERSONNEL: THIS IS AMANDA WALLER. I WANT MED TEAMS, A LIST OF THE DEAD AND CLEANUP ON EVERY LEVEL. DOUBLE-CHECK ALL CELL DOORS IMMEDIATELY.
CLICK
THE AUSTRALIAN'S LEGS KICK IN WILD DESPERATION.
AMUSING.

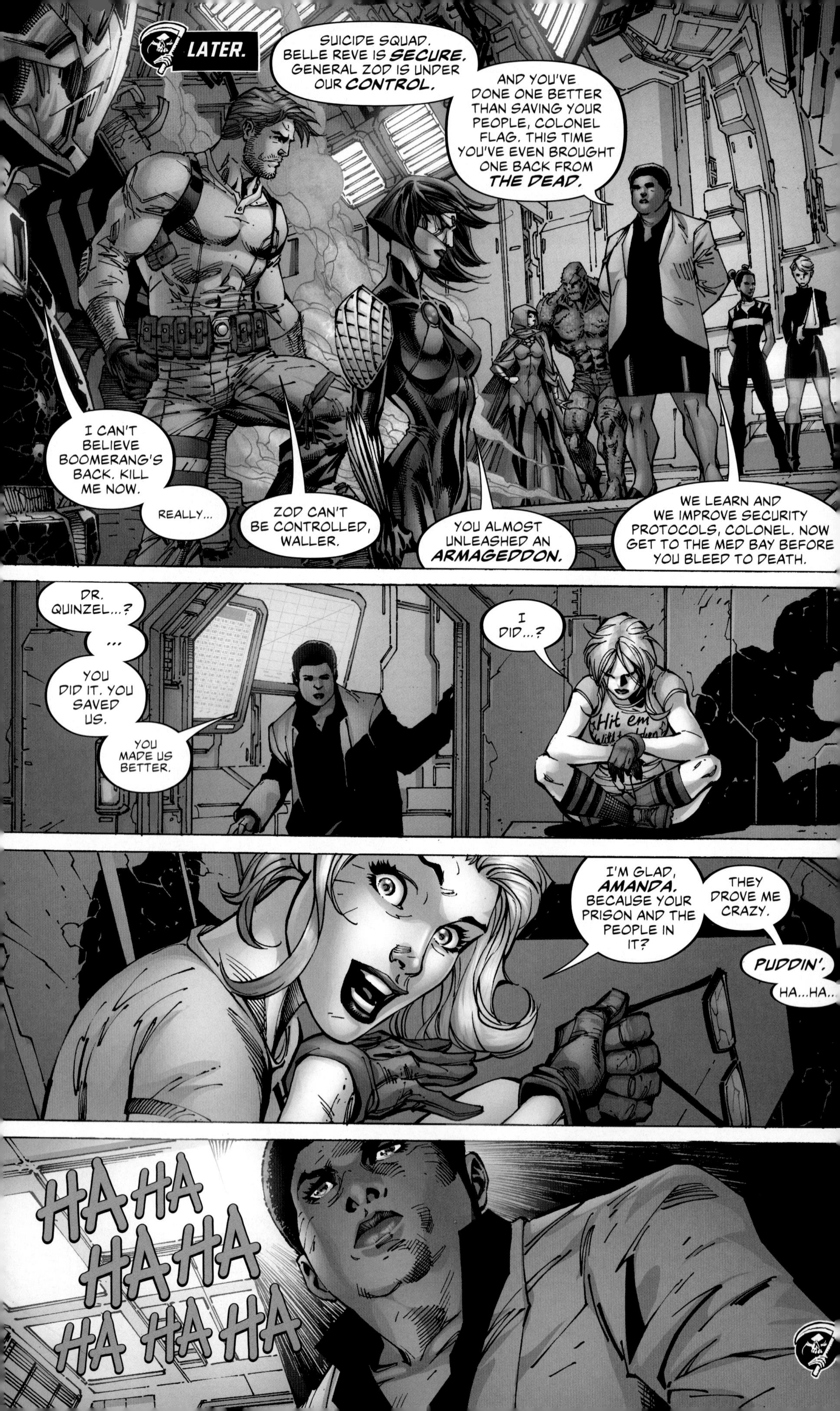
LATER.
SUICIDE SQUAD. BELLE REVE IS SECURE. GENERAL ZOD IS UNDER OUR CONTROL.
AND YOU'VE DONE ONE BETTER THAN SAVING YOUR PEOPLE, COLONEL FLAG. THIS TIME YOU'VE EVEN BROUGHT ONE BACK FROM THE DEAD.
I CAN'T BELIEVE BOOMERANG'S BACK. KILL ME NOW.
REALLY...
ZOD CAN'T BE CONTROLLED, WALLER.
YOU ALMOST UNLEASHED AN ARMAGEDDON.
WE LEARN AND WE IMPROVE SECURITY PROTOCOLS, COLONEL. NOW GET TO THE MED BAY BEFORE YOU BLEED TO DEATH.
DR. QUINZEL...?
...
YOU DID IT. YOU SAVED US.
YOU MADE US BETTER.
I DID...?
I'M GLAD, AMANDA. BECAUSE YOUR PRISON AND THE PEOPLE IN IT?
THEY DROVE ME CRAZY.
PUDDIN'.
HA...HA...
HA HA HA HA HA HA HA HA

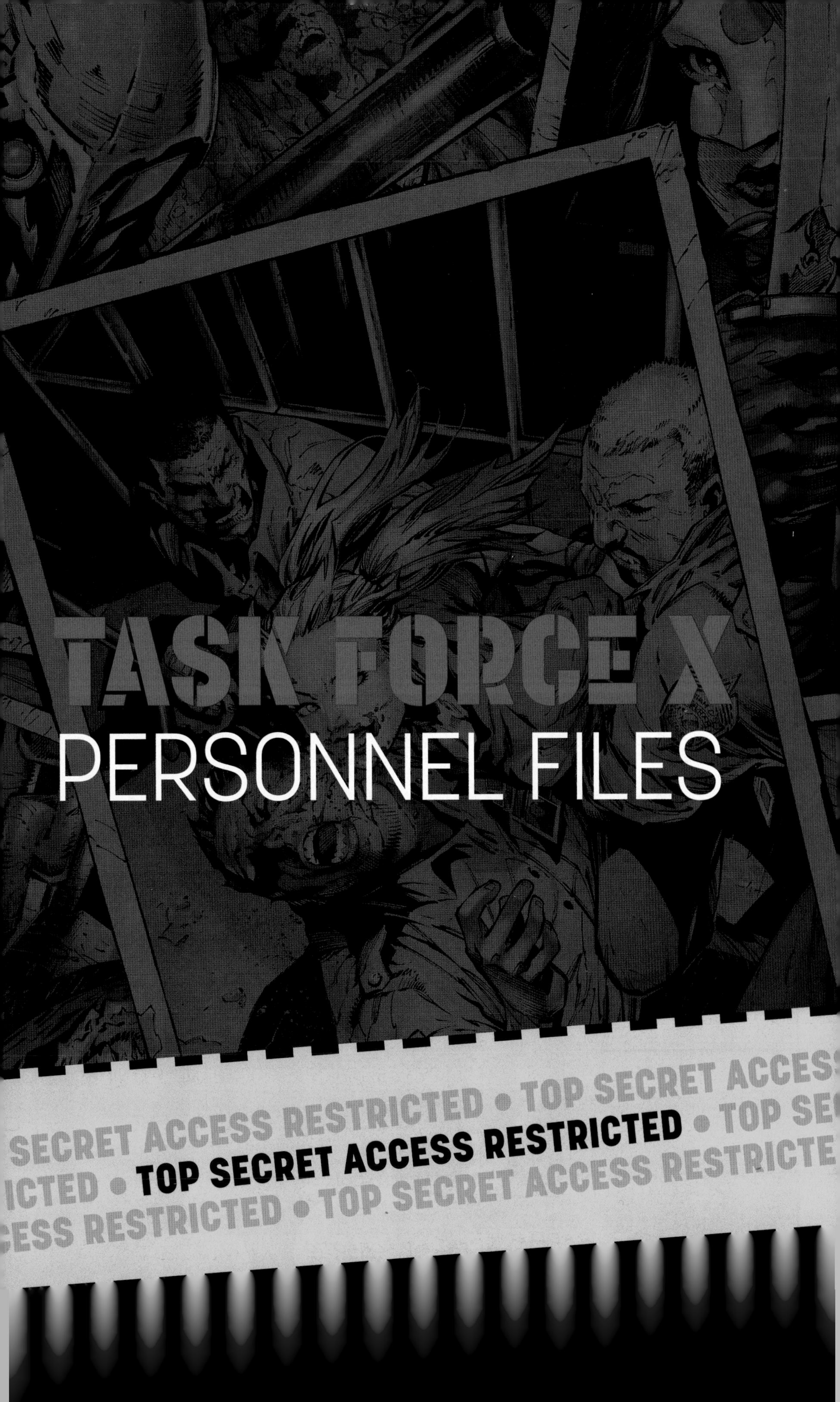
TASK FORCE X
PERSONNEL FILES
TOP SECRET ACCESS RESTRICTED

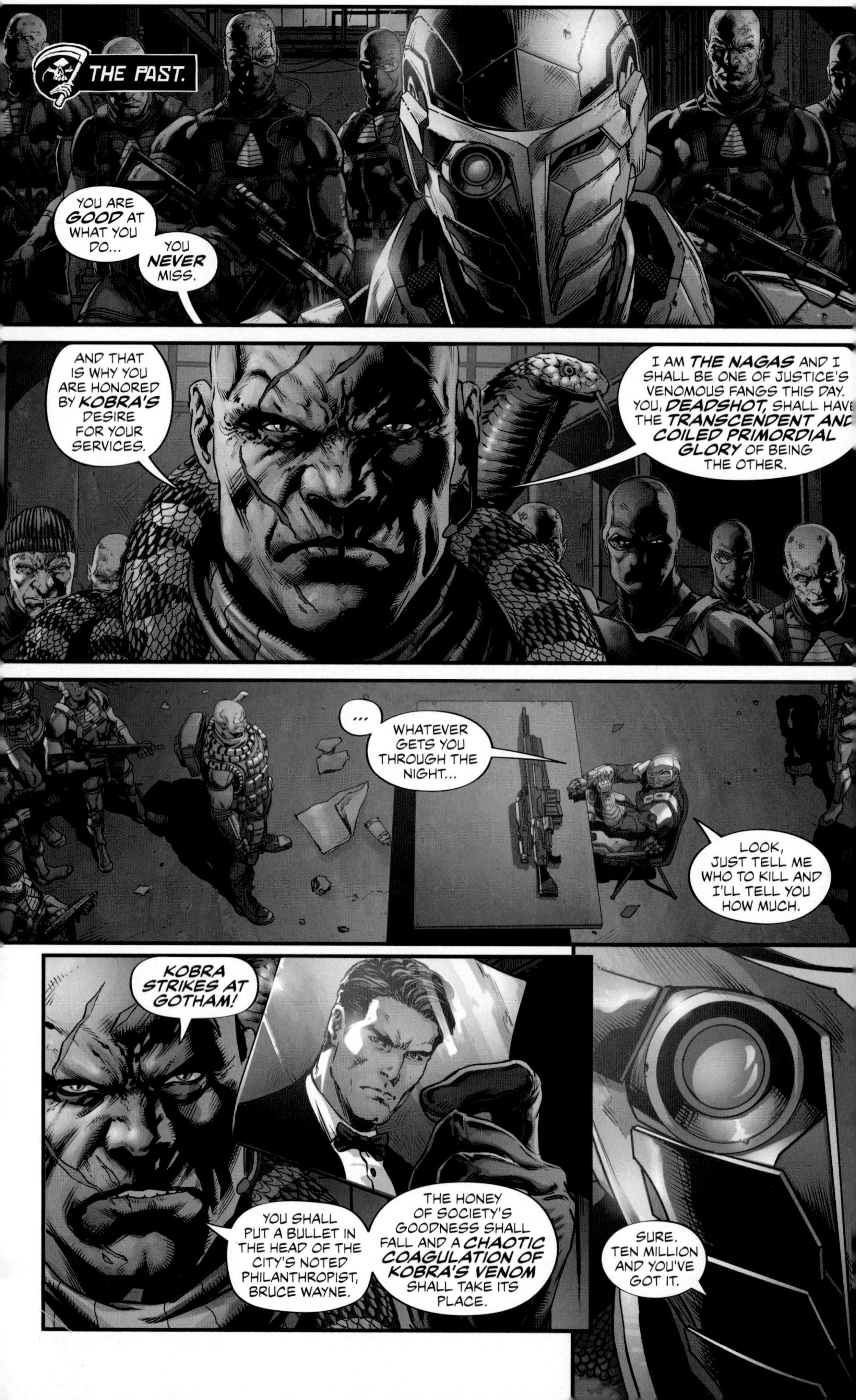
THE PAST.
YOU ARE GOOD AT WHAT YOU DO...
YOU NEVER MISS.
AND THAT IS WHY YOU ARE HONORED BY KOBRA'S DESIRE FOR YOUR SERVICES.
I AM THE NAGAS AND I SHALL BE ONE OF JUSTICE'S VENOMOUS FANGS THIS DAY. YOU, DEADSHOT, SHALL HAVE THE TRANSCENDENT AND COILED PRIMORDIAL GLORY OF BEING THE OTHER.
...
WHATEVER GETS YOU THROUGH THE NIGHT...
LOOK, JUST TELL ME WHO TO KILL AND I'LL TELL YOU HOW MUCH.
KOBRA STRIKES AT GOTHAM!
YOU SHALL PUT A BULLET IN THE HEAD OF THE CITY'S NOTED PHILANTHROPIST, BRUCE WAYNE.
THE HONEY OF SOCIETY'S GOODNESS SHALL FALL AND A CHAOTIC COAGULATION OF KOBRA'S VENOM SHALL TAKE ITS PLACE.
SURE. TEN MILLION AND YOU'VE GOT IT.

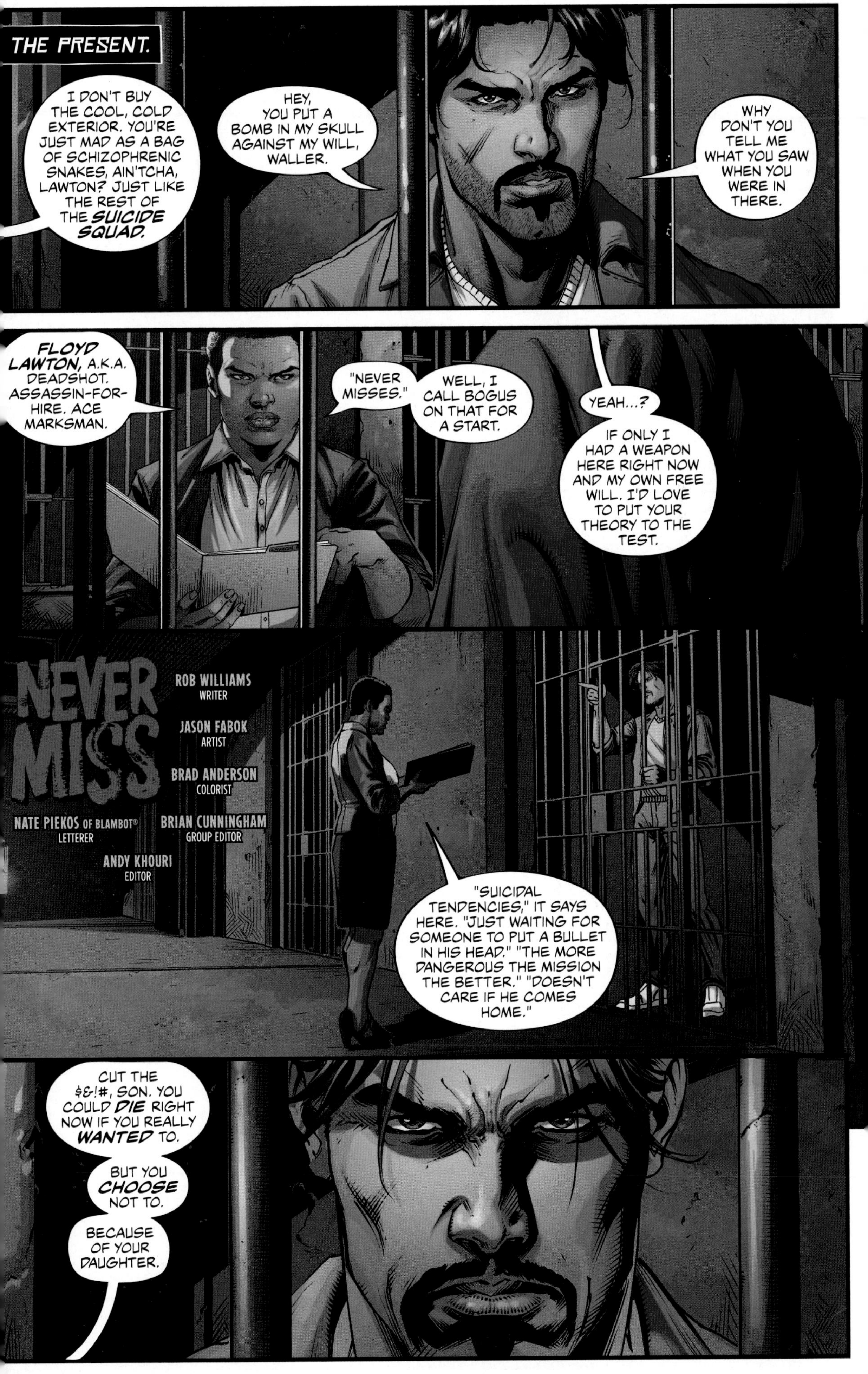
THE PRESENT.
I DON'T BUY THE COOL, COLD EXTERIOR. YOU'RE JUST MAD AS A BAG OF SCHIZOPHRENIC SNAKES, AIN'TCHA, LAWTON? JUST LIKE THE REST OF THE SUICIDE SQUAD.
HEY, YOU PUT A BOMB IN MY SKULL AGAINST MY WILL, WALLER.
WHY DON'T YOU TELL ME WHAT YOU SAW WHEN YOU WERE IN THERE.
FLOYD LAWTON, A.K.A. DEADSHOT. ASSASSIN-FOR-HIRE. ACE MARKSMAN.
"NEVER MISSES."
WELL, I CALL BOGUS ON THAT FOR A START.
YEAH...?
IF ONLY I HAD A WEAPON HERE RIGHT NOW AND MY OWN FREE WILL. I'D LOVE TO PUT YOUR THEORY TO THE TEST.
NEVER MISS
ROB WILLIAMS WRITER
JASON FABOK ARTIST
BRAD ANDERSON COLORIST
NATE PIEKOS OF BLAMBOT® LETTERER
BRIAN CUNNINGHAM GROUP EDITOR
ANDY KHOURI EDITOR
"SUICIDAL TENDENCIES," IT SAYS HERE. "JUST WAITING FOR SOMEONE TO PUT A BULLET IN HIS HEAD." "THE MORE DANGEROUS THE MISSION THE BETTER." "DOESN'T CARE IF HE COMES HOME."
CUT THE $&!#, SON. YOU COULD DIE RIGHT NOW IF YOU REALLY WANTED TO.
BUT YOU CHOOSE NOT TO.
BECAUSE OF YOUR DAUGHTER.

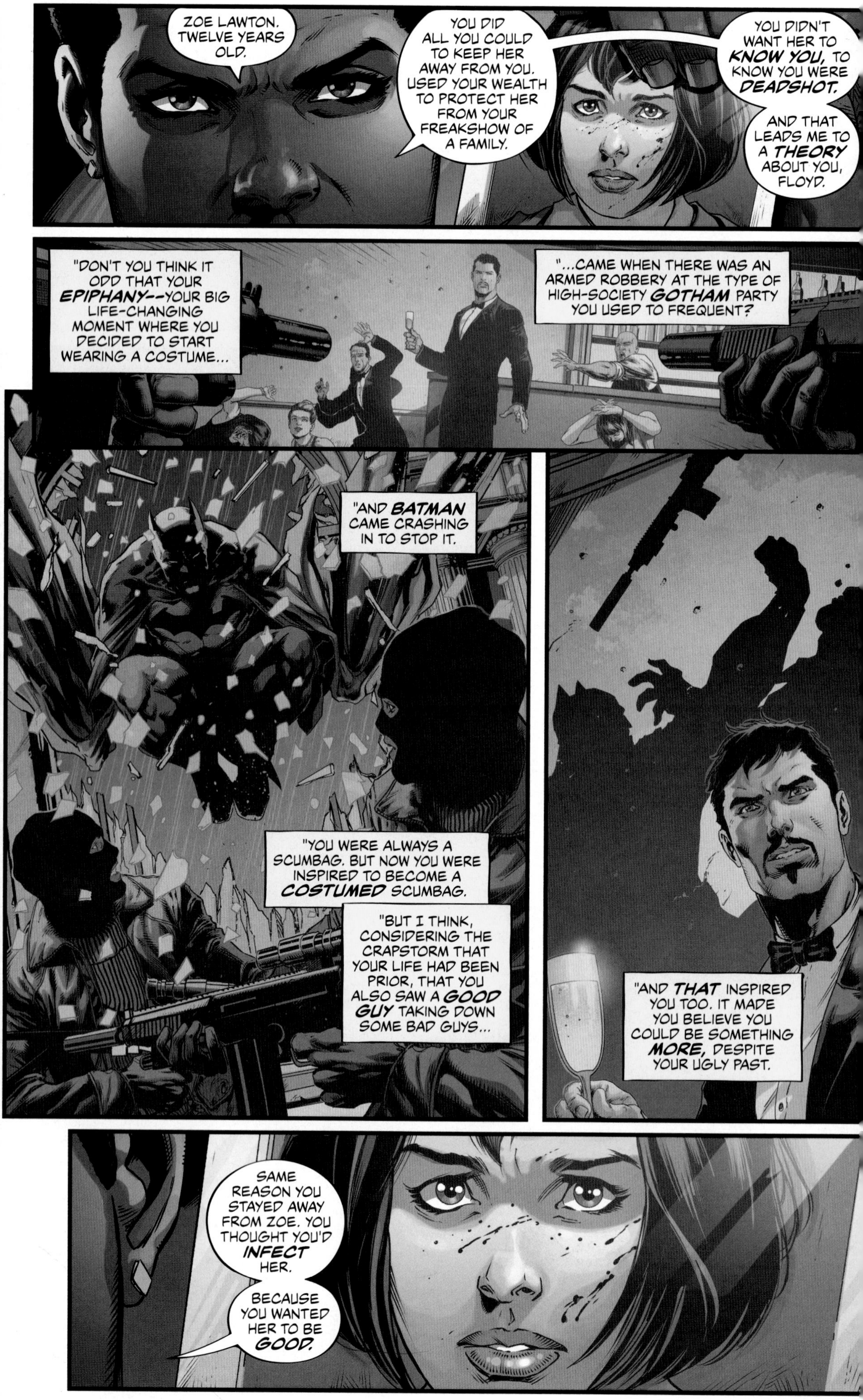
ZOE LAWTON. TWELVE YEARS OLD.
YOU DID ALL YOU COULD TO KEEP HER AWAY FROM YOU. USED YOUR WEALTH TO PROTECT HER FROM YOUR FREAKSHOW OF A FAMILY.
YOU DIDN'T WANT HER TO KNOW YOU, TO KNOW YOU WERE DEADSHOT.
AND THAT LEADS ME TO A THEORY ABOUT YOU, FLOYD.
"DON'T YOU THINK IT ODD THAT YOUR EPIPHANY--YOUR BIG LIFE-CHANGING MOMENT WHERE YOU DECIDED TO START WEARING A COSTUME...
"...CAME WHEN THERE WAS AN ARMED ROBBERY AT THE TYPE OF HIGH-SOCIETY GOTHAM PARTY YOU USED TO FREQUENT?
"AND BATMAN CAME CRASHING IN TO STOP IT.
"YOU WERE ALWAYS A SCUMBAG. BUT NOW YOU WERE INSPIRED TO BECOME A COSTUMED SCUMBAG.
"BUT I THINK, CONSIDERING THE CRAPSTORM THAT YOUR LIFE HAD BEEN PRIOR, THAT YOU ALSO SAW A GOOD GUY TAKING DOWN SOME BAD GUYS...
"AND THAT INSPIRED YOU TOO. IT MADE YOU BELIEVE YOU COULD BE SOMETHING MORE, DESPITE YOUR UGLY PAST.
SAME REASON YOU STAYED AWAY FROM ZOE. YOU THOUGHT YOU'D INFECT HER.
BECAUSE YOU WANTED HER TO BE GOOD.

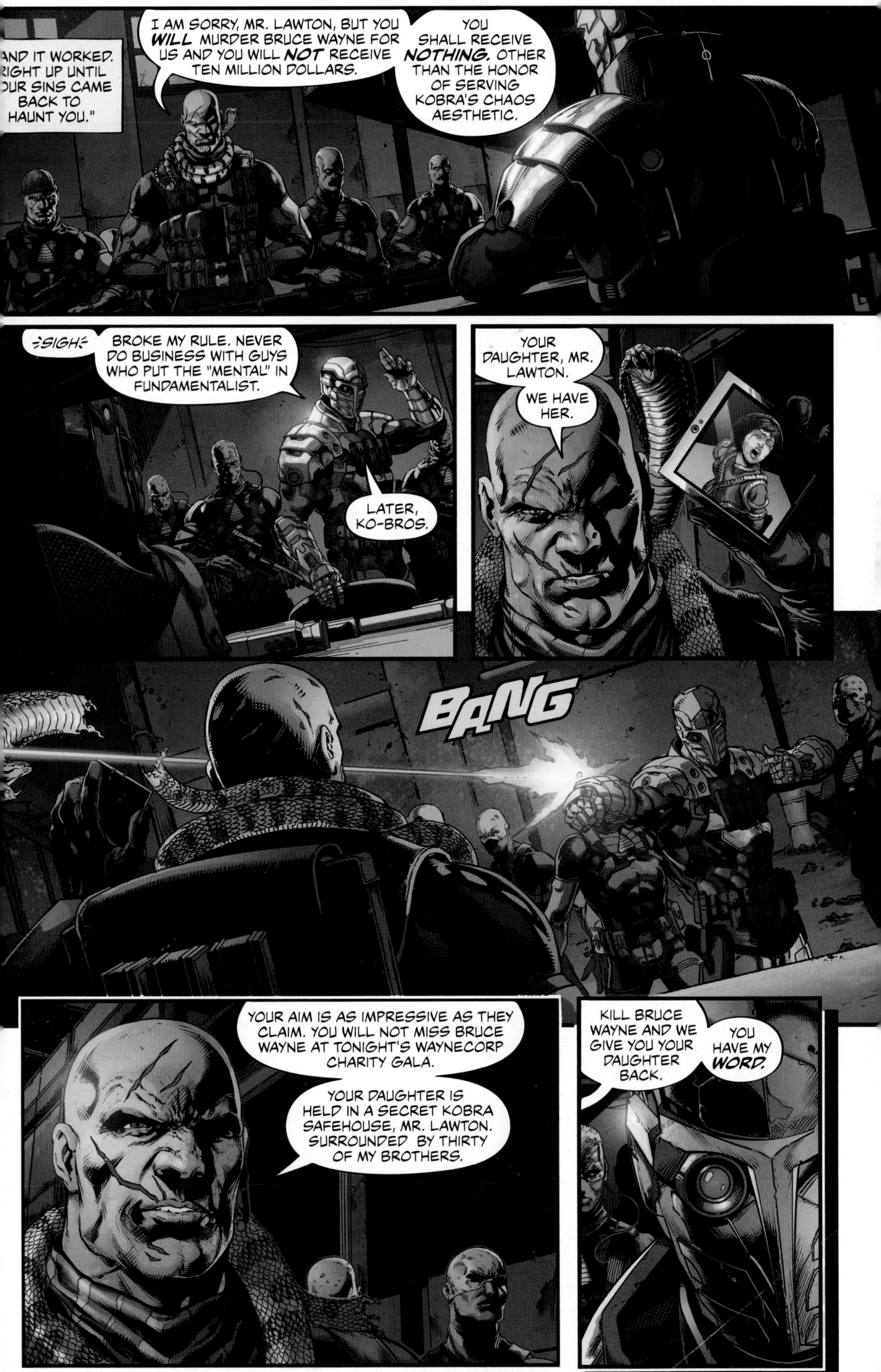
AND IT WORKED. RIGHT UP UNTIL YOUR SINS CAME BACK TO HAUNT YOU."
I AM SORRY, MR. LAWTON, BUT YOU WILL MURDER BRUCE WAYNE FOR US AND YOU WILL NOT RECEIVE TEN MILLION DOLLARS.
YOU SHALL RECEIVE NOTHING, OTHER THAN THE HONOR OF SERVING KOBRA'S CHAOS AESTHETIC.
SIGH
BROKE MY RULE. NEVER DO BUSINESS WITH GUYS WHO PUT THE "MENTAL" IN FUNDAMENTALIST.
LATER, KO-BROS.
YOUR DAUGHTER, MR. LAWTON.
WE HAVE HER.
BANG
YOUR AIM IS AS IMPRESSIVE AS THEY CLAIM. YOU WILL NOT MISS BRUCE WAYNE AT TONIGHT'S WAYNECORP CHARITY GALA.
YOUR DAUGHTER IS HELD IN A SECRET KOBRA SAFEHOUSE, MR. LAWTON. SURROUNDED BY THIRTY OF MY BROTHERS.
KILL BRUCE WAYNE AND WE GIVE YOU YOUR DAUGHTER BACK.
YOU HAVE MY WORD.

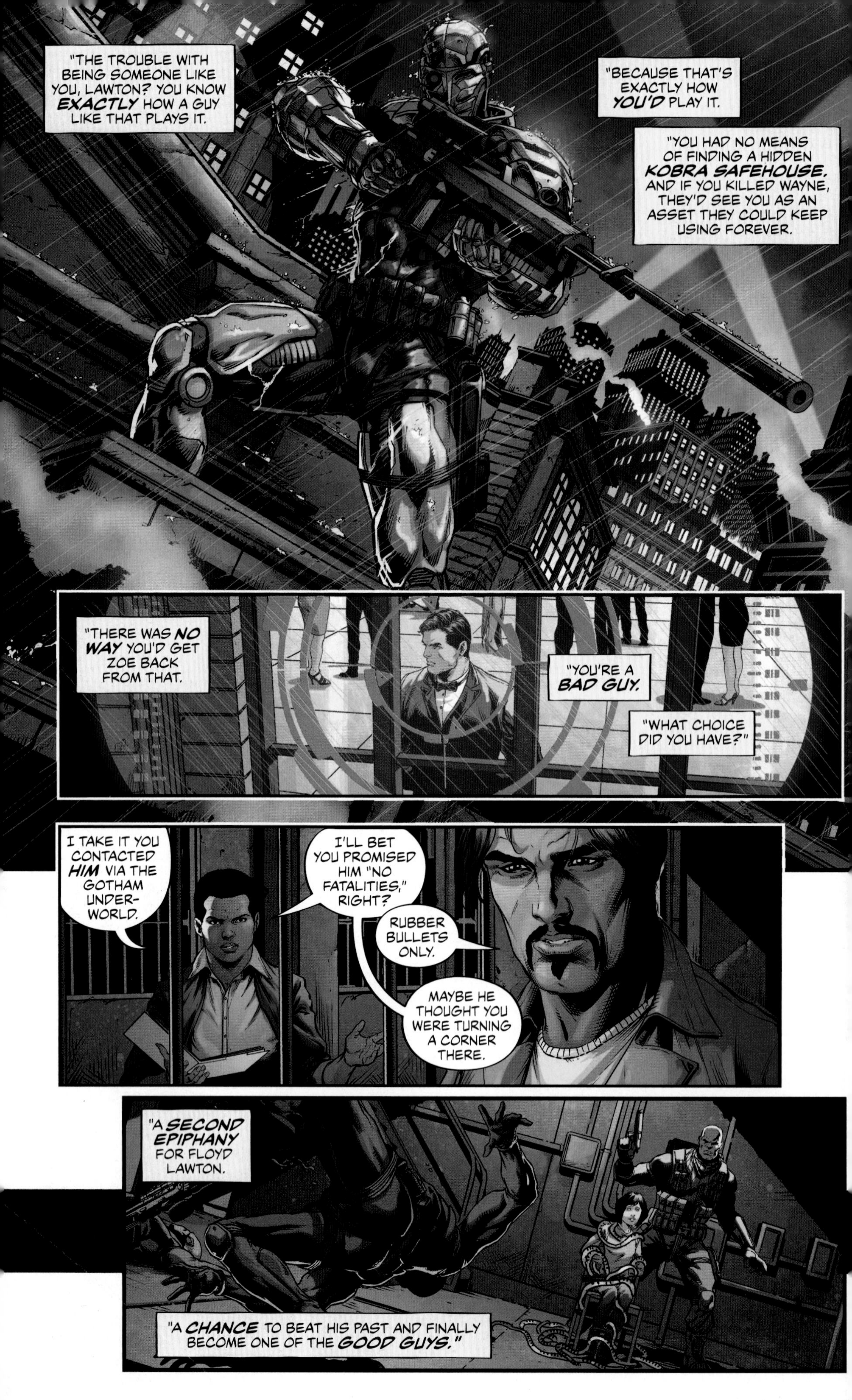
"THE TROUBLE WITH BEING SOMEONE LIKE YOU, LAWTON? YOU KNOW EXACTLY HOW A GUY LIKE THAT PLAYS IT.
"BECAUSE THAT'S EXACTLY HOW YOU'D PLAY IT.
"YOU HAD NO MEANS OF FINDING A HIDDEN KOBRA SAFEHOUSE. AND IF YOU KILLED WAYNE, THEY'D SEE YOU AS AN ASSET THEY COULD KEEP USING FOREVER.
"THERE WAS NO WAY YOU'D GET ZOE BACK FROM THAT.
"YOU'RE A BAD GUY.
"WHAT CHOICE DID YOU HAVE?"
I TAKE IT YOU CONTACTED HIM VIA THE GOTHAM UNDER-WORLD.
I'LL BET YOU PROMISED HIM "NO FATALITIES," RIGHT?
RUBBER BULLETS ONLY.
MAYBE HE THOUGHT YOU WERE TURNING A CORNER THERE.
"A SECOND EPIPHANY FOR FLOYD LAWTON.
"A CHANCE TO BEAT HIS PAST AND FINALLY BECOME ONE OF THE GOOD GUYS."

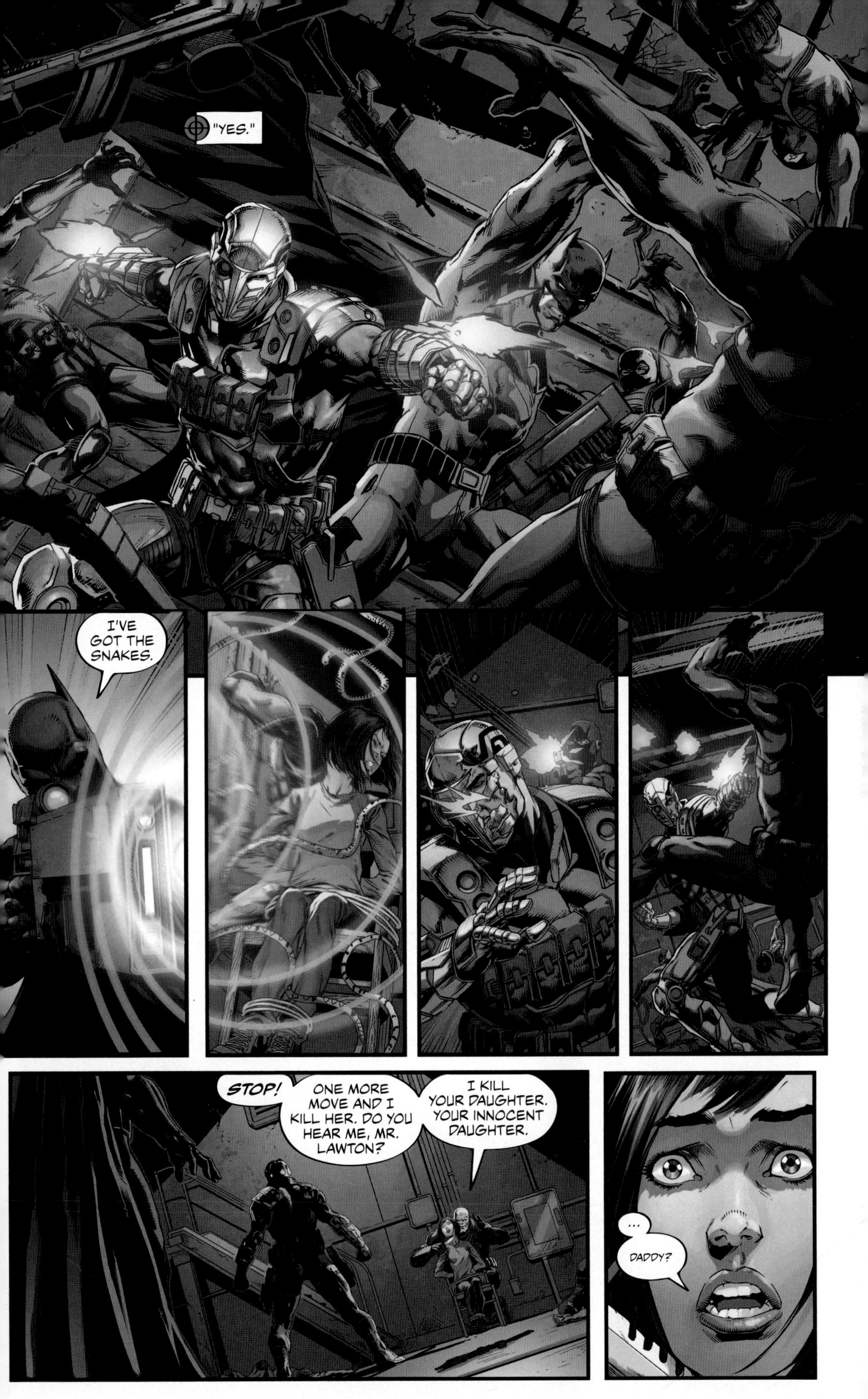
"YES."
I'VE GOT THE SNAKES.
STOP!
ONE MORE MOVE AND I KILL HER. DO YOU HEAR ME, MR. LAWTON?
I KILL YOUR DAUGHTER. YOUR INNOCENT DAUGHTER.
...
DADDY?

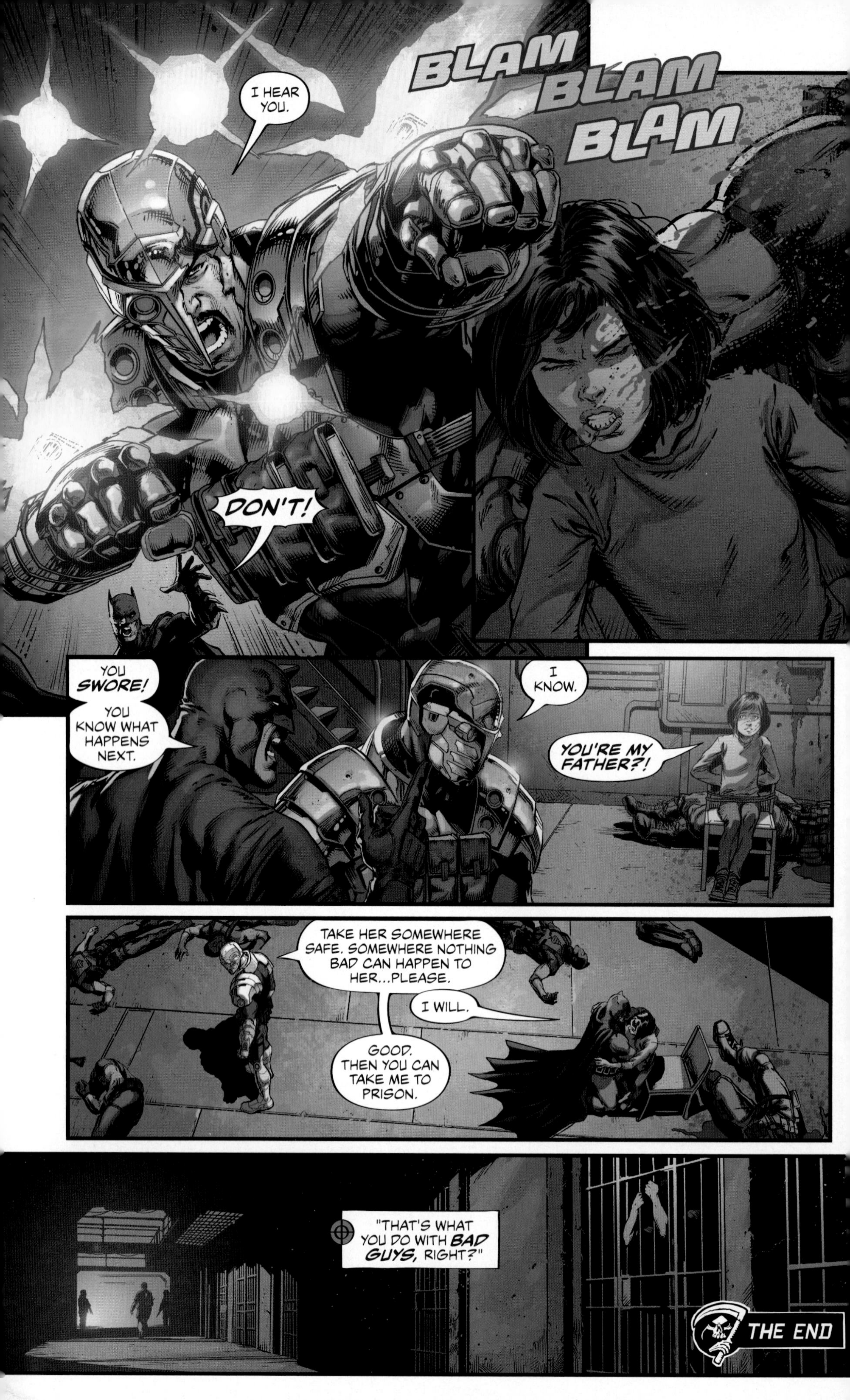
BLAM
BLAM
BLAM
I HEAR YOU.
DON'T!
YOU SWORE! YOU KNOW WHAT HAPPENS NEXT.
I KNOW.
YOU'RE MY FATHER?!
TAKE HER SOMEWHERE SAFE. SOMEWHERE NOTHING BAD CAN HAPPEN TO HER...PLEASE.
I WILL.
GOOD. THEN YOU CAN TAKE ME TO PRISON.
"THAT'S WHAT YOU DO WITH BAD GUYS, RIGHT?"
THE END

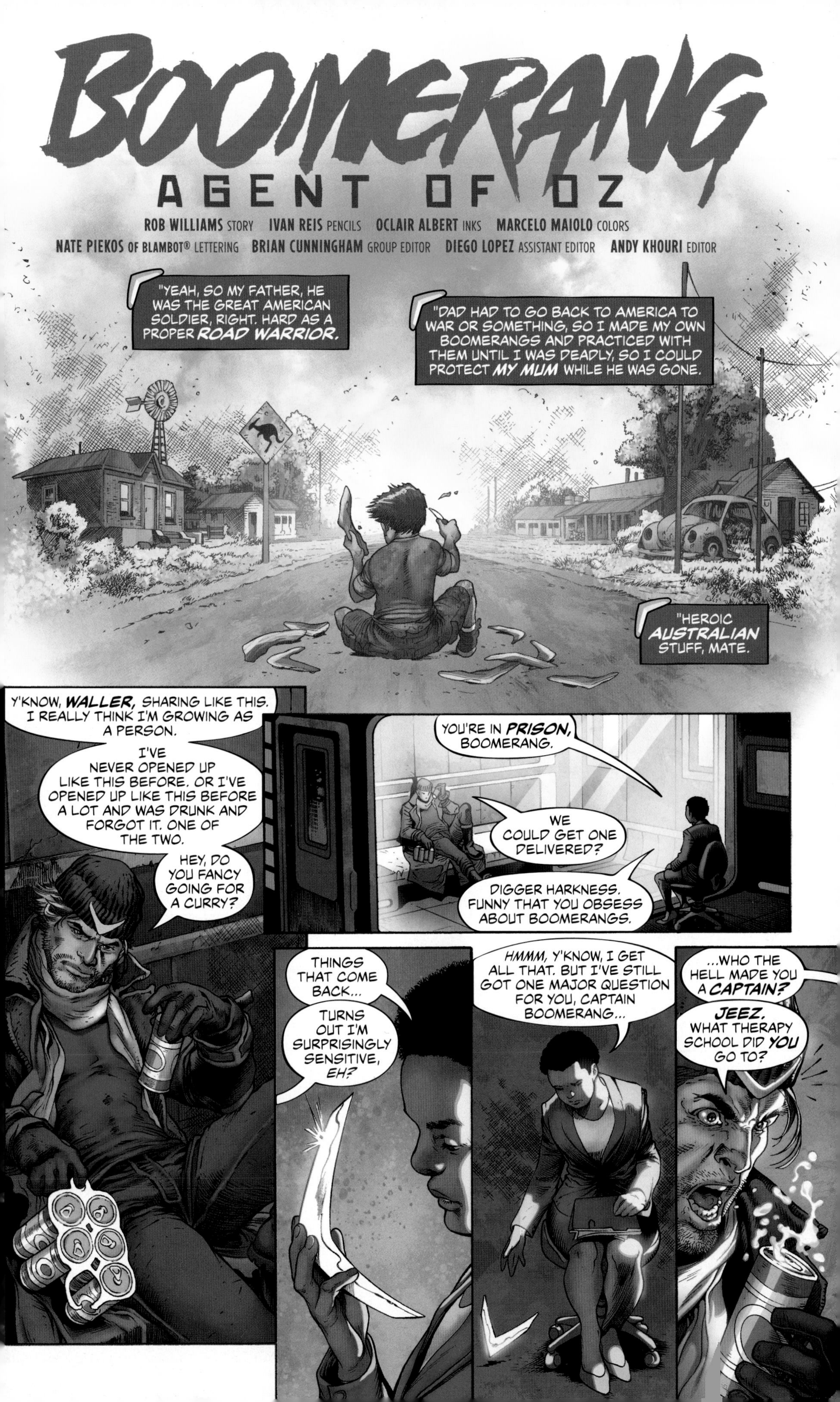
BOOMERANG
AGENT OF OZ
ROB WILLIAMS STORY IVAN REIS PENCILS OCLAIR ALBERT INKS MARCELO MAIOLO COLORS
NATE PIEKOS OF BLAMBOT® LETTERING BRIAN CUNNINGHAM GROUP EDITOR DIEGO LOPEZ ASSISTANT EDITOR ANDY KHOURI EDITOR
"YEAH, SO MY FATHER, HE WAS THE GREAT AMERICAN SOLDIER, RIGHT. HARD AS A PROPER ROAD WARRIOR.
"DAD HAD TO GO BACK TO AMERICA TO WAR OR SOMETHING, SO I MADE MY OWN BOOMERANGS AND PRACTICED WITH THEM UNTIL I WAS DEADLY, SO I COULD PROTECT MY MUM WHILE HE WAS GONE.
"HEROIC AUSTRALIAN STUFF, MATE.
Y'KNOW, WALLER, SHARING LIKE THIS. I REALLY THINK I'M GROWING AS A PERSON.
I'VE NEVER OPENED UP LIKE THIS BEFORE. OR I'VE OPENED UP LIKE THIS BEFORE A LOT AND WAS DRUNK AND FORGOT IT. ONE OF THE TWO.
HEY, DO YOU FANCY GOING FOR A CURRY?
YOU'RE IN PRISON, BOOMERANG.
WE COULD GET ONE DELIVERED?
DIGGER HARKNESS. FUNNY THAT YOU OBSESS ABOUT BOOMERANGS.
THINGS THAT COME BACK...
TURNS OUT I'M SURPRISINGLY SENSITIVE, EH?
HMMM, Y'KNOW, I GET ALL THAT. BUT I'VE STILL GOT ONE MAJOR QUESTION FOR YOU, CAPTAIN BOOMERANG...
...WHO THE HELL MADE YOU A CAPTAIN?
JEEZ. WHAT THERAPY SCHOOL DID YOU GO TO?

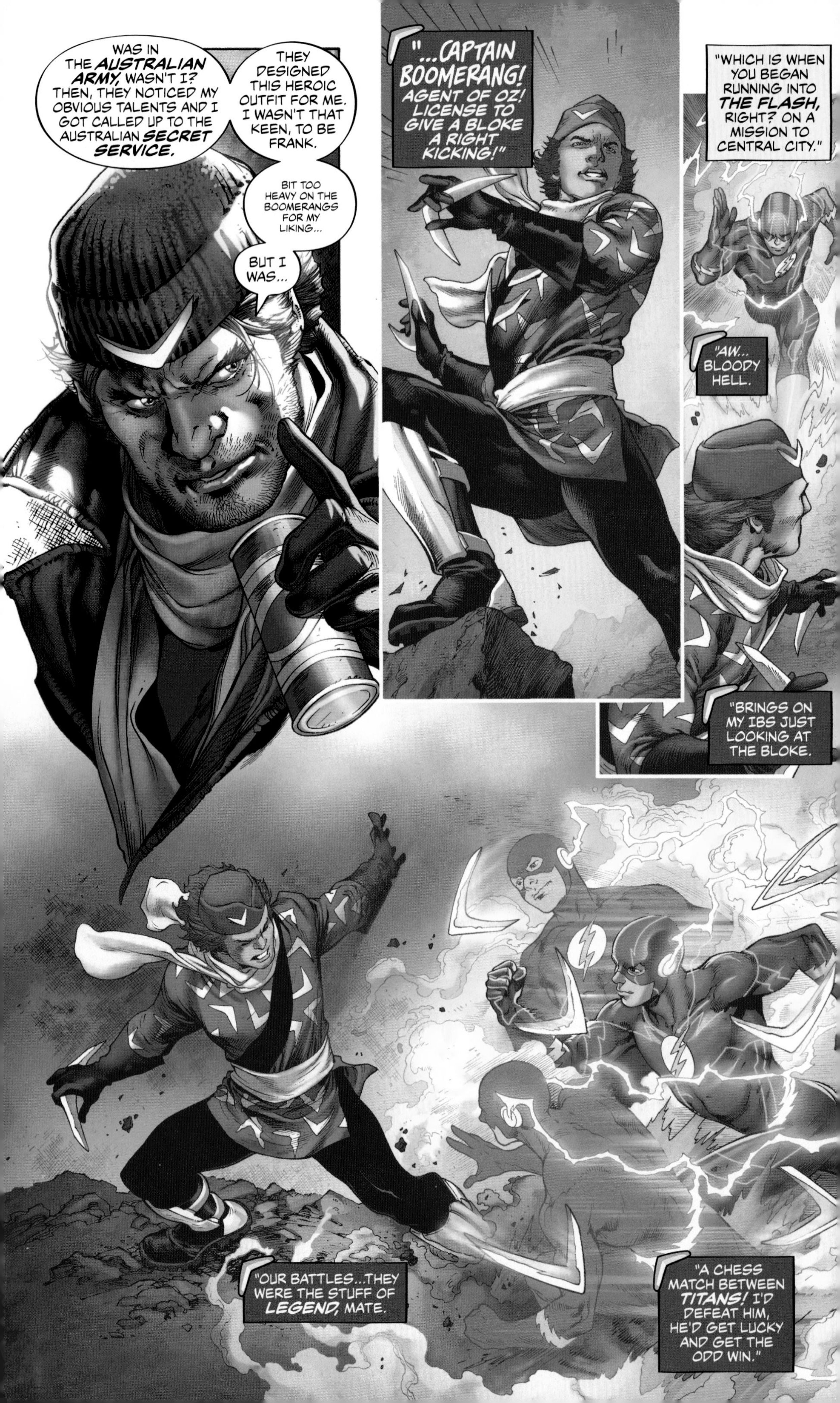
WAS IN THE AUSTRALIAN ARMY, WASN'T I? THEN, THEY NOTICED MY OBVIOUS TALENTS AND I GOT CALLED UP TO THE AUSTRALIAN SECRET SERVICE.
THEY DESIGNED THIS HEROIC OUTFIT FOR ME. I WASN'T THAT KEEN, TO BE FRANK.
BIT TOO HEAVY ON THE BOOMERANGS FOR MY LIKING...
BUT I WAS...
"...CAPTAIN BOOMERANG! AGENT OF OZ! LICENSE TO GIVE A BLOKE A RIGHT KICKING!"
"WHICH IS WHEN YOU BEGAN RUNNING INTO THE FLASH, RIGHT? ON A MISSION TO CENTRAL CITY."
"AW... BLOODY HELL.
"BRINGS ON MY IBS JUST LOOKING AT THE BLOKE.
"OUR BATTLES...THEY WERE THE STUFF OF LEGEND, MATE.
"A CHESS MATCH BETWEEN TITANS! I'D DEFEAT HIM, HE'D GET LUCKY AND GET THE ODD WIN."

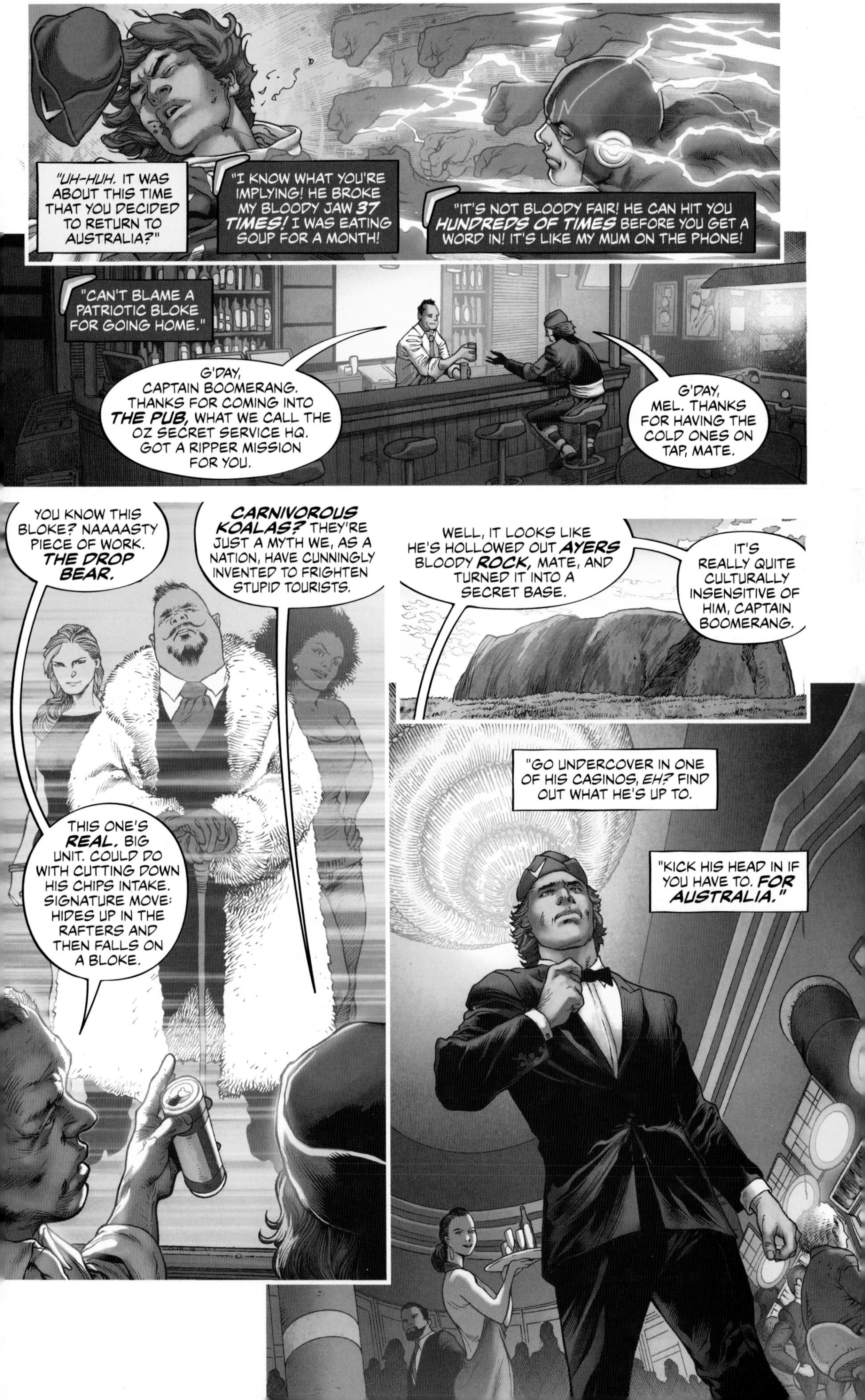
"UH-HUH. IT WAS ABOUT THIS TIME THAT YOU DECIDED TO RETURN TO AUSTRALIA?"
"I KNOW WHAT YOU'RE IMPLYING! HE BROKE MY BLOODY JAW 37 TIMES! I WAS EATING SOUP FOR A MONTH!
"IT'S NOT BLOODY FAIR! HE CAN HIT YOU HUNDREDS OF TIMES BEFORE YOU GET A WORD IN! IT'S LIKE MY MUM ON THE PHONE!
"CAN'T BLAME A PATRIOTIC BLOKE FOR GOING HOME."
G'DAY, CAPTAIN BOOMERANG. THANKS FOR COMING INTO THE PUB, WHAT WE CALL THE OZ SECRET SERVICE HQ. GOT A RIPPER MISSION FOR YOU.
G'DAY, MEL. THANKS FOR HAVING THE COLD ONES ON TAP, MATE.
YOU KNOW THIS BLOKE? NAAAASTY PIECE OF WORK. THE DROP BEAR.
CARNIVOROUS KOALAS? THEY'RE JUST A MYTH WE, AS A NATION, HAVE CUNNINGLY INVENTED TO FRIGHTEN STUPID TOURISTS.
THIS ONE'S REAL. BIG UNIT. COULD DO WITH CUTTING DOWN HIS CHIPS INTAKE. SIGNATURE MOVE: HIDES UP IN THE RAFTERS AND THEN FALLS ON A BLOKE.
WELL, IT LOOKS LIKE HE'S HOLLOWED OUT AYERS BLOODY ROCK, MATE, AND TURNED IT INTO A SECRET BASE.
IT'S REALLY QUITE CULTURALLY INSENSITIVE OF HIM, CAPTAIN BOOMERANG.
"GO UNDERCOVER IN ONE OF HIS CASINOS, EH? FIND OUT WHAT HE'S UP TO.
"KICK HIS HEAD IN IF YOU HAVE TO. FOR AUSTRALIA."

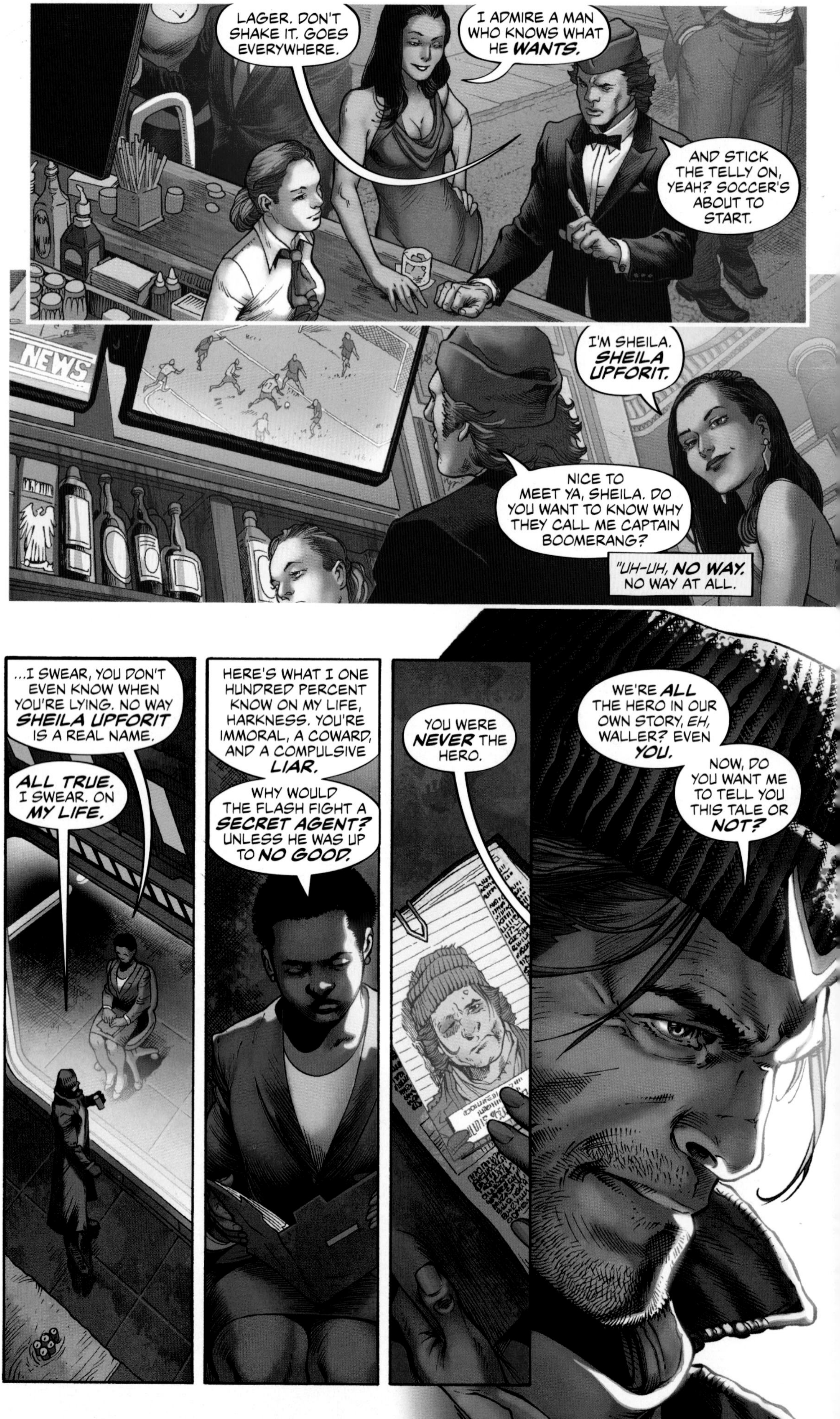
LAGER. DON'T SHAKE IT. GOES EVERYWHERE.
I ADMIRE A MAN WHO KNOWS WHAT HE WANTS.
AND STICK THE TELLY ON, YEAH? SOCCER'S ABOUT TO START.
NEWS
I'M SHEILA. SHEILA UPFORIT.
NICE TO MEET YA, SHEILA. DO YOU WANT TO KNOW WHY THEY CALL ME CAPTAIN BOOMERANG?
"UH-UH, NO WAY. NO WAY AT ALL.
...I SWEAR, YOU DON'T EVEN KNOW WHEN YOU'RE LYING. NO WAY SHEILA UPFORIT IS A REAL NAME.
ALL TRUE. I SWEAR. ON MY LIFE.
HERE'S WHAT I ONE HUNDRED PERCENT KNOW ON MY LIFE, HARKNESS. YOU'RE IMMORAL, A COWARD, AND A COMPULSIVE LIAR.
WHY WOULD THE FLASH FIGHT A SECRET AGENT? UNLESS HE WAS UP TO NO GOOD.
YOU WERE NEVER THE HERO.
WE'RE ALL THE HERO IN OUR OWN STORY, EH, WALLER? EVEN YOU.
NOW, DO YOU WANT ME TO TELL YOU THIS TALE OR NOT?

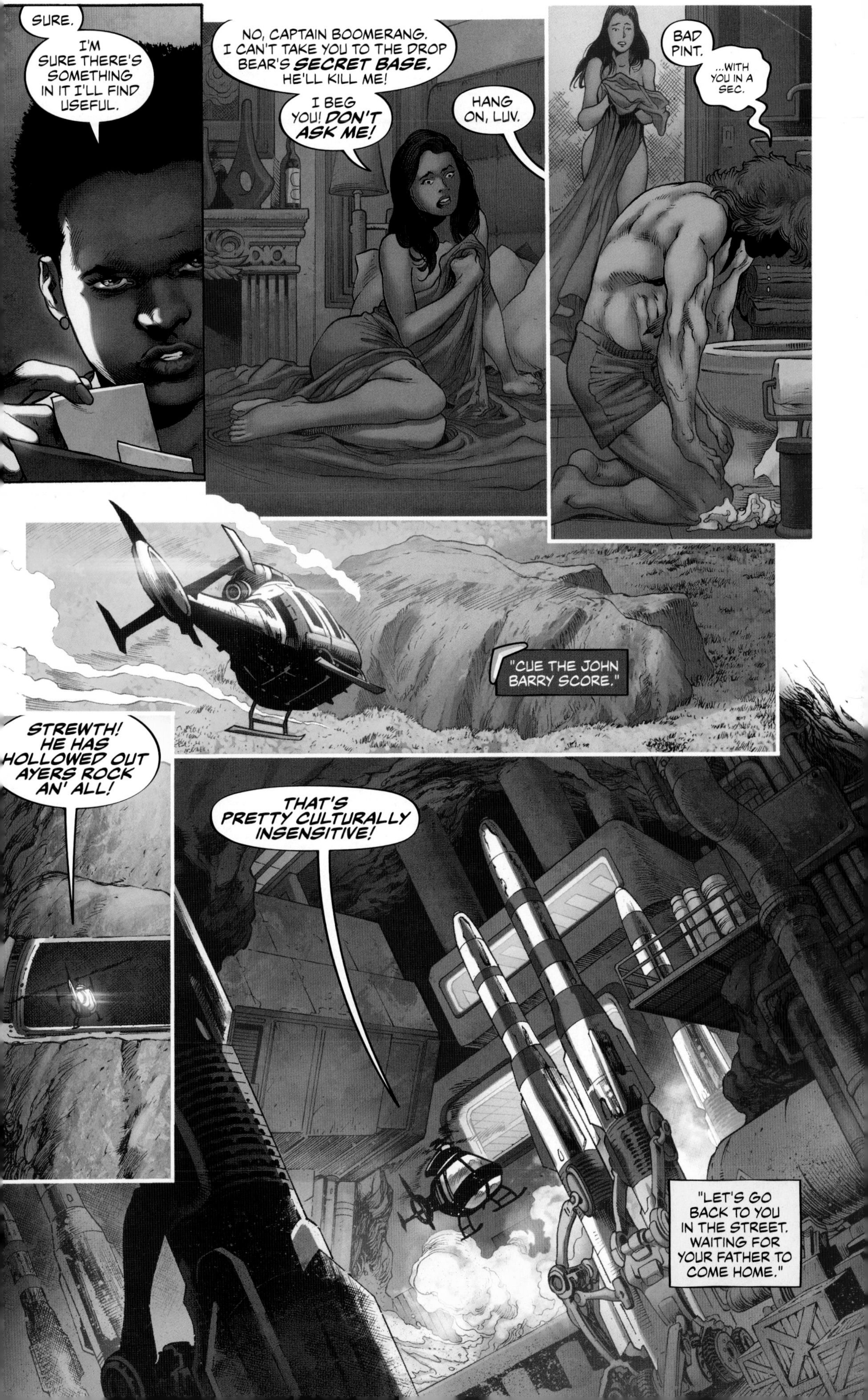
SURE.
I'M SURE THERE'S SOMETHING IN IT I'LL FIND USEFUL.
NO, CAPTAIN BOOMERANG. I CAN'T TAKE YOU TO THE DROP BEAR'S SECRET BASE. HE'LL KILL ME!
I BEG YOU! DON'T ASK ME!
HANG ON, LUV.
BAD PINT.
...WITH YOU IN A SEC.
"CUE THE JOHN BARRY SCORE."
STREWTH! HE HAS HOLLOWED OUT AYERS ROCK AN' ALL!
THAT'S PRETTY CULTURALLY INSENSITIVE!
"LET'S GO BACK TO YOU IN THE STREET. WAITING FOR YOUR FATHER TO COME HOME."

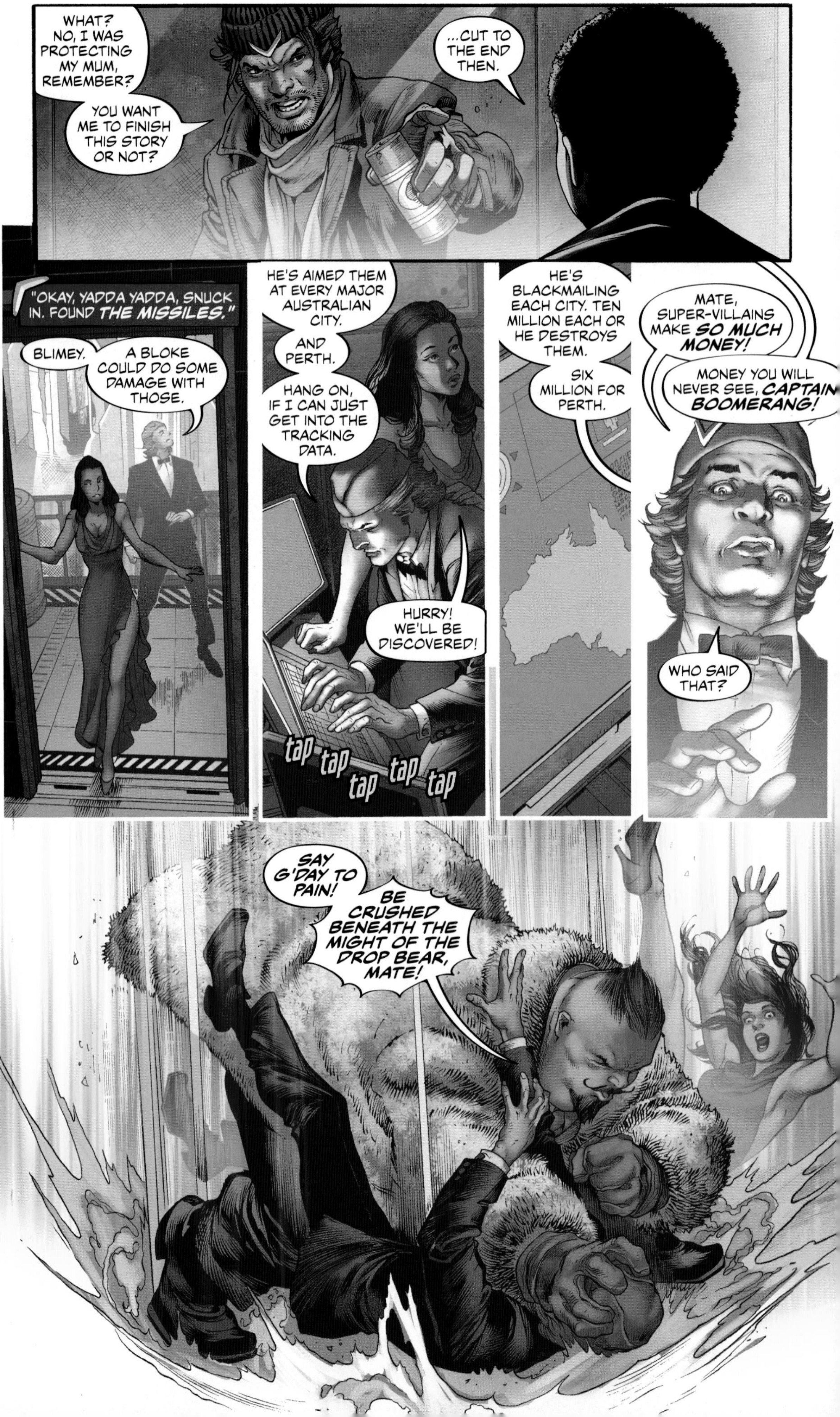
WHAT? NO, I WAS PROTECTING MY MUM, REMEMBER?
YOU WANT ME TO FINISH THIS STORY OR NOT?
...CUT TO THE END THEN.
"OKAY, YADDA YADDA, SNUCK IN. FOUND THE MISSILES."
BLIMEY.
A BLOKE COULD DO SOME DAMAGE WITH THOSE.
HE'S AIMED THEM AT EVERY MAJOR AUSTRALIAN CITY.
AND PERTH.
HANG ON, IF I CAN JUST GET INTO THE TRACKING DATA.
HURRY! WE'LL BE DISCOVERED!
tap tap tap tap tap
HE'S BLACKMAILING EACH CITY. TEN MILLION EACH OR HE DESTROYS THEM.
SIX MILLION FOR PERTH.
MATE, SUPER-VILLAINS MAKE SO MUCH MONEY!
MONEY YOU WILL NEVER SEE, CAPTAIN BOOMERANG!
WHO SAID THAT?
SAY G'DAY TO PAIN!
BE CRUSHED BENEATH THE MIGHT OF THE DROP BEAR, MATE!

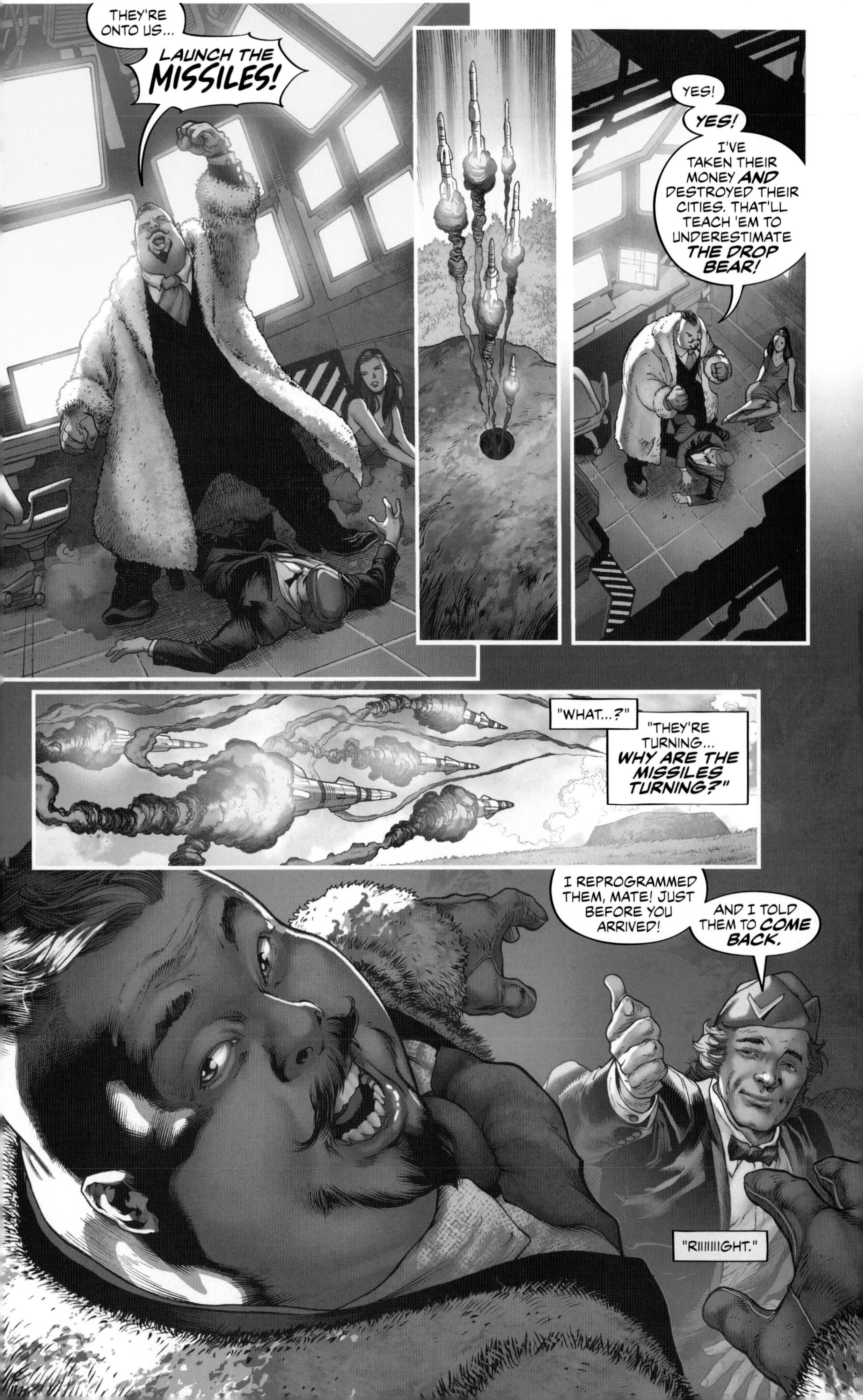
THEY'RE ONTO US... LAUNCH THE MISSILES!
YES!
YES!
I'VE TAKEN THEIR MONEY AND DESTROYED THEIR CITIES. THAT'LL TEACH 'EM TO UNDERESTIMATE THE DROP BEAR!
"WHAT...?"
"THEY'RE TURNING... WHY ARE THE MISSILES TURNING?"
I REPROGRAMMED THEM, MATE! JUST BEFORE YOU ARRIVED!
AND I TOLD THEM TO COME BACK.
"RIIIIIIGHT."

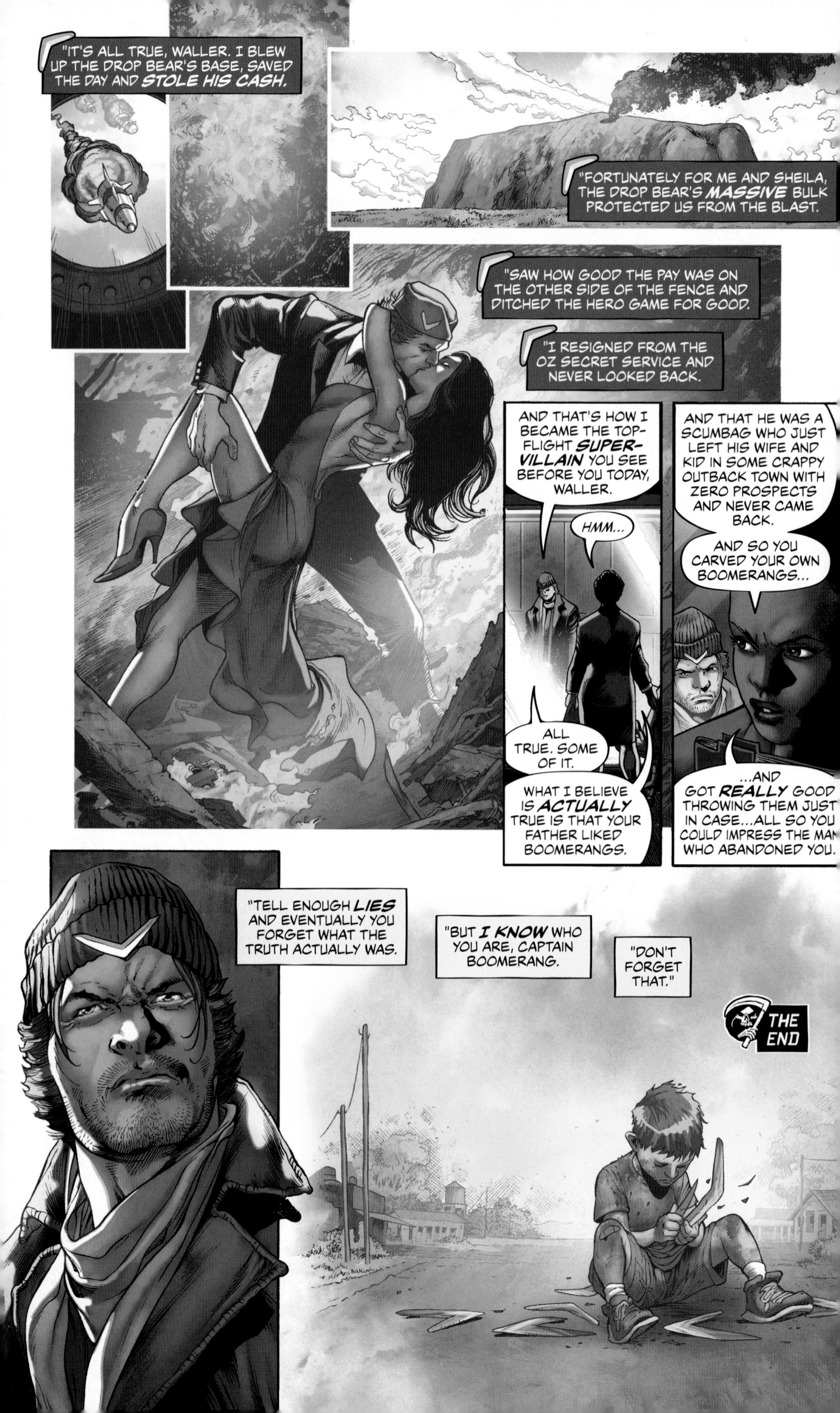
"IT'S ALL TRUE, WALLER. I BLEW UP THE DROP BEAR'S BASE, SAVED THE DAY AND STOLE HIS CASH.
"FORTUNATELY FOR ME AND SHEILA, THE DROP BEAR'S MASSIVE BULK PROTECTED US FROM THE BLAST.
"SAW HOW GOOD THE PAY WAS ON THE OTHER SIDE OF THE FENCE AND DITCHED THE HERO GAME FOR GOOD.
"I RESIGNED FROM THE OZ SECRET SERVICE AND NEVER LOOKED BACK.
AND THAT'S HOW I BECAME THE TOP-FLIGHT SUPER-VILLAIN YOU SEE BEFORE YOU TODAY, WALLER.
HMM...
ALL TRUE. SOME OF IT.
WHAT I BELIEVE IS ACTUALLY TRUE IS THAT YOUR FATHER LIKED BOOMERANGS.
AND THAT HE WAS A SCUMBAG WHO JUST LEFT HIS WIFE AND KID IN SOME CRAPPY OUTBACK TOWN WITH ZERO PROSPECTS AND NEVER CAME BACK.
AND SO YOU CARVED YOUR OWN BOOMERANGS...
...AND GOT REALLY GOOD THROWING THEM JUST IN CASE...ALL SO YOU COULD IMPRESS THE MA
WHO ABANDONED YOU.
"TELL ENOUGH LIES AND EVENTUALLY YOU FORGET WHAT THE TRUTH ACTUALLY WAS.
"BUT I KNOW WHO YOU ARE, CAPTAIN BOOMERANG.
"DON'T FORGET THAT."
THE END

"KATANA.

CHOOSE

ROB WILLIAMS WRITER   **PHILIP TAN** ARTIST   **ELMER SANTOS** COLORIST   **NATE PIEKOS** OF BLAMBOT® LETTERER

BRIAN CUNNINGHAM GROUP EDITOR   **HARVEY RICHARDS** ASSOC. EDITOR   **ANDY KHOURI** EDITOR

"YOU NEVER SAY A WORD.

"WHY IS THAT, DO YOU THINK?"

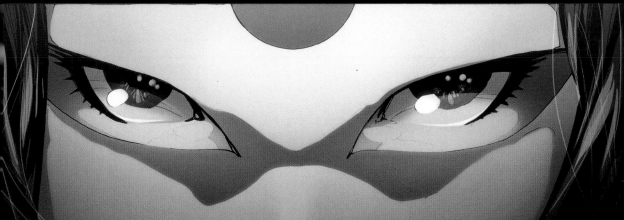

YEAH... NOT EXACTLY ABOUT THE BANTER, ARE YOU?

YOU VOLUNTEERED FOR TASK FORCE X, BUT I NEED TO BE SURE WE CAN *TRUST* YOU. TO BACK UP FLAG WHEN THE PSYCHOS TURN ON YOU BOTH IN THE FIELD.

I NEED TO *UNDERSTAND* YOU.

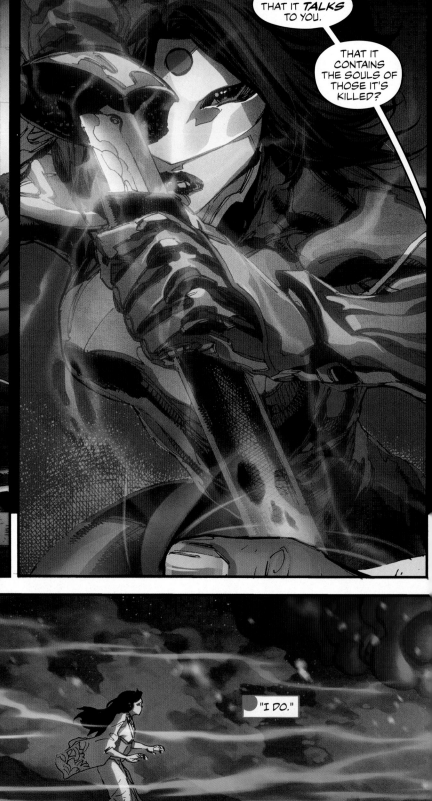

YOUR SWORD IS CALLED *SOULTAKER.*

YOU BELIEVE THAT IT *TALKS* TO YOU.

THAT IT CONTAINS THE SOULS OF THOSE IT'S KILLED?

"I DO."

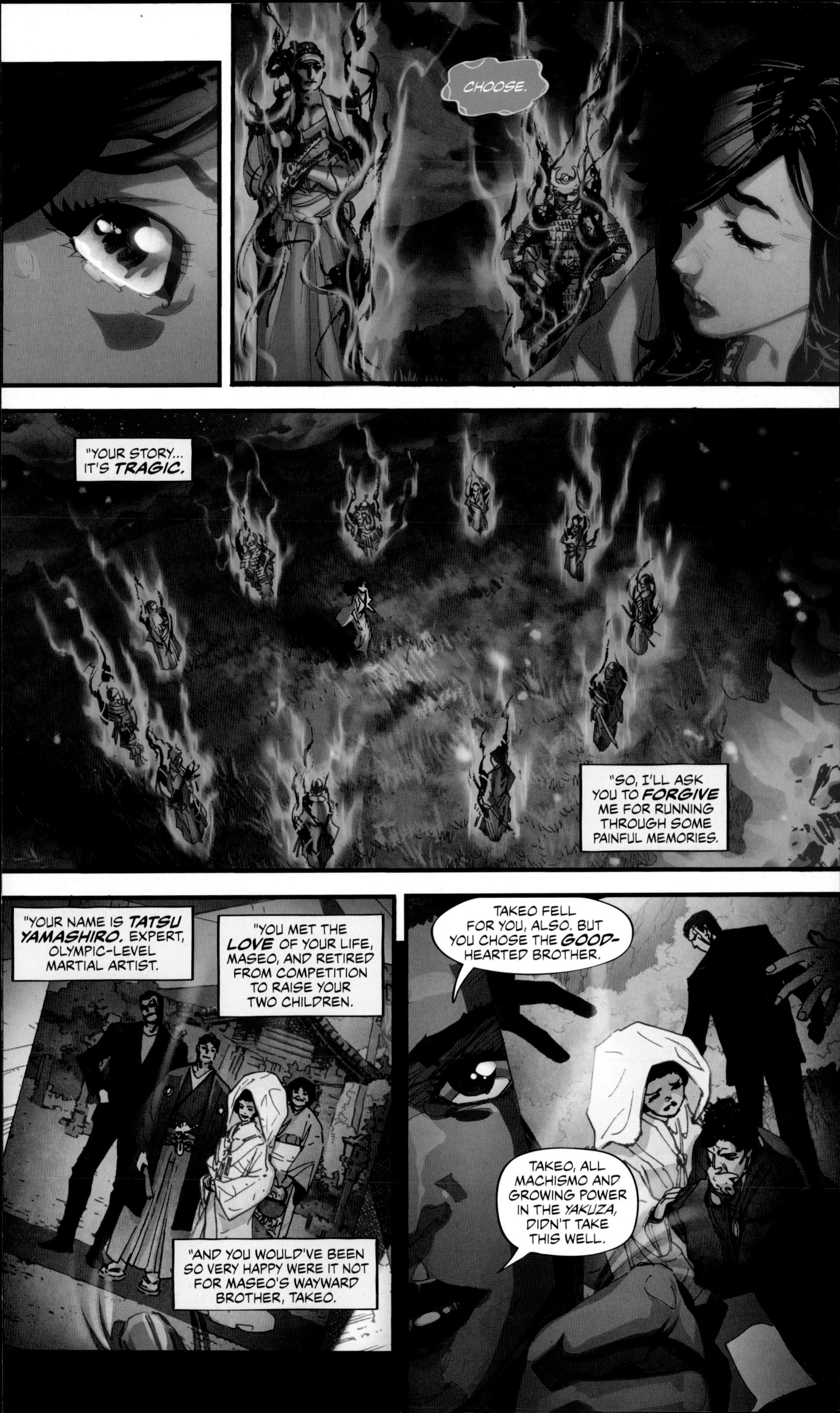
CHOOSE.
"YOUR STORY... IT'S TRAGIC.
"SO, I'LL ASK YOU TO FORGIVE ME FOR RUNNING THROUGH SOME PAINFUL MEMORIES.
"YOUR NAME IS TATSU YAMASHIRO. EXPERT, OLYMPIC-LEVEL MARTIAL ARTIST.
"YOU MET THE LOVE OF YOUR LIFE, MASEO, AND RETIRED FROM COMPETITION TO RAISE YOUR TWO CHILDREN.
"AND YOU WOULD'VE BEEN SO VERY HAPPY WERE IT NOT FOR MASEO'S WAYWARD BROTHER, TAKEO.
TAKEO FELL FOR YOU, ALSO. BUT YOU CHOSE THE GOOD-HEARTED BROTHER.
TAKEO, ALL MACHISMO AND GROWING POWER IN THE YAKUZA, DIDN'T TAKE THIS WELL.

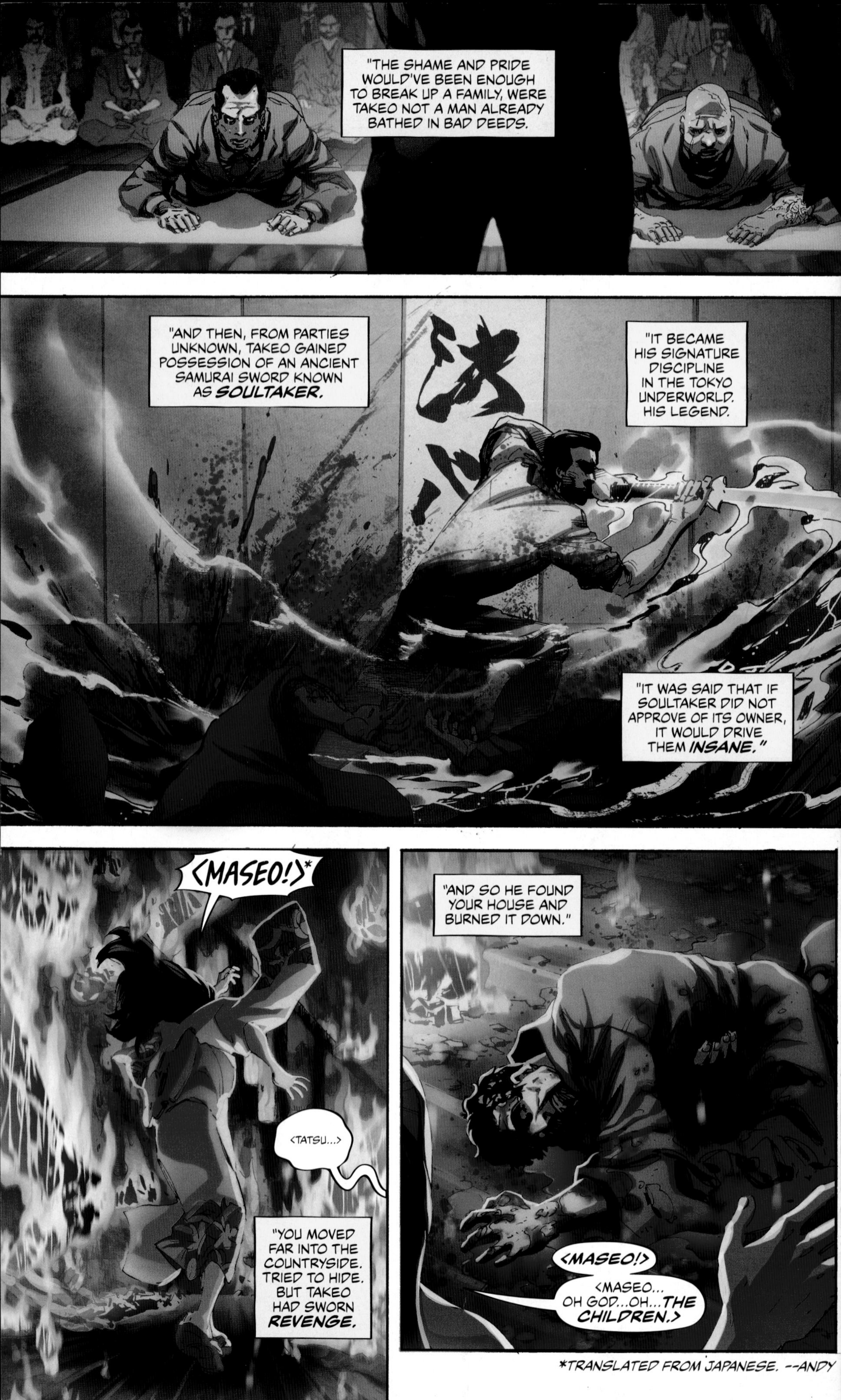
"THE SHAME AND PRIDE WOULD'VE BEEN ENOUGH TO BREAK UP A FAMILY, WERE TAKEO NOT A MAN ALREADY BATHED IN BAD DEEDS.
"AND THEN, FROM PARTIES UNKNOWN, TAKEO GAINED POSSESSION OF AN ANCIENT SAMURAI SWORD KNOWN AS SOULTAKER.
"IT BECAME HIS SIGNATURE DISCIPLINE IN THE TOKYO UNDERWORLD. HIS LEGEND.
"IT WAS SAID THAT IF SOULTAKER DID NOT APPROVE OF ITS OWNER, IT WOULD DRIVE THEM INSANE."
<MASEO!>*
<TATSU...>
"YOU MOVED FAR INTO THE COUNTRYSIDE. TRIED TO HIDE. BUT TAKEO HAD SWORN REVENGE.
"AND SO HE FOUND YOUR HOUSE AND BURNED IT DOWN."
<MASEO!>
<MASEO... OH GOD...OH...THE CHILDREN.>

*TRANSLATED FROM JAPANESE. --ANDY

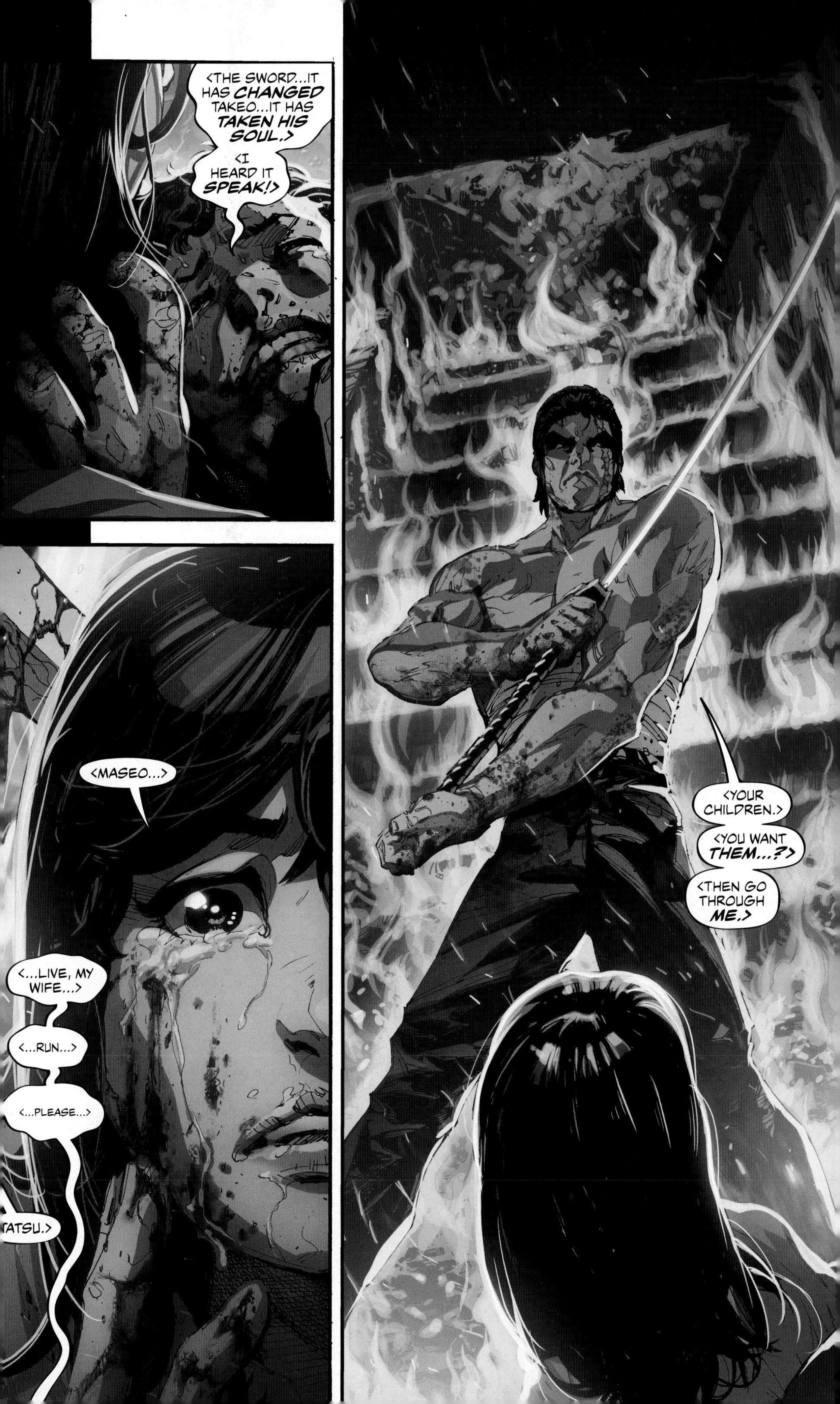
<THE SWORD...IT HAS CHANGED TAKEO...IT HAS TAKEN HIS SOUL.>
<I HEARD IT SPEAK!>
<MASEO...>
<...LIVE, MY WIFE...>
<...RUN...>
<...PLEASE...>
TATSU.>
<YOUR CHILDREN.>
<YOU WANT THEM...?>
<THEN GO THROUGH ME.>

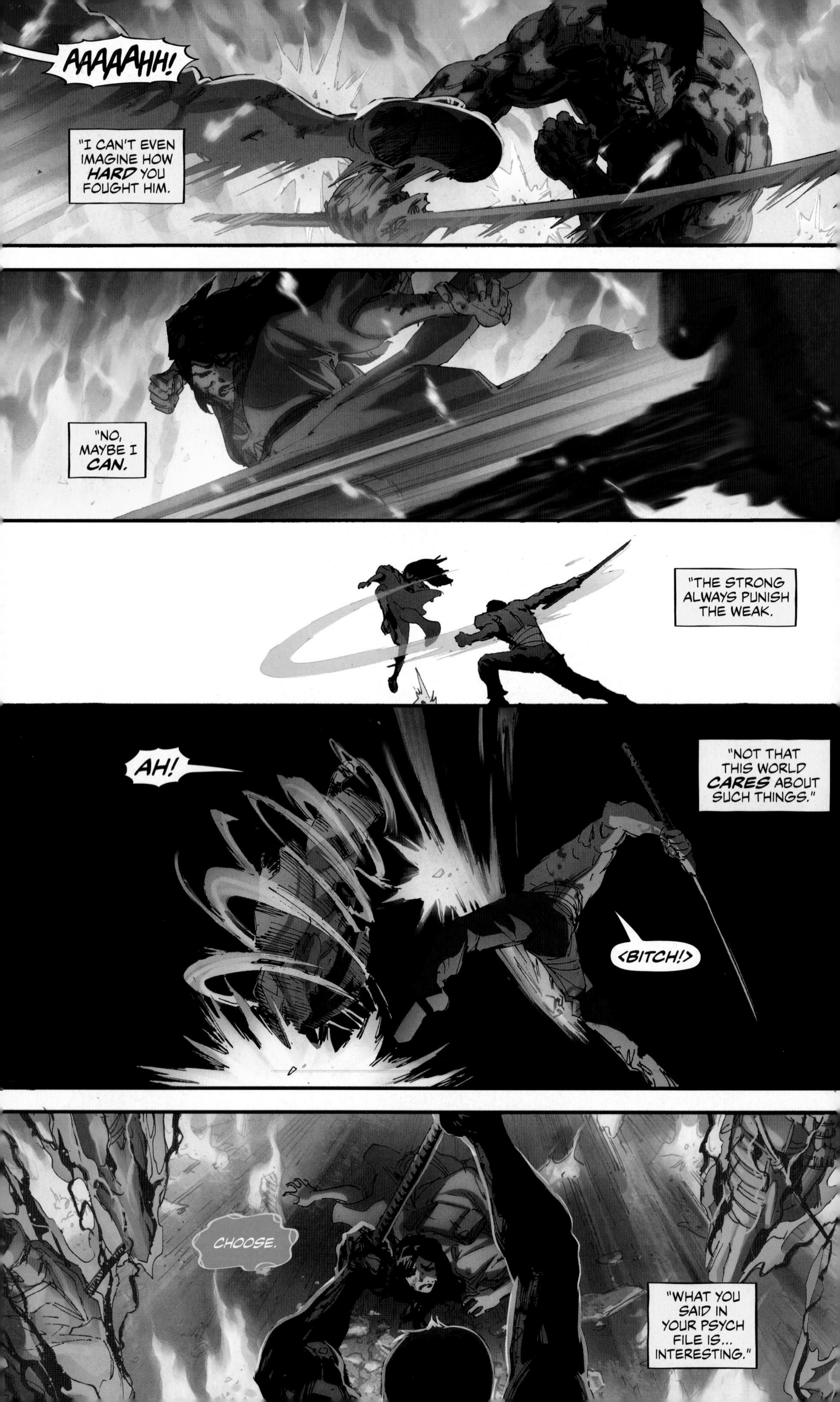

AAAAAHH!
"I CAN'T EVEN IMAGINE HOW HARD YOU FOUGHT HIM.
"NO, MAYBE I CAN.
"THE STRONG ALWAYS PUNISH THE WEAK.
AH!
"NOT THAT THIS WORLD CARES ABOUT SUCH THINGS."
<BITCH!>
CHOOSE.
"WHAT YOU SAID IN YOUR PSYCH FILE IS... INTERESTING."

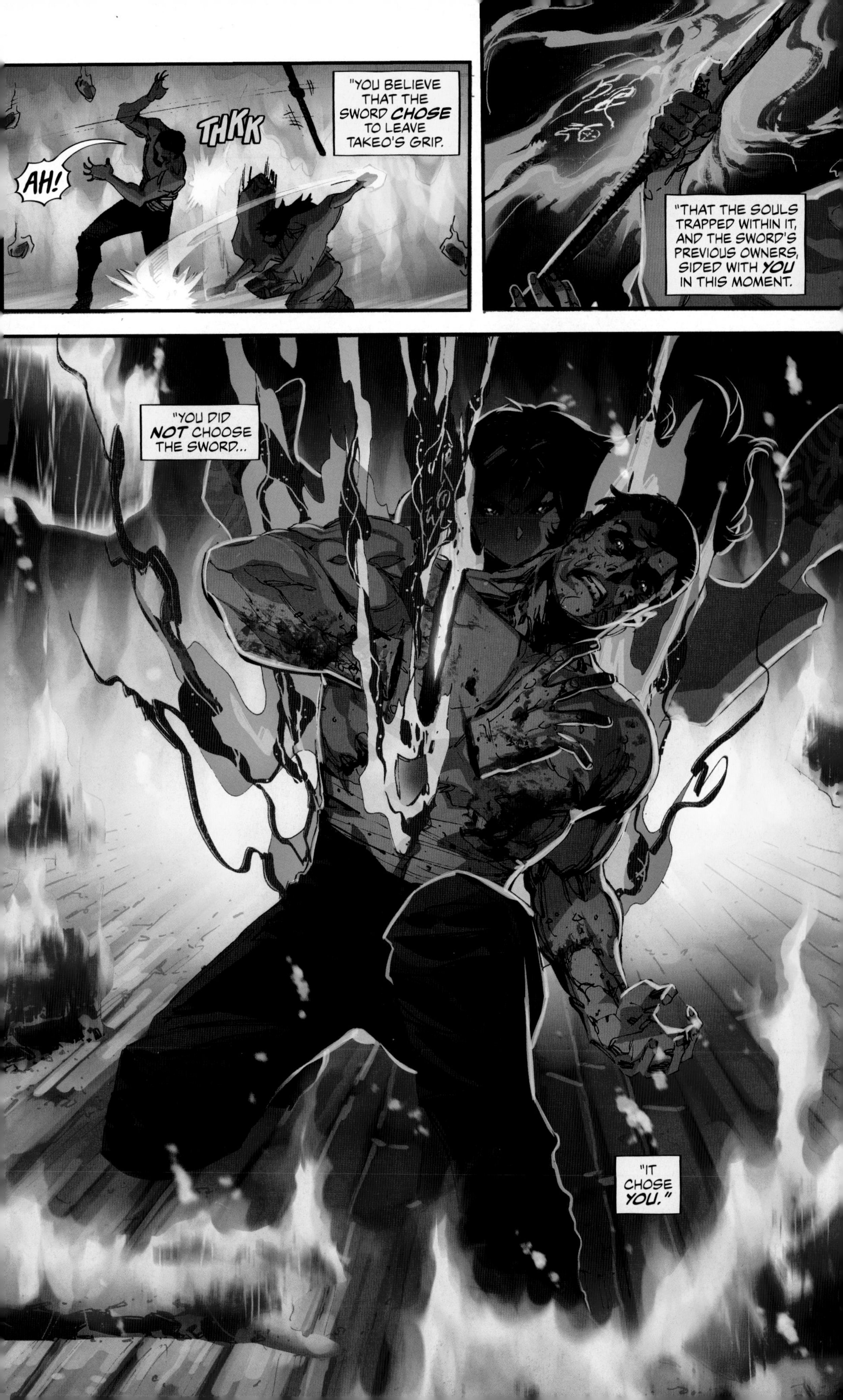
"YOU BELIEVE THAT THE SWORD CHOSE TO LEAVE TAKEO'S GRIP.
THKK
AH!
"THAT THE SOULS TRAPPED WITHIN IT, AND THE SWORD'S PREVIOUS OWNERS, SIDED WITH YOU IN THIS MOMENT.
"YOU DID NOT CHOOSE THE SWORD...
"IT CHOSE YOU."

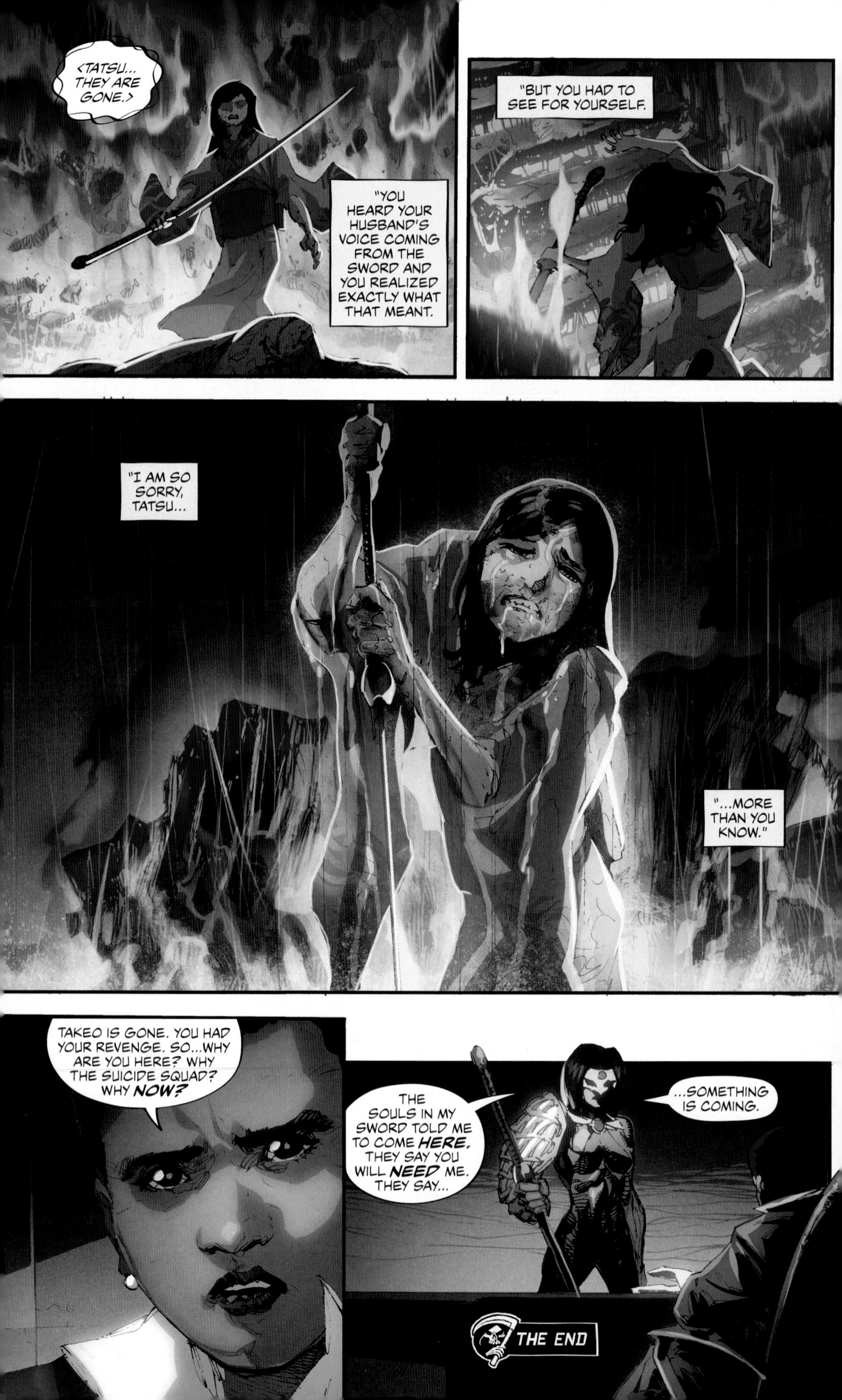

<TATSU... THEY ARE GONE.>
"YOU HEARD YOUR HUSBAND'S VOICE COMING FROM THE SWORD AND YOU REALIZED EXACTLY WHAT THAT MEANT.
"BUT YOU HAD TO SEE FOR YOURSELF.
"I AM SO SORRY, TATSU...
"...MORE THAN YOU KNOW."
TAKEO IS GONE. YOU HAD YOUR REVENGE. SO...WHY ARE YOU HERE? WHY THE SUICIDE SQUAD? WHY ***NOW?***
THE SOULS IN MY SWORD TOLD ME TO COME ***HERE.*** THEY SAY YOU WILL ***NEED*** ME. THEY SAY...
...SOMETHING IS COMING.
THE END

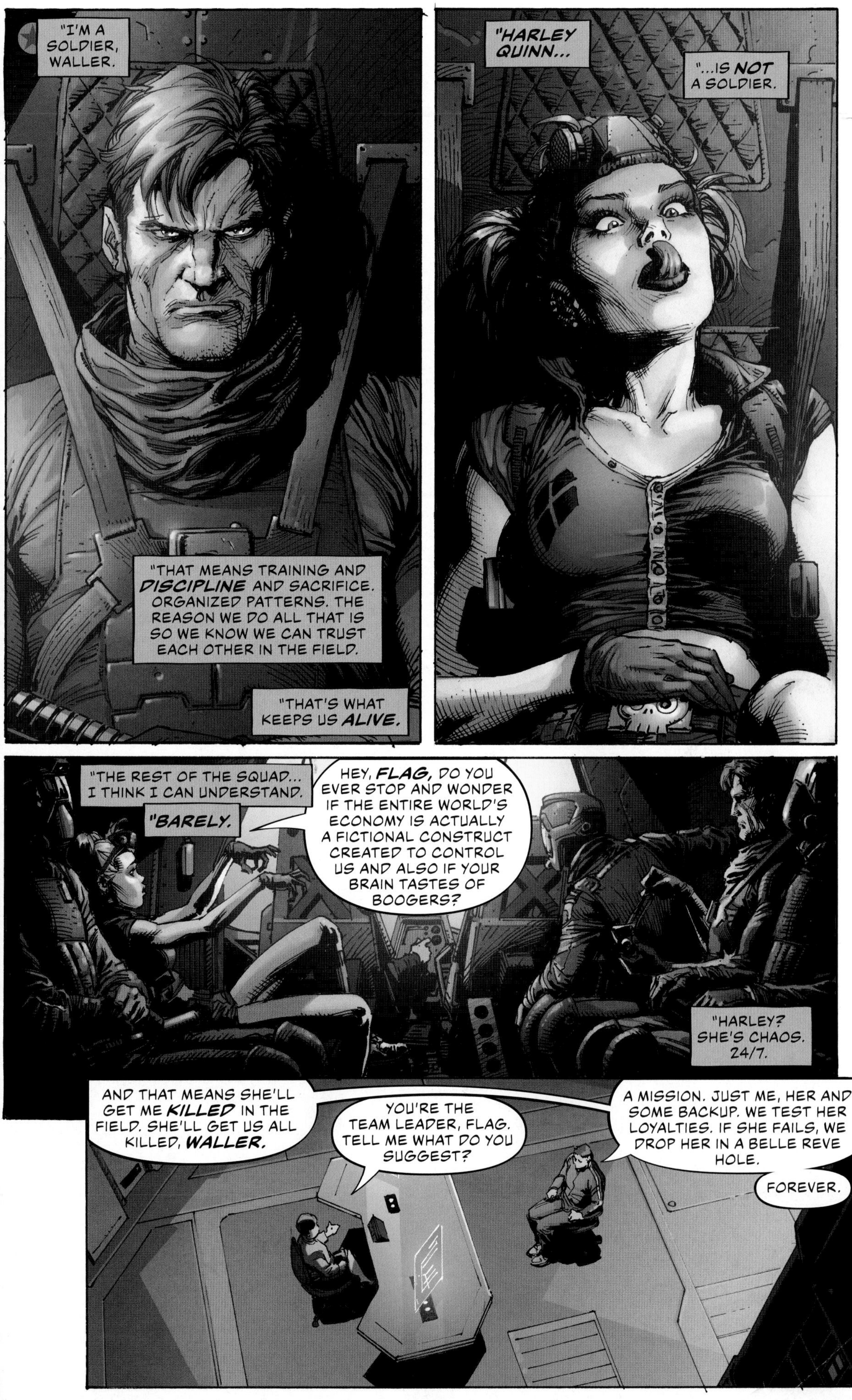

"I'M A SOLDIER, WALLER.
"THAT MEANS TRAINING AND DISCIPLINE AND SACRIFICE. ORGANIZED PATTERNS. THE REASON WE DO ALL THAT IS SO WE KNOW WE CAN TRUST EACH OTHER IN THE FIELD.
"THAT'S WHAT KEEPS US ALIVE.
"HARLEY QUINN...
"...IS NOT A SOLDIER.
"THE REST OF THE SQUAD... I THINK I CAN UNDERSTAND.
"BARELY.
HEY, FLAG, DO YOU EVER STOP AND WONDER IF THE ENTIRE WORLD'S ECONOMY IS ACTUALLY A FICTIONAL CONSTRUCT CREATED TO CONTROL US AND ALSO IF YOUR BRAIN TASTES OF BOOGERS?
"HARLEY? SHE'S CHAOS. 24/7.
AND THAT MEANS SHE'LL GET ME KILLED IN THE FIELD. SHE'LL GET US ALL KILLED, WALLER.
YOU'RE THE TEAM LEADER, FLAG. TELL ME WHAT DO YOU SUGGEST?
A MISSION. JUST ME, HER AND SOME BACKUP. WE TEST HER LOYALTIES. IF SHE FAILS, WE DROP HER IN A BELLE REVE HOLE.
FOREVER.

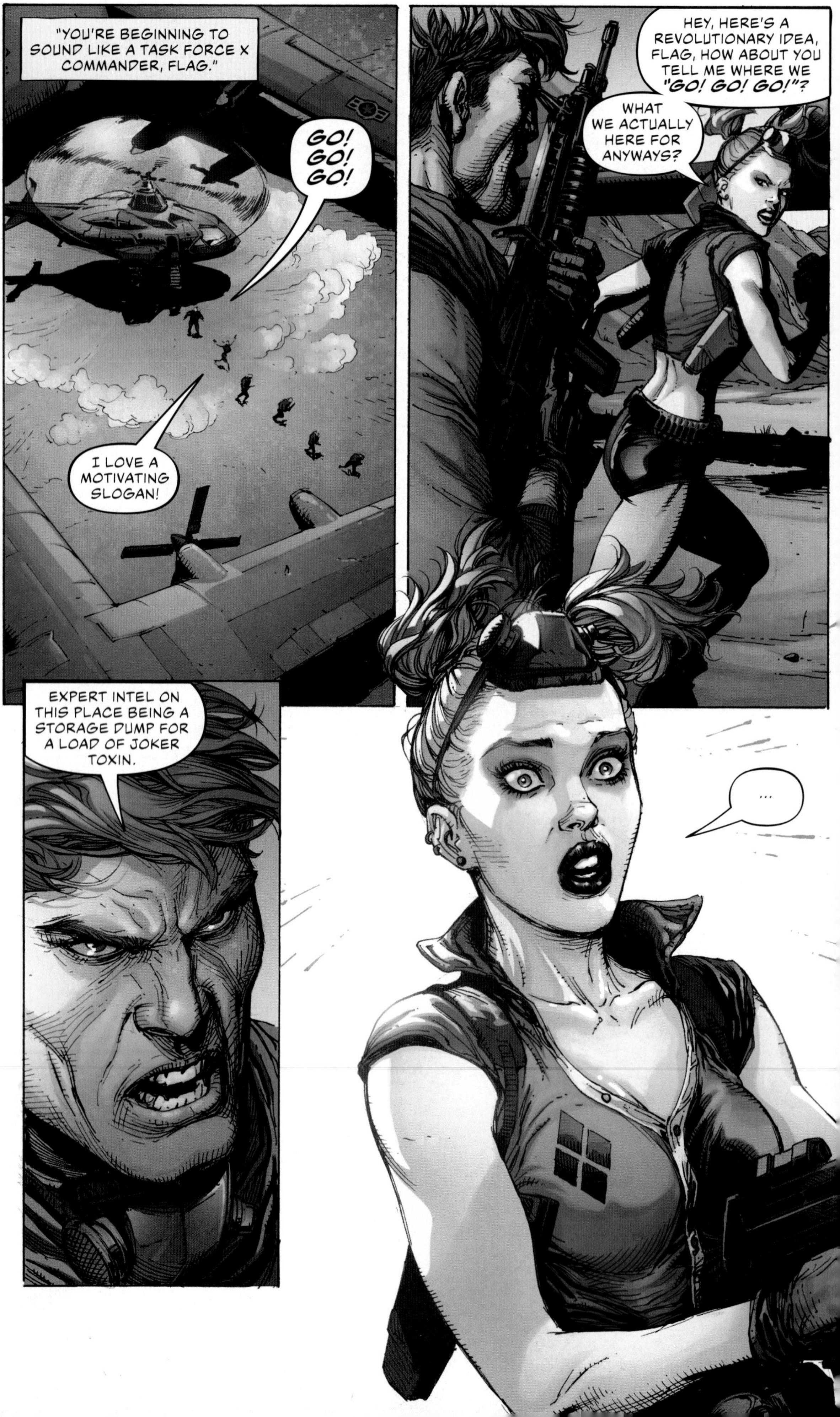
"YOU'RE BEGINNING TO SOUND LIKE A TASK FORCE X COMMANDER, FLAG."
GO! GO! GO!
I LOVE A MOTIVATING SLOGAN!
HEY, HERE'S A REVOLUTIONARY IDEA, FLAG, HOW ABOUT YOU TELL ME WHERE WE "GO! GO! GO!"?
WHAT WE ACTUALLY HERE FOR ANYWAYS?
EXPERT INTEL ON THIS PLACE BEING A STORAGE DUMP FOR A LOAD OF JOKER TOXIN.
...

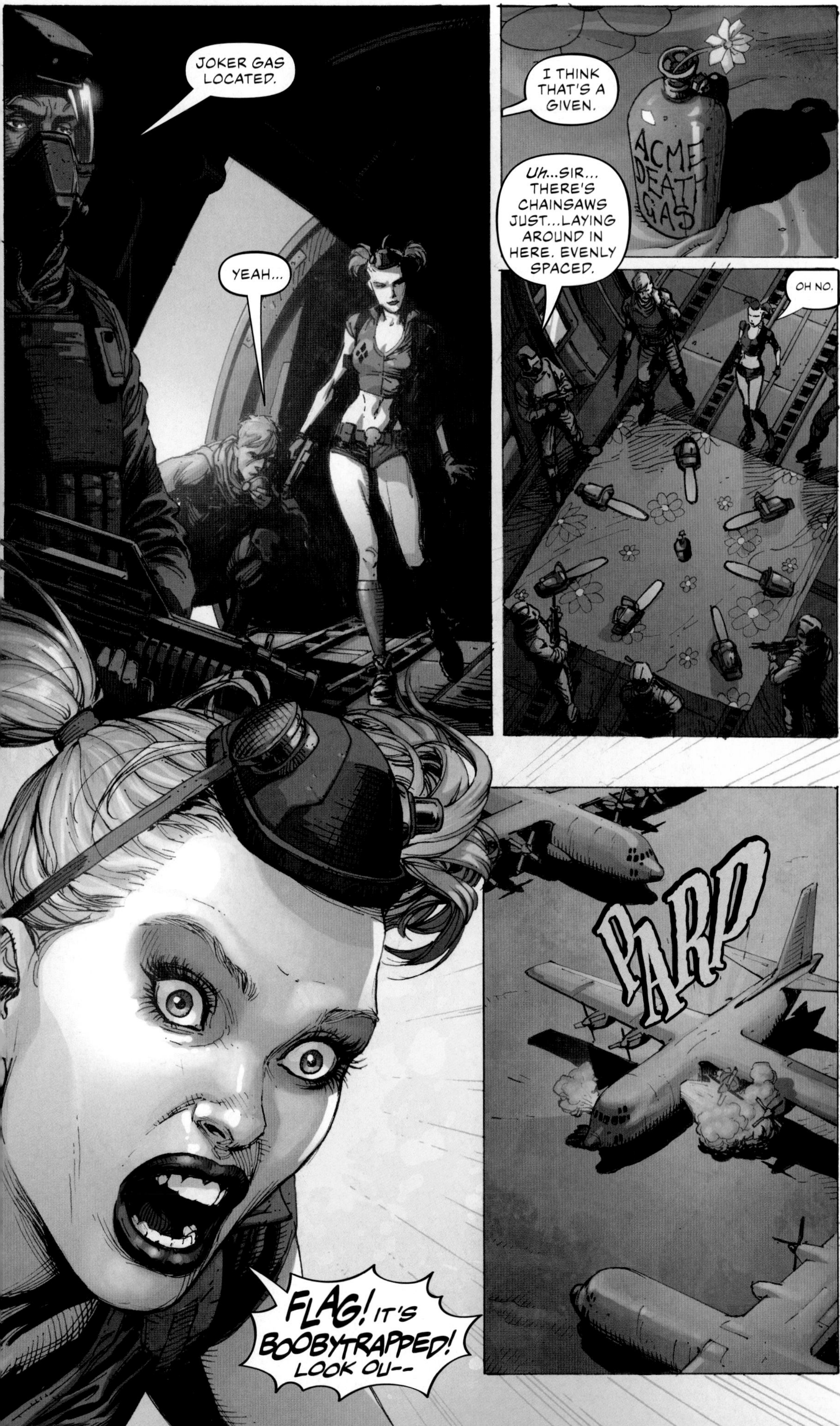
JOKER GAS LOCATED.
YEAH...
I THINK THAT'S A GIVEN.
ACME DEATH GAS
Uh...SIR... THERE'S CHAINSAWS JUST...LAYING AROUND IN HERE. EVENLY SPACED.
OH NO.
FLAG! IT'S BOOBYTRAPPED! LOOK OU--
PARP

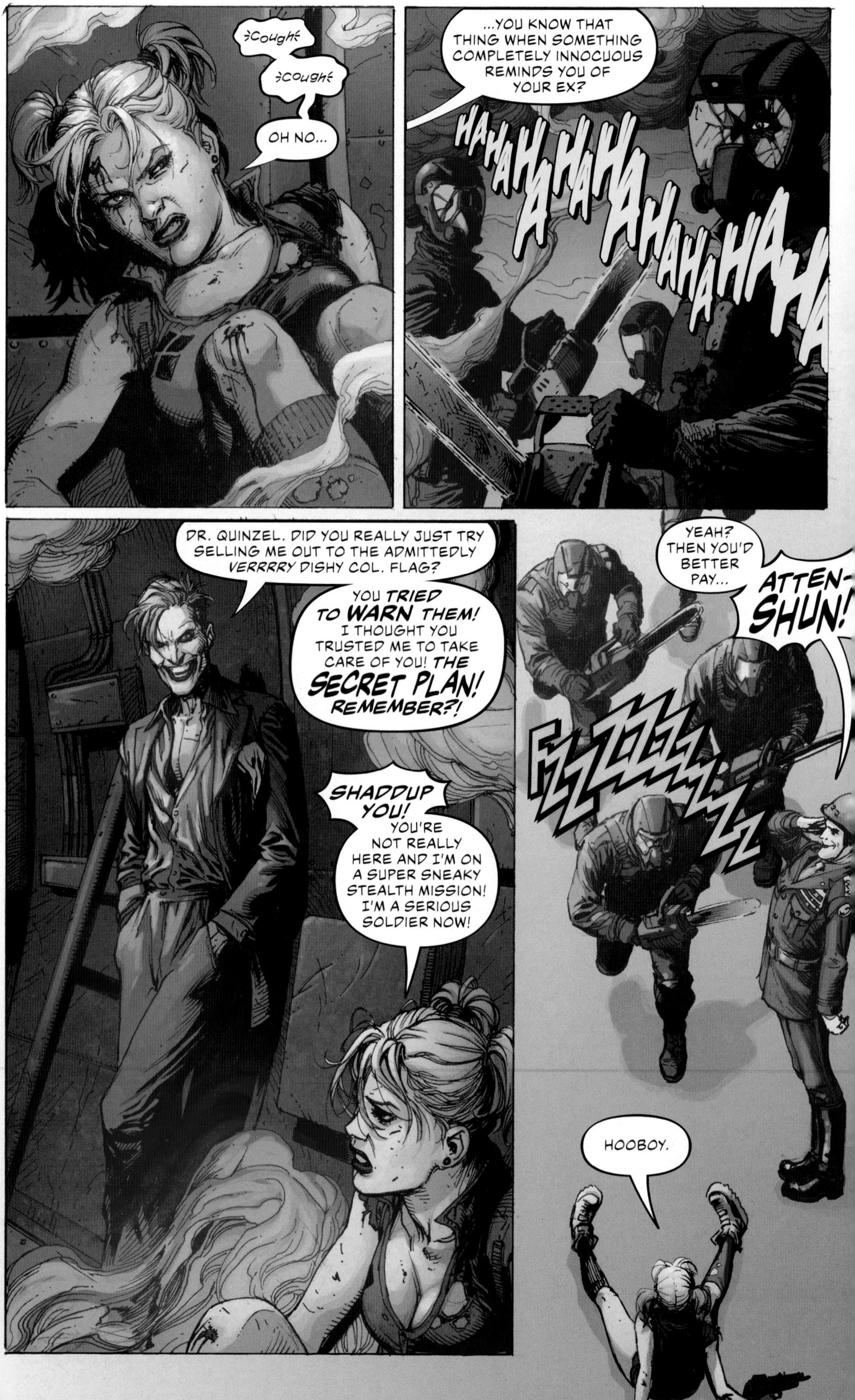

COUGH
COUGH
OH NO...
...YOU KNOW THAT THING WHEN SOMETHING COMPLETELY INNOCUOUS REMINDS YOU OF YOUR EX?
HAHAHAHAHAHAHAHAHAHAHAHAHAHAHAHAHA
DR. QUINZEL. DID YOU REALLY JUST TRY SELLING ME OUT TO THE ADMITTEDLY VERRRRY DISHY COL. FLAG?
YOU TRIED TO WARN THEM! I THOUGHT YOU TRUSTED ME TO TAKE CARE OF YOU! THE SECRET PLAN! REMEMBER?!
SHADDUP YOU! YOU'RE NOT REALLY HERE AND I'M ON A SUPER SNEAKY STEALTH MISSION! I'M A SERIOUS SOLDIER NOW!
YEAH? THEN YOU'D BETTER PAY...
ATTEN-SHUN!
FZZZZZZZZZ
HOOBOY.

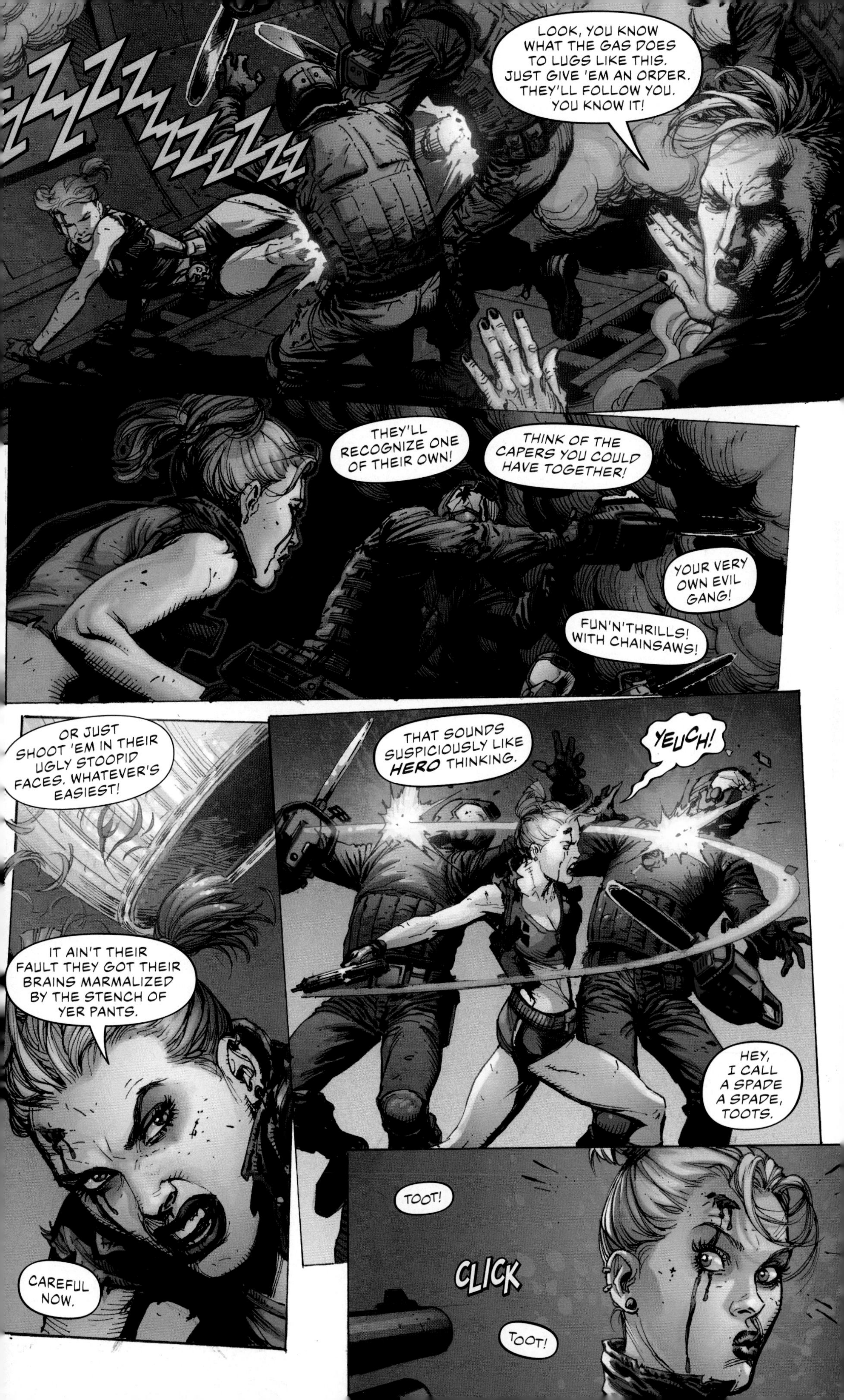
ZZZZZZZZZZZZZZZ
LOOK, YOU KNOW WHAT THE GAS DOES TO LUGS LIKE THIS. JUST GIVE 'EM AN ORDER. THEY'LL FOLLOW YOU. YOU KNOW IT!
THEY'LL RECOGNIZE ONE OF THEIR OWN!
THINK OF THE CAPERS YOU COULD HAVE TOGETHER!
YOUR VERY OWN EVIL GANG!
FUN'N'THRILLS! WITH CHAINSAWS!
OR JUST SHOOT 'EM IN THEIR UGLY STOOPID FACES. WHATEVER'S EASIEST!
IT AIN'T THEIR FAULT THEY GOT THEIR BRAINS MARMALIZED BY THE STENCH OF YER PANTS.
CAREFUL NOW.
THAT SOUNDS SUSPICIOUSLY LIKE HERO THINKING.
YEUCH!
HEY, I CALL A SPADE A SPADE, TOOTS.
TOOT!
CLICK
TOOT!

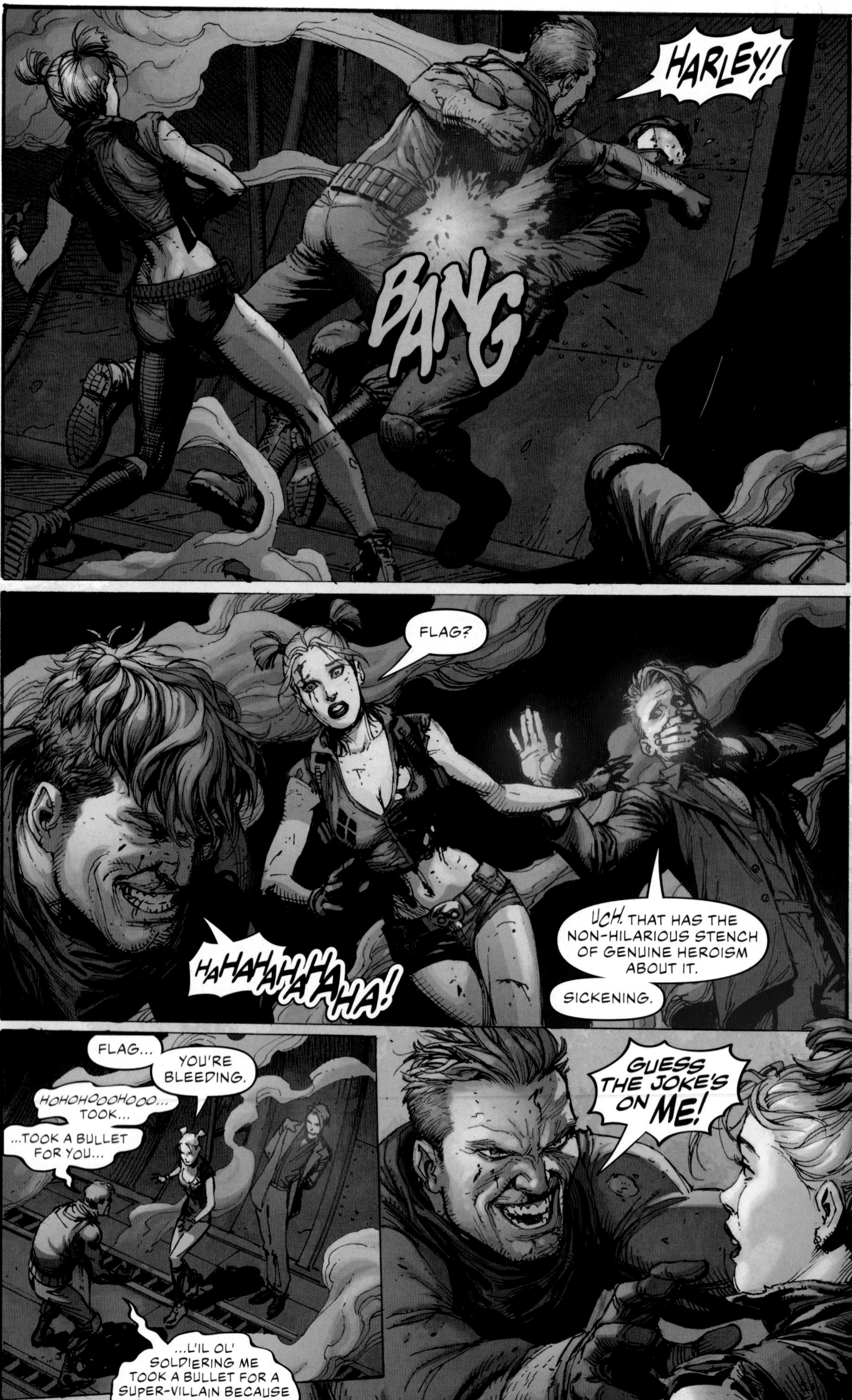
HARLEY!
BANG
FLAG?
UCH. THAT HAS THE NON-HILARIOUS STENCH OF GENUINE HEROISM ABOUT IT.
SICKENING.
HAHAHAHAHAHAHAHA!
FLAG...
YOU'RE BLEEDING.
HOHOHOOOHOOO... TOOK...
...TOOK A BULLET FOR YOU...
...L'IL OL' SOLDIERING ME TOOK A BULLET FOR A SUPER-VILLAIN BECAUSE SHE'S STILL PART OF MY SQUAD!
GUESS THE JOKE'S ON ME!

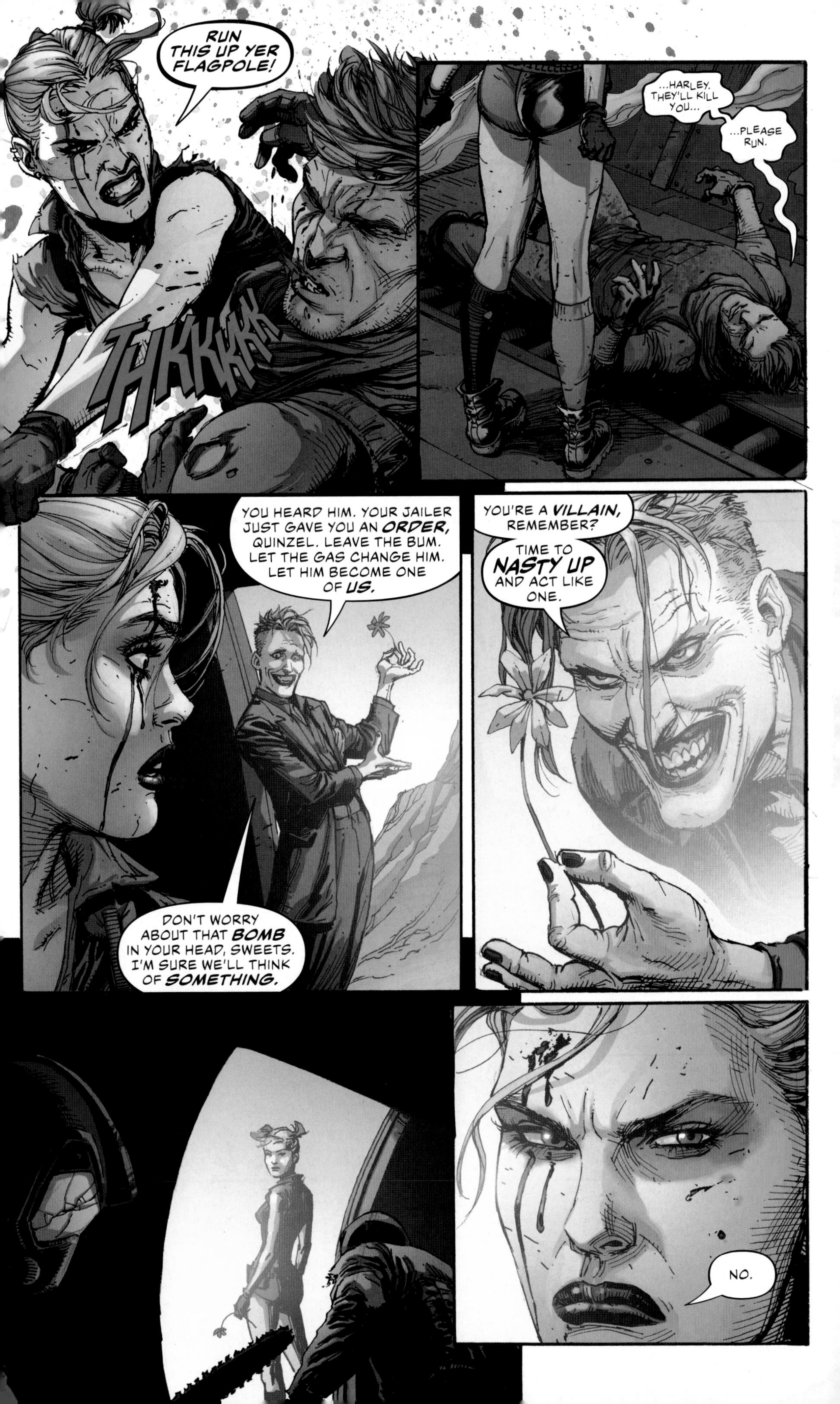
RUN THIS UP YER FLAGPOLE!
THKKKKK
...HARLEY. THEY'LL KILL YOU...
...PLEASE RUN.
YOU HEARD HIM. YOUR JAILER JUST GAVE YOU AN ORDER, QUINZEL. LEAVE THE BUM. LET THE GAS CHANGE HIM. LET HIM BECOME ONE OF US.
DON'T WORRY ABOUT THAT BOMB IN YOUR HEAD, SWEETS. I'M SURE WE'LL THINK OF SOMETHING.
YOU'RE A VILLAIN, REMEMBER?
TIME TO NASTY UP AND ACT LIKE ONE.
NO.

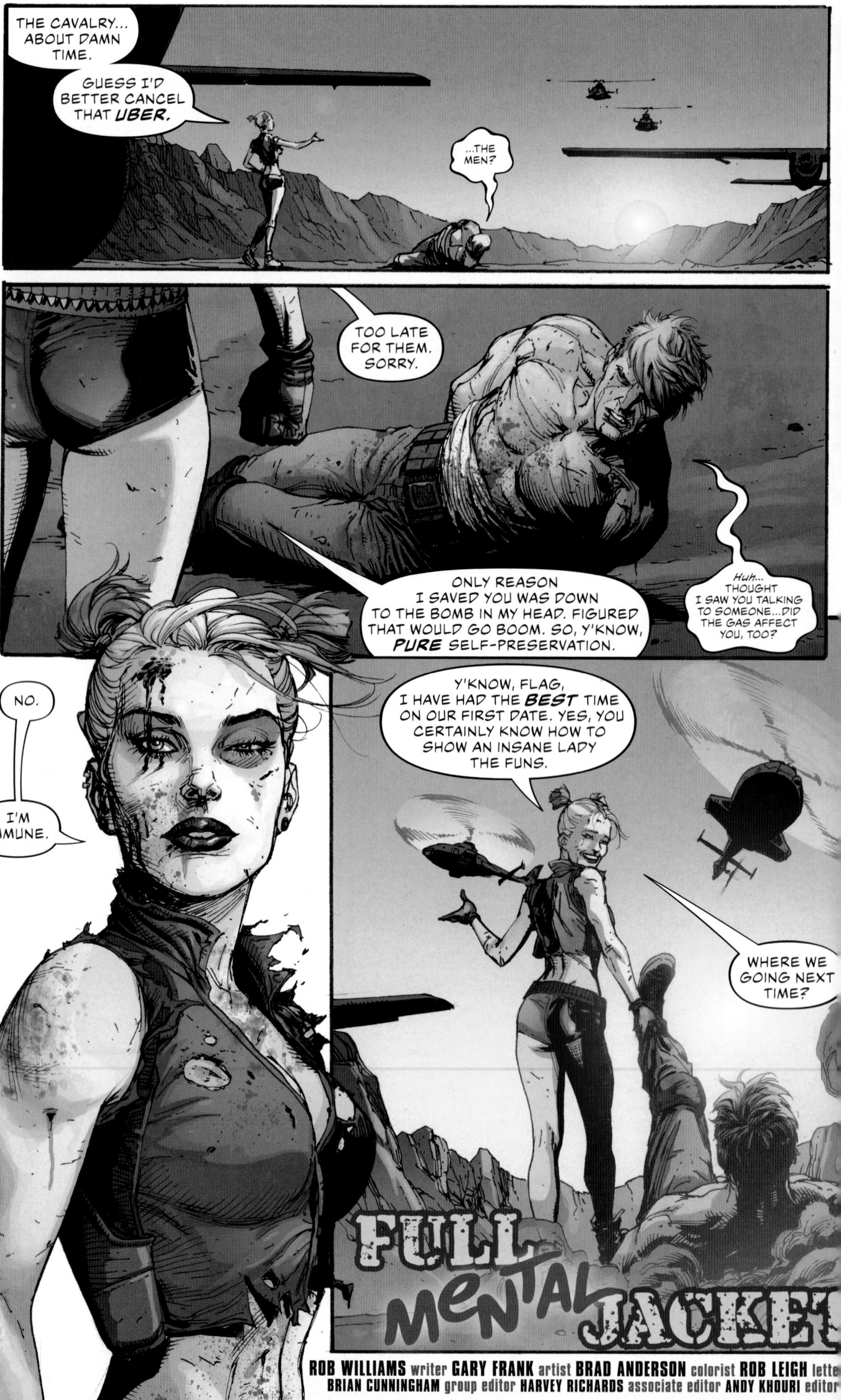

THE CAVALRY... ABOUT DAMN TIME.
GUESS I'D BETTER CANCEL THAT UBER.
...THE MEN?
TOO LATE FOR THEM. SORRY.
ONLY REASON I SAVED YOU WAS DOWN TO THE BOMB IN MY HEAD. FIGURED THAT WOULD GO BOOM. SO, Y'KNOW, PURE SELF-PRESERVATION.
Huh... THOUGHT I SAW YOU TALKING TO SOMEONE...DID THE GAS AFFECT YOU, TOO?
NO.
I'M IMMUNE.
Y'KNOW, FLAG, I HAVE HAD THE BEST TIME ON OUR FIRST DATE. YES, YOU CERTAINLY KNOW HOW TO SHOW AN INSANE LADY THE FUNS.
WHERE WE GOING NEXT TIME?
FULL MENTAL JACKET
ROB WILLIAMS writer GARY FRANK artist BRAD ANDERSON colorist ROB LEIGH lette
BRIAN CUNNINGHAM group editor HARVEY RICHARDS associate editor ANDY KHOURI editor

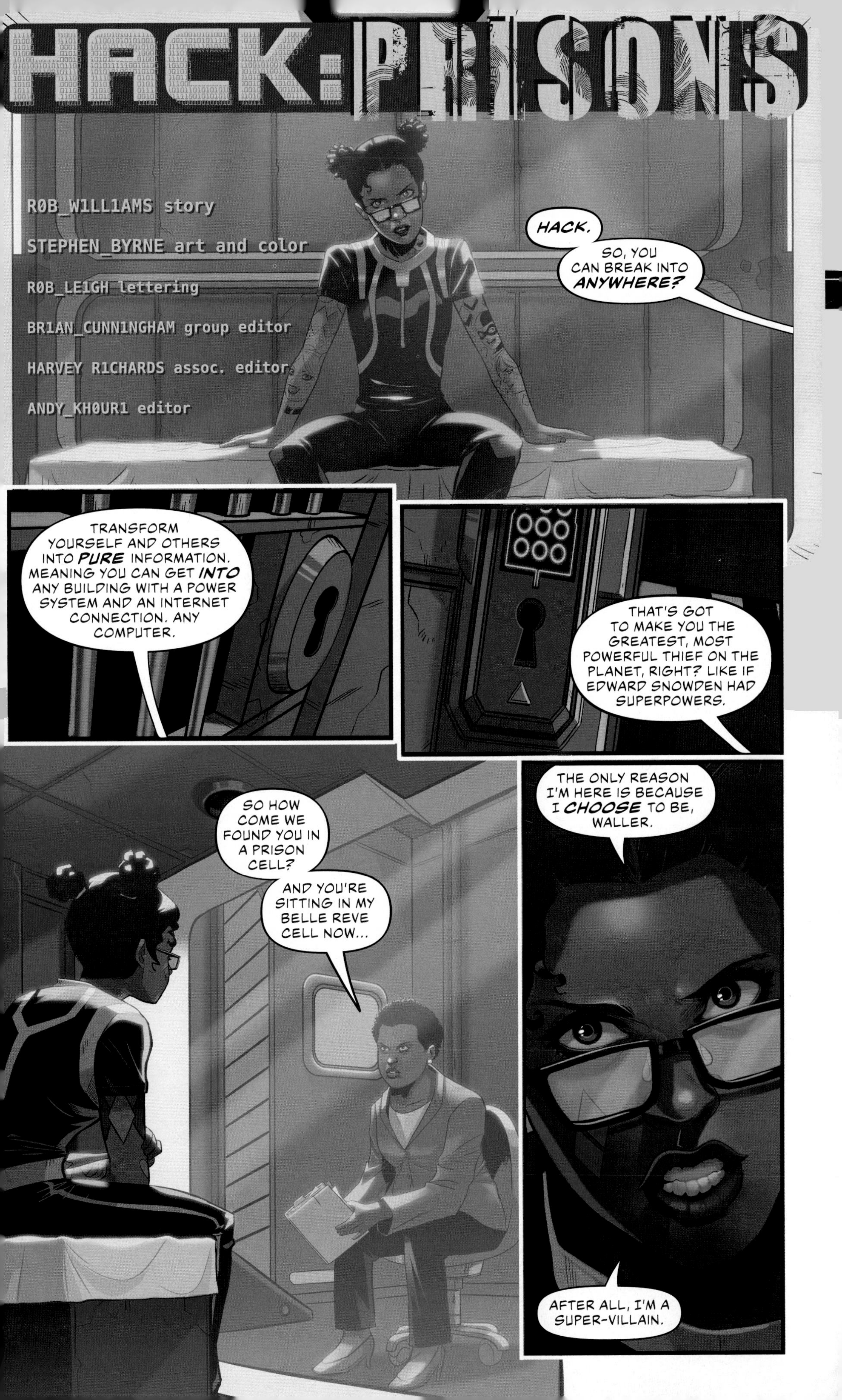
HACK: PRISONS
R0B_W1LL1AMS story
STEPHEN_BYRNE art and color
R0B_LE1GH lettering
BR1AN_CUNN1NGHAM group editor
HARVEY R1CHARDS assoc. editor
ANDY_KH0UR1 editor
HACK.
SO, YOU CAN BREAK INTO ANYWHERE?
TRANSFORM YOURSELF AND OTHERS INTO PURE INFORMATION. MEANING YOU CAN GET INTO ANY BUILDING WITH A POWER SYSTEM AND AN INTERNET CONNECTION. ANY COMPUTER.
THAT'S GOT TO MAKE YOU THE GREATEST, MOST POWERFUL THIEF ON THE PLANET, RIGHT? LIKE IF EDWARD SNOWDEN HAD SUPERPOWERS.
SO HOW COME WE FOUND YOU IN A PRISON CELL?
AND YOU'RE SITTING IN MY BELLE REVE CELL NOW...
THE ONLY REASON I'M HERE IS BECAUSE I CHOOSE TO BE, WALLER.
AFTER ALL, I'M A SUPER-VILLAIN.

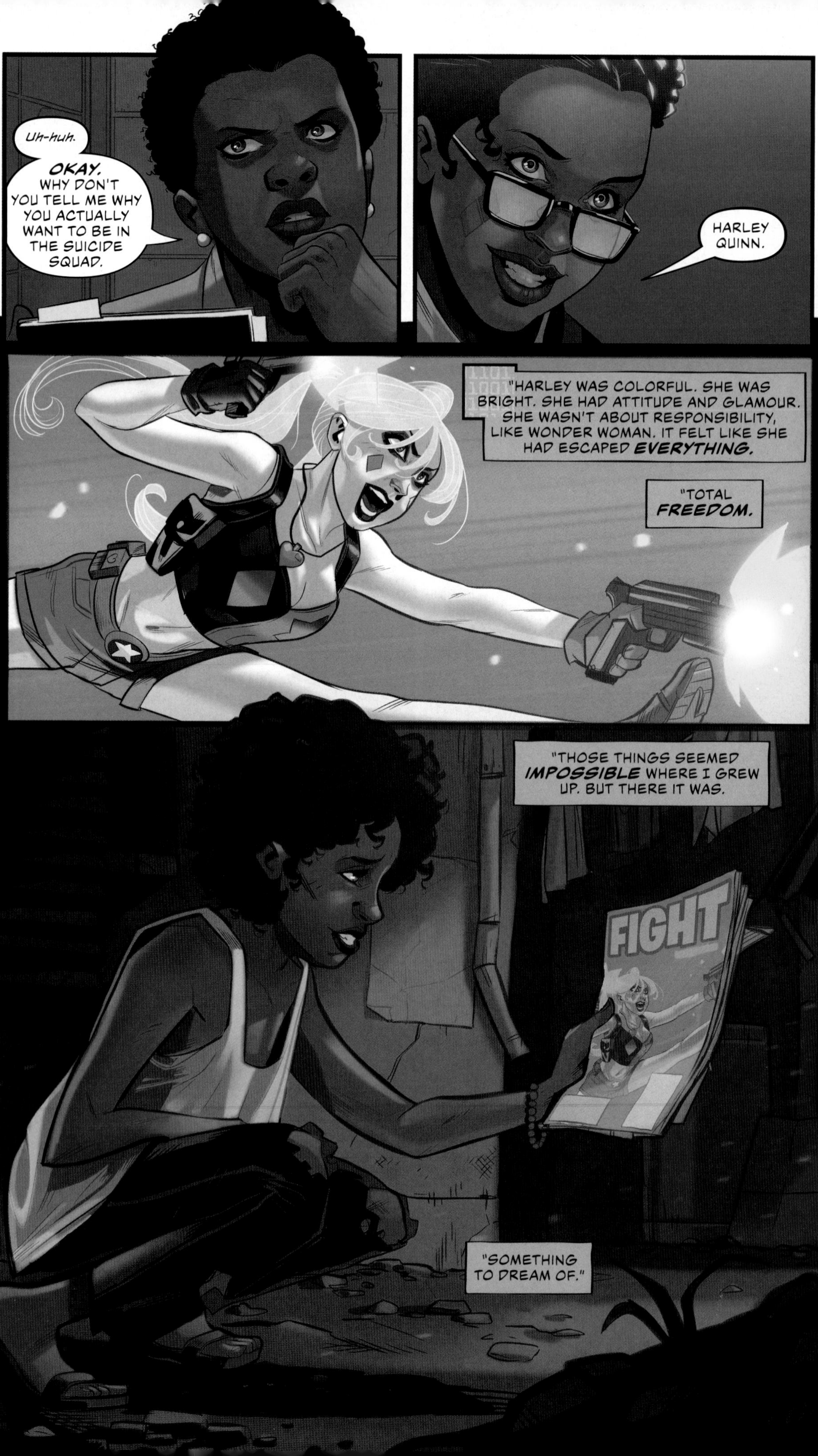

Uh-huh.
OKAY. WHY DON'T YOU TELL ME WHY YOU ACTUALLY WANT TO BE IN THE SUICIDE SQUAD.
HARLEY QUINN.
"HARLEY WAS COLORFUL. SHE WAS BRIGHT. SHE HAD ATTITUDE AND GLAMOUR. SHE WASN'T ABOUT RESPONSIBILITY, LIKE WONDER WOMAN. IT FELT LIKE SHE HAD ESCAPED EVERYTHING.
"TOTAL FREEDOM.
"THOSE THINGS SEEMED IMPOSSIBLE WHERE I GREW UP. BUT THERE IT WAS.
FIGHT
"SOMETHING TO DREAM OF."

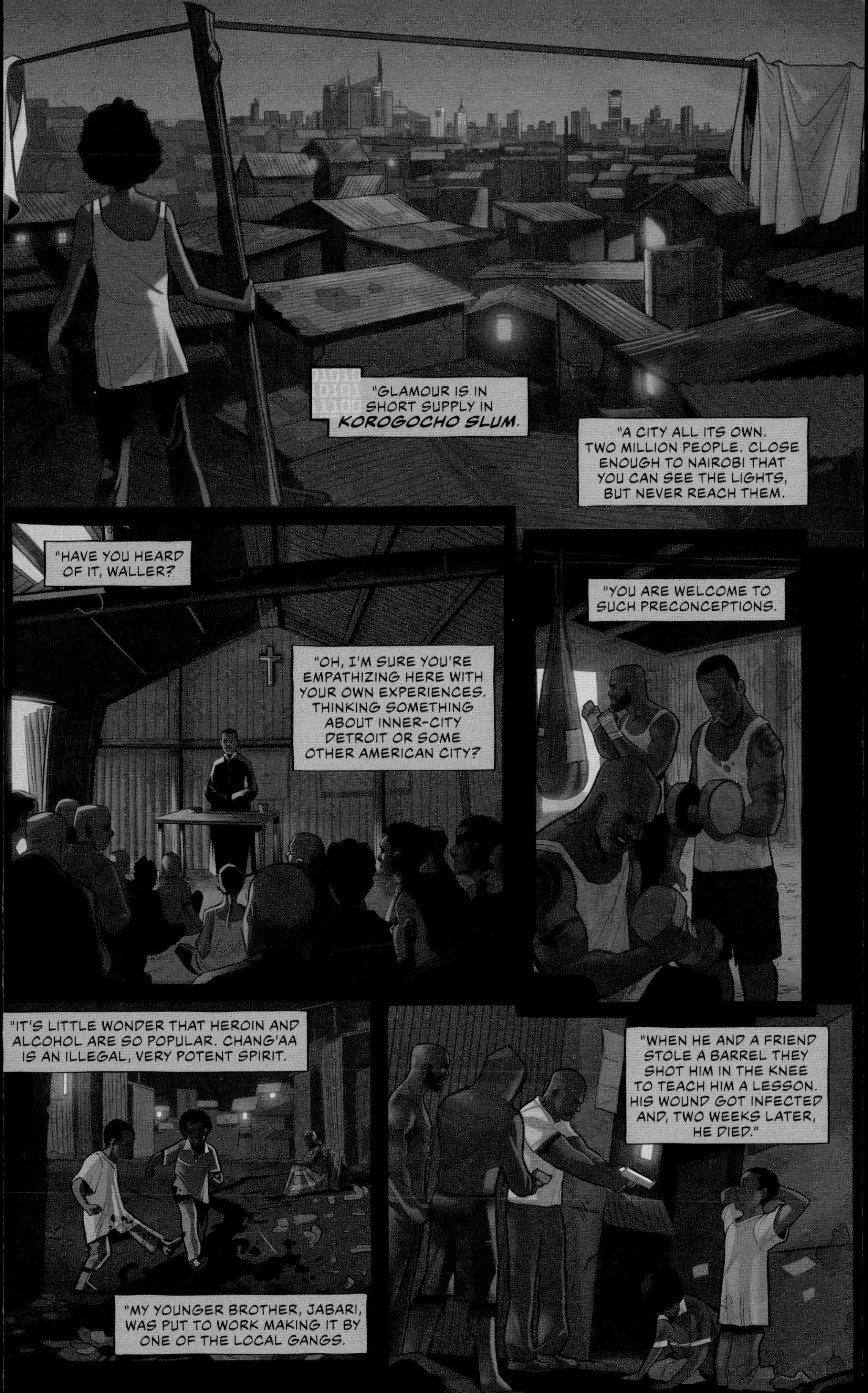

"GLAMOUR IS IN SHORT SUPPLY IN KOROGOCHO SLUM.
"A CITY ALL ITS OWN. TWO MILLION PEOPLE. CLOSE ENOUGH TO NAIROBI THAT YOU CAN SEE THE LIGHTS, BUT NEVER REACH THEM.
"HAVE YOU HEARD OF IT, WALLER?
"OH, I'M SURE YOU'RE EMPATHIZING HERE WITH YOUR OWN EXPERIENCES. THINKING SOMETHING ABOUT INNER-CITY DETROIT OR SOME OTHER AMERICAN CITY?
"YOU ARE WELCOME TO SUCH PRECONCEPTIONS.
"IT'S LITTLE WONDER THAT HEROIN AND ALCOHOL ARE SO POPULAR. CHANG'AA IS AN ILLEGAL, VERY POTENT SPIRIT.
"MY YOUNGER BROTHER, JABARI, WAS PUT TO WORK MAKING IT BY ONE OF THE LOCAL GANGS.
"WHEN HE AND A FRIEND STOLE A BARREL THEY SHOT HIM IN THE KNEE TO TEACH HIM A LESSON. HIS WOUND GOT INFECTED AND, TWO WEEKS LATER, HE DIED."

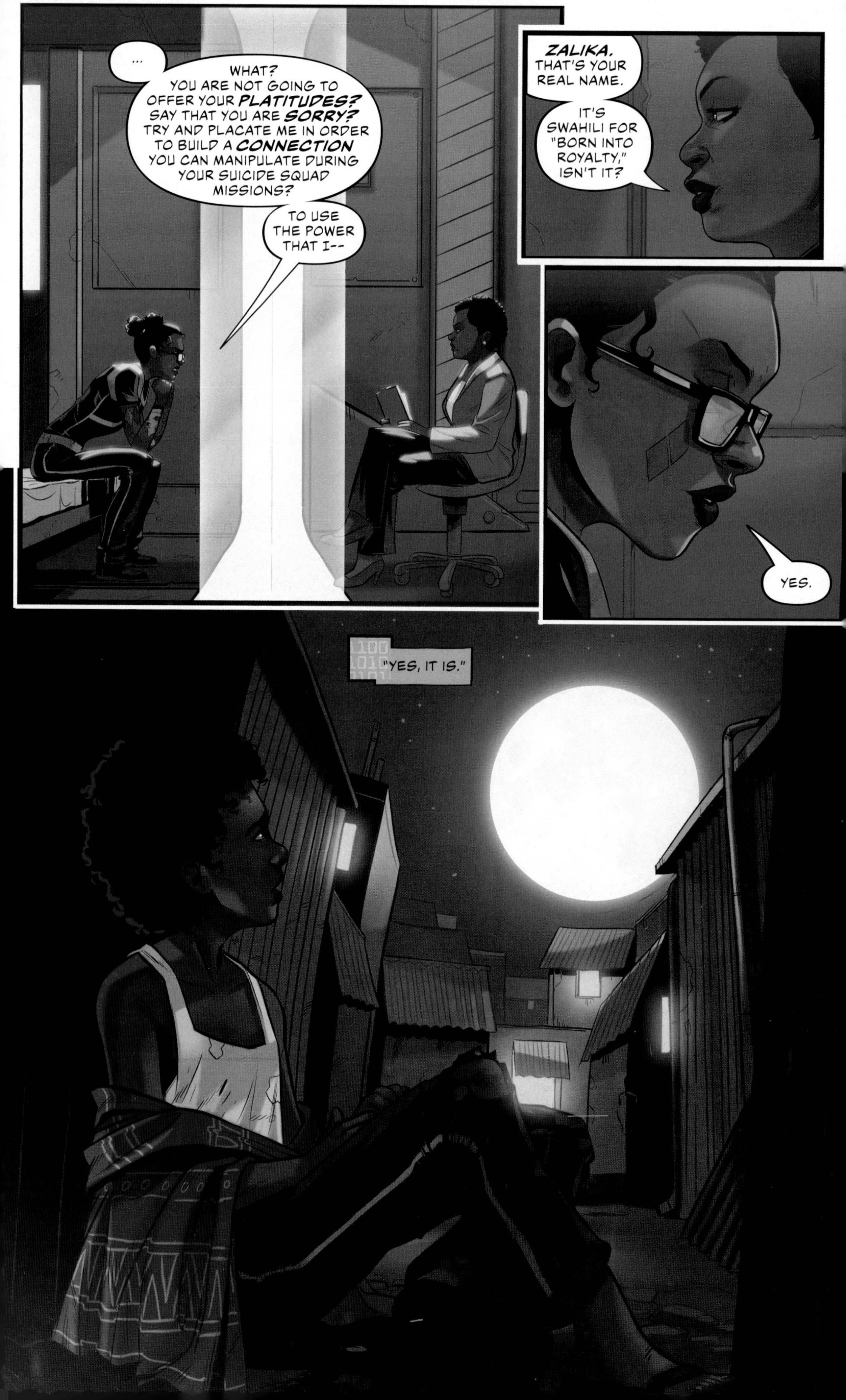
...
WHAT? YOU ARE NOT GOING TO OFFER YOUR PLATITUDES? SAY THAT YOU ARE SORRY? TRY AND PLACATE ME IN ORDER TO BUILD A CONNECTION YOU CAN MANIPULATE DURING YOUR SUICIDE SQUAD MISSIONS?
TO USE THE POWER THAT I--
ZALIKA. THAT'S YOUR REAL NAME.
IT'S SWAHILI FOR "BORN INTO ROYALTY," ISN'T IT?
YES.
"YES, IT IS."

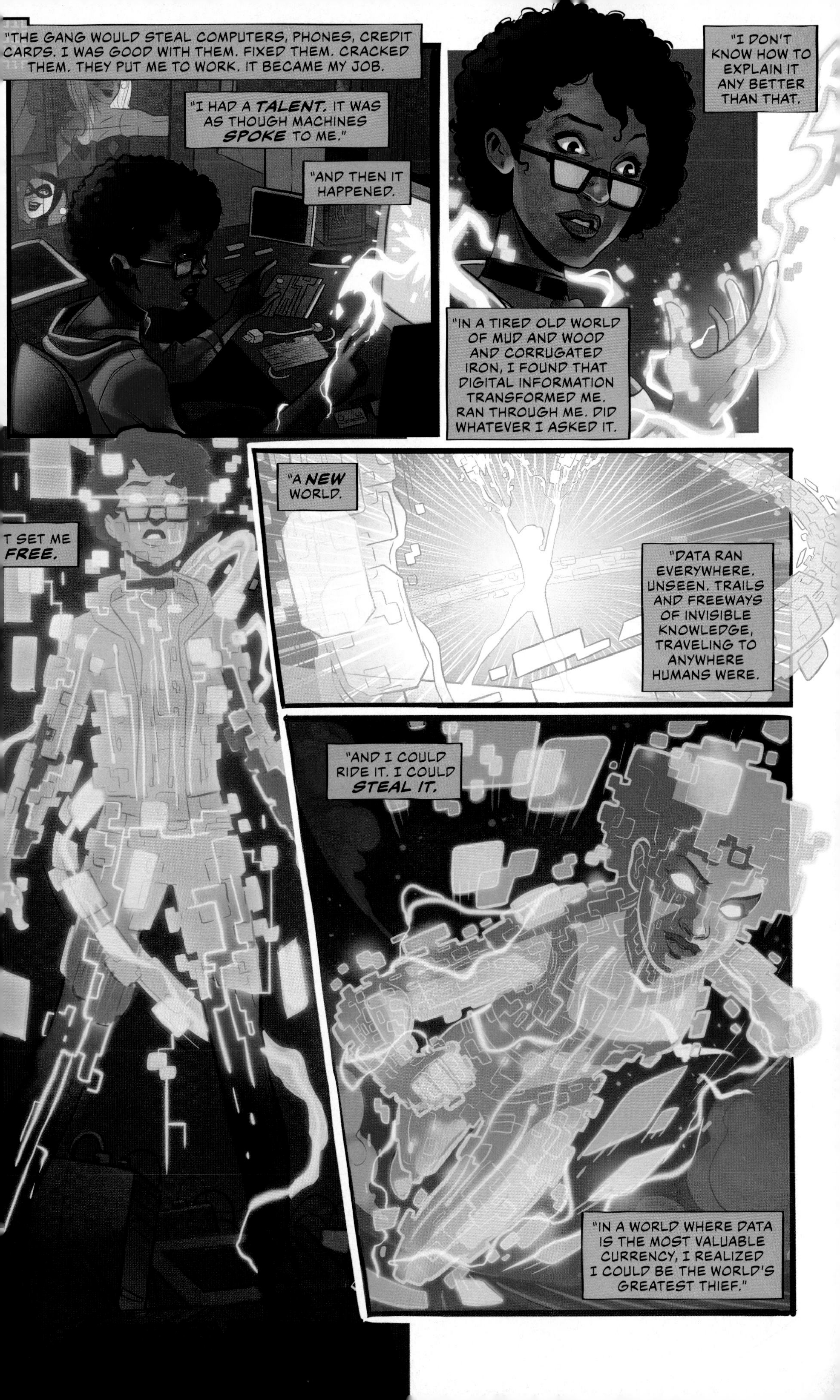
"THE GANG WOULD STEAL COMPUTERS, PHONES, CREDIT CARDS. I WAS GOOD WITH THEM. FIXED THEM. CRACKED THEM. THEY PUT ME TO WORK. IT BECAME MY JOB.
"I HAD A TALENT. IT WAS AS THOUGH MACHINES SPOKE TO ME."
"AND THEN IT HAPPENED.
"I DON'T KNOW HOW TO EXPLAIN IT ANY BETTER THAN THAT.
"IN A TIRED OLD WORLD OF MUD AND WOOD AND CORRUGATED IRON, I FOUND THAT DIGITAL INFORMATION TRANSFORMED ME. RAN THROUGH ME. DID WHATEVER I ASKED IT.
T SET ME FREE.
"A NEW WORLD.
"DATA RAN EVERYWHERE. UNSEEN. TRAILS AND FREEWAYS OF INVISIBLE KNOWLEDGE, TRAVELING TO ANYWHERE HUMANS WERE.
"AND I COULD RIDE IT. I COULD STEAL IT.
"IN A WORLD WHERE DATA IS THE MOST VALUABLE CURRENCY, I REALIZED I COULD BE THE WORLD'S GREATEST THIEF."

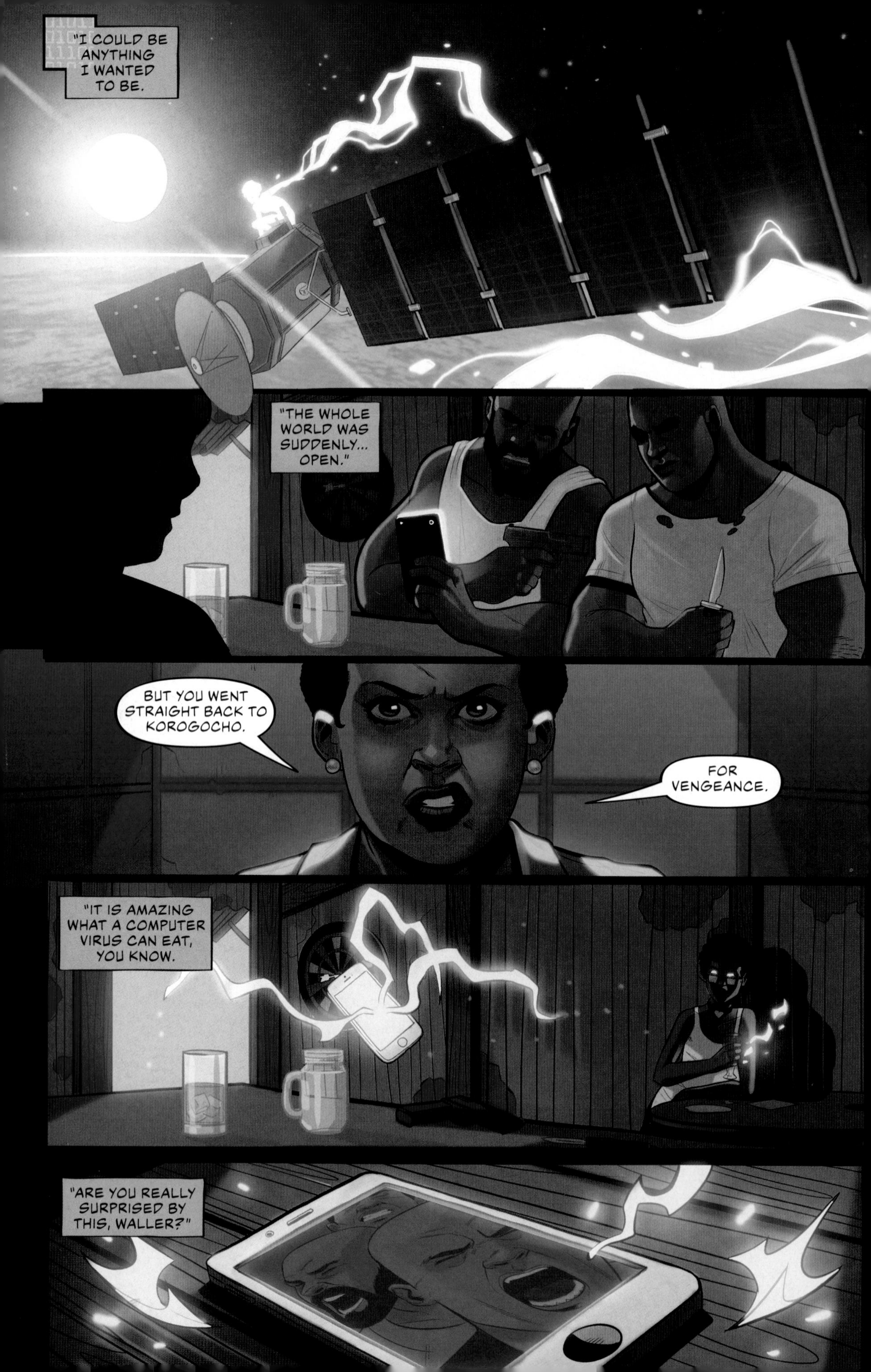
"I COULD BE ANYTHING I WANTED TO BE.
"THE WHOLE WORLD WAS SUDDENLY... OPEN."
BUT YOU WENT STRAIGHT BACK TO KOROGOCHO.
FOR VENGEANCE.
"IT IS AMAZING WHAT A COMPUTER VIRUS CAN EAT, YOU KNOW.
"ARE YOU REALLY SURPRISED BY THIS, WALLER?"

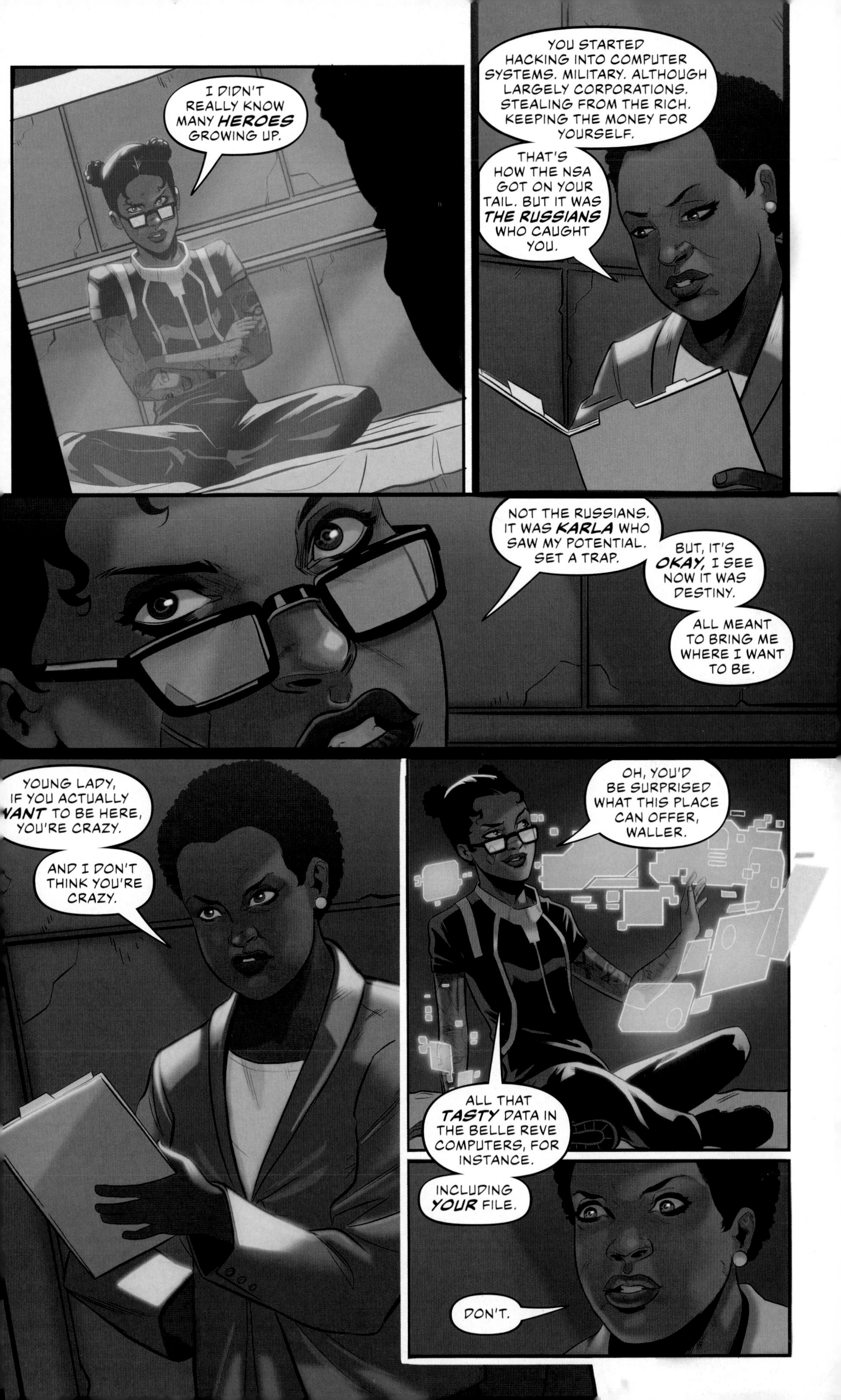

I DIDN'T REALLY KNOW MANY HEROES GROWING UP.
YOU STARTED HACKING INTO COMPUTER SYSTEMS. MILITARY. ALTHOUGH LARGELY CORPORATIONS. STEALING FROM THE RICH. KEEPING THE MONEY FOR YOURSELF.
THAT'S HOW THE NSA GOT ON YOUR TAIL. BUT IT WAS THE RUSSIANS WHO CAUGHT YOU.
NOT THE RUSSIANS. IT WAS KARLA WHO SAW MY POTENTIAL. SET A TRAP.
BUT, IT'S OKAY, I SEE NOW IT WAS DESTINY.
ALL MEANT TO BRING ME WHERE I WANT TO BE.
YOUNG LADY, IF YOU ACTUALLY WANT TO BE HERE, YOU'RE CRAZY.
AND I DON'T THINK YOU'RE CRAZY.
OH, YOU'D BE SURPRISED WHAT THIS PLACE CAN OFFER, WALLER.
ALL THAT TASTY DATA IN THE BELLE REVE COMPUTERS, FOR INSTANCE.
INCLUDING YOUR FILE.
DON'T.

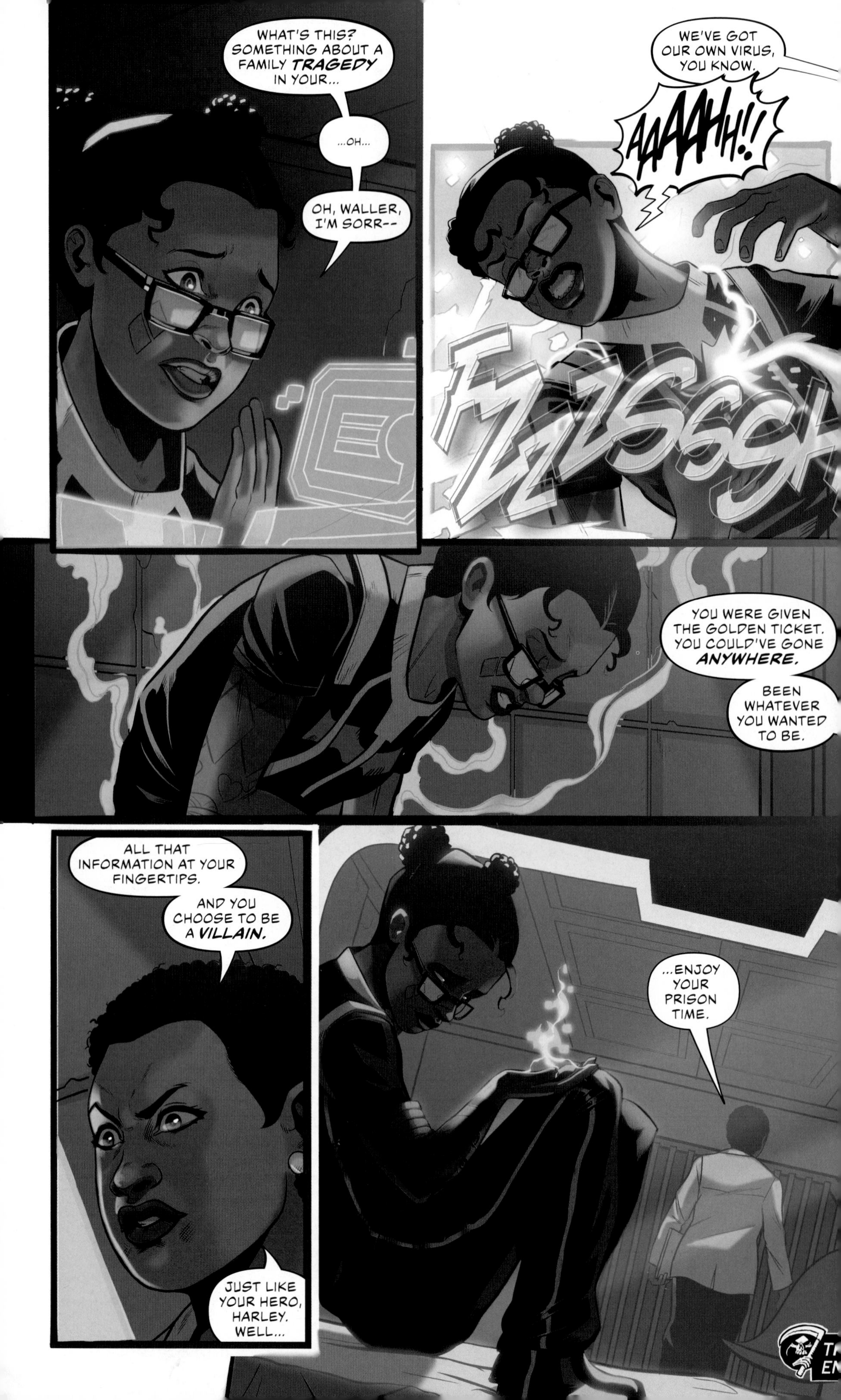
WHAT'S THIS? SOMETHING ABOUT A FAMILY TRAGEDY IN YOUR...
...OH...
OH, WALLER, I'M SORR--
WE'VE GOT OUR OWN VIRUS, YOU KNOW.
AAAAHH!!
FZZSSCH
YOU WERE GIVEN THE GOLDEN TICKET. YOU COULD'VE GONE ANYWHERE.
BEEN WHATEVER YOU WANTED TO BE.
ALL THAT INFORMATION AT YOUR FINGERTIPS.
AND YOU CHOOSE TO BE A VILLAIN.
JUST LIKE YOUR HERO, HARLEY. WELL...
...ENJOY YOUR PRISON TIME.

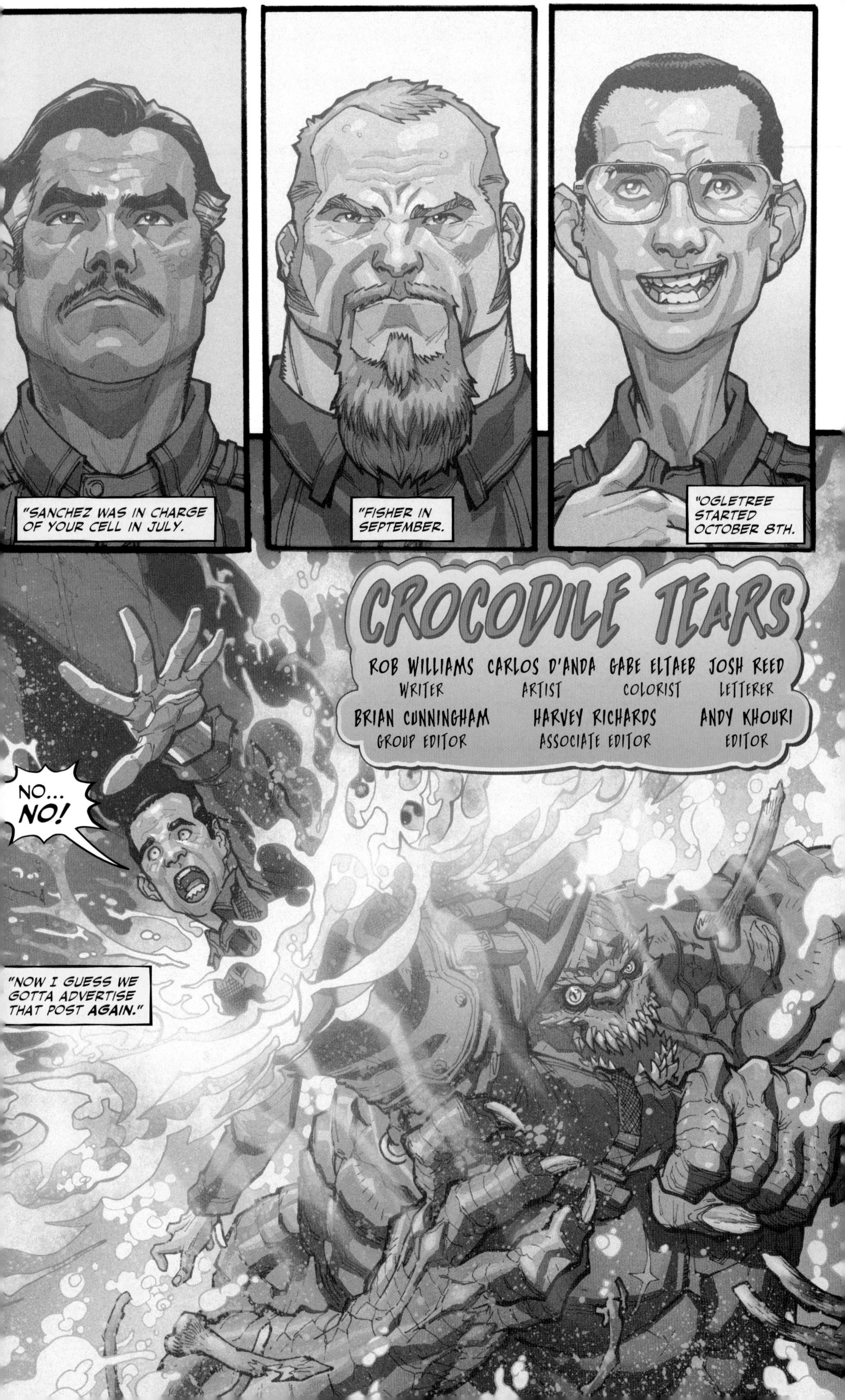
"SANCHEZ WAS IN CHARGE OF YOUR CELL IN JULY.
"FISHER IN SEPTEMBER.
"OGLETREE STARTED OCTOBER 8TH.
CROCODILE TEARS
ROB WILLIAMS WRITER
CARLOS D'ANDA ARTIST
GABE ELTAEB COLORIST
JOSH REED LETTERER
BRIAN CUNNINGHAM GROUP EDITOR
HARVEY RICHARDS ASSOCIATE EDITOR
ANDY KHOURI EDITOR
NO... NO!
"NOW I GUESS WE GOTTA ADVERTISE THAT POST AGAIN."

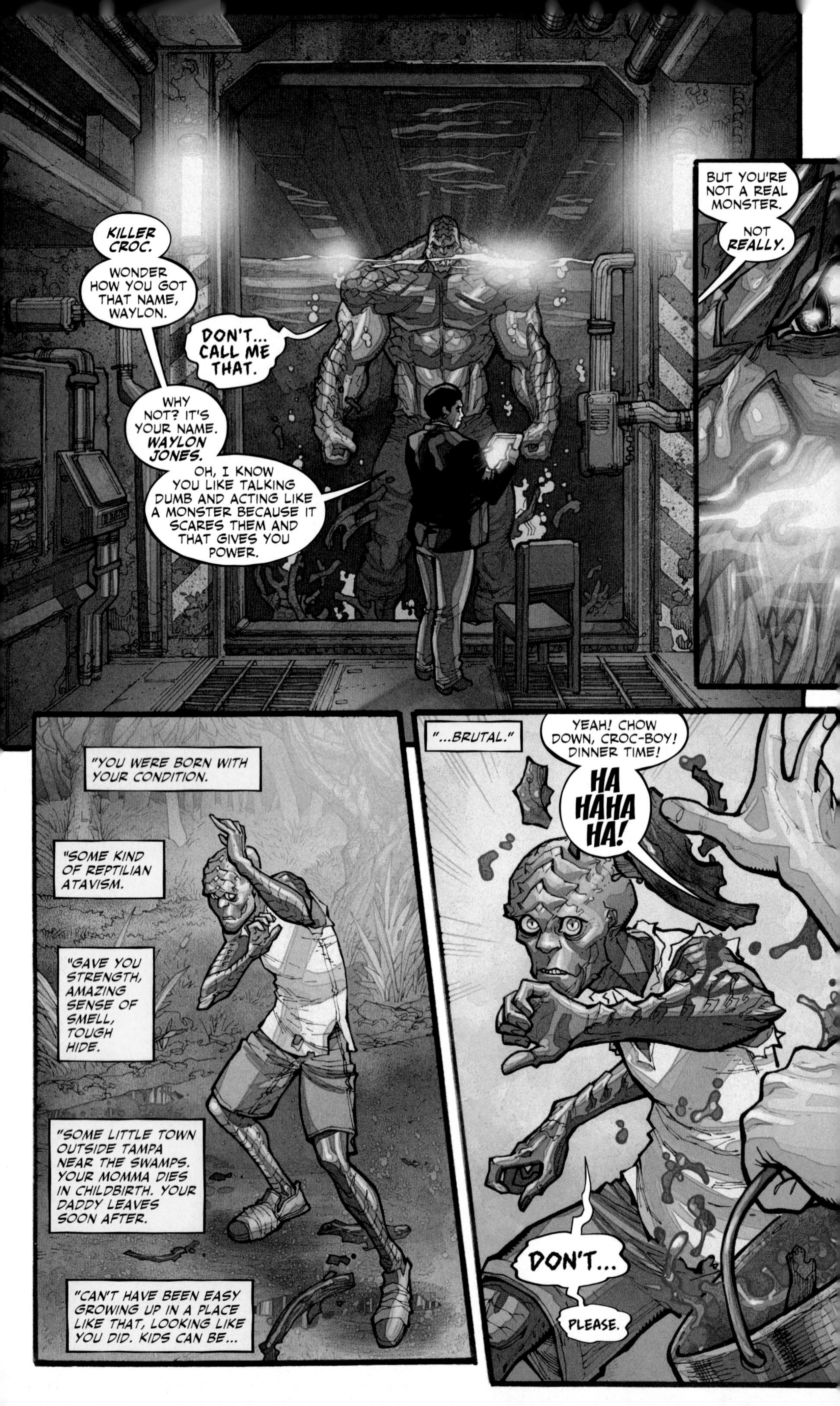

KILLER CROC.
WONDER HOW YOU GOT THAT NAME, WAYLON.
DON'T... CALL ME THAT.
WHY NOT? IT'S YOUR NAME. WAYLON JONES.
OH, I KNOW YOU LIKE TALKING DUMB AND ACTING LIKE A MONSTER BECAUSE IT SCARES THEM AND THAT GIVES YOU POWER.
BUT YOU'RE NOT A REAL MONSTER.
NOT REALLY.
"YOU WERE BORN WITH YOUR CONDITION.
"SOME KIND OF REPTILIAN ATAVISM.
"GAVE YOU STRENGTH, AMAZING SENSE OF SMELL, TOUGH HIDE.
"SOME LITTLE TOWN OUTSIDE TAMPA NEAR THE SWAMPS. YOUR MOMMA DIES IN CHILDBIRTH. YOUR DADDY LEAVES SOON AFTER.
"CAN'T HAVE BEEN EASY GROWING UP IN A PLACE LIKE THAT, LOOKING LIKE YOU DID. KIDS CAN BE...
"...BRUTAL."
YEAH! CHOW DOWN, CROC-BOY! DINNER TIME!
HA HAHAHA HA!
DON'T...
PLEASE.

FREAK! GONNA GET ME SOME OF THOSE EXPENSIVE CROCODILE SHOES! WHO WANTS SOME CROCODILE SHOES, BOYS?

YEAH! GET ME A BELT, TOO, ALEC!

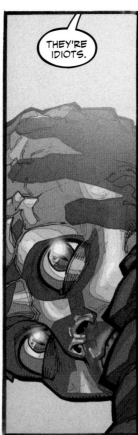

THEY'RE IDIOTS.

I'M EMMA. WHERE DO YOU LIVE? I CAN HELP YOU GET HOME.

"YOUR AUNT TAKES YOU IN."

"BUT SHE HAS HER OWN ISSUES."

THE GIRL WHO BEFRIENDED YOU. HER NAME WAS EMMA BRUC...

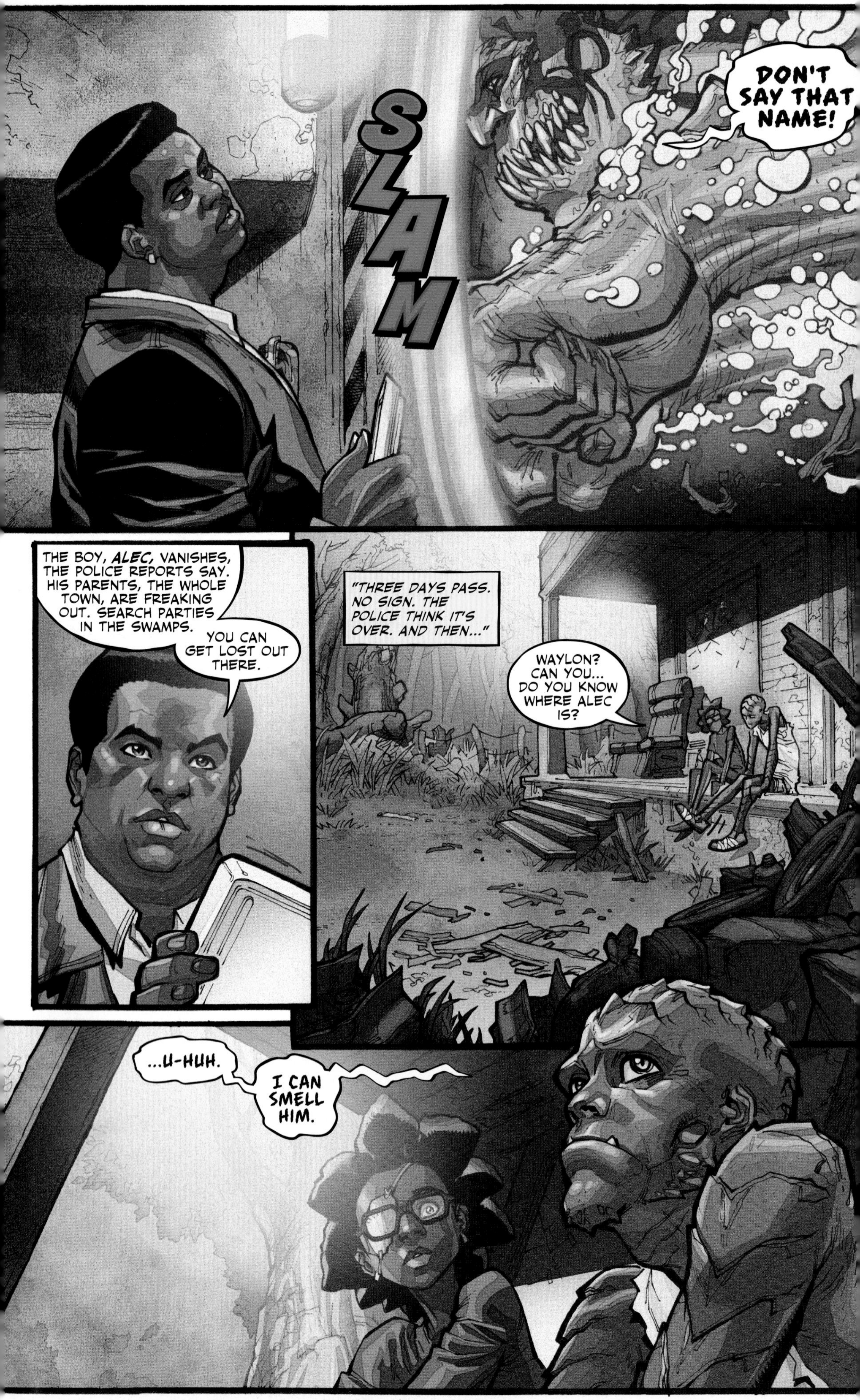
SLAM
DON'T SAY THAT NAME!
THE BOY, ALEC, VANISHES, THE POLICE REPORTS SAY. HIS PARENTS, THE WHOLE TOWN, ARE FREAKING OUT. SEARCH PARTIES IN THE SWAMPS.
YOU CAN GET LOST OUT THERE.
"THREE DAYS PASS. NO SIGN. THE POLICE THINK IT'S OVER. AND THEN..."
WAYLON? CAN YOU... DO YOU KNOW WHERE ALEC IS?
...U-HUH.
I CAN SMELL HIM.

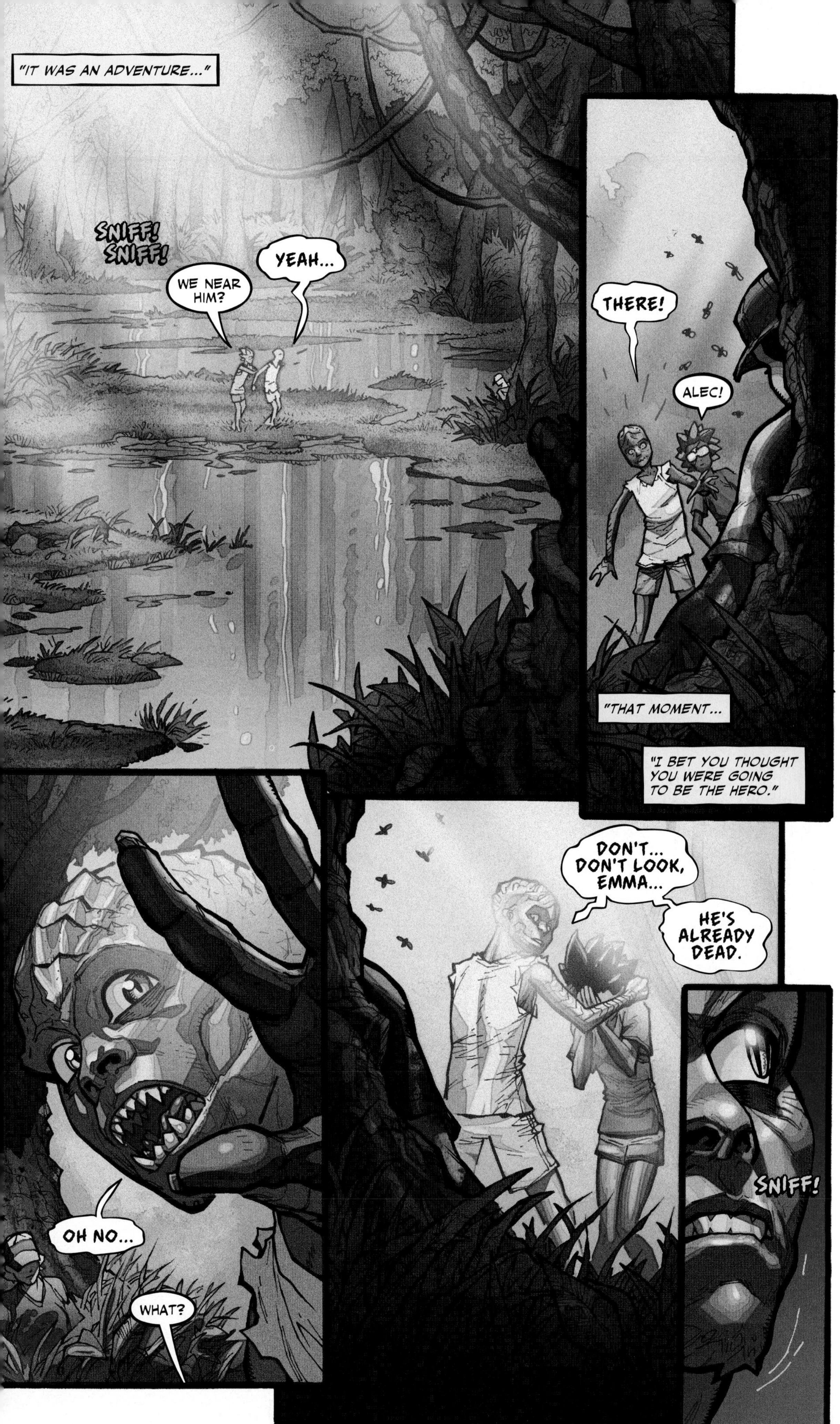
"IT WAS AN ADVENTURE..."
SNIFF! SNIFF!
WE NEAR HIM?
YEAH...
THERE!
ALEC!
"THAT MOMENT...
"I BET YOU THOUGHT YOU WERE GOING TO BE THE HERO."
OH NO...
WHAT?
DON'T... DON'T LOOK, EMMA...
HE'S ALREADY DEAD.
SNIFF!

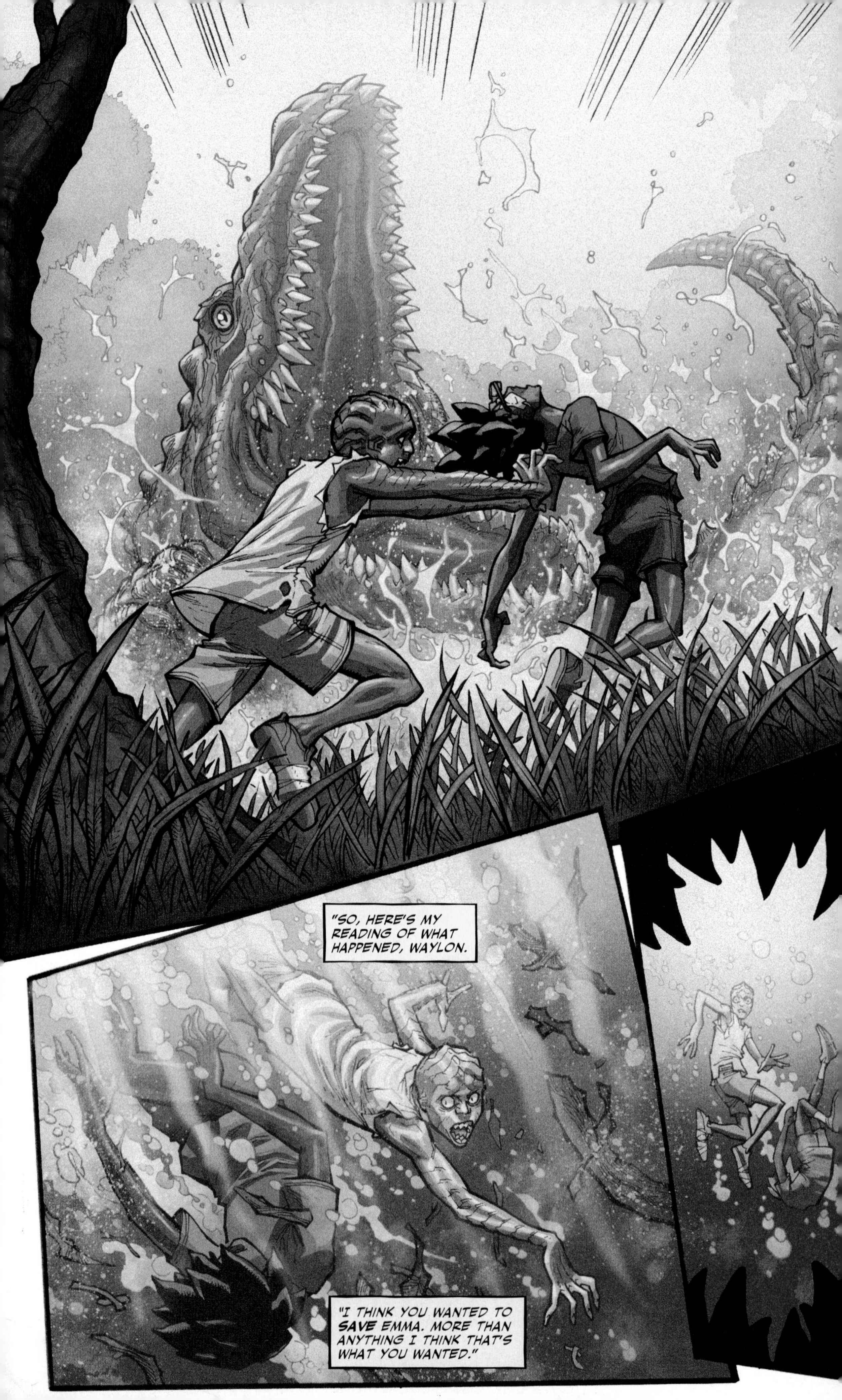
"SO, HERE'S MY READING OF WHAT HAPPENED, WAYLON.
"I THINK YOU WANTED TO SAVE EMMA. MORE THAN ANYTHING I THINK THAT'S WHAT YOU WANTED."

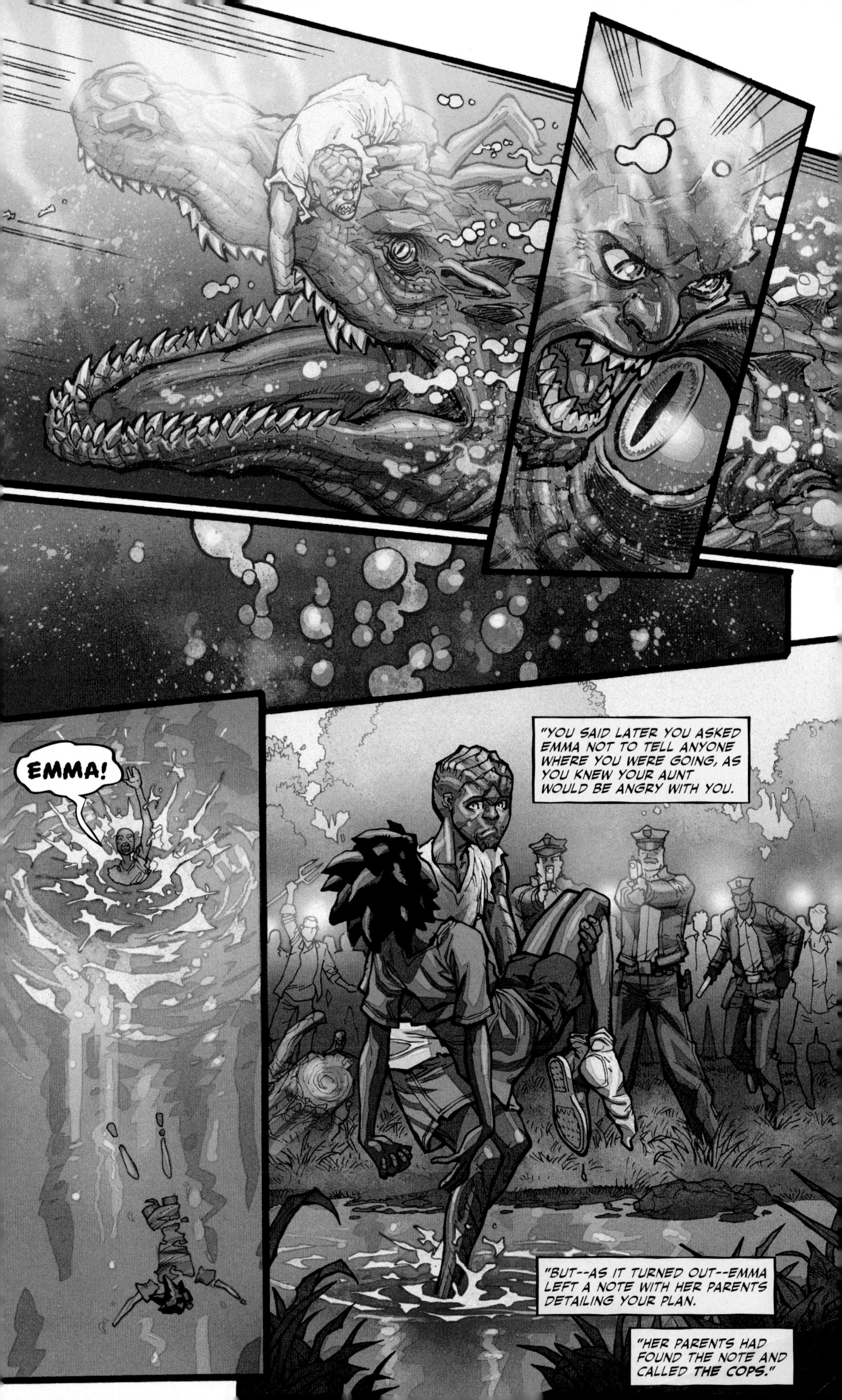
EMMA!
"YOU SAID LATER YOU ASKED EMMA NOT TO TELL ANYONE WHERE YOU WERE GOING, AS YOU KNEW YOUR AUNT WOULD BE ANGRY WITH YOU.
"BUT--AS IT TURNED OUT--EMMA LEFT A NOTE WITH HER PARENTS DETAILING YOUR PLAN.
"HER PARENTS HAD FOUND THE NOTE AND CALLED THE COPS."

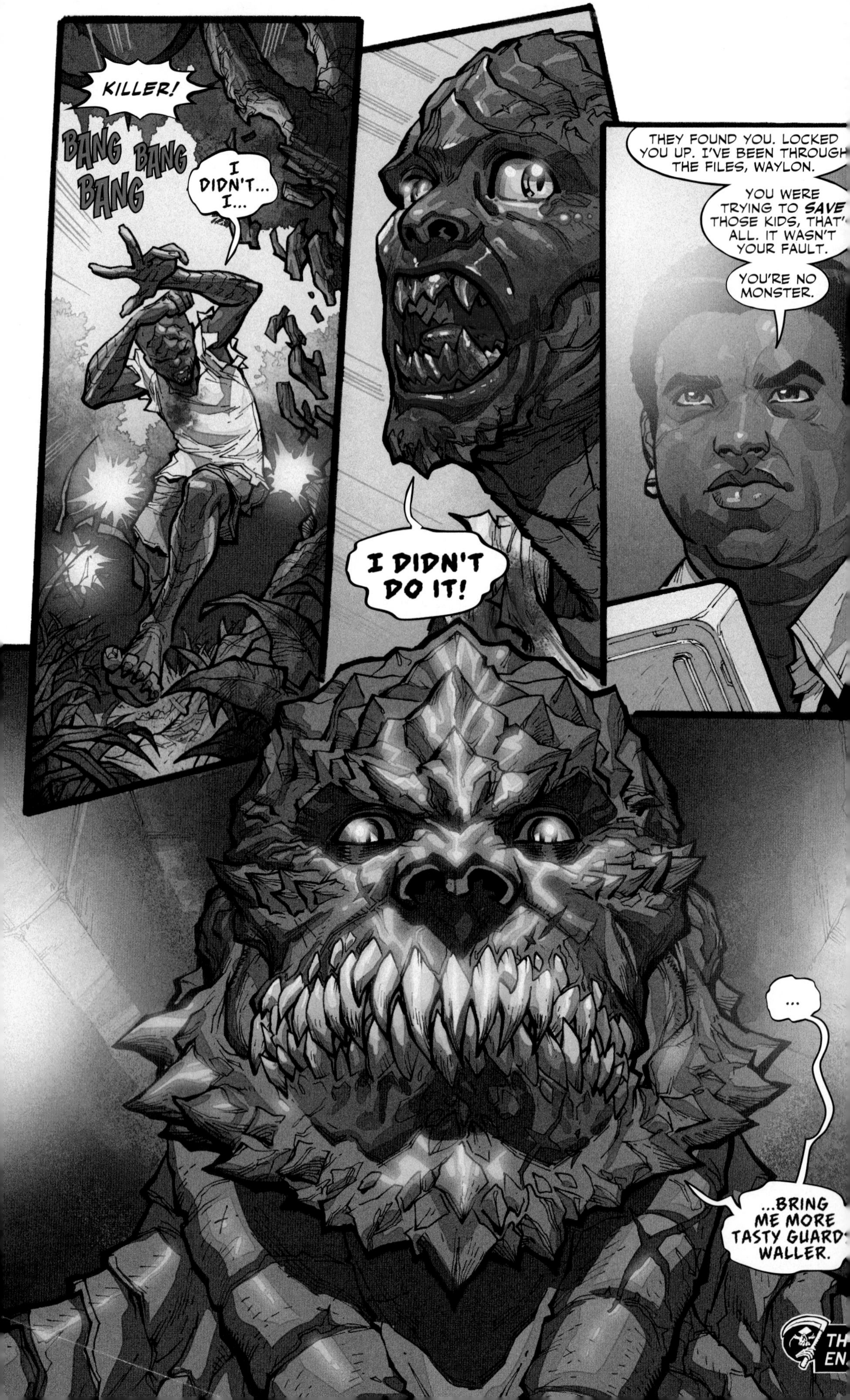

KILLER!
BANG BANG BANG
I DIDN'T... I...
I DIDN'T DO IT!
THEY FOUND YOU. LOCKED YOU UP. I'VE BEEN THROUGH THE FILES, WAYLON.
YOU WERE TRYING TO SAVE THOSE KIDS, THAT'S ALL. IT WASN'T YOUR FAULT.
YOU'RE NO MONSTER.
...
...BRING ME MORE TASTY GUARDS, WALLER.

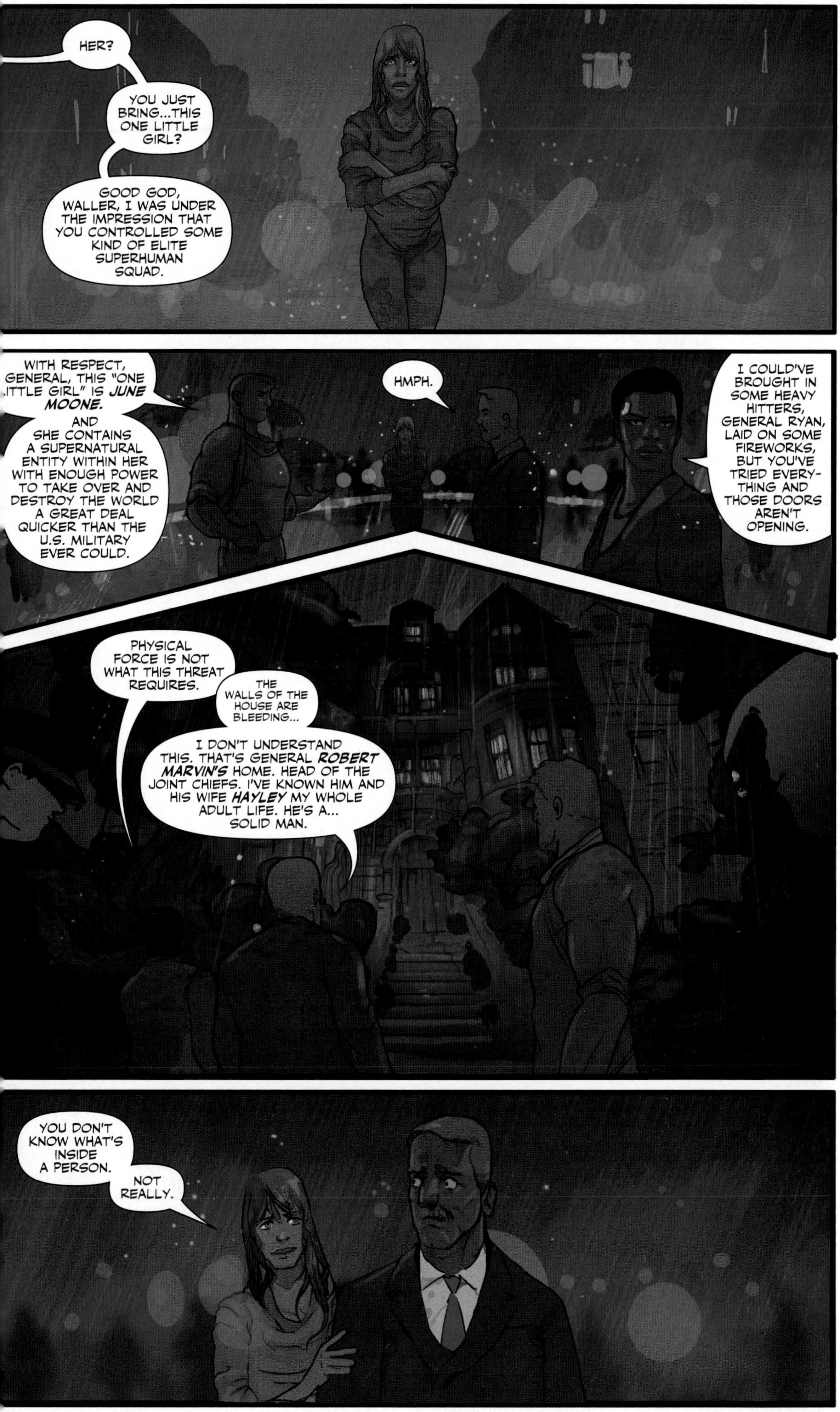
HER?
YOU JUST BRING...THIS ONE LITTLE GIRL?
GOOD GOD, WALLER, I WAS UNDER THE IMPRESSION THAT YOU CONTROLLED SOME KIND OF ELITE SUPERHUMAN SQUAD.
WITH RESPECT, GENERAL, THIS "ONE LITTLE GIRL" IS JUNE MOONE.
AND SHE CONTAINS A SUPERNATURAL ENTITY WITHIN HER WITH ENOUGH POWER TO TAKE OVER AND DESTROY THE WORLD A GREAT DEAL QUICKER THAN THE U.S. MILITARY EVER COULD.
HMPH.
I COULD'VE BROUGHT IN SOME HEAVY HITTERS, GENERAL RYAN, LAID ON SOME FIREWORKS, BUT YOU'VE TRIED EVERY-THING AND THOSE DOORS AREN'T OPENING.
PHYSICAL FORCE IS NOT WHAT THIS THREAT REQUIRES.
THE WALLS OF THE HOUSE ARE BLEEDING...
I DON'T UNDERSTAND THIS. THAT'S GENERAL ROBERT MARVIN'S HOME. HEAD OF THE JOINT CHIEFS. I'VE KNOWN HIM AND HIS WIFE HAYLEY MY WHOLE ADULT LIFE. HE'S A... SOLID MAN.
YOU DON'T KNOW WHAT'S INSIDE A PERSON.
NOT REALLY.

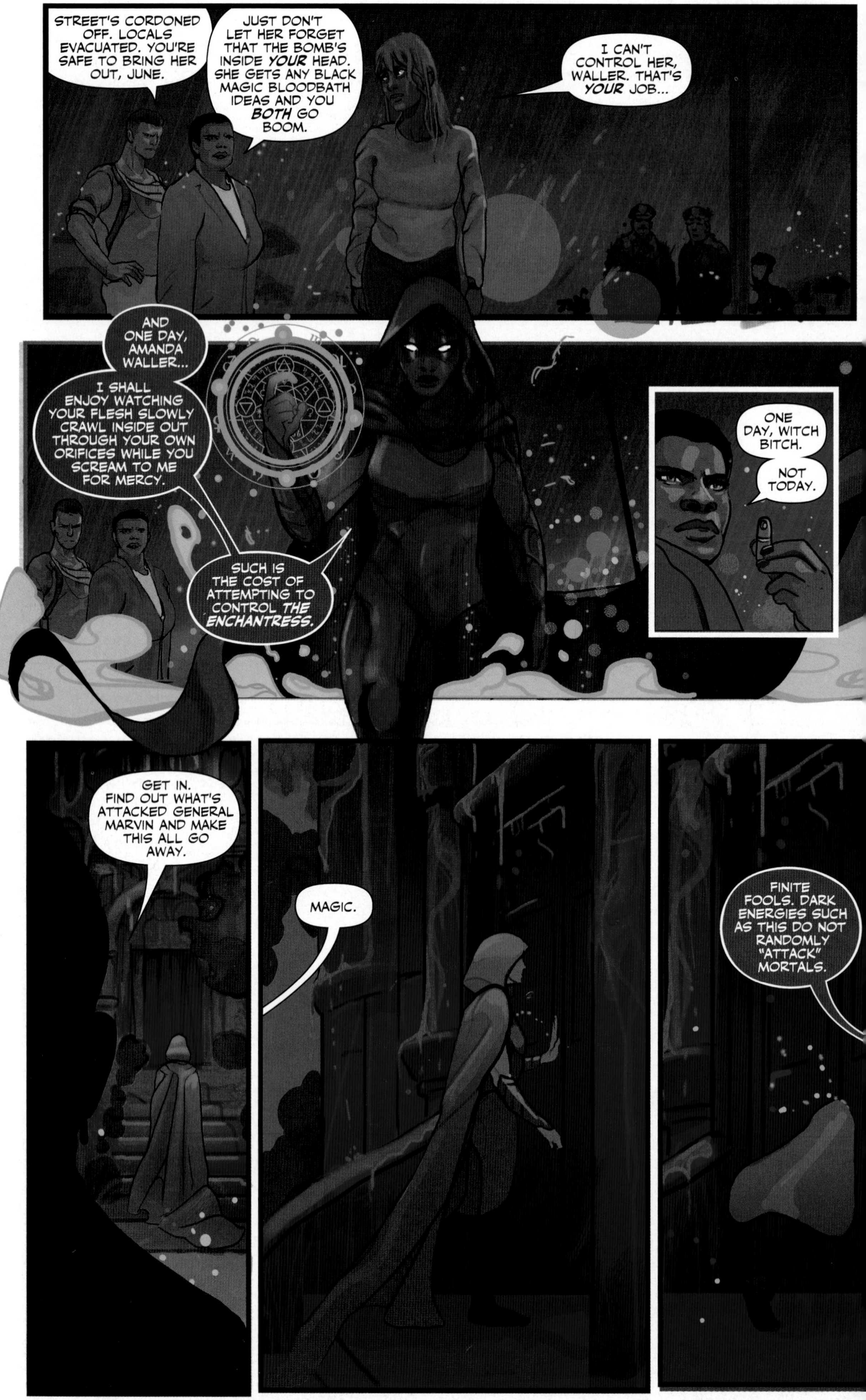
STREET'S CORDONED OFF. LOCALS EVACUATED. YOU'RE SAFE TO BRING HER OUT, JUNE.
JUST DON'T LET HER FORGET THAT THE BOMB'S INSIDE *YOUR* HEAD. SHE GETS ANY BLACK MAGIC BLOODBATH IDEAS AND YOU *BOTH* GO BOOM.
I CAN'T CONTROL HER, WALLER. THAT'S *YOUR* JOB...
AND ONE DAY, AMANDA WALLER...
I SHALL ENJOY WATCHING YOUR FLESH SLOWLY CRAWL INSIDE OUT THROUGH YOUR OWN ORIFICES WHILE YOU SCREAM TO ME FOR MERCY.
SUCH IS THE COST OF ATTEMPTING TO CONTROL *THE ENCHANTRESS.*
ONE DAY, WITCH BITCH.
NOT TODAY.
GET IN. FIND OUT WHAT'S ATTACKED GENERAL MARVIN AND MAKE THIS ALL GO AWAY.
MAGIC.
FINITE FOOLS. DARK ENERGIES SUCH AS THIS DO NOT RANDOMLY "ATTACK" MORTALS.

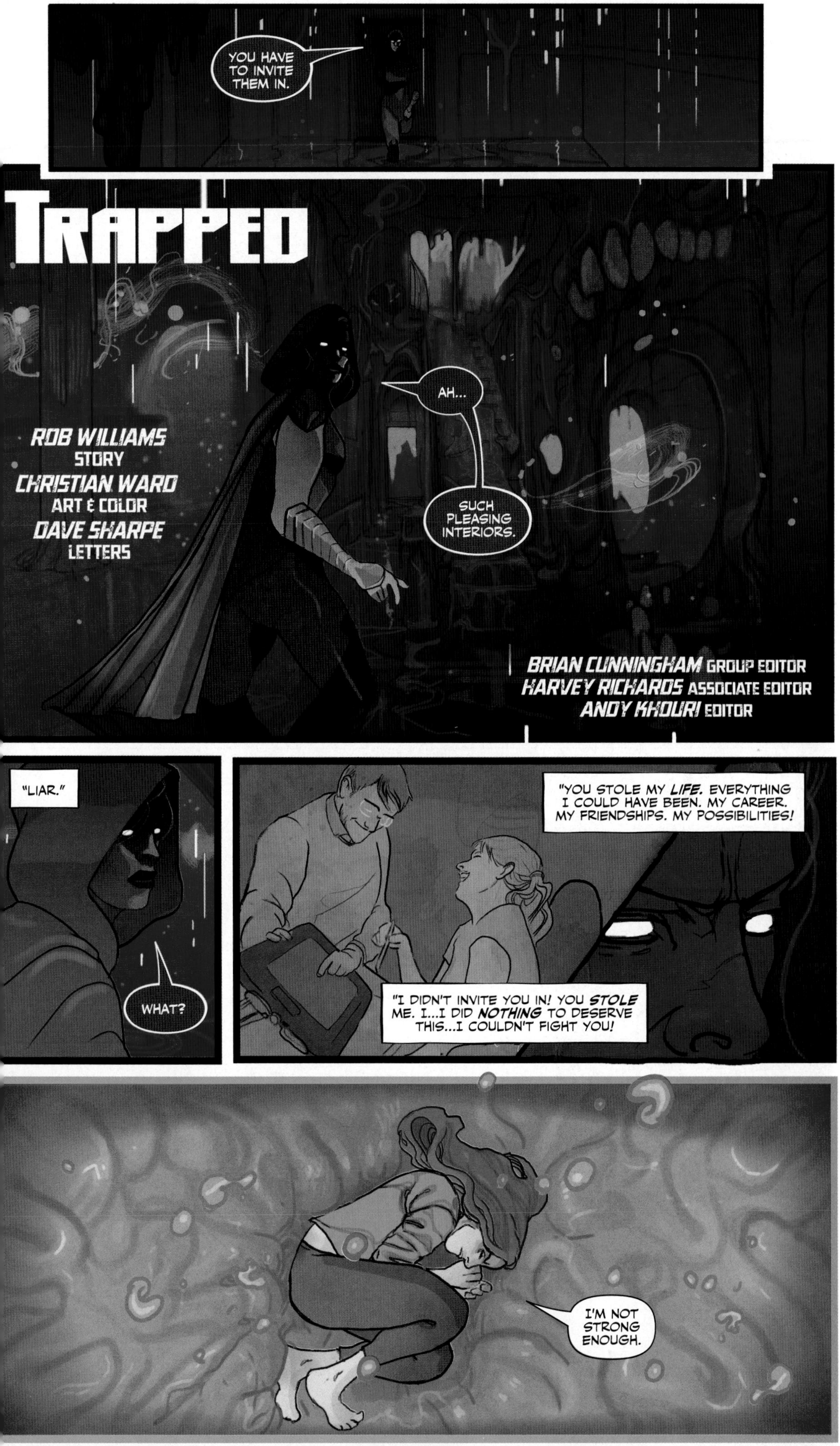
YOU HAVE TO INVITE THEM IN.
TRAPPED
AH...
SUCH PLEASING INTERIORS.
ROB WILLIAMS STORY
CHRISTIAN WARD ART & COLOR
DAVE SHARPE LETTERS
BRIAN CUNNINGHAM GROUP EDITOR
HARVEY RICHARDS ASSOCIATE EDITOR
ANDY KHOURI EDITOR
"LIAR."
WHAT?
"YOU STOLE MY LIFE. EVERYTHING I COULD HAVE BEEN. MY CAREER. MY FRIENDSHIPS. MY POSSIBILITIES!
"I DIDN'T INVITE YOU IN! YOU STOLE ME. I...I DID NOTHING TO DESERVE THIS...I COULDN'T FIGHT YOU!
I'M NOT STRONG ENOUGH.

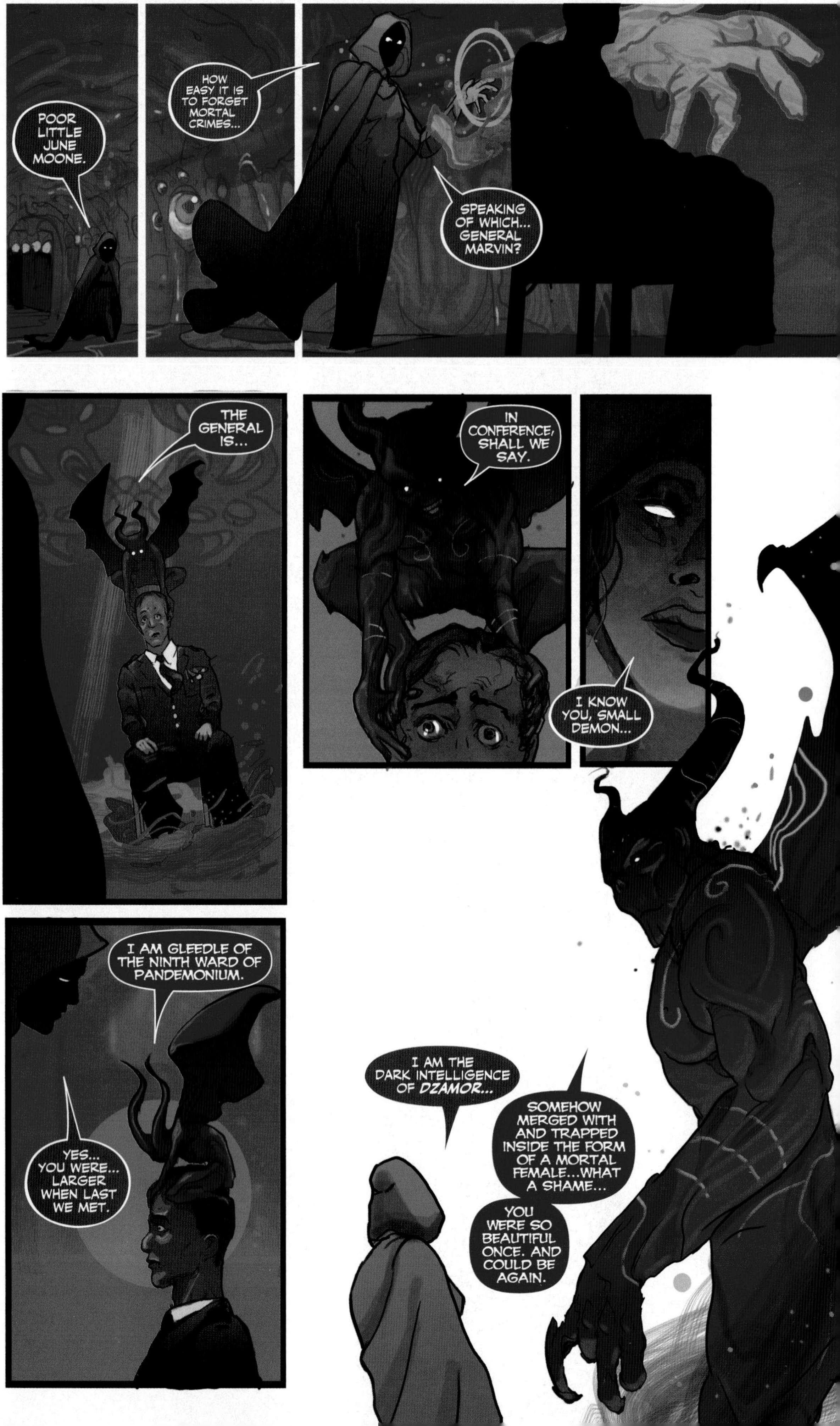
POOR LITTLE JUNE MOONE.
HOW EASY IT IS TO FORGET MORTAL CRIMES...
SPEAKING OF WHICH... GENERAL MARVIN?
THE GENERAL IS...
IN CONFERENCE, SHALL WE SAY.
I KNOW YOU, SMALL DEMON...
I AM GLEEDLE OF THE NINTH WARD OF PANDEMONIUM.
YES... YOU WERE... LARGER WHEN LAST WE MET.
I AM THE DARK INTELLIGENCE OF DZAMOR...
SOMEHOW MERGED WITH AND TRAPPED INSIDE THE FORM OF A MORTAL FEMALE...WHAT A SHAME...
YOU WERE SO BEAUTIFUL ONCE. AND COULD BE AGAIN.

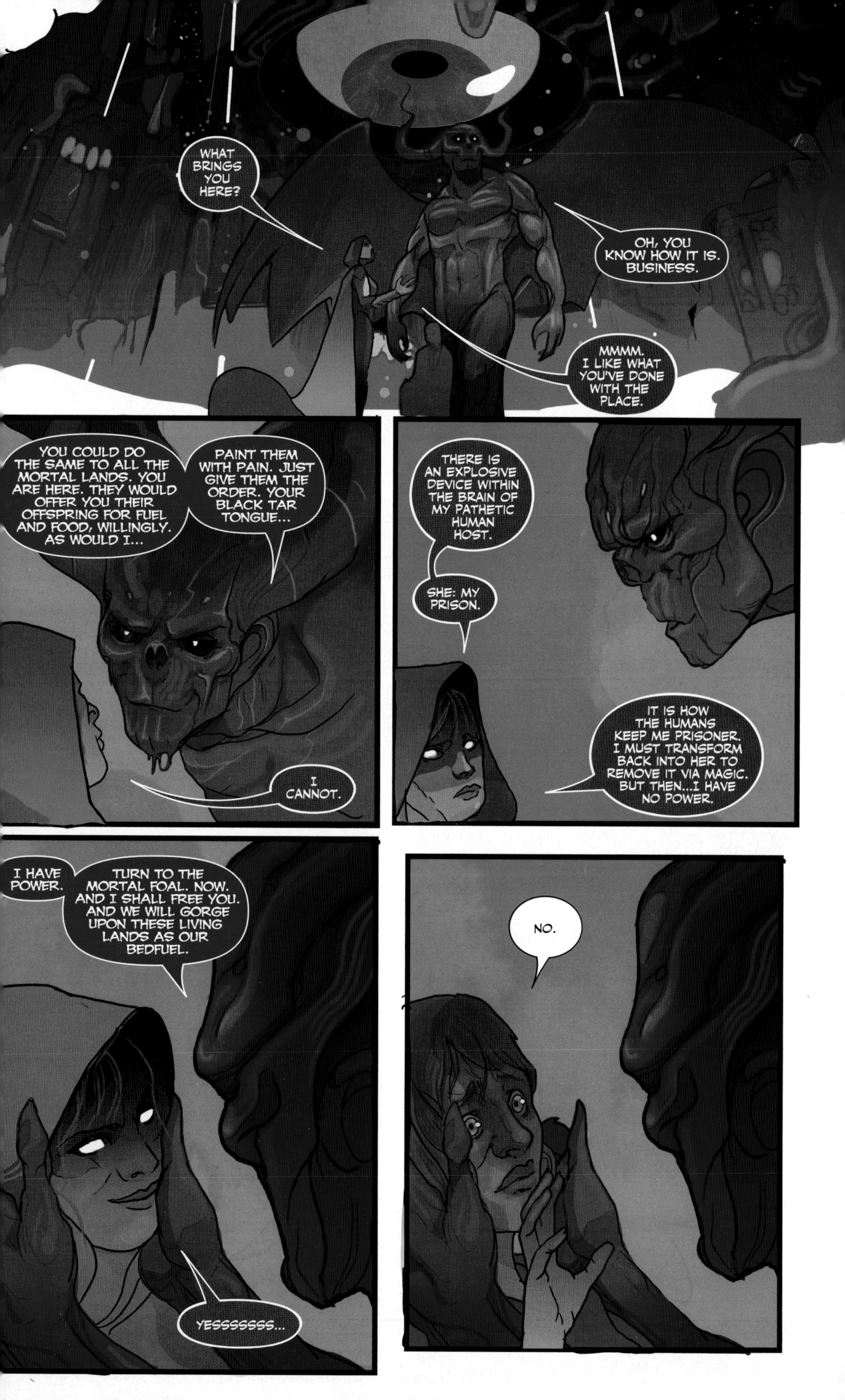
WHAT BRINGS YOU HERE?
OH, YOU KNOW HOW IT IS. BUSINESS.
MMMM. I LIKE WHAT YOU'VE DONE WITH THE PLACE.
YOU COULD DO THE SAME TO ALL THE MORTAL LANDS. YOU ARE HERE. THEY WOULD OFFER YOU THEIR OFFSPRING FOR FUEL AND FOOD, WILLINGLY. AS WOULD I...
PAINT THEM WITH PAIN. JUST GIVE THEM THE ORDER. YOUR BLACK TAR TONGUE...
I CANNOT.
THERE IS AN EXPLOSIVE DEVICE WITHIN THE BRAIN OF MY PATHETIC HUMAN HOST.
SHE: MY PRISON.
IT IS HOW THE HUMANS KEEP ME PRISONER. I MUST TRANSFORM BACK INTO HER TO REMOVE IT VIA MAGIC. BUT THEN...I HAVE NO POWER.
I HAVE POWER.
TURN TO THE MORTAL FOAL. NOW. AND I SHALL FREE YOU. AND WE WILL GORGE UPON THESE LIVING LANDS AS OUR BEDFUEL.
YESSSSSSS...
NO.

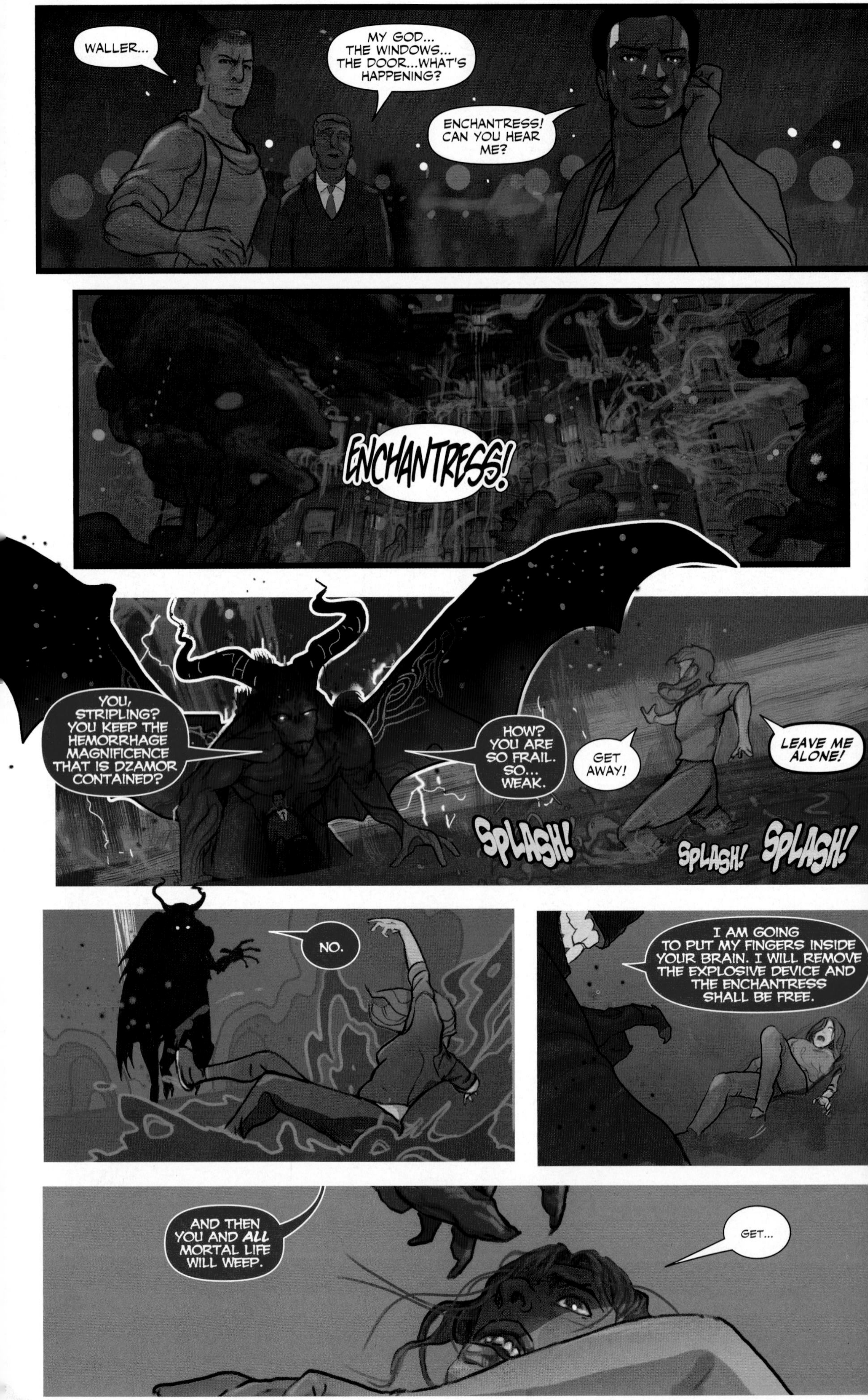

WALLER...
MY GOD... THE WINDOWS... THE DOOR...WHAT'S HAPPENING?
ENCHANTRESS! CAN YOU HEAR ME?
ENCHANTRESS!
YOU, STRIPLING? YOU KEEP THE HEMORRHAGE MAGNIFICENCE THAT IS DZAMOR CONTAINED?
HOW? YOU ARE SO FRAIL. SO... WEAK.
GET AWAY!
LEAVE ME ALONE!
SPLASH!
SPLASH!
SPLASH!
NO.
I AM GOING TO PUT MY FINGERS INSIDE YOUR BRAIN. I WILL REMOVE THE EXPLOSIVE DEVICE AND THE ENCHANTRESS SHALL BE FREE.
AND THEN YOU AND ALL MORTAL LIFE WILL WEEP.
GET...

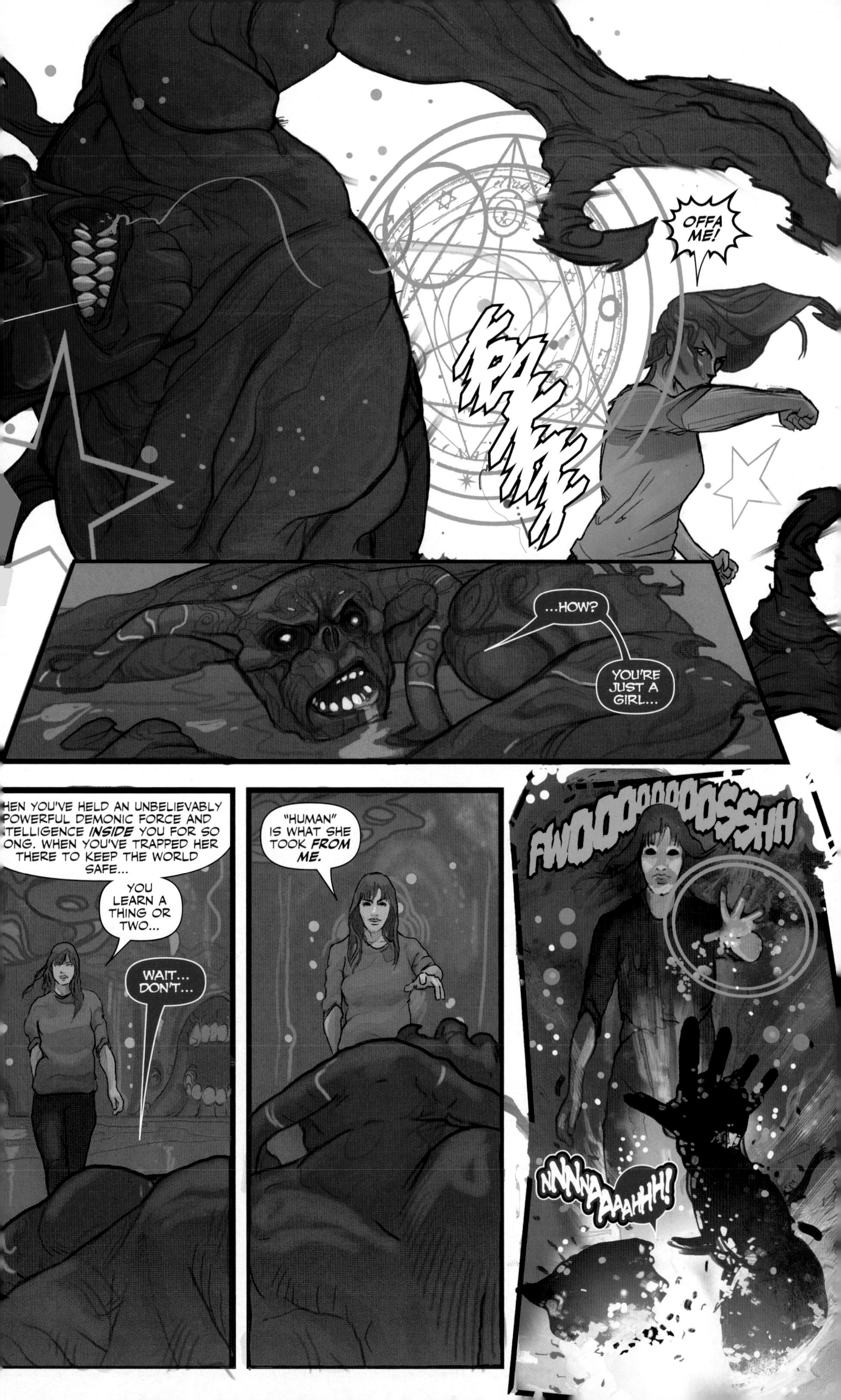
OFFA ME!
...HOW?
YOU'RE JUST A GIRL...
HEN YOU'VE HELD AN UNBELIEVABLY POWERFUL DEMONIC FORCE AND TELLIGENCE INSIDE YOU FOR SO ONG. WHEN YOU'VE TRAPPED HER THERE TO KEEP THE WORLD SAFE...
YOU LEARN A THING OR TWO...
WAIT... DON'T...
"HUMAN" IS WHAT SHE TOOK FROM ME.
FWOOOOOOOOSSHH
NNNNAAAAHHH!

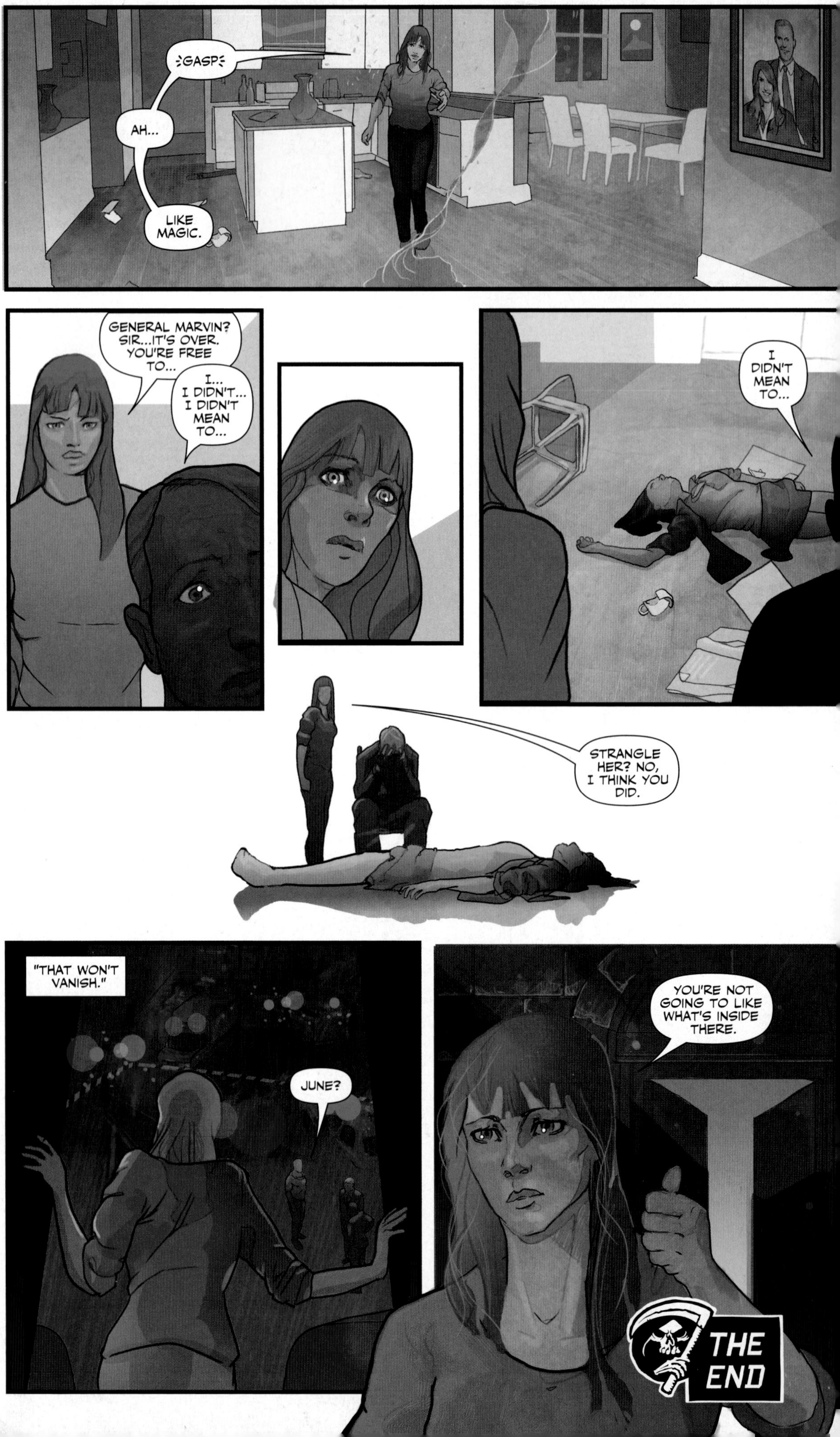

GASP
AH...
LIKE MAGIC.
GENERAL MARVIN? SIR...IT'S OVER. YOU'RE FREE TO...
I... I DIDN'T... I DIDN'T MEAN TO...
I DIDN'T MEAN TO...
STRANGLE HER? NO, I THINK YOU DID.
"THAT WON'T VANISH."
JUNE?
YOU'RE NOT GOING TO LIKE WHAT'S INSIDE THERE.
THE END

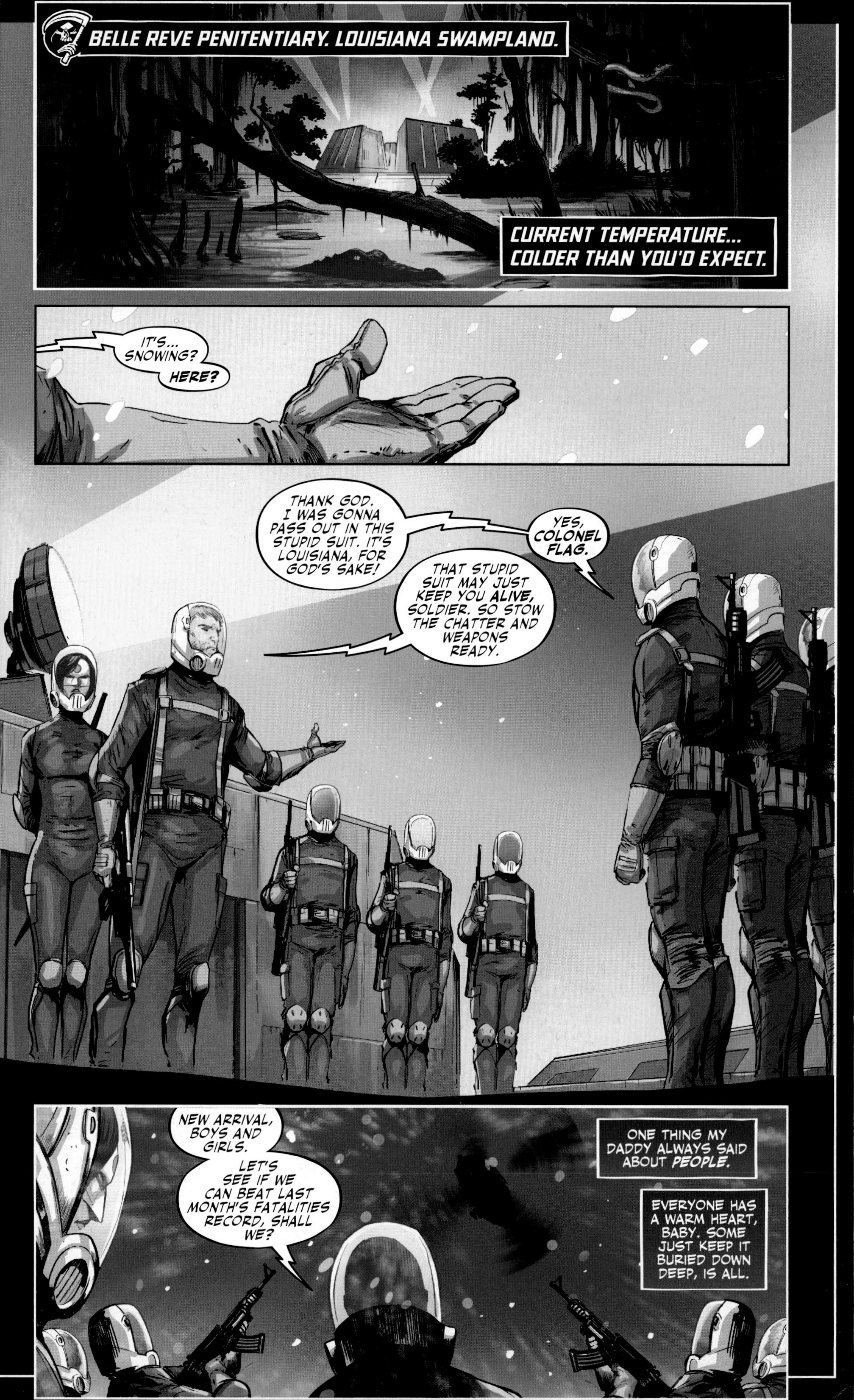
BELLE REVE PENITENTIARY. LOUISIANA SWAMPLAND.
CURRENT TEMPERATURE... COLDER THAN YOU'D EXPECT.
IT'S... SNOWING? HERE?
THANK GOD. I WAS GONNA PASS OUT IN THIS STUPID SUIT. IT'S LOUISIANA, FOR GOD'S SAKE!
THAT STUPID SUIT MAY JUST KEEP YOU ALIVE, SOLDIER. SO STOW THE CHATTER AND WEAPONS READY.
YES, COLONEL FLAG.
NEW ARRIVAL, BOYS AND GIRLS.
LET'S SEE IF WE CAN BEAT LAST MONTH'S FATALITIES RECORD, SHALL WE?
ONE THING MY DADDY ALWAYS SAID ABOUT PEOPLE.
EVERYONE HAS A WARM HEART, BABY. SOME JUST KEEP IT BURIED DOWN DEEP, IS ALL.

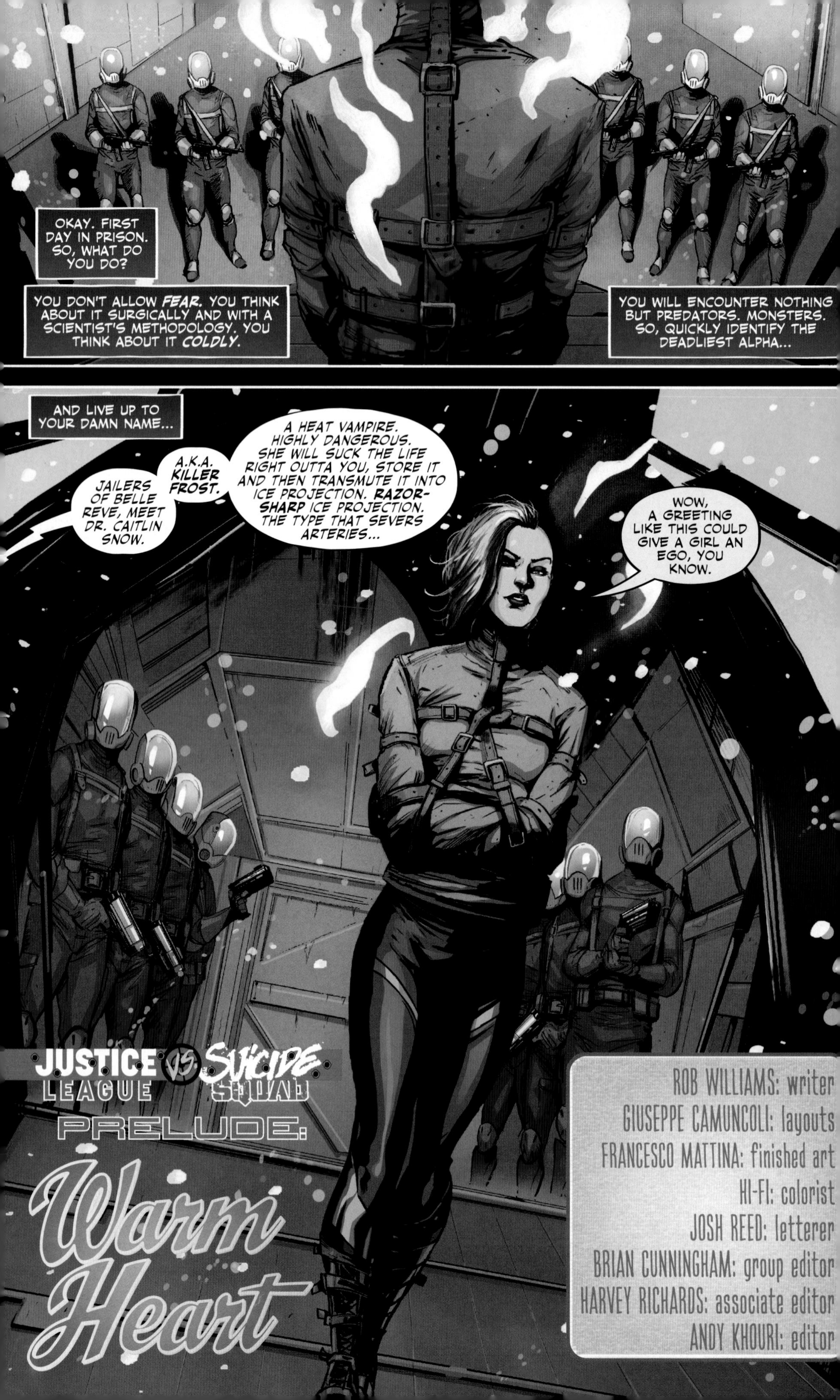
OKAY. FIRST DAY IN PRISON. SO, WHAT DO YOU DO?
YOU DON'T ALLOW FEAR. YOU THINK ABOUT IT SURGICALLY AND WITH A SCIENTIST'S METHODOLOGY. YOU THINK ABOUT IT COLDLY.
YOU WILL ENCOUNTER NOTHING BUT PREDATORS. MONSTERS. SO, QUICKLY IDENTIFY THE DEADLIEST ALPHA...
AND LIVE UP TO YOUR DAMN NAME...
JAILERS OF BELLE REVE, MEET DR. CAITLIN SNOW.
A.K.A. KILLER FROST.
A HEAT VAMPIRE. HIGHLY DANGEROUS. SHE WILL SUCK THE LIFE RIGHT OUTTA YOU, STORE IT AND THEN TRANSMUTE IT INTO ICE PROJECTION. RAZOR-SHARP ICE PROJECTION. THE TYPE THAT SEVERS ARTERIES...
WOW, A GREETING LIKE THIS COULD GIVE A GIRL AN EGO, YOU KNOW.
JUSTICE LEAGUE VS SUICIDE SQUAD
PRELUDE:
Warm Heart
ROB WILLIAMS: writer
GIUSEPPE CAMUNCOLI: layouts
FRANCESCO MATTINA: finished art
HI-FI: colorist
JOSH REED: letterer
BRIAN CUNNINGHAM: group editor
HARVEY RICHARDS: associate editor
ANDY KHOURI: editor

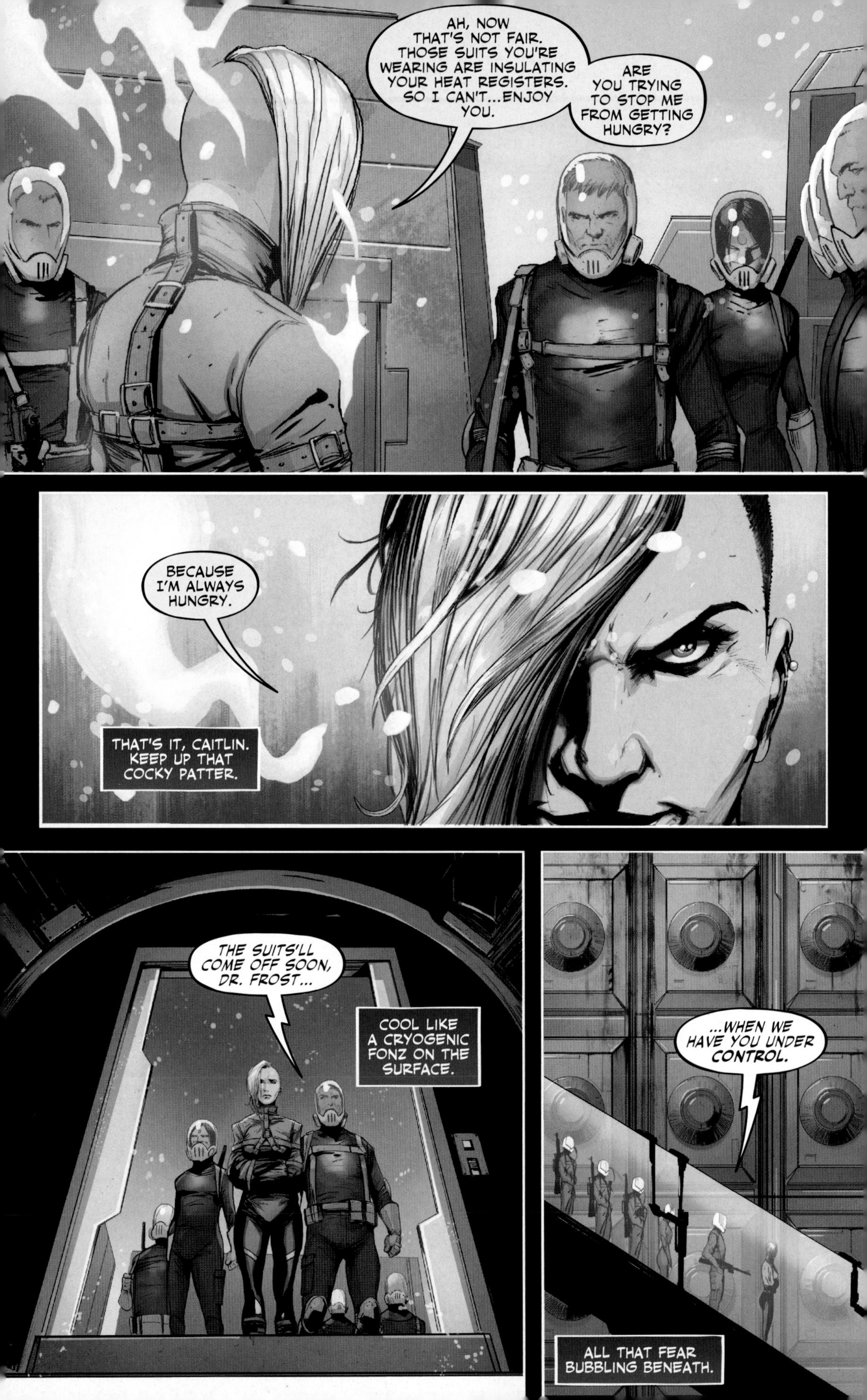
AH, NOW THAT'S NOT FAIR. THOSE SUITS YOU'RE WEARING ARE INSULATING YOUR HEAT REGISTERS. SO I CAN'T...ENJOY YOU.
ARE YOU TRYING TO STOP ME FROM GETTING HUNGRY?
BECAUSE I'M ALWAYS HUNGRY.
THAT'S IT, CAITLIN. KEEP UP THAT COCKY PATTER.
THE SUITS'LL COME OFF SOON, DR. FROST...
COOL LIKE A CRYOGENIC FONZ ON THE SURFACE.
...WHEN WE HAVE YOU UNDER CONTROL.
ALL THAT FEAR BUBBLING BENEATH.

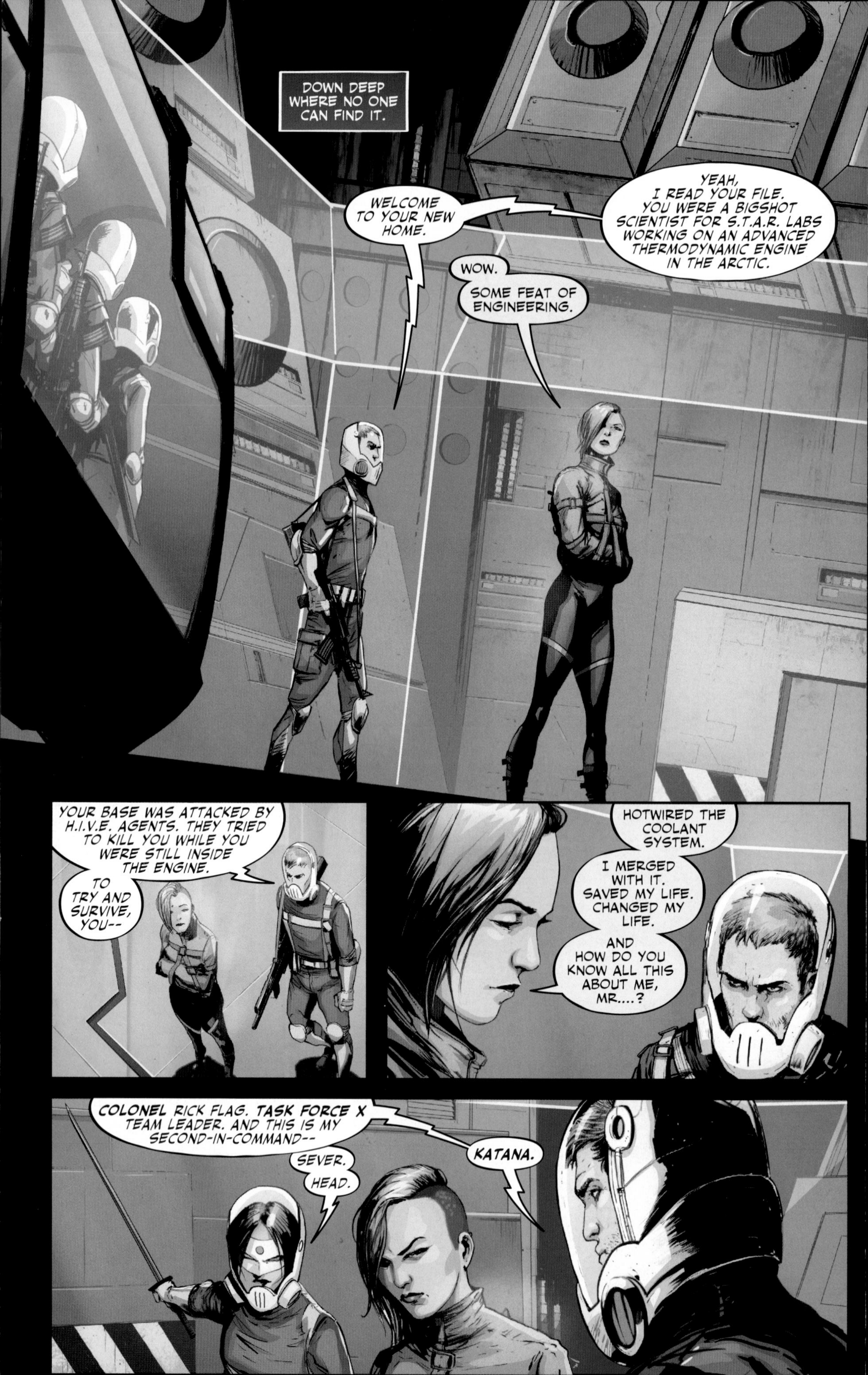
DOWN DEEP WHERE NO ONE CAN FIND IT.
WELCOME TO YOUR NEW HOME.
YEAH, I READ YOUR FILE. YOU WERE A BIGSHOT SCIENTIST FOR S.T.A.R. LABS WORKING ON AN ADVANCED THERMODYNAMIC ENGINE IN THE ARCTIC.
WOW.
SOME FEAT OF ENGINEERING.
YOUR BASE WAS ATTACKED BY H.I.V.E. AGENTS. THEY TRIED TO KILL YOU WHILE YOU WERE STILL INSIDE THE ENGINE.
TO TRY AND SURVIVE, YOU--
HOTWIRED THE COOLANT SYSTEM.
I MERGED WITH IT. SAVED MY LIFE. CHANGED MY LIFE.
AND HOW DO YOU KNOW ALL THIS ABOUT ME, MR....?
COLONEL RICK FLAG. TASK FORCE X TEAM LEADER. AND THIS IS MY SECOND-IN-COMMAND--
KATANA.
SEVER.
HEAD.

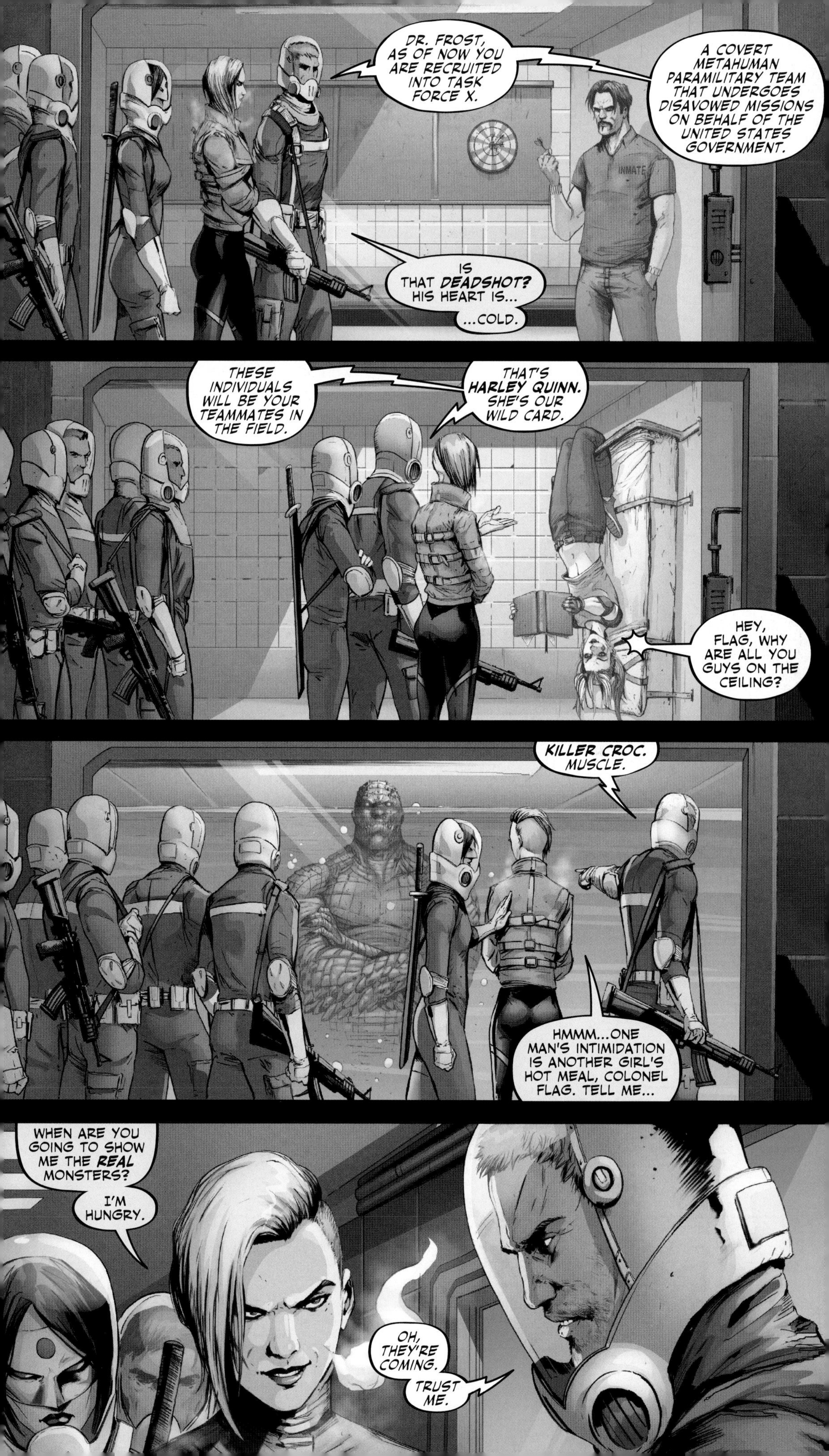
DR. FROST, AS OF NOW YOU ARE RECRUITED INTO TASK FORCE X.
A COVERT METAHUMAN PARAMILITARY TEAM THAT UNDERGOES DISAVOWED MISSIONS ON BEHALF OF THE UNITED STATES GOVERNMENT.
INMATE
IS THAT DEADSHOT? HIS HEART IS...
...COLD.
THESE INDIVIDUALS WILL BE YOUR TEAMMATES IN THE FIELD.
THAT'S HARLEY QUINN. SHE'S OUR WILD CARD.
HEY, FLAG, WHY ARE ALL YOU GUYS ON THE CEILING?
KILLER CROC. MUSCLE.
HMMM...ONE MAN'S INTIMIDATION IS ANOTHER GIRL'S HOT MEAL, COLONEL FLAG. TELL ME...
WHEN ARE YOU GOING TO SHOW ME THE REAL MONSTERS?
I'M HUNGRY.
OH, THEY'RE COMING.
TRUST ME.

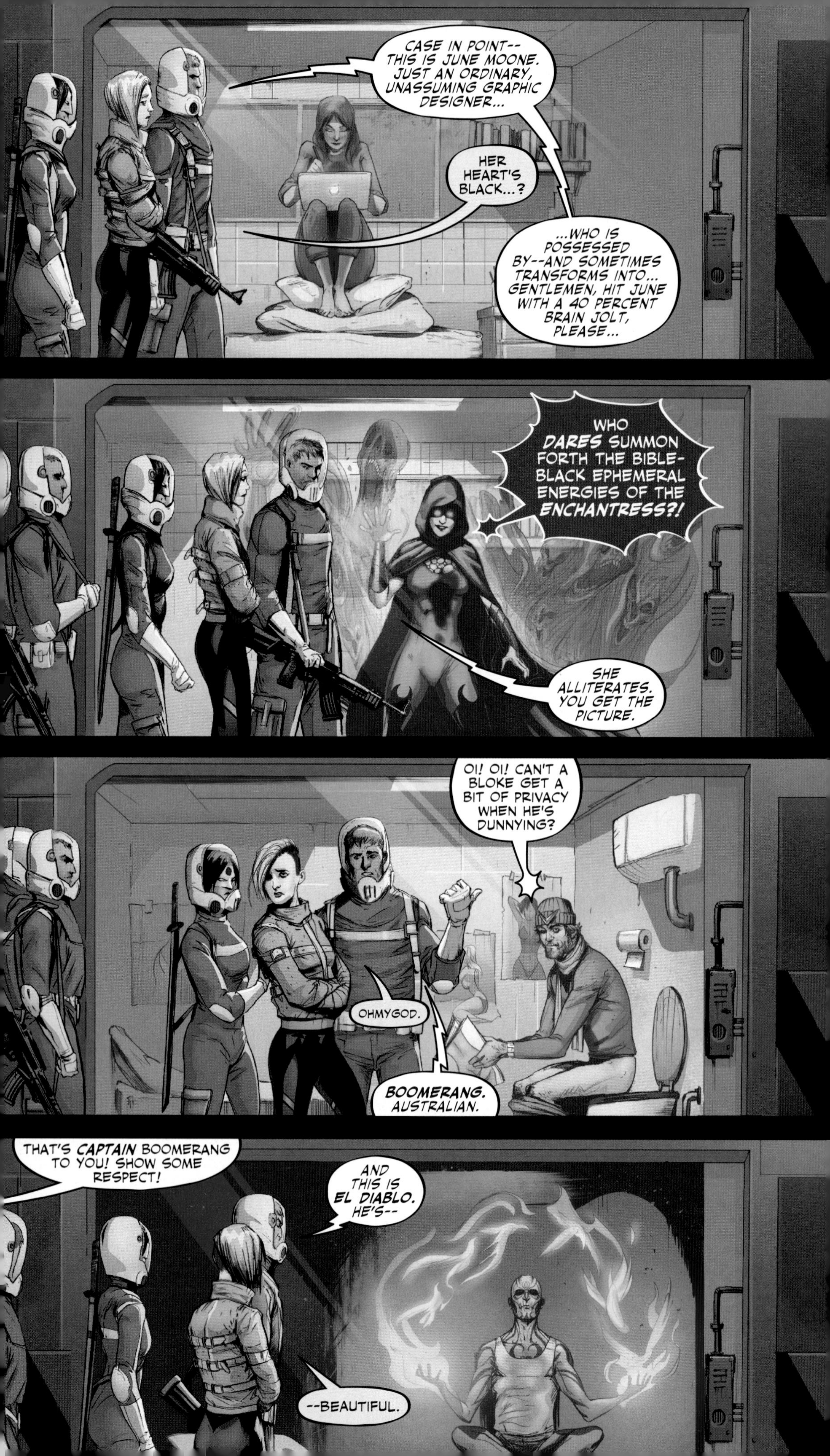
CASE IN POINT-- THIS IS JUNE MOONE. JUST AN ORDINARY, UNASSUMING GRAPHIC DESIGNER...
HER HEART'S BLACK...?
...WHO IS POSSESSED BY--AND SOMETIMES TRANSFORMS INTO... GENTLEMEN, HIT JUNE WITH A 40 PERCENT BRAIN JOLT, PLEASE...
WHO DARES SUMMON FORTH THE BIBLE-BLACK EPHEMERAL ENERGIES OF THE ENCHANTRESS?!
SHE ALLITERATES. YOU GET THE PICTURE.
OI! OI! CAN'T A BLOKE GET A BIT OF PRIVACY WHEN HE'S DUNNYING?
OHMYGOD.
BOOMERANG. AUSTRALIAN.
THAT'S CAPTAIN BOOMERANG TO YOU! SHOW SOME RESPECT!
AND THIS IS EL DIABLO. HE'S--
--BEAUTIFUL.

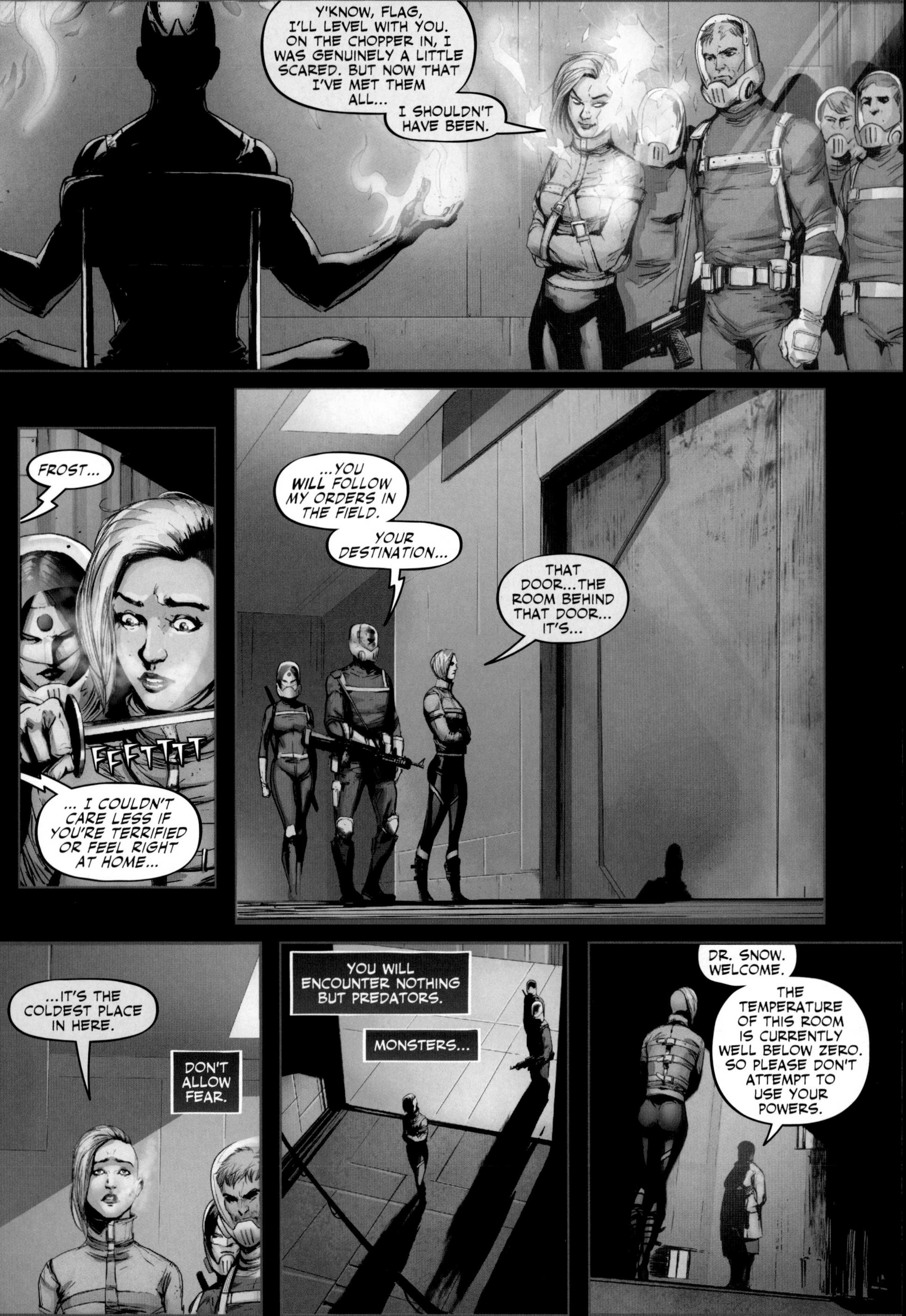
Y'KNOW, FLAG, I'LL LEVEL WITH YOU. ON THE CHOPPER IN, I WAS GENUINELY A LITTLE SCARED. BUT NOW THAT I'VE MET THEM ALL...
I SHOULDN'T HAVE BEEN.
FROST...
FFFTTTT
... I COULDN'T CARE LESS IF YOU'RE TERRIFIED OR FEEL RIGHT AT HOME...
...YOU WILL FOLLOW MY ORDERS IN THE FIELD.
YOUR DESTINATION...
THAT DOOR...THE ROOM BEHIND THAT DOOR... IT'S...
...IT'S THE COLDEST PLACE IN HERE.
DON'T ALLOW FEAR.
YOU WILL ENCOUNTER NOTHING BUT PREDATORS.
MONSTERS...
DR. SNOW. WELCOME.
THE TEMPERATURE OF THIS ROOM IS CURRENTLY WELL BELOW ZERO. SO PLEASE DON'T ATTEMPT TO USE YOUR POWERS.

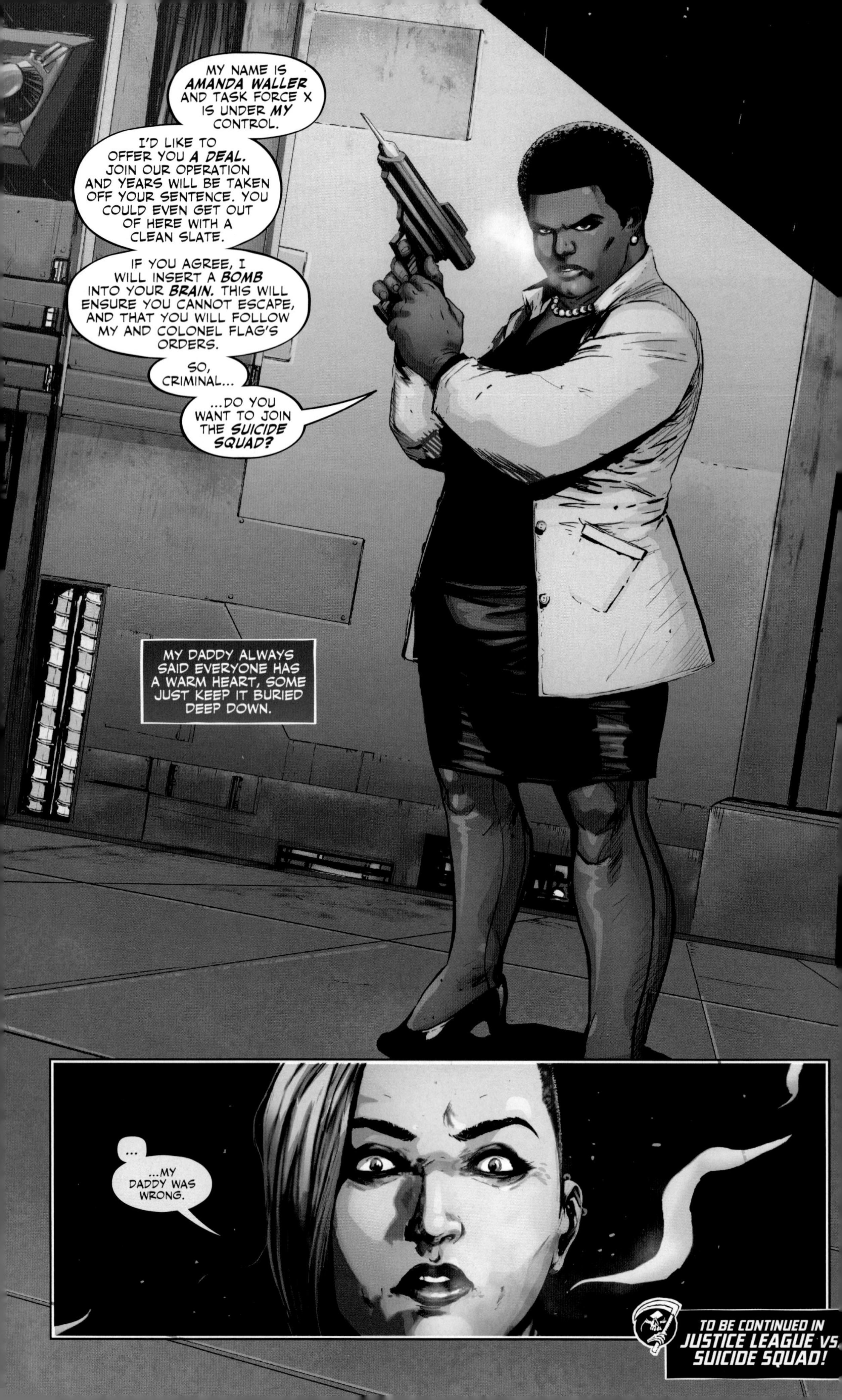

MY NAME IS AMANDA WALLER AND TASK FORCE X IS UNDER MY CONTROL.
I'D LIKE TO OFFER YOU A DEAL. JOIN OUR OPERATION AND YEARS WILL BE TAKEN OFF YOUR SENTENCE. YOU COULD EVEN GET OUT OF HERE WITH A CLEAN SLATE.
IF YOU AGREE, I WILL INSERT A BOMB INTO YOUR BRAIN. THIS WILL ENSURE YOU CANNOT ESCAPE, AND THAT YOU WILL FOLLOW MY AND COLONEL FLAG'S ORDERS.
SO, CRIMINAL...
...DO YOU WANT TO JOIN THE SUICIDE SQUAD?
MY DADDY ALWAYS SAID EVERYONE HAS A WARM HEART, SOME JUST KEEP IT BURIED DEEP DOWN.
...
...MY DADDY WAS WRONG.
TO BE CONTINUED IN JUSTICE LEAGUE VS. SUICIDE SQUAD!

SUICIDE SQUAD VARIANT COVER GALLERY

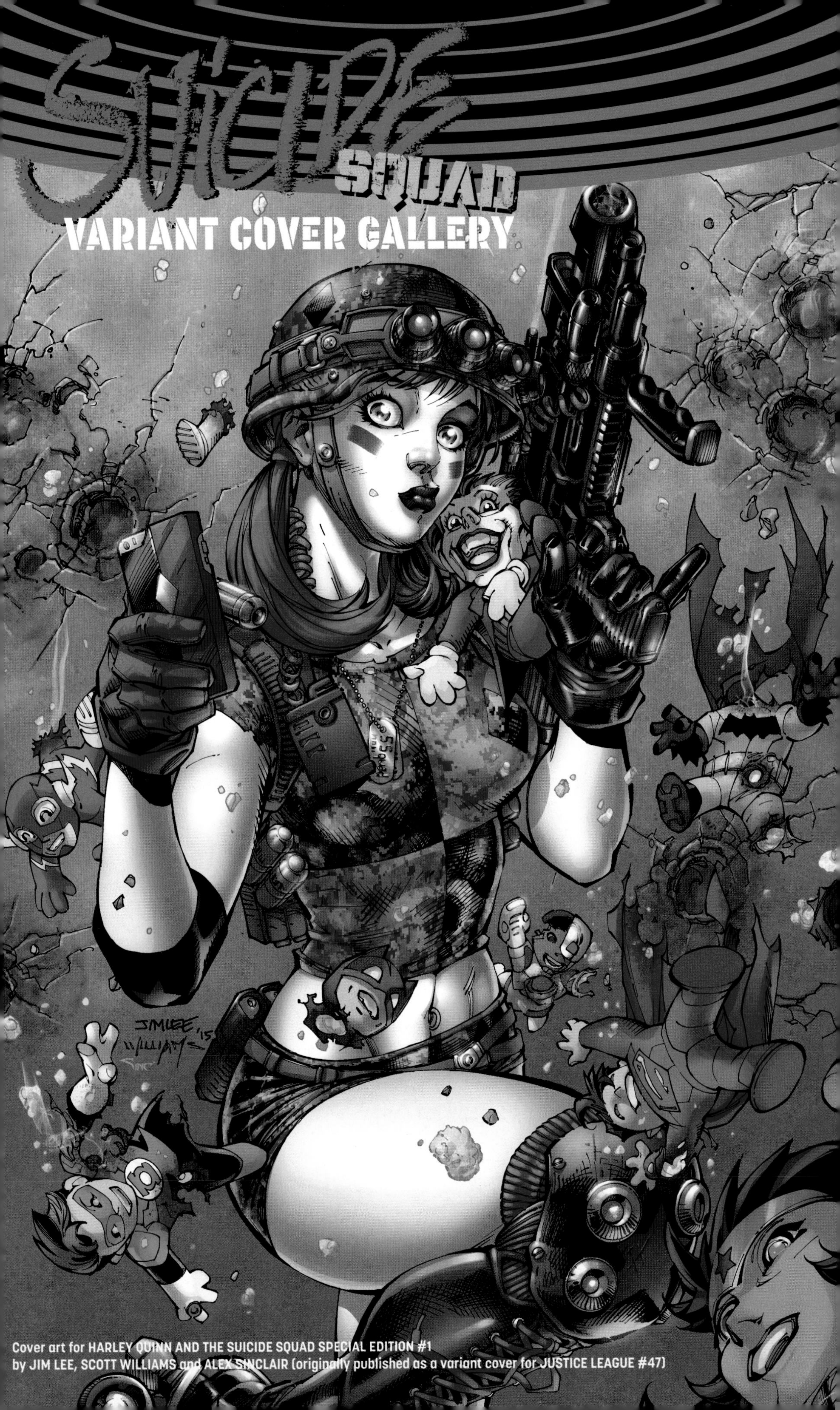

Cover art for HARLEY QUINN AND THE SUICIDE SQUAD SPECIAL EDITION #1 by JIM LEE, SCOTT WILLIAMS and ALEX SINCLAIR (originally published as a variant cover for JUSTICE LEAGUE #47)

Variant cover art for SUICIDE SQUAD: REBIRTH #1
by Amanda Conner and Paul Mounts

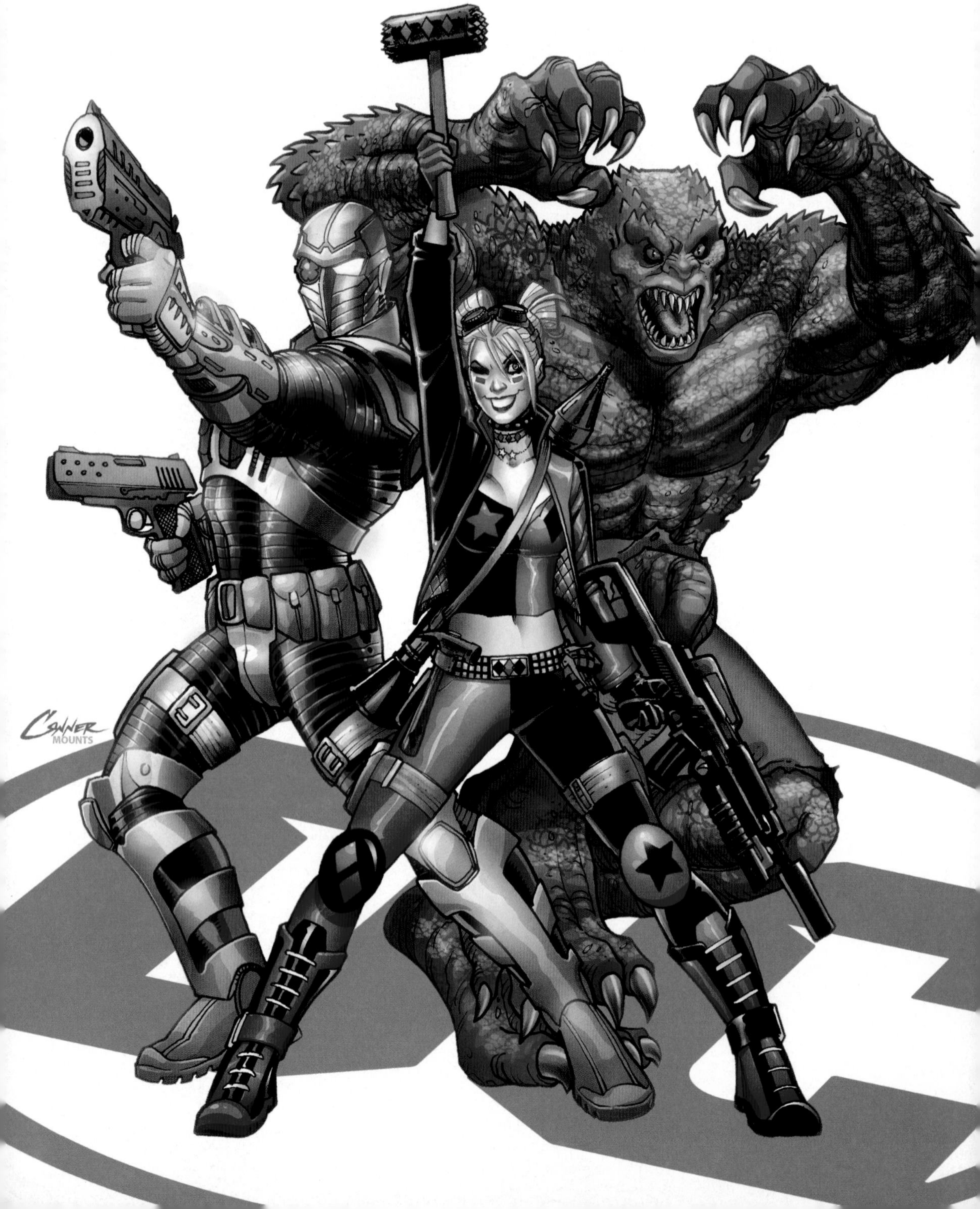
CONNER
MOUNTS

Limited-edition cover art for SUICIDE SQUAD: REBIRTH #1
by Philip Tan and Elmer Santos

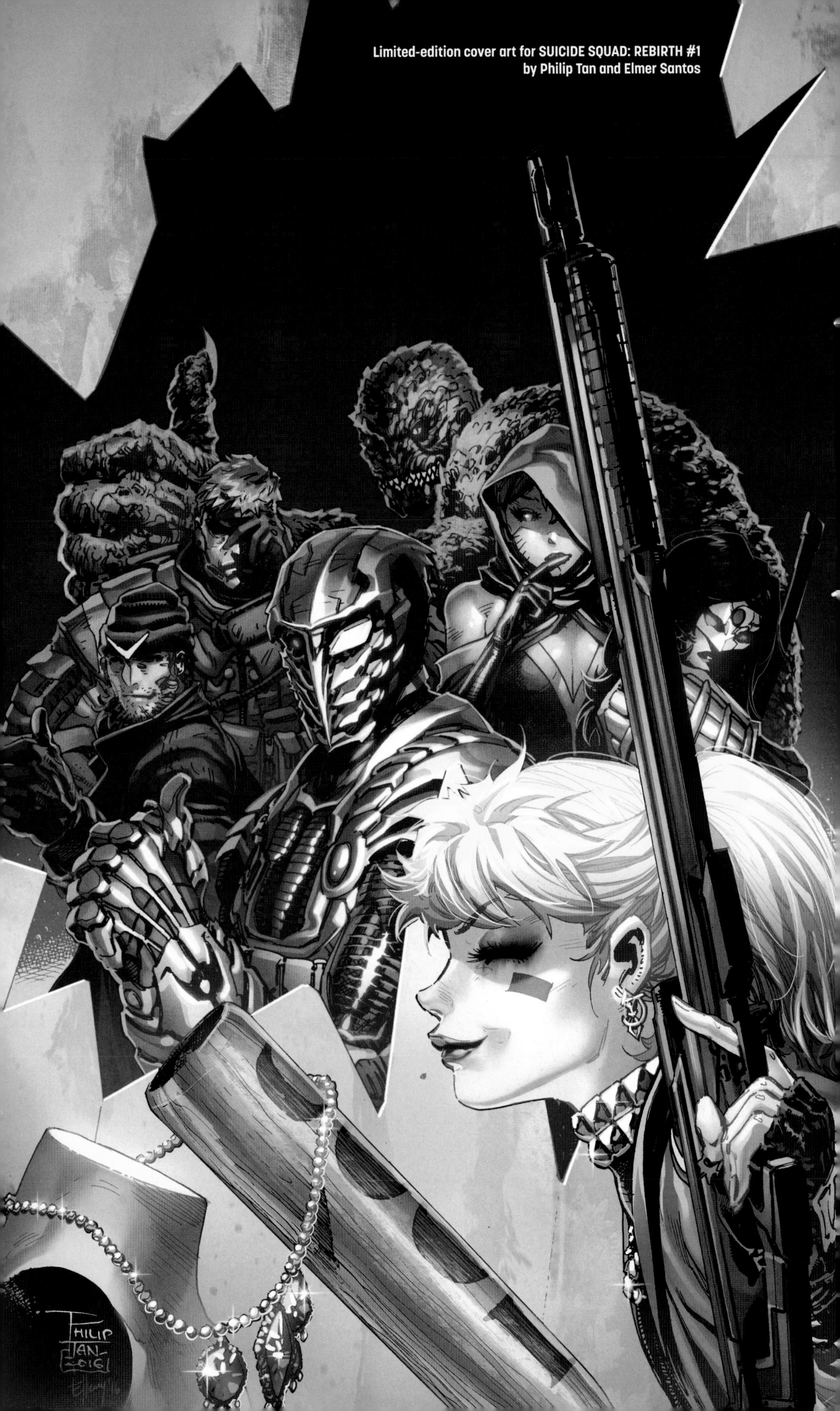
PHILIP TAN 2016

Variant cover art for SUICIDE SQUAD #1 by Lee Bermejo

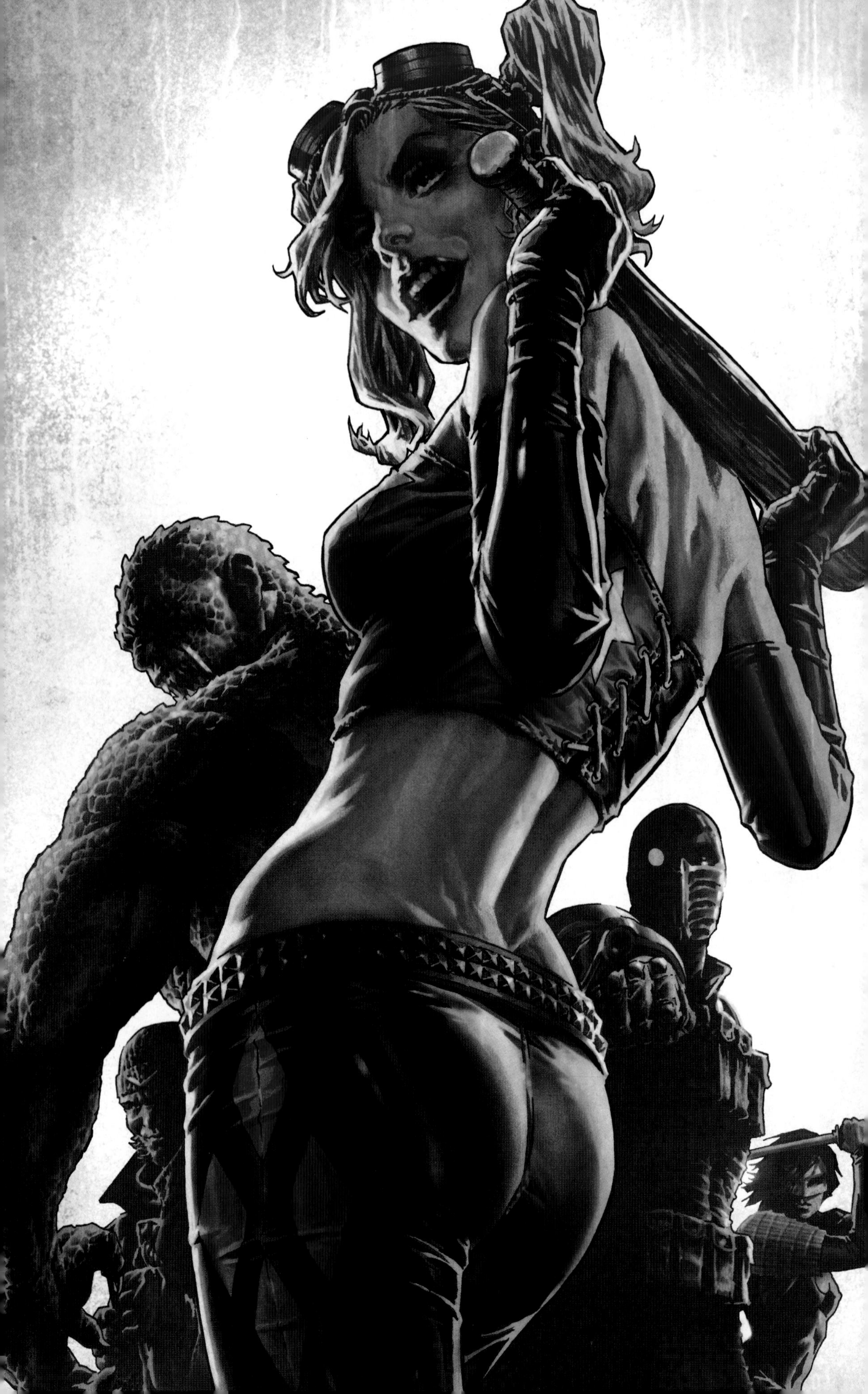

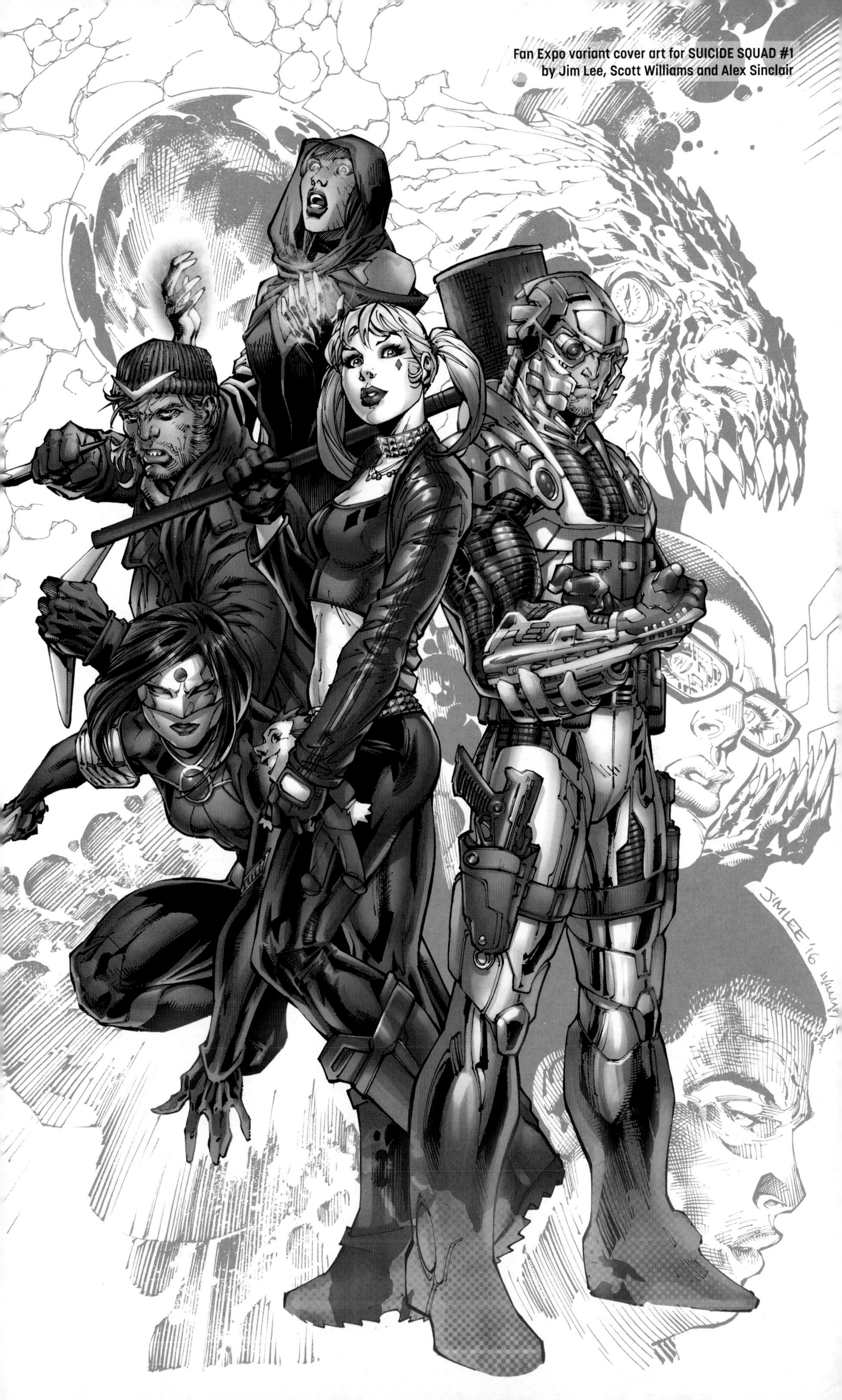

Fan Expo variant cover art for SUICIDE SQUAD #1
by Jim Lee, Scott Williams and Alex Sinclair

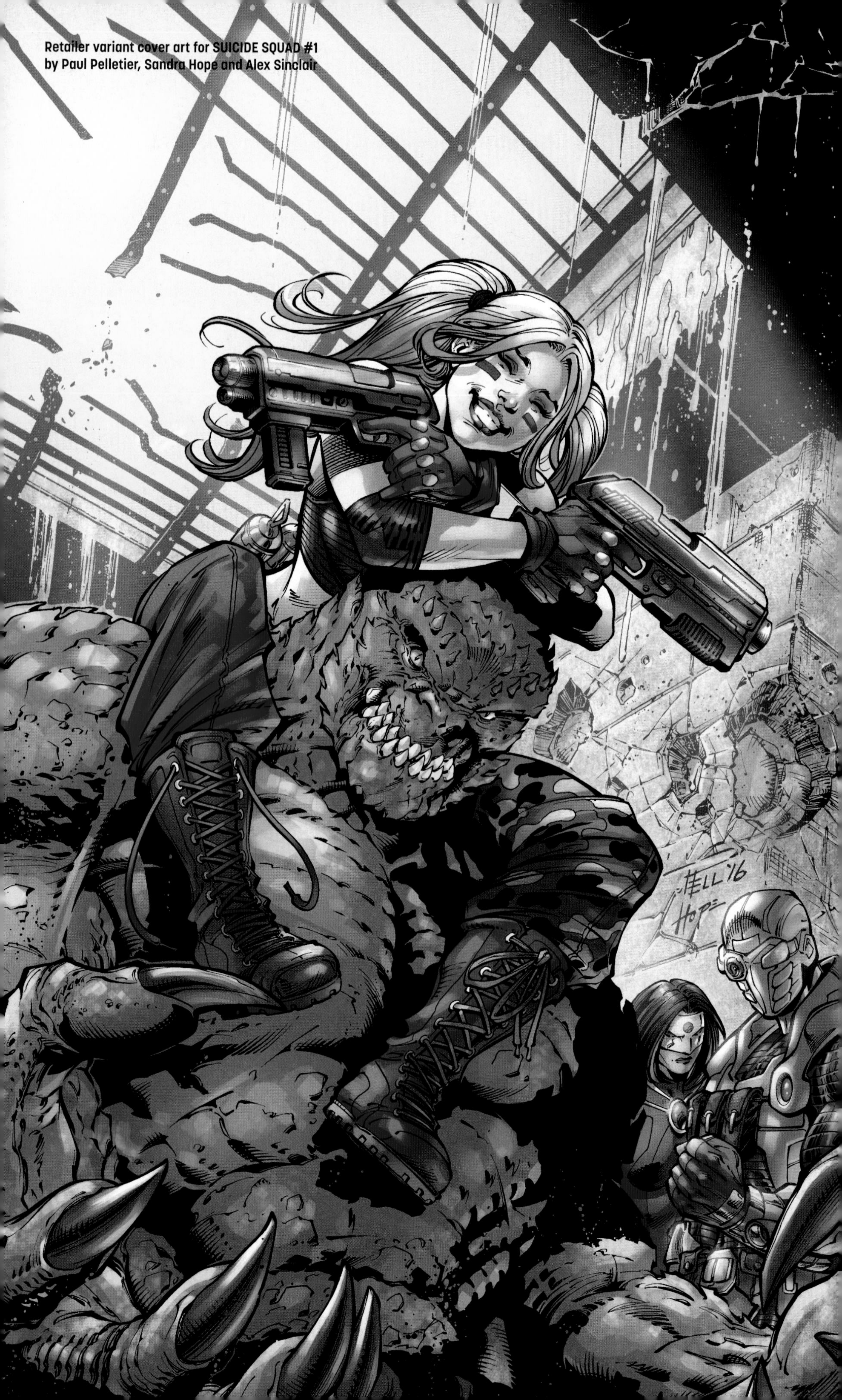

Retailer variant cover art for SUICIDE SQUAD #1
by Paul Pelletier, Sandra Hope and Alex Sinclair

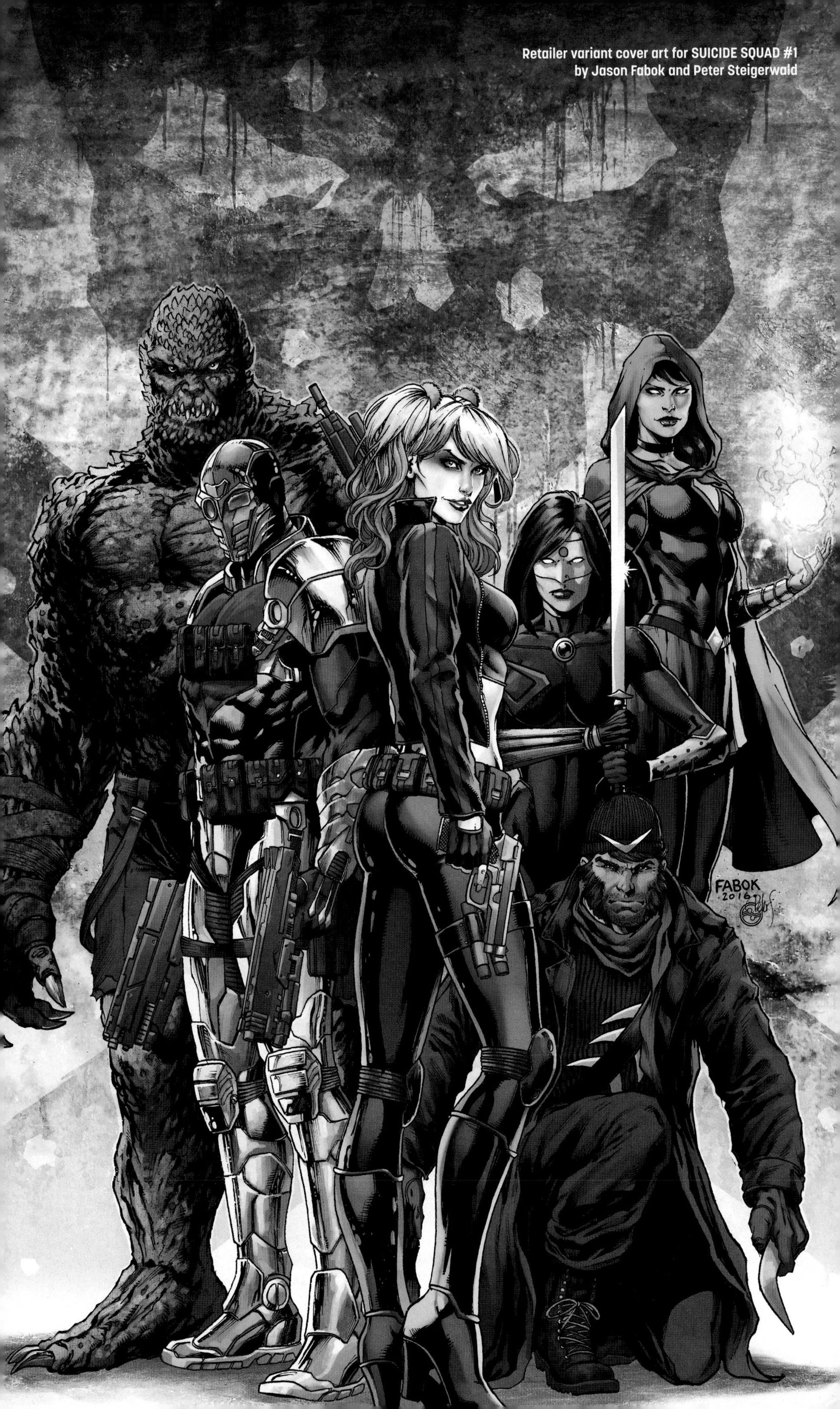
FABOK
2016

Retailer variant cover art for SUICIDE SQUAD #1
by Jason Fabok and Peter Steigerwald

Retailer variant cover art for SUICIDE SQUAD #1 by Joshua Middleton

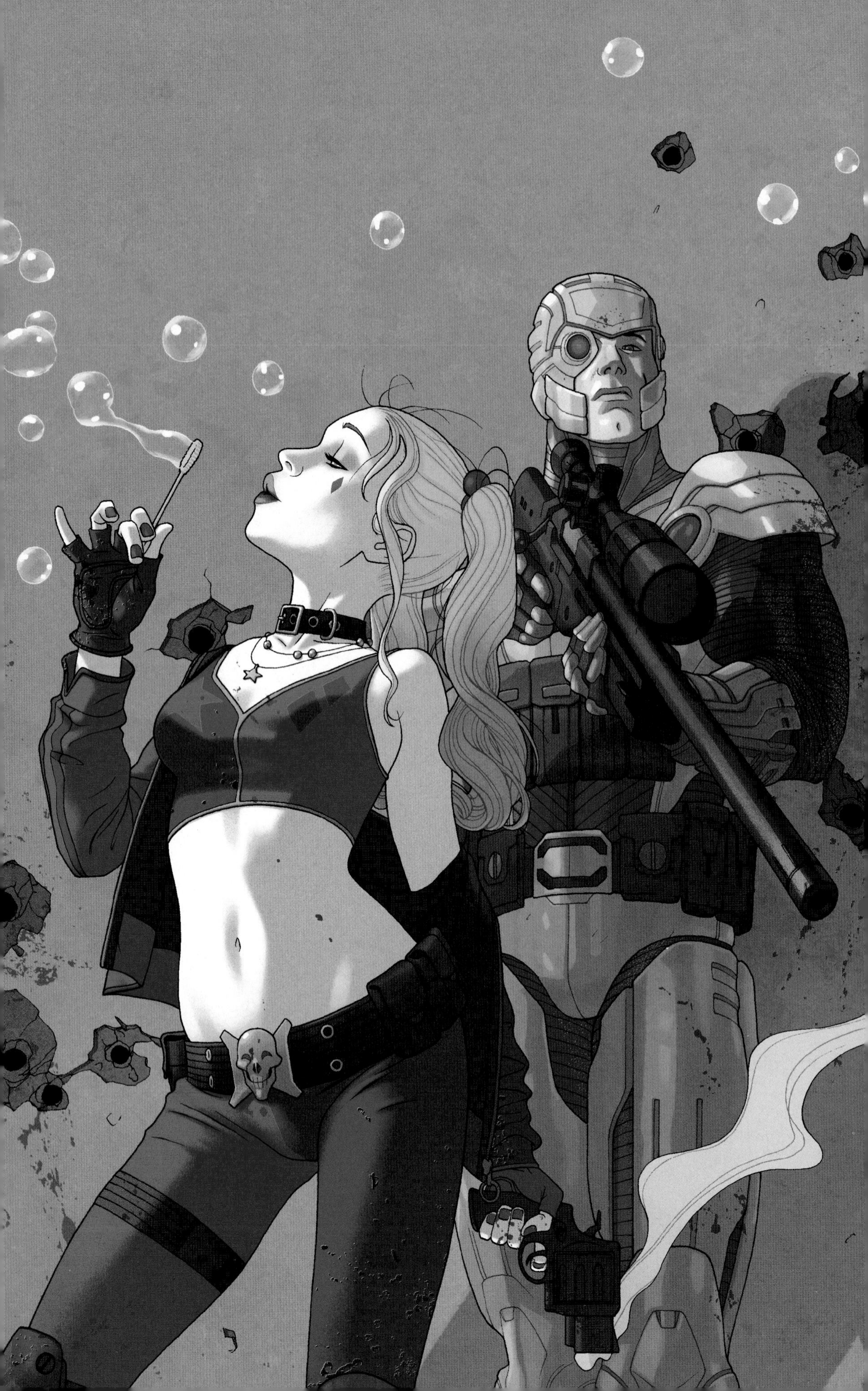

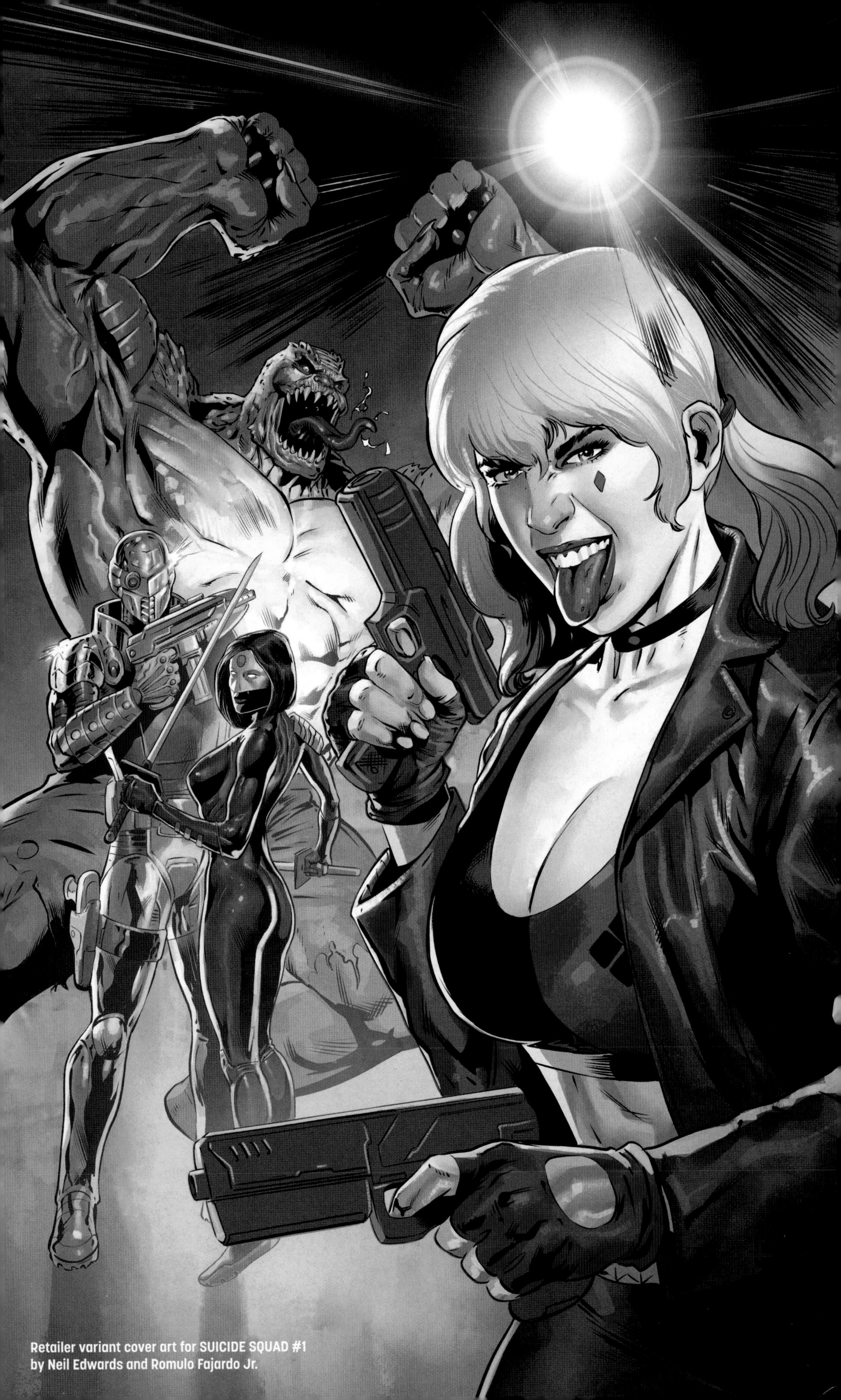

Retailer variant cover art for SUICIDE SQUAD #1
by Neil Edwards and Romulo Fajardo Jr.

Retailer variant cover art for SUICIDE SQUAD #1
by Liam Sharp and Alex Sinclair

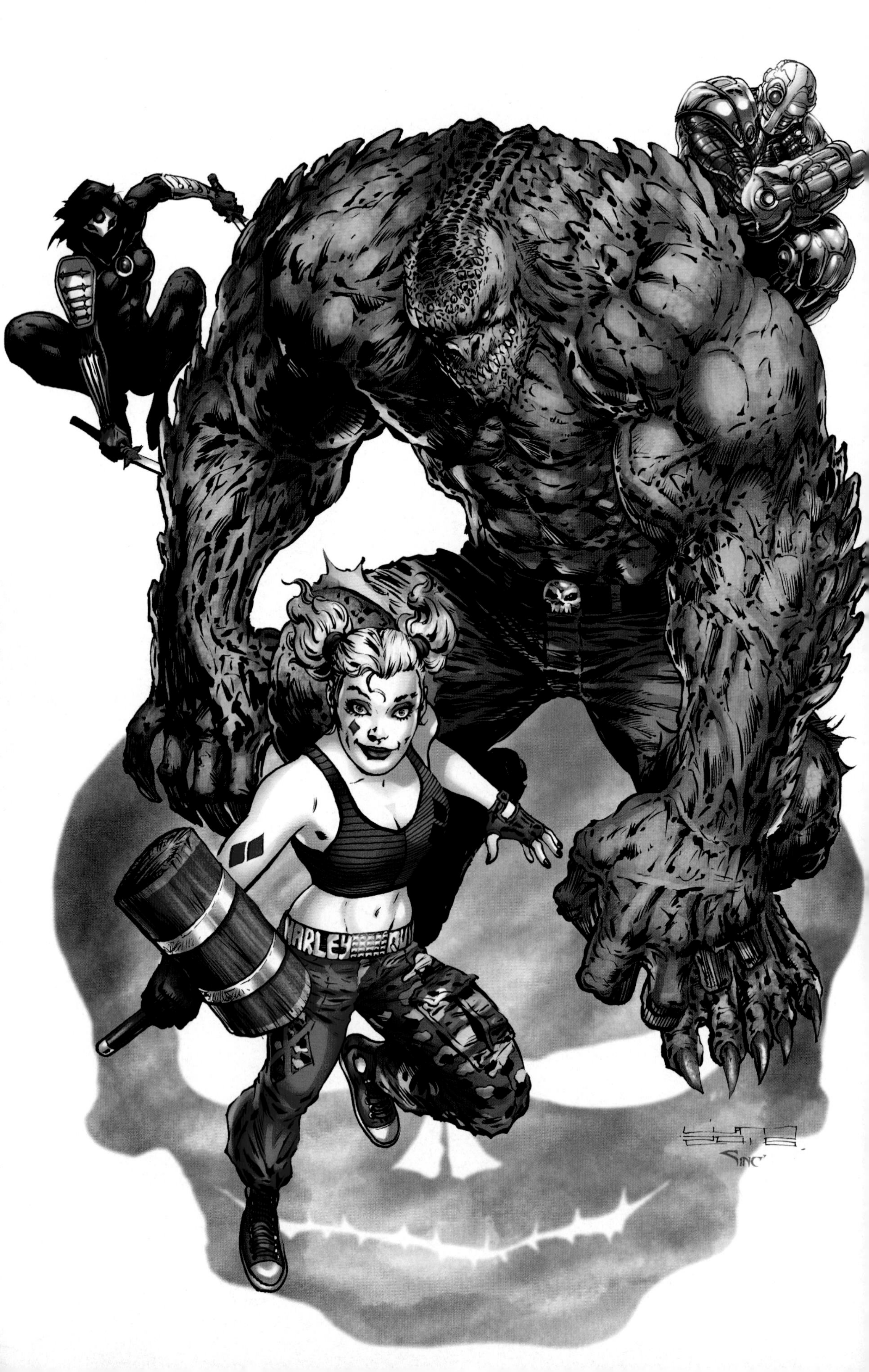
HARLEY

Retailer variant cover art for SUICIDE SQUAD #1
by Jay Anacleto and Romulo Fajardo Jr.

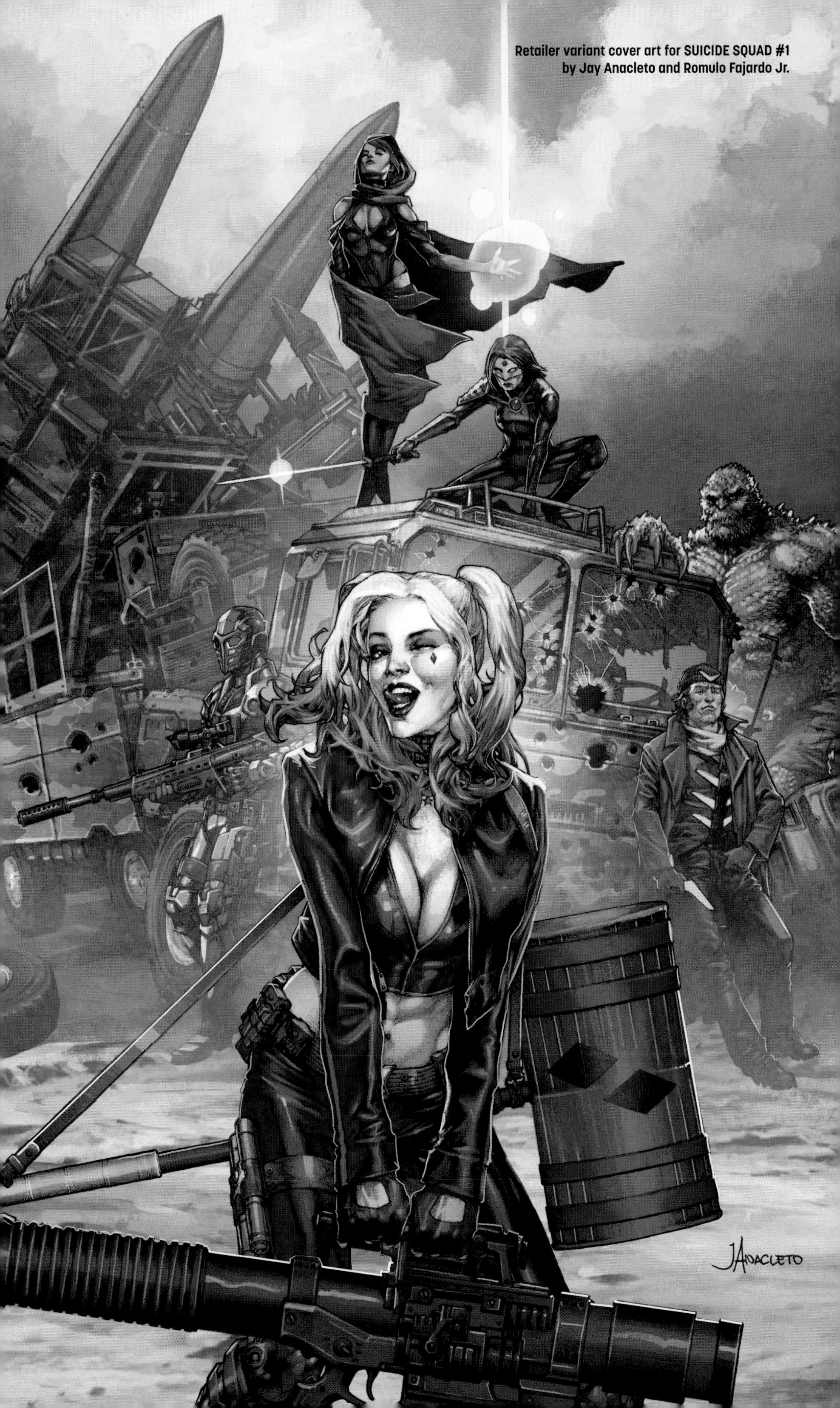

Retailer variant cover art for SUICIDE SQUAD #1
by Terry and Rachel Dodson

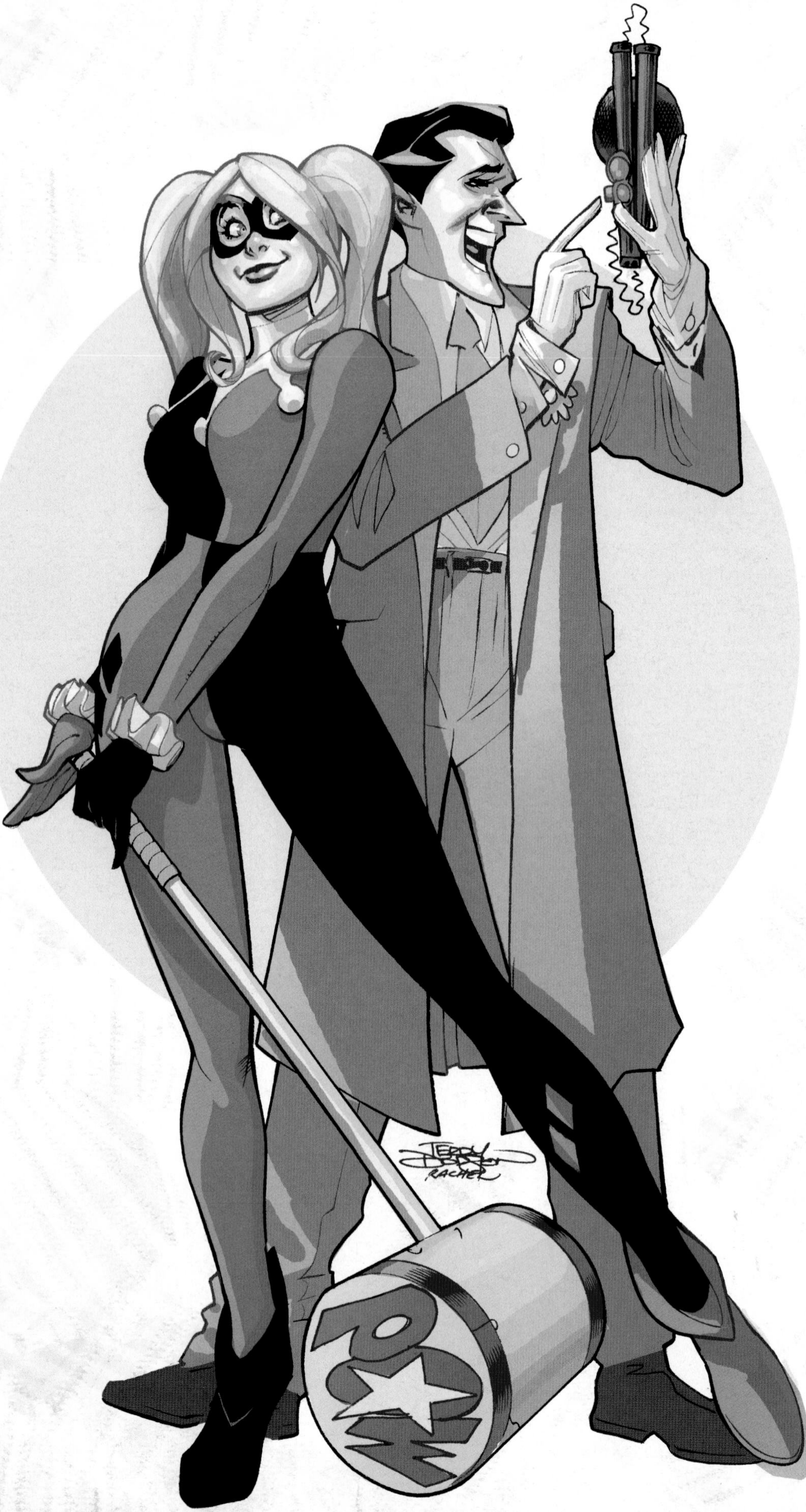
POW

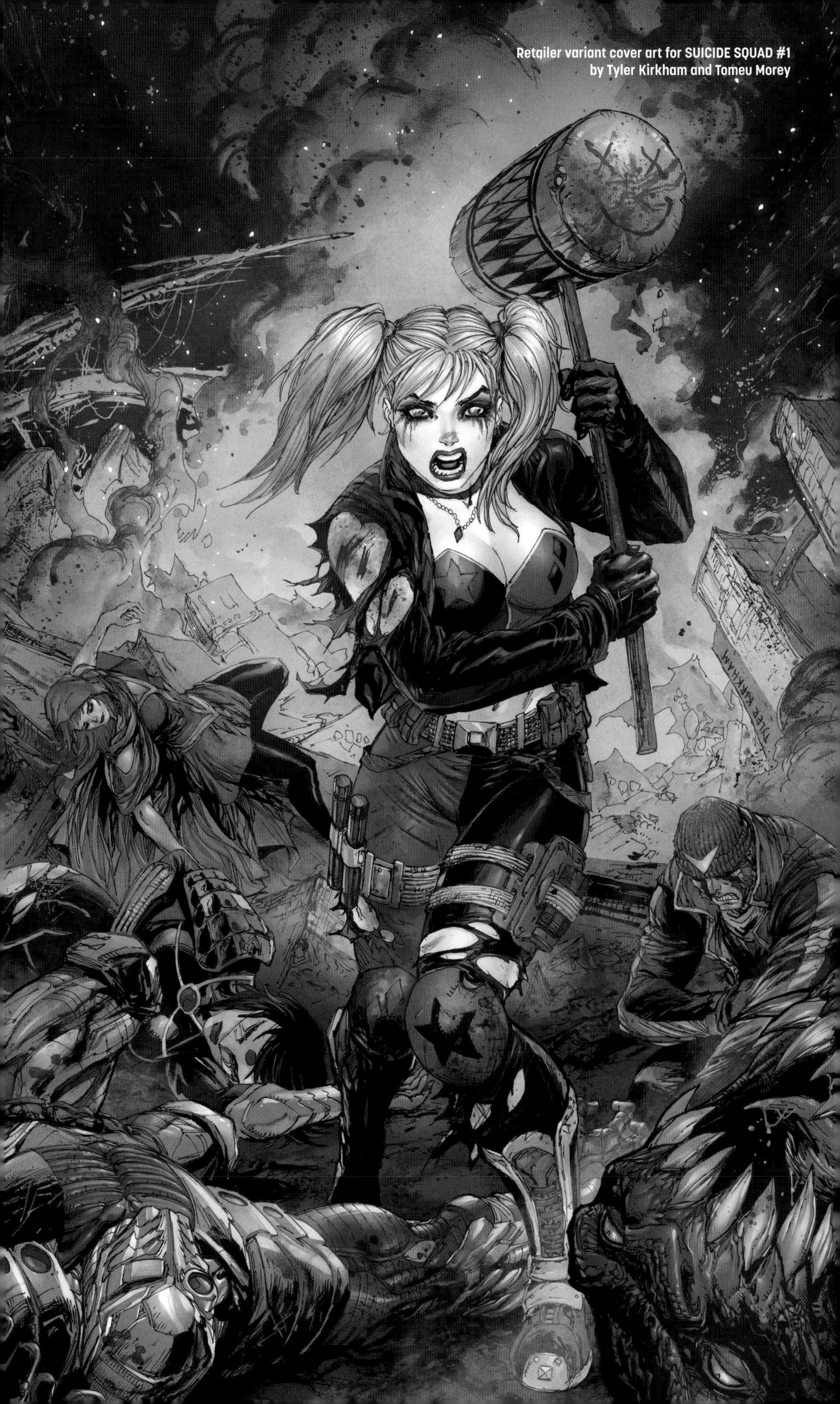

Retailer variant cover art for SUICIDE SQUAD #1
by Tyler Kirkham and Tomeu Morey

Retailer variant cover art for SUICIDE SQUAD #1 by Ben Oliver

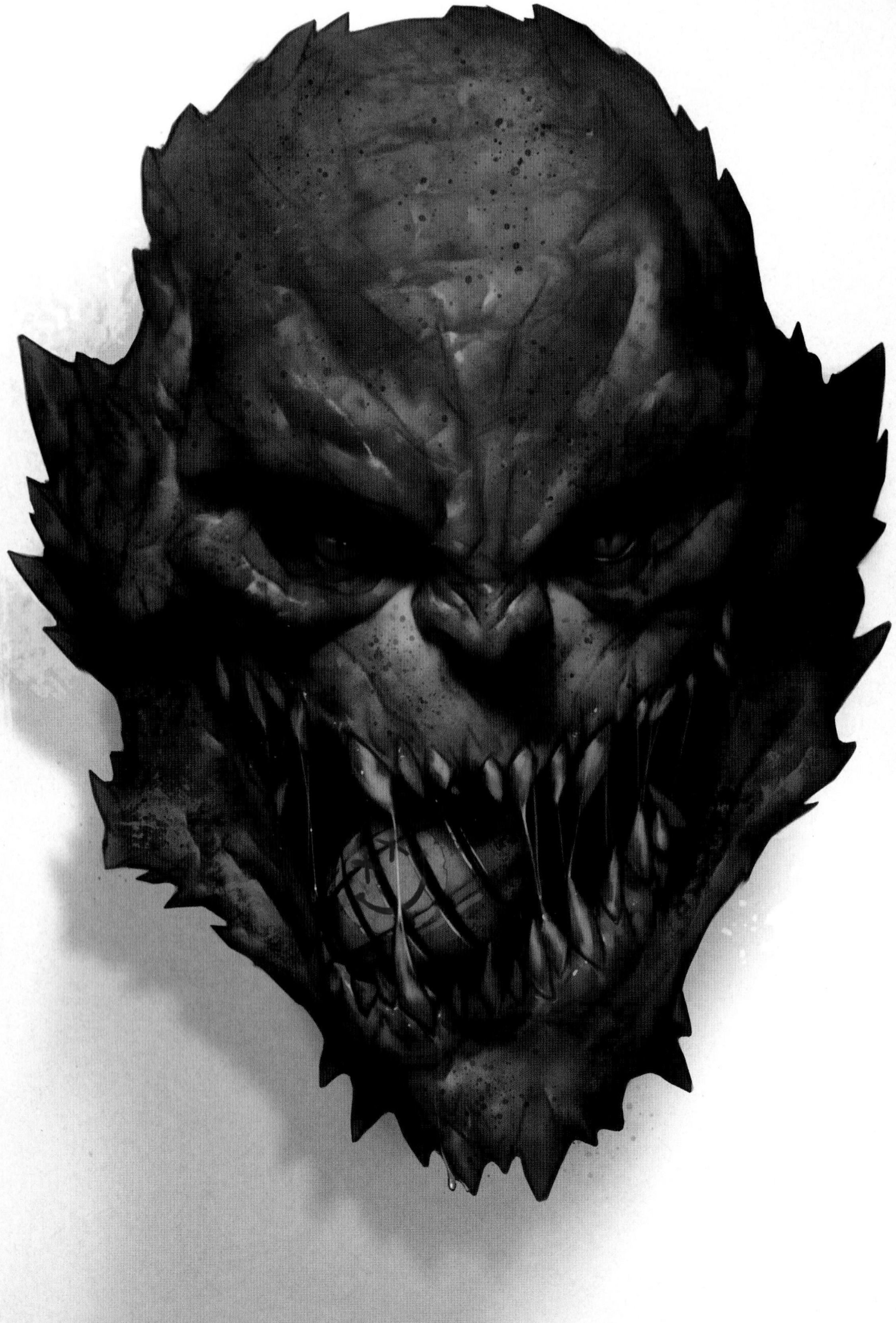

Retailer variant cover art for SUICIDE SQUAD #1 by Greg Tocchini

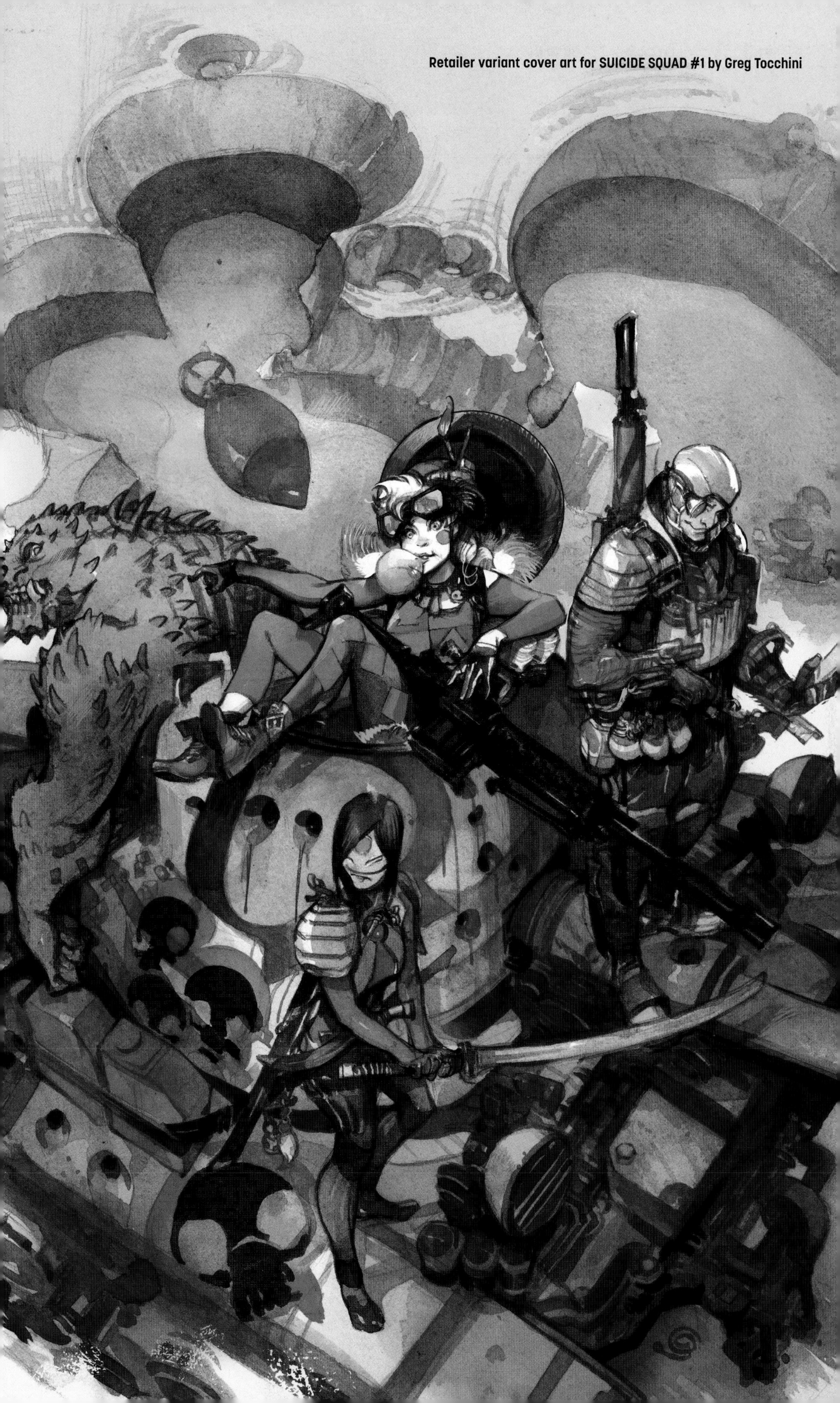

Retailer variant cover art for SUICIDE SQUAD #1
by Billy Tucci and Brian Miller

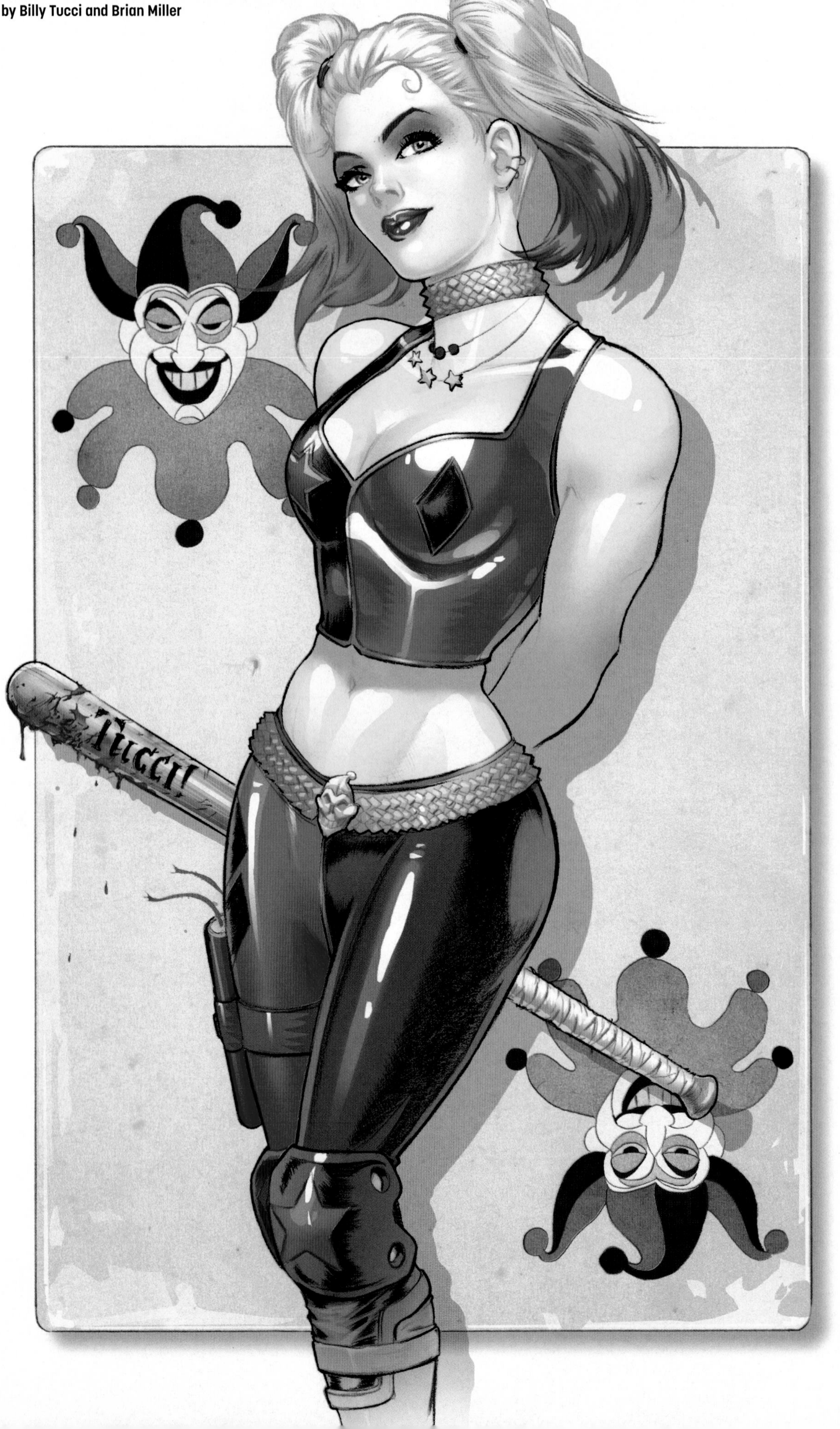
TUCCI!

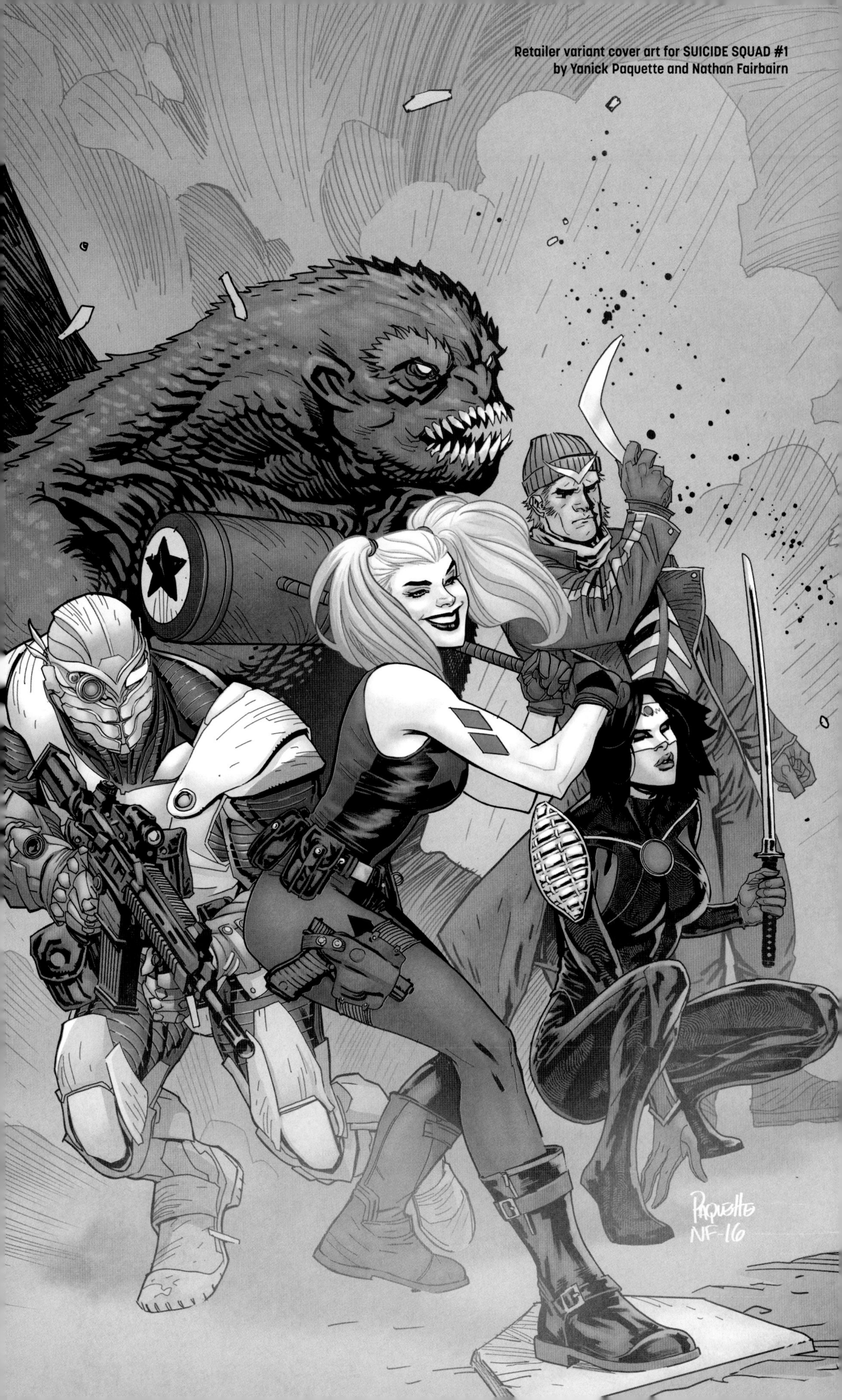

Retailer variant cover art for SUICIDE SQUAD #1
by Yanick Paquette and Nathan Fairbairn

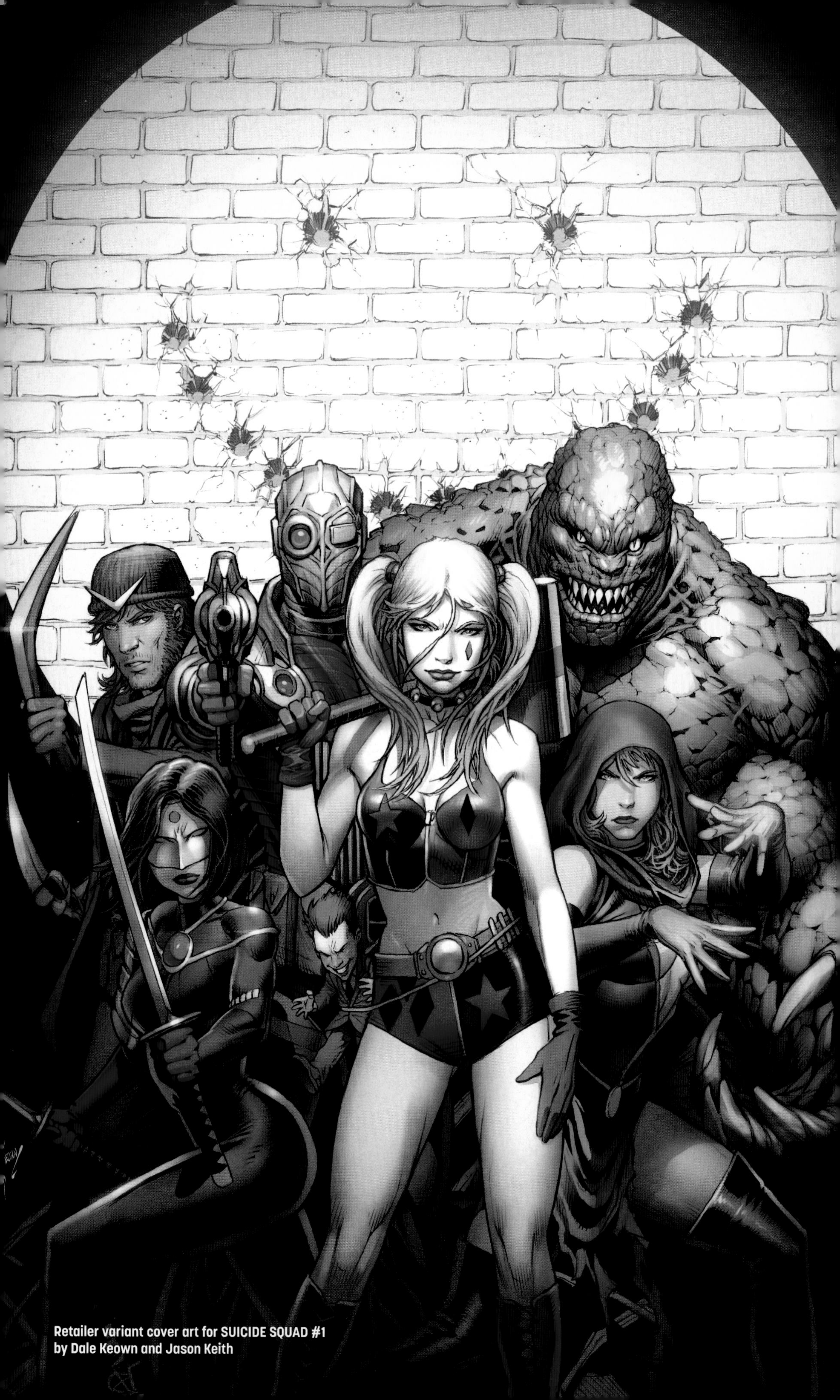

Retailer variant cover art for SUICIDE SQUAD #1
by Dale Keown and Jason Keith

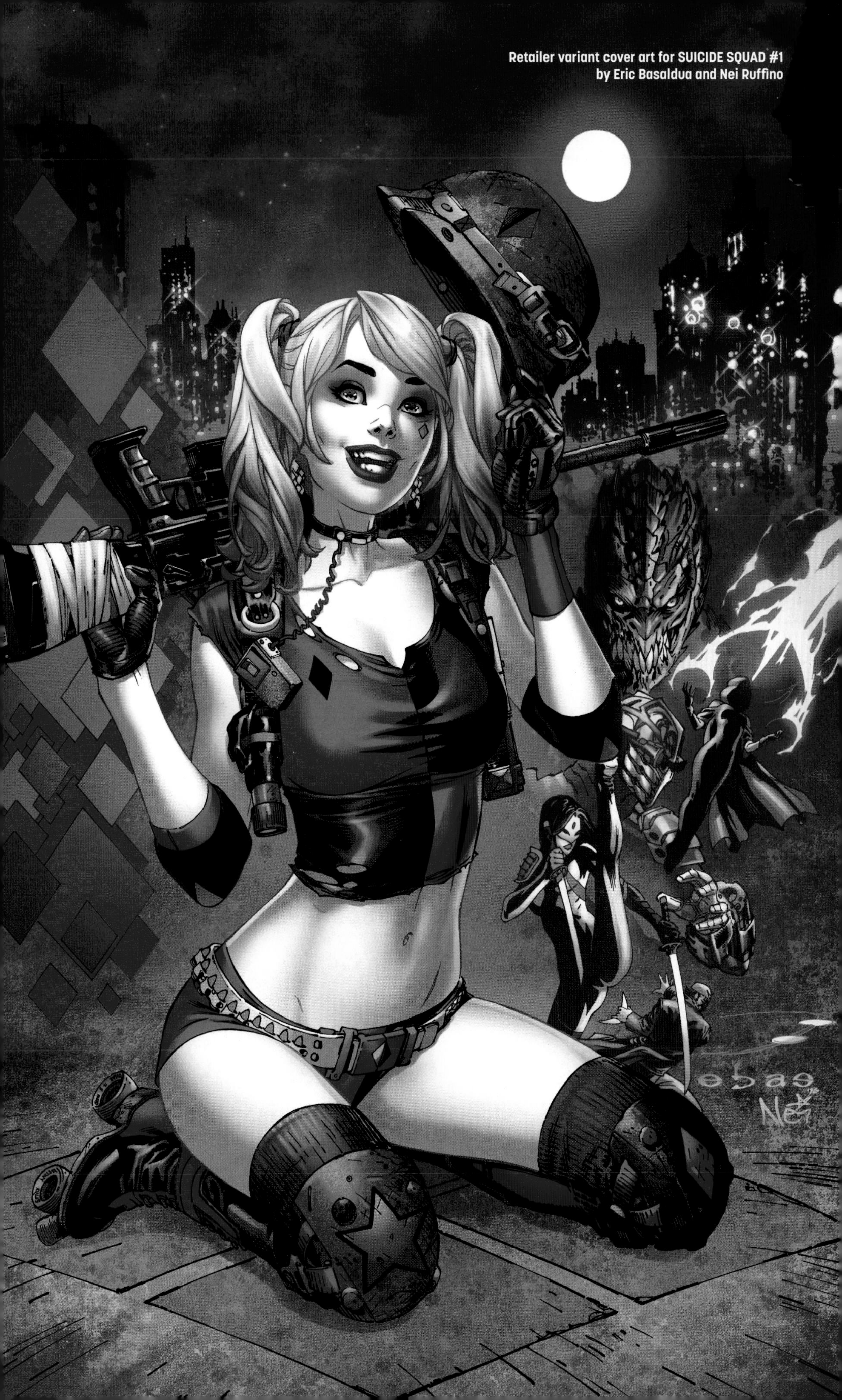

Retailer variant cover art for SUICIDE SQUAD #1
by Eric Basaldua and Nei Ruffino

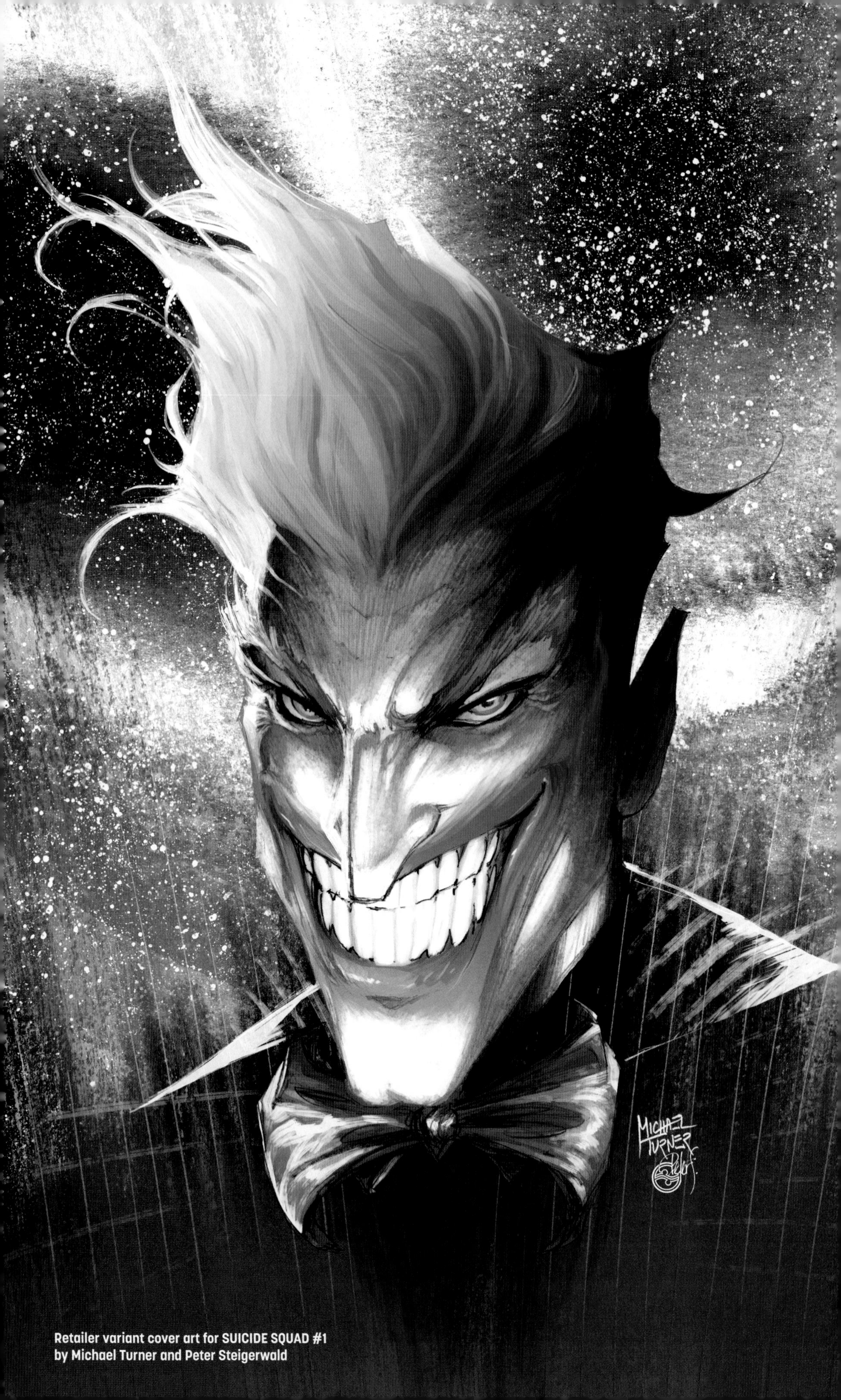
MICHAEL TURNER

Retailer variant cover art for SUICIDE SQUAD #1
by Michael Turner and Peter Steigerwald

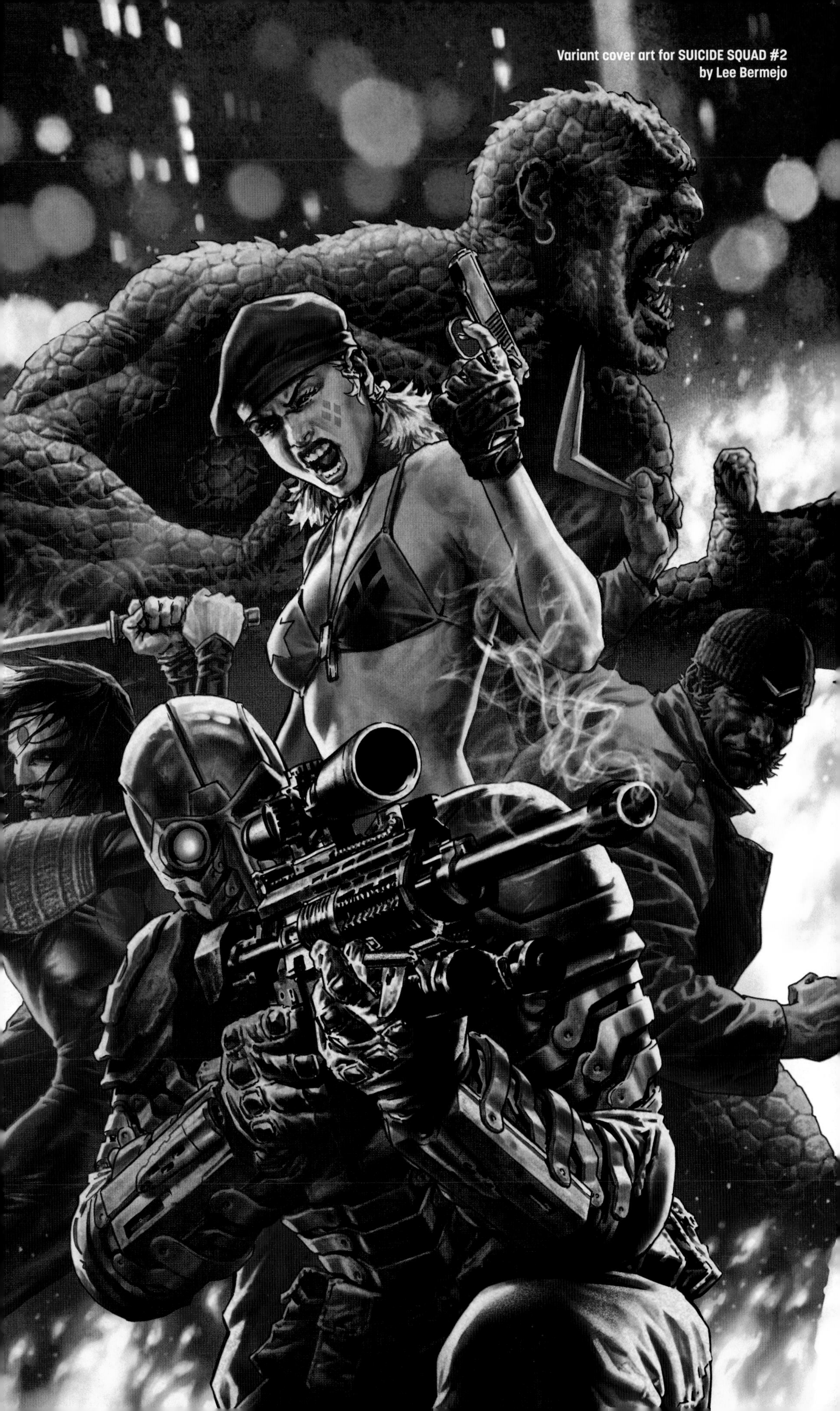

Variant cover art for SUICIDE SQUAD #2
by Lee Bermejo

Variant cover art for SUICIDE SQUAD #3
by Lee Bermejo

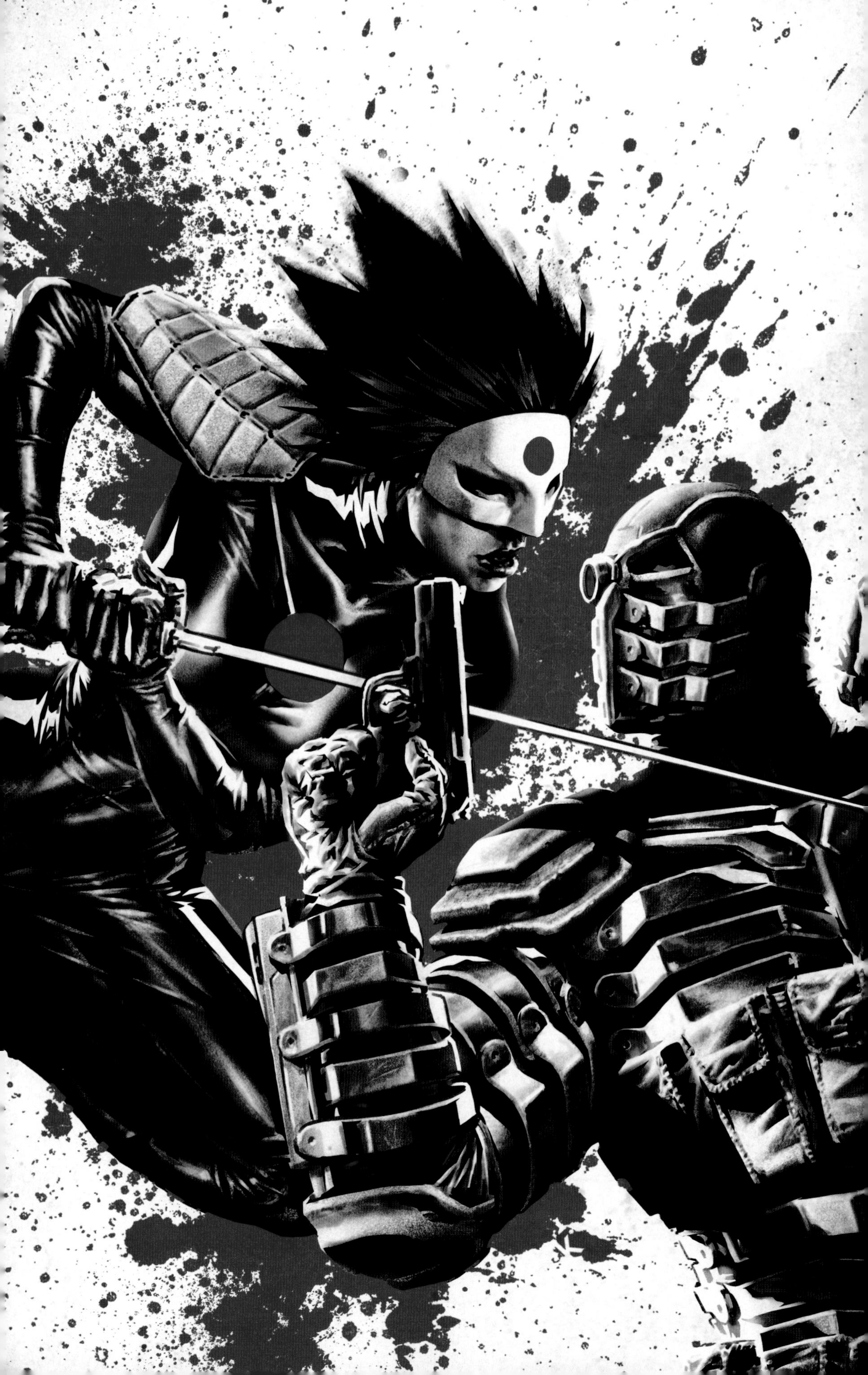

Variant cover art for SUICIDE SQUAD #4
by Lee Bermejo

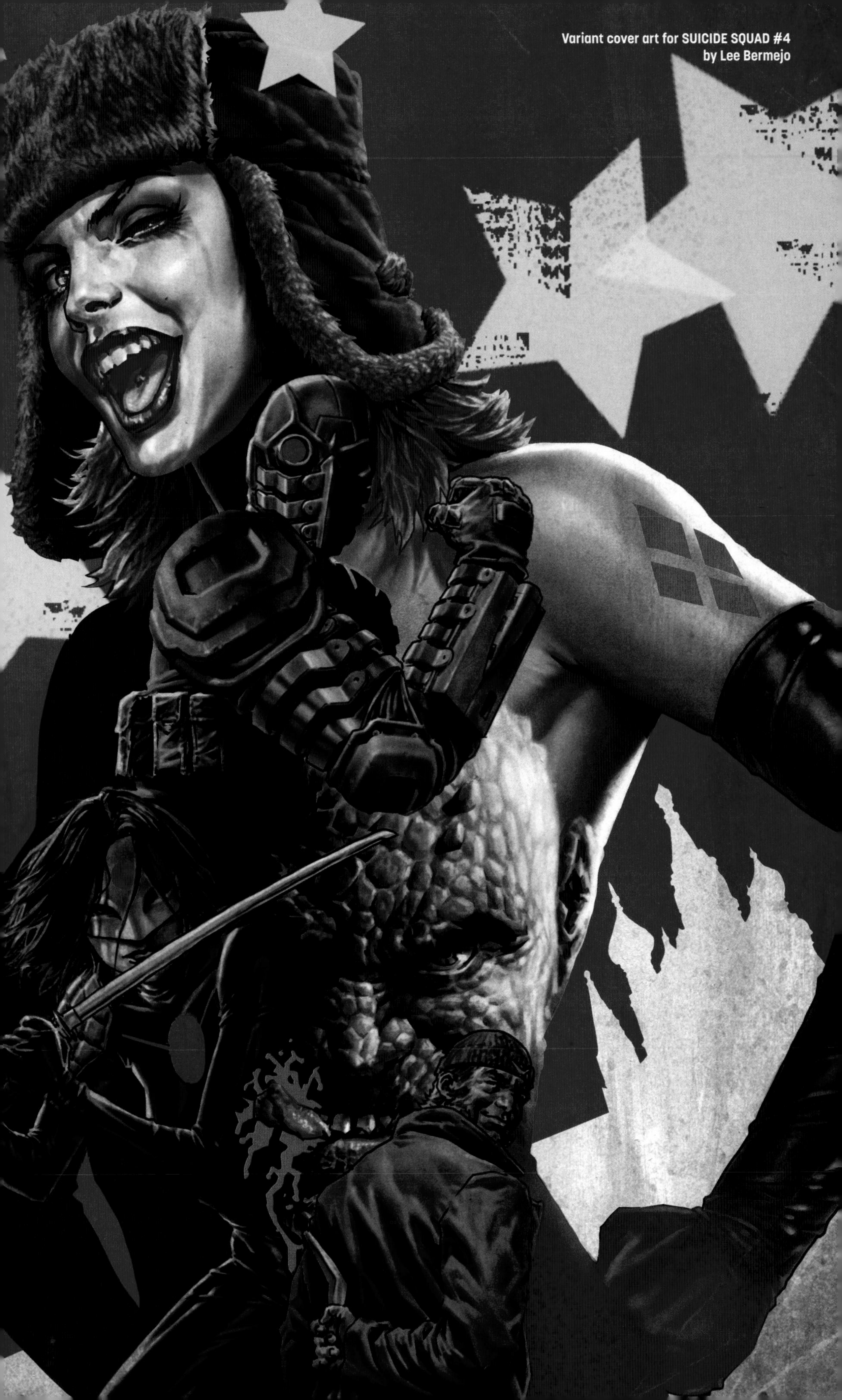

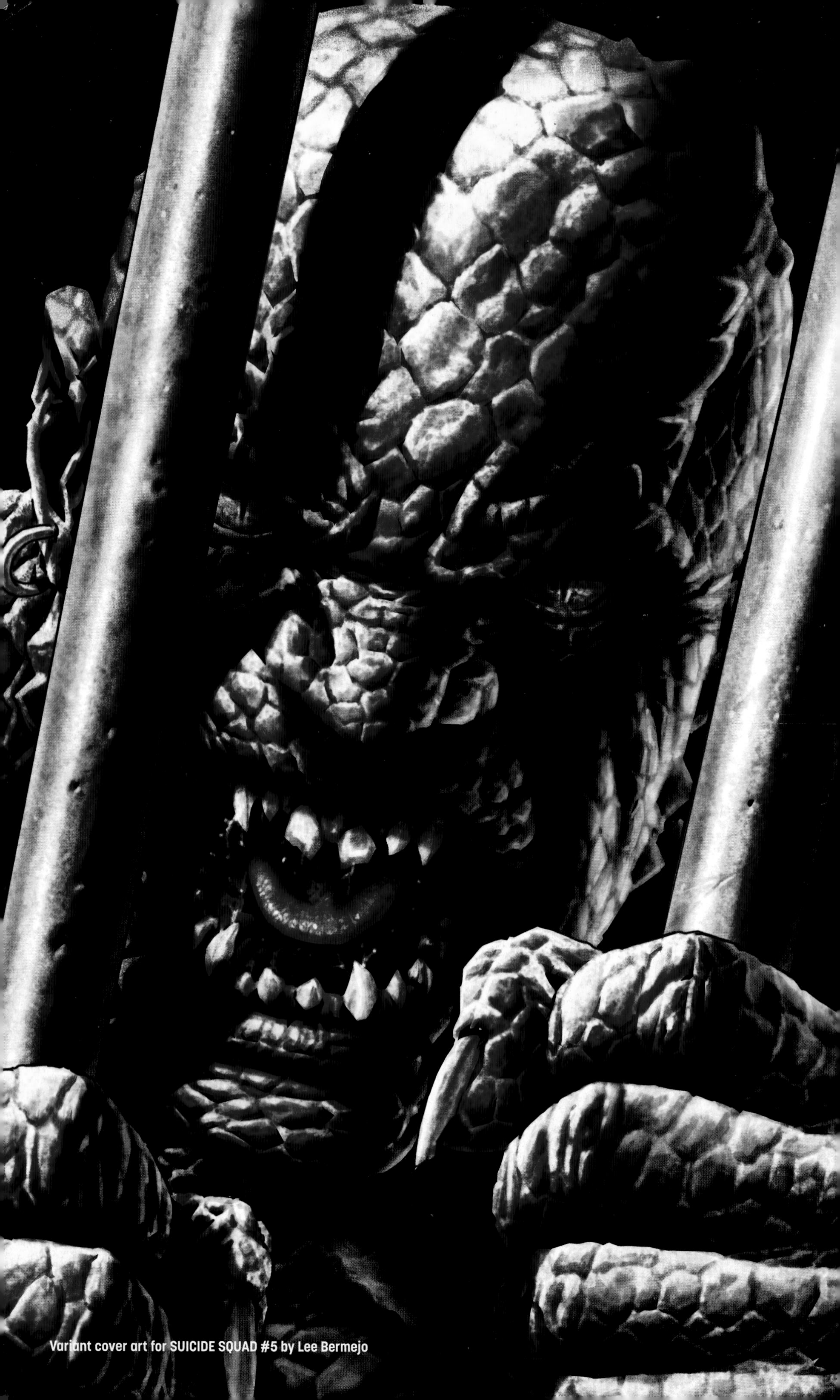

Variant cover art for SUICIDE SQUAD #5 by Lee Bermejo

Variant cover art for SUICIDE SQUAD #6 by Lee Bermejo

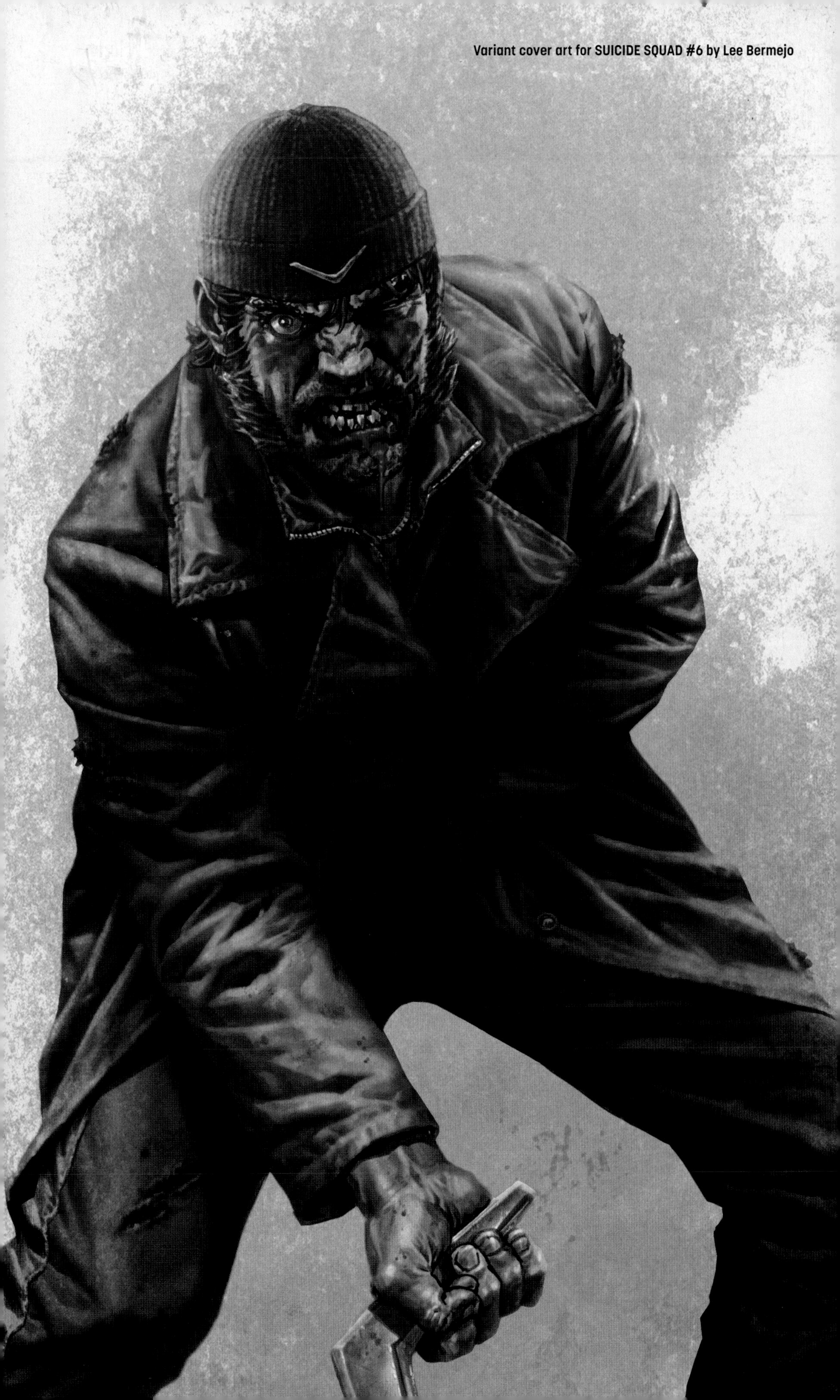

Variant cover art for SUICIDE SQUAD #7 by Lee Bermejo

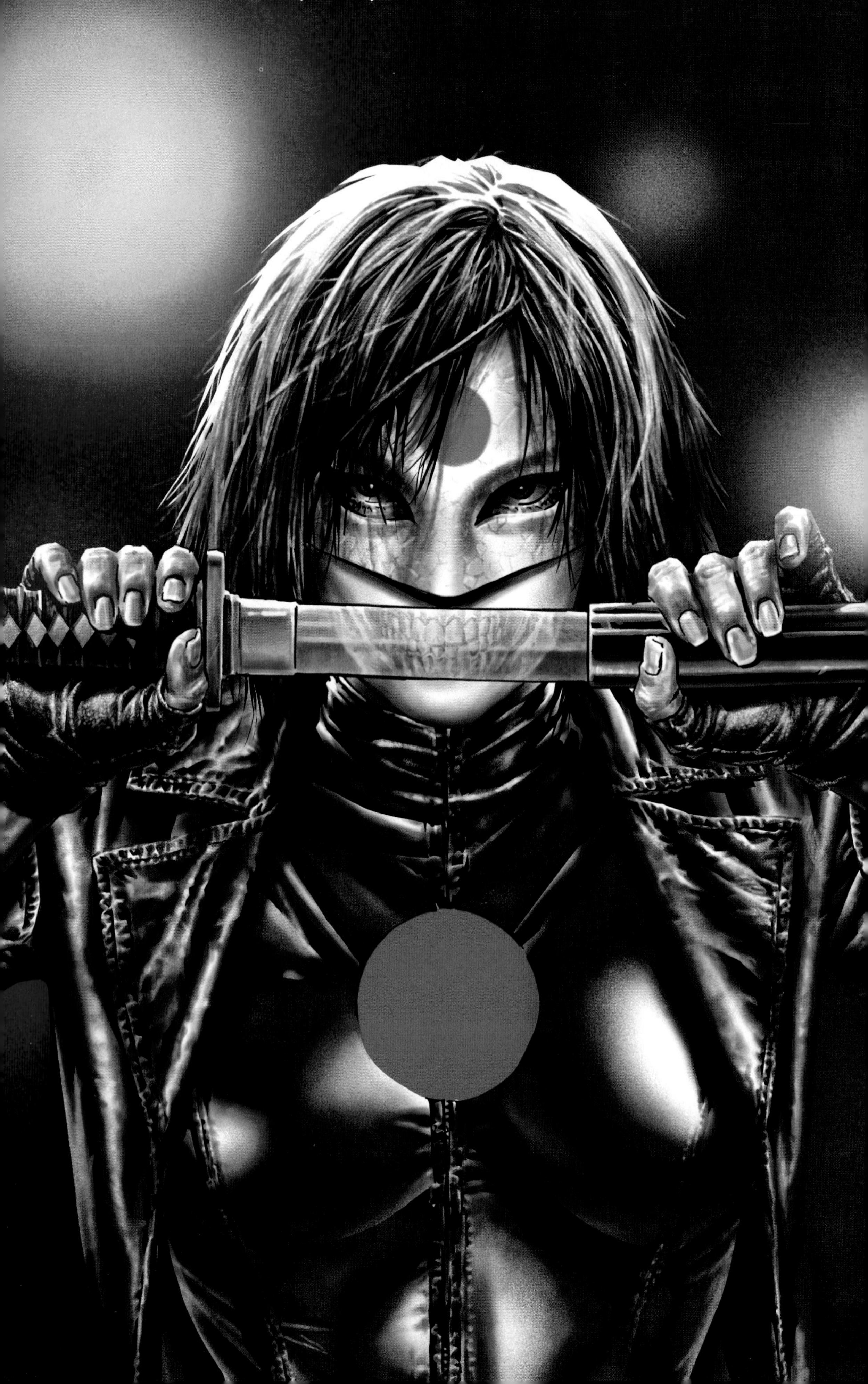

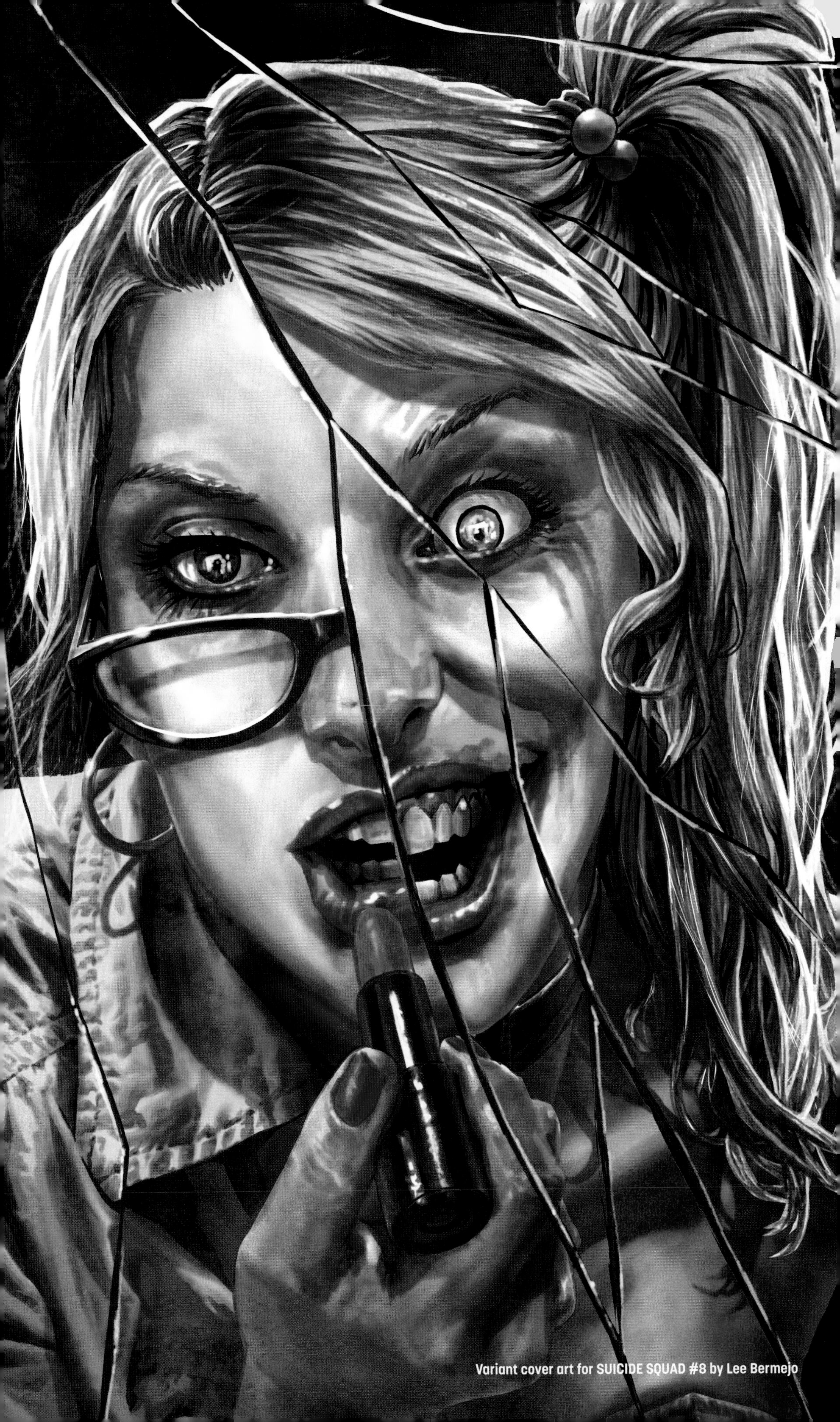

Variant cover art for SUICIDE SQUAD #8 by Lee Bermejo

SHADES OF GRAY

SUICIDE SQUAD pencil art by PHILIP TAN and JIM LEE

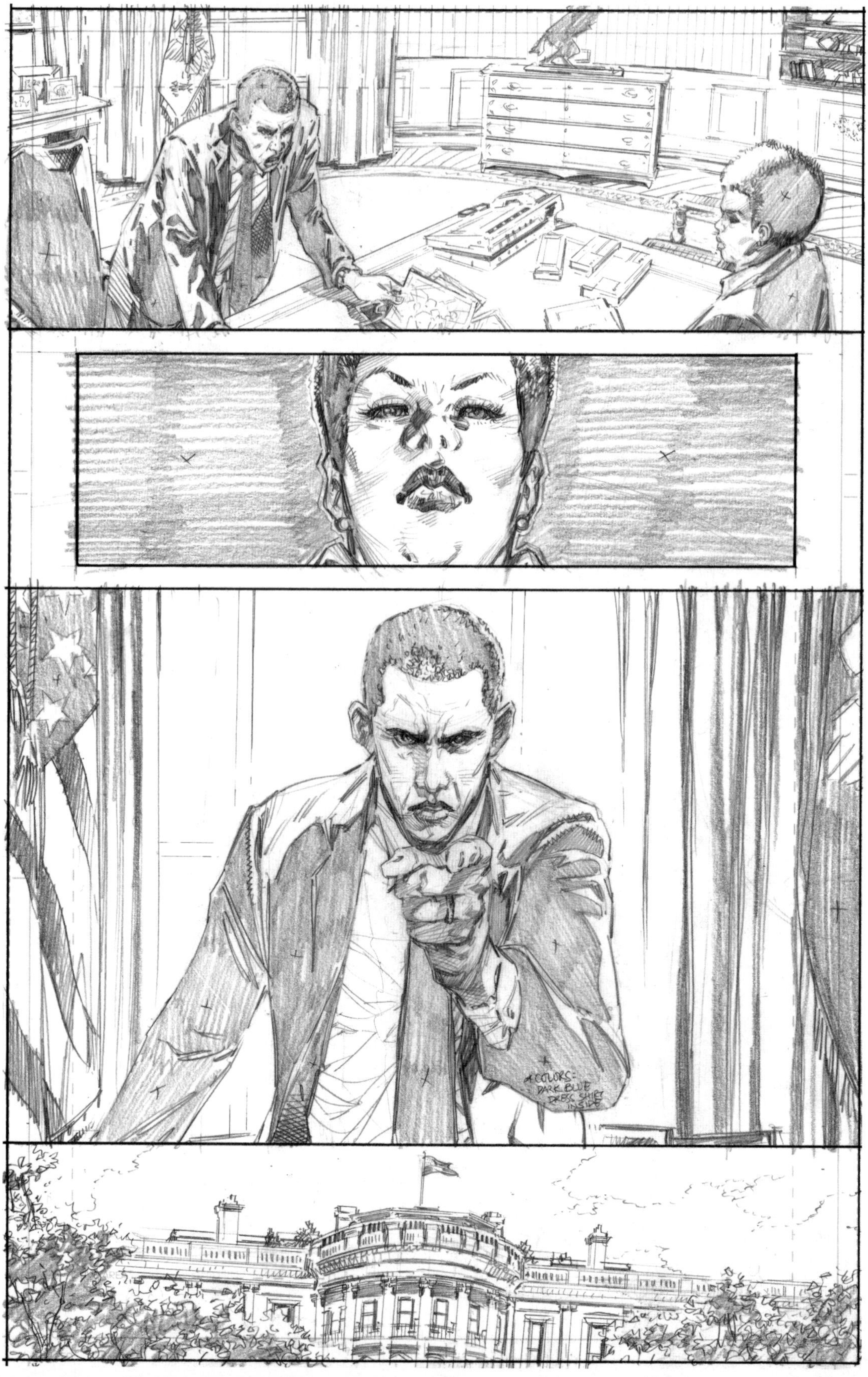
*COLORS: DARK BLUE DRESS SHIRT INSIDE

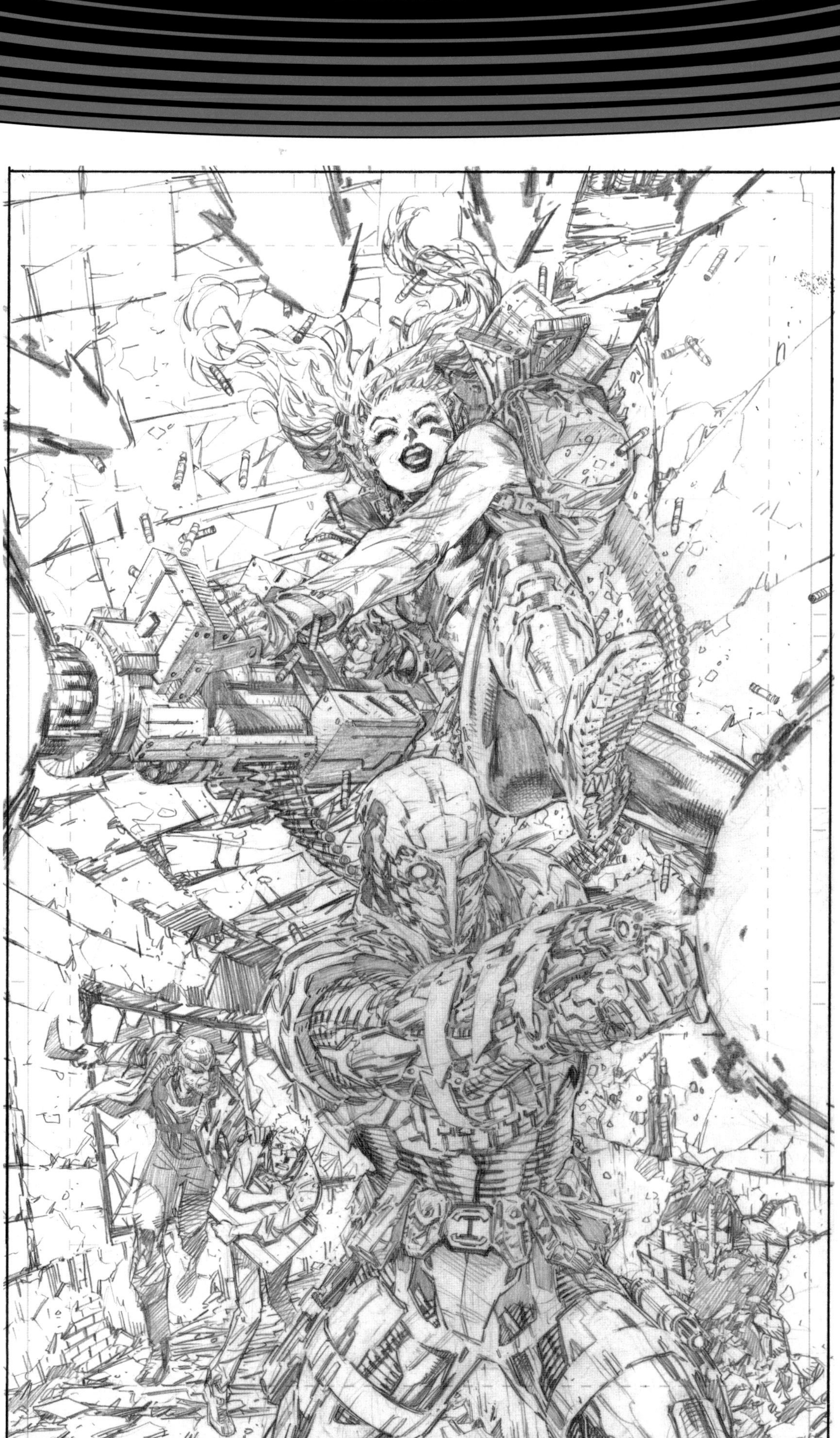

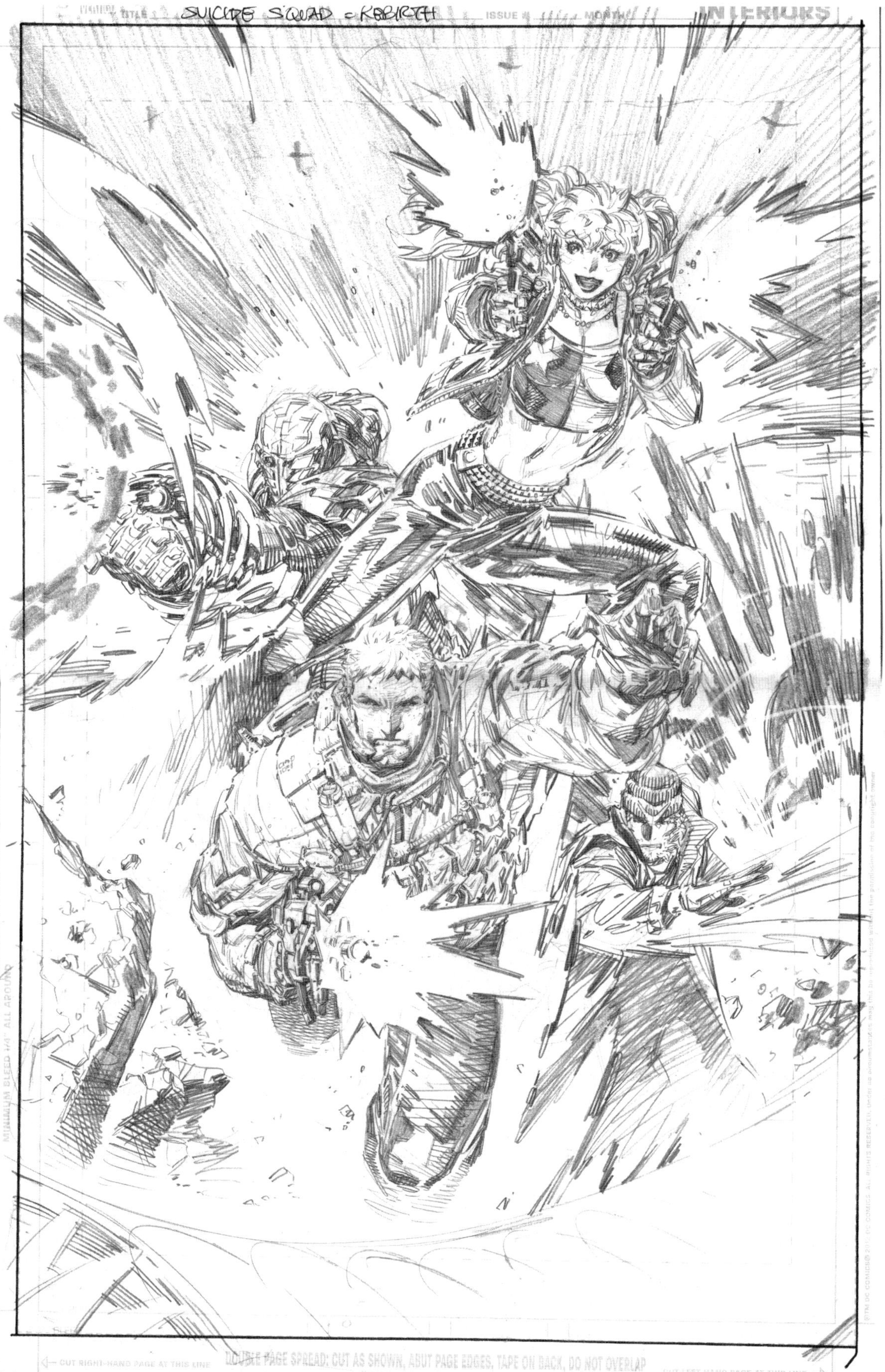
TITLE
SUICIDE SQUAD - REBIRTH
ISSUE #
MONTH
INTERIORS
MINIMUM BLEED 1/4" ALL AROUND
CUT RIGHT-HAND PAGE AT THIS LINE
DOUBLE PAGE SPREAD: CUT AS SHOWN, ABUT PAGE EDGES, TAPE ON BACK, DO NOT OVERLAP
CUT LEFT-HAND PAGE AT THIS LINE

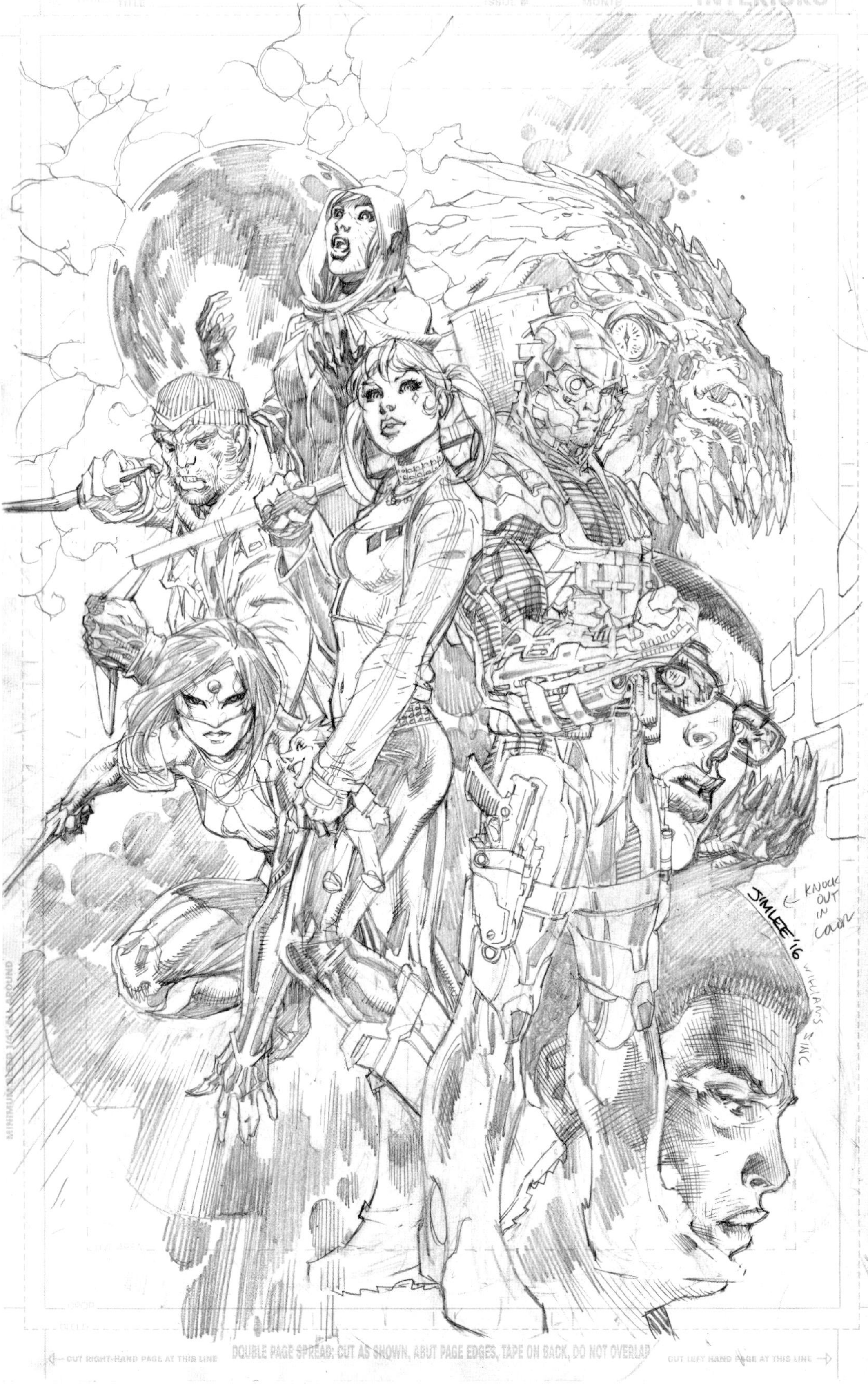

INTERIORS
JIM LEE '16
← KNOCK OUT IN COLOR
DOUBLE PAGE SPREAD: CUT AS SHOWN, ABUT PAGE EDGES, TAPE ON BACK, DO NOT OVERLAP
CUT RIGHT-HAND PAGE AT THIS LINE
CUT LEFT HAND PAGE AT THIS LINE

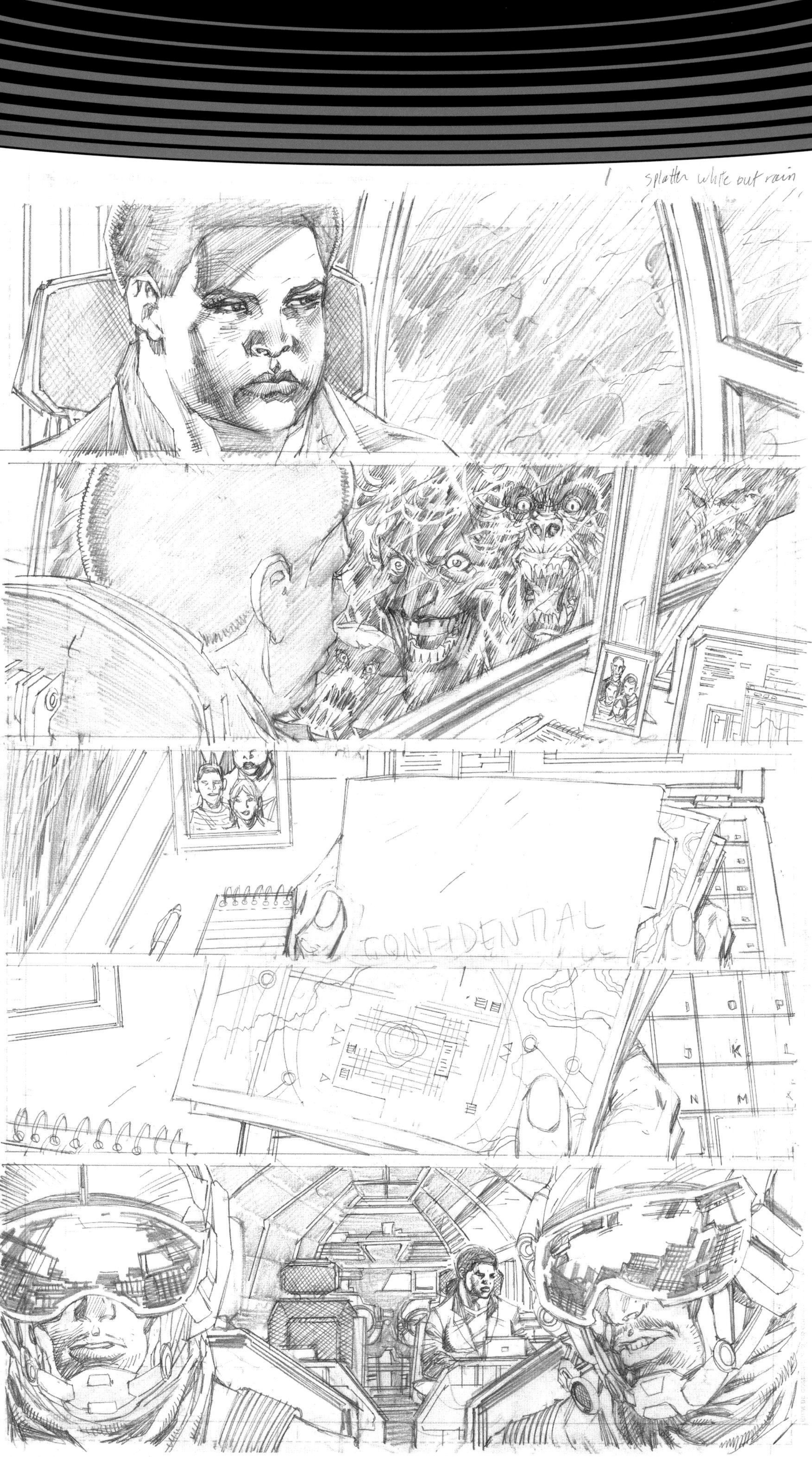
1 splatter white out rain
CONFIDENTIAL
O P
J K L
N M

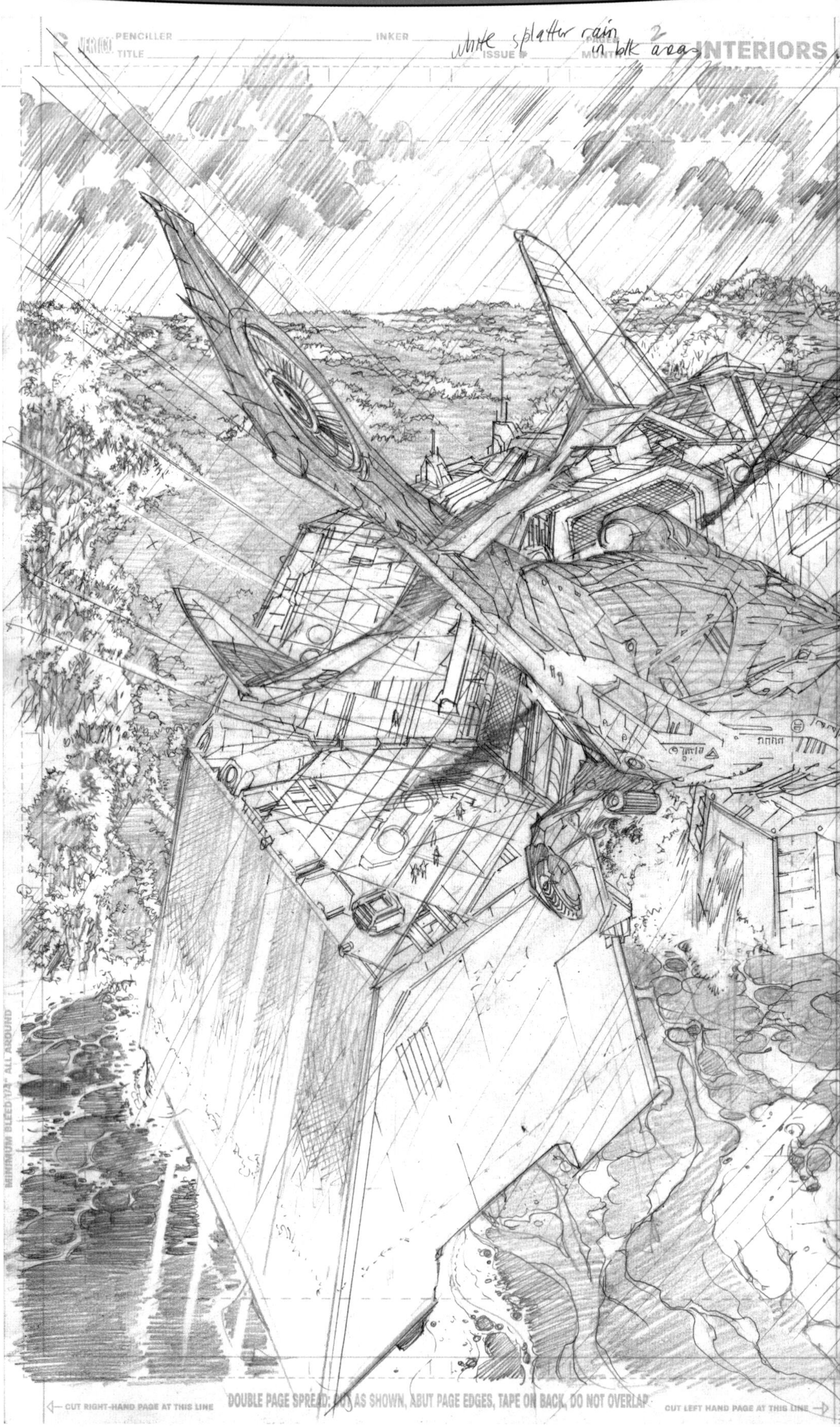
PENCILLER
INKER
TITLE
ISSUE #
MONTH
white splatter rain in blk areas
2
INTERIORS
MINIMUM BLEED 1/4" ALL AROUND
CUT RIGHT-HAND PAGE AT THIS LINE
DOUBLE PAGE SPREAD: CUT AS SHOWN, ABUT PAGE EDGES, TAPE ON BACK, DO NOT OVERLAP
CUT LEFT HAND PAGE AT THIS LINE

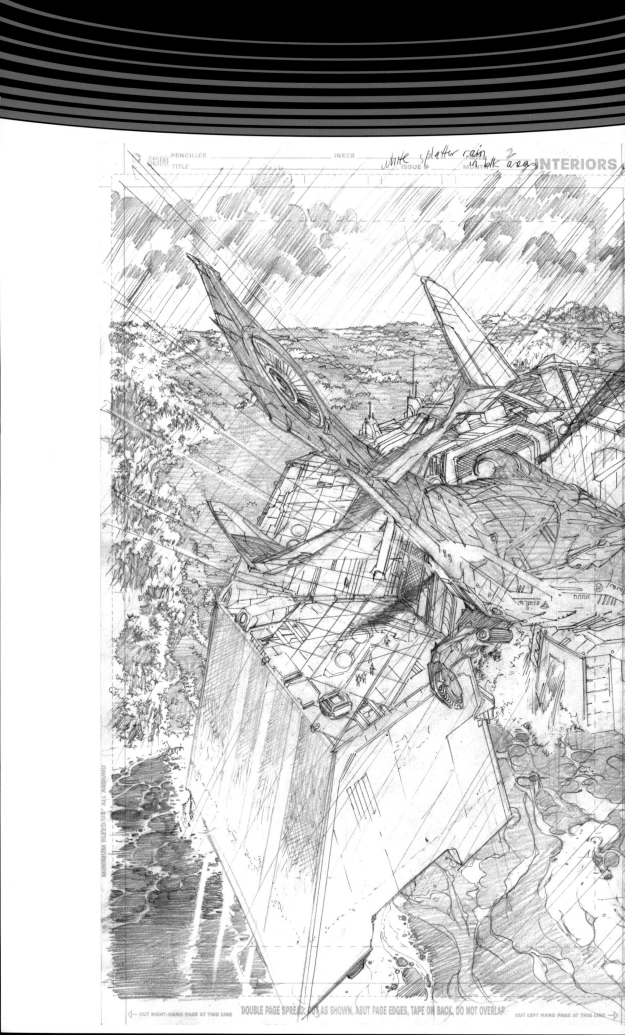

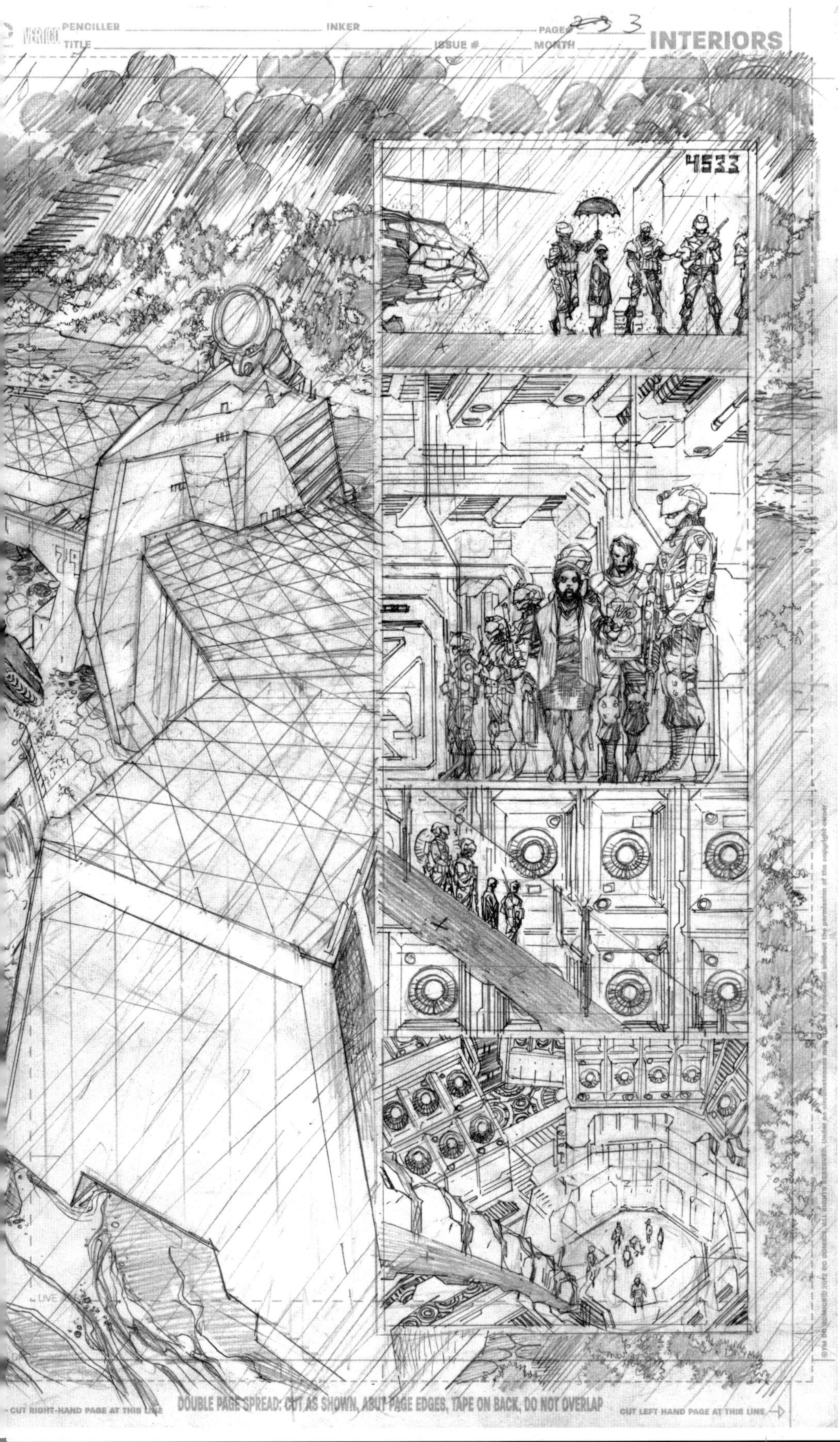
VERTIGO
PENCILLER
INKER
PAGE 3
TITLE
ISSUE #
MONTH
INTERIORS
4533
CUT RIGHT-HAND PAGE AT THIS LINE
DOUBLE PAGE SPREAD: CUT AS SHOWN, ABUT PAGE EDGES, TAPE ON BACK, DO NOT OVERLAP
CUT LEFT HAND PAGE AT THIS LINE

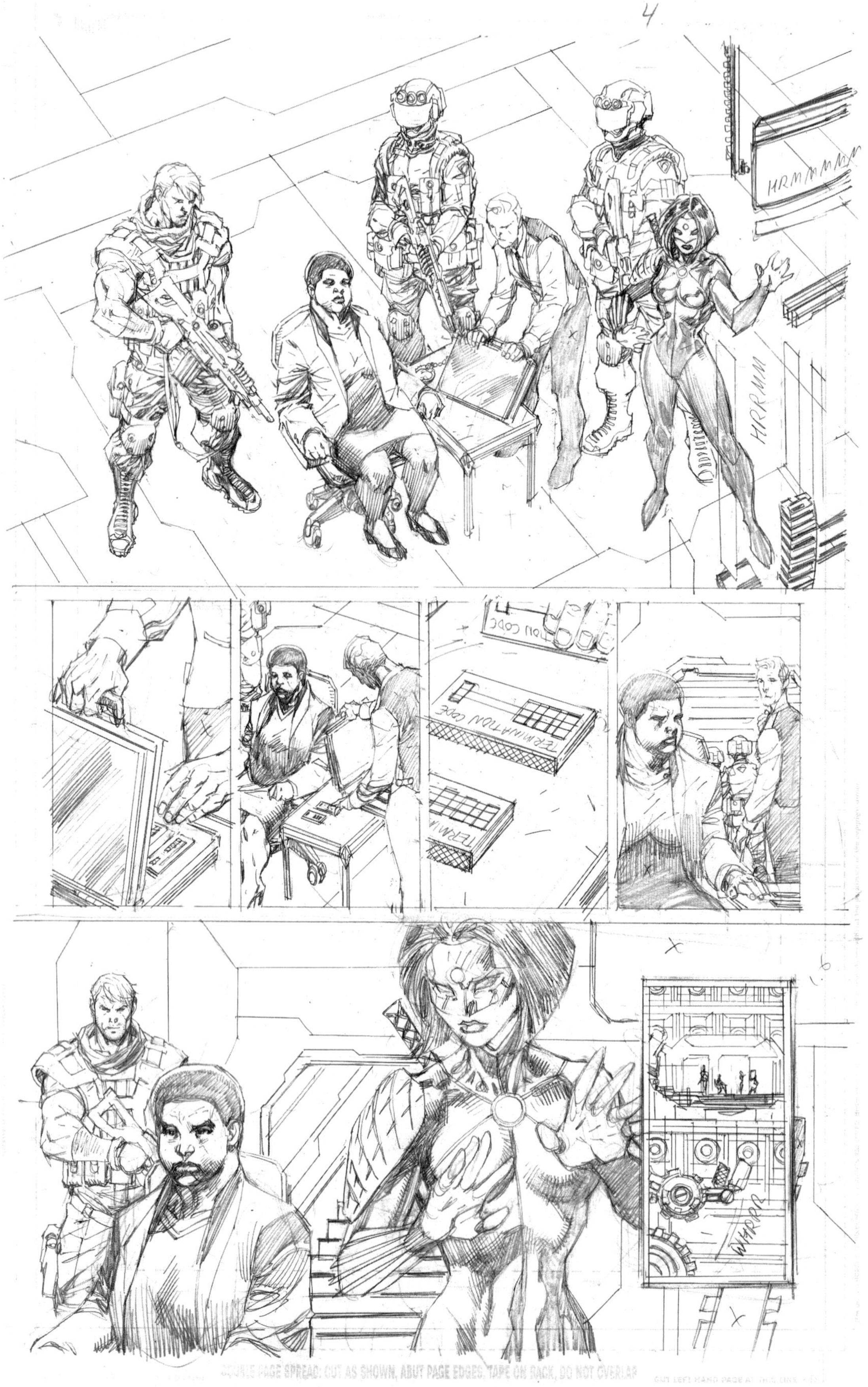
4
HRMMMMM
HRRMM
TERMINATION CODE
WHRRR
DOUBLE PAGE SPREAD: CUT AS SHOWN, ABUT PAGE EDGES, TAPE ON BACK, DO NOT OVERLAP

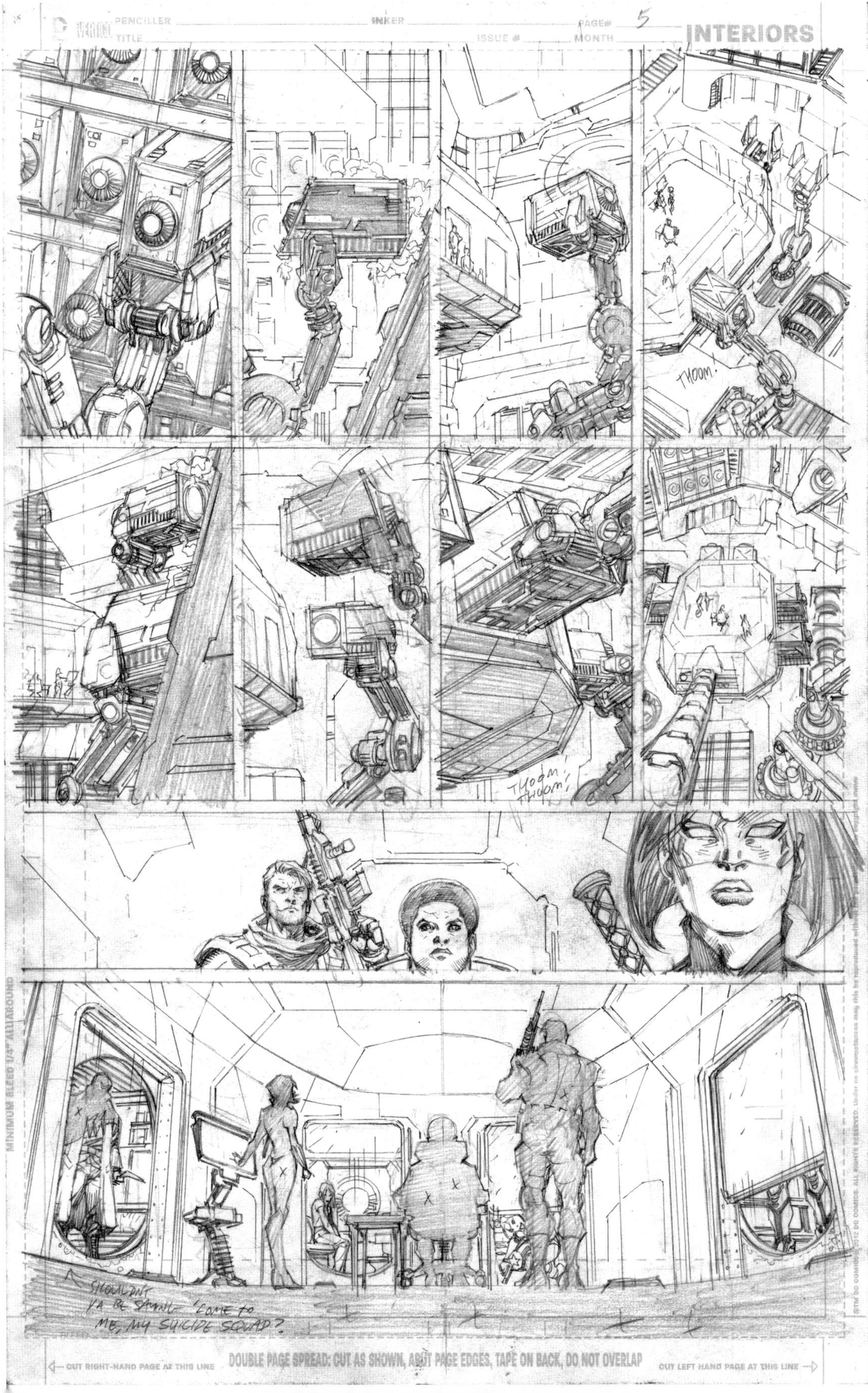
PENCILLER
INKER
PAGE# 5
INTERIORS
TITLE
ISSUE #
MONTH
THOOM!
THOOM! THOOM!
SHOULDN'T YA BE SAYING 'COME TO ME, MY SUICIDE SQUAD'?
MINIMUM BLEED 1/4" ALLAROUND
CUT RIGHT-HAND PAGE AT THIS LINE
DOUBLE PAGE SPREAD: CUT AS SHOWN, ABUT PAGE EDGES, TAPE ON BACK, DO NOT OVERLAP
CUT LEFT HAND PAGE AT THIS LINE

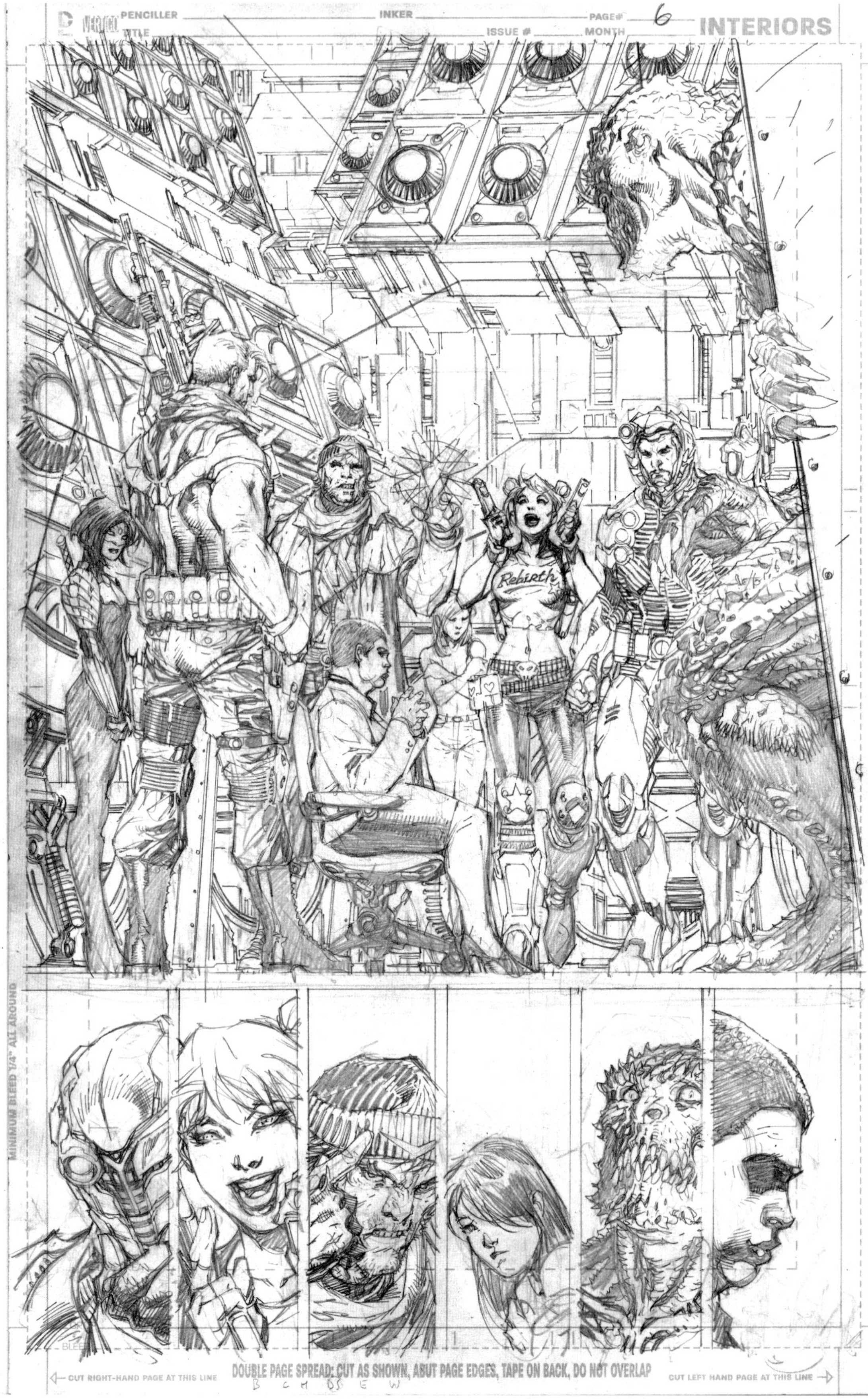
PENCILLER
INKER
PAGE# 6
TITLE
ISSUE #
MONTH
INTERIORS
Rebirth
MINIMUM BLEED 1/4" ALL AROUND
DOUBLE PAGE SPREAD: CUT AS SHOWN, ABUT PAGE EDGES, TAPE ON BACK, DO NOT OVERLAP
CUT RIGHT-HAND PAGE AT THIS LINE
CUT LEFT HAND PAGE AT THIS LINE

SPACE IN COLOR

SPACE IN COLOR

EARTH IN COLOR

KATANA

FLAGG

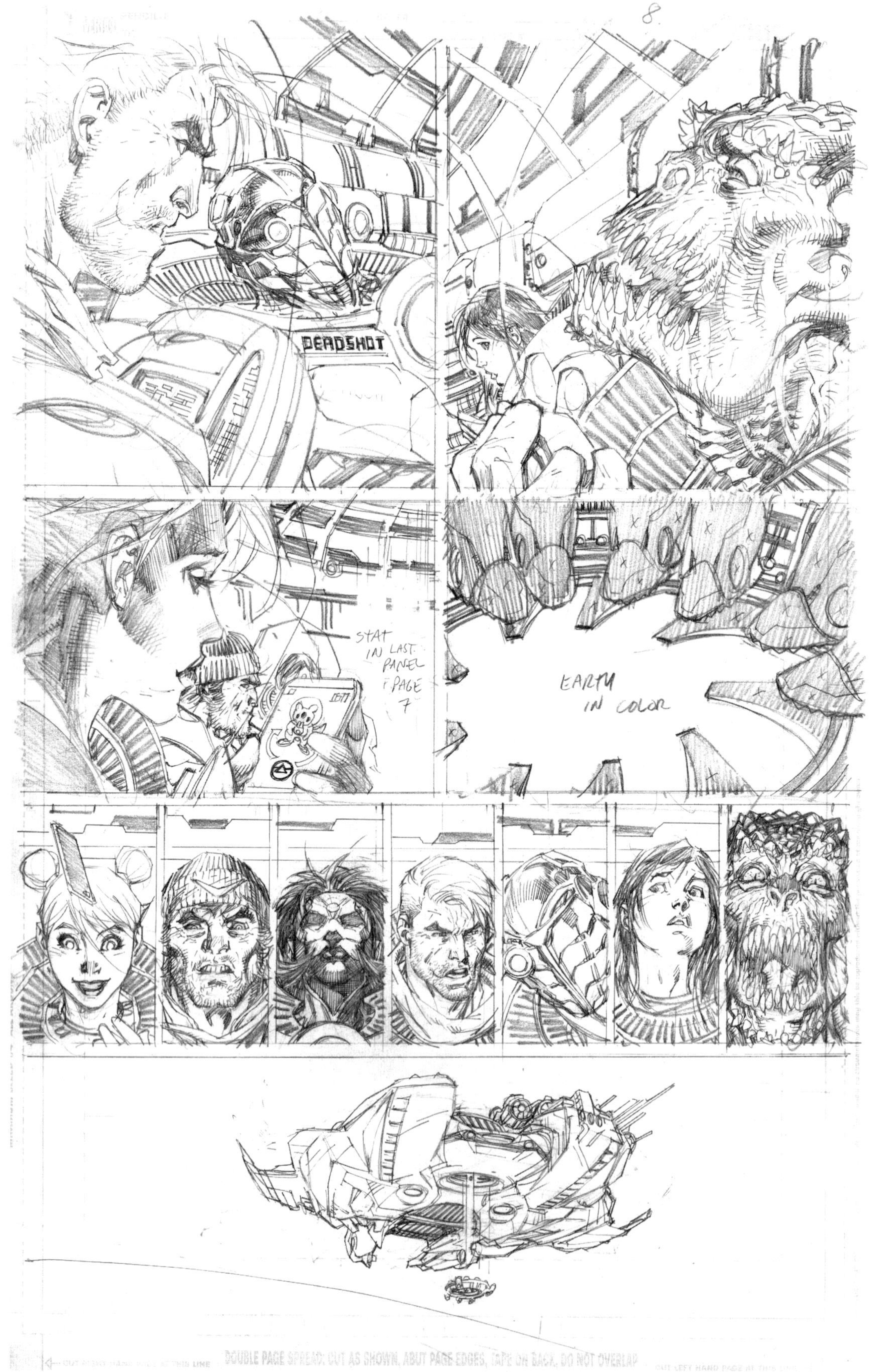
8.
DEADSHOT
STAT IN LAST PANEL F PAGE 7
EARTH IN COLOR
DOUBLE PAGE SPREAD: CUT AS SHOWN, ABUT PAGE EDGES, TAPE ON BACK, DO NOT OVERLAP

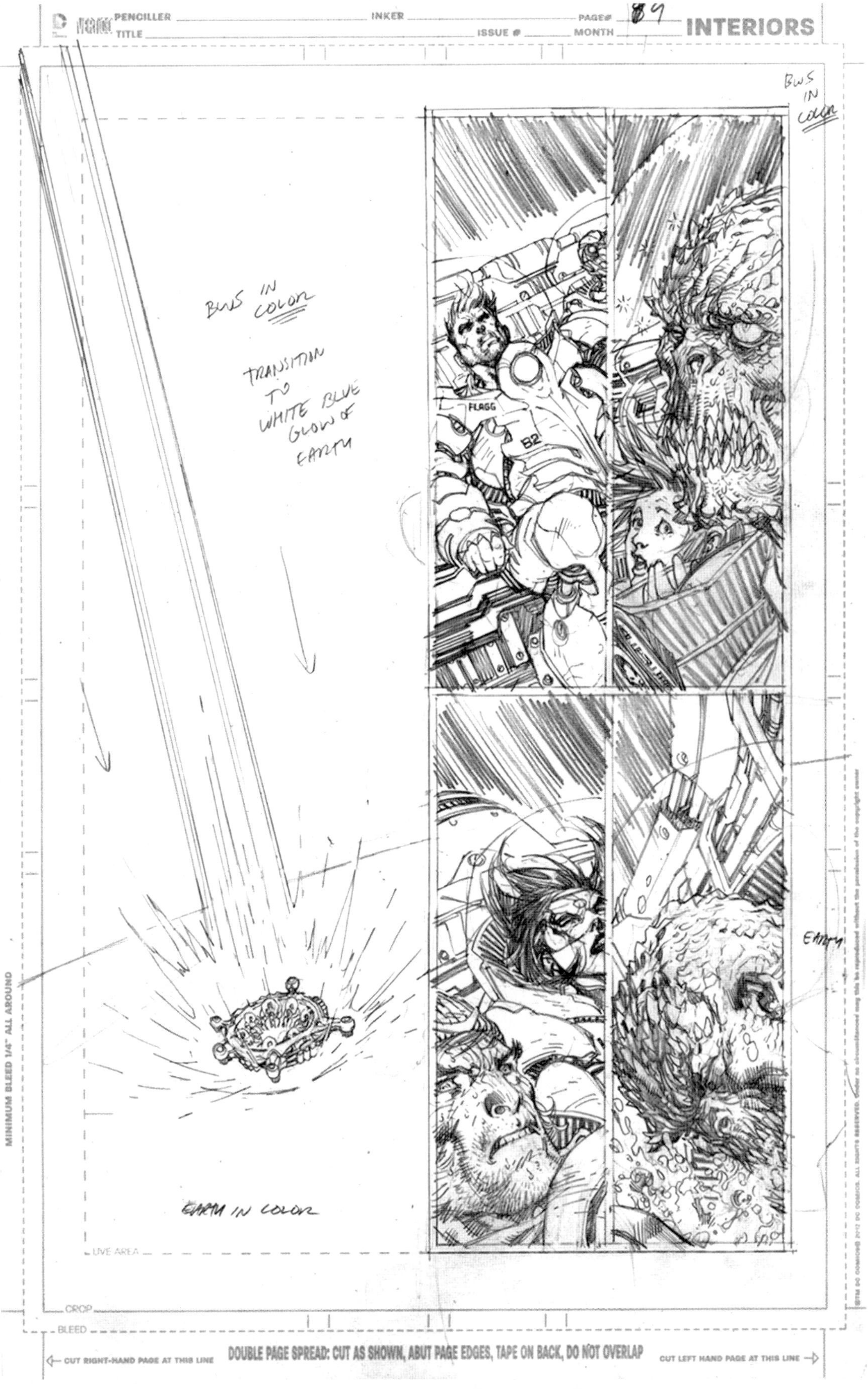
PENCILLER
INKER
PAGE# 84
TITLE
ISSUE #
MONTH
INTERIORS
BWS IN COLOR
TRANSITION TO WHITE BLUE GLOW OF EARTH
FLAGG
B2
EARTH
EARTH IN COLOR
LIVE AREA
CROP
BLEED
MINIMUM BLEED 1/4" ALL AROUND
CUT RIGHT-HAND PAGE AT THIS LINE
DOUBLE PAGE SPREAD: CUT AS SHOWN, ABUT PAGE EDGES, TAPE ON BACK, DO NOT OVERLAP
CUT LEFT HAND PAGE AT THIS LINE

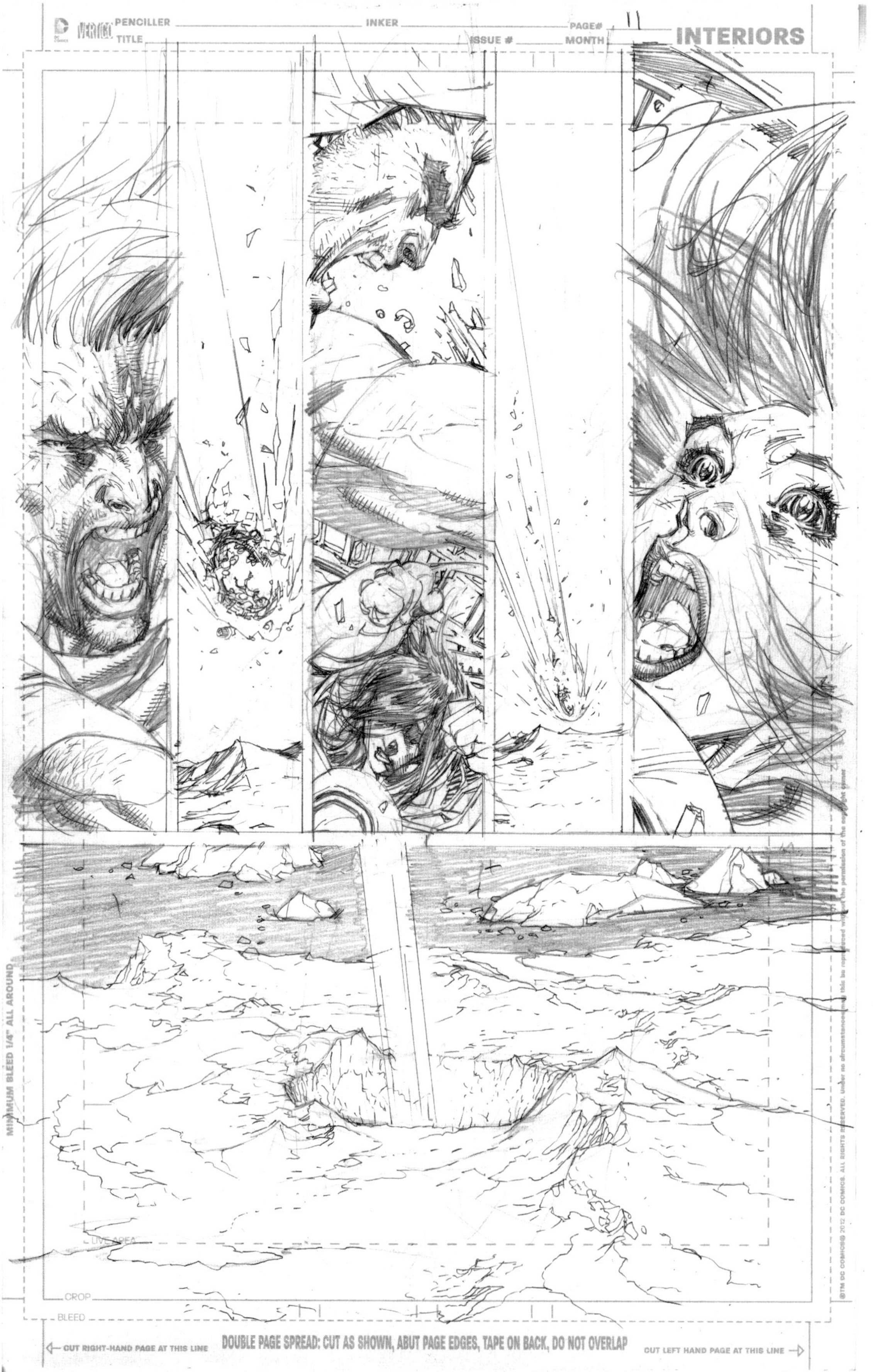PENCILLER
INKER
PAGE# 11
TITLE
ISSUE #
MONTH
INTERIORS
MINIMUM BLEED 1/4" ALL AROUND
LIVE AREA
CROP
BLEED
CUT RIGHT-HAND PAGE AT THIS LINE
DOUBLE PAGE SPREAD: CUT AS SHOWN, ABUT PAGE EDGES, TAPE ON BACK, DO NOT OVERLAP
CUT LEFT HAND PAGE AT THIS LINE

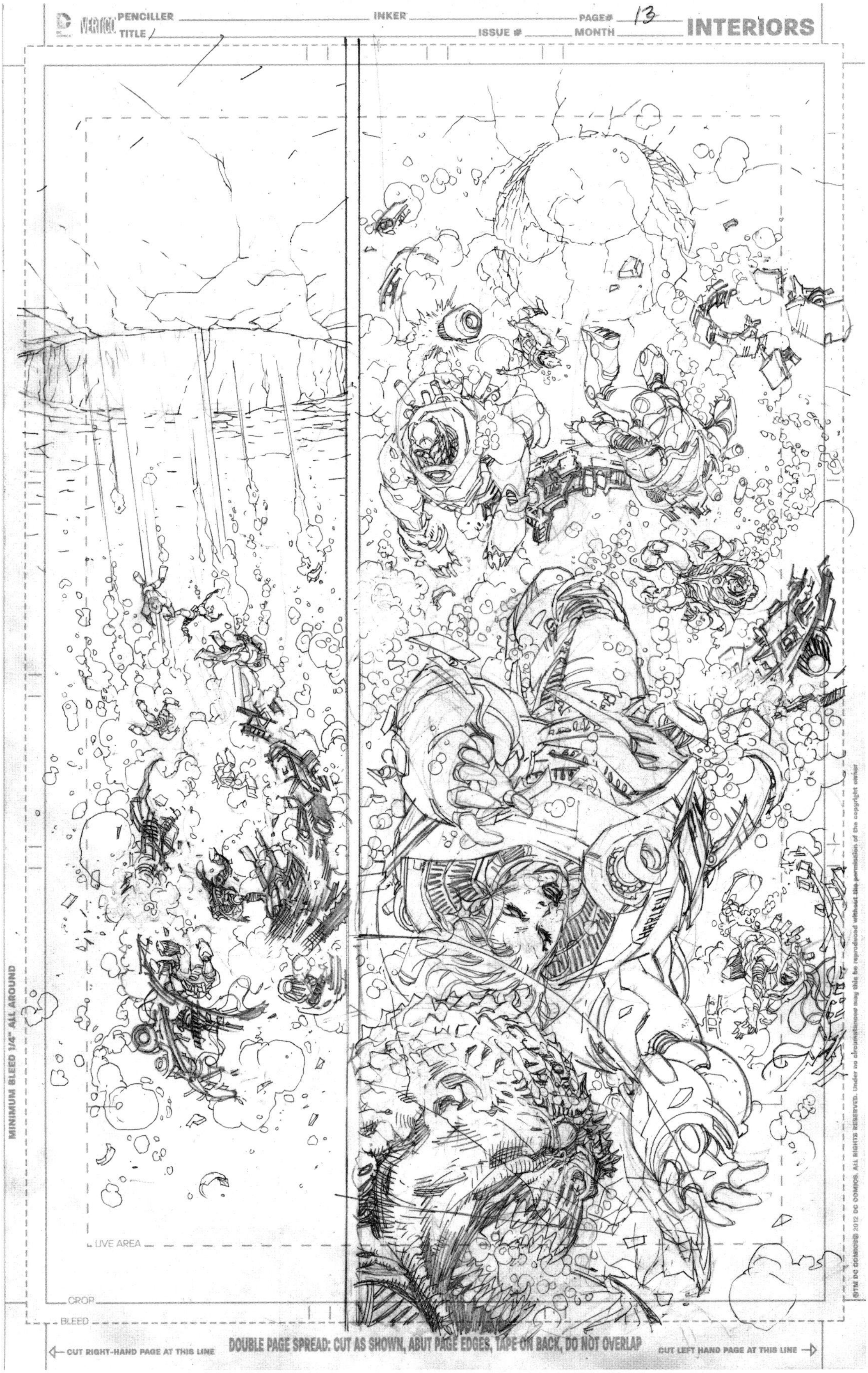
PENCILLER
INKER
PAGE# 13
INTERIORS
TITLE
ISSUE #
MONTH
LIVE AREA
CROP
BLEED
MINIMUM BLEED 1/4" ALL AROUND
DOUBLE PAGE SPREAD: CUT AS SHOWN, ABUT PAGE EDGES, TAPE ON BACK, DO NOT OVERLAP
CUT RIGHT-HAND PAGE AT THIS LINE
CUT LEFT HAND PAGE AT THIS LINE
©TM DC COMICS© 2012 DC COMICS. ALL RIGHTS RESERVED. Under no circumstances may this be reproduced without the permission of the copyright owner

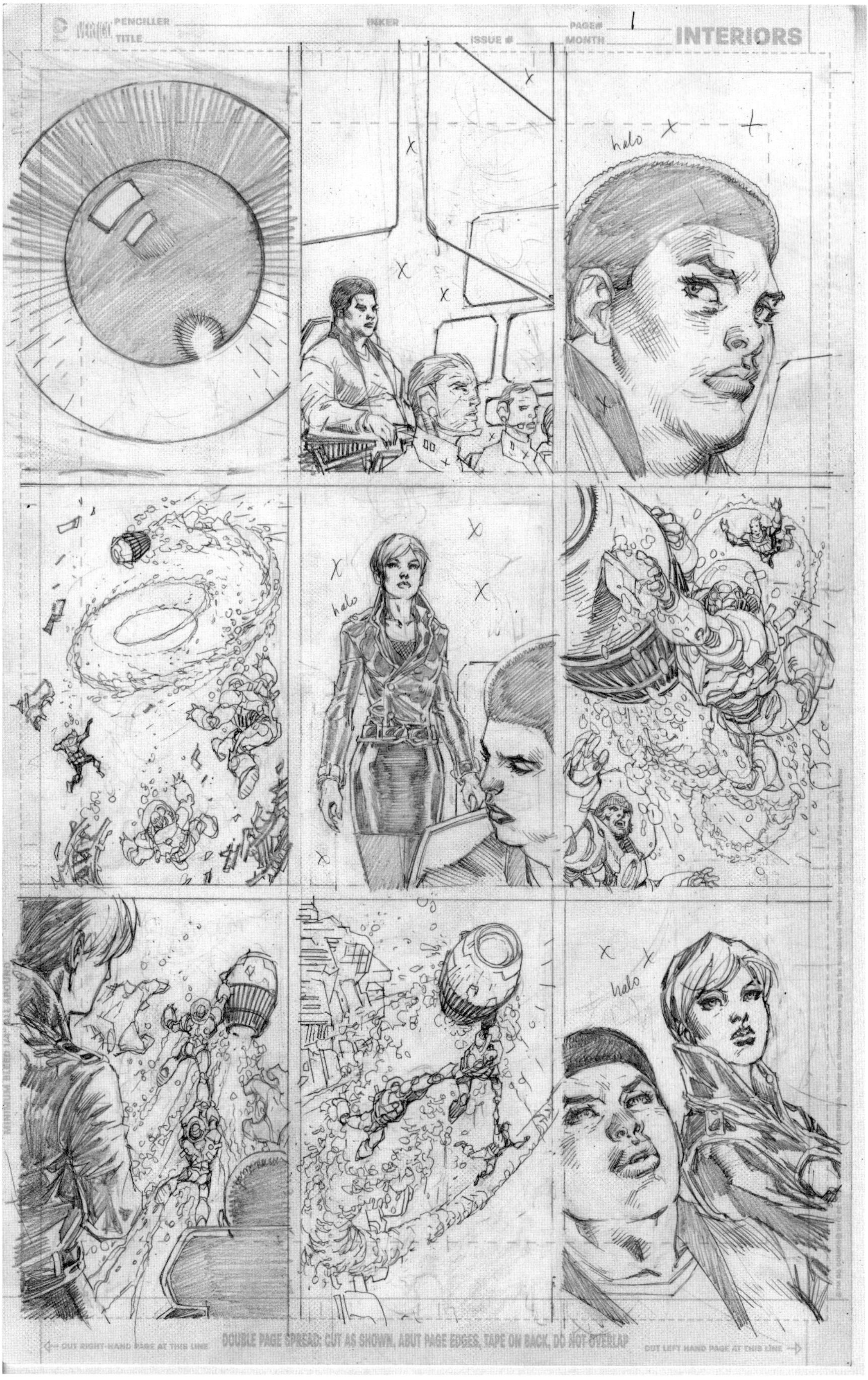
PENCILLER
INKER
PAGE# 1
INTERIORS
TITLE
ISSUE #
MONTH
halo
halo
halo
DOUBLE PAGE SPREAD: CUT AS SHOWN, ABUT PAGE EDGES, TAPE ON BACK, DO NOT OVERLAP
CUT RIGHT-HAND PAGE AT THIS LINE
CUT LEFT HAND PAGE AT THIS LINE

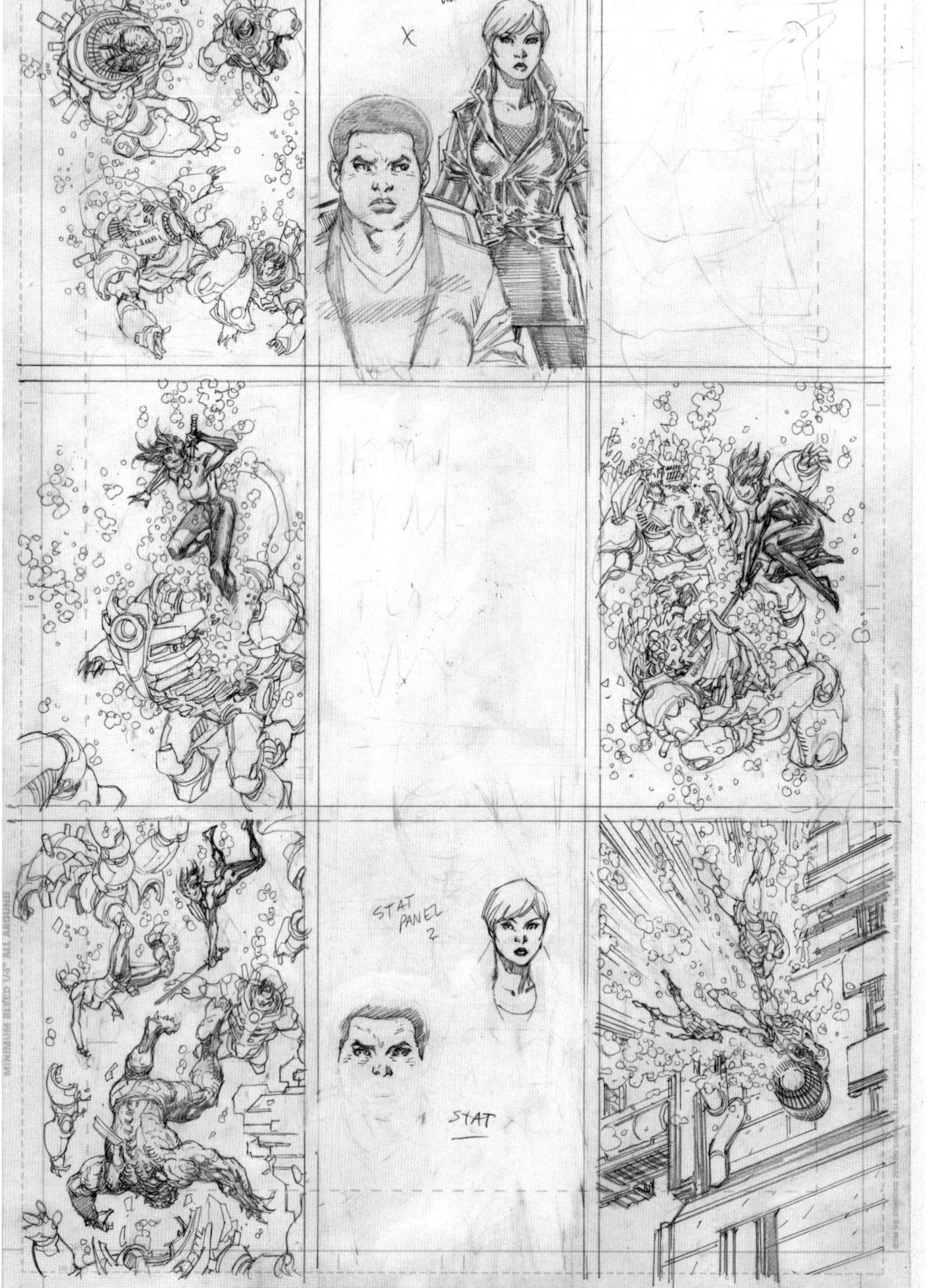
PENCILLER
TITLE
INKER
ISSUE #
PAGE# 2
MONTH
INTERIORS
halo X
X
STAT PANEL 2
STAT
MINIMUM BLEED 1/4" ALL AROUND
CUT RIGHT-HAND PAGE AT THIS LINE
DOUBLE PAGE SPREAD: CUT AS SHOWN, ABUT PAGE EDGES, TAPE ON BACK, DO NOT OVERLAP
CUT LEFT HAND PAGE AT THIS LINE

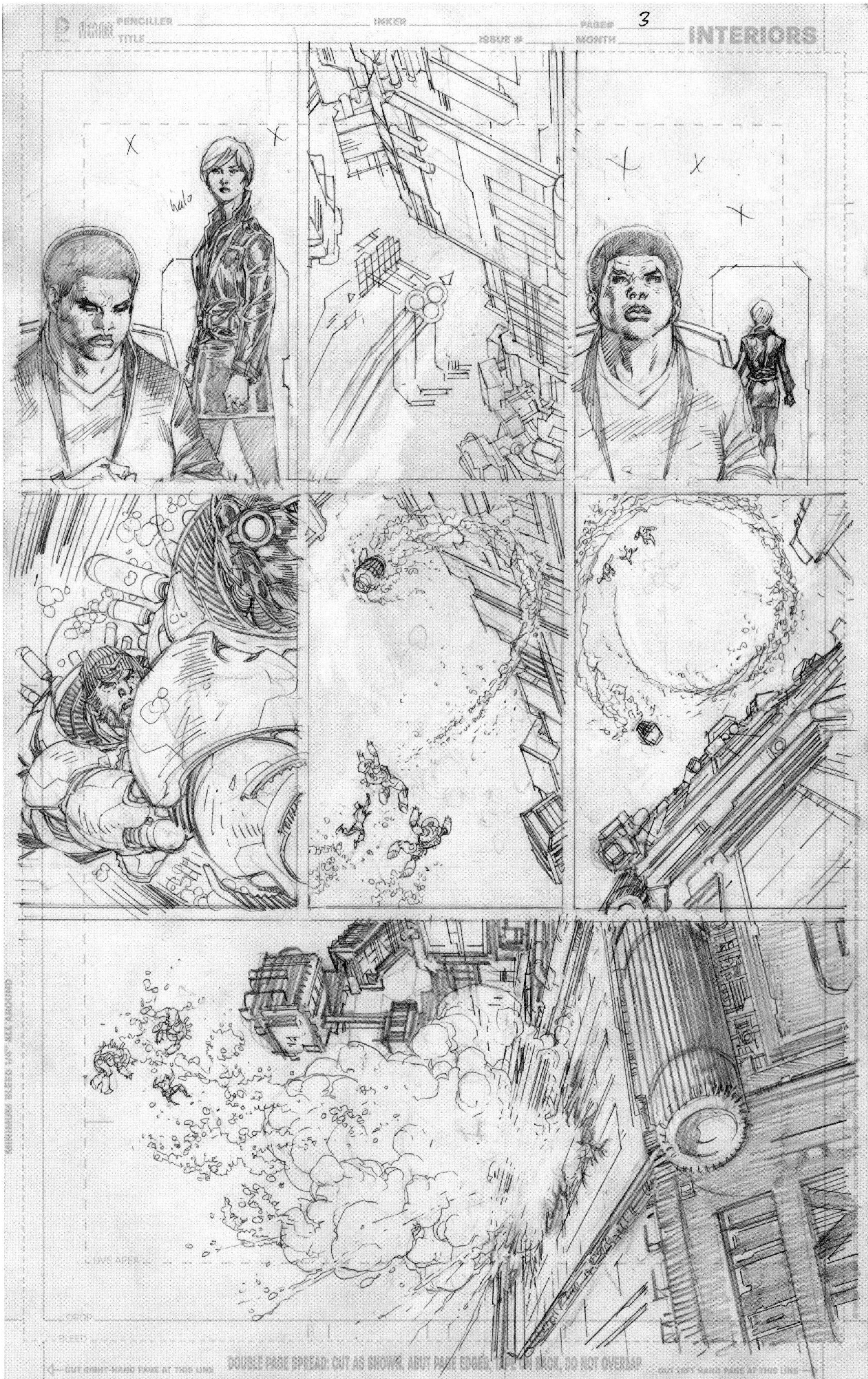
PENCILLER
INKER
PAGE# 3
TITLE
ISSUE #
MONTH
INTERIORS
halo
MINIMUM BLEED 1/4" ALL AROUND
LIVE AREA
CROP
BLEED
CUT RIGHT-HAND PAGE AT THIS LINE
DOUBLE PAGE SPREAD: CUT AS SHOWN, ABUT PAGE EDGES, TAPE ON BACK, DO NOT OVERLAP
CUT LEFT-HAND PAGE AT THIS LINE

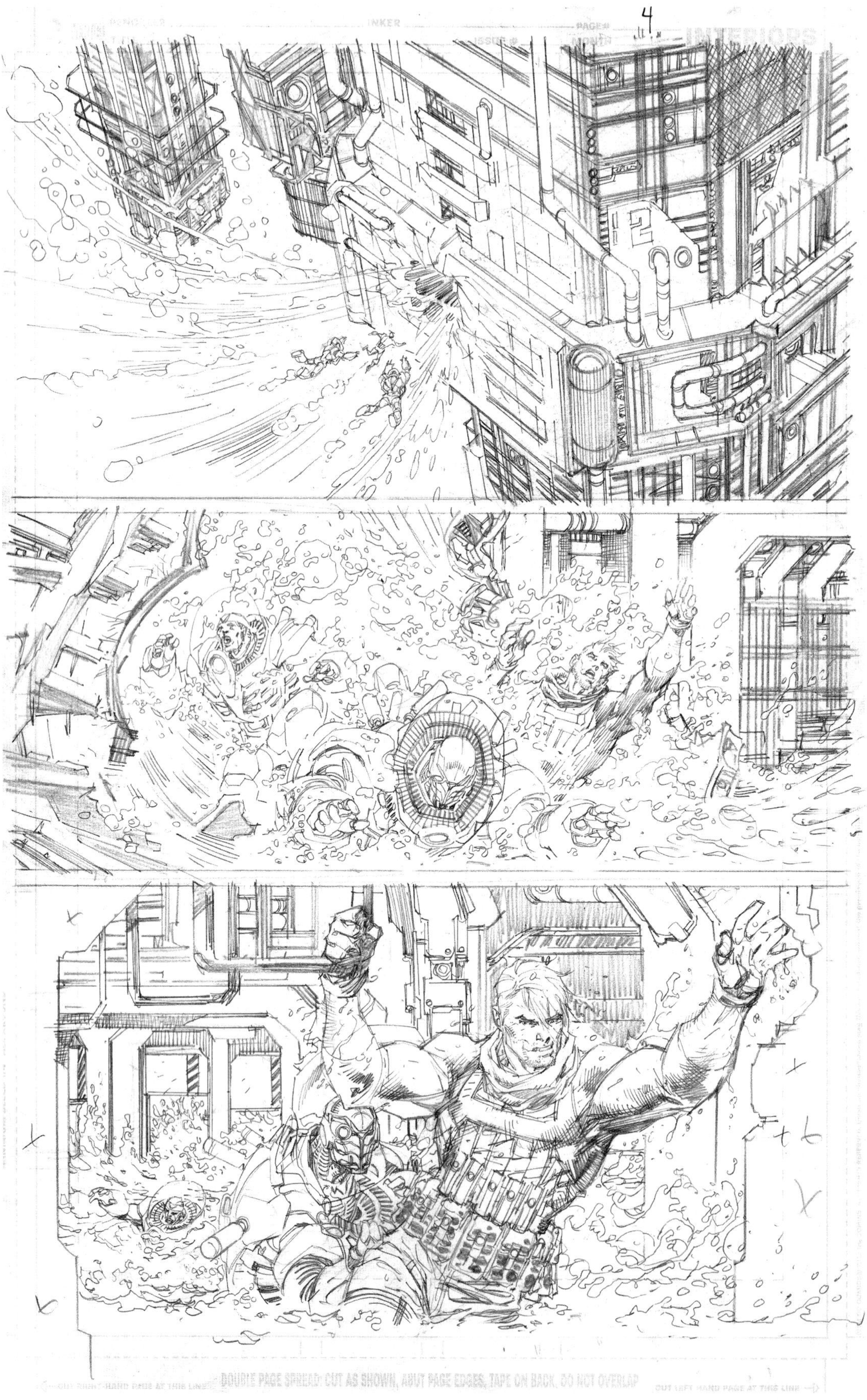
INKER
ISSUE #
PAGE#
4
INTERIORS
DOUBLE PAGE SPREAD: CUT AS SHOWN, ABUT PAGE EDGES, TAPE ON BACK, DO NOT OVERLAP

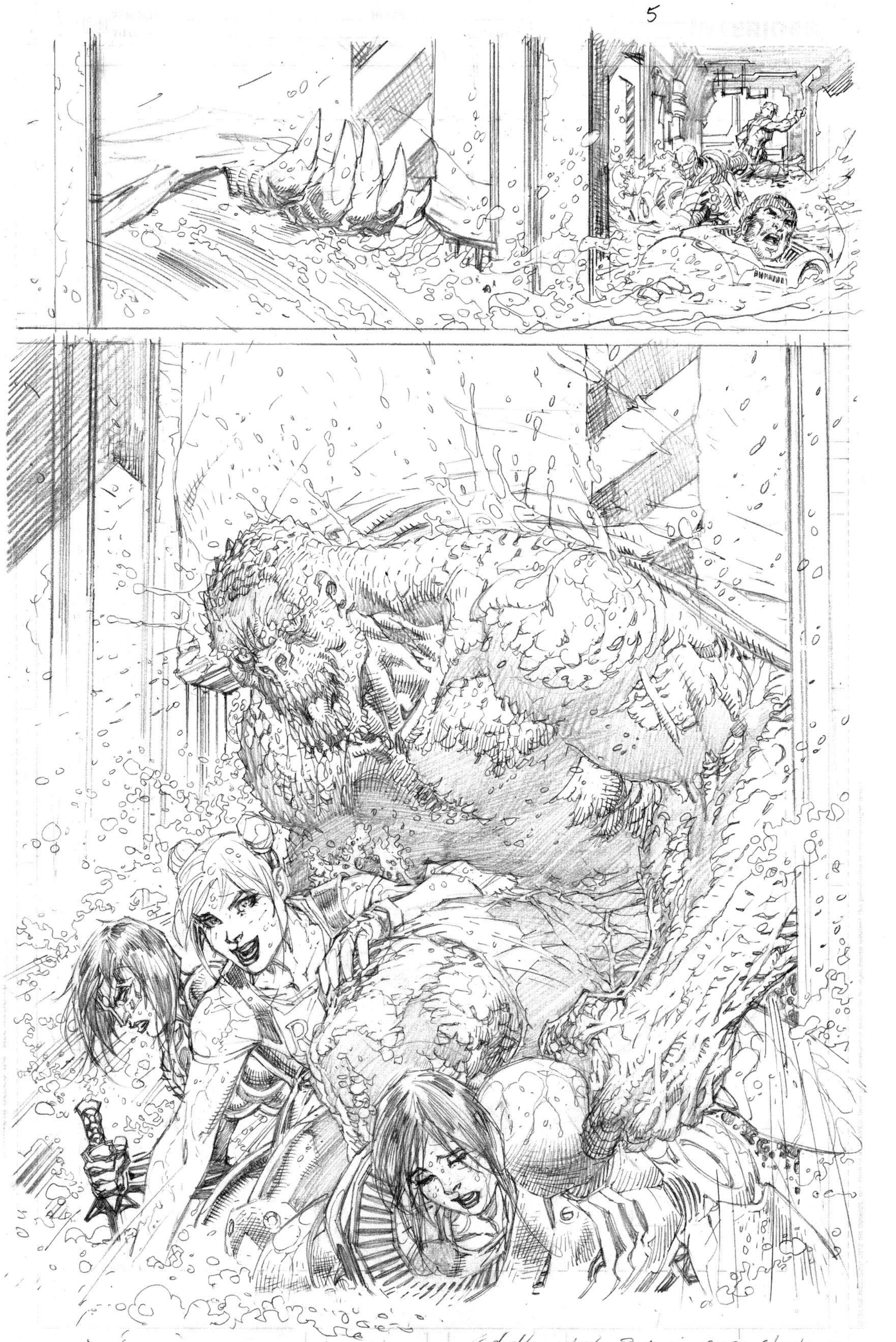
5
Splatter white out in core shadows
DOUBLE PAGE SPREAD: CUT AS SHOWN, ABUT PAGE EDGES, TAPE ON BACK, DO NOT OVERLAP

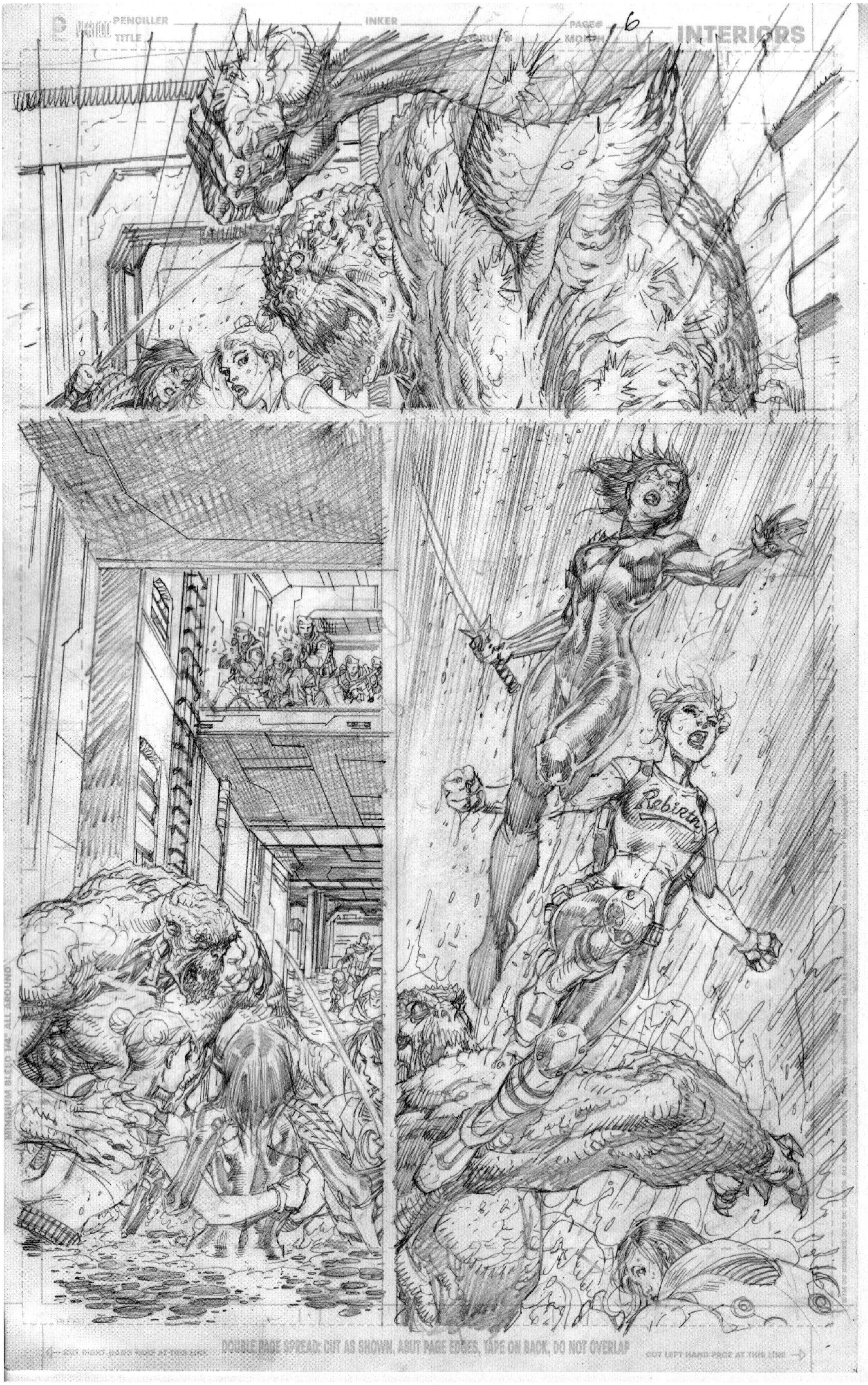
PENCILLER
INKER
PAGE# 6
TITLE
ISSUE#
MONTH
INTERIORS
Rebirth
MINIMUM BLEED 1/4" ALL AROUND
BLEED
CUT RIGHT HAND PAGE AT THIS LINE
DOUBLE PAGE SPREAD: CUT AS SHOWN, ABUT PAGE EDGES, TAPE ON BACK, DO NOT OVERLAP
CUT LEFT HAND PAGE AT THIS LINE

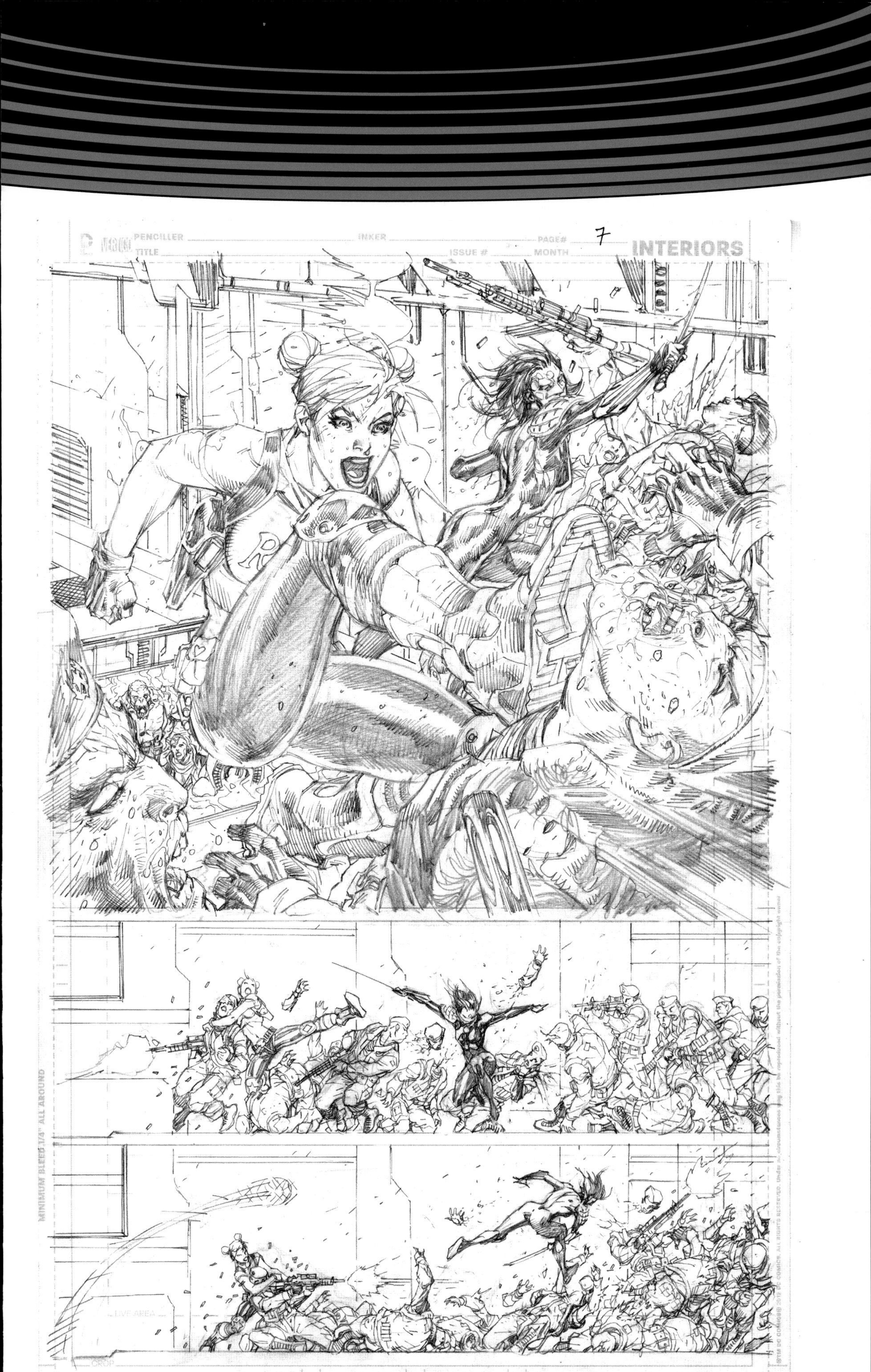

PENCILLER
INKER
PAGE# 7
INTERIORS
TITLE
ISSUE #
MONTH
MINIMUM BLEED 1/4" ALL AROUND
LIVE AREA
CROP
BLEED
KRAK!
DOUBLE PAGE SPREAD: CUT AS SHOWN, ABUT PAGE EDGES, TAPE ON BACK, DO NOT OVERLAP
CUT RIGHT-HAND PAGE AT THIS LINE
CUT LEFT HAND PAGE AT THIS LINE

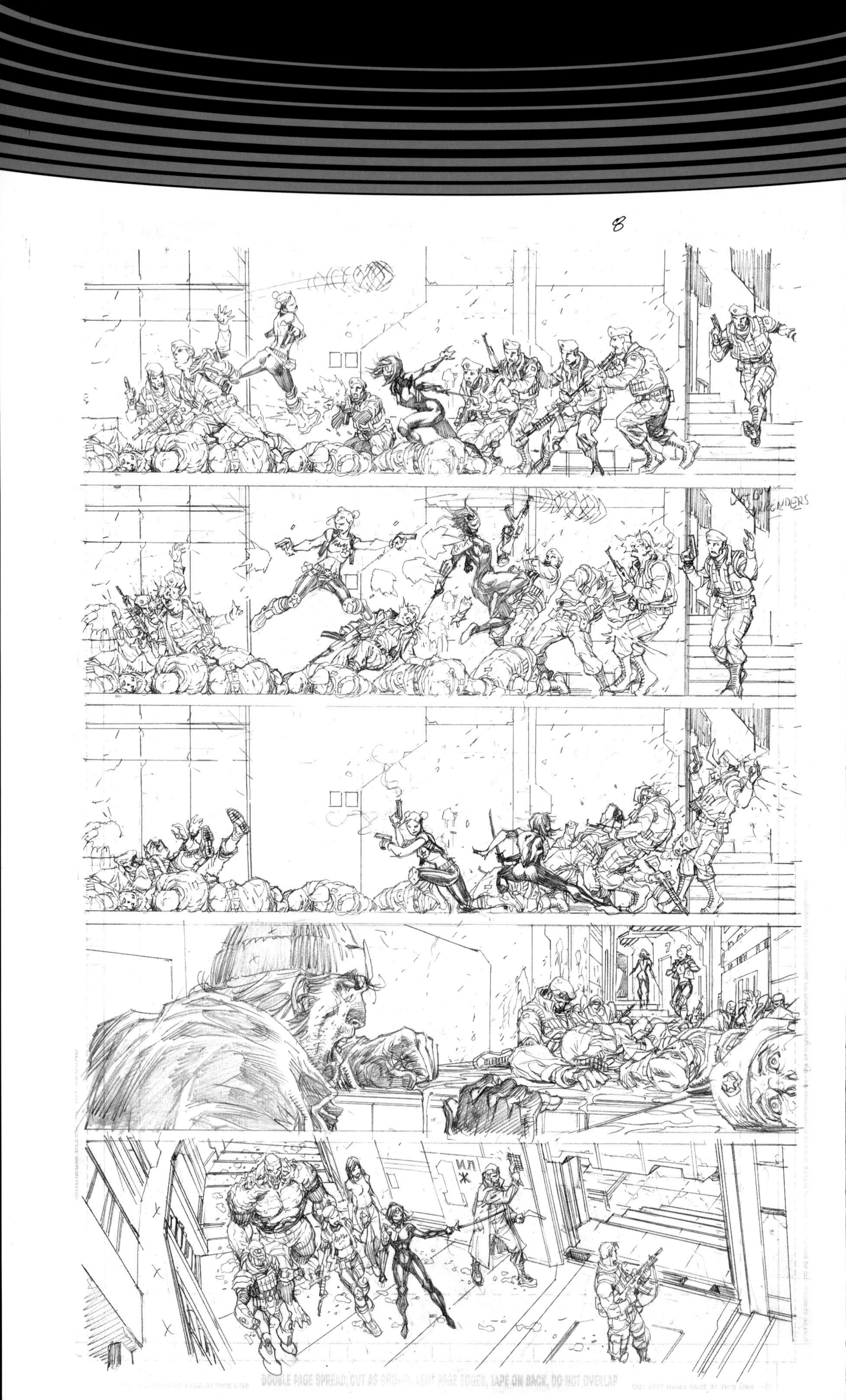
8
DOUBLE PAGE SPREAD: CUT AS SHOWN, ABUT PAGE EDGES, TAPE ON BACK, DO NOT OVERLAP

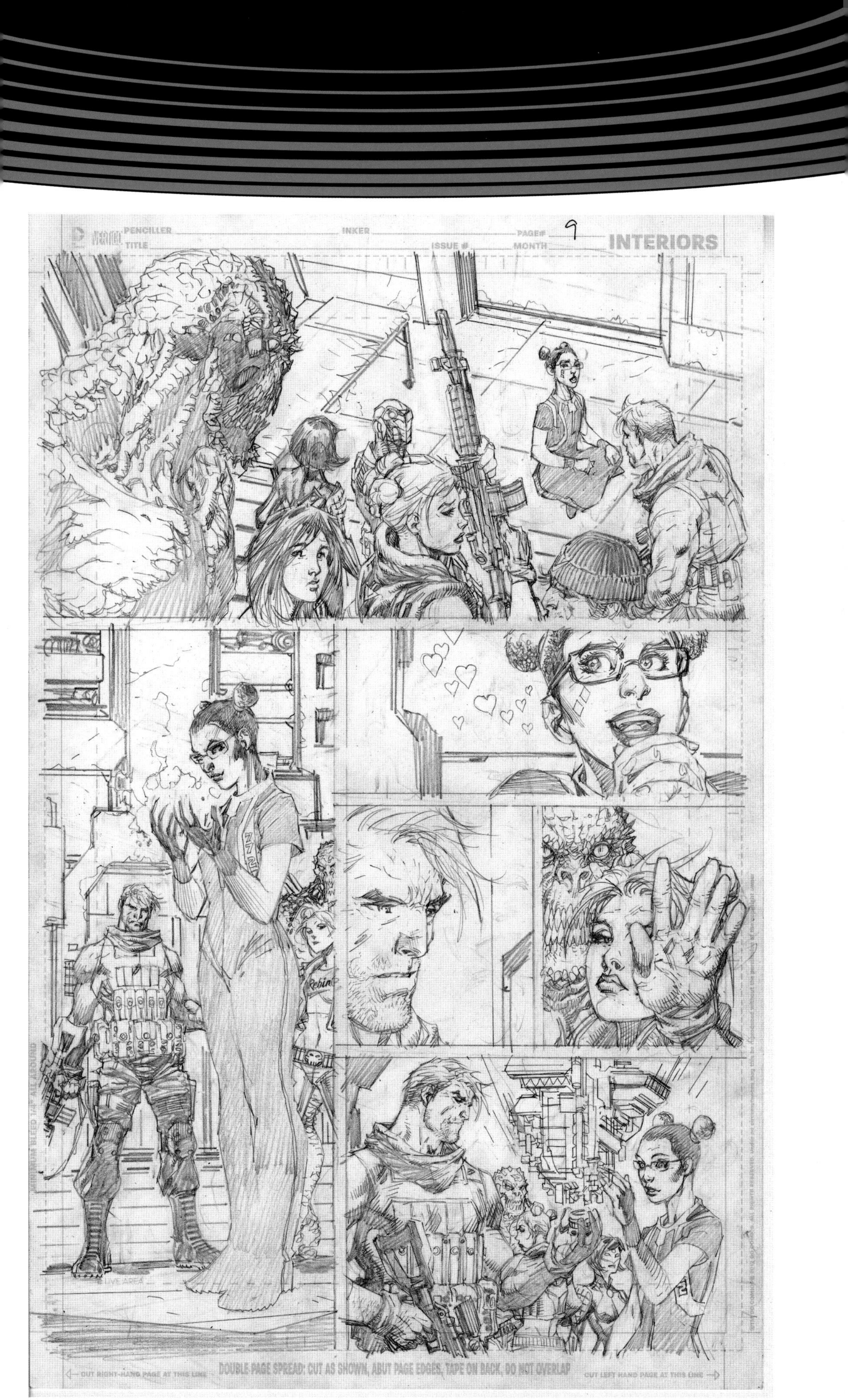
PENCILLER
INKER
PAGE# 9
TITLE
ISSUE #
MONTH
INTERIORS
CUT RIGHT-HAND PAGE AT THIS LINE
DOUBLE PAGE SPREAD: CUT AS SHOWN, ABUT PAGE EDGES, TAPE ON BACK, DO NOT OVERLAP
CUT LEFT HAND PAGE AT THIS LINE

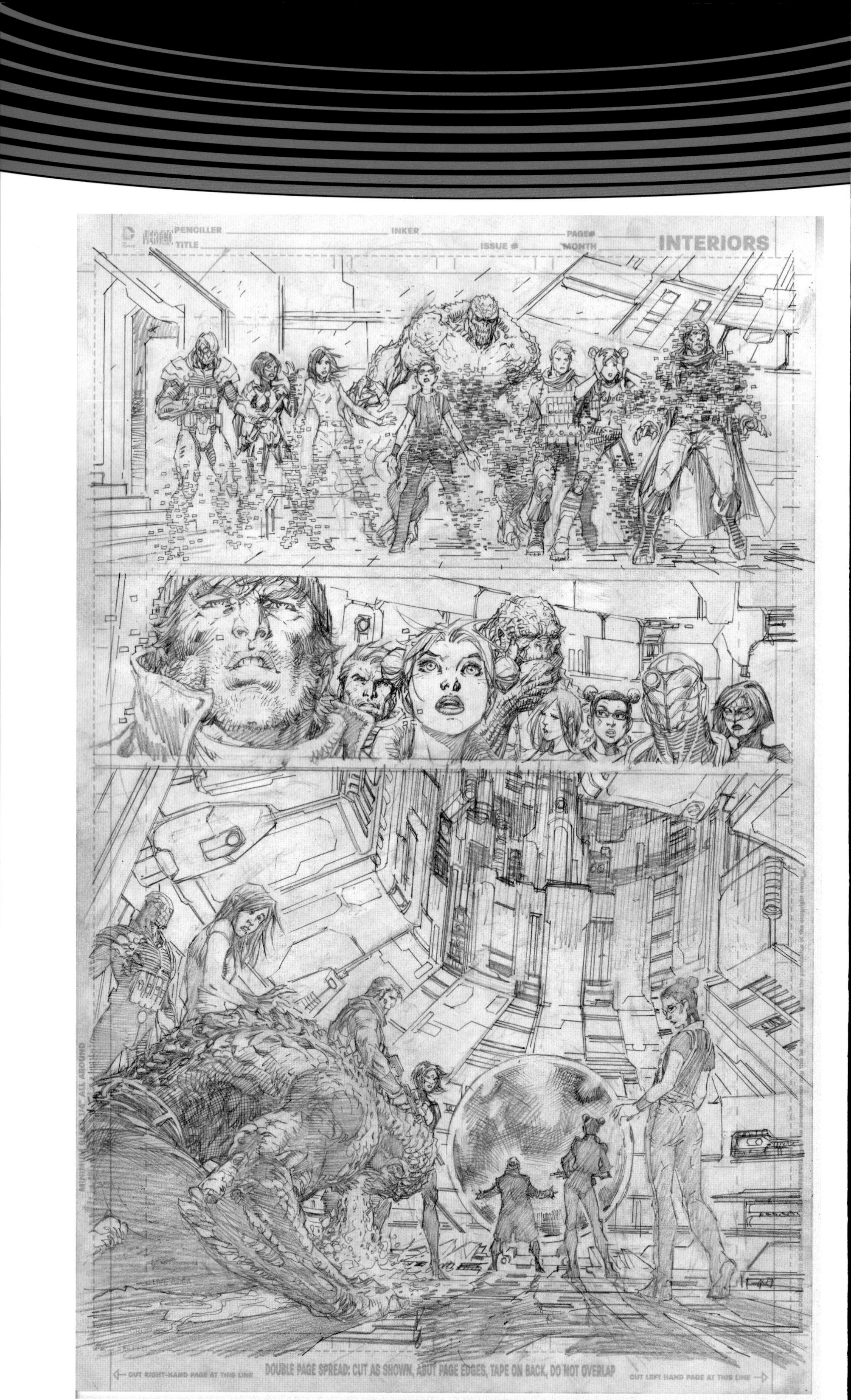
PENCILLER
INKER
PAGE#
TITLE
ISSUE #
MONTH
INTERIORS
CUT RIGHT-HAND PAGE AT THIS LINE
DOUBLE PAGE SPREAD: CUT AS SHOWN, ABUT PAGE EDGES, TAPE ON BACK, DO NOT OVERLAP
CUT LEFT HAND PAGE AT THIS LINE

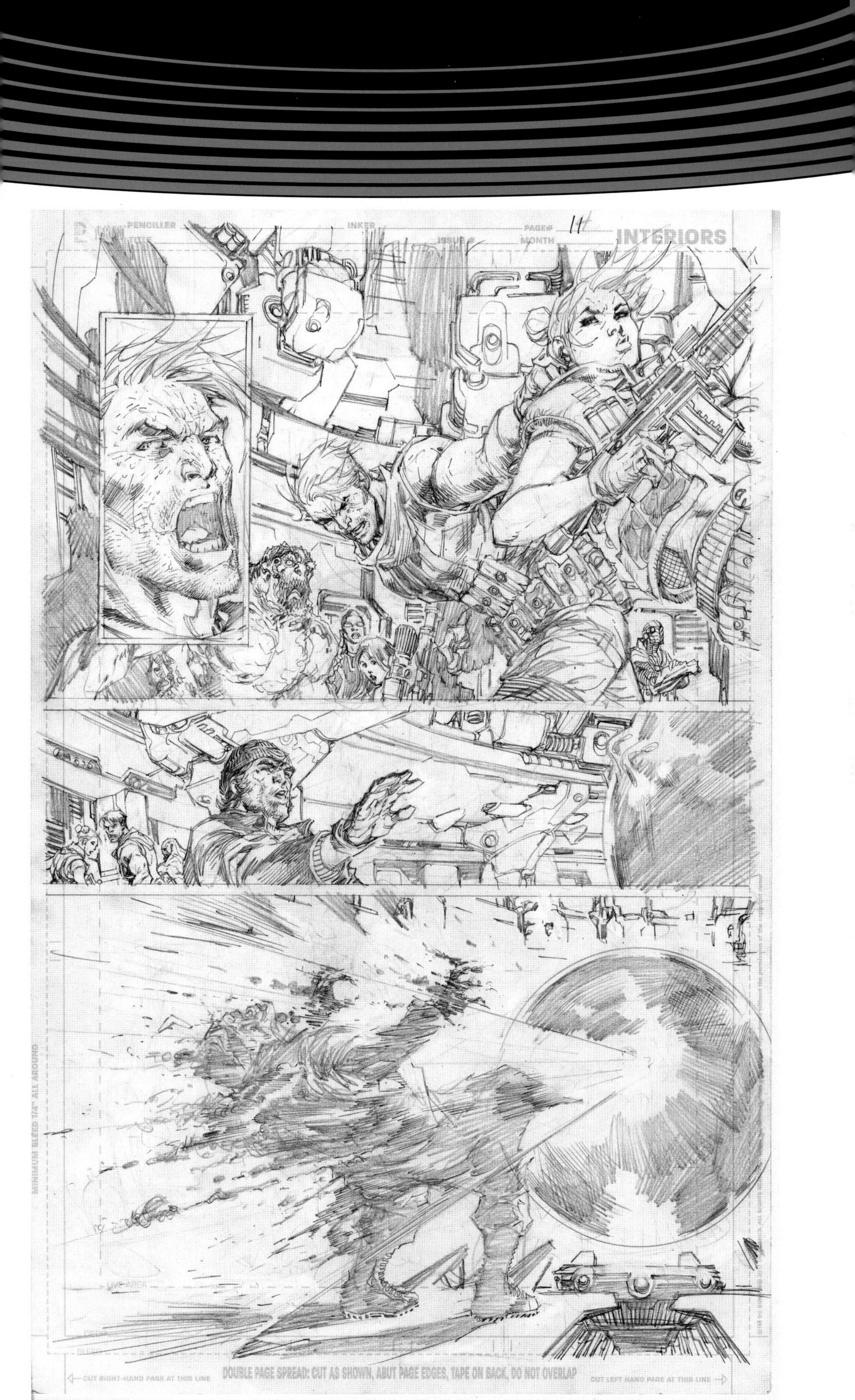
PENCILLER
INKER
PAGE# 11
TITLE
ISSUE #
MONTH
INTERIORS
MINIMUM BLEED 1/4" ALL AROUND
DOUBLE PAGE SPREAD: CUT AS SHOWN, ABUT PAGE EDGES, TAPE ON BACK, DO NOT OVERLAP
CUT RIGHT-HAND PAGE AT THIS LINE
CUT LEFT HAND PAGE AT THIS LINE

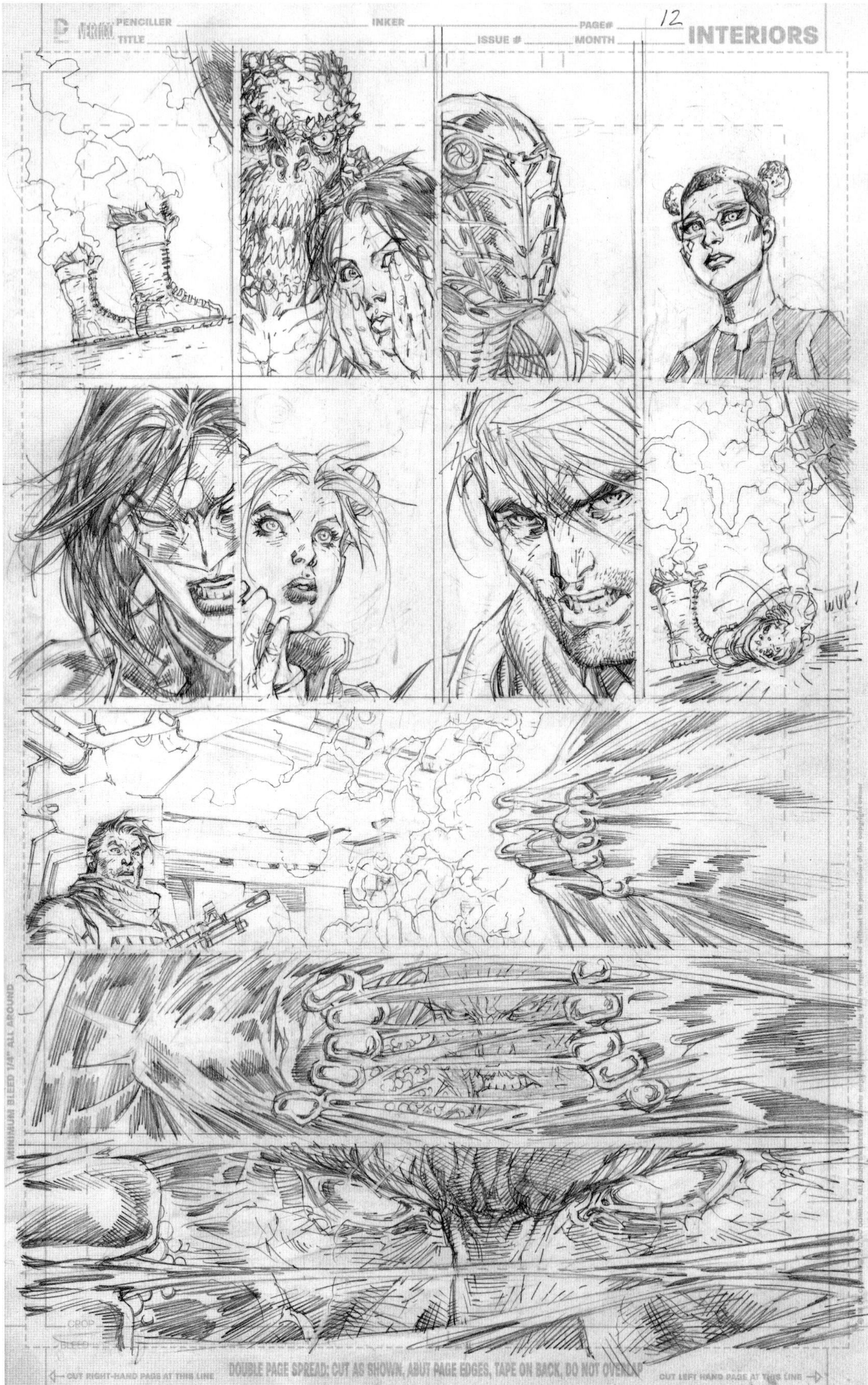
PENCILLER
INKER
PAGE#
12
TITLE
ISSUE #
MONTH
INTERIORS
WUP!
MINIMUM BLEED 1/4" ALL AROUND
CROP
BLEED
CUT RIGHT-HAND PAGE AT THIS LINE
DOUBLE PAGE SPREAD: CUT AS SHOWN, ABUT PAGE EDGES, TAPE ON BACK, DO NOT OVERLAP
CUT LEFT HAND PAGE AT THIS LINE

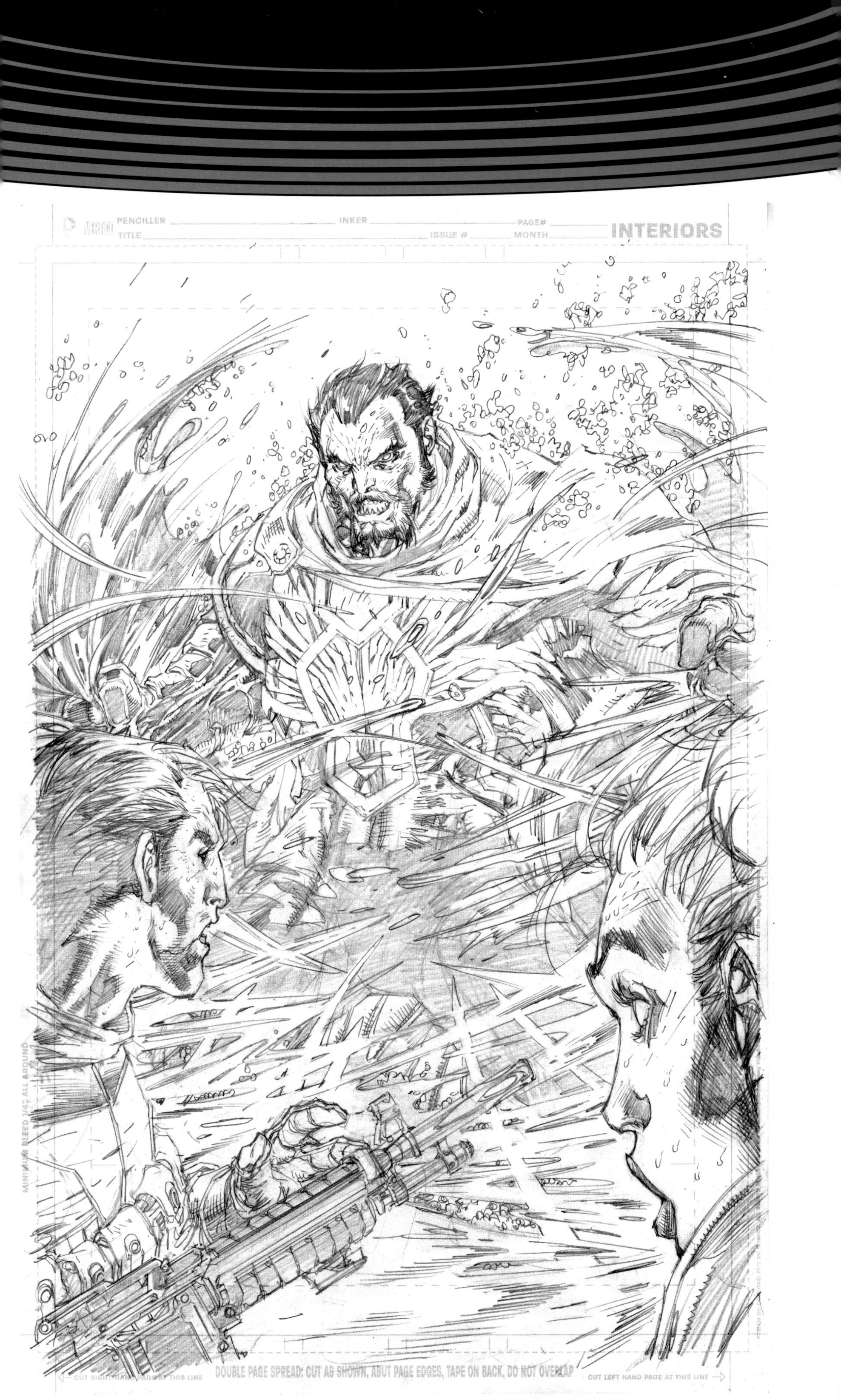
PENCILLER
INKER
PAGE#
TITLE
ISSUE #
MONTH
INTERIORS
MINIMUM BLEED 1/4" ALL AROUND
CUT RIGHT HAND PAGE AT THIS LINE
DOUBLE PAGE SPREAD: CUT AS SHOWN, ABUT PAGE EDGES, TAPE ON BACK, DO NOT OVERLAP
CUT LEFT HAND PAGE AT THIS LINE

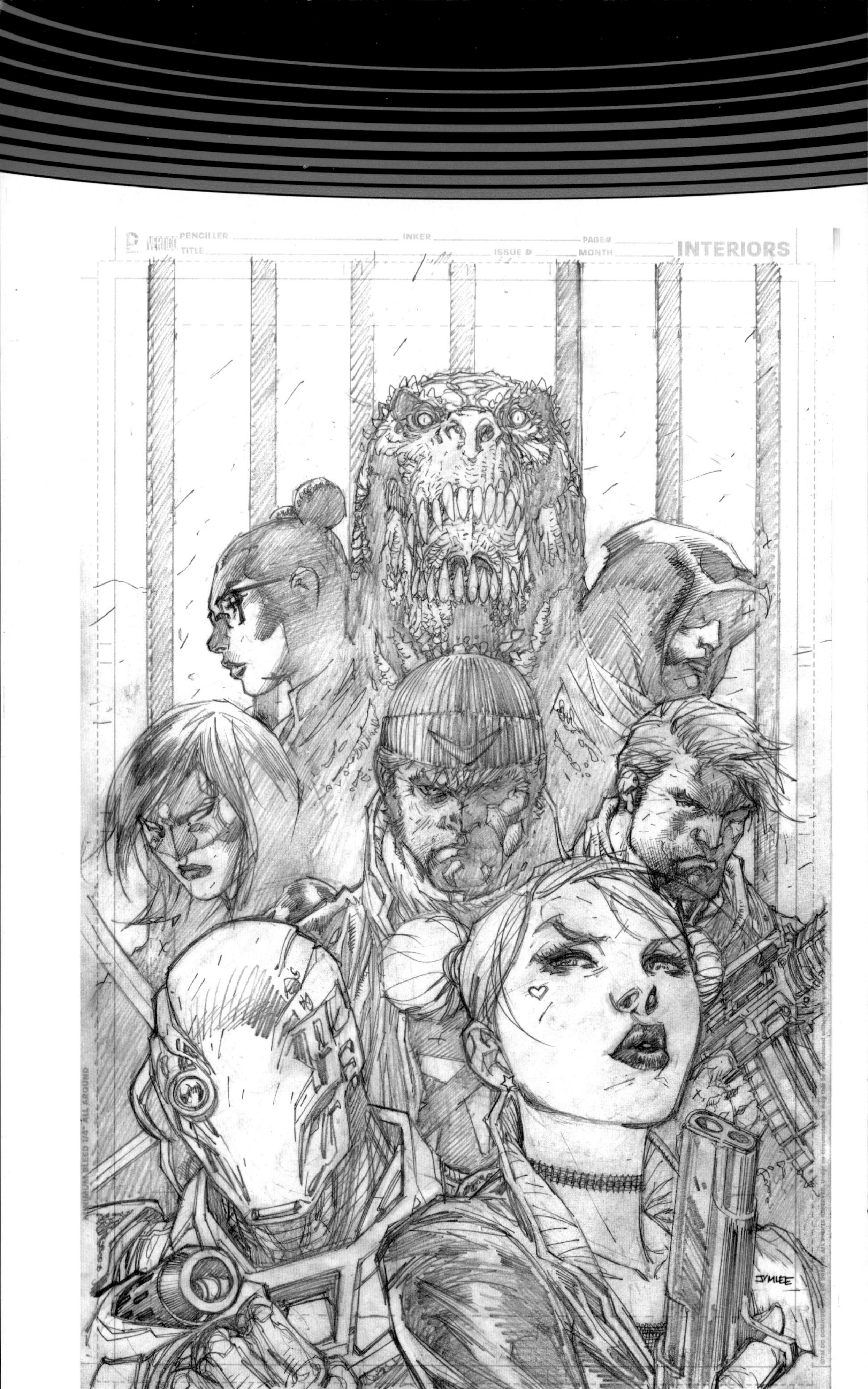
PENCILLER
INKER
PAGE#
TITLE
ISSUE #
MONTH
INTERIORS
JIMLEE